The
ECONOMIC INSTITUTIONS
of CAPITALISM

Firms, Markets, Relational Contracting

OLIVER E. WILLIAMSON
Yale University

THE FREE PRESS

To my teachers:

Kenneth J. Arrow
Alfred D. Chandler, Jr.
Ronald H. Coase
Herbert A. Simon

THE FREE PRESS
A Division of Simon & Schuster Inc.
1230 Avenue of the Americas
New York, NY 10020

THE FREE PRESS and colophon are trademarks
of Simon & Schuster Inc.

Manufactured in the United States of America

10 9

Library of Congress Cataloging-in-Publication Data

Williamson, Oliver E.
  The economic institutions of capitalism.

  Bibliography: p.
  Includes indexes.
  1. Institutional economics. I. Title.
[HB99.5.W55   1987]   338.7   87-11901
ISBN 0-02-934821-8 (pbk.)

Contents

Preface to the Paperback Edition

Transaction cost economics has helped to promote growing interest in the economics of organization. As compared with other work in this field, transaction cost economics is expressly concerned with issues at the interdisciplinary intersection of law, economics, and organization. After a tentative beginning, research on transaction cost economics has grown exponentially in the past fifteen years. Further work on the conceptual foundations remains to be done, additional phenomena await investigation, and further public policy applications have yet to be worked out. However, there is every reason to believe that substantial progress in all three areas will be made in the years ahead.

Although transaction cost economics is conceptually demanding, it repays the effort with interest. Any problem that can be formulated, directly or indirectly, as a contracting problem can be investigated to advantage in transaction cost terms. Not only does this approach make useful contact with a wide range of fascinating issues, but many disparate and puzzling phenomena turn out, upon examination, to have a very similar structure. Striking differences among labor markets, capital markets, intermediate product markets, corporate governance, regulation, and family organization notwithstanding, these are all variations on the very same underlying transaction cost economics theme. Different (sometimes rival, sometimes complementary) explanations for what had hitherto been regarded as settled issues have resulted. The economics research domain has been expanded in the process. Contacts with law, sociology, and political science are numerous and growing.

Thinking about problems of economic organization from a transaction cost economics point of view takes concerted effort. Once, however, a threshold of understanding is reached, the world of organization is "spontaneously" reordered. Applications abound. Experienced students of organization who had become accustomed to thinking about problems of organization in noneconomic ways now find that transaction cost features emerge and must be dealt with. The worldview of new students who get caught up in transaction cost reasoning is irreversibly altered.

What are the courses for which *The Economic Institution of Capitalism* is best suited? The "ideal" course is one on the Economics of Organization—an area of interest rapidly growing (as witnessed by the fact that courses of this kind have been appearing in the curricula of many leading universities and colleges). Established courses in Industrial Organization, Comparative Economic Systems, and Intermediate Microtheory can use the book as a complement to the basic text. The same is true for courses in Organization Theory, Corporate Strategy, Marketing, and Corporation Law. A growing dialogue between transaction cost economics and the study of political institutions and sociology of organization suggests applications in these disciplines as well.

Oliver E. Williamson

Preface

What is referred to herein as transaction cost economics is part of the revival of interest in the New Institutional Economics. Transaction cost economics owes its origins to striking insights—in law, economics, and organization—in the 1930s. As with many good ideas, operationalization came neither quickly nor easily. Grave skepticism over their tautological reputation notwithstanding, transaction cost explanations kept reappearing. The survival of this line of analysis was assured by the realization in the 1960s that "market failures" had transaction cost origins. As patterns recurred and commonalities were recognized, operationalization gradually began to take shape. The past decade has witnessed successive efforts to infuse transaction cost economics with greater operational content.

To be sure, the apparatus is still primitive and in need of refinement. Numerous applications of transaction cost reasoning have nevertheless been made. More are in prospect. Many of them turn out to be variations on a theme, which is consonant with Hayek's observation that "whenever the capacity of recognizing an abstract rule which the arrangement of these attributes follows has been acquired in one field, the same master mould will apply when the signs for those abstract attributes are evoked by altogether different elements."

A fully balanced treatment of economic organization is not herein attempted. To the contrary, economic organization is examined almost entirely, certainly preponderantly, through the lens of transaction cost economizing. Such a focused approach discloses the extraordinary degree to which economic organization is shaped by transaction cost economizing considerations. The wide range of phenomena to which such reasoning has application comes as a surprise even to those who, such as myself, are already persuaded that this is a fruitful orientation.

To be sure, transaction cost arguments are often best used in conjunction with, rather than to the exclusion of, other ways of examining the same phenomena. I therefore do not propose that a blinkered approach to economic organization proceed heedless of other alternatives. A comprehensive treatment will plainly take all of the relevant factors into account. Greater weight, however, will presumably be accorded to those approaches that make greater and more systematic headway.

My substantial excuse for proceeding in a narrowly focused way is that transaction cost economics is still in an early developmental stage. The potential scope and significance of the approach will be realized only upon relentless application of this type of reasoning. To be sure, there is a legitimate concern that such a focused analysis is given to excesses. The excesses are usually transparent, however, and I ask readers—both skeptics and others—to be on guard, to make allowances, and to restore perspectives.

Transaction cost economics is akin to orthodoxy in its insistence that economizing is central to economic organization. There are nevertheless real differences between a neoclassical production cost and the proposed governance cost orientation. But economizing, in any form whatsoever, is a purpose with which most economists agree and to which all can relate.

The proposed approach maintains that any issue that either arises as or can be recast as a problem of contracting is usefully examined in transaction cost terms. The recent ''mechanism design'' literature is similarly oriented to the study of contract. But there are real differences here as well. The mechanism design literature focuses on the *ex ante* (or incentive alignment) side of contract and assumes that disputes are routinely referred to and that justice is effectively (indeed, costlessly) dispensed by the courts. In contrast, transaction cost economics maintains that *the governance of contractual relations is primarily effected through the institutions of private ordering rather than through legal centralism.* Although the importance of *ex ante* incentive alignment is acknowledged, primary attention is focused on the *ex post* institutions of contract.

The behavioral assumptions I invoke in support of this approach to the study of contract are bounded rationality and opportunism. Both are intended as concessions to "human nature as we know it." Admittedly, the resulting conception of human nature is stark and rather jaundiced. Those who would emphasize more affirmative aspects of the human condition and wish to plumb features of economic organization that go beyond economizing will understandably chafe over such a choice of behavioral assumptions.

Those two behavioral assumptions support the following compact statement of the problem of economic organization: devise contract and governance structures that have the purpose and effect of economizing on bounded rationality while simultaneously safeguarding transactions against the hazards of opportunism. A relatively calculative orientation to economic organization unavoidably results—a constant concern of which is that calculativeness will be pushed to dysfunctional extremes. Subject to that caveat, I submit that any study of organization purporting to deal with economic realities must come to terms with this behavioral pair.

It is my great privilege to dedicate this book to my teachers, Kenneth Arrow, Alfred Chandler, Jr., Ronald Coase, and Herbert Simon. I had the pleasure of learning from Arrow and Simon in the classroom. Chandler and Coase have taught me mainly through their publications. Each has had a profound impact on my understanding of economic organization. This book would read very differently if the influence of any one of them were to be purged. It nevertheless goes without saying that they are neither individually nor collectively responsible for the result.

I have benefited greatly from the advice of scholars who have read various parts of the manuscript, sometimes in the form of earlier articles from which the book was shaped. Those who have read and advised me about the book in its near-final form include Henry Hansmann, Paul Joskow, Richard Nelson, and Roberta Romano. Those whose advice on parts of the manuscript or on earlier articles is acknowledged include William Allen, Masahiko Aoki, Erin Anderson, Banri Asanuma, Kenneth Arrow, William Baxter, Yoram Ben-Porath, Dennis Carlton, Frank Easterbrook, Donald Elliott, Victor Goldberg, Neal Gross, Sanford Grossman, Bengt Holmstrom, Alvin Klevorick, Benjamin Klein, Reinier Kraakman, David Kreps, Arthur Leff, Richard Levin, Paul MacAvoy, Scott Masten, Eitan Muller, Douglass North, William Ouchi, Thomas Palay, Robert Pollak, Michael Riordan, Mario Rizzo, David Sappington, Joseph Sax, Herbert Simon, Chester Spatt, Richard Stewart, David Teece, Lester Telser, Peter Temin, Gordon Winston, and Sidney Winter. I have also benefited from the reactions and advice of students during the past decade, especially those enrolled in a course on the Economics of Organization that I taught in the spring of 1984.

Although I did not realize it until much later, the book began to take shape while *Markets and Hierarchies* was still in galleys (Chapter 13, on franchise bidding, was in preparation at that time). Research during the intervening years benefited from a variety of research support—including grants from the National Science Foundation, a Guggenheim Fellowship, a year at the Center for Advanced Study in the Behavioral Sciences, the Sloan Foundation, and the Japanese Economic Research Foundation—for which I express my appreciation.

Many of the chapters are based on previously published research. They include articles and chapters of mine appearing in the *Journal of Law, Economics and Organization*, Vol. 1, Spring 1985 (Yale University Press, publisher) (Chapter 1); the *Journal of Institutional and Theoretical Economics*, Vol. 140, March 1984 (Chapters 1 and 2); the *Journal of Law and Economics*, Vol. 22, October 1979 (Chapter 3); the *American Journal of Sociology*, Vol. 87, November 1981 (© 1981 by The University of Chicago; all rights reserved; The University of Chicago, publisher), and the *University of Pennsylvania Law Review*, Vol. 127, April 1979 (Chapter 4); *Entrepreneurship* (1983), for which Joshua Ronen was the editor and Lexington Books, publisher (Chapter 5); *Weltwirtschaftliches Archiv*, December 1984 (Chapter 6); the *American Economic Review*, Vol. 73, September 1983 (Chapters 7 and 8); the *Journal of Economic Behavior and Organization*, Vol. 1, March 1980 (Chapter 9); *Firms, Organization and Labor* (1984), Frank Stephen, editor (Chapter 10); the *Journal of Economic Literature*, Vol. 19, December 1981 (Chapter 11); the *Yale Law Journal*, Vol. 88, June 1984, pp. 1183–1200 (reprinted by permission of The Yale Law Journal Company and Fred B. Rothman & Company) (Chapter 12); the *Bell Journal of Economics*, Vol. 7, Spring 1976 (Chapter 13); and *Industrial Organization, Antitrust and Public Policy* (1982), John Craven, editor (Chapter 14). I appreciate the permission of the publishers to elaborate and integrate these materials in this book.

The enterprise had the enthusiastic support of Ann Facciolo and Shelby Sola, who produced early and late versions of the manuscript, respectively. I express my thanks to both.

The involvement of Dolores and our children in the joint venture of which this book is a product defies description. Although each knows that I am enormously grateful, it bears repeating.

OLIVER E. WILLIAMSON

Prologue

Understanding the economic institutions of capitalism poses deep and enduring challenges to law, economics, and organization. The present study draws on and attempts to integrate earlier work of all three kinds. What is herein referred to as transaction cost economics is, by design, an interdisciplinary undertaking.

Contrary to earlier conceptions—where the economic institutions of capitalism are explained by reference to class interests, technology, and/or monopoly power—the transaction cost approach maintains that these institutions have the main purpose and effect of economizing on transaction costs. Legal and economic interpretations that were confidently advanced only ten and twenty years ago have had to be modified. Some have proved to be profoundly incorrect.

As the term suggests, transaction cost economics adopts a microanalytic approach to the study of economic organization. The focus is on transactions and the economizing efforts that attend the organization thereof. A transaction occurs when a good or service is transferred across a technologically separable interface. One stage of activity terminates and another begins. With a well-working interface, as with a well-working machine, these transfers occur smoothly. In mechanical systems we look for frictions: Do the gears mesh, are the parts lubricated, is there needless slippage or other loss of energy? The

1

economic counterpart of friction is transaction cost: Do the parties to the exchange operate harmoniously, or are there frequent misunderstandings and conflicts that lead to delays, breakdowns, and other malfunctions? Transaction cost analysis supplants the usual preoccupation with technology and steady-state production (or distribution) expenses with an examination of the *comparative costs of planning, adapting, and monitoring task completion under alternative governance structures.*

To be sure, complex organizations commonly serve a variety of economic and noneconomic purposes. That is plainly true of the economic institutions of capitalism, which are numerous, subtle, and continuously evolving. My emphasis on transaction cost aspects is not meant to suggest that transaction cost economizing is the only purpose served; but its importance has hitherto been neglected and/or undervalued. An effort to redress that circumstance is arguably warranted. I appeal to and push the logic of transaction cost economizing relentlessly—the object being to deepen our understanding and to develop the refutable implications that this point of view uniquely affords.

This book deals mainly with those aspects of transaction cost economics with which my own research has been concerned during the past decade,[1] but work on those and related matters goes back over fifty years. The decade of the 1930s is remarkable in this respect. Startling insights into the nature of economic organization were recorded in law, in economics, and in the study of organization. But the principal contributions were largely independent, and the unified concerns of the three literatures were not perceived. Partly for that reason, but mainly because neoclassical economics was such a formidable rival, transaction cost economics languished for the next thirty years.

1. Antecedents from the 1930s

1.1 *Economics*

A significant contribution to the study of economic organization that preceded the 1930s was Frank Knight's (1965) classic treatment of *Risk, Uncertainty, and Profit* in 1922. Knight plainly anticipated Percy Bridgeman's counsel to social scientists that ''the principal problem in understanding the actions of

---

[1]This book is a lineal descendant of *Markets and Hierarchies* (1975). Readers are referred to Chapter 1 of the earlier book for a related discussion of the intellectual antecedents to transaction cost economics.

men is to understand how they think—how their minds work" (1955, p. 450). Knight had earlier acknowledged the importance of studying "human nature as we know it" (1965, p. 270) and specifically identified "moral hazard" as an endemic condition with which economic organization must contend (1965, p. 260).[2]

Knight's keen behavioral insights never gained prominence, however. Attention was focused instead on the technical distinction between risk and uncertainty that he had introduced. This is partly explained by the fact that Knight's reference to moral hazard appeared in conjunction with his discussion of insurance, where the term has a well-defined technical meaning. Its more general relevance to the study of economic organization went unnoticed. Had Knight used a nontechnical term, such as "opportunism," that has broad and recognizable significance to social and economic organization quite generally, that result might have been avoided.[3]

Another economist whose deep understanding of economic organization went largely unrecognized except among a small core of institutionalists was John R. Commons. Commons advanced the proposition that the transaction is properly regarded as the basic unit of analysis (1934, pp. 4–8). The study of trading at a much more microanalytic level of analysis was thus indicated. Commons furthermore recognized that economic organization is not merely a response to technological features—economies of scale; economies of scope; other physical or technical aspects—but often has the purpose of harmonizing relations between parties who are otherwise in actual or potential conflict (Commons, 1934, p. 6). The proposition that economic organization has the purpose of promoting the continuity of relationships by devising specialized governance structures, rather than permitting relationships to fracture under the hammer of unassisted market contracting, was thus an insight that could have been gleaned from Commons. But the message made little headway against the prevailing view that the courts were the principal forum for conflict resolution.

Ronald Coase's classic 1937 article expressly posed the issue of eco-

[2]Internal organization sometimes appears as a consequence of this condition but should not be regarded as an organizational panacea. Among the internal problems of the corporation, for example, are "the protection . . . of members and adherents against each other's predatory propensities" (Knight, 1965, p. 254).

[3]Even Coase, whose credentials for studying economic organization are impeccable, mistakenly takes issue with Knight over the efficacy of markets for information. Thus whereas Knight implicitly recognized that internal organization could arise because of problems that attend the purchase and sale of information, Coase held instead: "We can imagine a system where all advice or knowledge was brought as required" (1952, p. 346). This statement disregards the serious hazards of opportunism to which information exchange is peculiarly subject (Arrow, 1971).

nomic organization in comparative institutional terms. Whereas markets were ordinarily regarded as the principal means by which coordination is realized, Coase insisted that firms often supplanted markets in performing these very same functions. Rather than regard the boundaries of firms as technologically determined, Coase proposed that firms and markets be considered alternative means of economic organization (1952, p. 333). Whether transactions were organized within a firm (hierarchically) or between autonomous firms (across a market) was thus a decision variable. Which mode was adopted depended on the transaction costs that attended each.

A crucial dilemma nevertheless remained. Unless the factors responsible for transaction cost differences could be identified, the reasons for organizing some transactions one way and other transactions another would necessarily remain obscure. The persistent failure to operationalize transaction costs was responsible for its tautological reputation (Alchian and Demsetz, 1972, p. 783).[4] Inasmuch as virtually any outcome could be explained by appeal to transaction cost reasoning, recourse to transaction costs gradually acquired "a well-deserved bad name" (Fisher, 1977, p. 322, n. 5). Headway on these matters thus unavoidably awaited operationalization.

1.2 Law

The legal literature to which I have reference deals mainly with contract law, although important labor law contributions have since been made. An especially important contribution is Karl Llewellyn's prescient treatment "What Price Contract?" in 1931. Llewellyn took exception to prevailing contract law doctrine, which emphasized legal rules, and argued that greater attention should be given to the purposes to be served. Less attention to form and more to substance was thus indicated—especially since being legalistic could sometimes stand in the way of getting the job done.[5] A concept of contract as framework was advanced. Llewellyn distinguished between "iron rules" and "yielding rules" (1931, p. 729) and held that

[4]Steven Cheung contends that "Coase's argument is . . . not tautological if one can identify different types of transactions and how they will vary under different circumstances" (1983, p. 4). That is correct. But the fact is that such a discriminating effort was not prescribed by Coase, and such a need went unrecognized until vertical integration was expressly explicated in transaction cost terms (Williamson, 1971). Indeed, full operationalization required additional effort and still continues (Williamson, 1975, 1979a, 1983; Klein, Crawford, and Alchian, 1978; Klein and Leffler, 1981; Masten, 1982; Riordan and Williamson, forthcoming).

[5]As Lon Fuller and William Perdue put it, "In the assessment of damages, the law tends to be conceived, not as a purposive ordering of human affairs, but as a kind of juristic mensuration" (1936, p. 52).

. . . the major importance of legal contract is to provide a framework for well-nigh every type of group organization and for well-nigh every type of passing or permanent relation between individuals and groups . . . —a framework highly adjustable, a framework which almost never accurately indicates real working relations, but which affords a rough indication around which such relations vary, an occasional guide in cases of doubt, and a norm of ultimate appeal when the relations cease in fact to work. [1931, pp. 736–37]

Such a concept of contract as framework is broadly consonant with process analysis of the type favored by Commons, where the study of working rules and continuity of exchange were emphasized. The convenient assumption, in both law and economics, that court ordering was routinely invoked to enforce contract was plainly challenged. The limited contractual role that Llewellyn assigned to litigation is a precursor to the more recent literature on "private ordering" (Galanter, 1981).

1.3 *Organizations*

The 1930s also witnessed the publication of Chester Barnard's important study *The Functions of the Executive* (1938). Whereas organization theorists had previously been preoccupied with creating "principles" of organization—which, it turned out, were often empirically vacuous (March and Simon, 1958, pp. 30–31)—Barnard was concerned instead with the processes of organization. The study of formal organization was emphasized, but not to the exclusion of informal organization. Cooperation was assigned a central place in the theory of organization that Barnard advanced. Express provision was made for tacit or personal knowledge.

Thus although Barnard approved of the extensive study by social scientists of "mores, folkways, political structures, institutions, attitudes, motives, propensities, instincts," he regretted that the study of formal organization had been relatively neglected (1938, p. ix); by formal organization he meant "that kind of cooperation among men that is conscious, deliberate, purposeful" (1938, p. 4). Barnard wanted greater emphasis placed on intended rationality, due allowance having been made for the limits imposed by physical, biological, and social factors (1938, pp. 12–45). What Herbert Simon subsequently referred to as "bounded rationality" (1957) was anticipated.

Effective adaptation was what distinguished successful cooperative systems from failures:

The survival of an organization depends upon the maintenance of an equilibrium of complex character in a continuously fluctuating environment of physical,

> biological, and social materials, elements, and forces which calls for readjust-
> ment of processes internal to the organization. We shall be concerned with the
> nature of the external conditions to which adjustment must be made, but the
> center of our interest is the process by which it is accomplished. [Barnard, 1938,
> p. 6]

Cooperation is jointly determined by social factors and incentive alignments: Inasmuch as the "social benefits [of cooperation] are limited . . . ,
efficiency depends in part on the distributive process in the cooperative system" (1938, p. 58). The study of formal organization needs to make provision, moreover, for the role of informal organization—"formal organizations
are vitalized and conditioned by informal organization . . . ; there cannot be
one without the other" (Barnard, 1938, p. 120). Informal organization facilitates communications, promotes cohesiveness, and serves to protect the personal integrity and self-respect of the individual against the disintegrating
effects of formal organization (1938, p. 122).

Finally, Barnard, in a very prescient passage, made explicit provision for
what Michael Polanyi (1962) later developed in the context of personal
knowledge. As Barnard put it:

> In the common-sense, everyday, practical knowledge necessary to the practice of
> the arts, there is much that is not susceptible of verbal statement—it is a matter of
> know-how. It may be called behavioral knowledge. It is necessary to doing
> things in concrete situations. It is nowhere more indispensable than in the execu-
> tive arts. [1938, p. 291]

Barnard's remarkable discussion of internal organization thus asserts or
develops the following: (1) Organization form—that is, formal organization—matters; (2) informal organization has both instrumental and humaniz-
ing purposes; (3) bounds on rationality are acknowledged; (4) adaptive, sequential decision-making is vital to organizational effectiveness; and (5) tacit
knowledge is important. Albeit lacking in comparative institutional respects—no firm or market comparison, for example, was attempted—a concept of the firm as governance structure was plainly contemplated.

The following propositions had thus been advanced and, in principle,
could have been joined in a concerted study of economic organization as of
1940: (1) Opportunism is a subtle and pervasive condition of human nature
with which the study of economic organization must be actively concerned
(Knight); (2) the transaction is the basic unit of organizational analysis
(Commons); (3) a central purpose of economic organization is to harmonize
exchange relations (Commons; Barnard); (4) the study of contract, broadly
conceived, is the legal counterpart to, and both stands to benefit from and can
help to inform the study of economic organization (Llewellyn); and (5) the

study of internal organization and market organization are not disjunct but are usefully joined within a common transaction cost economizing framework (Coase).

2. The Next Thirty Years

Those were auspicious beginnings. A sound basis for further advances had plainly been laid. The comparative institutional analysis of economic organization did not, however, flourish. Attention was concentrated elsewhere.

The prevailing orientation toward economic organization in the thirty-year hiatus between 1940 and 1970 was that technological features of firm and market organization were determinative. The allocation of economic activity as between firms and markets was taken as a datum; firms were characterized as production functions; markets served as signaling devices; contracting was accomplished through an auctioneer; and disputes were disregarded because of the presumed efficacy of court adjudication. The possibility that subtle economizing purposes are served by organizational variety does not arise within—indeed, is effectively beyond the reach of—this orthodox framework. Correspondingly, the prevailing public policy attitude toward unfamiliar or nonstandard business practices during that interval was deep suspicion and even hostility.

That state of affairs was lamented by Ronald Coase in his 1972 essay on the state of industrial organization. Although his 1937 paper, in which transaction rather than production costs were featured, was much cited, it was little used (Coase, 1972, p. 63). Discontent with exclusive reliance on neoclassical price theory was nevertheless building. Vernon Smith thus boldly declared, only two years later, that orthodoxy was dead and predicted that a new microtheory would arise which "will, and should, deal with the economic foundations of organization and institution, and this will require us to have an economics of information and a more sophisticated treatment of the technology of transacting" (1974, p. 321).[6]

Indeed, the main tradition notwithstanding, not everyone worked within the framework of received microtheory during the interval 1940 to 1970. To the contrary, significant dissents, of which transaction cost economics has been the special beneficiary, were continuing to appear in law, economics, and organization.

[6]Indeed, the seeds of a research response along these lines were already being sown. See Section 2.2 of Chapter 2.

2.1 Economics

Friedrich Hayek resisted the main tradition in his insistence that "the economic problem of society is mainly one of rapid adaptation to changes in particular circumstances of time and place" (1945, p. 524). How easy it is, he observed, "for an inefficient manager to dissipate the differentials on which profitability rests, and that it is possible, with the same technical facilities, to produce with a great variety of costs, are among the commonplaces of business experience which do not seem to be equally familiar in the study of the economist" (Hayek, 1945, p. 523).

Hayek further counseled that the study of adaptive systems will be facilitated not by focusing on statistical aggregates but by recognizing the importance of idiosyncratic knowledge—which, by its nature, cannot be summarized by statistical measures but nevertheless possesses great economic value, in that such knowledge serves as the basis for local adaptive action (Hayek, 1945, p. 523–24). If complexity is deep in the nature of things economic, then that ought to be acknowledged rather than suppressed (Hayek, 1967, chap. 2). An equilibrium approach to economics is thus only preliminary to the study of the main issues (Hayek, 1945, p. 530).

The postwar market failure literature served further to alert economists to the importance of information, its distribution among economic agents, and the difficulties attending its transmission and accurate disclosure.[7] Coase's treatment of social costs (1960) was especially noteworthy. Not only were market failures traced to transaction cost origins, but problems of economic organization were posed in a thoroughly comparative institutional way. The progressive development and refinement of this literature culminated with Kenneth Arrow's observation that "market failure is not absolute; it is better to consider a broader category, that of transaction costs, which in general impede and in particular cases block the formation of markets" (1969, p. 48)—where by transaction costs Arrow had reference to the "costs of running the economic system" (1969, p. 48).

[7]Armen Alchian's important contributions to the economics of property rights are also noteworthy. Nominal ownership analysis gives way to an examination of those who are in effective control of resources. The Berle and Means concern over the separation of ownership from control thus comes under renewed scrutiny in this way (Alchian, 1965). Efforts to curb managerial discretion—whether through the activation of the market for corporate control (Manne, 1965), internal reorganization of the firms so as to effect superior resource allocation (Alchian, 1969), or by other means—are also germane. The study of nonprofits and of socialist firms are usefully included within the property rights perspective (Furubotn and Pejovich, 1974). Steven Cheung's work on property rights (1969, 1983) is illustrative of the continuing vitality of this tradition. Also see Louis DeAlessi (1983).

That microanalytic orientation is reflected in a series of important contributions to the study of economic organization made by Arrow. Like Hayek, he emphasized that the needs of equilibrium and disequilibrium economics differ: "Traditional economic theory stresses the sufficiency of the price system as a source of information, and this is correct enough at equilibrium. In conditions of disequilibrium, [however], a premium is paid for the acquisition of information from sources other than the prices and quantities" to which the firm has direct access (Arrow, 1959, p. 47). Arrow subsequently described firms and markets as alternative instruments for organizing economic activity in his 1963 presidential address to the Institute of Management Sciences. He noted in that connection that the boundary of an organization is commonly defined by the line across which only price-mediated transactions take place, but he observed that the economic content of intraorganizational and price-mediated transactions are often similar (1971, p. 232). A common framework that applies to both is therefore indicated. He furthermore acknowledged that the hierarchical structure of internal organization is a decision variable (1971, pp. 226–27). An assessment of the efficacy of internal organization presumably needs to take this into account. Arrow's treatment of the economics of information disclosed that the "fundamental paradox" of information is traceable to opportunism—"its value for the purchaser is not known until he has the information, but then he has in effect acquired it without cost" (Arrow, 1971, p. 152).[8] Finally, Arrow insisted that the problem of economic organization be located in a larger context in which the integrity of trading parties is expressly considered (1974). The efficacy of alternative modes of contracting will thus vary among cultures because of differences in trust (Arrow, 1969, p. 62).

2.2 The Law and the Evolution of Private Ordering

Noteworthy developments in the law include assessments of the special attributes of collective bargaining contracts by Harry Shulman, Archibald Cox, and Clyde Summers. The relative merits of private ordering in relation to court ordering needed to be assessed in deciding on how to implement the Wagner Act. Shulman urged that the Act be interpreted as a "bare legal framework" within which private ordering between management and labor

[8]But for opportunism, the buyer could rely on the seller to charge him only the true value prior to disclosure, or the seller could depend on the buyer to pay full value upon disclosure. If neither party believes the other, the difficulties of exchange to which Arrow refers develop.

would operate (1955, p. 1000). The grievance and arbitration procedure was thus favored over judicial disposition of disputes because of the corrosive effects on continuing relationships that adversary proceedings encouraged (Shulman, 1955, p. 1024). Cox likewise held that the collective bargaining agreement should be understood as an instrument of governance, which is in the spirit of Commons, as well as an instrument of exchange: "The collective agreement governs complex, many-sided relations between large numbers of people in a going concern for very substantial periods of time" (1958, p. 22). Provision for unforeseeable contingencies is made by writing the contract in general, flexible terms and supplying the parties with a special arbitration machinery. "One simply cannot spell out every detail of life in an industrial establishment, or even of that portion which both management and labor agree is a matter of mutual concern" (Cox, 1958, p. 23).

The technical versus purposive distinction made earlier by Llewellyn was elaborated by Summers, who distinguished between "black letter law" on the one hand and a more circumstantial approach to law on the other. "The epitome of abstraction is the *Restatement,* which illustrates its black letter rules by transactions suspended in midair, creating the illusion that contract rules can be stated without reference to surrounding circumstances and are therefore generally applicable to all contractual transactions" (Summers, 1969, p. 566). Such a conception does not and cannot provide a "framework for integrating rules and principles applicable to all contractual transactions" (Summers, 1969, p. 566). A broader conception of contract, with emphasis on the affirmative purposes of the law and effective governance relations, is needed if that is to be realized. Summers conjectured in this connection that "the principles common to the whole range of contractual transactions are relatively few and of such generality and competing character that they should not be stated as legal rules at all" (1969, p. 527).

Other significant legal contributions include Stewart Macaulay's empirical studies of contract. Macaulay observed that contract execution is normally a much more informal and cooperative venture than legalistic approaches to contracting would suggest. He cited one businessman to the effect that "you can settle any dispute if you keep the lawyers and accountants out of it. They just do not understand the give-and-take needed in business" (1963, p. 61). More generally, Macaulay's studies of contractual practices support the view that contractual disputes and ambiguities are more often settled by private ordering than by appeal to the courts—which is in sharp contrast with the neoclassical presumptions of both law and economics. Transaction costs and comparative institutional analysis were prominently featured in Guido Calabresi's (1970) pathbreaking work on torts.

2.3 *Organization*

Important contributions in organization theory include Herbert Simon's semi-nal explication of the Barnard thesis in *Administrative Behavior* in 1947, Alfred Chandler's remarkable book *Strategy and Structure* (1962), and Michael Polanyi's treatment of *Personal Knowledge* (1962). Simon carries Barnard's rationality analysis forward and develops a more precise vocabu-lary in the process. He traces the central problem of organization to the joining of rational purposes with the cognitive limits of human actors: It "is precisely in the realm where human behavior is *intendedly* rational, but only *limitedly* so, that there is room for a genuine theory of organization and administration" (1957, p. xxiv). Intended rationality is responsible for the observed purposefulness of economic agents and economic organizations. Interesting economic and organizational choices arise only in a limited (or bounded) rationality context.

Simon makes repeated reference to the criterion of efficiency (1957, pp. 14, 39–41, 172–97), but he also cautions that organizational design should be informed by "a knowledge of those aspects of the social sciences which are relevant to the broader purposes of the organization" (1957, p. 246). A sensitivity to subgoal pursuit, wherein individuals identify with and pursue local goals at the possible expense of global goals (Simon, 1957, p. 13), and the "outguessing" or gaming aspects of human behavior (Simon, 1957, p. 252) are among those aspects.

Chandler's 1962 book had its origins in business history rather than organization theory. In many respects his historical account of the origins, diffusion, nature, and importance of the multidivisional form of organization ran ahead of contemporary economic and organization theory. Chandler clear-ly established that organization form had important business performance consequences, which neither economics nor organization theory had done (nor, for the most part, even attempted) before. The mistaken notion that economic efficiency was substantially independent of internal organization was no longer tenable after the book appeared.

Michael Polanyi's treatment of personal knowledge disclosed that to characterize the firm exclusively in technological terms was bankrupt:

> The attempt to analyze scientifically the established industrial arts has every-where led to similar results. Indeed even in the modern industries the indefinable knowledge is still an essential part of technology. I have myself watched in Hungary a new, imported machine for blowing electric lamp bulbs, the exact counterpart of which was operating successfully in Germany, failing for a whole year to produce a single flawless bulb. [Polanyi, 1962, p. 52]

That theme is carried forward in his discussion of craftsmanship. Polanyi observed that "an art which has fallen into disuse for the period of a generation is altogether lost. . . . It is pathetic to watch the endless efforts— equipped with microscopy and chemistry, with mathematics and electronics—to reproduce a single violin of the kind the half-literate Stradivarius turned out as a matter of routine more than 200 years ago" (Polanyi, 1962, p. 53). Idiosyncratic knowledge is likewise important with respect to language:

> To know a language is an art, carried on by tacit judgments and the practice of unspecifiable skills. . . . Spoken communication is the successful application by two persons of the linguistic knowledge and skill acquired by such apprenticeship, one person wishing to transmit, the other to receive, information. Relying on what each has learnt, the speaker confidently utters words and the listener confidently interprets them, while they mutually rely on each other's correct use and understanding of these words. A true communication will take place if, and only if, these combined assumptions of authority and trust are in fact justified. [1962, p. 206]

A coherent theory of economic organization that attempted to draw these several strands together nevertheless remained elusive. Neoclassical economic theories of firm and market organization and the neoclassical legal contracting tradition were left largely unscathed by these nonorthodox treatments. Meanwhile organization theory eschewed further development of the rationality approach in favor of nonrationality and power approaches to the study of organization (Williamson, 1981b, pp. 571–73). The upshot is that Coase's grim assessment of the state of comparative institutional analysis in 1972 was altogether warranted.

3. An Overview

The book successively sets out the rudiments of transaction cost economics, applies the basic arguments to a series of economic institutions over which there has been widespread disagreement or puzzlement, and develops public policy ramifications.

Chapter 1 provides an overview of the transaction cost economics approach to the study of economic organization. The behavioral assumptions on which transaction cost economics relies and the critical dimensions for distinguishing among transactions are developed in Chapter 2. Alternative approaches to the world of contract are described. What I refer to as the "Fundamental Transformation"—whereby a large-numbers condition at the outset (*ex ante* competition) is transformed into a small-numbers condition during contract execution and at contract renewal intervals (*ex post* competition)—

and its pervasive importance for the study of economic organization are developed.

Rather than characterize the firm as a production function, transaction cost economics maintains that the firm is (for many purposes at least) more usefully regarded as a governance structure. A comparative institutional approach to the governance of contractual relations is set out in Chapter 3.

Chapters 4 and 5 deal with vertical integration. Chapter 4 is concerned with theory and policy. Chapter 5 develops the evidence. Vertical integration is not only an important condition in its own right but equally because the transaction cost treatment of the decision to integrate is paradigmatic. Such apparently unrelated phenomena as the employment relation, aspects of regulation, certain nonstandard contracting practices, corporate governance, and even family organization are variations on a theme.

Chapter 6 attempts to fill a serious gap in the literature on economic organization. It examines the incentive and bureaucratic limits of internal organization in the context of the following dilemma: Why can't a large firm do everything a collection of small firms can do and more?

Chapters 7 and 8 deal with the uses of nonstandard contracting to effect credible commitments. Nonstandard contracting—customer and territorial restrictions, tie-ins, block booking, and related restraints—have been the source of much public policy consternation. This follows from the neoclassical view that transactions are properly assigned either to firms or to markets in accordance with some natural (mainly technological) order. Efforts to tamper with this natural order are thus presumed to have anticompetitive purpose and effect. The transaction cost approach discloses that this formulation is simplistic: Many nonstandard or unfamiliar contracting practices serve legitimate transaction cost economizing purposes. Often the parties are engaged in an effort to devise contractual safeguards that promote more efficient exchange. Commercial equivalents of hostages arise in this way.

The organization of work is addressed in Chapter 9. This chapter is partly responsive to the recent Radical Economics literature, which holds that hierarchy lacks redeeming economic purposes but operates entirely in the service of power (Marglin, 1974, 1984; Stone, 1974). This argument succeeds mainly by default: Inasmuch as neoclassical economics is preoccupied with production functions and is silent with respect to hierarchy, the existence—indeed the ubiquity—of hierarchy is presumably explained by other factors, of which power is the leading candidate. Addressing the economics of organization in transaction cost terms discloses that hierarchy also serves efficiency purposes and furthermore permits a variety of predictive statements regarding the organization of work to be advanced.

Chapter 10 deals with efficient labor organization. Unlike the preceding chapter, where the nature of the workers' status was a variable, here it is assumed that an authority relation prevails between workers and managers. The principal issue of interest is what governance structure supports will be crafted in response to job attributes of differing kinds. The ramifications of the argument for union organization are developed.

The modern corporation is the subject of Chapter 11. The transformation of the corporation from its traditional (unitary) form to its modern (multidivisional) form is traced, and the significance is assessed. Subsequent developments—the conglomerate and the multinational corporation—are shown to be extensions of the basic multidivisional structure, the object being to manage diversified product lines in the first instance and to facilitate technology transfer in the second.

Corporate governance issues are considered in Chapter 12. I argue that the board of directors is appropriately regarded as a governance structure response to those with diffuse and otherwise unprotected investments in the corporation. So regarded, it is principally an instrument of the stockholders.

Regulation is examined in Chapter 13. The proposition that franchise bidding can be used to supplant rate of return regulation in natural monopoly industries is disputed. Assessing this in transaction cost terms discloses that the argument goes through in some circumstances but not all. A discriminating approach to the use of franchise bidding is therefore proposed. A focused case study illustrating the contractual problems that beset franchise bidding is set out in an appendix.

Antitrust ramifications of transaction cost economics are summarized in Chapter 14. Transaction cost issues that arise in the context of contracting, merger, and strategic behavior are all addressed. The earlier preoccupation of antitrust with monopoly—to the virtual exclusion of economizing in non-technological forms—is challenged. Circumstances in which troublesome antisocial monopolizing arises are indicated.

The conclusions are set out in Chapter 15. The behavioral assumptions, the main arguments on which transaction cost economics relies, and the principal implications are summarized. The implied research agenda is sketched.

CHAPTER 1

Transaction Cost Economics

Firms, markets, and relational contracting are important economic institutions. They are also the evolutionary product of a fascinating series of organizational innovations. The study of the economic institutions of capitalism has not, however, occupied a position of importance on the social science research agenda.

Partly this neglect is explained by the inherent complexity of those institutions. But complexity can and often does serve as an inducement rather than a deterrent. The primitive state of our knowledge is at least equally explained by a reluctance to admit that the details of organization matter. The widespread conception of the modern corporation as a "black box" is the epitome of the noninstitutional (or pre-microanalytic) research tradition.

Merely to acknowledge that the microanalytic details of organization matter does not, however, suffice. The salient structural features of market, hierarchical, and quasi-market forms of organization need to be identified and linked to economic consequences in a systematic way. Lack of agreement on (or misconceptions regarding) the main purposes served by economic organization has also been an impediment to research progress.

A chapter in some yet unwritten history of economic thought will be needed to sort those matters out. Whatever the eventual explanation, the fact is that the study of economic institutions has witnessed a renaissance. Thus, whereas the study of institutional economics reached a nadir in the immediate postwar period, a renewal of interest in institutions and a reaffirmation of their economic importance can, with the benefit of hindsight, be traced to the early 1960s.[1] Operational content began to appear in the early 1970s.[2] A common characteristic of the new line of research is that the concept of firm as production function is supplanted (or augmented) by the concept of firm as governance structure. Research of the New Institutional Economics kind had reached a critical mass by 1975.[3] The ensuing decade has witnessed exponential growth.

Transaction cost economics is part of the New Institutional Economics research tradition. Although transaction cost economics (and, more generally, the New Institutional Economics) applies to the study of economic organization of all kinds, this book focuses primarily on the economic institutions of capitalism, with special reference to firms, markets, and relational contracting. That focus runs the gamut from discrete market exchange at the one extreme to centralized hierarchical organization at the other, with myriad mixed or intermediate modes filling the range in between. The changing character of economic organization over time—within and between markets and hierarchies—is of particular interest.

Although the remarkable properties of neoclassical markets, where prices serve as sufficient statistics, are widely conceded—as Friedrich Hayek put it, the market is a "marvel" (1945, p. 525)—opinions differ in assessing transactions that are organized within quasi-market and nonmarket modes of organization. At best the administrative apparatus and private ordering sup-

[1]The early contributions include Ronald Coase's reconceptualization of social costs (1960), Armen Alchian's pioneering treatment of property rights (1961), Kenneth Arrow's work on the troublesome economic properties of information (1962, 1963), and Alfred Chandler, Jr.'s contribution to business history (1962).

[2]These include my first efforts to recast the vertical integration problem in transaction cost terms (Williamson, 1971) and efforts to generalize that approach in the context of markets and hierarchies (Williamson, 1973); the treatments by Armen Alchian and Harold Demsetz of the "classical capitalist firm" in terms of team organization (1972) and their related work on property rights (1973); the proposed reformulation of economic history by Lance Davis and Douglass North (1971); the important work by Peter Doeringer and Michael Piore (1971) on labor markets; and Janos Kornai's provocative treatment of disequilibrium economics (1971).

[3]Some of this is described in the first chapter of *Markets and Hierarchies* (1975), which is titled "Toward a New Institutional Economics." The conference on "The Economics of Internal Organization" held at the University of Pennsylvania in 1974 (the papers from which were published in 1975 and 1976 in the *Bell Journal of Economics*) helped to redefine the research agenda. Many of the articles in the *Journal of Economic Behavior and Organization*, which first began publication in 1980, are in the New Institutionalist spirit. For recent commentary and contributions to this literature, see the March 1984 issue of the *Journal of Institutional and Theoretical Economics* and the forthcoming book of readings edited by Louis Putterman and Victor Goldberg.

ports that attend these transactions are messy. Some scholars decline even to deal with them. Others regard the deviations as evidence of a pervasive condition of "market failure." Until very recently the primary economic explanation for nonstandard or unfamiliar business practices was monopoly:[4] "[I]f an economist finds something—a business practice of one sort or another—that he does not understand, he looks for a monopoly explanation" (Coase, 1972, p. 67). That other social scientists should regard these same institutions as antisocial is unsurprising. The enforcement of antitrust from 1945 through 1970 reflected that orientation.

To be sure, a net negative social assessment is sometimes warranted. A more subtle and discriminating understanding of the economic institutions of capitalism has nevertheless been evolving. Many puzzling or anomalous practices have been cast into different relief in the process. This book advances the proposition that the economic institutions of capitalism have the main purpose and effect of economizing on transaction costs.

Main purpose is not, however, to be confused with sole purpose. Complex institutions commonly serve a variety of objectives. This is no less true here. The inordinate weight that I assign to transaction cost economizing is a device by which to redress a condition of previous neglect and undervaluation. An accurate assessment of the economic institutions of capitalism cannot, in my judgment, be reached if the central importance of transaction cost economizing is denied.[5] Greater respect for *organizational* (as against technological) features and for *efficiency* (as against monopoly) purposes is needed. This theme is repeated, with variation, throughout this book.

I submit that the full range of organizational innovations that mark the development of the economic institutions of capitalism over the past 150 years warrant reassessment in transaction cost terms. The proposed approach adopts a contracting orientation and maintains that any issue that can be formulated as a contracting problem can be investigated to advantage in transaction cost economizing terms. Every exchange relation qualifies. Many other issues which at the outset appear to lack a contracting aspect turn out, upon scrutiny, to have an implicit contracting quality. (The cartel problem is an example.) The upshot is that the actual and potential scope of transaction cost economics is very broad.

As compared with other approaches to the study of economic organiza-

---

[4]Important exceptions to this tradition—which, however, were widely ignored—are Lester Telser's (1965) and Lee Preston's (1965) treatments of restrictive trade practices.

[5]A balanced view of the economic institutions of capitalism will await more concerted attention to the sociology of economic organization, which, happily, is in progress. For recent work of this kind, see Harrison White (1981), Martha Feldman and James March (1981), Arthur Stinchcombe (1983), Mark Granovetter (forthcoming), and James Coleman (1982).

tion, transaction cost economics (1) is more microanalytic, (2) is more self-conscious about its behavioral assumptions, (3) introduces and develops the economic importance of asset specificity, (4) relies more on comparative institutional analysis, (5) regards the business firm as a governance structure rather than a production function, and (6) place greater weight on the *ex post* institutions of contract, with special emphasis on private ordering (as compared with court ordering). A large number of additional implications arise upon addressing problems of economic organization in this way. The study of the economic institutions of capitalism, as herein proposed, maintains that the transaction is the basic unit of analysis and insists that organization form matters. The underlying viewpoint that informs the comparative study of issues of economic organization is this: Transaction costs are economized by assigning transactions (which differ in their attributes) to governance structures (the adaptive capacities and associated costs of which differ) in a discriminating way.[6]

Given the complexity of the phenomena under review, transaction cost economics should often be used in addition to, rather than to the exclusion of, alternative approaches. Not every approach is equally instructive, however, and they are sometimes rival rather than complementary.

The nature of transaction costs is developed in section 1. A cognitive map of contract, in which alternative approaches to economic organization are described and with respect to which transaction cost economics is located, is set out in section 2. The relation between behavioral assumptions and alternative conceptions of contract is presented in section 3. A rudimentary contracting schema on which the argument in the book repeatedly relies is developed in section 4. Contractual issues that arise in organizing the company town are examined in section 5. Other applications are sketched in section 6. Concluding remarks follow.

1. Transaction Costs

1.1 *Frictionlessness*

Kenneth Arrow has defined transaction costs as the ''costs of running the economic system'' (1969, p. 48). Such costs are to be distinguished from production costs, which is the cost category with which neoclassical analysis

---

[6]Indeed, transaction cost economizing is central to the study of economic organization quite generally—in capitalist and noncapitalist economies alike.

has been preoccupied. Transaction costs are the economic equivalent of friction in physical systems. The manifold successes of physics in ascertaining the attributes of complex systems by assuming the absence of friction scarcely require recounting here. Such a strategy has had obvious appeal to the social sciences. Unsurprisingly, the absence of friction in physical systems is cited to illustrate the analytic power associated with "unrealistic" assumptions (Friedman, 1953, pp. 16–19).

But whereas physicists were quickly reminded by their laboratory instruments and the world around them that friction was pervasive and often needed to be taken expressly into account, economists did not have a corresponding appreciation for the costs of running the economic system. There is, for example, no reference whatsoever to transaction costs, much less to transaction costs as the economic counterpart of friction, in Milton Friedman's famous methodological essay (1953) or in other postwar treatments of positive economics.[7] Thus although positive economics admitted that frictions were important in principle, it had no language to describe frictions in fact.[8]

The neglect of transaction costs had numerous ramifications, not the least of which was the way in which nonstandard modes of economic organization were interpreted. Until express provision for transaction costs was made, the possibility that nonstandard modes of organization—customer and territorial restrictions, tie-ins, block booking, franchising, vertical integration, and the like—operate in the service of transaction cost economizing was little appreciated. Instead, most economists invoked monopoly explanations—be it of the leverage, price discrimination, or entry barriers kinds—when confronted with nonstandard contracting practices (Coase, 1972, p. 67). Donald Turner's views are representative: "I approach customer and territorial restrictions not hospitably in the common law tradition, but inhospitably in the tradition of antitrust."[9] As discussed below, the research agenda and public policy toward business were massively influenced by that monopoly predisposition. The prevailing view of the firm as production function was centrally implicated in that situation.

---

[7]Herbert Simon's treatments of decision-making in economics focus mainly on individual rather than institutional features of economic organization (1959; 1962).

[8]To be sure, the market failure literature was concerned with many of the relevant issues. But it rarely posed the issues in transaction cost terms. Arrow's remarks are thus prescient: "I contend that market failure is a more general category than externality. . . . [Moreover], market failure is not absolute; it is better to consider a broader category, that of transaction costs, which in general impede and in particular cases completely block the formation of markets" (1969, p. 48).

[9]The quotation is attributed to Turner by Stanley Robinson, 1968, N.Y. State Bar Association, Antitrust Symposium, p. 29.

1.2 *Explication*

Transaction cost economics poses the problem of economic organization as a problem of contracting. A particular task is to be accomplished. It can be organized in any of several alternative ways. Explicit or implicit contract and support apparatus are associated with each. What are the costs?

Transaction costs of *ex ante* and *ex post* types are usefully distinguished. The first are the costs of drafting, negotiating, and safeguarding an agreement. This can be done with a great deal of care, in which case a complex document is drafted in which numerous contingencies are recognized, and appropriate adaptations by the parties are stipulated and agreed to in advance. Or the document can be very incomplete, the gaps to be filled in by the parties as the contingencies arise. Rather, therefore, than contemplate all conceivable bridge crossings in advance, which is a very ambitious undertaking, only actual bridge-crossing choices are addressed as events unfold.

Safeguards can take several forms, the most obvious of which is common ownership. Faced with the prospect that autonomous traders will experience contracting difficulties, the parties may substitute internal organization for the market. This is not, to be sure, without problems of its own (see Chapter 6). Moreover, *ex ante* interfirm safeguards can sometimes be fashioned to signal credible commitments and restore integrity to transactions. The study of "nonstandard" contracting is centrally concerned with such matters.

Most studies of exchange assume that efficacious rules of law regarding contract disputes are in place and are applied by the courts in an informed, sophisticated, and low-cost way. Those assumptions are convenient, in that lawyers and economists are relieved of the need to examine the variety of ways by which individual parties to an exchange "contract out of or away from" the governance structures of the state by devising private orderings. Thus arises a division of effort whereby economists are preoccupied with the economic benefits that accrue to specialization and exchange, while legal specialists focus on the technicalities of contract law.

The "legal centralism" tradition reflects the latter orientation. It maintains that "disputes require 'access' to a forum external to the original social setting of the dispute [and that] remedies will be provided as prescribed in some body of authoritative learning and dispensed by experts who operate under the auspices of the state" (Galanter, 1981, p. 1). The facts, however, disclose otherwise. Most disputes, including many that under current rules could be brought to a court, are resolved by avoidance, self-help, and the like (Galanter, 1981, p. 2).

The unreality of the assumptions of legal centralism can be defended by reference to the fruitfulness of the pure exchange model. That is not disputed here. My concern is that the law and economics of private ordering have been pushed into the background as a consequence. That is unfortunate, since in "many instances the participants can devise more satisfactory solutions to their disputes than can professionals constrained to apply general rules on the basis of limited knowledge of the dispute" (Galanter, 1981, p. 4).[10]

The issues here are akin to those that were of concern to Karl Llewellyn in his discussion of contract in 1931 but have been systematically evaded since.[11] But for the limitations of legal centralism, the *ex post* side of contract can be disregarded. Given the very real limitations, however, with which court ordering is beset, the *ex post* costs of contract unavoidably intrude. Transaction cost economics insists that contracting costs of all kinds be accorded parity.

Ex post costs of contracting take several forms. These include (1) the maladaption costs incurred when transactions drift out of alignment in relation to what Masahiko Aoki refers to as the "shifting contract curve" (1983),[12] (2) the haggling costs incurred if bilateral efforts are made to correct *ex post* misalignments, (3) the setup and running costs associated with the governance structures (often not the courts) to which disputes are referred, and (4) the bonding costs of effecting secure commitments.

Thus suppose that the contract stipulates x but, with the benefit of hindsight (or in the fullness of knowledge), the parties discern that they should have done y. Getting from x to y, however, may not be easy. The manner in which the associated benefits are divided is apt to give rise to intensive, self-interested bargaining. Complex, strategic behavior may be elicited. Referring the dispute to another forum may help, but that will vary with the circumstances. An incomplete adaptation will be realized if, as a consequence of efforts of both kinds, the parties move not to y but to y'.

A complicating factor in all of this is that the *ex ante* and *ex post* costs of contract are interdependent. Put differently, they must be addressed simultaneously rather than sequentially. Also, costs of both types are often difficult

[10]Marc Galanter elaborates as follows: "The variability of preferences and of situations, compared to the small number of things that can be taken into account by formal rules . . . and the loss of meaning in transforming the dispute into professional categories suggest limits on the desirability of conforming outcomes to authoritative rules" (1981, p. 4).

[11]See "Prologue," Section 1.2.

[12]The *ex post* transaction costs are related to, but plainly differ from, what Michael Jensen and William Meckling refer to as agency costs, which they define as the sum of "(1) the monitoring expenditures of the principal, (2) the bonding expenditures by the agent, and (3) the residual loss" (1976, p. 308)—this last being a very expansive category.

to quantify. The difficulty, however, is mitigated by the fact that transaction costs are always assessed in a comparative institutional way, in which one mode of contracting is compared with another. Accordingly, it is the difference between rather than the absolute magnitude of transaction costs that matters. As Herbert Simon has observed, the comparison of discrete structural alternatives can employ rather primitive apparatus—''such analyses can often be carried out without elaborate mathematical apparatus or marginal calculation. In general, much cruder and simpler arguments will suffice to demonstrate an inequality between two quantities than are required to show the conditions under which these quantities are equated at the margin'' (1978, p. 6). Empirical research on transaction cost matters almost never attempts to measure such costs directly. Instead, the question is whether organizational relations (contracting practices; governance structures) line up with the attributes of transactions as predicted by transaction cost reasoning or not.

1.3 The Larger Context

This book concentrates on transaction cost economizing, but the costs need to be located in the larger context of which they are a part. Among the relevant factors—to which I sometimes (but not continuously) refer—are the following:

1. Holding the nature of the good or service to be delivered constant, economizing takes place with reference to the sum of production and transaction costs, whence tradeoffs in this respect must be recognized.
2. More generally, the design of the good or service to be delivered is a decision variable that influences demand as well as costs of both kinds, whence design is appropriately made a part of the calculus.
3. The social context in which transactions are embedded—the customs, mores, habits, and so on—have a bearing, and therefore need to be taken into account, when moving from one culture to another.[13]
4. The argument relies in a general, background way on the efficacy of competition to perform a sort between more and less efficient modes and to shift resources in favor of the former. This seems plausible, especially if the relevant outcomes are those which appear over inter-

---

[13]See Mark Granovetter (1983) for a discussion of the importance of embeddedness. Also see Douglass North (1981).

vals of five and ten years rather than in the very near term.[14] This intuition would nevertheless benefit from a more fully developed theory of the selection process. Transaction cost arguments are thus open to some of the same objections that evolutionary economists have made of orthodoxy (Nelson and Winter, 1982, pp. 356–70), though in other respects there are strong complementarities (pp. 34–38).

5. Whenever private and social benefits and costs differ, the social cost calculus should govern if prescriptive treatments are attempted.

2. A Cognitive Map of Contract

The field of specialization with which transaction cost economics is most closely associated is industrial organization. A number of the leading approaches to the study of industrial organization and the relation that transaction cost economics bears to them are examined here.

Industrial organization examines contract in terms of the purposes served. What are the parties trying to accomplish? Here as elsewhere in industrial organization, monopoly and efficiency purposes are usefully distinguished. The cognitive map shown in Figure 1–1 begins with this distinction.

2.1 The Monopoly Branch

All of the approaches to contract shown in Figure 1–1, monopoly and efficiency alike, are concerned with the same puzzle: What purposes are served by supplanting classical market exchange—whereby product is sold at a uniform price to all comers without restriction—by more complex forms of contracting (including nonmarket modes of economic organization)? The monopoly approaches ascribe departures from the classical norm to monopoly purpose. The efficiency approaches hold that the departures serve economizing purposes instead.

---

[14]This intuition is akin to that expressed by Michael Spence in his conjecture that entry barrier arguments give way to contestable markets in the long run (1983, p. 988). Although the long run for Spence probably exceeds five or ten years, some of the evolutionary phenomena of interest to me also span half a century. One way of putting it is that I subscribe to weak-form rather than strong-form selection, the distinction being that "in a relative sense, the *fitter* survive, but there is no reason to suppose that they are *fittest* in any absolute sense" (Simon, 1983, p. 69; emphasis in original).

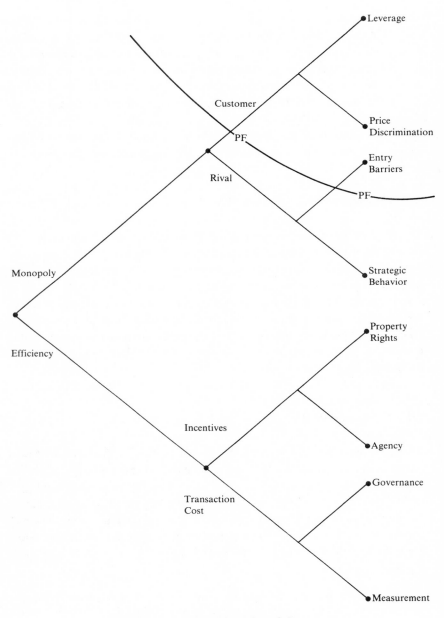

FIGURE 1–1. Cognitive Map of Contract

The four monopoly approaches to contract are grouped under two headings. The first examines the uses of customer and territorial restrictions, resale price maintenance, exclusive dealing, vertical integration, and the like in relation to buyers. The second is concerned with the impact of such practices on rivals.

The "leverage" theory of contract and the price discrimination interpretation of nonstandard contracting both focus on buyers. Richard Posner (1979) associates leverage theory with the (earlier) "Harvard School" approach and price discrimination with the "Chicago School" approach to antitrust economics. Leverage theory maintains that original monopoly power can be extended and that nonstandard contracting practices accomplish this. Although leverage theory is largely discredited among economists,[15] it maintains an appeal to many lawyers and continues to find its way into legal briefs[16] and court opinions.[17]

The price discrimination approach to nonstandard contracting maintains that original monopoly power is unchanged. Price discrimination is merely a means by which latent monopoly power is actualized. This interpretation of nonstandard contracting has been advanced by Aaron Director and Edward Levi (1956) in conjunction with tie-in sales and by George Stigler (1963) in relation to block booking. Tie-in sales and block booking are purportedly devices by which sellers are able to discover underlying product valuation differences among consumers and to monetize consumers' surplus.

The other two monopoly approaches examine nonstandard contracting practices in relation to rivals. They are expressly concerned with the enlargement of monopoly power by large established firms in relation to smaller actual or potential rivals. The barriers to entry literature, which is prominently associated with the work of Joe Bain (1956), is in that tradition. The early work in the area has come under considerable criticism, much of it originating

---

[15]The "main" leverage argument applies to the sale of complementary goods in the downstream market. Chicago maintains that tieing in these circumstances cannot extend monopoly power but merely represents an effort to effect price discrimination: "absent price discrimination, a monopolist will obtain no additional monopoly profits from monopolizing a complementary product" (Posner, 1976, p. 173). This assessment is widely conceded. Timothy Brennan and Sheldon Kimmel have since examined the special but interesting case where the tie occurs not in the downstream but in the upstream market. They show that a tie here can effect a monopoly in the second market if "economies of scope or demand conditions . . . [are] such that the producers cannot sell the second good profitably unless they sell the first good to the monopolist as well" (1983, p. 21).

[16]See, for example, the *amicus* brief prepared by Lawrence A. Sullivan in support of the respondent in *Monsanto Company* v. *Spray-Rite Service Corporation*.

[17]Although the majority opinion in *Jefferson Parish Hosp. Dist. No. 2* v. *Hyde* (44CCH S. Ct. Bull., P.) reaches the correct result, it also muddies the opinion by passing reference to leverage theory.

with the Chicago School. The main problems with the early work are that it was static and did not carefully identify the essential preconditions for entry barrier arguments to go through. The more recent literature on strategic behavior relieves many of the objections.[18] Investment and information asymmetries are expressly introduced. Intertemporal attributes are recognized; and reputation effect features are developed. The use of nonstandard contracting as a means of "raising rivals' costs" (Salop and Scheffman, 1983) is an especially intriguing possibility.

The recent strategic behavior literature excepted, all the monopoly approaches to contract work within the neoclassical framework, where the firm is regarded as a production function. Inasmuch as *the natural boundaries of the firm are therein defined by technology, any effort by the firm to extend its reach* by recourse to nonstandard contracting was presumed to have monopoly purpose and effect.[19] This "applied price theory" approach to industrial organization was the prevailing postwar orientation. As Coase observed (1972, p. 61), it informed both of the leading industrial organization texts—the one by Joe Bain (1958); the other by George Stigler (1968). The inhospitality approach to antitrust law enforcement, to which I referred in 1.1, was similarly oriented. Much of the strategic behavior literature, by contrast, is more closely associated with the governance structure conception of the enterprise (see Chapter 14). So as to highlight this important monopoly distinction, the dashed curve (denoted PF) in Figure 1–1 separates the earlier production function approaches from the more recent strategic conception of contract.

2.2 The Efficiency Branch

Most of what I refer to as the New Institutional Economics is located on the efficiency branch of contract. The efficiency branch of contract distinguishes between those approaches in which incentive alignments are emphasized and those which feature economies of transaction costs. The incentive alignment literature focuses on the *ex ante* side of contract. New forms of property rights and complex contracting are thus interpreted as efforts to overcome the incentive deficiencies of simpler property rights and contracting traditions. Ronald Coase (1960), Armen Alchian (1961; 1965), and Harold Demsetz (1967;

[18]See Chapter 14.

[19]To be sure, it can be argued that price discrimination is efficient, which it ordinarily is if it can be effected at zero transaction cost and if income distribution effects wash out. The zero transaction cost assumption is rarely warranted, however. Private and social valuations of price discrimination can yield contradictory results for this reason (Williamson, 1975, pp. 11–13).

1969) are prominently associated with the property rights literature.[20] Leonid Hurwicz (1972; 1973), Michael Spence and Richard Zeckhauser (1971), Stephen Ross (1973), Michael Jensen and William Meckling (1976), and James Mirrlees (1976) opened up the agency approach.[21]

The property rights literature emphasizes that *ownership matters,* where the rights of ownership of an asset take three parts: the right to use the asset, the right to appropriate returns from the asset, and the right to change the form and/or substance of an asset (Furubotn and Pejovich, 1974, p. 4). Upon getting the property rights straight, it is commonly assumed (often implicitly; sometimes explicitly) that asset utilization will thereafter track the purposes of its owners. This will obtain if (1) the legally sanctioned structure of property rights is respected and (2) human agents discharge their jobs in accordance with instructions.[22]

Thus, whereas the monopoly branch of contract interprets nonstandard forms of exchange as having monopoly purpose and effect, the property rights literature would inquire whether mistaken property rights assignments were responsible for resource misallocations. Redescribing property rights, possibly in complex (nonstandard) ways, is what explains contractual irregularities. Put differently, discrete market contracting is supplanted by more complex forms of contracting, because that is the way residual rights to control can be placed in the hands of those who can use those rights most productively.

The agency literature, particularly the early agency literature, emphasizes that principals contract in full awareness of the hazards that contract execution by agents poses. Thus although the separation of ownership from control attenuates profit incentives, that is anticipated at the time separation occurs and is fully reflected in the price of new shares (Jensen and Meckling, 1976). The future therefore holds no surprises; all of the relevant contracting action is packed into *ex ante* incentive alignments.

Actually, as Michael Jensen's influential survey points out (1983), the agency literature has developed in two parts. He refers to the one branch as the positive theory of agency. Here, "capital intensity, degree of specializa-

[20]For recent survey, see Louis De Alessi (1983). For an earlier survey, see Eirik Furubotn and Steve Pejovich (1974).

[21]For a recent survey, see Stanley Baiman (1982).

[22]The recent treatment of vertical integration by Sanford Grossman and Oliver Hart illustrates both of these propositions. Thus they view asset ownership as control over residual rights: "Each asset will have a single owner and that owner has the right to control the asset in the case of a missing [contractual] provision" (1984, p. 7). They further contend that the owner of physical assets "can order plant employees" to utilize these assets in accordance with his directions (1984, p. 17). Differences between market organization and vertical integration are thus entirely attributed to the asset ownership differences that distinguish them.

tion of assets, information costs, capital markets, and internal and external labor markets are examples of factors in the contracting environment that interact with the costs of various monitoring and bonding practices to determine the contractual forms" (Jensen, 1983, pp. 334–35). The positive branch repeatedly asserts that natural selection processes are reliably efficacious (Fama, 1980; Jensen, 1983, p. 331; Fama and Jensen, 1983, pp. 301, 327)—Armen Alchian's classic but highly nuanced and very cautious statement of the evolutionary approach to economics (1950) being cited as the main authority.

Jensen refers to the second type of agency literature as that of "principal–agent" (1983, p. 334). This relatively mathematical literature features *ex ante* incentive alignments in superlative degree. It has come to be known more recently as the mechanism design approach. This line of research is akin to the earlier contingent claims contracting literature[23] but moves beyond it by admitting contracting complications in the form of private information. Complex problems of incentive alignment are posed (which the contingent claims contracting literature had ignored) if full and candid disclosure of private information cannot be assumed. In other respects, however, the mechanism design and contingent claims contracting literatures are very similar: Both resolve all the relevant contracting issues in a comprehensive *ex ante* bargain;[24] and both assume that court ordering is efficacious.[25] Again, efficiency rather than monopoly purposes drive the argument.

The transaction cost literature also maintains the rebuttable presumption that nonstandard forms of contracting have efficiency purposes. Greater attention is shifted, however, to the contract execution stage. As shown in Figure

[23]Mervyn King characterizes the Arrow-Debreu model as follows:

. . . commodities are distinguished not only by physical and spatial characteristics, and by the date at which the commodity is made available, but also by the "state of the world" in which it is delivered. A "state of the world" is defined by assigning values to all the uncertain variables which are relevant to the economy . . . and comprises a complete list of all these variables. These states of the world are mutually exclusive, and together form an exhaustive set. . . . Commodities are now defined as contingent on the occurrence of certain events, and the market system comprises markets in all these contingent commodities. [1977, p. 128]

[24]The mechanism design literature assumes that the parties to a contract have the cognitive competence to craft contracts of unrestricted complexity. In the language of Chapter 2, the parties to a contract have unbounded rationality; see Bengt Holmstrom (1984). By contrast with the property rights literature, the mechanism design approach holds that "since each party's obligation to the other is completely specified for every state of nature, there are no residual rights of control over assets to be allocated" (Grossman and Hart, 1984, p. 7). Complex contracts are therefore not concerned with residual rights but with getting the obligations defined at the outset—due provision for private information having been acknowledged.

[25]See Baiman (1982, p. 168).

1–1, the transaction cost approach is split into a governance branch and a measurement branch. Of the two, this book places greater emphasis on the former. Both, however, are important and in fact are interdependent.

In common with the property rights literature, transaction cost economics agrees that ownership matters. It furthermore acknowledges that *ex ante* incentive alignments matter. But whereas the property rights and mechanism design approaches work within the tradition of legal centralism, transaction cost economics disputes that court ordering is efficacious. Attention is shifted instead to private ordering. What institutions are created with what adaptive, sequential decision-making and dispute settlement properties? To ownership and incentive alignment, therefore, transaction cost economics adds the proposition that the *ex post* support *institutions* of contract *matter*.

James Buchanan has argued that "economics comes closer to being a 'science of contract' than a 'science of choice' [on which account] the maximizer must be replaced by the arbitrator, the outsider who tries to work out compromises among conflicting claims" (1975, p. 229). The governance approach adopts the science of contract orientation but joins the arbitrator with an institutional design specialist. The object is not merely to resolve conflict in progress but also to recognize potential conflict in advance and devise governance structures that forestall or attenuate it.

Transaction cost economics maintains that it is impossible to concentrate all of the relevant bargaining action at the *ex ante* contracting stage. Instead, *bargaining is pervasive*—on which account the institutions of private ordering and the study of contracting in its entirety take on critical economic significance. The behavioral attributes of human agents, whereby conditions of bounded rationality and opportunism are joined, and the complex attributes of transactions (with special reference to the condition of asset specificity) are responsible for that condition.

The measurement branch of transaction cost economics is concerned with performance or attribute ambiguities that are associated with the supply of a good or service. The Alchian–Demsetz (1972) treatment of technological nonseparabilities (team organization) is an example. The issues have since been addressed by William Ouchi (1980b) in the context of work organization and Yoram Barzel (1982) with respect to the organization of markets. A recent interesting application is the study by Roy Kenney and Benjamin Klein (1983) of what they refer to as "oversearching." They take exception with Stigler's view that block booking has monopoly (price discrimination) purposes and argue instead that it serves to economize on measurement costs.

As indicated, this book deals mainly with the governance branch of transaction cost economics. Measurement aspects are also treated, however— as indeed they must be, as governance and measurement are interdependent.

3. The World of Contract

The world of contract is variously described as one of (1) planning, (2) promise, (3) competition, and (4) governance (or private ordering). Which of these descriptions is most applicable depends on the behavioral assumptions that pertain to an exchange and on the economic attributes of the good or service in question.

As developed more fully in Chapter 2, the study of economic organization turns critically on two behavioral assumptions. What cognitive competencies and what self-interest seeking propensities are ascribed to the human agents engaged in exchange? Transaction cost economics assumes that human agents are subject to bounded rationality, whence behavior is "*intendedly* rational, but only *limitedly* so" (Simon, 1961, p. xxiv), and are given to opportunism, which is a condition of self-interest seeking with guile. Transaction cost economics further maintains that the most critical dimension for describing transactions is the condition of asset specificity. Parties engaged in a trade that is supported by nontrivial investments in transaction-specific assets are effectively operating in a bilateral trading relation with one another. Harmonizing the contractual interface that joins the parties, thereby to effect adaptability and promote continuity, becomes the source of real economic value.

But for uncertainty, problems of economic organization are relatively uninteresting. Assume, therefore, that uncertainty is present in nontrivial degree and consider the ramifications for contract of differences in bounded rationality, opportunism, and asset specificity. Assume, in particular, that each of these conditions can take on either of two values: Either it is present in significant degree (denoted +) or it is presumed to be absent (denoted 0). Consider the three cases in which only one of these factors is presumed to be absent and then that in which all three are joined. Table 1–1 shows the four conditions to be compared and the contracting model that is associated with each.

The case where parties are opportunistic and assets are specific but economic agents have unrestricted cognitive competence essentially describes the mechanism design literature (Hurwicz, 1972; 1973; Meyerson, 1979; Harris and Townsend, 1981). Although the condition of opportunism requires that contracts be written in such a way as to respect private information, whence complex incentive alignment issues are posed, all the relevant issues of contract are settled at the *ex ante* bargaining stage. Given unbounded rationality, a comprehensive bargain is struck at the outset, according to which appropriate adaptations to subsequent (publicly observable) contingent

Table 1-1. Attributes of the Contracting Process

Behavioral Assumption		Asset Specificity	Implied Contracting Process
Bounded Rationality	Opportunism		
0	+	+	Planning
+	0	+	Promise
+	+	0	Competition
+	+	+	Governance

events are fully described. Contract execution problems thus never arise (or defection from such agreements is deterred because court adjudication of all disputes is assumed to be efficacious (Baiman, 1982, p. 168)). Contract, in the context of unbounded rationality, is therefore described as a world of planning.

Consider alternatively the situation where agents are subject to bounded rationality and transactions are supported by specific assets, but the condition of opportunism is assumed to be absent, which implies that the word of an agent is as good as his bond. Although gaps will appear in these contracts, because of bounded rationality, they do not pose execution hazards if the parties take recourse to a self-enforcing general clause. Each party to the contract simply pledges at the outset to execute the contract efficiently (in a joint profit maximizing manner) and to seek only fair returns at contract renewal intervals. Strategic behavior is thereby denied. Parties to a contract thus extract all such advantages as their endowments entitle them to when the initial bargain is struck. Thereafter contract execution goes efficiently to completion because promises of the above-described kind are, in the absence of opportunism, self-enforcing. Contract, in this context, reduces to a world of promise.

Consider, then, the situation where agents are subject to bounded rationality and are given to opportunism, but asset specificity is presumed to be absent. Parties to such contracts have no continuing interests in the identity of one another. This describes the world where discrete market contracting is efficacious, where markets are fully contestable,[26] and where franchise bid-

---

[26]Differences between transaction cost economics and "contestability theory" (Baumol, Panzer, and Willig, 1982) in asset-specificity respects are noteworthy. Both approaches to the study of economic organization acknowledge the importance of asset specificity, but they view it from opposite ends of the telescope. Thus contestability theory reduces asset specificity to insignificance, so that hit-and-run entry is easy. Transaction cost economics, by contrast, magnifies the condition of asset specificity. The existence of durable, firm specific assets is held to be widespread, and accordingly hit-and-run entry is often infeasible.

ding for natural monopoly goes through. Inasmuch as fraud and egregious contract deceits are deterred by court ordering,[27] contract, in this context, is described by a world of competition.

Each of the three devices fails when bounded rationality, opportunism, and asset specificity are joined. Planning is necessarily incomplete (because of bounded rationality), promise predictably breaks down (because of opportunism), and the pairwise identity of the parties now matters (because of asset specificity). This is the world of governance. Since the efficacy of court ordering is problematic, contract execution falls heavily on the institutions of private ordering. This is the world with which transaction cost economics is concerned. The organizational imperative that emerges in such circumstances is this: *Organize transactions so as to economize on bounded rationality while simultaneously safeguarding them against the hazards of opportunism.* Such a statement supports a different and larger conception of the economic problem than does the imperative "Maximize profits!"

4. A Simple Contracting Schema

Assume that a good or service can be supplied by either of two alternative technologies. One is a general purpose technology, the other a special purpose technology. The special purpose technology requires greater investment in transaction-specific durable assets and is more efficient for servicing steady-state demands.

Using k as a measure of transaction-specific assets, transactions that use the general purpose technology are ones for which $k = 0$. When transactions use the special purpose technology, by contrast, a $k > 0$ condition exists. Assets here are specialized to the particular needs of the parties. Productive values would therefore be sacrificed if transactions of this kind were to be prematurely terminated. The bilateral monopoly condition described above and elaborated in Chapter 2 applies to such transactions.

Whereas classical market contracting—"sharp in by clear agreement; sharp out by clear performance" (Macneil, 1974, p. 738)—suffices for transactions of the $k = 0$ kind, unassisted market governance poses hazards whenever nontrivial transaction-specific assets are placed at risk. Parties have an incentive to devise safeguards to protect investments in transactions of the latter kind. Let s denote the magnitude of any such safeguards. An $s = 0$ condition is one in which no safeguards are provided; a decision to provide safeguards is reflected by an $s > 0$ result.

[27]The assumption that court ordering is efficacious in a regime of bounded rationality and opportunism is plainly gratuitous, but it is the maintained assumption nonetheless.

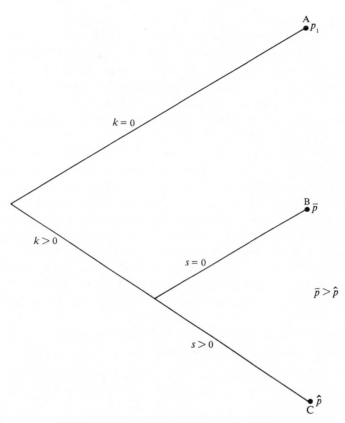

FIGURE 1–2. A Simple Contracting Schema

Figure 1–2 displays the three contracting outcomes corresponding to such a description. Associated with each node is a price. So as to facilitate comparison between nodes, assume that suppliers (1) are risk neutral, (2) are prepared to supply under either technology, and (3) will accept any safeguard condition whatsoever so long as an expected breakeven result can be projected. Thus node A is the general purpose technology ($k = 0$) supply relation for which a breakeven price of p_1 is projected. The node B contract is supported by transaction-specific assets ($k > 0$) for which no safeguard is offered ($s = 0$). The expected breakeven price here is $\bar{p}$. The node C contract also employs the special purpose technology. But since the buyer at this node provides the supplier with a safeguard, ($s > 0$), the breakeven price, $\hat{p}$, at node C is less than $\bar{p}$.

The protective safeguards to which I refer normally take on one or more of three forms. The first is to realign incentives, which commonly involves some type of severance payment or penalty for premature termination. A second is to create and employ a specialized governance structure to which to refer and resolve disputes. The use of arbitration, rather than litigation in the courts, is thus characteristic of node C governance. A third is to introduce trading regularities that support and signal continuity intentions. Expanding a trading relation from unilateral to bilateral exchange—through the concerted use, for example, of reciprocity—thereby to effect an equilibration of trading hazards is an example of that last.

This simple contracting schema, which will subsequently be elaborated, applies to a wide variety of contracting issues. It facilitates comparative institutional analysis by emphasizing that technology (k), contractual governance/safeguards (s) and price (p) are fully interactive and are determined simultaneously. Repeated reference to the schema will be made throughout the book. Indeed, it is gratifying that so many applications turn out to be variations on a theme. As Hayek observed, "whenever the capacity of recognizing an abstract rule which the arrangement of these attributes follows has been acquired in one field, the same master mould will apply when the signs for those abstract attributes are evoked by altogether different elements" (1967, p. 50).[28]

By way of summary, the nodes A, B, and C in the contractual schema set out in Figure 1–2 have the following properties:

1. Transactions that are efficiently supported by general purpose assets ($k = 0$) are located at node A and do not need protective governance structures. Discrete market contracting suffices. The world of competition obtains.
2. Transactions that involve significant investments of a transaction-specific kind ($k > 0$) are ones for which the parties are effectively engaged in bilateral trade.
3. Transactions located at node B enjoy no safeguards ($s = 0$), on which account the projected breakeven supply price is great ($\bar{p} > \hat{p}$). Such transactions are apt to be unstable contractually. They may revert to node A (in which event the special purpose technology would be replaced by the general purpose ($k = 0$) technology) or be relocated to node C (by introducing contractual safeguards that would encourage the continued use of the $k > 0$ technology).

[28]Although I was aware that the contractual approach to vertical integration on which I was working in 1971 would have other applications (including labor market organization and regulation), little did I imagine that nonstandard modes of contracting and corporate governance would also yield to the same type of analysis upon restating the issues in contracting terms.

4. Transactions located at node C incorporate safeguards ($s > 0$) and thus are protected against expropriation hazards.
5. Inasmuch as price and governance are linked, parties to a contract should not expect to have their cake (low price) and eat it too (no safeguard). More generally, it is important to study *contracting in its entirety*. Both the *ex ante* terms and the manner in which contracts are thereafter executed vary with the investment characteristics and the associated governance structures within which transactions are embedded.

5. Economic Organization of the Company Town

The company town is mainly regarded as a painful reminder of labor abuses associated with an earlier era. Surely there is nothing favorable, much less redeeming, that can be said about such a condition.

Still, company towns were the exception rather than the rule. The question, moreover, needs to be asked, why would anyone accept employment under patently unfavorable terms? More generally, what are the relevant contractual alternatives for which a comparative assessment is needed? Inasmuch as the study of extreme instances often helps to illuminate the essentials of a situation (Behavioral Sciences Subpanel, 1962, p. 5), an examination of the problems of organization faced by the company town may be instructive.

The issues are addressed in two stages. The first illustrates the advantages and the second the limitations of studying economic organization from the standpoint of "contracting in its entirety."

5.1 Contract Analysis

Assume the following: (1) A remote mineral source has been located, the mining of which is deemed to be economical; (2) the mineral can be mined only upon making significant investments in durable physical assets that are thereafter nonredeployable; (3) requisite labor skills are not firm-specific to any significant degree, but there are set-up costs associated with labor relocation; (4) the weather in the region is severe, which necessitates the provision of durable housing for protection from the elements; (5) the community of miners is too small to support more than one general store; and (6) the nearest city is forty miles away.

I wish to focus on two issues: Should the workers or the mining firm own the homes in the community? And how should the general store be owned and operated? So as to display the relevant features more clearly, two different mobility scenarios will be considered.

a. THE IMMOBILE SOCIETY

This is the pre-automobile era. The firm advertises for workers and describes the terms of employment. Given the remote location, workers will be concerned not merely with wages but also with housing and with the economic infrastructure.

Were the firm to decide to construct housing itself, it could then (1) sell the homes to the workers, (2) rent the homes to workers on short-term leases, (3) write long-term leases with severe penalties for early termination by the lessee, or (4) write long-term leases that bind the firm but permit easy termination by the lessee. Alternatively, the firm could (5) require workers to construct their own housing.

Given the thin market, workers who constructed their own homes would, in effect, be making firm-specific investments. Lacking contractual safe-guards—buy-back clauses (whereby the company guarantees a market in the event of layoff or termination), long-term employment guarantees, lump sum severance awards, death benefits, and the like—workers will agree to make such investments only if offered a sign-on bonus and/or a wage premium. Expressed in terms of the contractual schema in Figure 1–1, that last corresponds to a node B rather than a node C result (which is to say, a $\bar{w} > \hat{w}$ outcome).

Node B outcomes, however, are notoriously inefficient. The marginal costs of the firm will be driven up by a $\bar{w}$ wage bargain, whence the firm will make layoffs according to an inefficient criterion. Home designs chosen by the workers will likewise be compromised in consideration of the hazards. The advantages of concentrating all the specific investments on the mining firm are thus apt to be apparent to both parties at the outset (or will become obvious during negotiations). Accordingly, home ownership by the mining firm coupled with efficient lease terms ought to be observed. Option 4—long-term leases that bind the lessor but provide easy release for the lessee—have obvious attractions.[29]

Consider the general store. The leading possibilities here are: (1) The

---

[29]Whether the defects of the first three options described in the text exceed those of option (4) is left as an exercise for the reader. Rental arrangements are favored by assuming that occupants will exercise due care, which requires that deterrents for abuses that can be implemented to the satisfaction of the parties be included in the lease agreement. For a related discussion, see Alchian (1984, p. 40).

store is owned by the mining firm and (a) operated as a monopoly, (b) placed under a fair rate of return constraint, or (c) placed under a market basket (index number) constraint; (2) a multiyear franchise is awarded to the highest bidder, the receipts from which bidding competition are (a) paid to the company treasury, (b) divided among the initial group of workers, or (c) placed in a money market fund and paid out to customers over the life of the franchise in proportion to purchases; and (3) the store is owned and operated by the workers as a cooperative. Although none of these is unproblematic, options 2c and 3 have much to recommend them.[30] Whatever the determination, the more general point is this: The wage bargain to which the workers agree will be conditional on, rather than independent of, the way in which the general store is owned and operated if, as assumed, contract realizations reflect all of the salient features—of which the ownership and governance of the general store are plainly germane.

b. THE MOBILE SOCIETY

The appearance of the automobile, mobile homes, home freezers, mail order houses, and the like greatly relieve the contracting difficulties of the premobility era. The need for site-specific investments in homes is alleviated by the invention of suitable assets on wheels, which is what the mobile home option represents. Exclusive reliance on the general store is relieved by the possibility of shopping at a distance, which cheap transportation to the nearby city and purchases from mail order houses permit. Changes in markets and technology thus have sweeping contracting ramifications. In effect, a viable node A alternative has been introduced into what had previously been a contractually complicated node B/node C choice set.

To be sure, remote mining communities may present still other issues for which careful comparative institutional assessments will be needed. Plainly, however, contractual strains of the earlier era are greatly alleviated by the mobility that assets on wheels and competition permit.

5.2 *Some Reservations*

If contracting in its entirety reliably obtains, then an efficient configuration of wages, home ownership, company store operations, and the like will appear, whatever the mobility condition of the population. What then explains the widespread discontent with the organization of company towns in the premobility era?

---

[30]Again, this is left as an exercise for the reader.

There are two leading possibilities. One is that students of company towns have not performed the relevant comparative institutional tests. Rather than describe and evaluate the actual set of contractual choices from which company town organization is constrained to choose, company towns are compared instead with noncompany towns. Unsurprisingly, company towns fare poorly in the comparison. Inasmuch, however, as such a comparison is operationally irrelevant, it is wholly unhelpful to an understanding of the organizational problems with which the company town is faced.

The second possibility is that, especially in the context of labor market organization, contracting in its entirety is rarely realized. Company towns would be a good deal less objectionable if they were actually organized along efficient contracting principles. But what company store was ever organized as a cooperative? A chronic problem with labor market organization is that workers and their families are irrepressible optimists. They are taken in by vague assurances of good faith, by legally unenforceable promises, and by their own hopes for the good life. Tough-minded bargaining in its entirety never occurs or, if it occurs, comes too late. An objective assessment of employment hazards that should have preceded any employment agreement thus comes only after disappointment. "Demands" for redress in those circumstances are apt to be regarded as a bluff—based, as they are, on weakness. Collective organization may help, but it entails a struggle. Ensuing settlements may stanch the losses rather than effect a transfusion.

I submit that both factors contribute to the low opinion with which company towns are held. As stated at the outset, however, this book does not attempt a comprehensive treatment of all the relevant factors. Instead, I consistently assume that the parties to a contract are hard-headed and that the ramifications of alternative contracts are intuited if not fully thought through. This often sheds insights, but not without cost. Omissions and distortions sometimes result. Such costs are less severe, I believe, where commercial contracting practices (including vertical integration and supporting internal governance structures) are under review than when labor market organization is being studied. In any event, my emphasis on previously neglected transaction cost features is meant to redress an earlier imbalance. I fully concur that complex contracting will be better understood if examined from several well-focused perspectives.

6. Applications

The applications of transaction cost economics sketched here are developed more extensively in later chapters. The object is merely to motivate the proposition that transaction cost economics makés useful contact with many of the issues of central interest to applied microeconomics.

6.1 *Vertical Market Restrictions*

Whereas it was once common to approach customer and territorial restrictions and related forms of nonstandard contracting as presumptively anticompetitive, transaction cost economics maintains the rebuttable presumption that such practices have the purpose of safeguarding transactions. The contracting schema in section 4 discloses that firms in which specific assets are placed at hazard ($k > 0$) have an incentive to devise protective governance ($s > 0$), thereby to locate at node C. Many of the nonstandard practices, of which customer and territorial restrictions are examples, serve precisely this purpose.

Thus suppose that a firm develops a distinctive good or service and distributes it through franchisees. Assume further that the incentive to promote the good or service experiences externalities: Some franchisees may attempt to free-ride off of the promotional efforts of others; or franchisees that serve a mobile population may cut costs, allow quality to deteriorate, and shift the reputation effect onto the system. Franchisors thus have an incentive to extend their reach beyond the initial franchise award to include constraints on the condition of supply.

Transparent though that may be, it was not always so. Consider the position of the government in arguing the Schwinn case before the Supreme Court: A "rule that treats manufacturers who assume the distribution function more leniently than those who impose restraints on independent distributors merely reflects the fact that, although integration in distribution sometimes benefits the economy by leading to cost savings, agreements to maintain resale prices or to impose territorial restrictions of limited duration or outlet limitations of the type involved here have never been shown to produce comparable economies."[31] The clear preference for internal over market modes of organization is consonant with the then prevailing preoccupation with technological features and the associated disregard for the benefits of contractual safeguards.[32] In terms of the contracting schema set out in Figure 1–2, the government implicitly assumed that all trades were of a node A

---

[31]Brief for the United States at 58, *United States* v. *Arnold, Schwinn & Co.*, 388 U.S. 365 (1967).

[32]Lester Telser's insightful treatment of "abusive trade practices" (1965) was in the public domain but was simply disregarded.

kind—whence any efforts to impose restrictions were presumptively anticompetitive.

6.2 *Price Discrimination*

The Robinson-Patman Act has been interpreted as an effort "to deprive a large buyer of [discounts] except to the extent that a lower price could be justified by reason of a seller's diminished cost due to *quantity* manufacture, delivery, or sale, or by reason of the seller's good faith effort to meet a competitor's equally low price."[33] Again, this assumes a node A transaction. If, however, a seller is operating on the $k > 0$ branch and is selling to buyers one of which offers a contractual safeguard while the other refuses, it is unrealistic to expect that product will be sold to both at an identical price. Instead, the node B buyer must pay a premium ($\bar{p} > \hat{p}$) to reflect his refusal to safeguard the hazard.

6.3 *Regulation/Deregulation*

Monopoly supply is efficient where economies of scale are large in relation to the size of the market. But, as Friedman laments, "There is unfortunately no good solution for technical monopoly. There is only a choice among three evils: private unregulated monopoly, private monopoly regulated by the state, and government operation" (1962, p. 128).

Friedman characterized private unregulated monopoly as an evil because he assumed that private monopoly ownership implied pricing on monopoly terms. As subsequently argued by Demsetz (1968b), Stigler (1968), and Posner (1972), however, a monopoly price outcome can be avoided by using *ex ante* bidding to award the monopoly franchise to the firm that offers to supply product on the best terms. Demsetz advances the franchise bidding for natural monopoly argument by stripping away "irrelevant complications"—such as equipment durability and uncertainty (1968b, p. 57). Stigler contends that "customers can auction off the right to sell electricity, using the state as an instrument to conduct the auction. . . . The auction . . . consists of [franchise bids] to sell cheaply" (1968, p. 19). Posner agrees and furthermore holds that franchise bidding is an efficacious way by which to award and operate cable TV franchises.

Transaction cost economics recognizes merit in the argument but insists that both *ex ante* and *ex post* contracting features be examined. Only if

---

[33]*FTC* v *Morton Salt Co.*, 334 U.S. 37 (1948). Emphasis added.

competition is efficacious at *both* stages does the franchise bidding argument go through. The attributes of the good or service to be franchised are crucial to the assessment. Specifically, if the good or service is to be supplied under conditions of uncertainty and if nontrivial investments in specific assets are involved, the efficacy of franchise bidding is highly problematic. Indeed, the implementation of a franchise bidding scheme under those circumstances essentially requires the progressive elaboration of an administration apparatus that differs mainly in name rather than in kind from the sort associated with rate of return regulation. It is elementary that a *change in name lacks comparative institutional significance.*

This is not, however, to suggest that franchise bidding for goods or services supplied under decreasing cost conditions is never feasible or to imply that extant regulation or public ownership can never be supplanted by franchise bidding with net gains. Examples include local service airlines and, possibly, postal delivery. The winning bidder for each can be displaced without posing serious asset valuation problems, since the base plant (terminals, post office, warehouses, and so on) can be owned by the government, and other assets (planes, trucks, and the like) will have an active secondhand market. It is not, therefore, that franchise bidding is totally lacking in merit. On the contrary, it is a very imaginative proposal. Transaction cost economics maintains, however, that all contracting schemes—of which franchise bidding for natural monopoly is one—need to be examined microanalytically and assessed in a comparative institutional manner.

7. Concluding Remarks

Transaction cost economics relies on and develops the following propositions:

1. The transaction is the basic unit of analysis.
2. Any problem that can be posed directly or indirectly as a contracting problem is usefully investigated in transaction cost economizing terms.
3. Transaction cost economies are realized by assigning transactions (which differ in their attributes) to governance structures (which are the organizational frameworks within which the integrity of a contractual relation is decided) in a discriminating way. Accordingly:
   a. The defining attributes of transactions need to be identified.
   b. The incentive and adaptive attributes of alternative governance structures need to be described.
4. Although marginal analysis is sometimes employed, implementing

transaction cost economics mainly involves a comparative institutional assessment of discrete institutional alternatives—of which classical market contracting is located at one extreme; centralized, hierarchical organization is located at the other; and mixed modes of firm and market organization are located in between.

5. Any attempt to deal seriously with the study of economic organization must come to terms with the *combined* ramifications of bounded rationality and opportunism in conjunction with a condition of asset specificity.

Note, with respect to this last, that the main differences in the four concepts of contract that are discussed in the text can be traced to variations in one or more of these three conditions. Thus contract as comprehensive *ex ante* planning and contract as promise both make heroic assumptions about human nature—the absence of bounded rationality being featured by the one (planning); the absence of opportunism being presumed by the other (promise). By contrast, concepts of contract as competition and contract as governance make less severe demands in behavioral respects. Both accommodate and/or make express provision for bounds on rationality and the hazards of opportunism.

Thus it is the condition of asset specificity that distinguishes the competitive and governance contracting models. Contract as competition works well where asset specificity is negligible. This being a widespread condition, application of the competitive model is correspondingly broad. Not all investments, however, are highly redeployable. Use of the competitive model outside of the circumstances to which it is well-suited can be and sometimes is misleading.

Whereas the competitive model of markets has been developed to a refined degree, the formidable difficulties that attend contracting in the context of nonredeployable investments have only recently come under scrutiny. This is largely because the sources and economic importance of asset specificity had previously been undervalued. Extending the theory of economic organization to deal with asset specificity has been a central preoccupation of the New Institutional Economics research agenda. This book advances and employs a private ordering approach to economic organization in which the concept of contract as governance is featured.

CHAPTER 2

Contractual Man

Complex systems are usefully studied from several points of view. Among those that have been productively employed are economic man, working man, political man (Rawls, 1983, p. 13), and even hierarchical man. The approach to the study of economic organization employed in this book is that of contractual man.

As set out in Chapter 1, a variety of economic approaches have been employed in assessing contract. Those different approaches are distinguished by (1) the behavioral assumptions imputed to contractual man, (2) the attributes of transactions believed to be of economic importance, and (3) the degree to which the courts are relied upon for settling disputes. This chapter elaborates on the first two. The private ordering versus legal centralism issue is developed further in Chapter 3.

The behavioral assumptions on which transaction cost economics relies are described in section 1. The principal dimensions for characterizing transactions are examined in section 2. The "fundamental transformation," which is responsible for a widespread condition of bilateral contracting is discussed in section 3. Although there are no substantive results in this chapter, asset specificity and the fundamental transformation both play leading roles in the chapters that follow. Note should be taken of them, therefore, even by those who regard behavioral assumptions as unimportant.

1. Behavioral Assumptions

Many economists treat behavioral assumptions[1] as a matter of convenience. This reflects a widely held opinion that the realism of the assumptions is unimportant and that the fruitfulness of a theory turns on its implications (Friedman, 1953).[2] As noted earlier, however, Bridgeman urges that an understanding of the actions of men requires more self-conscious attention to the study of how the minds of men work (1955, p. 450). Iredell Jenkins concurs. He observes that "human institutions—including law—inherit their major problems and purposes from the general condition of man" and holds that the study of mind and of social process is needed to get at the roots (1980, p. 5). As Coase puts it, "Modern institutional economics should study man as he is, acting within the constraints imposed by real institutions. Modern institutional economics is economics as it ought to be" (1984, p. 231).

Transaction cost economics characterizes human nature as we know it by reference to bounded rationality and opportunism.[3] The first acknowledges limits on cognitive competence. The second substitutes subtle for simple self-interest seeking.

1.1 *Rationality*

Three levels of rationality are usefully distinguished. The strong form contemplates maximizing. Bounded rationality is the semistrong form.[4] The weak form is organic rationality.

[1]Beauty, it is said, is in the eye of the beholder. There is a sense in which the same is true of behavioral assumptions. Those who are impatient with such matters may therefore want to skip directly to Section 2. Plainly, however, many of differences among alternative approaches to the study of economic organization owe their origins to underlying differences in the behavioral assumptions (see Section 1.3).

[2]For a recent and informed critique of this "official methodology," see Donald McCloskey (1983). For a recent endorsement, see Baiman (1982, p. 177).

[3]I originally intended also to include a discussion of dignitarian values and how these influence economic organization. The effort was not successful, however. I regard this as a regretable shortfall and hope that it will be remedied. Occasional reference to dignity appears in the text (mainly in conjunction with the employment relation and informal organization), and the issues are discussed in a more general way in Chapter 15. A more complete and systematic treatment of the ramifications of dignity for economic organization is sorely needed. The possibility that economic organization is sometimes distorted by excesses of optimism is introduced in section 5.2 of Chapter 1. This too needs development.

[4]Note that this does not exhaust the rationality categories. Nonrationality and irrationality might also be included. Their exclusion here reflects the view expressed in Chapter 1 that the study of economic organization is better advised to focus on the purposes served.

a. MAXIMIZING

Neoclassical economics maintains a maximizing orientation. That is un-objectionable, if all of the relevant costs are recognized.[5] The maximizing tradition does not, however, encourage such recognitions. Instead, the role of institutions is suppressed in favor of the view that firms are production functions, consumers are utility functions, the allocation of activity between alternative modes of organization is taken as given, and optimizing is ubiquitous (DeAlessi, 1983). Contingent claims contracting of the Arrow–Debreu kind is an especially ambitious form of maximizing. The occasion to study alternative means of contracting vanishes upon assuming that comprehensive intertemporal trading of this kind is feasible. The world being reduced to a single gigantic once-for-all higgle-haggle (Meade, 1971, p. 166), technology, initial endowments, and risk preferences and perceptions are fully determinative.

b. BOUNDED RATIONALITY

Bounded rationality is the cognitive assumption on which transaction cost economics relies. This is a semistrong form of rationality in which economic actors are assumed to be *"intendedly* rational, but only *limitedly* so"* (Simon, 1961, p. xxiv). Note the simultaneous reference to both intended and limited rationality. That conjunction has been resisted by both economists and other social scientists, albeit for different reasons. Economists object to it because limits on rationality are mistakenly interpreted in nonrationality or irrationality terms. Regarding themselves as they do as the "guardians of rationality" (Arrow, 1974, p. 16), economists are understandably chary of such an approach. Other social scientists demur because reference to intended rationality makes too great a concession to the economists' maximizing mode of inquiry. The upshot is that bounded rationality invites attack from both sides.

Transaction cost economics acknowledges that rationality is bounded and maintains that both parts of the definition should be respected. An economizing orientation is elicited by the intended rationality part of the definition, while the study of institutions is encouraged by conceding that cognitive competence is limited.

---

[5]Not all skeptics of maximizing analysis would agree with this. I am nevertheless persuaded that most of the matters with which this book is concerned can be dealt with more formally. Often, however, formal efforts to introduce the relevant costs pull up short and/or do so in a way that lacks operational significance. Despite this, progress with formalization has occurred and is in prospect.

Comprehensive contracting is not a realistic organizational alternative when provision for bounded rationality is made (Radner, 1968). If mind is the scarce resource (Simon, 1978, p. 12), then economizing on claims against it is plainly warranted. Respect for limited rationality elicits deeper study of both market and nonmarket forms of organization. Given limited competence, how do the parties organize so as to utilize their limited competence to best advantage? Views to the contrary notwithstanding, the set of issues on which economic reasoning can usefully be brought to bear is enlarged rather than reduced when bounds on rationality are admitted.

Economizing on bounded rationality takes two forms. One concerns decision processes, and the other involves governance structures. The use of heuristic problem-solving—both in general (Simon, 1978) and in conjunction with specific problems, such as Rubic's cube (Heimer, 1983)—is a decision process response. Transaction cost economics is principally concerned, however, with the economizing consequences of assigning transactions to governance structures in a discriminating way. Confronted with the realities of bounded rationality, the costs of planning, adapting, and monitoring transactions need expressly to be considered. Which governance structures are more efficacious for which types of transactions? *Ceteris paribus,* modes that make large demands against cognitive competence are relatively disfavored.[6]

C.   ORGANIC RATIONALITY

The weak form of rationality is process or organic rationality, the type of rationality with which modern evolutionary approaches (Alchian, 1950;

---

[6]It is sometimes argued that bounded rationality is merely a convoluted way of stating that information is costly. Once this has been acknowledged, maximizing modes of analysis can deal with all of the issues with which bounded rationality is concerned. There is something to be said for this: As Simon observes, a large "plot of common ground is shared by optimizing and satisficing analysis" (1978, p. 8, n. 6). Although one might, on grounds of parsimony, recommend that "we prefer the postulate that men are reasonable to the postulate that they are supremely rational when either one of these assumptions will do" (Simon, 1978, p. 8), it is easy to understand how others can decide differently. Working within an extended neoclassical framework is not a benefit that will be sacrificed lightly.

As Richard Nelson and Sidney Winter argue, however, fundamental tensions remain:

> There is . . . a fundamental difference between a situation in which a decision maker is uncertain about the state X and a situation in which the decision maker has not given any thought to whether X matters or not, between a situation in which a prethought event judged of low probability occurs and a situation in which something occurs that never has been thought about. . . . Most complex models of maximizing choice do not come to grips with the problem of bounded rationality. Only metaphorically can a limited information model be regarded as a model of decision with limited cognitive abilities. [1982, pp. 66–67]

Evolutionary economics, of the kind with which Nelson and Winter are associated, relies less on intended rationality and more on the limits of rationality than do I.

Nelson and Winter, 1982) and Austrian economics (Menger, 1963; Hayek, 1967; Kirzner, 1973) are associated. But whereas Nelson and Winter deal with evolutionary processes within and between firms, the Austrian approach is concerned with processes of the most general kinds—the institutions of money, markets, aspects of property rights, and law being examples. As Louis Schneider puts it, such institutions "are not planned. A general blueprint of the institutions is not aboriginally in anyone's mind. [Indeed], there are situations in which ignorance . . . works more 'effectively' toward certain ends than would knowledge of and planning toward those same ends" (1963, p. 16). Although transaction cost economizing is surely an important contributor to the viability of the institutions with which Austrian economics is concerned, and a joinder of the two approaches would be useful, the research agenda of organic rationality and transaction cost economics are currently rather different. They are nevertheless complementary; each can expect to benefit from the insights of the other (Langlois, 1982, p. 50).

1.2 *Self-interest Orientation*

Three levels of self-interest seeking can also be distinguished. The strongest form, the one to which transaction cost economics appeals, is opportunism. The semistrong form is simple self-interest seeking. Obedience is the weak (really null) form.

a.   OPPORTUNISM

By opportunism I mean self-interest seeking with guile. This includes but is scarcely limited to more blatant forms, such as lying, stealing, and cheating. Opportunism more often involves subtle forms of deceit. Both active and passive forms and both *ex ante* and *ex post* types are included.

Ex ante and *ex post* opportunism are recognized in the insurance literature under the headings of adverse selection and moral hazard, respectively. The first is a consequence of the inability of insurers to distinguish between risks and the unwillingness of poor risks candidly to disclose their true risk condition. Failure of insureds to behave in a fully responsible way and take appropriate risk-mitigating actions gives rise to *ex post* execution problems. Both conditions are subsumed under the heading of opportunism.

More generally, opportunism refers to the incomplete or distorted disclosure of information, especially to calculated efforts to mislead, distort, disguise, obfuscate, or otherwise confuse. It is responsible for real or contrived conditions of information asymmetry, which vastly complicate problems of economic organization. Both principals and third parties (arbitrators, courts, and the like) confront much more difficult *ex post* inference problems as a consequence. It is not necessary, moreover, that all parties be given to opportunism in identical degree. Indeed, problems of economic organization are compounded if the propensity to behave opportunistically is known to vary among members of the contracting population, since now gains can be realized by expending resources to discriminate among types.

Nicholas Georgescu-Roegen's reference to behavior that deviates from the rules is consonant with this view of human nature. As he puts it:

> [O]bservation of what happens in the economic sphere of organizations, or between organizations and individuals, [reveals] phenomena that do not consist of tatonnement with given means toward ends *according to the rules*. They show beyond any doubt that in all societies the typical individual continually pursues also an end ignored by the standard framework: the increase of that [which] he can claim as his. . . . It is the pursuit of this end that makes the individual a true agent of the economic process. [1971, pp. 319–20; emphasis added]

Plainly, were it not for opportunism, all behavior could be rule governed. This need not, moreover, require comprehensive preplanning. Unanticipated events could be dealt with by general rules, whereby the parties agree to be bound by actions of a joint profit-maximizing kind. Thus problems during contract execution could be avoided by *ex ante* insistence upon a general clause of the following kind: I agree candidly to disclose all relevant information and thereafter to propose and cooperate in joint profit-maximizing courses of action during the contract execution interval, the benefits of which gains will be divided without dispute according to the sharing ratio herein provided.

It is noteworthy that Niccolò Machiavelli's efforts to deal with "men as they are" (Gauss, 1952, p. 14) makes prominent provision for opportunism. Upon observing that humans have a propensity to behave opportunistically, Machiavelli advised his prince that "a prudent ruler ought not to keep faith when by so doing it would be against his interest, and when the reasons which made him bind himself no longer exist. . . . [L]egitimate grounds [have never] failed a prince who wished to show colourable excuse for the promise" (Gauss, 1952, pp. 92–93). But reciprocal or preemptive opportunism is not the only lesson to be gleaned from an awareness that human agents are not fully trustworthy. Indeed, that is a very primitive response.

The more important lesson, for the purposes of studying economic organization, is this: Transactions that are subject to *ex post* opportunism will benefit if appropriate safeguards can be devised *ex ante*. Rather than reply to opportunism in kind, therefore, the wise prince is one who seeks both to give and to receive "credible commitments." Incentives may be realigned, and/or superior governance structures within which to organize transactions may be devised. The ramifications are developed more completely in subsequent chapters.

As discussed below, opportunism is a troublesome source of "behavioral" uncertainty in economic transactions—which uncertainty would vanish either if individuals were fully open and honest in their efforts to realize individual advantage or, alternatively, if full subordination, self-denial, and obedience could be presumed. Open or simple self-interest seeking is the motivational assumption on which neoclassical economics relies. It is the semistrong form of self-interest seeking. Obedience is tantamount to non-self-interest seeking.

b. SIMPLE SELF-INTEREST SEEKING

Although neoclassical man confronts self-interested others across markets, this merely presumes that bargains are struck on terms that reflect original positions. But initial positions will be fully and candidly disclosed upon inquiry, state of the world declarations will be accurate, and execution is oath- or rule-bound in the manner described above. Accordingly, whereas parties realize all advantages that their wealth, resources, patents, know-how, and so forth lawfully entitle them, those are all evident from the outset. Inasmuch as there are no surprises thereafter, a condition of simple self-interest seeking may be said to obtain. Issues of economic organization thus turn on technological features (e.g. scale economies), there being no problematic behavior attributable to rule deviance among human actors.[7]

c. OBEDIENCE

Obedience is the behavioral assumption that is associated with social engineering (Georgescu-Roegen, 1971, p. 348). Adolph Lowe puts it as follows: "One can imagine the limiting case of a monolithic collectivism in which the prescriptions of the central plan are carried out by functionaries who fully identify with the imposed macrogoals. In such a system the economically relevant processes reduce almost completely to technical manipulations" (1965, p. 142). The full identification to which Lowe refers contemplates stewardship of an extreme kind in which self-interestedness vanishes. Although it is a recurrent theme throughout utopian and related literatures, to

---

[7]As Peter Diamond puts it, standard economic models treat "individuals as playing a game with fixed rules which they obey. They do not buy more than they can pay for, they do not embezzle funds, they do not rob banks" (1971, p. 31).

project such "mechanistic orderliness" is even more unwarranted than "the basic position of standard economics" (Georgescu-Roegen, 1971, p. 348). Problems of economic organization would nevertheless be greatly simplified if that condition were satisfied or even closely approximated. Robots have the feature that they satisfy obedience requirements at zero social conditioning cost, albeit within a limited range of responsiveness.

1.3 Some Comparisons

The main behavioral assumptions which contingent claims, mechanism design, transaction cost economics, evolutionary (or organic) economics, team theory, and utopian approaches employ are summarized in Figure 2–1. Of special importance is that transaction cost economics pairs a semistrong form of cognitive competence (bounded rationality) with a strong motivational assumption (opportunism). Without *both,* the main problems of economic organization with which this book is concerned would vanish or be vastly transformed.

Thus there would be relatively little scope for organizational design and analysis if either high-powered or organic rationality prevailed. Comprehensive contracting would rule in the first instance, while conscious efforts give way to evolutionary processes in the second. Were it not for opportunism, moreover, the general clause device—whereby parties agreed to be bound by

	Behavioral Assumptions	
	Rationality	Self-Interest Orientation
Strong	CC; MD	TC;MD
Semi-strong	TC; T	CC
Weak	E	U; T

CC: CONTINGENT CLAIMS
MD: MECHANISM DESIGN
TC: TRANSACTION COST
E: EVOLUTIONARY
U: UTOPIAN
T: TEAM THEORY

FIGURE 2–1. Behavioral Assumptions of Alternative Approaches to Economic Organization

actions of a joint profit-maximizing kind—would also support ubiquitous contracting. There simply is no occasion to supplant market exchange by other modes of economic organization if promises to behave in a joint profit-maximizing way are self-enforcing and if sharing rules are agreed to at the outset. These issues are discussed further in the Appendix.

Mechanism design theory couples a variant of unbounded rationality with opportunism. The rationality variant is this: An information impactedness condition exists, whereby the principal and agent have knowledge of different and essentially private information and engage in complex contracting. Mechanism design theory is thus located between contingent claims contracting and transaction cost economics in rationality respects. Imputing high-powered computational capacity is consonant with the former, while an information asymmetry condition places it closer to the latter. With respect to self-interest seeking, however, mechanism design and transaction cost economics are wholly congruent. To be sure, there are language differences—mechanism design theory refers to the propensity of human agents to behave opportunistically as "moral hazard"—but both assume deep problems of veracity and truth revelation.[8] Inasmuch as information may be disclosed strategically rather than candidly upon request, initial information disparities between the parties will not be assuredly overcome by proposals that all relevant information be pooled. Instead, initial information asymmetries persist. Indeed, additional asymmetries develop as events unfold.

Team theory acknowledges bounded rationality but assumes that agents have identical preferences, which is equivalent to weak form self-interestedness (Marschak and Radner, 1972). Although interesting problems of informational decentralization are thereby posed, the presumed absence of opportunism simplifies matters considerably.

Utopian modes of organization are intendedly humanistic and are gener-

---

[8]I have resisted substituting the term "moral hazard" for opportunism for two reasons. For one thing, moral hazard is plainly distinguishable from adverse selection. Both are subsumed under opportunism. Second, and more important, reference to moral hazard sometimes discourages deeper inquiry.

To be sure, the term "moral hazard" may be legitimately extended to reach outside of its narrow insurance context—where it refers to the possibility that insureds will fail to take appropriate loss-mitigating actions in the insurance interval and will not candidly accept accountability—to include all failures of "due care." But it does not ordinarily elicit sensitivity to the full set of *ex ante* and *ex post* efforts to lie, cheat, steal, mislead, disguise, obfuscate, feign, distort, and confuse. If everyone who uses the term moral hazard both recognizes and is prepared to plumb the contractual ramifications of those attributes of human nature, the general term (opportunism) and the technical term (moral hazard) are interchangeable. To the extent, however, that moral hazard focuses attention narrowly on the analytically more tractable features of contracting, foreshortening can result. It is no accident that the formal principal–agent literature uses "moral hazard" while transaction cost economics uses "opportunism."

ally nonmarket. Whether they are democratic or hierarchical, utopian modes require deep commitment to collective purposes and commonly involve personal subordination. The history of social and economic organization records repeated efforts to craft such structures. But utopian societies are especially vulnerable to the pound of opportunism.[9]

The new man of socialist economics is endowed with a high level of cognitive competence (hence the presumed efficacy of planning) and displays a lesser degree of self-interestedness (a greater predisposition to cooperation) than his capitalist counterpart. The "cooperation and solidarity" on which socialism is based are "introduced by social planning", which "not only improves macroeconomic efficiency but [also adds these new qualities] to the economic process" (Horvat, 1982, p. 335).

2. Dimensions

Transaction cost economics maintains that there are rational economic reasons for organizing some transactions one way and other transactions another. But which go where and for what reason? A predictive theory of economic organization requires that the factors responsible for differences among transactions be identified and explicated.

The principal dimensions with respect to which transactions differ are asset specificity, uncertainty, and frequency. The first is the most important and most distinguishes transaction cost economics from other treatments of economic organization, but the other two play significant roles.

2.1 *Asset Specificity*

An awareness of the condition that is herein described as asset specificity can be traced at least to Alfred Marshall.[10] The contracting and organizational

---

[9]The experience of utopian societies is examined by Frank and Fritzie Manuel (1979). There is a brief discussion of the issues in Chapter 10 herein.

[10]Consider Marshall's discussion of idiosyncratic employment:

> The point of view of the employer . . . does not include the whole gains of the business: for there is another part which attaches to his employees. Indeed, in some cases and for some purposes, nearly the whole income of a business may be regarded as a quasi-rent, that is an income determined for the time by the state of the market for its wares, with but little reference to the cost of preparing for their work the various things and persons engaged in it. . . . Thus the head clerk in a business has an acquaintance with men and things, the use of which he could in some cases sell at a high price to rival firms. But in other cases it is of a kind to be of no value save to the business in which he already is; and then his departure

ramifications, however, went unremarked. Indeed, the quasi-rent condition to which Marshall referred played a lesser rather than a greater role as neo-classical economics progressed.

To be sure, Michael Polanyi's remarkable study of "personal knowledge" included several illustrations of industrial arts and craftsmanship in which the skills in question are so deeply embedded in the experienced workforce that they can be known or inferred by others only with great difficulty—if at all (Polanyi, 1962, pp. 52–53). Jacob Marschak likewise recognized that assets can be idiosyncratic and expressed concern with the readiness of economists to accept or employ assumptions of fungibility: "There exist almost unique, irreplaceable research workers, teachers, administrators: just as there exist unique choice locations for plants and harbors. The problem of unique or imperfectly standardized goods . . . has been indeed neglected in the textbooks" (Marschak, 1968, p. 14). It was widely believed that those uniqueness conditions were rare and/or unimportant, however. The nuances to which Polanyi and Marschak referred could thus safely be relegated to footnotes.

That viewpoint has been dramatically reversed in the past decade. Alchian, who once held otherwise,[11] now contends that "the whole rationale for the employer-employee status, and even for the existence of firms, rests on [asset specificity]; without it there is no known reason for firms to exist."[12]

The proposition that the idiosyncratic attributes of transactions have large and systematic organizational ramifications first appeared in conjunction with the study of vertical integration (Williamson, 1971). Transactions that are supported by investments in durable, transaction-specific assets experience "lock in" effects, on which account autonomous trading will commonly be supplanted by unified ownership (vertical integration). Thus although there may be large numbers of qualified bidders at the outset, if the "winner of an original contract acquires a cost advantage, say by reason of . . . unique

---

would perhaps injure it by several times the value of his salary, while probably he could not get half that salary elsewhere. [1948, p. 626]

The employees to whom Marshall refers are evidently specialized to the work of a particular firm. Discrete contracting is poorly suited for such transactions. Transaction cost economics predicts that contracts that have superior properties for safeguarding employment will appear.

[11]Alchian and Demsetz originally maintained that "neither the employee nor the employer is bound by any contractual obligations to continue their relationship. Long term contracts between employer and employee are not the essence of the organization we call a firm" (1972, p. 177). Alchian has since rejected this position (1984, pp. 38–39).

[12]Alchian, "First National Maintenance vs. National Labor Relations Board," unpublished manuscript, 1982, pp. 6–7. Alchian goes on generously to observe that "*Markets and Hierarchies* [is] by far the most elegant, though abstruse, statement of the [asset specificity] principle" (p. 7).

location or learning, including the acquisition of undisclosed or proprietary technical and managerial procedures and task-specific labor skills,'' bidding parity at contract renewal intervals will be upset—with the result that (comparative or remediable) *ex post* contracting strains predictably develop if discrete contracting is attempted (Williamson, 1971, p. 116).

a. EXPLICATION

Asset specificity arises in an intertemporal context. As set out in the contractual schema in Chapter 1, parties to a transaction commonly have a choice between special purpose and general purpose investments. Assuming that contracts go to completion as intended, the former will often permit cost savings to be realized. But such investments are also risky, in that specialized assets cannot be redeployed without sacrifice of productive value if contracts should be interrupted or prematurely terminated. General purpose investments do not pose the same difficulties. "Problems" that arise during contract execution can be solved in a general purpose asset regime by each party going his way. The following issue thus needs to be evaluated: Do the prospective cost savings afforded by the special purpose technology justify the strategic hazards that arise as a consequence of their nonsalvageable character?

A tradeoff is thus posed and needs to be evaluated. Unlike earlier treatments of economic organization, transaction cost economics is centrally concerned with that condition. Also, the nature of the tradeoff is not invariant but varies systematically with the governance structure to which the transactions in question are assigned. A comparative organizational assessment of tradeoffs is thus needed.

It is common to distinguish between fixed and variable costs, but this is merely an accounting distinction. More relevant to the study of contracting is whether assets are redeployable or not (Klein and Leffler, 1981). Many assets that accountants regard as fixed are in fact redeployable, for example, centrally located general purpose buildings and equipment. Durable but mobile assets such as general purpose trucks and airplanes are likewise redeployable. Other costs that accountants treat as variable often have a large nonsalvageable part, firm-specific human capital being an illustration. Figure 2–2 helps to make the distinction.

Thus costs are distinguished as to fixed (F) and variable (V) parts. But they are further classified as to the degree of specificity, of which only two kinds are recognized: wholly specific (k) and nonspecific (v). (That only two specificity classes are distinguished does not imply that assets must be entirely one kind or the other. Semi-specific assets involve a mixture of k and v.) The shaded region at the bottom of the figure is the troublesome one for purposes

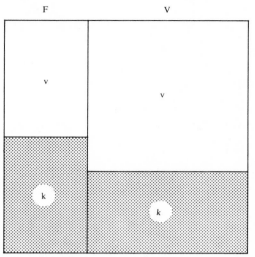

Accounting: Fixed (F) and Variable (V)
Contracting: Specific (k) and Nonspecific (v)

FIGURE 2–2.   Cost Distinctions

of contracting. That is where the specific assets are located. Such specificity is responsible for what is referred to as the "fundamental transformation" in Section 3 below.

At least four different types of asset specificity are usefully distinguished: site specificity; physical asset specificity; human asset specificity; and dedicated assets. The organizational ramifications, moreover, vary with each. The details are best developed in the context of specific organizational issues—vertical integration, nonstandard contracting, employment, corporate governance, regulation, and the like, which are the subjects of subsequent chapters. Suffice it to observe here that (1) asset specificity refers to durable investments that are undertaken in support of particular transactions, the opportunity cost of which investments is much lower in best alternative uses or by alternative users should the original transaction be prematurely terminated, and (2) the specific identity of the parties to a transaction plainly matters in these circumstances, which is to say that continuity of the relationship is valued, whence (3) contractual and organizational safeguards arise in support of transactions of this kind, which safeguards are unneeded (would be the source of avoidable costs) for transactions of the more familiar neoclassical (nonspecific) variety. Thus whereas neoclassical transactions take place within markets where "faceless buyers and sellers . . . meet . . . for an instant to exchange standardized goods at equilibrium prices" (Ben-Porath,

1980, p. 4), exchanges that are supported by transaction-specific investments are neither faceless nor instantaneous. The study of governance owes its origins to that condition.[13]

b. SIGNIFICANCE

The importance of asset specificity to transaction cost economics is difficult to exaggerate. Just as the absence of differential risk aversion would diminish if not vitiate much of the recent incentive work on contracting (Akerlof and Miyazaki, 1980; Bull, 1983), so would the absence of asset specificity vitiate much of transaction cost economics.[14] It is the source both of striking commonalities among transactions and of numerous refutable implications.

To be sure, asset specificity only takes on importance in conjunction with bounded rationality/opportunism and in the presence of uncertainty. It is nonetheless true that asset specificity is the big locomotive to which transaction cost economics owes much of its predictive content. Absent this condition, the world of contract is vastly simplified; enter asset specificity, and nonstandard contracting practices quickly appear. Neglect of asset specificity is largely responsible for the monopoly preoccupation of earlier contract traditions.

2.2 Uncertainty

a. GENERAL

Many of the interesting issues with which transaction cost economics is involved reduce to an assessment of adaptive, sequential decision-making. Contingent on the set of transactions to be effected, the basic proposition here is that governance structures differ in their capacities to respond effectively to

[13]Others who are persuaded of the importance of asset specificity include Klein, Crawford, and Alchian, who develop the argument in the context of what they refer to as "appropriable quasi-rents," where the quasi-rent value of an asset is the value in its next best use and the "potentially appropriable specialized portion of the quasi-rent is the portion, if any, in excess of its value to the second highest-valuing user" (1978, p. 298). Also see Klein (1980), Klein and Leffler (1981), Goetz and Scott (1981), and Alchian (1984).

[14]Markets are thoroughly contestable—in the sense of Baumol, Panzer, and Willig (1982)—if asset specificity is presumed to be absent. In this sense contestability theory and transaction cost economics are looking at the very same phenomenon—the condition of asset specificity—through opposite ends of the telescope.

disturbances. To be sure, those issues would vanish were it not for bounded rationality, since then it would be feasible to develop a detailed strategy for crossing all possible bridges in advance.[15] It would likewise be possible to adapt effectively using the "general rule" device described above were it not for opportunism. Confronted, however, by the need to cope with both bounded rationality and opportunism, comparative institutional assessments of the adaptive attributes of alternative governance structures must necessarily be made.

As Hayek maintained, interesting problems of economic organization arise only in conjunction with uncertainty: The "economic problem of society is mainly one of adaptation to changes in particular circumstances of time and place" (Hayek, 1945, p. 524). Disturbances, moreover, are not all of a kind. Different origins are usefully distinguished. Behavioral uncertainty is of special importance to an understanding of transaction cost economics issues.

Although there is a hint in the earlier discussions that uncertainty can have behavioral origins (Williamson, 1975, pp. 26–37), it generally goes unremarked. Even Tjalling Koopmans, whose distinction between primary and secondary uncertainty goes beyond most treatments and who describes the core problem of the economic organization of society as that of facing and dealing with uncertainty (1957, p. 147), does not deal with behavioral issues. Primary uncertainty is of a state-contingent kind, while secondary uncertainty arises "from lack of communication, that is from one decision maker having no way of finding out the concurrent decisions and plans made by others"— which Koopmans judges to be "quantitatively at least as important as the primary uncertainty arising from random acts of nature and unpredictable changes in consumer's preferences" (1957, pp. 162–63).

The secondary uncertainty to which Koopmans refers is of a rather innocent or nonstrategic kind, however. There is a lack of communication, but no reference is made to uncertainty that arises because of strategic nondisclosure, disguise, or distortion of information (note that information distortion involves not a lack of information but the conscious supply of false and misleading signals). Also, the plans to which Koopmans refers are merely unknown. The possibility that parties make strategic plans in relation to each

---

[15]Simon has taken the somewhat extreme position that the distinction between deterministic complexity and uncertainty is inessential. What is referred to as "uncertainty" in chess is "uncertainty introduced into a perfectly certain environment by inability—computational inability—to ascertain the structure of the environment. But the result of uncertainty, whatever its source, is the same: approximation must replace exactness in reaching a decision" (1972, p. 170).

other[16] that are the source of *ex ante* uncertainty and *ex post* surprises is nowhere suggested.

Uncertainty of a strategic kind is attributable to opportunism and will be referred to as *behavioral uncertainty*. Such uncertainty is presumably akin to what Ludwig von Mises refers to as case probability, where "case probability is a peculiar feature of our dealing with problems of *human action*. Here any reference to frequency is inappropriate, as our statements always deal with *unique events*" (1949, p. 112; emphasis added).[17] Thus even if it were possible to characterize the general propensity of a population to behave opportunistically in advance and perhaps even to screen for trustworthiness, knowing that one is dealing with a trader who comes from one part of the opportunism distribution rather than another does not fully describe the uncertainties that arise on this account. Those added uncertainties can be evaluated only upon projecting the devious responses (and own replies) that opportunism introduces. And those can be evaluated only in conjunction with the particulars of the contract. Even knowledge of particulars, moreover, does not preclude surprises. The capacity for novelty in the human mind is rich beyond imagination.[18] The issues here are nicely put by Leif Johansen, who observes that the study of economic behavior between motivationally complex economic agents is complicated by the fact that the "ranges of possible mes-

---

[16]The Holmes-Moriarity dilemma described by Oskar Morgenstern is an illustration:

> Sherlock Holmes, pursued by his opponent, Moriarity, leaves London for Dover. The train stops at a station on the way, and he alights there rather than travelling on to Dover. He has seen Moriarity at the railway station, recognizes that he is very clever and expects that Moriarity will take a faster special train in order to catch him in Dover. Holmes' anticipation turns out to be correct. But what if Moriarity had been still more clever, had estimated Holmes' mental abilities better and had foreseen his actions accordingly? Then, obviously, he would have travelled to the intermediate station. Holmes, again, would have had to calculate that, and he himself would have decided to go on to Dover. Whereupon, Moriarity would again have "reacted" differently. Because of so much thinking they might not have been able to act at all or the intellectually weaker of the two would have surrendered to the other in the Victoria Station, since the whole flight would have become unnecessary. [1976, pp. 173–74]

[17]G. L. S. Shackle likewise remarks that "in a great multitude and diversity of matters the individual has no record of a sufficient number of sufficiently similar acts, of his own or other people's, to be able to construct a valid frequency table of the outcomes of acts of this kind. Regarding these acts, probabilities are not available to him" (1961, p. 55). Georgescu-Roegen evidently agrees. He observes that "a measure for all uncertainty situations . . . has absolutely no meaning, for it can be obtained only by an intentionally mutilated representation of reality. We hear people almost every day speaking of 'calculated risk,' but no one yet can tell us how he calculated it so that we can check on his calculations" (1971, p. 83). Events that involve "novelty" cannot be described by probability distributions (Georgescu-Roegen, 1971, p. 122).

[18]"By saying that everybody was surprised at the announcement by President Johnson not to seek or accept the 1968 presidential nomination we do not simply mean that the ex ante belief in his move had been extremely small: we simply mean that nobody else had thought of it" (Georgescu-Roegen, 1971, p. 123).

sages, offers, threats, etc. which can be given during the process, including the timing of moves, are hard to delimit. Imagination and ability to surprise the opponents may be important points, and very often the 'agenda' will be expanded during the process'' (1979, p. 511). Surprise moves often elicit complex replies. Bounded rationality limits are quickly reached—since the entire decision tree cannot be generated for even moderately complex problems (Feldman and Kanter, 1965, p. 615).[19]

To be sure, behavioral uncertainties would not pose contractual problems if transactions were *known* to be free from exogenous disturbances, since then there would be no occasion to adapt and unilateral efforts to alter contracts could and presumably would be voided by the courts or other third party appeal. Insistence on original terms would thus everywhere be observed. The ease of enforcing contracts vanishes, however, once the need for adaptation appears (or can be plausibly asserted). Questions of the following kind arise: Should maladaptations to changed circumstances be tolerated lest efforts to effect an adaptation give rise to complex behavioral responses by opposite parties with the prospect of realizing net losses? Can a governance structure that attenuates such behavioral uncertainties be devised?[20] Such issues do not arise within the context of primary uncertainty but are nontheless germane to the study of economic organization.

b.   INTERACTION EFFECTS

The influence of uncertainty on economic organization is conditional. Specifically, an increase in parametric uncertainty is a matter of little consequence for transactions that are nonspecific. Since new trading relations are easily arranged, continuity has little value, and behavioral uncertainty is irrevelant. Accordingly, market exchange continues and the discrete contract-

---

[19]Inasmuch as a great deal of the relevant information about trustworthiness or its absence that is generated during the course of bilateral trading is essentially private information—in that it cannot be fully communicated to and shared with others (Williamson, 1975, pp. 31–37)—knowledge about behavioral uncertainties is very uneven. The organization of economic activity is even more complicated as a result.

[20]Stephen Littlechild's interesting discussion of the radical-subjectivist perspective introduces the possibility that governance structures will reflect behavioral uncertainties. He observes that "if uncertainty derives from the as yet undetermined actions of other agents, then it is necessary either to become privy to the decisions of those other agents (e.g., by agreement, collusion, merger, etc.) or to reduce one's dependence on them (e.g., by establishing or extending property rights)" (1983, p. 6). Jenkins likewise refers to the same condition when he observes that human relations are unstable because "men indicate by word or deed that they will act one way and then act in another" (1980, p. 18), to which he adds, "it is apparently only in the human context that disorder becomes a conspicuous feature; and it is only man who is at once challenged and equipped to deal purposely with it" (1980, p. 18).

ing paradigm holds across standardized transactions of all kinds, whatever the degree of uncertainty.

That is no longer so for transactions that are supported by idiosyncratic investments. Whenever assets are specific in nontrivial degree, increasing the degree of uncertainty makes it more imperative that the parties devise a machinery to "work things out"—since contractual gaps will be larger and the occasions for sequential adaptations will increase in number and importance as the degree of uncertainty increases. Also, and relatedly, concerns over the behavioral uncertainties referred to above now intrude.

A further discussion of the governance ramifications is best deferred to Chapter 3. Suffice it to observe here that (1) the interaction effects between uncertainty and asset specificity are important to an understanding of economic organization, and (2) empirical analysis of transaction cost features is complicated as a result.

2.3 *Frequency*

Adam Smith's famous theorem that "the division of labor is limited by the extent of the market" is mainly thought to have neoclassical cost ramifications. Investments in specialized production techniques the costs of which could be recovered in a large market may be unrecoverable if markets are small, whence general purpose plant and equipment and procedures will be observed in small markets. Similar reasoning carries over to the study of transaction costs. The basic proposition in the latter connection is this: Specialized governance structures are more sensitively attuned to the governance needs of nonstandard transactions than are unspecialized structures, *ceteris paribus*. But specialized structures come at a great cost, and the question is whether the costs can be justified. This varies with the benefits on the one hand and the degree of utilization on the other.

The benefits of specialized governance structures are greatest for transactions supported by considerable investment in transaction-specific assets. The reasons are those described previously. Whether the volume of transactions processed through a specialized governance structure utilizes it to capacity is then the remaining issue. The cost of specialized governance structures will be easier to recover for large transactions of a recurring kind. Hence the frequency of transactions is a relevant dimension. Where frequency is low but the needs for nuanced governance are great, the possibility of aggregating the demands of similar but independent transactions is suggested. Court ordering is commonly supplanted by arbitration in such circumstances: Both permit aggregation, but the latter is more oriented to the continuity needs of asset specific transactions.

More generally, the object is not to economize on transaction costs but to economize in both transaction and neoclassical production cost respects. Whether transaction cost economies are realized at the expense of scale economies or scope economies thus needs to be assessed. A tradeoff framework is needed to examine the production cost and governance cost ramifications of alternative modes of organization simultaneously. Rudimentary apparatus of this kind is developed in Chapter 4.

3. The Fundamental Transformation

Economists of all persuasions recognize that the terms upon which an initial bargain will be struck depend on whether noncollusive bids can be elicited from more than one qualified supplier. Monopolistic terms will obtain if there is only a single highly qualified supplier, while competitive terms will result if there are many. Transaction cost economics fully accepts this description of *ex ante* bidding competition but insists that the study of contracting be extended to include *ex post* features. Thus initial bidding merely sets the contracting process in motion. A full assessment requires that both contract execution and *ex post* competition at the contract renewal interval come under scrutiny.

Contrary to earlier practice,[21] transaction cost economics holds that a condition of large numbers bidding at the outset does not necessarily imply that a large numbers bidding condition will prevail thereafter. Whether *ex post* competition is fully efficacious or not depends on whether the good or service in question is supported by durable investments in transaction-specific human or physical assets. Where no such specialized investments are incurred, the initial winning bidder realizes no advantage over nonwinners. Although it may continue to supply for a long time, that is only because, in effect, it is continuously meeting competitive bids from qualified rivals. Rivals cannot be presumed to operate on a parity, however, once substantial investments in transaction-specific assets are put in place. Winners in such circumstances enjoy advantages over nonwinners, which is to say that parity is upset. Accordingly, what was a large numbers bidding condition at the outset is effectively transformed into one of bilateral supply thereafter. This fundamental transformation has pervasive contracting consequences.

---

[21]The earlier treatments of franchise bidding discussed in Chapter 13 illustrate contract analysis in which *ex post* features were ignored or effectively assumed away.

The reason why significant reliance investments in durable, transaction-specific assets introduces contractual asymmetry between the winning bidder on the one hand and nonwinners on the other is that economic values would be sacrificed if the ongoing supply relation were to be terminated. Faceless contracting is thereby supplanted by contracting in which the pairwise identity of the parties matters. Occasionally the identity of the parties is important from the very outset, as when a buyer induces a supplier to invest in specialized physical capital of a transaction-specific kind. Inasmuch as the value of that capital in other uses is, by definition, much smaller than the specialized use for which it has been intended, the supplier is effectively committed to the transaction to a significant degree. The effect is often symmetrical, moreover, in that the buyer cannot turn to alternative sources of supply and obtain the item on favorable terms, since the cost of supply from unspecialized capital is presumably great.

Ordinarily, however, there is more to idiosyncratic exchange than specialized physical capital. Human capital investments that are transaction-specific commonly occur as well. These evolve during contract execution. Specialized training and learning-by-doing economies in production operations are illustrations. Except when such investments are transferable to alternative suppliers at low cost, which is rare, the benefits can be realized only so long as the relationship between the buyer and seller is maintained.

Additional transaction-specific savings can accrue at the interface between supplier and buyer as contracts are successively adapted to unfolding events and as periodic contract renewal agreements are reached. Familiarity here permits communication economies to be realized: Specialized language develops as experience accumulates and nuances are signaled and received in a sensitive way. Both institutional and personal trust relations evolve. Thus the individuals who are responsible for adapting the interfaces have a personal as well as an organizational stake in what transpires. Where personal integrity is believed to be operative, individuals located at the interfaces may refuse to be part of opportunistic efforts to take advantage of (rely on) the letter of the contract when the spirit of the exchange is emasculated. Such refusals can serve as a check upon organizational proclivities to behave opportunistically.[22] Other things being equal, idiosyncratic exchange relations that

[22]Thorstein Veblen's remarks on the distant relation of the head of a large enterprise to transactions are apposite. He observes that in those impersonal circumstances the "mitigating effect which personal conduct may have in dealings between man and man is . . . in great measure eliminated. . . . Business management [then] has a chance to proceed . . . untroubled by sentimental considerations of human kindness or irritation or of honesty" (1927, p. 53). Veblen evidently assigns slight weight to the possibility that those to whom negotiating and execution responsibilities are assigned will themselves invest the transactions with integrity.

feature personal trust will survive greater stress and will display greater adaptability.

How to effect these adaptations poses a serious contracting dilemma, though it bears repeating that, absent the hazards of opportunism, the difficulties would vanish—since then the gaps in long-term, incomplete contracts could be faultlessly filled by recourse to the earlier described general clause device. Given, however, the unenforceability of general clauses and the proclivity of human agents to make false and misleading (self-disbelieved) statements, the following hazards must be confronted: Joined as they are in a condition of bilateral monopoly, both buyer and seller are strategically situated to bargain over the disposition of any incremental gain whenever a proposal to adapt is made by the other party. Although both have a long-term interest in effecting adaptations of a joint profit-maximizing kind, each also has an interest in appropriating as much of the gain as he can on each occasion to adapt. Efficient adaptations that would otherwise be made thus result in costly haggling or even go unmentioned, lest the gains be dissipated by costly subgoal pursuit. Governance structures that attentuate opportunism and otherwise infuse confidence are evidently needed.[23]

Thomas Palay's recent studies of transportation transactions suggest that Veblen erred—in that specialized transactions do enjoy the added safeguard of personal honor and integrity of the individuals who negotiate the terms (Palay, 1981, pp. 105, 117, 124). Ronald Dore's assessment of Japanese contracting practices also suggests that personal integrity matters (1983).

[23]Considering the importance of the fundamental transformation to the study of economic organization, the question arises as to why this condition was so long ignored. One explanation is that such transformations do not occur in the context of comprehensive, once-for-all contracting—which is a convenient and sometimes productive contracting fiction but imposes inordinate demands on limited rationality. A second reason is that the transformation will not arise in the absence of opportunism—which is a condition that economists have been loath to concede. Third, even if bounded rationality and opportunism are conceded, the fundamental transformation appears only in conjunction with an asset specificity condition, which is a contracting feature that has only recently been explicated.

Opportunism: A Digression

The behavioral assumption that human agents are given to opportunism elicits a variety of reactions, ranging from abhorrence through easy acceptance to an insistence that this is yet another case where there is nothing new under the sun. There are even those who regard opportunism as irrelevant.

Those who abhor the use of opportunism regard it as an unduly jaundiced view of human nature and/or are distressed with the theory of economic organization that it supports. I can appreciate both concerns. Note with respect to the first that I do not insist that every individual is continuously or even largely given to opportunism. To the contrary, I merely assume that some individuals are opportunistic some of the time and that differential trustworthiness is rarely transparent *ex ante*. As a consequence, *ex ante* screening efforts are made and *ex post* safeguards are created. Otherwise, those who are least principled (most opportunistic) will be able to exploit egregiously those who are more principled. (Even, moreover, in dealings among those who are known to be opportunistic, there are benefits in mutual restraint, as reflected in the aphorism that there is honor among thieves, although admittedly it invites a more complex interpretation than can be attempted here.)

One of the implications of opportunism is that "ideal" cooperative modes of economic organization, by which I mean those where trust and good intentions are generously imputed to the membership, are very fragile. Such organizations are easily invaded and exploited by agents who do not possess those qualities. "High-minded" organizational forms—those which presume trustworthiness, hence are based on nonopportunistic principles—are thus rendered nonviable by the intrusion of unscreened and unpenalized opportunists. Accordingly, those who would have cooperatives succeed must, of necessity, make organizational concessions to the debilitating effects of opportunism. Viable cooperatives will attempt to screen against, socially recondition, and otherwise penalize opportunistic invaders.

At the other extreme are those who maintain that opportunism has always been the operative behavioral assumption. Express reference to "self-interest-seeking with guile" is thus merely a gloss. My response comes in two parts. First, even if true, there are advantages in being more rather than less explicit about what we mean, especially in dealing with those who may be unfamiliar with oral traditions. But second, and more to the point, I seriously dispute that opportunism has been the operative behavioral assumption. Public goods, insurance, and oligopoly aside, there was little or no provision for opportunism in most textual and other treatments of economic organization as recently as 1970. Peter Diamond's remarks on the prevailing orientation toward self-interest seeking in the postwar era are pertinent: standard "economic models [treat] individuals as playing a game with fixed rules which they obey. They do not buy more than they know they can pay for, they do not embezzle funds, they do not rob banks" (1971, p. 31). Simple self-interest-seeking, rather than opportunism, was plainly the ruling view. Thus, circa 1970,

1. Vertical integration was not viewed as a problem of contracting but one of applied price theory and/or technology.
2. Labor union organization was treated almost entirely as a matter of monopoly, there being little or no reference to efficient governance and the attenuation of opportunism.
3. The efficiency benefits of nonstandard forms of contracting were almost wholly disregarded in favor of monopoly explanations for those conditions.
4. Regulatory solutions in which contracting complications attributable to opportunism were dismissed or suppressed were prescribed.
5. The study of contract doctrine relied (and still relies) almost entirely on assumptions of differential risk aversion, concerns over the hazards of opportunism having been suppressed.
6. Firms were regarded as production functions rather than governance structures.
7. More generally, the importance of process and of the institutions of governance to the study of economic organization were undervalued.

Indeed, if an appreciation for opportunism was widespread, what explains the dramatic impact of George Akerlof's treatment of the "lemons problem" in

1970? Or what explains Ronald Coase's uncontested claim that Industrial Organization, circa 1970, was a study in "applied price theory," whence neoclassical monopoly rather than efficient contracting considerations were predominant?

Consider finally the view that opportunism is irrelevant: All that matters is bounded rationality. That result is reached by observing that if unbounded rationality (of the most comprehensive kind, in which even all forms of private information were annihilated) were to obtain then comprehensive long-term contracting would be feasible and all of the problems purportedly due to "opportunism at contract renewal would be entirely eliminated at no cost. [Accordingly, the] reigning comparative-efficiency explanation for internal organization [opportunism] ultimately reduces to an explanation from imperfect structural knowledge [bounded rationality]" (Langlois, 1984, p. 33).

I agree that opportunism is of no account in the face of unbounded rationality. But I also insist that bounded rationality notwithstanding, contracting would be ubiquitous in the face of nonopportunism—that is, if simple self-interest-seeking is assumed. Thus although simple self-interest-seeking assures that all original bargaining advantages (e.g. monopoly ownership of resources) will be fully realized, it also permits *ex post* contracting problems to be annihilated by recourse to a "general clause" whereby parties to a contract promise to disclose all relevant information candidly and to behave in a cooperative fashion during contract execution and at contract renewal intervals.[1]

The general clause mechanics are discussed elsewhere (Williamson, 1975, pp. 27, 91–93). Suffice it to observe here that four cases must be

---

[1]That contracting works well in both of these cases does not mean that economies which initially differ only in the attributes of human agents—one has unboundedly rational but opportunistic agents (such agents, were they to be transported to a planet of boundedly rational agents, would thus take advantage of the indigenous population); the other economy has boundedly rational but nonopportunistic agents—will yield identical results. To the contrary, the latter economy will underperform the former: Some opportunities for improvements will not be perceived at all; some mistakes will be recognized only after the fact. Any "shortfalls" due to misperception or mistake will *not be remediable* by supplanting contract by vertical integration, however. This is the critical point.

Inasmuch as each agent can trust the other, delegation of decision responsibilities proceeds in a fully instrumental way in a community of nonopportunists. There being no strategic hazards, specialization of decision-making reflects tastes, differential information access, and differential decision-making competencies.

Agents who value decision participation will thus make this clear in the contracts they reach. All adaptations for which net gains can be projected will thereafter be realized without resistance within a community of nonopportunists. Should the nexus of contracts need to be expanded or otherwise altered—for insurance purposes, for example—this will come about by displaying the relevant data in a fully objective way. Reversals of decision roles, due to aging, learning, or the like, will simply come about whenever net gains are in prospect, the disposition of these gains being distributed according to the gainsharing rule negotiated at the outset.

distinguished and that contracting problems vanish for three of them. These are (1) unbounded rationality/nonopportunism—a condition of contractual utopia; (2) unbounded rationality/opportunism—a case where contracts can be made to work well by recourse to comprehensive contracting; (3) bounded rationality/nonopportunism—where contracting works well because of general clause protection against the hazards of contractual incompleteness; and (4) bounded rationality/opportunism—which I maintain accords with reality and is where all of the difficult contracting issues reside. The entries that appear in the following four-way classification of contract are offered as an overview.

Condition of Bounded Rationality

		Absent	Admitted
Condition of Opportunism	Absent	Bliss	"General clause" contracting
	Admitted	Comprehensive contracting	Serious contractual difficulties

CHAPTER 3

The Governance of Contractual Relations

The preceding chapters focused on alternative economic approaches to the study of contract. Alternative legal approaches to the study of contract also warrant review, and they are subject of the present chapter.

Contractual variety is the source of numerous puzzles with which the study of the economic institutions of capitalism is appropriately concerned. Transaction cost economics maintains that such variety is mainly explained by underlying differences in the attributes of transactions. Efficiency purposes are served by matching governance structures to the attributes of transactions in a discriminating way.

Ian Macneil's (1974; 1978) thoughtful and provocative three-way classification of contract is set out in section 1. A transaction cost interpretation is advanced in section 2. Issues of uncertainty and measurement are addressed in sections 3 and 4. The distribution of transactions within the spectrum of contract is discussed in section 5.

1. Contracting Traditions

There is widespread agreement that the discrete transaction paradigm— "sharp in by clear agreement; sharp out by clear performance" (Macneil,

1974, p. 738)—has served both law and economics well. But there is also increasing awareness that many contractual relations are not of this well-defined kind. A deeper understanding of the nature of contract has emerged as the legal-rule emphasis associated with the study of discrete contracting has given way to a more general concern with the contractual purposes to be served. Macneil's distinctions among classical, neoclassical, and relational law are instructive.

1.1 Classical Contract Law

As Macneil observes, any system of contract law has the purpose of facilitating exchange. What is distinctive about classical contract law is that it attempts to do so by enhancing discreteness and intensifying "presentiation" (1978, p. 862), where presentiation has reference to efforts to "make or render present in place or time; to cause to be perceived or realized at present" (1978, p. 863, n. 25). The economic counterpart to complete presentiation is contingent claims contracting, which entails comprehensive contracting whereby all relevant future contingencies pertaining to the supply of a good or service are described and discounted with respect to both likelihood and futurity.

Classical contract law endeavors to implement discreteness and presentiation in several ways. For one thing, the identity of the parties to a transaction is treated as irrelevant. In that respect it corresponds exactly with the "ideal" market transaction in economics.[1] Second the nature of the agreement is carefully delimited, and the more formal features govern when formal (for example, written) and informal (for example, oral) terms are contested. Third, remedies are narrowly prescribed so that, "should the initial presentiation fail to materialize because of nonperformance, the consequences are relatively predictable from the beginning and are not open-ended" (Macneil, 1978, p. 864). Additionally, third-party participation is discouraged (p. 864). The emphasis is thus on legal rules, formal documents, and self-liquidating transactions.

---

[1]As Lester G. Telser and Harlow N. Higinbotham put it:

> In an organized market the participants trade a standardized contract such that each unit of the contract is a perfect substitute for any other unit. The identities of the parties in any mutually agreeable transaction do not affect the terms of exchange. The organized market itself or some other institution deliberately creates a homogeneous good that can be traded anonymously by the participants or their agents. [1977, p. 997]

1.2 Neoclassical Contract Law

Not every transaction fits comfortably into the classical contracting scheme. In particular, for long-term contracts executed under conditions of uncertainty complete presentiation is apt to be prohibitively costly if not impossible. Problems of several kinds arise. First, not all future contingencies for which adaptations are required can be anticipated at the outset. Second, the appropriate adaptations will not be evident for many contingencies until the circumstances materialize. Third, except as changes in states of the world are unambiguous, hard contracting between autonomous parties may well give rise to veridical disputes when state-contingent claims are made. In a world where (at least some) parties are inclined to be opportunistic, whose representations are to be believed?

Faced with the prospective breakdown of classical contracting in such circumstances, three alternatives are available. One would be to forgo such transactions altogether. A second would be to remove those transactions from the market and organize them internally instead. Adaptive, sequential decision-making would then be implemented under unified ownership and with the assistance of hierarchial incentive and control systems. Third, a different contracting relation that preserves trading but provides for additional governance structure might be devised. This last brings us to what Macneil refers to as neoclassical contracting.

As Macneil observes, "Two common characteristics of long-term contracts are the existence of gaps in their planning and the presence of a range of processes and techniques used by contract planners to create flexibility in lieu of either leaving gaps or trying to plan rigidly" (1978, p. 865). Third-party assistance in resolving disputes and evaluating performance often has advantages over litigation in serving these functions of flexibility and gap filling. Lon Fuller's remarks on the procedural differences between arbitration and litigation are instructive:

> [T]here are open to the arbitrator . . . quick methods of education not open to the courts. An arbitrator will frequently interrupt the examination of witnesses with a request that the parties educate him to the point where he can understand the testimony being received. This education can proceed informally, with frequent interruptions by the arbitrator, and by informed persons on either side, when a point needs clarification. Sometimes there will be arguments across the table, occasionally even within each of the separate camps. The end result will usually be a clarification that will enable everyone to proceed more intelligently with the case. [1963, pp. 11–12]

A recognition that the world is complex, that agreements are incomplete, and that some contracts will never be reached unless both parties have confidence in the settlement machinery thus characterizes neoclassical contract law. One important purposive difference in arbitration and litigation that contributes to the procedural differences described by Fuller is that, whereas continuity (at least completion of the contract) is presumed under the arbitration machinery, that presumption is much weaker when litigation is employed.[2]

Patrick Atiyah's views regarding "the failure of classical law" are apposite:

> The modern commercial transaction is, in practice, apt to include provision for varying the terms of exchange to suit the conditions applicable at the time of performance. Goods ordered for future delivery are likely to be supplied at prices ruling at the time of delivery; rise and fall clauses in building or construction works are the rule and not the exception; currency-variation clauses may well be included in international transactions. And even where such provisions are not included in the contract itself, business people are in practice often constrained to agree to adjustments to contractual terms where subsequent events make the original contract no longer capable of performance on a fair basis. The rewards and penalties for guessing what the future will bring are no longer automatically thought of as being the natural consequences of success or failure in the skill and expertise of business activity. For example, in Government contracts, ex gratia payments are typically made in fixed price contracts, "where unforeseen circumstances have substantially raised costs and caused the contractor to suffer a loss." And conversely, contractors who make "excessive profits" in dealings with the Government may well discover that these are not regarded as the reward for abnormal skill and enterprise, but as the result of miscalculation by the Government which they will be compelled to hand over. Nor are such occurrences peculiar to Government or other public authorities. Even between private commercial organizations, the fact that business relationships are so often continuous means that the desire to maintain the goodwill of other contracting parties is often more important than the letter of a contract. [1979, pp. 714–15]

1.3 *Relational Contracting*

The pressures to sustain ongoing relations "have led to the spinoff of many subject areas from the classical, and later the neoclassical, contract law system, e.g., much of corporate law and collective bargaining" (Macneil, 1978, p. 885). Progressively increasing the "duration and complexity" of contract has thus resulted in the displacement of even neoclassical adjustment processes by adjustment processes of a more thoroughly transaction-specific, ongoing-administrative kind. The fiction of discreteness is fully displaced as the relation takes on the properties of a "minisociety with a vast array of norms

---

[2]As Lawrence Friedman observes, relationships are effectively fractured if a dispute reaches litigation (1965, p. 205).

beyond those centered on the exchange and its immediate processes'' (Macneil, 1978, p. 901). By contrast with the neoclassical system, where the reference point for effecting adaptations remains the original agreement, the reference point under a truly relational approach is the ''entire relation as it has developed [through] time. This may or may not include an 'original agreement'; and if it does, may or may not result in great deference being given it'' (Macneil, 1978, p. 890).

The spinoff to which Macneil refers notwithstanding, commercial law, labor law, and corporate law all possess striking commonalities.

2. Efficient Governance

As discussed above, the principal dimensions for describing transactions are asset specificity, uncertainty, and frequency. It will facilitate the argument in this section to assume that uncertainty is present in sufficient degree to pose an adaptive, sequential decision requirement and to focus on asset specificity and frequency. Three frequency classes—one-time, occasional, and recurrent—and three asset specificity classes—nonspecific, mixed, and highly specific—will be considered. To simplify the argument further, the following assumptions are made: (1) Suppliers and buyers intend to be in business on a continuing basis; thus the special hazards posed by fly-by-night firms can be disregarded. (2) Potential suppliers for any given requirement are numerous—which is to say that *ex ante* monopoly in ownership of specialized resources is assumed away. (3) The frequency dimension refers strictly to buyer activity in the market. (4) The investment dimension refers to the characteristics of investments made by suppliers.

Although discrete transactions are intriguing—for example, purchasing local spirits from a shopkeeper in a remote area of a foreign country one expects never again to visit or refer his friends—few transactions have such a totally isolated character. For those that do not, the difference between one-time and occasional transactions is not apparent. Accordingly, only occasional and recurrent frequency distinctions will be maintained. The two-by-three matrix shown in Figure 3–1 thus describes the six types of transactions to which governance structures must be matched. Illustrative transactions appear in the cells.

The question now is how Macneil's contracting classifications correspond to the description of transactions in Figure 3–1. Several propositions are suggested immediately: (1) Highly standardized transactions are not apt to require specialized governance structure. (2) Only recurrent transactions will

		Investment Characteristics		
		Nonspecific	Mixed	Idiosyncratic
Frequency	Occasional	Purchasing standard equipment	Purchasing customized equipment	Constructing a plant
	Recurrent	Purchasing standard material	Purchasing customized material	Site-specific transfer of intermediate product across successive stages

FIGURE 3–1.   Illustrative Transactions

support a highly specialized governance structure.[3] (3) Although occasional transactions of a nonstandardized kind will not support a transaction-specific governance structure, they require special attention nonetheless. In terms of Macneil's three-way classification of contract, classical contracting presumably applies to all standardized transactions (whatever the frequency), relational contracting develops for transactions of a recurring and nonstandardized kind, and neoclassical contracting is needed for occasional, nonstandardized transactions.

Specifically, classical contracting is approximated by what is described below as market governance, neoclassical contracting involves trilateral governance, and the relational contracts that Macneil describes are organized in bilateral or unified governance structures. Consider these seriatim.

2.1   Market Governance

Market governance is the main governance structure for nonspecific transactions of both occasional and recurrent contracting. Markets are especially

---

[3]Defense contracting may appear to be a counterexample, since an elaborate governance structure is devised for many defense contracts. This reflects in part, however, the special disabilities of the government to engage in own-production. But for that, many contracts would be organized in-house. Also, contracts that are very large and of long duration, as many defense contracts are, do have recurring character.

efficacious when recurrent transactions are contemplated, since both parties need only consult their own experience in deciding to continue a trading relationship or, at little transitional expense, turn elsewhere. Being standardized, alternative purchase and supply arrangements are presumably easy to work out.

Nonspecific but occasional transactions are ones for which buyers (and sellers) are less able to rely on direct experience to safeguard transactions against opportunism. Often, however, rating services or the experience of other buyers of the same good can be consulted. Given that the good or service is of a standardized kind, such experience rating, by formal and informal means, will provide incentives for parties to behave responsibly.

To be sure, such transactions take place within and benefit from a legal framework. But such dependence is not great. As S. Todd Lowry puts it, "the traditional economic analysis of exchange in a market setting properly corresponds to the legal concept of *sale* (rather than contract), since sale presumes arrangements in a market context and requires legal support primarily in enforcing transfers of title" (1976, p. 12). He would thus reserve the concept of contract for exchanges where, in the absence of standardized market alternatives, the parties have designed "patterns of future relations on which they could rely" (1976, p. 13).

The assumptions of the discrete contracting paradigm are rather well satisfied for transactions where markets serve as a main governance mode. Thus the specific identity of the parties is of negligible importance; substantive content is determined by reference to formal terms of the contract; and legal rules apply. Market alternatives are mainly what protect each party against opportunism by his opposite. Litigation is strictly for settling claims; concentrated efforts to sustain the relation are not made, because the relation is not independently valued.[4]

2.2 *Trilateral Governance*

The two types of transactions for which trilateral governance is needed are occasional transactions of the mixed and highly specific kinds. Once the principals to such transactions have entered into a contract, there are strong incentives to see the contract through to completion. Not only have spe-

---

[4]"Generally speaking, a serious conflict, even quite a minor one such as an objection to a harmlessly late tender of the delivery of goods, terminates the discrete contract as a live one and leaves nothing but a conflict over money damages to be settled by a lawsuit. Such a result fits neatly the norms of enhancing discreteness and intensifying . . . presentation" (Macneil, 1978, p. 877).

cialized investments been put in place, the opportunity cost of which is much lower in alternative uses, but the transfer of those assets to a successor supplier would pose inordinate difficulties in asset valuation.[5] The interests of the principals in sustaining the relation are especially great for highly idiosyncratic transactions.

Market relief is thus unsatisfactory. Often the setup costs of a transaction-specific governance structure cannot be recovered for occasional transactions. Given the limits of classical contract law for sustaining such transactions, on the one hand, and the prohibitive cost of transaction-specific (bilateral) governance, on the other, an intermediate institutional form is evidently needed.

Neoclassical contract law has many of the sought-after qualities. Thus rather than resorting immediately to court-ordered litigation—with its transaction-rupturing features—third-party *assistance* (arbitration) in resolving disputes and evaluating performance is employed instead. (The use of the architect as a relatively independent expert to determine the content of form construction contracts is an example (Macneil, 1978, p. 566).) Also, the expansion of the specific performance remedy in past decades is consistent with continuity purposes—though Macneil declines to characterize specific performance as the "primary neoclassical contract remedy" (1978, p. 879). The section of the Uniform Commercial Code that permits the "seller aggrieved by a buyer's breach . . . unilaterally to maintain the relation" is yet another example.[6]

2.3 Bilateral Governance

The two types of transactions for which specialized governance structure are commonly devised are recurring transactions supported by investments of the mixed and highly specific kinds. The fundamental transformation applies because of the nonstandardized nature of the transactions. Continuity of the trading relation is thus valued. The transactions' recurrent nature potentially permits the cost of specialized governance structures to be recovered.

Two types of transaction-specific governance structures for intermediate product market transactions can be distinguished: bilateral structures, where the autonomy of the parties is maintained, and unified structures, where the

---

[5]As discussed in Chapter 4, physical assets sometimes qualify as an exception.

[6]The rationale for this section of the Code is that "identification of the goods to the contract will, within limits, permit the seller to recover the price of the goods rather than merely damages for the breach . . . ([where the] latter may be far less in amount and more difficult to prove)" (Macneil, 1978, p. 880).

transaction is removed from the market and organized within the firm subject to an authority relation (vertical integration). Bilateral structures have only recently received the attention they deserve, and their operation is least well understood. The issues are elaborated in Chapters 7 and 8.

Highly idiosyncratic transactions are ones where the human and physical assets required for production are extensively specialized, so there are no obvious scale economies to be realized through interfirm trading that the buyer (or seller) is unable to realize himself (through vertical integration). In the case, however, of mixed transactions, the degree of asset specialization is less complete. Accordingly, outside procurement for those components may be favored by scale economy considerations.

As compared with vertical integration, outside procurement also maintains high-powered incentives and limits bureaucratic distortions (see Chapter 6). Problems with market procurement arise, however, when adaptability and contractual expense are considered. Whereas internal adaptations can be effected by fiat, outside procurement involves effecting adaptations across a market interface. Unless the need for adaptations has been contemplated from the outset and expressly provided for by the contract, which often is impossible or prohibitively expensive, adaptations across a market interface can be accomplished only by mutual, follow-on agreements. Inasmuch as the interests of the parties will commonly be at variance when adaptation proposals (originated by either party) are made, a dilemma is evidently posed.

On the one hand, both parties have an incentive to sustain the relationship rather than to permit it to unravel, the object being to avoid the sacrifice of valued transaction-specific economies. On the other hand, each party appropriates a separate profit stream and cannot be expected to accede readily to any proposal to adapt the contract. What is needed, evidently, is some way for declaring admissible dimensions for adjustment such that flexibility is provided under terms in which both parties have confidence. This can be accomplished partly by (1) recognizing that the hazards of opportunism vary with the type of adaptation proposed and (2) restricting adjustments to those where the hazards are least. But the spirit within which adaptations are effected is equally important (Macaulay, 1963, p. 61).

Quantity adjustments have much better incentive-compatibility properties than do price adjustments. For one thing, price adjustments have an unfortunate zero-sum quality, whereas proposals to increase, decrease, or delay delivery do not. Also, except as discussed below, price adjustment proposals involve the risk that one's opposite is contriving to alter the terms within the bilateral monopoly trading gap to his advantage. By contrast, a presumption that exogenous events, rather than strategic purposes, are responsible for quantity adjustments is ordinarily warranted. Given the idiosyncratic nature of the exchange, a seller (or buyer) simply has little reason to doubt the representations of his opposite when a quantity change is proposed.

Thus buyers will neither seek supply from other sources nor divert products obtained (at favorable prices) to other uses (or users)—because other sources will incur high setup costs and an idiosyncratic product is nonfungible across uses and users. Likewise, sellers will not withhold supply because better opportunities have arisen, since the assets in question have a specialized character. The result is that quantity representations for idiosyncratic products can ordinarily be taken at face value. Since inability to adapt both quantity and price would render most idiosyncratic exchanges nonviable, quantity adjustments occur routinely.

Of course, not all price adjustments pose the same degree of hazard. Those which pose few hazards will predictably be implemented. Crude escalator clauses that reflect changes in general economic conditions are one possibility. But since such escalators are not transaction-specific, imperfect adjustments often result when these escalators are applied to local conditions. Consider therefore whether price adjustments more closely related to local circumstances are feasible. The issue here is whether interim price adjustments can be devised for some subset of conditions such that the strategic hazards described above do not arise. What are the preconditions?

Crises facing either of the parties to an idiosyncratic exchange constitute one class of exceptions. Faced with a viability crisis that jeopardizes the relationship, *ad hoc* price relief may be permitted. More relevant and interesting, however, is whether there are circumstances whereby interim price adjustments are made routinely. The preconditions here are two: first, proposals to adjust prices must relate to exogenous, germane, and easily verifiable events; and second, quantifiable cost consequences must be confidently related thereto. An example may help to illustrate. Consider a component for which a significant share of the cost is accounted for by a basic material (copper; steel). Assume, moreover, that the fractional cost of the component in terms of this basic material is well specified. An exogenous change in prices of materials would in such a case pose few hazards if partial but interim price relief were permitted by allowing pass-through according to formula. A more refined adjustment than aggregate escalators would afford thereby obtains.

It bears emphasis, however, that not all costs so qualify. Changes in overhead or other expenses for which validation is difficult and which, even if verified, bear an uncertain relation to the cost of the component will not be passed through in a similar way. Recognizing the hazards, the parties will simply forgo relief of this kind.

2.4 Unified Governance

Incentives for trading weaken as transactions become progressively more idiosyncratic. The reason is that as human and physical assets become more specialized to a single use, and hence less transferable to other uses, economies of scale can be as fully realized by the buyer as by an outside supplier. The choice of organizing mode then turns entirely on which mode has superior adaptive properties. As discussed in Chapter 4, vertical integration will ordinarily appear in such circumstances.

The advantage of vertical integration is that adaptations can be made in a sequential way without the need to consult, complete, or revise interfirm agreements. Where a single ownership entity spans both sides of the transaction, a presumption of joint profit maximization is warranted. Thus price adjustments in vertically integrated enterprises will be more complete than in interfirm trading. And, assuming that internal incentives are not misaligned, quantity adjustments will be implemented at whatever frequency serves to maximize the joint gain to the transaction.

Unchanging identity at the interface coupled with extensive adaptability in both price and quantity is thus characteristic of highly idiosyncratic transactions. Market contracting gives way to bilateral contracting, which in turn is supplanted by unified contracting (internal organization) as asset specificity progressively deepens.[7]

The efficient match of governance structures with transactions that results from the foregoing is shown in Figure 3–2.

---

[7]Note that this transaction cost rationale for internal organization is very different from that originally advanced by Coase. He argued that there are two factors that favor organizing production in the firm as compared with the market: the cost of "discovering what the relevant prices are" is purportedly lower, and the "costs of negotiating and concluding a separate contract for each exchange transaction which takes place on a market" are reduced (Coase, 1952, p. 336). His 1972 treatment of the main differences between firms and markets invokes precisely these same two factors (Coase, 1972, p. 63). Expressed in terms of the behavioral assumptions on which I rely, Coase (implicitly) acknowledges bounded rationality but makes no reference to opportunism. Indeed, to contend, as he does, that Knight offers no reason for superseding the price system, since "[w]e can imagine a system where all advice or knowledge was bought as required" (Coase, 1952, p. 346), is essentially to deny that markets for information are beset by opportunism. Coase is not only silent on the contracting hazards and maladaptations on which I rely to explain nonstandard contracting, but he makes no mention of the need to dimensionalize transactions, which is the key to the discriminating approach. Those differences notwithstanding, the debts of transaction cost economics to Coase's early work are beyond adequate acknowledgment.

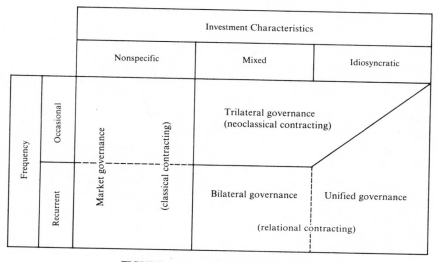

FIGURE 3–2. Efficient Governance

3. Uncertainty

The proposed match of governance structures with transactions considers only two of the three dimensions for describing transactions: asset specificity and frequency. The third dimension, uncertainty, is assumed to be present in sufficient degree to pose an adaptive, sequential decision problem. The occasion to make successive adaptations arises because of the impossibility (or costliness) of enumerating all possible contingencies and/or stipulating appropriate adaptations to them in advance. The effects on economic organization of increases in uncertainty above that threshold level have not, however, been considered.

As indicated earlier, nonspecific transactions are ones for which continuity has little value, since new trading relations can be easily arranged by both parties. Increasing the degree of uncertainty does not alter this. Market governance (classical contracting) thus holds across standardized transactions of all kinds, whatever the degree of uncertainty.

Matters change when asset specificity is introduced. Since continuity now matters, increasing the degree of parametric uncertainty makes it more imperative to organize transactions within governance structures that have the capacity to ''work things out.'' Failure to support transaction-specific assets with protective governance structures predictably results in costly haggling and maladaptiveness. Efforts to restore a position on the shifting contract curve may be forgone for this reason. The intrusion of behavioral uncertainty, which is associated with unique events, compounds the difficulties.

Indeed, though it is extreme and even implausible in many trading situations, it is not strictly essential for the original disturbance to which an adaptation is sought to have exogenous origins. As discussed in Chapter 7, Section 4, one of the parties to a bilateral trade can contrive to introduce a disturbance that alters the profit prospects of the other. An even more blatant example would be for one party to make false state of the world declarations. Thus suppose that a contract stipulates that X will be delivered under θ_1 and $X + \delta$ under θ_2, where θ_1 and θ_2 refer to state realizations. If it is difficult for third parties to discern which state actually obtains, buyers may falsely assert that θ_2 obtains. Although such blatant opportunism may be rare, it nevertheless illustrates the problems that arise when trading parties possessing the behavioral attributes of human nature as we know it are joined, by reason of asset specificity, in a bilateral trading situation.

Transactions with mixed investment attributes pose especially interesting organizational problems. Unless an appropriate market-assisted governance structure can be devised, such transactions may ''flee'' to one of the polar extremes as the degree of uncertainty increases. One possibility would be to sacrifice valued design features in favor of a more standardized good or service. Market governance would then apply. Alternatively, the valued design features could be preserved (perhaps even enhanced) and the transaction assigned to internal organization instead. Sometimes, however, it will be feasible to devise nonstandard contracts of the kinds discussed in Chapters 7 and 8. Where that is done (and is not prohibited by public policy), bilateral contracting relations between nominally autonomous contracting agents can often survive the stresses of greater uncertainty.

Reductions in uncertainty, of course, warrant shifting transactions in the opposite direction—although such shifts may be delayed if the assets in question are long-lived. To the extent that uncertainty decreases as an industry matures, which is the usual case, the benefits that accrue to internal organization (vertical integration) presumably decline. Accordingly, greater reliance on market procurement is commonly feasible for transactions of recurrent trading in mature industries.

4. Measurement

The cognitive map of contract set out in Figure 1–1 (Chapter 1) distinguishes between two branches of transaction cost economics: the governance branch and the measurement branch. The former is concerned mainly with organizing transactions in such a way as to facilitate efficient adaptations. The latter is concerned with the ways by which better to assure a closer correspondence between deeds and awards (or value and price). To be sure, these are not independent. The difference in emphasis is nevertheless real and needs to be highlighted. It is furthermore noteworthy that problems of governance and measurement both vanish if *either* bounds on rationality *or* opportunism are presumed to be absent.

Thus assume that parties to a trade do not experience bounded rationality. Assume, moreover, that this implies the absence of private information and that this competence extends to impartial arbiters. Governance problems then vanish, since comprehensive contracting is feasible. Opportunistic inclinations are simply of no account. Measurement problems likewise vanish, since a world of unbounded rationality is one in which measurement costs are zero. An opportunistic propensity to exploit private information is vitiated in these circumstances.

Assume instead that parties experience bounded rationality but are not opportunistic. Incomplete contracting does not then pose a governance issue, since the general clause device assures that appropriate adaptations will be implemented without resistance by either party to a bilateral trade. Similarly, costly measurement is not a problem if neither party to a trade attempts to exploit private information to the disadvantage of the other—which neither will do if opportunism is absent.

Repeated reference to bounded rationality and opportunism does not, however, without more, direct attention to the particular problems of economic organization that are most severe. Some transactions test bounded rationality limits more severely. Some pose greater hazards of opportunism. Which are they?

Just as the study of governance has benefited by efforts to identify the critical dimensions with respect to which transactions differ in governance respects, so likewise will the study of measurement benefit by efforts to develop the underlying microanalytics. Although the measurement branch of transaction cost economics has made considerable headway during the past decade (Barzel, 1982; North, 1982; Kenney and Klein, 1983), the relevant dimensions for ascertaining where the measurement difficulties reside remain somewhat obscure. Be that as it may, an effort to examine some of the underlying features will nevertheless be attempted.

4.1 *Ex Ante Problems*

The adverse selection problem referred to above is an illustration of an *ex ante* condition where one party to the trade has private information that it can choose selectively to disclose, which asymmetry the other party cannot overcome except at great cost. The condition is a manifestation of a more general problem that is responsible for measurement difficulties, namely, idiosyncratic information. Many of the problems that George Akerlof (1970) treats in the context of "lemons" are precisely attributable to such an *ex ante* valuation condition. The seller of a used car can thus be presumed to have deeper knowledge than the buyer, which asymmetry introduces distortions into this market. And Groucho Marx's refusal to join a club that would admit him reflects a condition of bilateral asymmetry: if they really knew what he was like, they wouldn't admit him; and since they don't know, they presumably have admitted many others of dubious reputation earlier.

The recent Kenney and Klein (1983) treatment of "oversearching" in the market for gem-quality uncut diamonds is another illustration of the phenomenon. Despite classification into more than two thousand categories, significant quality variation in the stones evidently remained. How can such a market be organized so that oversearching expenses are not incurred and each party to the trade has confidence in the other? The "solution" that Kenney and Klein describe entails more than just accumulating experience upon which to base "trust". By assembling groups of diamonds—or "sights"— and subjecting the exchange to special trading rules, hazards of opportunism are more reliably attenuated.

4.2 *Contract Execution*

Information asymmetries of two kinds can be distinguished at the contract execution stage. The more familiar is where one party to the trade has more knowledge over the particulars than does the other. For example, a salesman's success depends jointly on his sales efforts and stochastic state realizations. Although the salesman knows the former, he cannot be relied upon accurately to report them. Accordingly, if the producer can observe only output alone, then compensation is based entirely on sales. (That is the classic agency problem, where $X = X(a,\theta)$, where X denotes output, a is effort, and θ is the state realization.) Complex incentive alignment problems are thereby posed (Holmstrom, 1979).

A second, less widely recognized type of asymmetry takes the form of King Solomon problems. Here each party to the transaction knows the full truth of what has occurred, but it is costly to disclose the facts to anyone other than an on-site observer. Those are the issues with which Alchian and Demsetz (1972) were concerned in their discussion of team organization. If two or more workers must work coordinately and if their separate contributions cannot be ascertained by an *ex post* examination of the work product, then assignment of someone to oversee the work may be needed. Supervision purportedly arises in this way.

Unsurprisingly, many of the most interesting problems of economic organization involve both asset specificity and information asymmetry issues. Indeed, as Alchian has argued, the two are often inseparable (1984, p. 39).

5. The Distribution of Transactions

The study of contractual relations plainly involves more than an examination of discrete markets on the one hand and hierarchical organization on the other. As Llewellyn observed in 1931, the exchange spectrum runs the full gamut from pure market to hierarchy and includes complex "future deals" located between market and hierarchy extremes (1931, p. 727). Similarly, George Richardson remarks that "what confronts us is a continuum passing from transactions, such as those on organized commodity markets, where the cooperation element is minimal, through intermediate areas in which there are linkages of traditional connection and good will, and finally to those complex and interlocking clusters, groups and alliances which represent cooperation fully and formally developed" (1972, p. 887). Both Richardson's examples and those more recently developed and discussed by Arthur Stinchcombe (1983) demonstrate that activity in the middle range is extensive. Stewart Macaulay's empirical examination of commercial contracting practices (1963) confirms this.

Suppose that transactions were to be arrayed in terms of the degree to which parties to the trade maintained autonomy. Discrete transactions would thus be located at the one extreme, highly centralized, hierarchical transactions would be at the other, and hybrid transactions (franchising, joint ventures, other forms of nonstandard contracting) would be located in between. What would the resulting distribution of transactions look like?

The three leading candidates are (1) the bimodal distribution, where most transactions cluster at one or the other extreme, (2) the normal distribution, whence the extremes are rare and most transactions display an intermediate degree of interdependence, and (3) the uniform transaction. Whereas I was earlier of the view that transactions of the middle kind were very difficult to organize and hence were unstable, on which account the bimodal distribution was more accurately descriptive (Williamson, 1975), I am now persuaded that transactions in the middle range are much more common. (Such transactions have, moreover, been the object of increasing attention in the economic,[8]

---

[8]See especially Chapters 7, 8, 10, and 13 and the numerous references to the recent economic literature therein.

legal,[9] and organizations[10] literatures.) But inasmuch as standardized commodity transactions are numerous and as administrative organization is similarly widespread, the tails of the distribution are thick. By a process of elimination, the uniform distribution appears most nearly to correspond with the world of contract as it is. Whatever the empirical realities, greater attention to transactions of the middle range will help to illuminate an understanding of complex economic organization. If such transactions flee to the extremes, what are the reasons? If such transactions can be stabilized, what are the governance processes?

[9]Macaulay (1963); Macneil (1974); Clarkson, Miller, and Muris (1978); Atiyah (1979); Goetz and Scott (1983); Palay (1984); Masten (1984); and Kronman (1985) are examples.

[10]Stinchcombe (1983), Harrison White (1981), and Robert Eccles (1981), and Granovetter (1983) are examples.

CHAPTER 4

Vertical Integration: Theory and Policy

The law and economics of vertical integration have long been subject to controversy. Roger Blair and David Kaserman's recent review of the issues employs the language of warfare—battleground, skirmishes, campaigns, and the like—to set the stage (1983, p. 1). Contests of two kinds can be distinguished. The earlier ones took place within the monopoly domain, the disputes having reference to whether vertical integration was principally an instrument of price discrimination, was designed to check successive marginalization, or had entry barrier purposes. More recently monopoly and efficiency explanations have been paired off. Vigorous resistance notwithstanding, the technological orientation and monopoly presumptions of an earlier era have gradually made way for an interpretation in which efficiency purposes are more prominently featured. By comparison with the 1968 Vertical Merger Guidelines, those issued by the Justice Department in 1982 make significant allowances for efficiency. Indeed, the 1984 Merger Guidelines even make provision for an efficiency defense (Chapter 14).

To be sure, as with most complex forms of organization, vertical integration can and sometimes does serve a variety of economic purposes.[1] I focus here on what I consider to be the main purpose served: economizing on

[1]Paul Kleindorfer and Gunter Knieps (1982, p. 1) offer the following summary statement on the purposes of vertical integration:

transaction costs. A brief discussion of strategic purposes, however, is also included.

The commonsense explanation for vertical integration is that it has technological origins.[2] That explanation is disputed in section 1. The main factor to which I attribute a decision to integrate is a condition of asset specificity. A simple model in which asset specificity is featured and in which the tradeoffs between transaction costs and production costs are displayed is developed in section 2. Further implications of this approach are developed in section 3. Vertical Merger Guidelines are examined in section 4.

1.   Technological Determinism

Ours is indisputably a technologically advanced society. That complex organization is needed to serve a complex technology is surely common sense. In particular, comprehensive integration—backward into materials, laterally into components, and forward into distribution—is widely believed to be the organizational means by which complex products and services are created, produced, and efficiently brought to market.

That conception is supported by the firm-as-production-function orientation. Large, integrated firms, wherein production is accomplished by joining fungible inputs to yield outputs according to the engineering specifications, are supposedly the rule rather than the exception. Reference to "physical or technical aspects" sometimes buttresses this nonmarket presumption. The standard example is the integration of iron and steel making, where the

---

The most popular [explanation] has been that when economies of scope between successive stages due to technological organizational interrelationships are strong enough, these activities should be provided under joint ownership (e.g., Chandler [1966]). Other arguments for Vertical Integration have been the avoidance of factor distortions in monopolized markets (e.g., Vernon and Graham [1971], Warren-Boulton [1974], Schmalensee [1973]); uncertainty in the supply of the upstream good with the consequent need for information by downstream firms (Arrow [1975]); and the transfer of risks from one section of the economy to another (Crouhy [1976], Carlton [1979]). Furthermore, it has been pointed out that transaction costs might create important incentives for vertical integration (e.g., Coase [1937], Williamson [1971, 1975]).

Omitted from this list is the incentive to use vertical integration as an organization shell to evade taxes on intermediate products (Stigler, 1951) or as a device, through judicious use of transfer pricing, to take advantage of differences among tax jurisdictions (that arise, for example, between states). Jerry Green's recent examination of information externalities (1984) also warrants inclusion. Yoram Barzel (1982) and Douglass North (1978) trace vertical integration to difficulties of measurement.

[2]The recent book by Roger Blair and David Kaserman (1983) provides an expansive survey and assessment of the literature.

realization of thermal economies is said to require integration (Bain, 1958, p. 381). Even, moreover, if tight technological linkages of that kind are missing, existing configurations of assets are widely believed to reflect technological principles. Especially among noneconomists, more integration is thought to be preferable to less. Only in such rare circumstances where outside suppliers have patents or where economies of scale or scope are very large would outside procurement be seriously contemplated.

All of the above is plausible, which is to say that vertical integration appears to be the unproblematic result of a natural technological order. I submit, however, that intermediate product market transactions are much more numerous than the conventional wisdom would suggest.[3] The marvels of the market to which Hayek referred in 1945 apply equally today. I furthermore contend that decisions to integrate are rarely due to technological determinism but are more often explained by the fact that integration is the source of transaction cost economies.

One way of putting it is as follows: Technology is fully determinative of economic organization only if (1) there is a single technology that is decisively superior to all others and (2) that technology implies a unique organization form. Rarely, I submit, is there only a single feasible technology, and even more rarely is the choice among alternative organization forms determined by technology.

Recall in this connection the contracting schema in Chapter 1, where general purpose and special purpose technologies are distinguished. Recall further that the parties to the transactions so described have the option of crafting governance structures responsive to their contracting needs. Only as market-mediated contracts break down are the transactions in question removed from markets and organized internally. The presumption that "in the beginning there were markets" informs this perspective.

This market-favoring premise has two advantages. One is that it helps to flag a condition of bureaucratic failure that has widespread economic importance but goes little remarked. (The issues here are briefly introduced in section 3 and are more fully developed in Chapter 6.) Second, it encourages the view, which I believe to be correct, that technological separability between successive production stages is a widespread condition—that sepa-

[3]Absent good measures of change in the amount of vertical integration, it is often inferred from the observed increases in firm size over time that the degree of vertical integration has increased. But such increases in firm size are often a result of radial expansion, whereby the firm grows to serve larger markets but the composition of activity is unchanged, or of diversification. It is evident that few consumer product firms are comprehensively integrated backward into raw materials. And many manufacturers decline to integrate forward into distribution. Lateral integration into components is also incomplete—as an examination of the automobile industry (General Motors, Ford, Chrysler, Toyota) discloses (Monteverde and Teece, 1982).

rability is the rule rather than the exception.[4] It thus becomes easy and even natural to regard the transaction as the basic unit of analysis. As between alternative feasible modes for organizing transactions, which has superior efficiency properties and why? Once that orientation is adopted, internal organization is seen less as a consequence of technology and more as the result of a comparative assessment of markets and hierarchies.

A useful strategy for explicating the decision to integrate is to hold technology constant across alternative modes of organization and to neutralize obvious sources of differential economic benefit, such as transportation cost savings. Thus consider two separable manufacturing operations in which the output of one stage feeds the next. An entrepreneur has decided to enter stage II activity and is considering alternative ways of organizing stage I. One possibility is to solicit bids from qualified suppliers to produce to his needs. A second is to integrate backward and do the work himself.

Assume that the same stage I technology will be employed whether the entrepreneur makes or buys. One factor that would appear to favor own-manufacture over procurement is that transportation cost economies may be realized. That is superficial, however, since an independent stage I supplier can locate in the same cheek-by-jowl relation to stage II as can an integrated owner. Accordingly, transportation (and related inventory cost savings) are neutralized. What is it, then, that favors one of the modes in relation to the other?

Although this query is one to which a theory of the firm might reasonably be expected to speak, mundane vertical integration of this kind is a subject on which the orthodox view of the firm as production function is curiously silent. Given that the two stages in question are technologically separable, and given that factor price, tax, and related distortions are not obviously posed, there is no compelling neoclassical reason to prefer integration over market procurement.

The notion that an independent stage I supplier would be willing to locate in cheek-by-jowl proximity to the stage II buyer nevertheless runs contrary to intuition. Surely there are undisclosed hazards in such an association? If so, does this have organizational ramifications?

---

[4]The view that technological nonseparability is a common condition and is primarily responsible for the appearance of the "classical capitalist firm" and its successor was advanced by Armen Alchian and Harold Demsetz (1972). The principal example they offered in support of their view was that of manual freight loading, whereby two men need to work coordinately in order to load a truck. Such team relations are restricted to relatively small groups, however. The symphony orchestra is the largest such group of which I am aware. See Karl Marx, Vol. 1, chap. 13, for an early insightful discussion of nonseparability. Interesting though such a condition is, nonseparabilities do not explain the appearance and viability of very large-scale organization. Alchian (1984) now holds that complex organization owes its origin to transaction costs.

Note that reference to hazards introduces nonproduction (transaction cost) considerations. Of special importance in this connection, and the distinct contribution of transaction cost economics, is the following proposition: The magnitude of the hazards depends on the attributes of the assets and on the characteristics of the contracting relation.

Thus suppose that stage I requires an investment in durable, general purpose equipment that is mounted "on wheels," hence can be costlessly relocated. Contractual problems between independent buyer and supplier are here limited since contracts can be terminated and productive resources relocated at negligible cost. Given the unspecialized nature of the investments and the mobility that has been ascribed to them, neither buyer nor supplier operates at the sufferance of the other. Problems arise, however, if stage I involves durable specialized investments or if, once put in place, relocation of general purpose assets is thereafter very costly. Here the parties must face issues such as the following: Can the complex contract be written and implemented at low cost whereby independent parties assuredly adapt their relation efficiently to changing circumstances? What are the hazards of incomplete contracting? In consideration of the fundamental transformation to which autonomous contracting is subject in these circumstances, ought unified ownership of the two stages be elected instead? Adaptive, sequential decision-making of the combined stages would then be implemented under the administrative aegis rather than in a recurring bargaining context.[5]

To be sure, this is a highly simplified and stylized example. But the basic argument applies quite generally: Technology is not determinative of economic organization if alternative means of contracting can be described that can feasibly employ, in steady state respects at least, the same technology. I submit that several alternative modes commonly qualify, whence technology is more usefully regarded as a factor that delimits the set of feasible modes— the final choice thereafter turning on a transaction cost assessment. Distinguishing among transactions according to their attributes is essential for final mode selection purposes.

Even that, however, is too simple. It assumes a sequential process whereby technology is selected first and choice among feasible organizational modes is made thereafter. This convenient expository device is used in section 2, below. In fact, however, technology and organizational modes ought to be treated symmetrically; they are decision variables whose values are determined simultaneously. The issues here are addressed elsewhere (Masten, 1982; Riodan and Williamson, forthcoming). Suffice it to observe that, albeit

---

[5]The limits of fiat also need to be addressed. Suffice it to observe here that common ownership of successive stages attenuates incentives for managers to suboptimize, since they do not appropriate separate profit streams. But the issues are more complex. See Chapter 6.

qualified, the main arguments survive when formulated in a more general framework.

2. A Heuristic Model

As discussed in earlier chapters and sketched in section 1 above, the principal factor to which transaction cost economics appeals to explain vertical integration is asset specificity. Without it, market contracting between successive production stages ordinarily has good economizing properties. Not only can production economies be realized by an outside supplier who aggregates orders, but the governance costs of market procurement are negligible—since neither party has a transaction-specific interest in the continuity of the trade. As asset specificity increases, however, the balance shifts in favor of internal organization.

The argument is developed in two parts. First, output is held constant and economies of scale and scope are assumed to be negligible (or the firm in question is of sufficient size to exhaust them). Choice between firm and market thus turns entirely on governance cost differences. Second, economies of scale and scope are admitted, but output is constrained to be the same.[6]

2.1 *Governance Costs and Economic Organization*

The main differences between market and internal organization are these: (1) Markets promote high-powered incentives and restrain bureaucratic distortions more effectively than internal organization; (2) markets can sometimes aggregate demands to advantage, thereby to realize economies of scale and scope; and (3) internal organization has access to distinctive governance instruments. The differences between market and internal organization in incentive and control respects are developed in Chapter 6. For my purpose here, I take these as given.

Consider, therefore, the decision of a firm to make or buy a particular good or service. Suppose that it is a component that is to be joined to the mainframe and that the quantity to be supplied is fixed.[7] Economies of scale and scope are assumed to be negligible, so the critical factors that are deter-

---

[6]As I acknowledge above, a more complete and general model would treat output, asset specificity, and organization form as decision variables.

[7]Assume that the component is used in fixed proportions and represents a negligible fraction of the total cost.

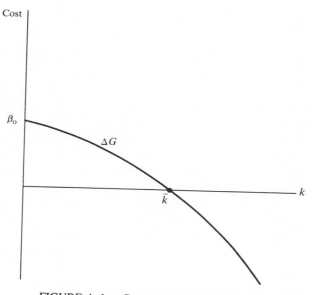

FIGURE 4-1. Comparative Governance Cost

minative in the decision to make or buy are production cost control and the ease of effecting intertemporal adaptation.

The high-powered incentives of markets manifest themselves in both respects: They favor tighter production cost control but, as the bilateral dependency of the relation between the parties builds up, they impede the ease of adaptation. The latter effect is a consequence of the fundamental transformation that occurs as a condition of asset specificity deepens. Let $\beta(k)$ be the bureaucratic costs of internal governance and $M(k)$ the corresponding governance costs of markets, where k is an index of asset specificity. Assume that $\beta(0) > M(0)$, by reason of the above described cost control effects. Assume further, however, that $M' > \beta'$ evaluated at every k. This second is a consequence of the comparative disability of markets in adaptability respects. Letting $\Delta G = \beta(k) - M(k)$, the relation shown in Figure 4-1 obtains.

Thus market procurement is the preferred supply mode where asset specificity is slight—because of the incentive and bureaucratic disabilities of internal organization in production cost control respects. But internal organization is favored where asset specificity is great, because a high degree of bilateral dependency exists in those circumstances and high-powered incentives impair the ease with which adaptive, sequential adjustments to disturbances are accomplished. As shown, the switchover value, where the choice between firm and market is one of indifference, occurs at $\bar{k}$.

2.2 Economies of Scale and Scope

The foregoing assumes that economies of scale and scope are negligible, so that the choice between firm and market rests entirely on the governance cost differences. Plainly that oversimplifies. Markets are often able to aggregate diverse demands, thereby to realize economies of scale and scope. Accordingly, production cost differences also need to be taken into account.[8]

Again it will be convenient to hold output unchanged. Let $\triangle C$ be the steady state production cost difference between producing to one's own requirements and the steady state cost of procuring the same item in the market. (The steady state device avoids the need for adaptation.) Expressing $\triangle C$ as a function of asset specificity, it is plausible to assume that $\triangle C$ will be positive throughout but will be a decreasing function of k.

The production cost penalty of using internal organization is large for standardized transactions for which market aggregation economies are great, whence $\triangle C$ is large where k is low. The cost disadvantage decreases but remains positive for intermediate degrees of asset specificity. Thus although dissimilarities among orders begin to appear, outside suppliers are nevertheless able to aggregate the diverse demands of many buyers and produce at lower costs than can a firm that produces to its own needs. As goods and services become very close to unique (k is high), however, aggregation economies of outside supply can no longer be realized, whence $\triangle C$ asymptotically approaches zero. Contracting out affords neither scale nor scope economies in those circumstances. The firm can produce without penalty to its own needs.

[8]The argument assumes that the firm produces to and services only its own needs. If diseconomies of scale or scope are large, therefore, technological features will deter all but very large firms from supplying to their own needs.

Plausible though this appears, neither economies of scale nor scope are, by themselves, responsible for decisions to buy rather than make. Thus, suppose that economies of scale are large in relation to a firm's own needs. Absent prospective contracting problems, the firm could construct a plant of size sufficient to exhaust economies of scale and sell excess product to rivals and other interested buyers. Or suppose that economies of scope are realized by selling the final good in conjunction with a variety of related items. The firm could integrate forward into marketing and offer to sell its product together with related items on a parity basis—rival and complementary items being displayed, sold, and serviced without reference to strategic purposes.

That other firms, especially rivals, would be willing to proceed on this basis is surely doubtful. Rather than submit to the strategic hazards, some will decline to participate in such a scheme (Williamson, 1975, pp. 16–19, 1979c, pp. 979–80). The upshot is that *all* cost differences between internal and market procurement ultimately rest on transaction cost considerations. Inasmuch, however, as the needs of empirical research on economic organization are better served by making the assumption that firms which procure internally supply exclusively to their own needs, whence technological economies of scale and scope are accorded independent importance (see, for example, the study of Walker and Weber [1984], which is briefly discussed in Section 3.2 of Chapter 5), I employ this assumption here.

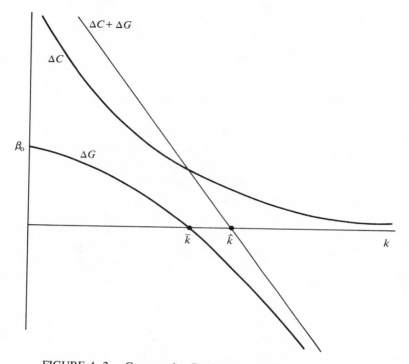

FIGURE 4–2. Comparative Production and Governance Costs

This $\triangle C$ relation is shown in Figure 4–2. The object, of course, is not to minimize $\triangle C$ or $\triangle G$ taken separately but, given the optimal or specified level of asset specificity, to minimize the sum of production and governance cost differences. The vertical sum $\triangle G + \triangle C$ is also displayed. The crossover value of k for which the sum $(\triangle G + \triangle C)$ becomes negative is shown by $\hat{k}$, which value exceeds $\bar{k}$. Economies of scale and scope thus favor market organization over a wider range of asset specificity values than would be observed if steady state production cost economies were absent.

More generally, if $k*$ is the optimal degree of asset specificity,[9] Figure 4–2 discloses:

1. Market procurement has advantages in both scale economy and governance respects where optimal asset specificity is slight ($k* << \hat{k}$).

[9]Reference to a single "optimal" level of k is an expository convenience: The optimal level actually varies with organization form. The intuition for this is set out in footnote 13, below. For a more complete treatment, see Scott Masten (1982) and Riordan and Williamson (forthcoming).

2. Internal organization enjoys the advantage where optimal asset specificity is substantial ($k^* >> \hat{k}$). Not only does the market realize little aggregate economy benefits, but market governance, because of the "lock-in" problems that arise when assets are highly specific, is hazardous.

3. Only small cost differences appear for intermediate degrees of optimal asset specificity. Mixed governance, in which some firms will be observed to buy, others to make, and all express "dissatisfaction" with their current procurement solution, are apt to arise for these. Accidents of history may be determinative. Or nonstandard contracts of the types discussed briefly in Chapter 3 and examined more fully in Chapters 7 and 8 may arise to serve these.

4. More generally, it is noteworthy that, inasmuch as the firm is everywhere at a disadvantage to the market in production cost respects ($\triangle C > 0$ everywhere), the firm will never integrate for production cost reasons alone. Only when contracting difficulties intrude does the firm and market comparison support vertical integration—and then only for values of k^* that exceed $\hat{k}$.

Additional implications may be gleaned by introducing quantity (or firm size) and organization form effects. Thus consider firm size (output). The basic proposition here is that diseconomies associated with own-production will be everywhere reduced as the quantity of the component to be supplied increases. The firm is simply better able to realize economies of scale as its own requirements become larger in relation to the size of the market. The curve $\triangle C$ thus everywhere falls as quantity increases. The question then is what happens to the curve $\triangle G$. If this twists about $\bar{k}$, which is a plausible construction,[10] then the vertical sum $\triangle G + \triangle C$ will intersect the axis at a value of $\bar{k}$ that progressively moves to the left as the quantity to be supplied increases. Accordingly:

5. Larger firms will be more integrated into components than will smaller, *ceteris paribus*.

Finally, although this anticipates arguments developed more fully in Chapter 11, the bureaucratic disabilities to which internal organization is subject vary with the internal structure of the firm. Multidivisionalization,

---

[10]Assume that $\beta(k,X) = I(k)X$, where $I(0) > 0$ and $I(k)$ is the internal governance cost per unit of effecting adaptations. Assume further that $M(k,X) = M(k)X$, where $M(0) = 0$ and $M(k)$ is the corresponding governance cost per unit of effecting market adaptions. Then $\triangle G = [I(k) - M(k)]X$, and the value at which $\triangle G$ goes to zero will be independent of X. The effect of increasing X is to twist $\triangle G$ clockwise about the value of $\bar{k}$ at which it goes to zero.

assuming that the M-form is feasible, serves as a check against the bureaucratic distortions that appear in the unitary form (U-form) of enterprise. Expressed in terms of Figure 4–2, the curve $\triangle G$ falls under multidivisionalization as compared with the unitary form organization. Thus, assuming $\triangle C$ is unchanged:

6. An M-form firm will be more integrated than its U-form counterpart, *ceteris paribus.* [11]

3. Further Implications

3.1 *Asset Specificity Distinctions*

Additional implications of a transaction cost economizing kind can be derived by recognizing that asset specificity takes a variety of forms and that the organizational ramifications vary among these. Four types of asset specificity are usefully distinguished: site specificity—e.g. successive stations that are located in a cheek-by-jowl relation to each other so as to economize on inventory and transportation expenses; physical asset specificity—e.g. specialized dies that are required to produce a component; human asset specificity that arises in a learning-by-doing fashion; and dedicated assets, which represent a discrete investment in generalized (as contrasted with special purpose) production capacity that would not be made but for the prospect of selling a significant amount of product to a specific customer. The organizational ramifications of each are as follows:

1. *Site specificity.* Unified ownership is the preponderant response to an asset specificity condition that arises when successive stages are located in close proximity to one another. Such specificity is explained by an asset immobility condition, which is to say that the setup and/or relocation costs are great. Once such assets are located, therefore, the parties are thereafter operating in a bilateral exchange relation for the useful life of the assets.

2. *Physical asset specificity.* If assets are mobile and the specificity is attributable to physical features, market procurement may still be feasible by concentrating the ownership of the specific assets (e.g. specialized dies) on the buyer and putting the business up for bid. Lock-in problems are avoided, because the buyer can reclaim the dies and reopen the bidding should

---

[11]There are, however, offsetting considerations. U-form managers may be better able to implement their preferences for empire-building, which could take the form of vertical integration. See Chapter 6.

contractual difficulties develop.[12] Thus *ex post* competition is efficacious, and internal organization is unneeded.

3. *Human asset specificity.*   Any condition that gives rise to substantial human asset specificity—be it learning-by-doing or chronic problems of moving human assets in team configurations—favors an employment relation over autonomous contracting. Common ownership of successive stages is thus predicted as the degree of human asset specificity deepens.

4. *Dedicated Assets.*   Investments in dedicated assets involve expanding existing plant on behalf of a particular buyer. Common ownership in these circumstances is rarely contemplated. Trading hazards are nevertheless recognized and are often mitigated by *expanding* the contractual relation to effect symmetrical exposure. Paradoxically, greater aggregate hazard exposure can be mutually preferred to less if, as a consequence, hazard "equilibration" is thereby realized. (The issues here are developed more fully in Chapters 7 and 8.)

Yet another implication of transaction cost reasoning is that where firms are observed both to make and to buy an identical good or service, the internal technology will be characterized by greater asset specificity than will the external technology, *ceteris paribus*.[13] No other approach to the study of vertical integration generates this set of implications.

3.2   *Efficient Boundaries*

The foregoing treats every separable stage of production as one for which a careful assessment of make-or-buy is warranted. In fact, matters are often simpler than that. There are some stages for which integration is not apt to be seriously considered. Backward integration into raw materials is infeasible for many firms. Moreover, there are other stages for which common ownership will appear to be natural. James Thompson's references to a "core technology" (1967, pp. 19–23) presumes that some stages will be consolidated. Site specificity is commonly associated with these. More interesting is the

---

[12]See Teece (1981) for an earlier discussion of this point.

[13]Assume that the optimal level of k is very large, whichever mode of organization is employed. Internal procurement is thus favored in these circumstances. Assume that this is done but that the firm thereafter opens a second plant (of identical size) in a different geographic region for which it is constrained to procure the component in the market. The optimum level of k in these two cases will not be identical. To the contrary, the choice of k in the second (nonintegrated) case will be less than in the first (integrated) case. The reason is that lower k will permit the market to realize aggregation economies and mitigate the governance costs of market procurement, whereas internal organization is denied the same aggregation benefits (see, however, the introductory remarks in Chapter 6) and has superior governance features. For a more general discussion, see Riordan and Williamson (forthcoming). Also see Scott Masten (1982), who was the first rigorously to demonstrate this point.

procurement of items for which off-site production experiences little or no penalty. When is such a component bought, and when is it made?

All these issues can be pulled together in the context of the "efficient boundaries" problem.[14] Thus consider the organization of three distinct production stages, which, for site-specificity reasons, are all part of the same firm. That is the technological core. Suppose that raw materials are distinct and are naturally procured from the market. Suppose further that two things occur at each production stage: There is a physical transformation, and components are joined to the "mainframe." And suppose, finally, that the firm has a choice between own distribution and market distribution.

Let the core production stages be represented by $S1$, $S2$, $S3$, and draw these as rectangles. Let raw materials be represented by R and draw this as a circle. Let component supply by represented by $C1$-B, $C2$-B, $C3$-B if the firm buys its components, and $C1$-O, $C2$-O, $C3$-O if it makes its own components. Draw these as triangles. Let distribution be given by D-B if the firm uses market distribution, and D-O if the firm uses own distribution. Draw these as squares. Finally, let a solid line between units represent an actual transaction and a dashed line a potential transaction, and draw the boundary of the firm as a closed curve that includes those activities that the firm does for itself.

Given the core technology presumptions, stages $S1$ through $S3$ will be organized internally and raw materials will be purchased. Components $C1$ through $C3$ and stage D thus remain to be evaluated with respect to the tradeoffs set out in subsection 2.2 above. Assume that the firm determines on this basis to make component $C2$ and engage in own distribution. The efficient boundary of the firm is thus given by the closed curve in Figure 4–3 that includes, in addition to the technical core, component $C2$ and the distribution stage, D. Components $C1$ and $C3$ and raw material are procured in the market.

Obviously this is arbitrary and merely illustrative. It also oversimplifies greatly. It is relatively easy, however, to elaborate the schema to add to the

---

[14]The term was first introduced by William Ouchi (1980a). One way of answering the question of whether drawing the boundary of the firm one way rather than another makes any difference is to ask a series of related questions. Consider the following:

   A. Production aspects
      1. Would economies of scale be mainly exhausted if the firm were to produce its own requirements?
      2. Are economies of scope significant and can they be realized within the firm?
   B. Design and asset aspects
      1. Does the item in question have special design features? Should it?
      2. Are steady state economies realized by producing the item with the use of a special purpose technology?
   C. Contracting aspects
      1. Are contracting parties prospectively locked into a bilateral exchange relation?
      2. Are there frequent needs to adapt the exchange relation to unanticipated disturbances?

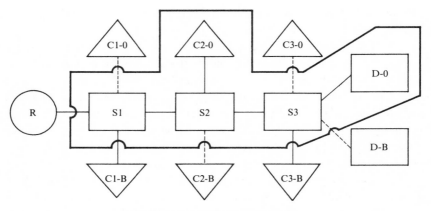

FIGURE 4–3.   Efficient Boundary

core, to consider additional components, to include several raw material stages and consider backward integration into them, to break down distribution, and so on. But the central points would remain unchanged, namely: (1) The common ownership of some stations—the core—is sufficiently obvious that a careful, comparative assessment is unneeded (site specificity will often characterize these transactions); (2) there is a second set of transactions in which own supply is manifestly uneconomic, hence market supply is indicated (many raw materials are commonly of this kind); but (3) there is a third set of activities for which make-or-buy decisions can be made only after assessing the production and transaction cost consequences of alternative modes. The efficient boundary is the inclusive set of core plus additional stages for which own supply can be shown to be the efficient choice.

The basic orientation that informs the transaction cost approach to vertical integration is that integration should be *selective*. Contrary to what is sometimes argued, more integration is not always better than less. The data bear this out (see Chapter 5).

4.   Vertical Merger Guidelines

The cognitive map of contract set out in Chapter 1 (Figure 1–2) identifies two main approaches to the study of contract: monopoly and efficiency. Of the two, the monopoly approach was the more fully developed and more widely favored through the early 1970s (Coase, 1972). Vertical integration is one of the areas to which the monopoly branch of contract was thought to have relevance.

Leverage theory and entry barrier arguments were especially prominent. Vertical integration was believed to permit monopoly power in one area to be magnified through acquisition of another (the leverage theory hypothesis) or to impair the condition of entry (the entry barrier hypothesis).[15] Lacking a "physical or technical aspect" (Bain, 1968, p. 381), whereupon technological cost savings were plausibly associated with vertical integration, anticompetitive purpose was thought to be the driving force. It was easy, therefore, to conclude that public policy concern was warranted whenever vertical integration involved an "appreciable degree of market control at even one stage of the production process" (Stigler, 1955, p. 183). Specifically, Stigler stated that when a firm had at least 20 percent of an industry's output, its acquisition of more than 5 percent of the output capacity of firms to which it sells or from which it buys can be presumed to violate the antitrust laws (Stigler, 1955, pp. 183–84).

The 1968 Vertical Merger Guidelines, which set the limits on acquiring firm and acquired firm market shares at 10 and 6 percent respectively, were plainly in this monopoly/technological spirit. The Guidelines were either informed by and reflected this line of scholarship, or the correspondence between the two is a remarkable coincidence. Given the prevailing firm-as-production-function framework, an affirmative rationale for vertical integration that did have technological origins was not evident. There being no transaction cost economies to realize, even the slightest degree of monopoly power was thought to be responsible for decisions to integrate. The threshold level for imputing monopoly power and purpose to the acquiring firm was set at 20 percent by Stigler and was subsequently reduced to 10 percent in the 1968 Guidelines.

Transaction cost economics takes issue with that in two respects. First, the possibility that vertical integration is driven by transaction cost economies needs to be taken into account where parties are operating in a bilateral trading context. Second, the slightest degree of monopoly power will not elicit integration if, as developed more fully in Chapter 6, internal organization is beset by incentive difficulties. Slight degrees of monopoly power at one stage are not, without more, sufficient to warrant internal procurement.

This is not to say that vertical integration is wholly unproblematic in antitrust respects, however. To the contrary, integration by dominant firms can place smaller rivals at a strategic disadvantage. Interestingly, such anticompetitive effects also have transaction cost origins.

---

[15]Robert Bork (1954) expressly took exception with this, but his views were not widely heeded.

Entry impediments of two types can arise where the leading firms in stage I integrate (backward or forward) into what could otherwise be a competitively organized stage II activity. For one thing, the residual (nonintegrated) sector of the market may be so reduced that only a few firms of efficient size can service the stage II market. Firms that would otherwise be prepared to enter stage I may be discouraged from coming in by the prospect of having to engage in small-numbers bargaining, with all the hazards this entails, with those few nonintegrated stage II firms. Additionally, if prospective stage I entrants lack experience in stage II related activity, and thus would incur high capital costs were they to enter both stages themselves, integrated entry may be rendered unattractive. The integration of stages I and II by leading firms is then anticompetitive, in entry aspects at least, if severing the vertical connections would permit a competitive (large-numbers) stage II activity to develop without loss of scale economies.[16]

Vertical integration in industries with low or moderate degrees of concentration does not, however, pose the same problems. Here a firm entering into either stage can expect to strike competitive bargains with firms in the other stage whether they are integrated or nonintegrated. The reasons are that no single integrated firm enjoys a strategic advantage with respect to such transactions and that collusion by the collection of integrated firms (in supply or demand respects) is difficult to effectuate. Vertical integration rarely poses an antitrust issue, therefore, unless the industry in question is highly concentrated or, in less concentrated industries, collective refusals to deal are observed. But for such circumstances, vertical integration is apt to be of the efficiency promoting kind.

The 1982 Merger Guidelines hold that vertical mergers are unlikely to pose troublesome antitrust issues unless the Herfindahl index in the acquired firm's market exceeds 1800 (this corresponds, roughly, to a four-firm concentration ratio of 70 percent) and the market share of the acquired firm exceeds 5 percent. The presumption is that nonintegrated stage I firms can satisfy their stage II requirements by negotiating competitive terms with stage

---

[16]Although Posner now concedes that the above-described cost of capital effects can have entry barrier effects (1979, p. 946), he evidently regards this as a very special case. As Steven Salop and David Scheffman point out, however, this is only one of a series of actions that dominant firms can take whereby differential cost penalities can be imposed on actual or potential rivals (1983, p. 267). Among the tactics that they describe are (1) selective group boycotts (where they offer the *Klor's* case as an illustration), (2) industrywide wage contracts, where wage increases have a disproportionate impact on the labor-intensive fringe (my treatment of the *Pennington* case is an example; Williamson, 1968a), (3) vertical price squeezes, and (4) backward integration by a dominant firm such that the downstream price to rivals of the affected input is raised differentially (Salop and Scheffman, 1983).

II firms where the HHI is below 1800. The 1982 Vertical Merger Guidelines thus focus exclusively on the monopolistic subset, which is congruent with transaction cost reasoning. It is furthermore noteworthy that the anticompetitive concerns to which the Guidelines refer—regarding costs of capital,[17] (contrived) scale diseconomies, and the use of vertical integration to evade rate regulation—are all consonant with transaction cost reasoning.[18] Also, the 1982 Guidelines expressly acknowledge that investments in the secondary market are risky in the degree to which "capital assets in the secondary market are long-lived and specialized to that market."[19] This core proposition plainly has transaction cost economics origins.

Despite this striking correspondence, the 1982 Guidelines are not fully consonant with transaction cost reasoning throughout. The transaction cost rationale for challenging a 5 percent acquisition whenever the HHI exceeds 1800 is not transparent. Furthermore, it was not until 1984 that the Guidelines made provision for an economies defense. To be sure, there are hazards in allowing an economies defense, especially if economic evidence must be presented in court.[20] These hazards can be mitigated, however, if the Justice Department declines to bring cases where economies are clearly driving organizational outcomes (Kauper, 1983, pp. 519–22).[21]

Whatever is decided in economies defense respects, the fact is that the

---

[17]To its credit, the Justice Department observes that the need for additional capital, by itself, does not constitute a barrier to entry into the primary market (here, stage I), as long as the necessary funds are available at a cost commensurate with the level of risk in the secondary market. But the Department correctly recognizes that the risk in the secondary market is not independent of structure. Integrated entry that includes an unfamiliar stage is apt to carry a risk premium. This is because lenders "doubt that would-be entrants to the primary market have the necessary skills and knowledge to succeed in the secondary market and, therefore, in the primary market" (Guidelines, Sec. iv [B] [1] [b] [i]). The 1982 Guidelines further note that this problem is exacerbated when a high percentage of the capital assets in the secondary market are long-lived and specialized to that market, and are therefore difficult to recover in the event of failure. Transaction cost reasoning plainly informs the 1982 reforms.

[18]The concern is that the regulator will be unable to evaluate the reasonableness of the costs incurred and prices charged by an integrated supplier because the relevant information is costly to obtain and difficult to evaluate. Such concerns would vanish were regulators comprehensively knowledgeable (not subject to bounded rationality) or if regulated firms would disclose all relevant information candidly (not subject to opportunism).

[19]Guidelines, Sec. iv (B) (1) (b).

[20]Some of these are discussed in Williamson (1977).

[21]Refusal to consider compelling evidence that the parties to a transaction are proposing a vertical merger because of the contracting difficulties that attend antonomous trading would constitute a serious breach of rationality. General Motors' acquisition of Fisher Body after a contracting relationship experienced strain is described by Klein, Crawford, and Alchian (1978). See also Bain (1958, p. 658).

1982/1984 Vertical Merger Guidelines reflect a genuine sensitivity to transaction cost features—and are much more permissive than their predecessors as a consequence. Although there are those who counsel otherwise (Schwartz, 1983), public policy is arguably more informed and has been made more consonant with the public interest.

CHAPTER 5

Vertical Integration: Some Evidence

The evidence on vertical integration reported below is often crude, and some of the interpretations can be disputed. I nevertheless submit that, taken in the aggregate, the evidence supports the proposition that vertical integration—backward, forward, and lateral—is more consistent with transaction cost economizing than with the leading alternatives. In particular, the condition of asset specificity is the main factor to which a predictive theory of vertical integration must appeal.

The contention that transaction cost economizing is the main factor responsible for decisions to integrate does not preclude that there are other factors, several of which sometimes operate simultaneously. If, however, transaction cost economizing is really central, then the other factors are reduced to supporting roles. This is the basic argument.

The types of evidence germane to an assessment of transaction cost issues are discussed in section 1. The mundane integration of core technologies is briefly discussed in section 2. Forward vertical integration out of manufacturing into distribution is considered in section 3. Lateral integration into components is examined in section 4. Backward integration into raw materials is discussed in section 5. Some remarks about Japanese manufacture appear in section 6. Alternative explanations for vertical integration are briefly treated in section 7. Concluding remarks follow.

1. Types of Evidence

There is no single correct unit of analysis for addressing issues of economic organization. Which units are most appropriate depends on the questions being asked. The issues of interest in this book require a semi-microanalytic level of analysis—more microanalytic than received price theory, but less microanalytic than many sociological and social psychological studies of organizational behavior.

Accounting data, even rather detailed accounting data, are often poorly suited for the needs of transaction cost economics. The principal reason is that the usual fixed cost–variable cost distinction does not get to the core issues. As discussed and developed in the preceding chapters, the more important distinction is between redeployable and nonredeployable costs (see Figure 2–2). Those costs in turn are a reflection of the condition of asset specificity.

Several types of microanalytic studies can be and have been done to assess the condition of asset specificity and its contracting consequences. They include:

1. Statistical models (utilizing, for example, probit techniques) in which the attributes of transactions are associated with organization form. The study of vertical integration in the automobile industry by Kirk Monteverde and David Teece (1982) is an example.
2. Bivariate tests for association between attributes of transactions and contracting modes. The studies of aerospace and transportation contracting by Scott Masten (1984) and by Thomas Palay (1984; 1985) are examples.
3. The examination of contractual vignettes, some of which arise in antitrust proceedings. The Canadian study referred to in Chapter 8 is an illustration.
4. Focused case studies: The CATV study in Chapter 13 is an example.
5. Studies of the contractual features and governance structure of long-term contracts, of which recent studies of long-term coal contracts are examples (Goldberg and Erickson, 1982; Joskow, 1985).
6. Other studies of nonstandard contracting—of which R&D and, more generally, defense contracting are illustrative.
7. Focused industry studies, of which John Stuckey's remarkable treatment of vertical integration and joint ventures in the aluminum industry (1983) is noteworthy.
8. An examination of changing organization practices as reported in the business history literature. Chandler's work (1962; 1977) is especially important.

The common feature of all of these is that they deal with more micro-analytic features of economic organization than is customary in the field of industrial organization. A breadth (more observations) for depth (greater detail) tradeoff is commonly implied. I am persuaded that greater depth is needed and even essential if the study of economic organization is to progress. A second common characteristic of these studies is that direct measures of transaction costs are rarely attempted. Instead, the comparative institutional issue of interest is whether transactions, which differ in their attributes, are supported by governance structures in conformity with the predictions of the theory.

2. Mundane Integration

Vertical integration, and the evidence that relates thereto, of two kinds is usefully distinguished. The first, which I will refer to as mundane vertical integration, involves integration of successive stages within the core technology. (These are the on-site stages referred to as S1, S2, and S3 in Figure 4–3.) The second, which is more exotic, involves integration of peripheral or off-site activities—backward integration into basic materials, lateral integration into components, forward integration into distribution, and the like. Most discussions of vertical integration pass over the first and focus entirely on the second. But for the present brief discussion, this chapter also follows this practice.

It bears repeating, however, that integration of the core technology—stages that are located in a cheek-by-jowl association with one another, thereby to save on transportation and inventory expense, realize thermal economies, and the like—is not so unproblematic that this should be taken for granted. It also bears remark that the orthodox theory of the firm has no explanation for why successive stages in the core technology should be under unified ownership rather than each owned autonomously.

Inasmuch as there is overwhelming evidence that successive cheek-by-jowl stages are integrated, failure for a theory of the firm to explain this condition constitutes a serious lapse. Theories which do, by contrast, offer consistent explanations for both on-site and off-site types of integration are presumably to be credited (or, as the case may be, discredited) with evidence of both kinds.

The evidence that successive on-site stations are predominantly integrated is abundant. What is everywhere taken for granted is not, however, beyond review. The integration of flow process operations is especially thought to be obvious. Consider, for example, the ownership and operation of successive stages within a petroleum refinery.

Although it is common to assume that a refinery is an indecomposable technological unit, whence the interesting questions of integration involve assessments of backward vertical integration into crude oil supply or forward integration into distribution of refined product, this technological presumption is incorrect. Numerous separable stages within the petroleum refinery can be identified, the organization of which is problematic. How should the storage tanks for intermediate and finished product be owned and operated? Should the asphalt unit be franchised to the highest bidder? Should the quality control laboratory be independently owned and operated? Such queries are rarely posed, but they are plainly matters to which a theory of economic organization might reasonably be asked to speak.

One of the reasons, I submit, why these mundane matters go unremarked is because most of us have reasonably good transaction cost intuitions. Nevertheless, transaction cost economics asks that these intuitions be probed by examining the attributes of transactions, with special emphasis on the condition of asset specificity. Potentially troublesome transactions are ones where the parties are effectively operating in a bilateral exchange relation to each other and need to adapt the interface at recurrent intervals. These are precisely the circumstances where asset specificity, uncertainty, and frequency are joined.

The storage tank and asphalt unit stages described above are almost certainly characterized by a high degree of site specificity. Recovery value that exceeds scrap is unlikely for the storage tanks; and the asphalt unit can be redeployed to alternative use or users only at great expense. The redeployability of the quality control laboratory might conceivably be preserved by siting it, albeit at added expense, on wheels. In the degree to which idiosyncratic knowledge of the refinery has quality control importance, however, a human asset specificity condition intrudes.

Vertical integration is thus the predicted response for both storage tank and asphalt units. Unless the physical and human assets of the laboratory can be moved at slight sacrifice, moreover, integration is the preponderant response to the issue of laboratory organization as well. Transaction cost economics further predicts that if, for regulatory or other reasons, prohibitions or penalties against vertical integration for these transactions are posed, then long-term contracts will be devised in which bilateral (private ordering) safeguards are carefully crafted (Joskow, 1985).

Suppose, *arguendo,* that the capacity of transaction cost economics to reach and deal with mundane integration is granted. Forward, lateral, and backward integration are surely more problematic, however. How does it fare in these respects? Consider these *seriatim.*

3. Forward Integration into Distribution

3.1 *The Observed Transformation*

The principal development that induced forward vertical integration into distribution to occur in the second half of the nineteenth century was the appearance of the railroads (Porter and Livesay, 1971, p. 55). To be sure, there were other significant technological developments, including the telegraph (Chandler, 1977, p. 189), the development of continuous processing machinery (Chandler, 1977, pp. 249–53), the refinement of interchangeable parts manufacture (Chandler, 1977, pp. 75–77), and other technological developments that supported mass manufacture (Chandler, 1977, chap. 8). Without the low cost, reliable, all-weather transportation afforded by the railroad, however, the incentive to integrate forward would have been much less.[1]

The extensive forward integration from manufacturing into distribution that occurred during the last thirty years of the nineteenth century was, however, highly varied. The differences are the conditions to be explained. From least to most, integration into distribution varied as follows: (1) none, in which case the prevailing wholesale and retail structure continued; (2) integration into wholesale but not retail; and (3) retail (which usually included wholesale). A temporal dimension is useful to bear in mind in all of this, since the factors that favor integration at one point in time may not continue indefinitely. Also, mistaken forward integration warrants attention. Presumably such integration errors are less likely to be imitated or renewed and for this reason will be less widely reported. But a predictive theory of forward integration should explain both failures and successes.

a. UNCHANGED DISTRIBUTION

The sectors of the American economy where independent wholesalers continued to serve as distributors of goods to independent retailers included "the complex of goods sold through retail outlets such as grocery, drug, hardware, jewelry, liquor, and dry goods stores" (Porter and Livesay, 1971, p. 214). Whether independent wholesalers and retailers provided the full set

[1]Not only did the railroad have a significant impact on the distribution of manufactured goods, but the organization of the railroad posed distinctive problems of its own (Chandler, 1977, chap. 3), and servicing the supply needs of the growing railway industry had a direct impact on the organization of the iron and steel industry (Porter and Livesay, 1971, pp. 55–62).

of support services, however, or whether manufacturers performed some of these depended on product differentiation. As discussed below, the role of the middleman was reduced for branded products.

b. WHOLESALING

Manufacturer involvement in wholesaling functions of three kinds can be distinguished: preselling, inventory management, and facility ownership. The cigarette was the "orphan" of the American tobacco industry until 1880. The appearance of the Bonsack machine for the continuous processing of cigarettes in 1881 and its adoption by James Duke quickly changed that (Chandler, 1977, pp. 249–50). Duke cut the prices of cigarettes drastically to reflect manufacturing economies and coupled this with massive advertising (Chandler, 1977, pp. 290–92). Although Duke continued to sell through jobbers and retailers, he also organized a network of sales offices in the larger American cities in which salaried managers worked to coordinate marketing and distribution (Chandler, 1977, p. 291). The appearance of continuous processing machinery and attendant economies of scale also gave rise to branding and subsequent efforts to presell product and manage distribution in "matches, flour, breakfast cereals, soup and other canned products, and photographic film" (Chandler, 1977, p. 289).

Whitman's decision to use two different methods to merchandise candy is noteworthy. Wholesalers were bypassed in the sale of high-grade, packaged candies. Small, inexpensive bar and packaged candies, by contrast, were sold through the usual jobber and wholesale grocer network. Control of the wholesaling function for the former was arguably more important for quality control purposes. The high-grade items were "sold directly to retailers so that the company could regulate the flow of the perishable items and avoid alienating customers" (Porter and Livesay, 1977, p. 220), who were presumably prepared to pay a premium to avoid stale candy.

Ownership of wholesaling was reserved for products that required special handling, mainly refrigeration. Meatpacking and beer are examples (Chandler, 1977, pp. 299–302). Gustavus Swift was the leading innovator in meatpacking. He recognized that the practice of shipping live beef east involved considerable waste and proposed to eliminate this by slaughtering and dressing cattle in the Midwest and shipping the beef east in refrigerated cars. Implementing this transformation, however, was not easy. It met with resistance both from Eastern butchers, packers, and jobbers (Porter and Livesay, 1971, p. 169) and from the railroad interests (Chandler, 1977, p. 300). In order to execute his strategy, Swift had to build his own refrigerator cars and ice houses and construct a network of branch houses that provided "refrigerated storage space, a sales office, and a sales staff to sell and deliver the meat to the retail butchers, grocers, and other food shops'' (Chandler, 1977, p. 300).

c. RETAILING

Integration into final sales and service represented a more ambitious variety of forward integration. Three classes of products can be distinguished: specialized consumer nondurables; consumer durables requiring information aids, credit, and follow-on service; and producer durables requiring the same.

Kodak photographic film is an example of the first kind. George Eastman developed a paper-based film to replace the glass plates then in use in the early 1880s. The film required a special camera, however, and developing the film was complex. Meeting little success among professional photographers, Eastman and his associates set themselves to developing the amateur market. "To sell and distribute his new camera and film and to service their purchasers, Eastman . . . created a worldwide marketing network" (Chandler, 1977, p. 297). He explained his decision to eliminate independent wholesalers as follows:

> The wholesaler or jobber is a detriment to our business because a large proportion of it is in sensitized goods which are perishable. . . . We have organized our distribution facilities so as to get the goods into the hands of the consumer as quickly as possible. Our sensitized goods carry an expiration date. Our own retail houses . . . have been educated to control their stocks very accurately so that the goods are kept moving. [Porter and Livesay, 1971, p. 178]

Consumer durables for which forward integration into retailing was attempted were sewing machines and, later, automobiles. Upon resolution of the legal contests over patents in 1854, sewing machine patents were released to twenty-four manufacturers. Only three attempted to integrate forward, however, and only they remained major factors in the industry. The pattern adopted by Singer in the fourteen branches that it had opened by 1859 was to staff each with "a female demonstrator, a mechanic to repair and service, and a salesman or canvasser to sell the machine, as well as a manager who supervised the others and handled collections and credits" (Chandler, 1977, p. 303).

Although automobiles were mainly sold through franchised dealers rather than company-owned outlets, the Ford Motor Company and others required their dealers to "supply full demonstrations and instructions for customers unschooled in the operation of the new vehicles. Furthermore, the dealers agreed to instruct consumers in the proper methods of caring for the cars and to keep on hand a supply of parts and a force of mechanics capable of repairing the autos'' (Porter and Livesay, 1971, p. 195). And, of course, independent wholesalers were eliminated entirely from the distribution process.

Alfred P. Sloan's explanation of why the automobile manufacturers decided to use franchises rather than own dealerships is interesting. He observes that

. . . automobile manufacturers could not without great difficulty have undertaken to merchandise their own product. When the used car came into the picture in a big way in the 1920s as a trade-in on a new car, the merchandising of automobiles became more a trading proposition than an ordinary selling proposition. Organizing and supervising the necessary thousands of complex trading institutions would have been difficult for the manufacturer; trading is a knack not easily fit into the conventional type of a managerially controlled scheme of organization. So the retail automobile business grew up with the franchised-dealer type of organization. [1964, p. 282]

Not only, therefore, did the retail sale and service of automobiles require that transaction-specific investments be incurred, but it also required, especially as trade-ins became more common, that judgments based on idiosyncratic local information be made. Centralized ownership reduced the incentive to exercise that judgment in a discriminating way and posed severe monitoring problems. Rather, therefore, than integrate fully into the retail sale of automobiles, an intermediate form, the franchised dealership, evolved instead.

Producer durables were distributed through two networks. Small, standardized machinery was sold through commission merchants and jobbers. For products that were of special design, technologically complex, and quite expensive and for which installation and repair required special expertise, however, integrated marketing systems were developed (Porter and Livesay, 1971, pp. 183–84). Examples include Cyrus McCormick, who pioneered the development of integrated distribution for farm equipment and set the stage for others thereafter to imitate (Livesay, 1979, chap. 3). Office machines were another case where demonstration, sales, and service required specialized expertise for which franchised dealers were instrumental to success (Porter and Livesay, 1971, pp. 193–94).

The manufacture of textile machinery, sugar mill machinery, industrial boilers, and large, stationary steam engines also favored direct contact between buyer and seller (Porter and Livesay, 1971, pp. 181–82). The sale of electrical machinery posed special problems for customers that had ''special needs and requirements that made standardization extremely difficult in the industry's early years'' (Porter and Livesay, 1971, p. 187). The sale, installation, and service of electric generators and related central station equipment required even closer attention. Forward integration in all of those areas was correspondingly extensive (Porter and Livesay, 1971, pp. 180–92).

d. MISTAKEN INTEGRATION

Forward integration mistakes are not widely reported and, if reported, are not always recorded as mistakes. An exception is American Tobacco's effort to use integration into the wholesaling and retailing of cigars as a device by which to expand its position in this market. Porter and Livesay record the effort as follows:

> [American Tobacco] had much success in the nineties in extending its dominance from the cigarette business into other lines in the tobacco industry, including smoking tobacco, plug tobacco, and snuff. The cigar trade, however, proved much more difficult to conquer, primarily because it . . . was not subject to economies of scale in production. American Tobacco [turned instead, therefore, to forward integration]. . . . These efforts to move into the wholesale and even the retail end of the [cigar] industry proved very expensive, and American Tobacco endured substantial losses in its war on the cigar trade. [1971, p. 210]

Porter and Livesay also report that the "American Sugar Refining Co. engaged in a similar effort to drive its competitor John Arbuckle out of business by buying into wholesale and retail houses to discourage the sale of Arbuckle's sugar. The attempt failed miserably and proved very costly" (1971, p. 211, n. 52).

Pabst Brewing, Schlitz, and other large brewers purchased saloons in the late 1800s and rented them to operators as outlets for their brands of beer (Cochran, 1948, pp. 143–46). Whatever the merits it might have had at the time—which, except as a short-run expedient, appear doubtful (Cochran, 1948, p. 199)—the shift from kegs to bottled beer rendered it nonviable.

3.2 *Transaction Cost Interpretation*

Chandler (1977, pp. 287, 302) and Porter and Livesay (1971, pp. 166, 171, 179) refer repeatedly to the "inadequacies of existing marketers" in explaining forward integration by manufacturers into distribution in the late 1800s and early 1900s. Presumably the same would be said of marketers in the 1950s when IBM integrated forward in the sale and service of computers. But to what do those inadequacies refer? Judging from the differential response, the nature or degree of severity evidently varied considerably.

The explanation advanced here is at best suggestive. It appears, however, that scale economy, scope economy, and transaction cost factors are operative. In addition, a hitherto unremarked factor also appears: externalities.[2]

Recall that the cognitive map of contract breaks transaction cost economizing into two parts: the governance branch and the measurement branch. The governance branch is preoccupied with problems of harmonizing and adapting exchange where *ex post* bilateral trading is supported by investments in specific assets. Although the measurement branch plays a less substantial role in the analysis of problems dealt with in this book (partly because the problems selected for study have a bilateral trading quality), it is nevertheless important. The contracting complications posed by externalities have measurement origins.

Externality concerns arise in conjunction with a branded good or service that is subject to quality debasement. Whereas a manufacturer can inspect, thereby better to control, the quality of components and materials it purchases from earlier stage and lateral suppliers, it is less easy to exercise continuing quality controls over items sold to distributors.[3] That is not a special problem if the demands of individual distributors are independent of one another. If, however, the quality enhancement (debasement) efforts of distributors give rise to positive (negative) interaction effects, the benefits (costs) of which can be incompletely appropriated by (assigned to) the originators, failure to extend quality controls over distribution will result in suboptimization.

Whereas scale economies accrue when cost savings are realized by adding apples to apples—formally, $C(X_1 + X_2) < C(X_1) + C(X_2)$—economies of scope accrue if cost savings result when apples and oranges are joined—formally, $C(X,Y) < C(X) + C(Y)$. Economies of scale are probably less relevant to a decision to integrate forward into distribution than are economies of scope. To be sure, firms that are very large in relation to the size of the market may be able to justify own distribution where smaller firms cannot—Kodak's processing of film being an example.[4] Often, however, retail goods are sold by independent retail outlets, even where producer market shares are very great—breakfast cereals and diamonds being examples.

[2] Externalities also have transaction cost origins (Arrow, 1969; Williamson, 1975, pp. 5–6). It seems useful to examine distribution externalities of the free-rider kind separately, however, as they are a common reason for exercising controls over the distribution process.

[3] As discussed below, this can sometimes be overcome by incurring additional packaging or other expense—for instance, placing the item in a hermetically sealed container with an inert atmosphere—rather than by extending control over distributors.

[4] Actually, independent photo-finishers flourished after Kodak signed a 1954 consent decree with the Department of Justice whereby its tie-in sales of color film and processing were terminated. So long, however, as the residual (nonintegrated) photo-finishing market was very small, potential film entrants could view that condition as in impediment to successful entry.

Breakfast cereals, soup, bread, meat, and milk are thus sold from a noninte-grated grocery store. Diamonds are sold with other jewelry. Economies of scope (and/or the incentive deficiencies of integration) are evidently very large in relation to any prospective gains that would accrue to forward integra-tion in such circumstances.

In consideration of the potential economies of scope to which market distribution modes have access, decisions to integrate forward presumably turn on benefits—or, inasmuch as our emphasis throughout has been on costs, on transaction cost savings—that market modes are unable to realize. The governance cost problems that arise in conjunction with specialized assets, including those associated with the wasteful dissipation of valued firm-specif-ic reputation effects (which is the externality effect referred to above), thus warrant examination. Do they bear any systematic relation to the types of forward integration decisions reached by manufacturers in the late nineteenth century?

I submit that they do. Specifically, the forward integration decisions reported by Chandler take on the pattern shown in Table 5–1, where + + denotes considerable, + denotes some, ~ indicates uncertain, and 0 is negli-gible. The observed degree of forward integration is shown on the left column and the relative importance of economies of scope, externalities, and asset specificity are shown in each of the next three columns.

Thus forward integration is never observed if externalities and asset specificity are negligible (Class I), or if it does occur it is mistaken (Class VIII) and will be eventually undone. There simply are no governance or measurement purposes to be served in those circumstances. Limited integra-

Table 5–1. Forward Integration into Distribution

Degree of Forward Integration	*Economies of Scope*	*Externalities*	*Asset Specificity*
I. None	+ +	0	0
Wholesale			
II. (1) Preselling	+	+	0
III. (2) Inventory management	+	+ +	0
IV. (3) Ownership	0	+	+ +
Retail			
V. (1) Consumer nondurables	~	+	+
VI. (2) Consumer durables	0	+	+ +
VII. (3) Producer durables	0	+	+ +
VIII. (4) Mistaken	+	0	0

tion into wholesaling occurs in response to coordination and inventory management needs (Classes II and III), but comprehensive integration is not observed until specialized investments, especially refrigeration, are required (Class IV).

Integration into final sales and service is mainly observed for consumer and producer durables where considerable knowledge is imparted at point of sale and specialized follow-on service is required (Classes VI and VII). Some products involve complicated incentive issues, of which the decision to sell automobiles through franchised dealers rather than an employee network is an example. The issues here are discussed more fully in Chapter 6.

To be sure, the foregoing is a highly provisional assessment. The qualitative assignments (from + + through 0) are judgmental and based on description; other factors that have a bearing on forward integration have been ignored (see, however, section 7, below); and temporal elements, including customer learning, which may reduce the need for sales and service assistance, have been ignored. Often, however, refined assessments are not needed to evaluate discrete structural alternatives (Simon, 1978, p. 6)—which is to say that crude assignments are often adequate for pattern-seeking purposes.

4. Lateral Integration

The distinction between lateral and backward integration is somewhat arbitrary. I shall include in the former the supply of components, body panels, and the like and reserve backward integration for more basic materials.

4.1 A Case Study

Klein, Crawford, and Alchian's (1978, pp. 308–10) treatment of the bilateral exchange relationship between Fisher Body and General Motors in the 1920s is illustrative of lateral integration. The basic facts are these:

1. In 1919 General Motors entered a ten-year contractual agreement with Fisher Body whereby General Motors agreed to purchase substantially all its closed bodies from Fisher.

2. The price of delivery was set on a cost-plus basis and included provisions that General Motors would not be charged more than rival automobile manufacturers. Price disputes were to be settled by compulsory arbitration.

3. The demand for General Motors' production of closed body cars increased substantially above that which had been forecast. As a consequence

General Motors became dissatisfied with the terms under which prices were to be adjusted. It furthermore urged Fisher to locate its body plants adjacent to GM assembly plants, thereby to realize transportation and inventory economies. Fisher Body resisted.

4. General Motors began acquiring Fisher stock in 1924 and completed a merger agreement in 1926.

The contracting relation between General Motors and Fisher Body thus moved through three stages. More or less autonomous contracting evidently worked to the satisfaction of the parties in the wooden body era. Specialized physical assets were needed, however, to support the distinctive body designs that attended the shift to the metal body era. A condition of greater bilateral dependency thereby resulted. Efficient contracting principles required that a new contracting structure be crafted in response. Price adjustment by formula and dispute settlement by arbitration were thus expressly provided. Unanticipated demand and cost realizations nevertheless placed this bilateral contracting relation under strain. Additional strains were in prospect, moreover, if Fisher Body were to accede to General Motors' request that site-specific investments be undertaken. Faced with the prospect that both operating and investment decisions would be out of alignment during much of the rapid growth stage of development, bilateral governance eventually gave way to unified governance.

To be sure, transaction cost reasoning does not predict this sequence in detail. The observed succession of changes—from classical through bilateral to unified contracting—in response to the progressive deepening of transaction-specific investments, during a period when adaptive needs were great, is nonetheless consistent with the overarching argument. The transaction cost hypothesis would have been contradicted, moreover, had the contracting relation remained constant in the face of these changes. Rival theories of economic organization are mainly silent on these matters.

4.2 *Statistical Model Estimations Using Field Data*

Kirk Monteverde and David Teece (1982) have recently studied the degree to which General Motors and Ford are integrated backward into components and the economic factors that are responsible. They examined 133 component groupings, which, they observe, "include most of the major items that go into a complete vehicle" (1982, p. 207). Probit techniques are used to estimate a log likelihood function with eight independent variables, the most important of which are (1) engineering effort in designing the ith component; (2) a binary variable indicating whether the component is specific to the manufacturer or not; (3) a dummy variable for the company (Ford or GM); and (4) a series of subsystem dummies (engine, chassis, ventilation, electrical, body). Their principal findings were: (1) "the variable chosen as a proxy for transaction-specific skills ('engineering') is highly significant"; (2) "components specific to a single supplier [are] candidates for vertical integration"; (3) "General Motors is more integrated into component production than is Ford"; and (4) the subsystem dummies were not significant taken alone, but taken together "significantly contributed to the explanatory power of the model" (1982, p. 212). They concluded that transaction cost considerations, especially industrial knowhow that is specialized to a particular firm, are important in defining the efficient boundaries in the two corporations.

An independent study by Gordon Walker and David Weber partially confirms and extends this assessment. Their sample consisted entirely of relatively simple parts that are inputs to the initial assembly stage of automobile manufacture (1984, p. 381). They examined the effects of asset specificity (measured, albeit, rather indirectly), uncertainty, and scale economies. Their data consisted of sixty decisions made by a component division for which a committee met to evaluate the merits of make or buy. Microanalytic observations from component purchasing, manufacturing engineering, product engineering, and sales were elicited. The data were then analyzed using the unweighted least squares procedure of Jöreskog and Sörbom (1982). Although they interpret their results as "mixed" in transaction cost terms and attribute most of the explanatory power to "comparative production costs," they acknowledge that this may be due to limitations in both the data and the model for which subsequent work is indicated (Weber and Walker, 1984, p. 387). Further efforts to plumb the factors that are responsible for comparative production cost differences between buyer and supplier will, I submit, disclose added transaction cost features. (Diseconomies of small scale in an integrated firm are often explained by the contracting difficulties that an integrated firm experiences in selling product to rivals.)

Erin Anderson and David Schmittlein (1984) examine the organization of marketing. They examine whether or not the sales force in the electronic components industry is integrated by estimating a logistic function. They likewise obtain mixed effects: "integration is associated with increasing levels of asset specificity, difficulty of performance evaluation, and the combination of these two factors," but frequency and uncertainty measures turn out not to be significant (Anderson and Schmittlein, 1984, p. 385). One of the ramifications of both the Walker and Weber and the Anderson and Schmittlein articles is that added theory is necessary if the needs of empirical studies of transaction cost issues are to be met.

Thomas Palay has recently studied transportation transactions between manufacturers and railroads. Although most rail shipments are unexceptionable, in that shippers are contracting for standardized services, some pose special railroad car design and/or handling problems. An example is the "high cube" cars that are specialized to automobile parts shipment. The cars, larger and more expensive than standard box cars, are transferable among automobile manufacturers without sacrifice of value. However, the racks used to secure auto parts in transit, at a rack cost of between five thousand and fifteen thousand dollars per boxcar, are designed to the needs of each manufacturer, hence are nonredeployable. Although initially the carriers owned both the high cube cars and the racks, problems developed with respect to the latter. Consonant with the theory, racks are now mainly owned by the shippers (Palay, 1981, pp. 117–18).

Tank cars and covered hoppers to move chemicals were the most specialized and required the greatest investment of the transportation transactions that Palay examined:

> This equipment is generally built to the particular substances being moved. . . . Glass or rubber lining, specialized pressure volumes, and damage control equipment are but a few examples of the unique equipment employed. . . . Utilization patterns simply make it too costly to attempt to modify a car to handle a new product each trip, and cleaning involves expensive facilities and technologies. The cost of specialized tank cars ranged from 50 to 100 thousand dollars. [1981, pp. 129–30]

The "highly idiosyncratic nature of the rail equipment has led to shipper ownership of its own tank and covered hopper cars" (Palay, 1981, p. 134).

Scott Masten's recent examination of the organization of production in the aerospace industry and of the government's procurement policies is similarly corroborative:

> Overall, the data on the aerospace system support the contention that design specificity and complexity are necessary, if not sufficient, conditions for the breakdown of cooperation in market-mediated exchanges and the subsequent integration of production within the firm. In addition, the procurement policies professed by the government provide supportive detail not yet available in the formal analysis, such as the effects of uncertainty on the scope of contractual agreements and the relevance of the absolute value of investments on the need for specialized governance structures. [Masten, 1984, p. 417]

Finally, Paul Joskow's (1985) ambitious study of vertical integration and long-term contracts for the supply of coal for coal-burning electric utilities demonstrates that governance structures line up with the needs of transactions in a discriminating way. The correspondence between transaction cost reasoning and microanalytic economic organization in practice is strongly borne out by Pablo Spiller's (1985) empirical study of vertical mergers as well.

5. Backward Integration

Backward integration into raw materials may occur for three main reasons: (1) to realize prospective transaction cost economies; (2) for strategic purposes; or (3) for mistaken reasons. Transaction cost economies will warrant integration where the parties are tightly joined in a bilateral exchange relation, making problems of harmonizing the interface crucial, and where integration does not sacrifice economies of aggregation. The acquisition of the Mesabi iron ore deposits by steel companies may qualify (Parsons and Ray, 1975), though others favor a strategic explanation (Wall, 1970). Acquisitions of coal and limestone deposits by steel companies appear to lack either transaction cost or strategic purpose and were possibly mistaken. As Joskow's recent study discloses, however, detailed knowledge of the feasible contracting options is needed (Joskow, 1985).

An illustration of what was held to be strategic backward integration, undertaken for the purpose of forestalling rivalry, is Alcoa's acquisition of bauxite deposits and hydroelectric sites. Allegations to this effect were made in conjunction with the famous antitrust suit in which the Justice Department charged Alcoa with monopoly and monopolization.[5] The definitive assessment of backward integration into bauxite deposits has since been made by John Stuckey (1983). In very gross terms, the cost difference of processing a mixed-hydrate bauxite, which is efficiently processed with a high-temperature technology, in a low-temperature refinery instead, comes to almost 100 percent (Stuckey, 1983, pp. 53–54). But the details also matter. Bauxite storage covers are needed for some ores and not for others (p. 49); residue processing costs vary greatly (p. 53); and air pollution equipment is tailored to the attributes of the bauxite (p. 60). Moreover, although smelting is less idiosyncratic, there is, nevertheless, an "art part of smelting," which is upset if the aluminum supply is varied (p. 63).

Stuckey refers to both physical and site specificity in his summary assessment:

> The bilateral-monopoly nature of bauxite-exchange relationships results from several largely immutable technical and structural factors. First, bauxite is a heterogeneous commodity, and the ore in any deposit has unique chemical and physical properties. The efficient processing of a given bauxite usually requires a tailor-made refinery with specially designed technologies for chemical processing, materials handling and waste disposal. Once a mine and its associated infrastructure is developed, and its appropriately designed refinery is constructed, the two plants are locked together to the economic extent of their technical complementarity. The evidence indicates that, in economic terms, the

[5]*United States* v. *Aluminum Company of America,* 148 F. 2d 416 (2d Cir. 1945).

complementarity is often strong, meaning that within a wide range of bauxite transaction prices the mine and refinery are wedded together economically.

A second set of factors locking mines and refineries together includes the wide geographical spread of the world's major bauxite deposits, the vast distances between the deposits and primary smelters, the low value of bauxite at the mine front door relative to freight rates, and the over 50-percent reduction in material volume during refining. The last three factors encourage the back-to-back location of mines and refineries for transport cost reasons. [1983, p. 290]

Stuckey also notes that information asymmetries regarding the quality and extent of bauxite deposits complicate problems of long-term contracting (pp. 291–92).

The incentive to integrate because of asset specificity of both physical plant and site specificity kinds is thus reinforced by information asymmetry considerations. The upshot is that backward integration from refining into bauxite is an altogether predictable outcome from a transaction cost economics standpoint—which presumably explains why this is the preponderant organizational form.

Manufacturers appear sometimes to have operated on the mistaken premise that more integration is always preferable to less. From a transaction cost point of view, the following examples of backward integration would appear to be mistakes (and, I conjecture, have mainly been abandoned as renewal decisions have presented themselves): (1) backward integration by Pabst Brewing into timberland and barrel-making plants (Chandler, 1977, p. 301); (2) backward integration by Singer Sewing Machine into timber, an iron mill, and some transportation (Chandler, 1977, p. 305); (3) backward integration by the McCormick Company into timberlands, mines, twine factories, and hemp plantations (Chandler, 1977, p. 307); and (4) Ford Motor Company's "fully integrated behemoth at River Rouge, supplied by an empire that included ore lands, coal mines, 700,000 acres of timberland, sawmills, blast furnaces, a glass works, ore and coal boats, and a railroad" (Livesay, 1979, p. 175).

To be sure, managers, like others, are reluctant to concede mistakes. Accordingly, mistaken integration may not quickly be undone. Moreover some, like "the River Rouge behemoth," involve the construction of facilities in cheek-by-jowl proximity to each other. Such site specificity forces the parties into a bilateral trading relation and for this reason is apt to be continued. Distant twine factories, by contrast, can be sold off or closed down with ease.

Site preemption issues aside, backward integration that lacks a transaction cost rationale or serves no strategic purposes will presumably be recognized and will be undone.[6] The discontinuation or sale of mistaken integration activities will occur more rapidly if the firm is confronted with active rivalry.

6. Some Remarks About Japanese Manufacture

The Japanese rely much more extensively on subcontracting than is true in the United States. The experience of Toyota Motor Company, which has crafted an unusual relationship with its parts suppliers, is frequently cited in this connection. What explains Toyota's success with subcontracting? What is the Japanese experience more generally? Definitive answers to neither question are attempted here. Some perspective is nevertheless attempted.[7]

6.1 Toyota

As remarked earlier, the "study of extreme instances often provides important leads to the essentials of the situation."[8] In particular, case studies are often selected not because they are believed to be representative but because they permit the issues in question to be illustrated in a particularly dramatic way.[9] That is the spirit in which the Toyota experience with its subcontractors should be interpreted. Among large Japanese corporations, Toyota has been especially successful in forging a mutually profitable and durable relation with its subcontractors. Some features of that situation are noteworthy:

a. LONG HISTORY

Toyota began manufacturing automobiles in 1937, and its relations with many of its present subcontractors go back to the very earliest years. The fact that the automobile industry was well established by 1937 meant that state of the art technology could be borrowed and contracting relations crafted accord-

---

[6]Backward integration into the buying and storage of agricultural products were undertaken by American Tobacco and by Campbell Soup and Heinz (Chandler, 1977, pp. 291, 295). Assuring a "steady supply" of tobacco, vegetables, and other perishables is reported to be the reason, but more detail would be needed to assess the nature of the market breakdown (if such there was).

[7]These remarks are based on interviews I had with Japanese business firms (including Toyota and its suppliers) during a visit to Japan from April through July 1983.

[8]Behavioral Sciences Subpanel, President's Science Advisory Committee, *Strengthening the Behavioral Sciences, Washington, D.C.,* 1962, p. 5. For a discussion of the uses of extreme instances in economics research, see Williamson (1964, pp. 86–89).

[9]The franchise bidding case study reported in Chapter 13 has these attributes.

ingly. The initial conditions facing Toyota were thus different from those confronting earlier entrants to the industry.

b. COMMON DESTINY

Toyota emphasized from the outset that the parent company, its subsidiaries, and its subcontractors face a "common destiny." The parties were thus encouraged to regard the relation as a long-term one. A presumption that relations would be continued and differences would be worked out was maintained.

c. TWO VENDOR POLICY

A pervasive aura of goodwill notwithstanding, transaction cost reasoning is nevertheless respected. Both strategic investments and those of a highly specific kind are undertaken by Toyota. Contract renewals for work done by outside contractors are never automatic, moreover. Annual contracts are always subject to the discipline of competitive bidding. Exclusive reliance is avoided by adherence to a "two-vendor policy," whereby Toyota divides the work between two or more suppliers. Occasionally, Toyota both makes and buys, though that is rare.

d. GOVERNANCE

Many Toyota subcontractors sell almost their entire annual product to Toyota. Their dependence is reinforced by the site-specific nature of the investment, which is especially significant. Thus although the plant, equipment, and most of the labor force of the subcontractors are not highly specialized, the location of the plants in the immediate neighborhood of Toyota assembly plants makes them remote from other manufacturing.[10] Those suppliers are therefore exposed to an expropriation risk.

As will be developed in Chapter 7, it is commonly in the *mutual* interest of trading parties to devise safeguards against opportunism. One type of safeguard is to develop a machinery whereby reputation effects are more accurately and reliably recorded and experiences shared among interested parties. Collective organization can and often does serve this purpose. Interestingly, Toyota and its subcontractors evidently recognize this and have organized supplier associations in response. Whatever their original intent, those associations now serve reputation effect purposes—among others.[11]

[10]The Toyota plants are located in Toyota City, which is near to but outside of Nagoya.

[11]The largest of the supplier organizations is the Kyohokai. This is made up of 224 manufacturers of auto parts and components. The Seihokai (23 manufacturers of molds, gauges, jigs, and the like) and the Eihokai (37 contractors for plant facilities) were first organized in 1962 and were

e. POSSIBLE STRAIN

Toyota's growth in the postwar period is remarkable. The company produced its millionth car in 1962. The cumulative total reached 20 million in 1976 and 40 million in 1983. Toyota suppliers shared in that growth and in the attendant prosperity.

Recent strains, however, have begun to develop as the growth of the world auto market has slowed and domestic content pressures on imported automobiles have increased in the United States and elsewhere. Although a serious divergence of interest has not developed, the presumption of identical interest is no longer as strong. Toyota, for example, did not consult its supplier organizations before reaching a joint venture agreement with General Motors to manufacture cars in GM's then idle Fremont, California plant. (Indeed, it apprised its leading suppliers only hours before making the agreement public.) Although its suppliers recognize the need to adapt to changed circumstances, they also feel some unease. Toyota, moreover, has recently expressed concern lest its suppliers attempt to maintain their growth by selling parts in which Toyota has a design or other proprietary interest to rival automobile firms.

The strength of a relationship is tested when it is put to strain. Although Toyota and its suppliers appear to recognize the benefits of continuing their cooperation, and the famed Kanban system does not appear to be in jeopardy, future relationships between Toyota and its suppliers should not be projected as a simple extrapolation of the past.

6.2 *Subcontracting More Generally*

Although the Japanese reliance on subcontracting is great, the same principles that inform make or buy decisions in the United States and in other Western countries also apply in Japan.[12] What differs are the margins. The hazards of trading are less severe in Japan than in the United States because of cultural and institutional checks on opportunism.

---

merged in 1983. Those associations serve as important communication and planning links. The organized contact of the suppliers among each other as well as with the client company also assures that experience is quickly and accurately shared.

[12]This point came out repeatedly in discussions that I had with purchasing specialists in Japanese firms, especially those who had international experience. By contrast, many of the production people in Japanese firms believed that their contracting practices and principles were unique.

a. DEALING

Zentaro Kitagawa, a leading contract law specialist, describes the Japanese negotiating process as follows: "Japanese businessmen place more emphasis on building up a personal relationship than on drafting a detailed contract; all decisions are made by the group rather than the individual; lawyers are usually not consulted during the negotiations" (1980, p. 1–24). A greater sense of commitment to see the contract through to completion and to accommodate to the needs of the other is believed to result.

b. LITIGATION

The propensity to litigate is vastly smaller in Japan than in the United States. As Frank Gibney observes, "The total number of civil actions in Japan in one year (1980) was about 500,000—about half the number of cases of California. On a per capita basis, there is one lawsuit in Japan for every twenty in the United States" (1982, p. 106). The Japanese emphasis on harmony in relation to justice helps to explain that condition. Gibney contends that compromise is preferred by the Japanese to confrontation and that "the process of discussion and consultation is in itself often more important than the precise kind of decision that may be reached" (1982, p. 108). Accordingly, although Japanese courts are formally committed to dispense justice, they are more interested than an American court in restoring harmony (Gibney, 1982, p. 109). The fact that the number of lawyers in Japan is deliberately kept small serves further to preserve this nonlitigous tradition.[13]

Whether U.S. firms can or will improve their record in contracting respects is problematic. The issues are examined in Chapter 7. Suffice it to observe here that there is growing dissatisfaction with the prevailing adversary approach to law (Bok, 1983; Gilson, 1984). Public policy attitudes toward complex interfirm contracting are regarded more sympathetically today than was true only a decade earlier.

7. Some Alternative Explanations

The leading alternative theories that have been offered to explain organizational changes are domination theory, market power, technology, life cycle, pecuniary economies, and strategic behavior. I shall consider them seriatim.

[13]The small number of lawyers in Japan is explained by the fact that of the tens of thousands of law graduates annually, of which some 30,000 take the examinations for admission to the National Legal Training and Research Institute, only 500 annual appointments to the Institute are made (Gibney, 1982, p. 113). All lawyers, prosecutors, and judges must be graduates of the Institute.

7.1 Domination Theory

Domination theory focuses on human actors. There are those who possess economic power and those who do not. The organization of economic activity is under the control of those who possess power. The reason why one mode is chosen over another is that it permits those who are in control to extend and perfect their power.

This theory of organizational innovation presumably applies to the relations both between capitalists and workers and among capitalists themselves. The thesis that work is hierarchically organized so as to prevent workers from gaining power is examined in Chapter 9. Consider, therefore, whether power theory explains confrontations in intermediate product markets between capitalists. Porter and Livesay report that during the "first two centuries after the initial English settlement on the North American continent, urban merchants dominated" (1971, p. 5). Those "urban merchant capitalists . . . were the wealthiest, best informed, and most powerful segment of early American society" (p. 6). The all-purpose merchant nevertheless gave way to the specialized merchant early in the nineteenth century, which merchants then became "the most important men in the economy" (p. 8). The specialized merchant in turn found his functions sharply cut back by the rise late in the 1800s of the integrated manufacturer: "The long reign of the merchant had finally come to a close. In many industries the manufacturer of goods had also become their distributor. A new economy dominated by the modern, integrated manufacturing enterprise had arisen" (1971, p. 12).

Power theory must confront two troublesome facts in explaining those changes. First, why would the general purpose and later the special purpose merchants ever permit economic activity to be organized in ways that removed power from their control? Second, why did power leak out selectively—with the merchant role being appropriated extensively by some types of manufacturers but not by others? As developed above, the transaction cost approach explains both in terms of efficiency.

To be sure, this does not preclude the possibility that power is also operative. For example, entrenched interests may sometimes be able to delay organizational transformations. Power enthusiasts have not, however, demonstrated that significant organizational innovations—those in which large transaction cost sayings are in prospect—are regularly defeated by established interests. There is abundant evidence to the contrary. Within the economic arena,[14] therefore, if not more generally, I submit that organizational innova-

---

[14]The political arena is another thing. Although established firms have not blocked the development of the conglomerate form, they have slowed its spread. Much of the legislation passed by states to impede takeovers was done at the behest of the managements of established

tions for which nontrivial efficiency gains can be projected will find a way to subdue (or otherwise will be accommodated by) opposed interests. Power is relegated to a secondary role in such a scheme of things.

7.2 *Market Power*

Market power arguments can be brought to bear on organizational innovation in two ways. One is that possessors of market power simply prefer certain organizational arrangements. The second is that organization is used strategically as an impediment to rivals.

The latter is considered in subsection 7.6, below. Porter and Livesay appear to appeal to the former in explaining why manufacturers integrated into distribution in some industries and not in others. Thus they observe that the "incidence of oligopoly and large size was much less frequent" among manufacturers that did not integrate forward than among those that did (1971, p. 214). It is noteworthy, however, that a number of large firm/concentrated industry groups are included among those nonintegrators: breakfast cereals, hand soaps, soup, and razor blades, to name a few. Those industries would presumably be prime candidates for forward integration if oligopolistic preferences rather than efficiency were driving the organizational outcomes.

7.3 *Technology*

The argument that technological imperatives explain organizational outcomes is an old one. As explained earlier, however, the common ownership of two stages that are operating in a cheek-by-jowl association with each other is to be understood as a solution to a troublesome bilateral bargaining relation. Steady state thermal economies can always be realized by placing autonomous blast furnaces and rolling mills alongside one another, whatever the ownership structure. Choice among structures thus turns on how to mediate the interface in response to disturbances. This is a transaction cost issue.

Although forward integration into distribution is an anomaly if addressed in terms of physical or technical aspects, Chandler has come forward with an alternative technological explanation for that condition. While acknowledging that successful organizational innovations serve, among other things, to econ-

---

firms (Cary, 1969; Winter, 1978, p. 43). Unable to suppress conglomerates by exercising economic power in the market place, incumbent managements turned to the political process instead. Possibly it is in that forum that power theory has the most to offer.

omize on transaction costs (1977, p. 256), the main factor on which he relies in explaining forward integration is what he refers to as "economies of speed" (pp. 281, 298; Chandler and Daems, 1979, pp. 30–31). According to Chandler and Daems, such economies

> . . . could only be realized . . . if a managerial hierarchy carefully scheduled the flows. . . . Therefore, when and where a new technology permitted mass production and when or where new markets permitted mass distribution, such administrative coordination turned out to be more efficient than when the movement of goods *between* units was a result of a multitude of market transactions. [1979, p. 31]

Although economies of speed remain unspecified, appeal to an intuitive notion of such economies leads to a number of anomalous results. Why didn't manufacturers comprehensively integrate into distribution for the sale of cigarettes, beer, and branded packaged goods? Why were small, standardized producer durables sold through independent distributors while manufacturers sold and serviced large, unique producer durables themselves? I submit that fungible human assets were employed for the retail sale and service of cigarettes, other packaged goods, and standardized producer durables, while that was not the case for large, unique producer durables. It is this (together with the economies of scope available for the former set of products and not for the latter plus the diseconomies of bureaucracy that attend forward integration) rather than "economies of speed" differentials that explain the pattern.

7.4 *Life Cycle*

George Stigler (1951) has advanced a theory of vertical integration in which life cycle features are prominent. Extensive integration is favored at both the early and late stages of an industry's development and less integration occurs at the intermediate stages. Integration in the textile industry is held to be consistent with the hypothesis (Stigler, 1951).[15]

Both Porter and Livesay (1971, p. 132) and Chandler (1977, p. 490) read the evidence differently. Specifically, Porter and Livesay contend that "while large firms may pass through the three stages described by Stigler, they frequently engage in reintegration as a result of rising, not declining, demand" (Porter and Livesay, 1971, p. 132). The predicted stage two reduction

---

[15]Although the textile mills were the first to introduce large factories to the United States, the industry is not the bellwether that many have thought it to be (Chandler, 1977, p. 72). Factory organization, with its emphasis on the technology of production, simply falls well short of business organization, which deals with the organization of the firm.

in vertical integration is not borne out in the aluminum industry either (Stuckey, 1983, pp. 26–46).

I submit that life cycle analysis needs to be joined with transaction costs in order for observed patterns of vertical integration to be explained. More interesting, moreover, than the disputed demand features referred to above is the following life cycle phenomenon: As customers and independent middlemen become more knowledgeable of the technology and as reliability of an item increases (so that service requirements decrease), the transaction cost incentive to maintain a forward market presence by a manufacturer decreases. Accordingly, items that were once marketed by an integrated sales and service organization can often be returned to the market in the later stages of a product's life cycle.

That has numerous ramifications, among which is the viability of discount houses for selling mature products. Also, public policy toward forward integration ought to make allowances for life cycle features. The likelihood that forward integration is justified by transaction cost considerations is much greater for products that are sold before maturity sets in. The possibility that such integration is continued at mature stages because it serves strategic entry impeding purposes likewise deserves consideration.

Those issues have a bearing on the differential performance of firms whose complex products are technologically on a parity but which follow different early stage marketing strategies. The success of IBM in relation to Sperry-Rand (and, later, RCA and GE) may well turn on the intensive sales and support that IBM offered for its relatively unfamiliar but complex product in the 1950s, which were critical formative years in the computer industry's history.

7.5 *Pecuniary Economies*

Vertical integration may be adopted as a device by which to avoid excise taxes (Coase, 1937; Stigler, 1951). Whether this has been an important factor in explaining vertical integration in the United States has never been established. I conjecture that it has been of minor significance in relation to the real transaction cost savings reported above.

Corporate taxes (and tax credits) have been a factor for some mergers, but probably more for conglomerate than for vertical mergers in the United States—especially in the period following World War II (although this remains to be investigated). Plainly tax considerations played a principal role in the early postwar acquisitions of Royal Little (Sobel, 1974, p. 356). And they continue to influence conglomerate acquisitions to this day, the attempted takeover of the Mead Corporation by Occidental Petroleum being a recent example.[16] Whether such assets, once acquired, will be effectively managed is an organization form issue (see Chapter 11). Whatever the immediate incentives to integrate, therefore, transaction cost issues still must be addressed. (Those conglomerates that adopted a holding company rather than an M-form structure would presumably be less well suited to deal with complexity and adversity and would be shakeout candidates as events progressed.)

7.6   Strategic Behavior

Strategic behavior has reference to efforts by dominant firms to take up and maintain advance or preemptive positions and/or to respond punitively to rivals. The object in both instances is to deter rivalry. An example of the first kind would be forward integration into distribution where the resulting transaction cost savings are negligible. Punitive strategic behavior is illustrated by predatory pricing. These troublesome issues are discussed more fully in an antitrust context in Chapter 14. Suffice it to observe here that strategic behavior mainly has relevance in dominant firm or tightly oligopolistic industries. Since most of the organizational change reported above occurred in nondominant firm industries, appeal to strategic considerations is obviously of limited assistance in explaining the reorganization of American industry over the past 150 years.[17]

None of the six alternative theories of organizational structure/innovation treated here makes more than a piecemeal contribution to an understanding of the reshaping of the American economy, and some are plainly misconceived. Transaction cost economizing, by contrast, not only applies broadly—to the changing governance of intermediate product markets, labor markets, corporate governance, and regulation—but also helps to explain many of the microanalytic details and some of the general movements of vertical integration.

[16]*Mead Corp.* v. *Occidental Petroleum Corp.,* No. C-3-78-241 (S.D. Ohio, filed Aug. 18, 1978) and *United States* v. *Occidental Petroleum Corp.,* No. C-3-78-288 (S.D. Ohio, complaint dismissed without prejudice Apr. 4, 1979).

[17]It nonetheless applies selectively—if not in the decision to integrate forward, then in the decision to maintain a forward presence after the industry has matured and the original transaction cost incentives to integrate have weakened or vanished. This is a matter requiring separate investigation.

8. Concluding Remarks

Although characterizing the firm as a production function is a convenient and useful abstraction, such an approach suppresses much of the interesting action that accounts for the high performance features of an enterprise economy. It facilitates marginal analysis within a given institutional framework at the expense of organization and comparative institutional features. The firm as governance structure approach maintains an economizing orientation but makes express provision for organizational innovation and relies more on comparative institutional than on marginal analysis in assessing the alternatives.

Schumpeter, Porter and Livesay, Chandler, Cochran, Cole, and Davis and North have argued persuasively that the American economy has witnessed numerous and significant organizational innovations during the past 150 years. This chapter accepts that judgment and takes the argument a step further. I argue that transaction cost economizing is the previously neglected but key concept for understanding organizational innovation in general and vertical integration in particular.

The study of transaction cost economizing entails an examination of alternative ways by which to govern exchange interfaces. Firms, markets, and mixed modes are recognized as alternative instruments of governance. Which is best suited for mediating a transaction (or related set of transactions) depends on the underlying characteristics of the transaction(s) in question. Dimensionalizing transactions, with special attention to their asset specificity features, is crucial to the exercise. Since tradeoffs between scale and scope economies on the one hand and transaction cost economies on the other are sometimes important, provision for tradeoffs has to be made.

While many of the benefits of successful organizational innovations originally redound to the advantage of the firms that originate them, the benefits accrue to society at large as the competitive process unwinds. That Andrew Carnegie profited greatly and sometimes at the expense of others from the reorganization of steel is undeniable. Of greater economic significance, however, is that the steel industry was rationalized to advantage with lasting benefits realized by society.[18] The process of "handing on" always works "through a fall in the price of the product to the new level of costs" (Schumpeter, 1947, p. 155) whenever rivals are alert to new opportunities and are not prevented by purposive restrictions from adopting them.

Natural selection forces do not always operate quickly, however. Firms

---

[18]This does not imply that all efforts to reorganize the steel industry yielded social benefits. Important changes made by Carnegie and Frick are described and interpreted in Chapter 10.

that are buffered against product market rivalry, as appears to have been the case in Europe prior to the 1968 tariff reductions within the European Economic Community (Franko, 1972), and against capital market discipline, as was the Ford Motor Company with its concentrated ownership and $600 million Depression bank account (Livesay, 1979, p. 179), can postpone the reckoning. But those would appear to be the exception rather than the rule. Where incumbent managements are not pressed to adopt the new procedures by economic events, successor managements, often in conjunction with the appointment of a new chief executive, commonly will (Chandler, 1962, chap. 7).

The transaction cost approach to the study of vertical integration yields numerous refutable implications, many of which are unique to this approach. The cumulative evidence, which includes mundane, forward, lateral, and backward integration, is broadly corroborative.[19] Additional studies are nevertheless needed. For one thing, the theoretical apparatus on which transaction cost economics relies is primitive and in need of refinement. The basic tradeoffs need more fully to be worked out; the basic attributes with respect to which transactions differ need more fully to be explicated.

Also, and related, empirical assessments of vertical integration need to acknowledge the complex nature of this condition. If vertical integration is commonly the product of multiple factors, empirical studies ought to make more adequate provision for this.

These precautions notwithstanding, the vertical integration dialogue has been permanently altered by the infusion of transaction cost reasoning. The custom of paying lip service to transaction cost issues—by acknowledging them in principle, thereafter to ignore them in fact (Coase, 1972, p. 63)—has become much less common and, in the judgment of some (e.g. Alchian, 1984; Joskow and Schmalensee, 1983; Stuckey, 1983; Joskow, 1985), even untenable.

---

[19]Although disparate studies using different data and methods are often more convincing than the econometric result from a single "crucial experiment" (Mayer, 1980, p. 173), I do not mean to suggest that the cumulative evidence is dispositive.

CHAPTER 6

The Limits of Firms: Incentive and Bureaucratic Features

Why can't a large firm do everything that a collection of small firms can do and more? That is a variant of a question asked many times before for which an adequate answer has never been devised—to wit, what is responsible for limitations in firm size? Yet another way of putting the same issue is this: Why not organize everything in one large firm?

The tradeoff model in Chapter 4 offers two reasons why a firm would eschew integration: economies of scale and scope may be sacrificed if the firm attempts to make for itself what it can procure in the market; and the governance costs of internal organization exceed those of market organization where asset specificity is slight. Expressed in terms of Figures 4–1 and 4–2 (Chapter 4), those possibilities correspond to $\triangle C > 0$ and $\triangle G > 0$ conditions, respectively. The first is not a thoroughly comparative explanation. If economies of scale are realized by the outside supplier, then the same economies can be preserved upon merger by instructing the supplier to service the market in the future just as it has in the past.[1] The fundamental limitation to firm size thus must turn on the governance cost disabilities of internal organi-

[1]Actually, rivals of a firm that has acquired its supplier may be loath to place orders with the (integrated) supply stage. Accordingly, the supplier may not be able to continue business as usual. To be sure, that defect could be remedied by merging all the firms with which the supplier did business into one big firm. This escalates the assessment and hence will be set aside.

zation where asset specificity is insubstantial. But wherein do the firm's comparative disabilities in those governance cost ($\triangle G > 0$) respects reside? Why is the intercept (β_o) of the $\triangle G$ curve positive?

The shortcomings of earlier treatments of the firm size puzzle are briefly sketched in section 1. A comparative institutional assessment of the incentive effects of acquiring an owner-managed supplier is set out in section 2. I argue that efforts to preserve high-powered incentives in the integrated status have unwanted side effects—where by high-powered incentives I have reference to residual claimant status whereby an agent, either by agreement or under the prevailing definition of property rights, appropriates a net revenue stream, the gross receipts and/or costs of which stream are influenced by the efforts expended by the economic agent. Acquisition of a supplier in which ownership and management are already separated is examined in section 3. A symmetrical treatment will consider not merely the effects of introducing marketlike (high-powered) incentives into firms but will also examine the use of firmlike (low-powered, e.g. cost plus) incentives in markets. That is the subject of section 4. Bureaucratic costs of internalizing the incremental trans-action are discussed in section 5. Several examples illustrating the limits of high-powered incentives in firms are described in section 6. Concluding re-marks follow.

1. A Chronic Puzzle

Frank Knight made early reference to the limitations to firm size puzzle when, in 1921, he observed that the "diminishing returns to management is a subject often referred to in economic literature, but in regard to which there is a dearth of scientific discussion" (1965, p. 286, n. 1). And in 1933 he elaborated as follows:

> The relation between efficiency and size of firm is one of the most serious problems of theory, being, in contrast with the relation for a plant, largely a matter of personality and historical accident rather than of intelligible general principles. But the question is peculiarly vital, because the possibility of monop-oly gain offers a powerful incentive to *continuous and unlimited* expansion of the firm, which force must be offset by some equally powerful one making for decreased efficiency. [1965, p. xxiii; emphasis in original]

Tracy Lewis's recent remarks that large established firms will always realize greater value from inputs than small potential entrants are apposite:

> The reason is that the leader can at least use the input *exactly* as the entrant would have used it, and earn the same profits as the entrant. But typically, the leader can *improve* on this by coordinating production from his new and existing inputs.

Hence the new input will be valued more by the dominant firm. [1983, p. 1092, emphasis added]

If the dominant firm can use the input in exactly the same way as the smaller entrant, then the larger firm can do everything the smaller firm could. If it can improve on the input usage, it can do more. Accordingly, industries are not everywhere organized as monopolies solely because of public policy vigilance and restraints.

A different way of posing the issue is in terms not of horizontal but of vertical integration. Thus Ronald Coase inquired, "Why does the entrepreneur not organize one less transaction or one more?" (1952, p. 339). More generally the issue is, "Why is not all production carried on in one big firm?" (p. 340).

Various answers have been advanced. They all suffer, however, from a failure to adopt and maintain the relevant comparative institutional standard. Thus consider Knight's response: "The question of diminishing returns from entrepreneurship is really a matter of the amount of uncertainty present. To imagine that a man could adequately manage a business enterprise of indefinite size and complexity is to imagine a situation in which effective uncertainty is entirely absent" (1965, pp. 286–87). In effect, Knight attributes limitations upon entrepreneurship to a condition of bounded rationality. As uncertainty increases, problems of organization become increasingly complex, and bounds on cognitive competence are reached. But he does not address the issues in a genuinely comparative manner.

Thus suppose that two firms are competing. In principle, net gains ought always to be available by merging the two. Economies of scale can be more fully exploited. Certain overhead and rivalry expenses can be curtailed. And product prices may improve—at least temporarily. Joining the two does not increase the aggregate uncertainty. Since the gaming moves and replies of rivalry have been removed, uncertainty has arguably been reduced. Moreover—and this is the really critical point—decisions need not be forced to the top but can always be assigned to the level at which the issues are most appropriately resolved. Specifically, by conferring semiautonomous status on what had previously been fully autonomous firms in the premerger period, the best of both worlds can presumably be realized. If, for example, demand or cost inter-action effects are such that net gains can be had by moving decisions to the top, it will be done. Those decisions, however, that are most efficiently made at operating levels will remain there. Intervention at the top thus always occurs *selectively*, which is to say only upon a showing of expected net gains. The resulting combined firm can therefore do everything that the two autonomous firms could do previously *and more*. The same argument applies, moreover, not merely to horizontal mergers but also to vertical and conglomerate mergers.[2] The upshot is that, possible public policy restraints (against monopoly, vertical integration, or aggregate size) aside, a compelling reason to explain why all production is not concentrated in one large firm is not reached by Knight's argument.

Although other efforts to explain limitations on firm size have since been made, none addresses the issues in the way I have just posed it. And none really disposes of the puzzle. Thus consider my treatment of limits on firm size in terms of the "control loss" phenomenon (Williamson, 1967b). It involved the application to hierarchical organization of what F. C. Bartlett referred to as the serial reproduction effect in transmitting messages or images between individuals. His experiments involved the oral transmission of descriptive and argumentive passages through a chain of serially linked individuals. Bartlett concluded from a number of such studies:

> It is now perfectly clear that serial reproduction normally brings about startling and radical alterations in the material dealt with. Epithets are changed into their opposites; incidents and events are transposed; names and numbers rarely survive intact for more than a few reproductions; opinions and conclusions are reversed—nearly every possible variation seems as if it can take place, even in a relatively short series. At the same time the subjects may be very well satisfied with their efforts, believing themselves to have passed on all important features with little or no change, and merely, perhaps, to have omitted unessential matters. [1932, p. 175]

Bartlett illustrated this graphically with a line drawing of an owl which, when redrawn successively by eighteen individuals, each sketch based on its immediate predecessor, ended up as a recognizable cat; and the farther from the initial drawing one moved, the greater the distortion experienced (1932, pp. 180–81).

I applied the same argument to the firm size dilemma by invoking bounded rationality and noting that limited spans of control are thereby implied. If any one manager can deal directly with only a limited number of subordinates, then increasing firm size necessarily entails adding hierarchical levels. Transmitting information across these levels experiences the losses to which Bartlett referred, which are cumulative and arguably exponential in form. As firm size increases and successive levels of organization are added, therefore, the effects of control loss eventually exceed the gains. A limit upon radial expansion is thus reached in this way.

---

[2]To be sure, conglomerate benefits may sometimes be small. Ordinarily, however, there will be something—perhaps cash management—for which the combined entity can, in principle, do better. If autonomy is retained by the division in all other respects and the combined firm realizes a net gain in this one respect, an aggregate gain upon merger will obtain, *ceteris paribus*.

Plausible though the argument seemed at the time, it does not permit selective intervention of the kind described above. Rather, the entire firm is managed from the top. All information that has a bearing on decisions is transmitted across successive levels from bottom to top; all directives follow the reverse flow down.

The scenario thus contemplates comprehensive (unselective) linkages between stages. Internal organization need not, however, adopt this structure. Suppose instead that the parent firm deals with each of its parts by exercising forebearance with respect to those activities where no net gains are in prospect (in which event the parent directs the operating part to replicate small firm behavior) and intervenes wherever coordination yields net gains. The puzzle to which I referred at the outset is evidently restored—or at least the serial reproduction loss "solution" does not apply—if such selective intervention is admitted.

The same is true, moreover, of arguments that firm size is limited by growth (Penrose, 1959) or by organization capital (Prescott and Visscher, 1980). Both arguments ignore the possibility that merger may be coupled with selective intervention. Thus if a series of small firms can grow rapidly, or if small firms can acquire valued organizational capital, a merger of those very same firms can selectively do the same and more.

An important recent paper by John Geanakoplos and Paul Milgrom (1984) traces firm size limitations to the "deadlines and delays" that attend hierarchical modes of organization. But the alternative mode of organization with respect to which hierarchy experiences a cost disadvantage is nowhere described. If the set of activities to be organized is held constant, and if internal organization can intervene selectively, the purported disability of hierarchy in relation to a collection of small firms does not withstand scrutiny.

The upshot is that limitations on firm size of a comparative institutional kind have yet to be described.[3]

2. Integration of an Owner-Managed Supply Stage

The obvious answer to the puzzle of why firms do not comprehensively integrate is that selective intervention is not feasible. But why should that be? If the reasons were obvious, the puzzle of what is responsible for limitations on firm size would not persist.

I attempt here to identify some of the main reasons why selective inter-

---

[3]See, however, Kenneth Arrow (1974) and my discussion of the limits of vertical integration in Williamson (1975, chap. 7).

vention breaks down. So as to facilitate the argument, assume that an owner-managed supplier is acquired by the buyer.[4] Assume that this ownership change is accomplished as follows:

1. A price at which the assets are transferred is agreed to.
2. The formula for determining the price at which product is to be transferred from the supply division to the buying division is stipulated.
3. So as to encourage cost economizing, the high-powered incentives that characterize markets are carried over into the firm. Accordingly, the supply division is advised that it will appropriate its net revenues—which are defined as gross revenues less the sum of operating costs, user charges (for asset maintenance and depreciation), and other relevant expenses (e.g. for R & D).
4. Selective intervention will obtain. Accordingly, the supply division is advised to conduct business as usual with the following exception: The supplier will accede to decisions by the buyer to adapt to new circumstances, thereby to realize collective gains, without resistance.[5] Failure to accede is cause for and gives rise to termination.

Unified ownership of the assets of the two stages thus (1) preserves high-powered incentives (rule 3), (2) provides for selective intervention (rule 4), and (3) precludes costly haggling (rule 4). The last two features permit adaptive sequential decision-making economies to be realized by merging what had previously been nonintegrated stages of organization.

Implicit in the argument is the assumption that the two stages are operating in a bilateral exchange relation with each other by reason of investments in

[4]Readers familiar with the recent examination of the costs of vertical integration by Sanford Grossman and Oliver Hart (1984) will recognize that they, like I, trace these costs to incentive impairments that attend unified ownership of successive stages. Their work on these matters and mine were contemporaneous, but I have nevertheless benefited from their treatment and specifically recommend it to those who wish to see these issues developed in a more formal way.

Despite similarities, their work and mine differ in the following significant respects: (1) they ignore the very factors—asset malutilization; accounting contrivances—that I regard as central to incentive distortions in firms; (2) they deny that internal and market organization differ in auditing respects; (3) their "even-handed" insistence that high-powered (transfer pricing) incentives apply in all ownership regimes asymmetrically denies adaptability advantages to integration that weaker (e.g. cost plus) incentives coupled with unified ownership would support; and (4) they disregard the bureaucratic consequences of internal organization. My discussion in this section features asset utilization and accounting effects. Auditing differences are treated in section 4. Salaried management in the preacquisition supply stage is the subject of section 3, and bureaucratic features are addressed in section 5.

[5]This does not preclude consultation between the two divisions, thereby to settle upon superior courses of action. In the event of conflict, however, the purchasing division's preferences are determinative.

transaction-specific assets. Such specificity can take at least four forms: site specificity, physical asset specificity, human asset specificity, and dedicated assets. It will be convenient here to consider only physical asset specificity.

Indeed, given rule 4 above, human asset specificity is effectively ruled out. As developed more fully in Chapter 10, it is in the mutual interests of firm and worker to safeguard the employment relation against abrupt termination (by either party) wherever labor develops firm specific skills and knowledge during the course of its employment. Accordingly, the rule do this/do that or terminate is maladapted to the needs of the parties where firm-specific human assets are considerable.[6] The argument here therefore assumes that the bilateral exchange relation is due entirely to a condition of physical asset specificity. Rule 4 thus applies, whereunder failure to accede to any order to adapt will be cause for termination. Upon realization that successor managements can always be brought in to implement change orders as requested, the incumbent management always acquiesces.[7]

Were this the end of the story, selective intervention with net gains would presumably obtain. In fact, however, numerous measurement difficulties stand in the way of implementing a merger agreement that is attended by high powered incentives. Some of them operate to the disadvantage of the buyer, some work to the disadvantage of the supplier, and others impose losses on both.

2.1 Asset Utilization Losses

The former owner-manager of the supply stage becomes the manager of the supply division upon sale of the supply stage assets to the buyer. The change of status has immediate and serious incentive effects if the high-powered incentive rules described above are employed. For one thing, the manager

---

[6]Suppose that the physical assets at the supply stage are of a general purpose kind but that the human assets display considerable specificity. The purchasing firm agrees to buy the physical assets of the supply stage and advises the supply division that product will thereafter be traded according to a transfer pricing rule; that the managers of the supply division will appropriate all of the net receipts that this transfer pricing rule supports; and that the supply division will be operated under the direction of the purchasing unit in the postacquisition period.

That last is a King Canute provision. Ownership of the physical assets is without content in those circumstances. The human agents who embody the relevant asset specificity are the critical units with which a deal must be struck. Given that those human agents are in a position to bargain—and, indeed, will continue to bargain, given the high-powered incentives to which they remain subject—they are scarcely subject to the purchasing unit's ''orders'' in any usual command and control respect. Accordingly, common ownership of the physical assets of both stages accomplishes precisely no adaptive gains whatsoever.

[7]Grossman and Hart (1984), in their interesting recent treatment of the limits of vertical integration, proceed similarly. Unlike the studies referred to in section 1, their analysis is

who appropriates the net receipts associated with the supply division no longer has the same incentives to utilize equipment with equivalent care and to incur identical preventive maintenance. Since, by assumption, the manager has no firm-specific human assets at stake, the manager behaves myopically with respect to the enterprise. The object being to maximize immediate net receipts, labor costs will be saved by utilizing equipment intensively, and maintenance expense will be deferred to a successor management. Having been paid for his assets upon giving up ownership status, the manager of the supply division proceeds to run them into the ground and leaves the firm to invest his augmented net receipts elsewhere.

To be sure, there are checks against asset abuses of both kinds. The new asset owner may insist that certain utilization and maintenance procedures be observed and furthermore monitor the supply division for compliance. Note, however, that added monitoring costs—unneeded in the nonintegrated state—have now been introduced. Additionally, reputation effects can deter managers from behaving irresponsibly. These, however, are imperfect. Some managers may shrug them off if the immediate gains are large enough and if they cannot be required to disgorge their ill-gotten gains. (Swiss bank accounts have attractive features in that respect.)

The upshot is that efficient asset utilization and the use of high-powered incentives experience tensions in an integrated firm—tensions that do not arise when the two production stages are independent. Contrary to the type of selective intervention that I postulated in section 1, the integrated firm *cannot* wholly replicate outside procurement in "business as usual" respects. Instead, there are *unavaoidable side effects*.

2.2 *Accounting Contrivances*

The price at which a supplier agrees to sell his assets to the buyer will vary with the stream of net receipts that he projects in the post merger period. Given the high-powered incentives described above, that stream will vary with (1) revenues, (2) costs, and (3) continued employment.

One hazard is that the supplier will be "promised" a favorable net receipt stream, hence accept a low price for transferring asset ownership, only to learn to his dismay that his employment has been terminated. Suppose, out

---

genuinely comparative. They ascribe incentive limitations to firms, however, rather than examine the underlying microanalytic factors responsible for those limitations.

of awareness of such a hazard, the supplier demands and receives a guarantee of continued employment. Such guarantees accomplish little, however, if the net receipts of the supply division can be altered substantially through the exercise of accounting discretion. Expropriation can then be accomplished by indirection.

Net receipts can be squeezed in either or both of two ways. For one, revenues can be reduced by cutting transfer prices. For another, cost imputations can be raised. The supply division is vulnerable in both respects.

Given the impossibility of comprehensive contracting, the transfer pricing rule that is stipulated at the outset will necessarily be incomplete. So as to correct against misalignments, prices will need to be reset periodically to reflect changing circumstances. This can be done by consulting the market if asset specificity is zero. Complications intrude, however, when even a slight degree of asset specificity appears. Thus although the terms under which product is traded between autonomous parties are disciplined by the credible threat that the supplier will retire his specialized assets, rather than use them to support the supplier's specialized procurement needs, if mutually acceptable terms are not reached, the manager of the supply division in the integrated firm does not have the same option. If push comes to shove, the physical assets are no longer his to retire (or, more generally, redeploy). Employment guarantees notwithstanding, the manager of the supply division can, if he refuses to accept the proposed terms, be brushed aside. (He is simply "reassigned.") Upon merger, therefore, the determination of transfer prices has, in effect, become a decision for the purchasing division (which now owns the assets of both parts) to reach unilaterally. The hazard is obvious: Despite assurances to the contrary, prices will be set so as to squeeze the net receipts of the supply stage.

Cost determination is problematic, moreover, whatever the degree of asset specificity. Whereas each stage determines its own accounting practices in the pre-merger regime, that is no longer permitted—indeed, is wholly implausible—upon merger. Instead, responsibility for the accounting rules will be concentrated on the asset owner.[8] Explicit agreements that limit accounting discretion notwithstanding, the supply stage runs the risk that costs will be reset to its disadvantage.[9]

---

[8]These costs could be made subject to repeated bargaining in the *ex post* period. But that defeats the notion that governance costs are reduced by merger.

[9]Conceivably the courts can be employed to safeguard the interests of the supply stages in transfer pricing and cost accounting respects. Plainly, however, this is a highly imperfect and costly forum to which to appeal decisions of that kind. Note, moreover, that while spot prices can be used to define transfer prices in the limiting case where $k = 0$, a corresponding market standard is not available to define cost imputations.

The upshot is that the supply stage is better advised to discount very heavily any promise that favorable net receipt streams are in prospect and to realize its full bargaining advantage by extracting maximum asset valuation terms at the outset—because a squeeze is in prospect thereafter. But there is more to it. If the use of high-powered incentives in firms is inherently subject to corruption, then the notion that the integrated firm can do everything that the nonintegrated parts could accomplish is a fiction. Instead, the integrated firm does better in some respects and worse in others.

2.3 *Incentive Ramifications and* β_o

High-powered incentives in firms give rise to difficulties of two kinds: The assets of the supply stage are not utilized with due care, and the net revenue stream of the supply stage is subject to manipulation. Upon realization that high-powered incentives in firms experience such disabilities, lower-powered incentives are apt to be introduced instead. Were the supply stage management to be compensated mainly by salary and become subject to periodic monitoring (decision review, auditing, and the like), the supply stage would have less need to be concerned with accounting chicanery, and the asset owner's concern with asset dissipation would be lessened.

Low-powered incentives have well-known adaptability advantages. That, after all, is what commends cost plus contracting. But such advantages are not had without cost—which explains why cost plus contracting is embraced reluctantly (Williamson, 1967a). Our first explanation for why firms do not everywhere supplant markets thus is that (1) firms cannot mimic the high-powered incentives of markets without experiencing added costs; (2) although recourse by firms to lower-powered incentives is thereby indicated, that too comes at a cost; and (3) those added costs of internal organization are not offset by comparative adaptability gains under circumstances where $k = 0$, since those are precisely the conditions under which the identity of the parties does not matter, whence classical market contracting works well. The net governance costs of acquiring an owner-operated supply stage are thus positive where asset specificity is slight. A $\beta_o > 0$ condition thereby obtains.

More generally, the argument is this: Incentives and controls are adapted to the attributes of each organizational alternative. To attempt to "hold the rules as nearly constant as possible," on the theory that what works well in one regime ought to apply equally to another, is thus mistaken. The powers and limits of each form of organization must be discovered and respected.

2.4 *Innovation*

The foregoing makes no reference to innovation. Implicitly, product and process innovations are unimportant. Transactions are moved from markets to hierarchies as asset specificity builds up because the high-powered incentives in firms operate as a disability when adaptations to stochastic or other disturbances are attempted in a tightly bilateral trading context.

How, if at all, is the assignment of transactions to markets and hierarchies altered by the introduction of process or product innovations? Unfortunately, the study of innovation is enormously complex (Phillips, 1970; Nelson, 1984). Some large corporations maintain that innovation can be and has been successfully bureaucratized: "We employ many people who, if left to their own devices, might not be research-minded. In other words, we hire people to be curious as a group. . . . We are undertaking to *create* research capability by the sheer pressure of money."[10] As discussed in subsection 6.4 below, however, there appear to be some projects for which the use of high-powered incentives elicits superior research results. How do nonintegrated and integrated supply stages compare in supplying incentives for innovation?

The issues are many-sided. An obvious advantage of integration is that research and development cooperation between stages may be easier to elicit. But there are at least two incentive-impairing effects.

a.   CAUSAL AMBIGUITY

As discussed in subsection 4.2, below, reasoning systems are expected to behave in reasoning ways. Administrative boundaries are much easier to breach than are market boundaries when demands for reason are expressed.

Thus if a supply division in an integrated firm is largely but not wholly responsible for the success (failure) of an innovative effort, it may be difficult to concentrate the benefits (costs) in such a way as to reflect that condition. To illustrate, suppose that the purchasing stage proposes that the supply stage consider a process or product innovation. Contrast the results if the supply stage is integrated or independent and if the proposal is successful or not. Assume in any event that the supply stage incurs nontrivial costs in conducting the necessary research and development.

Ownership autonomy in the nonintegrated regime will serve to concentrate the net benefits of both failures and successes on the independent supply stage. The uncorrupted use of high-powered incentives in firms would do the

---

[10]The quotation is attributed to the research coordinator of Standard Oil of Ohio by Daniel Hamburg (1963, p. 107).

same. But whereas the requests of an independent purchaser are apt to be dismissed should it ask for its "fair share" of the gains, an integrated purchasing stage is much more likely to prevail in asking that its significant contribution to the project be acknowledged. Not only does fairness dictate that the rewards be shared, but to do otherwise would result in large compensation disparities between the two stages. Those in turn would thereafter give rise to invidious comparisons. Since the firm has the discretion to remedy the disparities by administrative decision, and since to do otherwise poses severe strains, the high-powered incentives of markets are apt to be compromised.

The *ex post* weakening of incentives for innovation does not, however, come without cost. The management of the supply division will anticipate that similar pressures will arise in the future—which is to say that, the rules notwithstanding, high-powered incentives in firms are subject to degradation.[11]

b. GENERAL OFFICE INTRUSION

Even if the division of benefits between supply and purchasing stages could be decided objectively, there is serious doubt that an *ex ante* agreement to distribute a pro rata share of the rewards will be respected. Instead, a redistribution away from the operating parts in favor of the ownership is apt to be effected by manipulation of the transfer pricing and cost accounting rules.

To be sure, the management of an independent supply stage also runs the risk that the ownership will keep two sets of books. True performance results could thus be disguised. The relevant question, however, is one of degree. If integration ordinarily permits greater accounting discretion, which it arguably does (see subsection 2.2 above), then the results of innovation are more easily obfuscated in the integrated state.

Moreover, even if the ownership of an integrated firm were to resist manipulation of that kind, high-powered incentives to innovate need not obtain. The problem is one of information asymmetry/impactedness. If it is very costly to prove that manipulation has not occurred, then, ownership promises of good behavior notwithstanding, managers will be continuously suspect that it will occur—in which case their incentives are unavoidably impaired.

---

[11]Similar arguments apply where a research and development project fails. Here the independent supply stage bears the costs almost entirely. The buyer when asked to share simply declines. By contrast, the integrated supply stage is apt to ask for and receive relief. After all, it undertook the project at the purchasing stage's request. *Ex post* cost sharing between the integrated stages will thus be ordered.

C. A PROVISIONAL MATCH

The introduction of innovation plainly complicates the earlier-described assignment of transactions to markets or hierarchies based entirely on an examination of their asset specificity qualities. Indeed, the study of economic organization in a regime of rapid innovation poses much more difficult issues than those addressed here. Nevertheless, it may be instructive to examine a narrow construction of the problem.

Thus consider a firm that has the need for the continuing supply of goods and services that differ not merely in asset specificity respects but also in terms of their innovative potential, where the latter has reference to the degree to which a good or service is susceptible to cost-saving improvements. The earlier argument—that goods and services that are supported by nonspecific assets will be procured in the market and that the balance shifts in favor of vertical integration as asset specificity deepens—remains intact in circumstances where the innovative potential is slight. Differences, therefore, if there are any, are concentrated in the regime where innovative potential is great.

It is useful in this connection to distinguish between cost savings that are generic and those that are proprietary. Generic cost savings are ones that are quickly recognized and easily imitated by rival suppliers. Patents, copyrights, trade secrets, and the like afford little protection for these. Those that are proprietary, by contrast, are ones for which the benefits of innovation can be appropriated.

In principle, both generic and proprietary cost savings can be supported by assets of either nonspecific or specific kinds. Easy imitation, however, is ordinarily associated with nonspecific investments. Accordingly, market procurement of goods or services of the generic cost-saving kind will usually pose little bilateral dependency or profit strain, whence market procurement is normally indicated. The procurement of items for which cost savings are proprietary, especially those that are supported by transaction specific assets, is another matter.

The tension here is that while the buyer will want both to participate in the benefits of innovation and to encourage supply stage investments of an efficient (transaction specific) kind, the supplier's incentives to innovate (which entails the realization of cost savings of a subtle, nonobvious, and often noncomparable kind) will be diminished if the supply stage is integrated.[12] A complex tradeoff situation is thus posed when the potential incen-

---

[12]The incentive limitations of large firms for rewarding innovation are suggested by the following story in the *Wall Street Journal,* May 15, 1984, p. 1:

tive benefits are great and the transaction is characterized by substantial asset specificity. New hybrid forms of organization may appear in response to such a condition. (Innovative organizational forms in the semiconductor industry are illustrative [Levin, 1982]. Although the discussion of hybrid forms in Chapters 7 and 8 is apposite, the examples in subsection 6.4 below are closer to the point. Much more study of the relations between organization and innovation is needed.)

3. Acquisition of a Supply Stage in Which Ownership and Management Are Separated

Suppose, *arguendo*, that vertical integration *of the kind described above* experiences the incentive disabilities that are ascribed to it. It is nevertheless noteworthy that the conditions described above are very special. In particular I have assumed that ownership and management are joined in the preacquisition supply stage. What if that condition does not obtain?

Suppose that an independent supplier undergoes an ownership change before an acquisition of the supplier is even contemplated. Suppose, in particular, that what had been a closely held, owner-managed firm becomes a diffusely held firm in which none of the management has a significant equity interest.

The hazards of using high-powered (net receipt) incentives to compensate the management of this firm will be evident to owners and managers alike. Owners will recognize the asset dissipation hazards, and managers will be concerned that owners will retain influence over accounting, thus posing a risk that net receipt realizations will be manipulated. When those consequences are foreseen, high-powered incentives in this now diffusely owned

---

Cash awards for employee ideas grow in number and size of the top prizes.

Commerica Inc. will start its Great Idea program July 5 to solicit money-saving tips from workers. In a trial, it got 3,000 suggestions. Top prizes are $10,000. General Motors recently doubled its top award to $20,000 and now includes some salaried employees. Also, first-line supervisors can win up to $1,000 for ideas. Previously, such workers didn't have incentives.

Pitney Bowes Business Systems raised its top prize to $50,000 paid over two years from $30,000 paid over three years. Ford Motor now allows groups of hourly workers instead of just an individual to win its top award of $6,000. Eastman Kodak paid $3.6 million in awards last year, up 8.7% from 1982, and figures it saves $16 million from the suggestions.

In the overall scheme of things, however, these awards are peanuts. The big prizes for innovation always accrue to entrepreneurship. The issues are nevertheless complicated. For a discussion, see Williamson (1975, chapter 10).

firm will give way to incentives of a lower-powered kind. Salaried compensation will therefore obtain.

The critical question is whether, in view of the above-described changes that attend the change in ownership of the premerger supply stage, merger incurs any added costs. If it does not, then the acquisition by a purchasing stage of a supply stage in which the ownership has already been sold off would offer the prospect of gain without cost. The gains would presumably take the same form as those ascribed to merger previously: Subgoal pursuit by the supply stage management would be attenuated, so that coordination between the two stages would be accomplished more easily and effectively in the postmerger period when common ownership obtains.

The firm size dilemma to which I referred at the outset would then be restored with only a minor change. The puzzle would now read as follows: Why are not all *diffusely owned* production stages placed under unified ownership, thereby to be organized and operated as one large firm? Unless undisclosed costs of merger are discovered, we are mainly back where we started. Put differently, section 2 is an explication of the Berle and Means problem and does not provide an explanation for limits on vertical integration outside of that special context.

Unremarked merger consequences of three kinds warrant consideration. For one thing, to observe that ownership and management are separated does not establish that ownership is thereafter wholly lacking in control. Differential control effects within merged and nonmerged entities is thus one possibility. Second, the fact that managements in both pre- and postmerger regimes are salaried does not necessarily imply that compensation is disconnected from net receipts. Finally, the possibility that integration affects the internal politics of the corporation with systematic performance consequences warrants scrutiny. The first two consequences are considered here. The third is addressed in section 4.

3.1 Ownership Effects

The absence of continuous (hands-on) control permits those to whom decision powers are delegated to exercise discretion. But a total absence of control is not thereby implied. To the contrary, if ownership control is reasserted when performance approaches or falls below threshold standards, then the relevant questions are ones of thresholds and competence to intervene. *Ceteris paribus,* weak standards imply greater opportunities for managerial discretion. Ownership interests are commonly activated, however, before bankruptcy becomes imminent.

The issues here are akin to those that arise in the M-form corporation, where operating and strategic decisions are separated. Thus even if, as discussed in Chapter 11, middle managers are "ostensibly" free from oversight during the operating interval, the absence of oversight should not be implied if (1) strategic management can and does intervene when a crisis occurs—which is to say, when the "essential variables" fall outside of prescribed limits— and (2) the operating plans are periodically renegotiated (say, at annual budget review intervals).

Albeit attenuated, the ownership bears a similar oversight relation to the strategic management. The relevant comparative institutional question is whether differential performance between integrated and nonintegrated regimes arises on that account. The main difference, if there is one, is that ownership oversight generally operates on more aggregate performance measures. Divisional performance thus generally escapes scrutiny. A tradeoff thus obtains whereby ownerhip oversight at the divisional level is somewhat less intensive in the integrated regime. The issues here, however, relate mainly to the costs of bureaucracy and are treated more fully in section 4.

3.2 *Contingent Compensation*

The compensations of salaried managers and other employees who work for wages are ostensibly disconnected from performance. That is superficial, however, if in fact salaries are adjusted at contract renewal intervals and promotions are made with reference to past or promised performance. More generally, to model the employment relation entirely with reference to piece rate/flat rate distinctions is warranted only if intertemporal reputation and commitment features are absent (or are otherwise constant) across such classifications. That is rarely the case.

a. SALARY

Assume that salary tracks reported net receipts with a lag. The question then is whether the net receipts of the supply division are independent of the pre- and postmerger status. One possible difference is that the postmerger management of the supply division may be more subject to accounting manipulation of reported net receipts than was the same management when the firm was an independent supplier. If, as seems plausible, the managers in the acquiring stage have a greater postmerger say over the accounting procedures, then net receipts in the postacquisition period will be tilted in the acquiring stage's favor. Transfer prices in the postmerger regime are apt to be (comparatively) distorted as a result.

b. PROMOTIONS

If promotions are made not on the basis of seniority, rotation, a coin toss, or some other event over which the managers have no discretionary control, then the way in which the promotion process operates in the pre- and postmerger periods also warrants examination. Merger can effect promotions in two respects: Promotions within the supply stage may be made on a different basis as a result of the merger; and promotions out of the supply stage into the management of the combined entity now become feasible. If the postmerger promotion process becomes more highly politicized in either or both of those respects, the fact of salaried compensation in both pre- and postmerger regimes does not constitute incentive neutrality.

That managers playing in the larger (postmerger) game will conduct themselves differently from their behavior in the smaller (premerger) game is, at very least, plausible. Thus whereas promotions might be expected to go to those who presented themselves as effective advocates at the trading interface in the premerger period, the advantage is more apt to accrue to those who are effective conciliators postmerger. Chester Barnard's remarks are apposite:

> The general method of maintaining an informal executive organization is so to operate and select and promote executives that a general condition of compatibility of personnel is maintained. Perhaps often and certainly occasionally, men cannot be promoted or selected, or even must be relieved, because they cannot function, because they ''do not fit,'' where there is no question of formal competence. [1938, p. 224]

To be sure, efforts can be made to insulate the promotion process from those effects. For example, managers in the supply division might be advised that they are ineligible for promotion to the general office. But such a policy may be ineffective and/or ill-advised. Ineffectiveness will result if such policies are unaccompanied by credible commitments. Adverse side effects will occur if such policies engender resentment. Beyond that, moreover, is the question of whether, even if supply stage managers are denied advancement, they are in a position to delay or even block the promotion of others.

The upshot is that promotion differences between the nonintegrated and integrated regimes are unavoidable. If the promotional balance is tilted away from merit in favor of politics in the process, which would appear to be the likely result, incentive impairments in the postmerger condition will obtain[13]—in which event, the adaptive benefits that integration potentially affords notwithstanding, integration is always attended by added costs. Selective intervention—gain without cost—is simply not a member of the feasible set.

---

[13]The text emphasizes the negative politicizing consequences that a merger has on promotion. This does not, however, exhaust the possibilities. Benefits can obtain if managers who

4. The Costs of Bureaucracy

The costs of acquisition discussed in section 2 are mainly ones that will accrue to any separation of ownership from control, merger-related or otherwise. Although the costs of acquisition discussed in section 3 are not confounded in ownership and control respects, they are also more speculative in nature and are probably weaker in effect. The question thus arises as to whether there are other costs of merger that have yet to be identified. In particular, are there undisclosed "costs of bureaucracy" that obtain when successive production stages are joined?

Philip Selznick contends that "the most important thing about [nonmarket] organizations is that, though they are tools, each nevertheless has a life of its own" (1949, p. 10). Instrumental intentions notwithstanding, formal structures can "never succeed in conquering the nonrational dimensions of organizational behavior" (Selznick, 1948, p. 25). Richard Scott summarizes the argument as follows:

> [O]rganizational rationality is constrained by "the recalcitrance of the tools of action": persons bring certain characteristics to the organization and develop other commitments as members that restrict their capacity for rational action; organizational procedures become valued ends in themselves; the organization strikes bargains with its environment that compromise present objectives and limit future possibilities. [1981, p. 91]

What are the ramifications of such views for economic approaches to the study of organization? One possible economic response is to regard the conditions to which Selznick, Scott, and others refer as noise. Aberrations from rationality are thus treated as error terms. A stronger response is to deny that such behavior even exists. Neither is proposed here. Instead, an informed economic approach to the study of organization will display an interest in and *thereafter make provision for* all regularities of whatever kind. If the behavior in question is systematic, allowance can be made for it in making comparative institutional choices and in organizational design respects. Thus, if some forms of organization are less subject to bureaucratic distortions than others, this will be taken into account in assessing alternative modes. Within modes where distortions are especially severe, moreover, it may be possible to mitigate such conditions by devising checks or organizational reforms.

---

otherwise have dead-end prospects are presented with new opportunities for advancement by a merger.

The condition of premerger promotion prospects thus warrants scrutiny. Where they are sharply circumscribed (the market for managers is poorly developed; the firm is growing slowly; senior managers are far from retirement), a more sympathetic assessment of the effects of a merger on managerial incentives is warranted.

By comparison with the market failure literature, the literature on bureaucratic failure is relatively underdeveloped. The discussion here merely attempts to identify some of the main life cycle features that beset internal organization. As compared with market organization, internal organization displays a differential propensity to manage complexity, to forgive error, and to engage in logrolling.

4.1 *The Propensity to Manage*

A propensity to manage seems to characterize all forms of bureaucratic organization. To be sure, the public sector is widely thought to be especially culpable in this respect—and probably is. Charles Morris captures the spirit in his reference to "the cost of good intentions". What he characterizes as "the new rationalist style in government" was based on "a confident optimism that the most intractable problems would give way before the resolute assault of intelligent, committed people" (1980. p. 23). But the same attitude also characterizes the private sector (Feldman and March, 1981).

Actually, the propensity to manage has two parts rather than just one. The part to which Morris refers is the *instrumental* propensity: Decision-makers project a capacity to manage complexity that is repeatedly refuted by events. Although such a propensity is well-intentioned, problems regularly turn out to be more difficult and/or managerial competence more limited than managers of complexity originally project (Perrow, 1983). Counterexamples to the contrary notwithstanding, this is the main opinion.

The second type of propensity is more reprehensible. It is the *strategic* propensity to use the resources of the organization to pursue subgoals. If, for the reasons given in section 2, pecuniary incentives in firms are weaker than those in markets, then political games and preferences have greater sway. Efforts to tilt the organization, often through greater hands-on management, commonly result.

Odysseus-type solutions are often attractive where *ex ante* resolve is known regularly to break down in the face of recurrent exigencies/temptations. Out of awareness that the call of the Sirens would be well-nigh irresistible, Odysseus instructed that he should be bound to the mast. As Jon Elster points out, "binding oneself is a privileged way of resolving the problem of weakness of will" (1979, p. 37). Such self-denial benefits can be realized within the firm if mergers for which the advocates can identify only limited prospective benefits are refused. The uncounted, but nevertheless predictable, costs attributable to the future propensity to manage will thereby assuredly be avoided.

4.2 *Forgiveness*

Systems of justice vary systematically with organization. Families are ordinarily presumed to have deep knowledge of the transactions that occur between or impinge on the membership, to employ long time horizons, and to be relatively forgiving.[14] Markets, in contrast, are presumed to have less knowledge of idiosyncratic circumstances, employ shorter time horizons, and are relatively severe (unforgiving).

For the reasons given in section 5, internal organization enjoys comparative auditing advantages. Accordingly, the integrated firm has greater capacity to reach informed decisions on the merits than do nonintegrated trading entities. The confounding of risks and decisions, which complicates market assessments, can thus be unpacked with greater precision and confidence internally. In principal, therefore, internal asset managers can better ascertain whether to continue funding a project than could the capital market.

But there are at least two further consequences. First, the prospect of penalty can and often does elicit inordinate energies. The market is a severe taskmaster. Unless escalator clauses have been expressly agreed to from the outset, unexpected cost increases are absorbed rather than passed through when transactions are mediated by the market. By contrast, unexpected cost increases that occur in trades within the firm are apt to be negotiable. The justification for such increases can be examined more fully within the firm, and the hazards of misrepresentation are less severe than in the market. But internal organization is thereby denied access to the supranormal energies that the market is able to mobilize. It is unrealistic to expect that such efforts will be expended if reasoned or plausible explanations can be advanced to support the cost increases in question: Reasoning systems are expected to behave in reasoning ways. (Academics, being the ultimate reasoners, are often unsuited for administrative positions on that account.)

Second, the net benefit calculus employed by firm and market differ. Indeed, a useful definition of forgiveness, at least for purposes of evaluating commercial transactions, is whether "excuses" are evaluated strictly with reference to a pecuniary net benefit calculus or not. As between the two, the market is expected to employ a stricter pecuniary net benefit calculus than is the firm. In this sense, it is less forgiving. A leading reason for this is that the firm maintains greater separability among transactions with the market than it can for transactions that are organized internally.

---

[14]Of these three aspects, which are all related, forgiveness is the most important and distinctive.

It is thus easy for a firm to terminate a supplier of a good or service that is supported by nonspecific assets ($k = 0$) at the first indication of failure. Were this same transaction to be organized internally, however, the firm would conduct an inquiry and consider second chances. Partly this is a manifestation of the aforementioned auditing advantage of internal organization. But it is also the case that the firm is unable to treat each internal transaction in a fully separable way. In effect, internal transactions of the $k=0$ kind benefit from an association with other internal transactions for which $k > 0$.

Thus whereas continuity of transactions of the latter kind is valued from a pecuniary net benefit standpoint, the same is not true for the former. Firms that internalize transactions of both kinds are unable, however, to treat each in a fully discriminating way. A rational decision to "work things out" when things go wrong for $k > 0$ transactions spills over and infects transactions of the $k = 0$ kind. It is unacceptable, both to insiders and to interested observers, for the firm to behave differently. Simple regard for human dignity demands that due process be respected. Barnard's remarks about informal organization are apposite: One of the purposes served by informal organization is that of "maintaining the personality of the individual against certain effects of formal organizations which tend to disintegrate the personality" (Barnard, 1938, p. 122).

Thus whereas extreme market outcomes can be accepted as the luck of the draw, administrative actions are interpreted by all of the affected parties, including interested outsiders (associates, family, friends, and so forth), as merit choices. That places a severe burden of due process on internal organization. A plausible case will not do; a preponderance of evidence is needed if severe penalties are to be meted out. Out of awareness that they operate under the protection of a norm of internal due process, individuals are able to exploit the internal organization in minimum performance respects, and some do.

To be sure, the above described weakening of incentives applies strictly to $k = 0$ activities. The possibility that a merit choice environment intensifies incentives within the firm, as compared with the market, for $k > 0$ activities is not denied. It suffices, however, for the purposes of the argument, that due process spillovers are responsible for incentive attentuation for the $k = 0$ condition.

4.3 *Logrolling*

Again the issue is not whether internal organization experiences costs but whether differential costs are incurred in moving from nonintegrated to integrated status. I submit that internal operating and investment decisions are more subject to politicization.

a. OPERATING DECISIONS

Alvin Gouldner contends that the norm of reciprocity is as important and universal as the incest taboo (1961). It finds expression throughout human society—across cultures and degrees of development and over time. Opportunities to give effect to reciprocity, however, vary with the circumstances. In general those opportunities are greater within more highly integrated organizations than in less. Moreover, those opportunities are apt to be given expression—which is a manifestation of the earlier described tendency for internal traders to be more accommodating than autonomous traders. This is not necessarily a bad thing; the prospect of such accommodation is a factor that weighs favorably in evaluating trades that are supported by specific assets. The possibility that it will go beyond the objective merits to include reciprocal managerial back-scratching is, however, a matter for concern and is appropriately taken into account in the decision to internalize incremental transactions.

b. INVESTMENT RENEWAL BIASES

An internal procurement bias is supported by a number of factors.[15] For one thing, the internal supplier that produces mainly for internal uses may be judged to be at a relative disadvantage in the market place. The internal supplier may lack both the large and experienced marketing organization and the established customer connections to which nonintegrated external suppliers have access. In consideration of such conditions, and if fixed costs are nonredeployable, a "preference" for internal procurement might seem appropriate—at least so long as the external price exceeds the variable cost of internal supply.

This may be a specious argument, however, since the nonredeployability of assets may easily be overstated (there may be a secondhand market for the machinery in question) and individual equipment renewal decisions ought eventually to be made with reference to the long-run viability of the internal facility. Managers are notably reluctant, however, to abolish their own jobs, even in the face of employment guarantees. The problems with such guarantees are that while continued employment may be secure, assurances that status will be maintained when a position is eliminated, and that promotion prospects will not be upset upon removal from a known promotion ladder are unenforceable. A preference for internal supply is thus to be expected and may manifest itself by urging that each equipment replacement decision be made serially, in semi-independent fashion. A fundamentally nonviable internal capability may be uncritically preserved in this way.

[15]The discussion here is based on Williamson (1975, p. 119).

4.4 *Further Remarks*

The main benefits of vertical integration, according to the transaction cost economics point of view adopted here, take the form of governance rather than production cost savings. They are discerned by examining the problems that attend autonomous contracting when the parties to a trade are operating in a bilateral exchange relation. The main costs of vertical integration are more difficult to discover, however. They are plainly not of a neoclassical production function kind. Neither are differential governance cost features transparent. Analysis at a more microanalytic level is evidently needed.

That is an analytic inconvenience, to say the least—made all the more so by the underdeveloped state of the bureaucratic failure literature. One possibility, when the economic realities do not line up with the analytic conveniences, is to pretend otherwise. Just as transaction cost reasoning and the examination of microanalytic phenomena has helped to illuminate the factors responsible for market failure, however, I conjecture that similar headway can be made against the subject of bureaucracy if a concerted effort is made here as well.

To be sure, undiscovered production cost features may appear that vitiate the need for such an effort. Or unremarked contractual difficulties that attend vertical integration may still emerge. I will be surprised, however, if the principal limits to vertical integration turn out to have nonbureaucratic origins. A difficult road ahead is in prospect.

5. Low-Powered Incentives in Markets

A symmetrical treatment of economic organization will examine not merely the strains that result when the high-powered incentives associated with markets are introduced into firms, but will also consider whether the low-powered incentives employed by firms can be introduced without strain into markets. The latter question is the matter of concern here.

Assume, for the purposes of this section, that the innovative tensions discussed in 2.4, above, are slight. Assume further that the amount of physical asset specificity at the supply stage is great. Integration is thus the indicated form of organization.

Suppose, as a consequence of the factors discussed in subsections 2.1 and 2.2, that the integrated firm decides to transfer product between divisions on the cost plus terms. The supply division thus accedes to requests from the procurement division that it adapt the quantity or quality of the product without resistance.[16] Lest costs be permitted to escalate or economizing opportunities go unnoticed or be forgone, however, the supply division is periodically reviewed in cost and decision respects. Suppose, *arguendo,* that the resulting performance is judged to be satisfactory.

If such low-powered incentives coupled with periodic auditing have advantages in firms, why not replicate the same with markets? That is a different way of putting the question that I posed at the outset—only here the question is why can't the market replicate the firm? It will be useful to address the question by examining the following more operational statement of the problem: What are the consequences of cost plus contracting between autonomous firms?

Interfirm and intrafirm cost plus contracting differ in at least two significant respects. Both are related to the fact that an autonomous firm has an added degree of freedom that an integrated division does not: It can take its assets and flee. The first difference is that an independent supplier has an incentive to incur costs for strategic purposes that the internal supply division did not. The second is that interfirm auditing cannot be presumed to be as effective as intrafirm auditing.

The strategic difference is this: The independent firm has a stronger incentive to make investments for which reimbursements can plausibly be claimed—in plant and equipment and in human capital—if they give it an added capability to compete for other business. To be sure, both external supplier and the internal supply division can be advised (and may agree) that they are to supply exclusively to the needs of the procurement division. But enforcing such a provision against an independent supplier is apt to be much more difficult. Court ordering is much less effective than administrative fiat in effecting preferences on these matters.[17]

It is sometimes argued that interfirm and intrafirm audits are indistinguishable. Thus Sanford Grossman and Oliver Hart "assume that integration in itself does not make any new variable observable to both parties. Any audits which an employer can have done of her subsidiary are also feasible when the subsidiary is a separate company" (1984, p. 5). I submit that there are reasons to believe otherwise. Specifically, market and internal organization differ in "informal organization" respects. Chester Barnard put the argument as follows:

> Since the efficiency of organization is affected by the degree to which individuals assent to orders, denying the authority of an organization communication is a

---

[16]This oversimplifies. The supply division will resist cutbacks, lest it drop below some minimum viable level of activity and be shut down altogether.

[17]Firms do, after all, breach contracts, and courts are often loath to enforce exclusive dealing agreements between firms. But courts would not ordinarily deign to deal with a firm's internal decision to supply exclusively to its own needs.

threat to the interests of all individuals who derive a net advantage from their connection with the organization, unless the orders are unacceptable to them also. Accordingly, at any given time there is among most of the contributors an active personal interest in the maintenance of the authority of all orders which to them are within the zone of indifference. The maintenance of this interest is largely a function of informal organization. [1938, p. 169]

Although Armen Alchian does not make reference to informal organization, he nevertheless acknowledges that "anyone vulnerable to [a] threat of loss [if the coalition is impaired] will seek to preserve not only the coalition but also to reduce the possibility of that threat from the other members of the coalition" (1983, p. 9). If a stronger mutual interest in organizational integrity can be presumed among members of an integrated organization than would exist between independent trading units—because their destinies are more closely tied in the former than in the latter case—then internal auditors can expect to receive greater cooperation, including even hints as to where the "dead bodies lie," than can be presumed when auditing across an autonomous ownership boundary is attempted.[18]

Indeed, the external auditor can ordinarily anticipate only perfunctory cooperation. Since if "our" costs are disallowed then "our" profits will decline and "our" viability may be jeopardized, the employees of the independent supply stage will engage in cost justification and cover up.

To be sure, divisions also engage in obfuscation and cover-up against internal auditors. Division managements cannot, however, take the physical assets they have accumulated through cost overruns and flee. Termination with and without assets makes a difference. If, therefore, heads must roll in an integrated division where cost excesses have become great, and if guilty and innocent in these circumstances go down together, then it is easy to understand how those who are not implicated in malfeasance will collaborate early and actively with internal auditors.

The upshot is that cost plus contracting in markets cannot be presumed to be identical to cost plus contracting in firms. Transferring a transaction out of the firm and into the market therefore will rarely occur on unchanged cost plus terms but will instead be attended by incentive and governance realignments.

This repeats the argument advanced earlier: Incentives and governance structures that are observed to work well in one organizational milieu do not

[18]I do not, however, mean to suggest that internal audits are unproblematic. As the sociologists have repeatedly observed and reported, internal auditing is subject to corruption (Dalton, 1957; Granovetter, forthcoming). But these same sociologists fail to offer a comparative perspective. Thus although it is instructive to know that internal organization is flawed, it is equally important to know whether the flaws are remediable or not. If all the relevant organizational alternatives are equally or more severely flawed, the observation that internal audits are imperfect lacks comparative institutional significance.

transfer uncritically to others. To the contrary, organization form, incentive instruments, and governance safeguards must be derived simultaneously.[19]

6. Illustrative Examples

Evidence on the incentive limits of firms is not well developed. For one thing, firms are understandably chary of admitting administrative strains that may be interpreted as managerial failures. Additionally, the incentive limits of firms has eluded analytic scrutiny. There is simply no place, within the production function framework in which a profit maximization objective is prescribed, for incentive limits to appear.

The six examples discussed below are merely suggestive. At best they confirm that all the incentive limits discussed so far find real world counterparts. But a much more systematic development of the relevant microanalytic data is needed.

6.1 *Inside Contracting*

The use of high-powered incentives in firms was attempted in New England manufacturing firms at the turn of the century. What has been referred to as the inside contracting system has been described as follows:

> Under the system of inside contracting, the management of a firm provided floor space and machinery, supplied raw material and working capital, and arranged for the sale of the final product. The gap between raw material and finished product, however, was filled not by paid employees arranged in [a] descending hierarchy . . . but by [inside] contractors, to whom the production job was delegated. They hired their own employees, supervised the work process, and received a [negotiated] piece rate from the company. [Buttrick, 1952, pp. 201–2]

As I have discussed elsewhere, the inside contracting system was beset with a number of contractual difficulties (Williamson, 1975, pp. 96–97):

1. Equipment was not utilized and maintained with appropriate care.
2. Process innovations were (a) biased in favor of labor-saving, as against material-saving, innovations and (b) regularly delayed until after contract renewal terms had been reached.
3. Incentives for product innovation were weak.

---

[19]To extrapolate the eventual convergence of capitalist and socialist enterprise because they already display strong commonalities is, therefore, unwarranted. Equally important is that each mode has displayed and will continue to display distinctive features, the transfer of which, even if feasible, experiences strain.

4. Contractor incomes were sometimes thought to be excessive in relation to those of the capitalist, in which event the capitalist sought redress at contract renewal intervals.

Inside contracting can thus be regarded as an effort to implement rules 1 through 4, as described in section 2 above, the main difference being that the inside contractor could be replaced not at will but only at contract renewal intervals. This imaginative effort to preserve high-powered incentives in firms presumably encouraged economizing on variable costs. But those same high-powered incentives also evidently gave rise to asset malutilization and were responsible for distortions in the innovation process. Intertemporal income strains between capitalist and contractor also appeared. Those (and perhaps other) disabilities are presumably responsible for the demise of inside contracting, although vestiges of that form of organization continue in the construction industry, where, however, work is done on a project rather than on a continuing supply basis (Eccles, 1981).

6.2 *Automobile Franchise Dealership*

Recall Alfred P. Sloan's explanation (see Chapter 5, section 4) for why the automobile manufacturers did not integrate forward into automobile sales and service but used franchises instead. A principal complicating factor was the trade-in. Many hundreds of thousands of such transactions needed to be negotiated at geographically dispersed locations. Considerable judgment was evidently required to assess the highly variable quality of the cars presented for trade-in. A generous used car valuation would help to sell new cars, but a net loss would be recorded upon resale of the traded item. An undervaluation of an automobile proposed in trade would not meet the market and thus would not move new autos.

To be sure, the automobile manufacturer could insist that every transaction be split into two parts: The owner of a used car would strike his own best deal elsewhere and use the proceeds to buy a new car. The sale of the new car would then be more of what Sloan referred to as "an ordinary selling proposition" rather than a "trading proposition" (1964, p. 282). But inasmuch as large numbers of customers were evidently attracted to bilateral trade, the relevant question was how to respond. Sloan explains that managers in large firms lack the "knack" for trading, but I submit that the fundamental difficulty resides in the incentives of the large, managerially controlled enterprise. Supervisors and salesmen in such an organization lack confidence that they will fully appropriate the gains when highly profitable deals are struck. And those same supervisors and salesmen cannot be held fully accountable if losses are incurred (firing them is an imperfect solution if employees can secure employment elsewhere without bearing a full reputation-effect penalty). A means by which to concentrate incentive effects more effectively is evidently needed. That, rather than the incapacity to support the knack of trading, is what explains the franchised dealership response.

6.3 *Acquisitions, Incentives, and Internal Equity*

Tenneco, Inc., is the nation's largest conglomerate. Its employees number almost 100,000 and its annual sales exceed $15 billion. Tenneco acquired Houston Oil and Minerals Corporation late in 1980. Houston was a relatively small company with premerger sales of $383 million, 1,200 employees, and an aggressive reputation for oil exploration.

In hopes of retaining Houston's experienced oil exploration people, Tenneco offered special salary, bonuses, and benefits that others at Tenneco did not enjoy. Tenneco also "agreed to keep Houston Oil intact and operate it as an independent subsidiary" rather than consolidate the new acquisition (Getschow, 1982, p. 17).

Despite initial enthusiasm, Houston's managers and its geologists, geophysicists, engineers, and landsmen left in droves during the ensuing year. One complaint was the excessive bureaucratic delays in getting the compensation package defined (Getschow, 1982, p. 17). There were also bureaucratic restraints: As Tenneco's vice president for administration observed, "We have to ensure internal equity and apply the same standard of compensation to everyone" (Getschow, 1982, p. 17), which is to say that the differential treatment could not be sustained. By October 1981 Tenneco "had lost 34% of Houston Oil's management, 25% of its explorationists, and 19% of its production people, making it impossible to maintain it as a distinct unit" (p. 17). The offers by independent producers, which evidently have fewer or different burdens and restraints, of "stock options, production bonuses and, especially, royalty interests in the oil they discover—[incentives] that the majors have been unwilling or unable to offer to match" (p. 1) were principally responsible for the unraveling. Despite their best efforts, large firms are not always able to replicate small firms in all relevant respects.

6.4 *Hybrid Modes*

One way of joining large and small firms in the innovation process is this: Concentrate the initial development and market testing to be performed by independent inventors and small firms (perhaps new entrants) in an industry, the successful developments then to be acquired, possibly through licensing or merger, for subsequent development by a large multidivisional firm. But that is not the only systems solution permitting high-powered incentives to be concentrated at the early innovative stages of the R&D process. A recent *Business Week* report on how to "tap innovations created at small companies" begins as follows:

> In 1982, Ramtek Corp. wanted to add an advanced graphics machine to its line of computer peripherals. Despite its hefty research and development budget—nearly 11% of sales, well above its industry's average—the Santa Clara (Calif.) company decided against developing the system on its own. Instead, it funneled $2 million into Digital Productions Inc., of Los Angeles, which had a big lead in the technology. But this was no acquisition. Rather, Ramtek invested in the tiny company specifically so Digital would develop the software for a powerful new imaging system that Ramtek now expects will be a big success.
>
> Ramtek's experience represents an important shift in the way established companies are tapping the technology of smaller, entrepreneurial ones. In the past, big companies typically bought up little ones when they wanted their expertise. But in many cases, the acquiring corporations mismanaged their new property and lost the very people and creative environment that attracted them in the first place. [*Business Week,* June 25, 1984, p. 40]

The report subsequently goes on to observe that such arrangements are increasing rapidly, from 30 in 1980 to 140 in 1983—"established firms, although strong in both long-term research and marketing clout, are finding out they are better off relying on entrepreneurial companies for nearer-term innovations" (p. 41). As General Motors explained of its purchase of 11 percent of Teknowledge in 1984, "If we purchased such a company outright, we would kill the goose that laid the golden egg" (p. 41).

To be sure, such partial ownership positions are not without hazards. It is nevertheless instructive that, at least for many projects that do not require an enormous research commitment, large companies are becoming increasingly aware that the bureaucratic apparatus they use to manage mature products is less well-suited to supporting early stage entrepreneurial activity. Hybrid forms of organization result.

6.5 *Auditing Limits of Interfirm Organization*

The experience of the railroads in the late nineteenth century is germane. As reported by Alfred Chandler, Jr. (1977), efforts by the railroads to effect interfirm coordination regularly broke down. Informal alliances gave way to federations, which in turn were supplanted by merger. Among the many

problems with which the federations had to contend were "false billing regarding weight or amounts shipped or distances sent and improper classification of freight moved" (Chandler, 1977, p. 141). Auditing checks were
attempted, but the unenforceability of cartel agreements encouraged continued defection (pp. 141–44).

Cartel experience in the telegraph industry ran a similar course. Limited
cooperative arrangements in the 1850s proved ineffective. Market division
was then attempted by creating six operating regions, with one company
assigned to each. Business was pooled where the lines overlapped, but implementation problems arose. The six firms were reduced first to three and then,
in 1866, to a single company, Western Union (Chandler, 1977, p. 197).

Manufacturers in the 1870s and 1880s used trade associations to devise
"increasingly complex techniques to maintain industrywide price schedules
and production quotas" (Chandler, 1977, p. 317). When those failed, the
manufacturers resorted to the purchase of stock in each others' companies,
which "permitted them to look at the books of their associates and thus better
enforce their cartel agreement." But they could not be certain that the company accounts to which they were given access were accurate. As with rail
and telegraph, effective control required the next step, merger (Chandler,
1977, pp. 317–19). Auditing limits were evidently a contributing factor.

6.6 Socialist Enterprise

Internal organization in socialist firms likewise experiences strain when asked
to deliver on promises of high-powered incentives. Branko Horvat reports the
following incident:

> . . . there was a Computer Center that could not cover its costs. We decided to
> introduce an incentive scheme whereby the members of the center would share in
> all positive and negative differences in business results compared with those of
> previous years. Improvement did not appear very likely and, in any case, the
> incentive differences were very modest. The new manager of the center turned
> out to be an exceptionally capable man, however, and at the time of the annual
> business debate, the center could boast of phenomenal improvements. Instead of
> giving full recognition to what had been achieved, the council decided to ignore
> its own decision of a year earlier, proclaimed the incentive scheme inapplicable,
> and distributed the surplus in an arbitrary fashion. . . . We did not know they
> could do so well, was the [explanation], and it cannot be tolerated that they
> should earn more than others. The center lapsed into losses again. [1982, p. 256]

The incident is noteworthy in two respects. For one thing, both socialist
and capitalist managers are evidently responsive to pecuniary incentives.
Exhortation can be helpful in both (indeed, may be wholly adequate in some

circumstances), but the realization of potential cost savings is sometimes promoted by the introduction of high-powered incentives. Second, both socialist and capitalist firms are known to renege if the savings realization/profit participation from high-powered incentives is "excessive." Put differently, both socialist and capitalist "promises" need to be backed by credible commitments of the kinds discussed in Chapters 7 and 8.

7. Concluding Remarks

Why can't a large firm do everything that a collection of small firms can do and more? The basic argument of this chapter is this: Selective intervention, whereby integration realizes adaptive gains but experiences no losses, is not feasible. Instead, the transfer of a transaction out of the market into the firm is regularly attended by an impairment of incentives. It is especially severe in circumstances where innovation (and rewards for innovation) are important. But it appears in all transactions of the non-Nirvana kind to which Austin Robinson (1934, p. 250) made early reference. The market is a marvel, therefore, not merely because of its remarkable signaling properties (under the requisite preconditions), but also because of its remarkable capacity to present and preserve high-powered incentives.

Although the argument is especially transparent in the case where a preacquisition owner-manager is reduced to mere manager status upon acquisition, incentive consequences also attend mergers in which preacquisition managers hold no significant ownership position. The problem in the former case is that postmerger efforts to preserve high-powered incentives give rise to distortions and are apt to be corrupted, as a consequence of which low-powered incentives are instituted in their place. The problem in the latter case is that even low-powered (salaried) compensation schemes have contingent reward features in both payment and promotion respects. Those are likewise subject to impairment in the postacquisition condition.

Efforts to "hold incentives constant," thereby to effect incentive neutrality, thus turn out to be delusional. The problem is that none of the following is costlessly enforceable: promises by division managers to utilize assets with "due care"; promises by owners to reset transfer prices and exercise accounting discretion "responsibly"; promises to reward innovation in "full measure"; promises to preserve promotion prospects "without change"; and agreements by managers to "eschew politics." Internalizing the incremental transaction leads to incentive disabilities in all of those respects, and as a consequence transactions are apt to be organized in an altogether different way upon merger.

Thus although it is useful to think of markets and hierarchies as alternative modes with many common features, it is also essential to recognize that distinctive strengths and weaknesses are associated with each. Both incentive and governance features have to be acknowledged. As compared with internal transactions, market mediated transactions rely more on high-powered incentives and less on the administrative process (including auditing) to accomplish the same result.

CHAPTER 7

Credible Commitments I: Unilateral Applications

The transactions of interest in this chapter and the next are those supported by nontrivial investments in specific assets. Although integration (unified ownership) of successive stages has the *ex post* contractual advantages ascribed to it in earlier chapters, the advantages do not come without a cost. For one thing, economies of scale or scope may be sacrificed upon removing transactions from markets and organizing them internally. (Recall that the asset specificity switchover value, $\hat{k}$, is one where the advantages of the market in production cost respects is just offset by the disadvantage of the market in governance cost respects.)[1] Also, as discussed in Chapter 6, internal organization experiences serious incentive and bureaucratic disabilities.

The integration decision is thus beset by tradeoffs. In consideration of those, might it be possible to craft intermediate structures, located between discrete market contracting at the one extreme and hierarchical organization on the other, whereby the hazards of bilateral contracting are attenuated with less severe sacrifices in the aforementioned incentive and scale/scope economy respects? Put differently, can the parties to a bilateral trade create credible commitments, whereby each will have confidence in trading with the other, such that (expressed in terms of the contractual schema set out in Figure 1–2) the transaction is moved from node B to node C?

[1]See Figure 4–2 in Chapter 4.

My analysis of these matters assumes that there are many qualified suppliers at the outset and that suppliers are risk neutral, hence will produce to any contract whatsoever for which an expected breakeven result can be projected. Suppliers are furthermore assumed to be farsighted. The differential hazards of breach that arise under different investment and contracting scenarios are thus recognized. Given that suppliers assess contracts in this way, buyers choose the contractual terms that best suit their needs. Posing the issues this way discloses that the parties have a *mutual* interest in forging an exchange relationship in which both have confidence. More generally, the analysis illustrates the pitfalls of focusing on either the *ex ante* or the *ex post* conditions of contract. Instead, contracts need to be assessed "in their entirety."

The merits of the legal centralism versus private ordering approaches to contract, which were briefly discussed in Chapter 2, are developed more fully in section 1. Credible commitments are examined in section 2. The hostage model is set out in section 3. Problems of engaging the supplier are treated in section 4. Applications to unilateral trading are sketched in section 5. The Schwinn case is interpreted in section 6. Applications to bilateral trading are developed in the next chapter.

1. Private Ordering

As indicated earlier, the legal centralism tradition maintains that the courts are well suited for administering justice whenever contract disputes arise. If few cases are brought to the courts for disposition, that is only because contracts are carefully drawn and/or because the law of contract is fully nuanced and the relevant facts are easy to display. Litigated disputes rarely arise, because the parties can anticipate their disposition and will quickly effect settlement themselves. The exceptions—that is, the cases that appear in court—merely prove the rule that court ordering is efficacious.

The private ordering approach disputes that view. It maintains instead that contracts should be regarded as framework and as a basis for ultimate appeal (Llewellyn, 1931). All contracts, but especially long-term contracts, are incomplete and imperfect documents. Consider the following "general clause" that appears in the thirty-two-year coal supply agreement between the Nevada Power Company and the Northwest Trading Company:

> It is the intent of the Parties hereto that this Agreement, as a whole and in all of its parts, shall be equitable to both Parties throughout its term. The Parties recognize that omissions or defects in the Agreement beyond control of the

Parties or not apparent at the time of its execution may create inequities or hardships during the term of the Agreement, and further, that supervening conditions, circumstances or events beyond the reasonable and practicable control of the Parties, may from time to time give rise to inequities which impose economic or other hardships upon one or both of the Parties. In the event an inequitable condition occurs which adversely affects one Party, it shall be the joint and equal responsibility of both Parties to act promptly and in good faith to determine the action required to cure or adjust for the inequity and effectively to implement such action. Upon written claim of inequity served by one Party upon the other, the Parties shall act jointly to reach an agreement concerning the claimed inequity within sixty (60) days of the date of such written claim. An adjusted base coal price that differs from market price by more than ten percent (10%) shall constitute a hardship. The Party claiming inequity shall include in its claim such information and data as may be reasonably necessary to substantiate the claim and shall freely and without delay furnish such other information and data as the other Party reasonably may deem relevant and necessary. If the Parties cannot reach agreement within sixty (60) days the matter shall be submitted to arbitration. [1980, pp. 10–11]

Unlike a comprehensive contract, this contract contemplates omissions, drafting defects, and unanticipated contingencies. Contrary to legal centralism, bilateral and trilateral (arbitration) efforts will be used to settle disputes rather than have immediate recourse to court ordering.

Hobbes's interesting discussion of oaths and promises in *The Leviathan* is pertinent:

The force of words, being, as I have formerly noted, too weak to hold men to the performance of their covenants; there are in man's nature, but two imaginable helps to strengthen it. And those are either fear of the consequence of breaking their word; or a glory, or pride in appearing not to break it. The latter is a generosity too rarely found to be presumed on, especially in the pursuers of wealth, command, or sensual pleasure; which are the greatest part of mankind. . . . So that before the time of civil society . . . there is nothing can strengthen a covenant of peace agreed on, against the temptations of avarice, ambition, lust, or other strong desire, but the fear that invisible power, which they every one worship as God; as fear as a revenger of their perfidy. [Hobbes, 1928, pp. 92–93]

Accordingly, Hobbes concluded that "there must be some coercive power, to compel men equally to perform their covenants" (1928, p. 94). That legal centralism solution has had widespread appeal to many lawyers and social scientists. Jerold Auerbach's recent examination of the incapacity of private parties to order their affairs effectively is illustrative.

Auerbach observes that the "success of non-legal dispute settlement has always depended on a coherent community vision" (1983, p. 4). Although religious communities provided the necessary coherence within early colonial settlements in America, recourse to litigation in the courts became common and permissible as religious intensity waned (p. 5). The fundamental dilemma is that the benefits of individualism to which Americans aspire are realized only by relying extensively on the "legal system" (pp. 10, 146).

Auerbach nevertheless acknowledges that "business interests" may be an exception. The communitarian value that he ascribes to business is "a community of profit. . . . Selfish and secular to the core, they nevertheless have emerged among the most persistent American defenders of alternative dispute settlement" (1983, p. 6). He thus records the paradox that "the pursuit of self-interest and profit generated its own communitarian values, which commercial arbitration expressed. The competitive individualism of the marketplace was checked by the need for continuing harmonious relations among men who did business with each other" (p. 44).

The paradox to which he refers derives from the view that private ordering is possible only if supported by communitarian values, which values are presumed to be alien to a business relationship. Assuming that the term "communitarian" is given its ordinary signification, such baggage is both unneeded and unhelpful. The study of economic organization is better served, I submit, by focusing on the purposes served. As Philip Wicksteed put it

> We enter into business relations with others, not because our purposes are self-ish, but because those with whom we deal are relatively indifferent to them. . . . There is surely nothing degrading or revolting to our higher sense in this fact of our mutually furthering each others purposes because we are interested in our own. . . . [The nexus of exchange] indefinitely expands our freedom of com-bination and movement; for it enables us to form one set of groups linked by cohesion of [diverse] faculties and resources, and another set of groups linked by community of purpose, without having to find the "double coincidence" which would otherwise be necessary. [Robbins, 1933, pp. 179–80]

Extensive recourse to private ordering is hardly a paradox if the limits of contract and of the courts are recognized from the outset and if the issues of organization are posed comparatively. Inasmuch, moreover, as the benefits of "continuing harmonious relations" to which Auerbach refers are not unique to business but apply to organizations of all kinds, while the limits of courts for dealing with complex problems are everywhere severe, greater attention to the ways by which conflict is mitigated *ex ante* and to the range of formal and informal devices by which disputes are settled *ex post* is needed. The pos-sibility that "credible commitments" play a larger role in the making and execution of contracts than has hitherto been recognized is among the matters that warrant study.

2. Credible Commitments

2.1 *Commitments versus Threats*

Credible commitments and credible threats share this common attribute: Both appear mainly in conjunction with irreversible, specialized investments. But whereas credible commitments are undertaken in support of alliances and to promote exchange, credible threats appear in the context of conflict and rivalry.[2] The former involve reciprocal acts designed to safeguard a relationship, while the latter are unilateral efforts to preempt an advantage. Efforts to support exchange generally operate in the service of efficiency; preemptive investments, by contrast, are commonly antisocial. Both are plainly important to politics and economics, but the study of credible commitments is arguably the more fundamental of the two.

Interest in credible threats is much more widespread, and the credible threat literature is more fully developed,[3] however, than is the interest and economic literature dealing with credible commitments. The disparity is consistent with the treatment accorded to each in Thomas Schelling's classic essay (1956) on bargaining, where the main emphasis is placed on tactics by which one party can realize an advantage in relation to a rival by credibly "tying one's hands." But Schelling also, albeit briefly, addresses the matter of promise. He observes in this connection: "Bargaining may have to concern itself with an 'incentive' system as well as the division of gains" (p. 300) and adds in a footnote that the exchange of hostages served incentive purposes in an earlier age (p. 300, n. 17).

That the study of credible commitments has been relatively neglected is explained by the aforementioned assumption, common to both law and eco-

[2]It should be noted that I use the terms threat and commitment differently from Curtis Eaton and Robert Lipsey (1981). They distinguish between empty and credible threats and use the term commitment to refer to the latter. I submit that the language of rivalry is well served by reference to threats; and I suggest that the term commitment be reserved to describe exchange. Thus both credible and noncredible commitments are distinguished in evaluating exchange.

Alliances complicate matters in that they are organized in relation to another party. That could be wholly beneficial, but it need not be. Thus suppliers could form an alliance in relation to buyers, with possible antisocial results. Credible commitments that simultaneously support exchange and promote alliances thus sometimes pose tradeoffs.

[3]Recent applications within economics involve investments in specific capital undertaken for the purpose of impeding new entry (Dixit, 1979, 1982; Eaton and Lipsey, 1981; Schmalensee, 1981). For discussion of reputation effects and quasi-credibility in the economics literature, see David Kreps and Robert Wilson (1982), Paul Milgrom and John Roberts (1982), and Chapter 14 herein.

nomics, that the legal system enforces promises in a knowledgeable, sophisticated, and low-cost way. Albeit instructive, this convenient assumption is commonly contradicted by the facts—on which account additional or alternative modes of governance have arisen. Bilateral efforts to create and offer hostages are an interesting and, as it turns out, economically important illustration. Absent a recognition of and appreciation for the merits of private ordering, the suggestion that hostages are used to support contemporary exchange is apt to be dismissed as fanciful. I submit, however, that not only are the economic equivalents of hostages widely used to effect credible commitments, but failure to recognize the economic purposes served by hostages has been responsible for repeated policy error.

To be sure, pure private ordering is extreme. As Robert Mnookin and Lewis Kornhauser put it, private ordering invariably operates in "the shadow of the law" (1979).[4] As between contracting fictions, however, the private ordering fiction is at least as instructive as is that of legal centralism. Indeed, for purposes of studying transaction cost issues, it is more so. (A more balanced view, however, will make shadow of the law provisions.)

2.2 Self-enforcing Agreements

Lester Telser characterizes a self-enforcing agreement as one which, if "one party violates the terms the only recourse of the other is to terminate the agreement" (1981, p. 27). Contrary to legal centralism, the courts and other third parties are assumed away. Benjamin Klein and Keith Leffler are explicit on this: "[W]e assume throughout . . . that contracts are not enforceable by the government or any third party" (1981, p. 616). Commercial contract law in late-nineteenth-century Taiwan evidently approximated this condition (Brockman, 1980). Stewart Macaulay's remarks about the informality of contract in buiness are likewise in this spirit: "Often businessmen do not feel they have 'a contract'—rather they have 'an order.' They speak of 'cancelling the order' rather than 'breaching our contract' " (1963, p. 61).

Both this chapter and the next adopt that orientation. Also, although hostages can have both *ex ante* (screening) and *ex post* (bonding) effects, the *ex post* contract execution consequences are of principal interest to the self-enforcing agreement literature and are the main focus here. Additionally, like both Telser and Klein and Leffler, the intertemporal contracts of concern here feature both uncertainty and transaction-specific capital. But whereas Telser

---

[4]Galanter suggests that a better way to characterize the study of contract is "law in the shadow of indigenous ordering" (1981, p. 23). There is a good deal to be said for this. The main point is that a place for law is properly provided in any comprehensive study of contract.

deals with "a sequence of transactions over time such that the ending date is unknown and uncertain" (1981, p. 30), because any finite sequence of transactions using his model will unravel (p. 29), the transactions I consider can be (indeed, normally are) finite. The Klein and Leffler analysis also maintains that self-enforcing contracts are of indefinite rather than finite duration. A further difference between the hostage model and Klein and Leffler's very insightful treatment of quality assurance problems is that theirs applies to final product markets while the main applications of the hostage model are in intermediate product markets (at least those are the main applications herein described). The efficiency sacrifice that Klein and Leffler associate with quality assurance, moreover, is avoided.[5]

3. The Hostage Model

The simple hostage model serves to illuminate both unilateral and bilateral exchange, permits the concept of specific capital to be extended beyond earlier uses, and clarifies how costs should be described in assessing exchange. While it is primitive and suggestive, rather than refined and definitive, it serves as a paradigmatic wedge by which the importance of private ordering is exposed and is easily made the vehicle for further analysis.

3.1 *Technologies and Costs*

The assessment of alternative contracts will be facilitated by assuming that the product in question can be produced by either of two technologies. One is a general purpose technology; the second is a special purpose technology. The special purpose technology requires greater investment in transaction-specific durable assets and, as described below, is more efficient for servicing steady state demands.

The distinction introduced in Chapter 2 (see especially Figure 2–2) between redeployable and nonsalvageable investments will be employed here. Rather, therefore, than use the convention of fixed and variable costs, the two technologies in question will be described in value realization terms.[6] The

---

[5]Klein and Leffler's "fundamental theoretical result" involves the assurance of quality through the sacrifice of "minimum-cost production techniques" (1981, pp. 618, 628–29), while the hostage model involves no such sacrifice (indeed, the use of hostages to support exchange encourages investment in specific asset technologies that have *lower* expected costs).

[6]Only the nonsalvageable part of an advance commitment is appropriately regarded as sunk (Klein and Leffler, 1981, p. 619).

value that can be realized by redeploying variable and fixed costs will be given by v. The nonsalvageable value of advance commitments will be denoted by k. The two technologies in question can be described as:

T_1: The general purpose technology, all advance commitments of which are salvageable, the redeployable unit operating costs of which are v_1.

T_2: The special purpose technology, the nonsalvageable value of advance commitments of which are k and the redeployable unit operating costs of which are v_2.

3.2 Contracting

There are two periods. Orders are placed in the first, and production, if any, occurs in the second. Buyers can either take delivery or refuse it. Demand is stochastic. The gross value to buyers is assumed to be uniformly distributed over the interval 0 to 1, and the quantity demanded at every price will be assumed to be constant, which it will be convenient to set equal to unity. Sunk costs, if any, are incurred in the first period. Inasmuch as sunk costs are incurred for certain while the decision to incur redeployable costs is contingent on the buyer's decision to confirm or cancel an order, a choice between technologies is interesting only if $k + v_2 < v_1$. The demand and cost relations are set out in Figure 7–1.

a. NET BENEFITS

The criterion by which decisions to take or refuse delivery will be evaluated is joint profit maximization. Feasibility and/or bureaucratic disabilities aside, vertical integration assuredly accomplishes the joint profit maximization result. Thus the reference condition for evaluating contracts will be an integrated firm with two divisions, a producing division and a marketing division. The producing division has access to the same two technologies

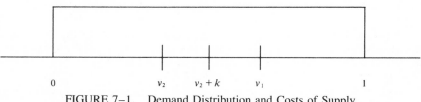

FIGURE 7–1. Demand Distribution and Costs of Supply

described above, one of which involves specific assets, the other of which does not. Whichever technology is employed, product is transferred between divisions at marginal cost.

That $k + v_2 < v_1$ does not establish that the special purpose technology (T_2) is more efficient. Whether it is or not depends on a net benefit calculation. The expected net benefits of using the general purpose technology (T_1) are given by the product of the probability that the integrated firm will decide to produce and the average net benefits that are realized when product is supplied. The integrated firm will decide to produce only if the realized demand price exceeds marginal costs, whence the probability of production under T_1 is $1 - v_1$. The mean net benefits during production periods are $(1 - v_1)/2$, whence the expected net benefits for technology T_1 are:

$$(1) \qquad b_1 = (1 - v_1)(1 - v_1)/2 = \frac{(1 - v_1)^2}{2} .$$

The expected net benefits for the specific asset technology (T_2) are found similarly. Again, the integrated firm will produce whenever realized demand price exceeds marginal costs. Expected net receipts, however, must be reduced by the amount of the earlier investment in specific assets, k, in computing expected net benefits. Thus we have:

$$(2) \qquad b_2 = (1 - v_2)(1 - v_2)/2 - k = \frac{(1 - v_2)^2}{2} - k$$

where the first term is the expected excess of revenue over out-of-pocket costs.

The specific asset technology will be selected only if $b_2 > b_1$, which requires that

$$(3) \qquad k < \frac{(1 - v_2)^2}{2} - \frac{(1 - v_1)^2}{2}$$

b. AUTONOMOUS CONTRACTING

Assume that the inequality in (3) holds and consider the case of autonomous contracting between a buyer, who services final demand, and a producer, who manufactures the product. Assume that demand and production technologies are as described above. Efficient contracting relations are those that replicate the vertical integration result, namely, (1) select the specific asset technology and (2) produce and sell product whenever realized demand price exceeds v_2. Assume that both parties are risk-neutral and that the production side of the industry is competitively organized. Whatever contracting relation is described, producers will be willing to supply if a breakeven condition (expressed in expected value terms) can be projected.[7]

Recall that orders are placed in the first period. Specific assets, if any, are committed in the first period in anticipation of second period supply. Whether second period production actually occurs, however, is contingent on demand realizations. Buyers have the option of confirming or canceling orders in the second period. Consider three contracting alternatives:

I. The buyer purchases specific assets and assigns them to whichever seller submits the lowest bid, $\bar{p}$.

II. The producer makes the specific asset investment himself and receives a payment of $\bar{p}$ in the second period if the buyer confirms the order but nothing otherwise.

III. The producer makes the specific asset investment himself and receives $\hat{p}$ from the buyer if the buyer confirms the order, is paid αh, $0 \leq \alpha \leq 1$, if the order is canceled while the buyer pays $\hat{p}$ upon taking delivery and experiences a reduction in wealth of h if second period delivery is canceled.

The third scenario can be thought of as one where the buyer posts a hostage, that he values in amount h, which hostage is delivered to the producer, who values it in amount αh, if the order is canceled.

The producer will break even under contracting relation I if he is compensated in amount v_2, which is his out-of-pocket cost, for each unit demanded. The low bidder will thus offer to supply product for $\bar{p} = v_2$. Since the buyer's net benefits are maximized if he invests in the specific assets, and since product is transferred on marginal cost terms, the contract replicates the vertical integration relation. Contracts of type I are feasible, however, only if the specialized assets are mobile and the specificity is attributable to physical features (e.g. specialized dies). Market procurement can then service the needs of the parties without posing holdup problems by concentrating the ownership of the specific assets on the buyer (who then assigns them to the low bidder). Inasmuch as the buyer can reclaim the dies and, without cost, solicit new bids should contractual difficulties develop, type I contracts yield an efficient result.[8]

Attention hereafter will be focused on contracts II and III, the assump-

---

[7]There is no problem in principle in allowing suppliers to extract positive profits as a condition of supply. The salient features of the hostage model are all preserved if, instead of an expected breakeven condition, the supplier was assumed to realize some target level of expected profits on each contract. Although final demands will be choked off as a consequence, the main features of the contractual argument survive.

[8]This ignores the possibility that suppliers will abuse the dies if ownership resides with the buyer.

tion being that asset specificity is of the human, site specific, or dedicated asset kinds. The autonomous buyer will confirm an order under contract II whenever realized demand price exceeds $\bar{p}$ but not otherwise. The producer will thus break even if $(1 - \bar{p})\bar{p} - [(1 - \bar{p})v_2 + k] = 0$, whence

(4) $$\bar{p} = v_2 + \frac{k}{1-\bar{p}} \ .$$

Product will thus be exchanged at a price that exceeds marginal cost under this contracting scenario.[9] Plainly if $\bar{p} \geq v_1$, the buyer is better off to scuttle contract II and purchase instead from producers who utilize the (inferior) variable cost technology T_1 (and will break even by supplying product on demand for a price of v_1).

The buyer will confirm an order under contract III whenever the realized demand price exceeds $\hat{p} - h$. Let $\hat{p} - h$ be denoted by m. The seller will then break even when $(1 - m)\hat{p} + m \, \alpha \, h - [(1 - m)v_2 + k] = 0$, whence

(5) $$\hat{p} = v_2 + \frac{k - m \, \alpha \, h}{1 - m} \ .$$

The case where $h = k$ and $\alpha = 1$ is one where the buyer gives up wealth in amount of the investment in specific assets in cancellation states, and this is delivered to the producer, who values it in amount k. Under these circumstances, (5) becomes

(5') $$\hat{p} = v_2 + k \ .$$

Since the buyer places an order whenever demand exceeds $m = \hat{p} - h$, this yields the result that $m = v_2$, whence orders will be placed whenever demand exceeds v_2—which is the efficient (marginal cost) supply criterion.

The buyer's net benefits under contracting scheme III are

(6) $$b_3 = (1 - m)[(m + \frac{1 - m}{2} - \hat{p}] - mh$$

where $(1 - m)$ is the probability of placing an order, $m + (1 - m)/2$ is the expected demand price for all orders that are placed, $\hat{p}$ is the payment in demand confirmation states to the producer, and h is the wealth sacrifice in

---

[9]Conceivably $\bar{p}$ will exceed v_1, in which event the buyer who is contemplating contract II will prefer instead to purchase from sellers who use the general purpose technology. The comparison in the text implicitly assumes that $\bar{p} < v_1$. Also note that a standby technology that can be costlessly switched into and out of the product in question could effectively truncate demand at v_1. This would be true if potential middlemen could place orders to take product at v_1 from general purpose manufacturers, which orders could be costlessly canceled (and general purpose assets redeployed) if demands fell below this value. I will arbitrarily assume that this is not feasible. The problem could, however, be reformulated by describing demand as uniformly distributed over the interval 0 to v_1 with a spike at v_1 carrying a probability mass of $1 - v_1$.

cancellation states (which occur with probability m). Under the assumptions that $h = k$ and $\alpha = 1$, this reduces to

$$(6') \qquad\qquad b_3 = \frac{(1 - v_2)^2}{2} - k$$

which is identical to the net benefit calculation for technology T_2 under the vertical integration reference condition (see equation [2]).

Accordingly, contracting scheme III accompanied by the stipulations that $h = k$ and $\alpha = 1$ replicates the efficient investment and supply conditions of vertical integration. Problems arise, however, if $h < k$ or $\alpha < 1$. The disadvantage, moreover, accrues entirely to the buyer—since the seller, by assumption, breaks even whatever contracting relation obtains. Thus although *after* the contract has been made the buyer would prefer to offer a lesser valued hostage and cares not whether the hostage is valued by the producer, at the time of the contract he will wish to assure the producer that a hostage of k for which the producer realizes full value ($\alpha = 1$) will be transferred in nonexchange states. Failure to make that commitment will result in an increase in the contract price. Thus, whereas producers who are concerned only with *ex ante* screening can tolerate values of α less than one—see the discussion of ugly princesses in section 4 below—this is not the case at all when *ex post* opportunism is the concern. If the producer is not indifferent, as between two princesses, each of whom is valued identically by the buyer, the producer's preferences now need to be taken into account.[10]

To summarize, therefore, we observe that contract I mimics vertical integration, but only under special asset specificity conditions; contract II is inferior; and contract III yields the vertical integration result if $h = k$ and $\alpha = 1$. Furthermore, note that an important feature of contract III is that the buyer takes delivery in all demand states for which realized demand exceeds $m = \hat{p} - h$. Since the supplier is always paid $\hat{p}$ upon execution, the buyer sometimes takes delivery when his realized receipts (upon resale of the product) are less than $\hat{p}$. This does not, however, signal inefficiency, since orders are never confirmed when realized demand price falls below marginal cost (v_2). Indeed, it is precisely because of the hostage feature that efficiency is realized and contract III is superior to contract II.

The above has a bearing on the contracting schema discussed in Chapter 1, to which recurrent reference is made throughout this book. For conve-

[10]Placing an upper bound of unity on α precludes the possibility that the supplier values that hostage more than does the buyer. Potential gains from trade would exist for all hostages for which α exceeds unity. A case for negatively valued hostages could be made in the context of ugly princesses (see subsection 4.1).

nience, the basic contracting choices are reproduced (with minor changes) in Figure 7–2. That the (breakeven) prices at nodes A, B, and C should differ was evident at the outset: The technologies differ and, as between nodes B and C, the hazards differ. But there is a further difference between nodes B and C that can be ascertained only by working through the net benefits, as set out in the text: Namely, a node C contract leads to superior asset utilization.

The fact that suppliers are indifferent as between nodes B and C, because an expected breakeven result can be projected under each condition, does not therefore mean that the two outcomes can be regarded with a shrug. On the contrary, both buyers and society have an interest in seeing a node C outcome realized. That applies not merely to intermediate product, which is the focus of this chapter and the next, but also to the organization of labor (Chapter 10) and the supply of capital (Chapter 12).

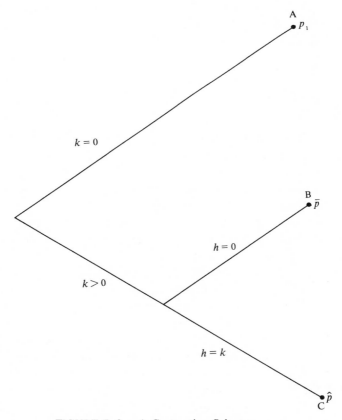

FIGURE 7–2. A Contracting Schema

4. Engaging the Supplier

Suppliers are passive instruments in this model. They are indifferent among contracts, since their expected profits are the same (zero) whichever choice the buyer makes. What drives the argument is that buyers can secure better terms only by relieving producers of demand cancellation losses. Buyers cannot have their cake (product supplied by the efficient technology at a price of $\hat{p}$) and eat it too (cancel without cost). Price reductions are not awarded gratuitously.

Inasmuch as optimality is realized if $h = k$ and $\alpha = 1$, the ideal hostage would appear to be an offer of generalized purchasing power: money. A security bond in amount $h = k$ would serve this purpose. The reason the argument does not terminate here is that such an arrangement does not assuredly engage the interests and cooperation of the supplier. Three reasons can be adduced for this condition: contrived cancellation, uncertain valuation, and incomplete contracting. All are a consequence of joining bounded rationality with opportunism.

4.1 Contrived Cancellation

The issue of contrived cancellation has been addressed by Kenneth Clarkson, Roger Miller, and Timothy Muris in their discussion of refusal of the courts to enforce stipulated damage clauses where breach has been deliberately induced (1978, pp. 366–72). Induced breach could arise where a party intentionally withholds relevant information, yet complies with the letter of the contract. Or it might involve perfunctory fulfillment of obligations where more resourceful cooperation is needed (pp. 371–72). In either case, induced breach is costly to detect and/or prove (p. 371).

This explanation for selective enforcement of liquidated damage clauses has troubled other legal scholars (Posner, 1979, p. 290), but a more satisfactory explanation has yet to be advanced. At the very least, the Clarkson et al. treatment reflects a sensitivity to the subtleties of opportunism—on which account private ordering is more complicated than the bare bones hostage model would suggest. Among other things, the expropriation hazard to which they refer may explain the use of ugly princesses.

Thus suppose that demand uncertainties are negligible, whence order cancellation hazards can be disregarded. Suppose further, however, that buyers differ in credit risk respects and that producers would, if they could, refuse sales to poor risks. Assuming that the difference between good and poor risks is sufficiently great that a separating equilibrium is feasible,[11] producers could demand hostages (or, put differently, good risks could offer hostages) as a way by which to screen. Given, moreover, that the only use to which hostages are put is as a screen, a value of $\alpha = 0$ would accomplish that purpose without exposing the buyer to an expropriation hazard (based, say, on a legal technicality). Specifically, a king who is known to cherish two daughters equally and is asked, for screening purposes, to post a hostage is better advised to offer the ugly one.

4.2 Uncertain Valuation

The model assumes that the value of the specific investment (k) is well specified. This need not be the case. Indeed, it may be difficult for buyers to ascertain whether the investments made in response to first period orders are of the amount or the kind that producers claim. That is not a serious problem if the production side of the market is competitively organized and fly-by-night concerns can be disregarded. Where, however, this cannot be presumed, the possibility that buyers will be expropriated arises. Producers may feign delivery competence (claim to have invested in specific assets in amount k but only committed $k' < k$) and expropriate bonds for which $h = k$ by contriving breach or invoking a technicality.

The hazard is especially great if the producer, who retains possession of the assets for which specificity is claimed, can preserve asset values by integrating forward into the buyer's market upon taking possession of the hostage. Even though the producer is poorly suited to performing successor stage functions, the possession of specialized stage I assets effectively reduces the costs that would otherwise attend *de novo* stage II entry.

To be sure, the buyer who offers a hostage and recognizes a risk of contrived expropriation will adjust the original terms to reflect the risk. Specifically, contracts supported by hostages for which expropriation risks are believed to be great will command less than those where the same hazards are believed to be lower. But this is to concede that, absent additional safeguards, neither the transfer of product on marginal cost terms nor the efficient level and kind of investment will assuredly attend contracts of type III. Deeper governance issues than those contemplated by the simple model are evidently posed.

[11]Ex ante screening attributes are briefly examined in Williamson (1982, pp. 6–9). The assessment of a screening equilibrium is complex, however, and is not central to the main argument. See Michael Rothschild and Joseph Stiglitz (1976) and John Riley (1979a, and 1979b) for a discussion of screening equilibrium issues.

4.3 Incomplete Contracts/Haggling

Complex contracts are invariably incomplete, and many are maladaptive. The reasons are two: Many contingencies are unforeseen (and even unforeseeable), and the adaptations to those contingencies that have been recognized for which adjustments have been agreed to are often mistaken—possibly because the parties acquire deeper knowledge of production and demand during contract execution than they possessed at the outset (Nelson and Winter, 1982, pp. 96–136). Instrumental gap filling thus is an important part of contract execution. Whether it is done easily and effectively or, instead, reaching successive agreements on adaptations and their implementation is costly makes a huge difference in evaluating the efficacy of contracts.

Thus even if contrived breach hazards could be disregarded, producers who are entirely open and candid about contract execution may nevertheless be in a position to haggle—thereby to expropriate sellers—because contracts are incomplete or maladaptive. Specialized governance structures that have the purpose and effect of promoting harmonious adaptations and preserving the continuity of exchange relations arise in response to that condition. Use of knowledgeable third parties (arbitration) and reciprocal exposure of specialized assets are two possibilities.

4.4 Safeguards in Kind

The above-described difficulties with pecuniary bonding do not alter the proposition that buyers can purchase product from suppliers on better terms if they offer assurances than if they do not. But it raises the possibility that assurances will take forms other than bonding.

Assume that the buyers in question are not merely conduits but incur production and distribution expenses before making deliveries to customers. Assume further that buyers have access to two technologies, one fully general purpose while the other requires investments in specific capital that has value only in conjunction with servicing final demands for the product in question. Assume finally that the redeployable costs (v) of the special purpose technology are lower than those of the general purpose technology.

It then follows that suppliers will sell product at a lower price to buyers whose investments in sales and service are more specific than it will to those whose specific investments are less—even if no hostage exchange is made upon cancellation of an order. That is because such buyers will thereafter confirm orders in more adverse demand states than those who do not. Put differently, buyers who drive their redeployable costs down by making transaction-specific investments present the supplier with a more favorable demand scenario that those who do not. In this sense, forward specific investments constitute a credible commitment. The resulting contract will not, however, yield the efficient marginal cost pricing result. That will come about only if compensation is paid to suppliers upon order cancellation.

Such a defect does not imply that hostage transfers should always attend unilateral trading. Such a rule suffers from the aforementioned expropriation hazard. More generally, all feasible trading alternatives may be flawed. A comparative institutional assessment of the main organizational alternatives would presumably include consideration of the following:

1. Full compensation upon order cancellation, in which event buyers are exposed to expropriation hazards.
2. Buyers invest in specific assets but refuse compensation, which creates a more favorable demand scenario but still exposes suppliers to a (reduced) risk of uncompensated losses.
3. As a compromise, suppliers create credible commitments and make partial but incomplete hostage payments upon order cancellation.
4. The contractual relation is expanded by developing suitable reciprocity arrangements.
5. The transaction is consolidated under common ownership, which is the vertical integration alternative.

Whether options 4 and 5 are feasible will vary with the circumstances. Reciprocity is examined in Chapter 8, while the tradeoffs that attend vertical integration were examined in Chapter 4. Here as elsewhere, informed choice among complex alternatives requires detailed knowledge of the institutional realities of economic life (Koopmans, 1957, p. 145). The attributes of the trading parties, the technologies to which they have access, and the markets in which they operate all have to be assessed.

5. Unilateral Trading Applications

The technologies and contractual options discussed above are displayed schematically in Figure 7–2. If $\hat{p} < p_1 < \bar{p}$, then the relevant nodes are A and C: The buyer will either ask the supplier to employ the general purpose technology and will pay p_1 upon delivery of product for which orders are confirmed, or he will ask that the supplier make specific investments for which the buyer offers safeguards. If instead $\hat{p} < \bar{p} < p_1$, then the relevant nodes are B and C: Only the special purpose technology will be employed, with respect to which some buyers will offer safeguards while others will not.

The argument that buyers can affect the terms and manner of supply by offering (or refusing to offer) hostages has ramifications for Robinson-Patman price discrimination and to an understanding of franchising and two-part pricing.

5.1 Robinson-Patman

The Robinson-Patman Act has been interpreted as an effort ''to deprive a large buyer of [discounts] except to the extent that a lower price could be justified by reason of a seller's diminished costs due to *quantity* manufacture, delivery, or sale, or by reason of the seller's good faith effort to meet a competitor's equally low price.''[12] Plainly, that $\hat{p}$ is less than $\bar{p}$ in the hostage model has neither quantity nor meeting competition origins. Neither is it contrary to the public interest. Indeed, it would be inefficient and unwarranted for a producer to charge the same price to two customers who order an identical amount of product, but only one of which offers a hostage, if (1) investments in specialized assets are required to support the transactions in question, or (2) if, because of a refusal to make a credible commitment, transactions of the second kind are produced with a general purpose (but high-cost) technology.

The missing ingredients, plainly, are the differential commitment to buy (as reflected by the willingness to offer hostages) and the differential incentives to breach once hostages have been posted. The confusion is explained by the propensity to employ conventional (steady state) microtheory to the neglect of transaction cost aspects. Rectifying that involves examination of the microanalytics of transactions, with special reference to asset specificity and the hazards thereby posed, and evaluation of alternative contracts with respect to a *common reference condition,* prospective breakeven being a useful standard. Once that is done, a different understanding of many nonstandard or unfamiliar contracting practices, many of which are held to be presumptively unlawful, frequently emerges.[13]

5.2 Franchising

Klein and Leffler (1981) argue that franchisees may be required to make investments in transaction specific capital as a way by which to safeguard the

[12]*FTC* v. *Morton Salt Co.,* 334 U.S. 37 (1948); emphasis added.

[13]Note that the argument applies only to $\hat{p}$ versus $\bar{p}$ comparisons in trades where specific assets are involved. The efficiency properties of customer price differentials that do have such origins are not contemplated by this argument.

franchise system against quality shading. As Klein (1980) puts it, franchisers can better

> . . . assure quality by requiring franchisee investments in specific . . . assets that upon termination imply a capital loss penalty larger than can be obtained by the franchisee if he cheats. For example, the franchiser may require franchisees to rent from them short term (rather than own) the land upon which their outlet is located. This lease arrangement creates a situation where termination can require the franchisee to move and thereby impose a capital loss on him up to the amount of his initial nonsalvageable investment. Hence a form of collateral to deter franchisee cheating is created. [p. 359]

The arrangement is tantamount to the creation of hostages to restore integrity to an exchange.

That logic notwithstanding, the use of hostages to deter franchisees from exploiting demand externalities is often regarded as an imposed (top down) solution. Franchisees are "powerless"; they accept hostage terms because no others are available. Such power arguments are often based on *ex post* reasoning. That the use of hostages to support exchange can be and often is an efficient systems solution, hence is independent of who originates the proposal, can be seen from the following revised sequence.[14]

Suppose that an entrepreneur develops a distinctive, patentable idea that he sells outright to a variety of independent, geographically dispersed suppliers, each of which is assigned an exclusive territory. Each supplier expects to sell only to the population located within its territory, but all find to their surprise (and initially to their delight) that sales are also made to a mobile population. Purchases by the mobile population are based not on the reputation of individual franchisees but on customers' perceptions of the reputation of the system. A demand externality arises in this way.

Thus, were sales made only to the local population, each supplier would fully appropriate the benefits of its promotional and quality enhancement efforts. Population mobility upsets this: Because the cost savings that result from local quality debasement accrue to the local operator while the adverse demand effects are diffused throughout the system, suppliers now have an incentive to free ride off of the reputation of the system. Having sold the exclusive territory rights outright, the entrepreneur who originated the program is indifferent to those unanticipated demand developments. It thus remains for the collection of independent franchisees to devise a correction themselves, lest the value of the system deteriorate to their individual and collective disadvantage.

The franchisees, under the revised scenario, thus create an agent to

---

[14]The idea that this is a useful way to pose the franchise issue evolved out of discussions I had with Jeffrey Goldberg. For a more complete development, see Goldberg (1982).

police quality or otherwise devise penalties that deter quality deterioration. One possibility is to return to the entrepreneur and hire him to provide such services. Serving now as the agent of the franchisees, the entrepreneur may undertake a program of quality checks (certain purchasing restraints are introduced, whereby franchisees are required to buy only from qualified suppliers; periodic inspections are performed). The incentive to exploit demand externalities may further be discouraged by requiring each franchisee to post a hostage and by making franchises terminable.[15]

This indirect scenario serves to demonstrate that it is the *system* that benefits from the control of externalities. But this merely confirms that the normal scenario in which the franchisor controls the contractual terms is not an arbitrary exercise of power. Indeed, if franchisees recognize that the demand externality exists from the outset, if the franchisor refuses to make provision for the externality in the original contract, and if it is very costly to reform the franchise system once initial contracts are set, franchisees will bid less for the right to a territory than they otherwise would. It should not therefore be concluded that perceptive franchisors, who recognize the demand externality in advance and make provision for it, are imposing objectionable *ex ante* terms on unwilling franchisees. They are merely taking steps to realize the full value of the franchise. Here as elsewhere, contracts must be examined in their entirety.

5.3 Two-Part Pricing

Victor Goldberg and John Erickson describe an interesting two-part pricing scheme that they observed in the sale of coke. The producer both sold coke to the calciner and owned and leased the land upon which the plant of the calciner was built. Inasmuch as the coke was sold for "about one-quarter the current market price of equivalent quality coke" (1982, p. 25), Goldberg and Erickson conjecture that "the rental rate was above the fair market rate and that the contract was designed to ensure that the calciner would continue to perform" (p. 25). Assuming that marginal costs are much less than average, such an arrangement can be interpreted as one by which the parties are attempting to strike efficient pricing terms that approximate those of the hostage model.

---

[15]Termination is a credible threat only if the franchisee who cheats on the system bears a capital loss. This is the basic Klein and Leffler (1981) message. It would not do, therefore, if the terminated franchisee were permitted to sell the franchise to a highest bidder unless the investment in specific capital took the form of the franchisee's specialized knowledge of the system, and the terminated franchisee were thereafter prohibited from participating in owner, adviser, or employee status.

The pricing of utility services, whereby *ex ante* installation fees are paid by subscribers, also has interesting two-part pricing attributes.[16] The risk that sellers will expropriate buyers upon receipt of advance payment can be mitigated by creating a specialized third party, which for convenience may be referred to as a regulatory commission (Goldberg, 1976a). Utilization of utility services can be priced so as to more nearly approximate marginal cost.

More generally, Goldberg and Erickson conjecture that nonlinear pricing schemes are much more widespread than is commonly believed. They further point out that such arrangements are often very subtle and will require detailed knowledge of contracts to investigate (1982, pp. 56–57).

6. Schwinn

Although issues posed in *Schwinn*[17] are not precisely the same as the franchise matters discussed above, they are nevertheless closely related. Inasmuch as this case displays pretransaction cost type reasoning, it is instructive to consider the government's arguments against the franchise restrictions employed by Schwinn and then to consider an alternative construction.

6.1 *The Objections*

Arnold, Schwinn & Co. is a longtime producer of quality bicycles. It decided to impose restrictions on its franchisers in 1951, at which time its U.S. market share was 22 percent. Authorized dealers, who had previously been required to provide minimum services (advertising, assembly, maintaining a stock of bicycles and replacement parts, providing qualified repair personnel, and the like), were now prohibited from reselling Schwinn bicycles to nonauthorized dealers. The restriction was designed to deny access of Schwinn product to discount houses. Although its market share thereafter fell steadily (to 13 percent in 1961), Schwinn enforced that restriction over the next decade. The government brought suit, claiming that the restriction was anticompetitive. Its jurisdictional statement advanced the following theory of the case:

> In industries in which products are highly differentiated, a particular brand—like Schwinn bicycles—often has a market of its own, within which [intrabrand] competition is highly important to the consumer and should be preserved. . . . Schwinn's strenuous efforts to exclude unauthorized retailers from selling its

[16]This possibility was suggested to me by Alvin Klevorick.

[17]*United States* v. *Arnold, Schwinn & Co.*, 388 U.S. 365 (1967).

bicycles suggest that, absent these restraints, there would be a broader retail distribution of these goods with the resulting public benefits (including lower price) of retail competition.[18]

Similar views were repeated in the government's brief:

> The premise of the Schwinn franchising program is that Schwinn is a distinctive brand which commands a premium price—that it enjoys, in other words, a margin of protection from the competition of other brands. To the extent that this premise is sound, it is clear that the only fully effective control upon the retail price of Schwinn bicycles is that imposed by competition among Schwinn dealers and distributors.[19]

The government also disclosed the animosity with which it regarded product differentiation:

> Either the Schwinn bicycle is in fact a superior product for which the consumer would willingly pay more, in which event it should be unnecessary to create a quality image by the artificial device of discouraging competition in the price of distributing the product; or it is not of premium quality, and the consumer is being deceived into believing that it is by its high and uniform retail price. In neither event would the manufacturer's private interest in maintaining a high-price image justify the serious impairment on competition that results.[20]

And the government expressed its view about the merits of vertical integration as compared with vertical restraints:

> Even if the threat to integrate were not wholly lacking in credibility in the circumstances of this case, we would urge that it was not a proper defense to the restraint of trade charge. In the first place, a rule that treats manufacturers who assume the distribution function themselves more leniently than those who impose restraints on independent distributors merely reflects the fact that, although integration in distribution may sometimes benefit the economy by leading to cost savings, agreements to maintain resale prices or to impose territorial restrictions of unlimited duration or outlet limitations of the type involved here have never been shown to produce comparable economies.[21]

The government's views on product differentiation and franchise restraints thus can be reduced to the following three propositions: (1) Differentiated products can be classed as those for which a price premium is warranted and those for which such a premium is not; (2) whether differentiation is real or contrived, intrabrand price competition is essential to the protection of

[18]Jurisdictional Statement for the United States at 14, *United Staves* v. *Arnold, Schwinn & Co.*, 388 U.S. 365 (1967).

[19]Brief for the United States at 26, *United States* v. *Arnold, Schwinn & Co.*, 388 U.S. 365 (1967).

[20]*Ibid.*, 47.

[21]*Ibid.*, 50.

consumer interests; and (3) although vertical integration sometimes yields economies, the same cannot be said for vertical restraints.[22]

6.2 An Alternative Interpretation

The possibility that Schwinn had identified a viable niche in a competitive industry and that the restraints it had introduced were needed to preserve the viability of the niche went completely unnoticed by the government. Instead, the government turned all its powers of advocacy to the description of an imagined anticompetitive offense. It ignored possible differences among customers and their marketing ramifications. Such a simplistic formulation is not satisfactory.

The buyers that will be most attracted by Schwinn will presumably be those for whom the opportunity cost of time is great or who are relatively inept at self-assembly and service. Thus, high-priced lawyers and other consultants who bill clients on an hourly basis will pay several times the going rate for a haircut, by patronizing barber shops that cut hair by appointment, rather than joining the queue at a wait-your-turn establishment (Becker, 1965, p. 493). The argument generalizes to the procurement of consumer durables. Time is economized if the customer does not have to search for a brand possessing the requisite properties and is easily able to locate and visit an outlet where the brand is stocked. And additional time is saved if the item comes preassembled, is reasonably trouble-free, and is reliably serviced at convenient outlets.

Such a brand of bicycle will also be attractive to customers who, though their unit opportunity cost of time may be below average, are particularly inept at self-assembly and repairs. In such a situation, despite low unit costs, the total opportunity cost is great, being the product of unit cost and time expended. Thus, two classes of customers will respond positively to the

---

[22]Richard Posner, who acknowledges briefing and arguing the *Schwinn* case for the government, contends that his analysis of the issues at that time "reflected the then prevailing thinking of the economics profession on restricted distribution" (Posner, 1977, p. 3). Although I agree that there was (and is) economic thinking congenial to the views set out in the *Schwinn* brief, I would hesitate to characterize it as that of the economics profession. Inasmuch as the brief is inexplicit about sources of its economic reasoning (Preston's is the only economics article dealing with vertical restraints that is cited in the brief (Brief for the United States at 49, *United States* v. *Arnold, Schwinn & Co.*, 388 U.S. 365 [1967]), since Preston expressly discusses a series of legitimate economic purposes that can be served by vertical restraints (Preston, 1965, pp. 507–19), because Telser's work on the rationality of restraints was in the public domain at that time (Telser, 1960, 1965), and because I expressly took exception with the brief while it was in preparation, Posner's attribution sweeps too broadly.

Schwinn image: Those who are mechanically inept and those who, although capable, have a high per-unit opportunity cost of time.

All that merely establishes, however, that franchised sales of Schwinn bicycles will appeal to some customers. It does not reach the question whether Schwinn should sell to all comers, allowing dealers to determine whether or not to offer the set of services that would qualify them as franchisees. Were Schwinn to do so, customers who have the above-described attributes would presumably go to the franchised outlet; those who do not could go elsewhere. Because in a world of unbounded rationality more degrees of freedom—in this instance, more methods of merchandising—are necessarily better than less, the natural policy inclination would be to let customers decide the question for themselves.

Several justifications, however, can be articulated in support of franchise restrictions: First, the Schwinn quality image may be debased without sales restraints; second, even if quality images are not impaired, the viability of franchises may hinge on sales restraints; third, the costs of enforcing the distribution contracts are increased in a mixed distribution system.[23] The quality image of Schwinn turns partly on objective considerations: Schwinn bicycles bought from authorized dealers come with an assured set of sales and service attributes. But the image may also be affected by information exchanged by word of mouth. If potential customers are told, "I bought a Schwinn bike and it was a lemon," but are not advised that the bicycle was bought from a discount house and misassembled, and that Schwinn's guarantees were thereby vitiated, customer confidence in Schwinn is easily impaired. Put differently, quality reputation may be preserved only if goods and services are sold under conditions of constraint.[24] Note in this connection that the incentive to invest in commercial reputation by surrounding transactions with institutional infrastructure occurs only in a world of bounded rationality.

Even if the quality image of franchise sales is unimpaired by non-

---

[23]Although arguably not applicable to the Schwinn case, a fourth justification can be based on unfair allocation of demonstration costs: Customers might shop for Schwinn bicycles at the franchised dealer—deciding on what model, features, and so on, to buy—and then make their purchase at the discount house, where the costs of demonstration are largely avoided. That may be a more serious concern when more expensive items, such as automobiles, are being marketed.

[24]The fact that 20 percent of Schwinn's authorized sales were made by outlets—B. F. Goodrich, hardware, and department stores—which did not provide service might be taken as "proof" that the above hazard is insubstantial. See Brief for the United States at 43–44, *United States* v. *Arnold, Schwinn & Co.*, 388 U.S. 365 (1967). But there are three mitigating considerations: (1) While 20 percent nonserviced sales may be permissible, 40 percent may not be; (2) the outlets described have reputation attributes rather different from discount houses, and hence may "stand behind" sales more completely; and (3) business judgment on such matters is entitled to a certain degree of undisputed respect.

franchise selling, the commercial viability of franchisees, which hinges on volume considerations, should be examined. Suppose that it is determined that a franchised dealer needs to sell a minimum number of bicycles in order to break even. Suppose further that Schwinn carefully locates its franchisees cognizant of those breakeven needs.[25] Finally, suppose that the system is initially viable but that discount sales subsequently appear. Marginal franchise operators shortly thereafter become nonviable. As a consequence the assurance of convenient Schwinn service outlets is jeopardized. Customer interest declines and other viable franchisees become marginal. The deterioration, taken together with the impaired quality image described above, creates the risk that the franchise mode will become nonviable, and customers for whom such differentiation yields net gains will be able to deal only in the undifferentiated market.

The third justification for franchise restrictions involves policing costs. The argument here is that it is less costly to police simple systems than it is to police more complicated ones. Causality (responsibility) is difficult to trace (attribute) in complex systems. If few "excuses" can be offered, fewer veracity checks have to be made. Although I do not suggest that this was a primary consideration for Schwinn, it could be relevant to the design of other marketing systems. Again, it is a problem only in a world of bounded rationality, because frictionless systems are self-policing.

Consider finally whether Schwinn will integrate forward into retailing if restrictions on sales to nonfranchised outlets are prohibited. If Schwinn's costs of integrated sales were identical with those of its franchisees, that presumably would occur. There are several reasons, however, to believe the case to be otherwise. First, franchised dealers were not exclusively engaged in the sales and service of Schwinn bicycles; other brands were also handled.[26] Also, many franchisees were engaged in nonbicycle sales. Assuming that multiple brand and multiple product sales are necessary for distributors to break even, forward integration would require Schwinn to engage in unwanted and possibly unavailable sales activities. Diversification into other products with which Schwinn had no expertise or familiarity is the unwanted activity. Stocking other brands, moreover, might pose difficulties of availability, as other bicycle manufacturers might suspect, with cause, that their brands would be slighted and demeaned if sold by Schwinn employees.

---

[25]This is altogether to be expected. Franchisors will ordinarily auction off franchise locations where greater than competitive returns are expected unless such auctions are costly to run.

[26]Schwinn required its franchisees to display Schwinn bicycles "with position equal to and as prominent as that of any competitive bicycle." Brief for Arnold, Schwinn & Co., Appendix 1, at 57 n. 89, *United States* v. *Schwinn & Co.*, 388 U.S. 365 (1967).

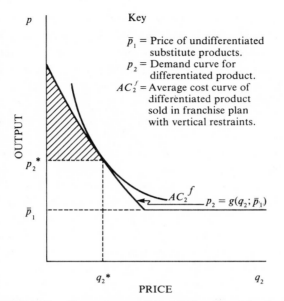

FIGURE 7–3. Consequences of Prohibiting Franchise Restraints

Furthermore, even if disabilities of those kinds did not exist, the question still remains whether Schwinn could provide incentives for managers of integrated sales outlets that promote performance equal to that when franchising is used. Both carrot and stick considerations must be addressed. The incentive disabilities associated with bureaucratic modes of organization stand as a further impediment to forward integration by Schwinn (see Chapter 6).

The upshot is that if the worst consequences obtain (namely, the franchise system collapses, Schwinn is unable to integrate forward economically, and the Schwinn brand image vanishes), prohibiting franchise restraints gives rise to real economic losses of the kind shown in Figure 7–3. The demand curve for Schwinn bicycles is here given by $p_2 = g(q_2; \bar{p}_1)$, where $\bar{p}_1$ is the price at which other bicycles sell (which is taken as given). The curve AC_2^f is the average cost of sales and service for franchised outlets. As drawn, franchising just breaks even (covers all of its costs, including a fair rate of return) at a price and quantity of p_2^*, q_2^*, respectively. Assuming that the costs of supplying nondifferentiated bicycles are not increased by Schwinn franchising, the net welfare gains (losses) realized by offering (withdrawing) the Schwinn brand will be given by the shaded consumer surplus region.

The government's case, which eschewed transaction cost features in favor of the firm-as-production-function construction, missed a great deal of what was relevant in order to reach an accurate economic assessment of what was at stake.[27] Schwinn illustrates the over-reaching that occurred during the inhospitablity era of antitrust enforcement. There being no place for the nonstandard (or, in Coase's terms, "ununderstandable" [1972, p. 67]) contracting practices within the applied price theory tradition, the merits of these practices were rejected or dismissed.

[27]If customers were fully knowledgeable or could be apprised without cost of all relevant attributes of all products, Schwinn could simply announce that it was supplying a bicycle that had these properties, the announcement would be registered among potential buyers, customers could verify that these conditions existed (though verification is a redundant operation in a world of complete knowledge), and those who valued the attributes could judge whether the premium was justified. Product differentiation in a world of unbounded rationality would thus proceed in a smooth and faultless manner.

Consumers, however, do not have those high-powered attributes: Their capacity to receive, store, recover, and process information is limited. In the light of those limitations, not only does Schwinn face the problem of transmitting its distinctive qualities, but it faces the problem of having its image believed. Thus, if consumers are occasionally misled, in that they are sometimes told one thing and learn to their dismay that it is incorrect, and if instances of fraud or deception are not known without cost to other potential buyers, so that reputations are not instantly and accurately updated, consumers will be wary when sellers apprise them that their brand has "superior" qualities.

In a market of boundedly rational consumers, Schwinn is faced with three interrelated information problems. First, it needs to bring to the attention of consumers the distinctive attributes that it purports to supply. Second, it needs to provide an institutional infrastructure that will prevent these attributes from being degraded. Third, it needs to accomplish both goals in an economical fashion. The government appears to have perceived none of this.

CHAPTER 8

Credible Commitments II: Bilateral Applications

The hostage model developed in the preceding chapter is applied here to bilateral trading. The concern is the same as that addressed earlier: In consideration of the expropriation hazards of bonding, buyer and seller may seek to *expand* the contractual relation beyond its "natural" limits, thereby creating a *mutual reliance relation*.

One way to safeguard transactions in which suppliers make specific investments is for buyers to invest in transaction-specific assets at the forward stage. *Ceteris paribus*, more favorable demand projections are signaled to suppliers in that way. A residual risk of uncompensated cancellation losses nevertheless remains. Forward investments in a unilateral trading regime do not therefore suffice to realize full trading optimality. Although it is not always feasible or efficacious, unilateral trading is sometimes supplanted by bilateral trading for that reason. As described below, such an expansion of the contractual relation can sometimes yield (or more nearly approximate) full optimality.

Reciprocity and exchange (swaps) are examined in section 1. The simple hostage model is extended to bilateral trading in section 2. Petroleum exchanges are examined in section 3. Concluding remarks, applying to both this and the preceding chapter, are set forth in section 4.

1. Reciprocity

1.1 *General*

Reciprocity transforms a unilateral supply relation—where A sells X to B—into a bilateral one, whereby A agrees to buy Y from B as a condition for making the sale of X and both parties understand that the transaction will be continued only if reciprocity is observed. The resulting contractual relation is thereby expanded. Although reciprocal selling is widely held to be anticompetitive (Stocking and Mueller, 1957; Blake, 1973), others regard it more favorably. George Stigler offers the following affirmative rationale for reciprocity:

> The case for reciprocity arises when prices cannot be freely varied to meet supply and demand conditions. Suppose that a firm is dealing with a colluding industry which is fixing prices. A firm in this collusive industry would be willing to sell at less than the cartel price if it can escape detection. Its price can be reduced in effect by buying from the customer-seller at an inflated price. Here reciprocity restores flexibility of prices.[1]

Inasmuch, however, as many industries do not satisfy the prerequisites for oligopolistic price collusion (Posner, 1969; Williamson, 1975, chap. 12), and reciprocity is sometimes observed among them, reciprocity presumably has other origins as well. Tiebreaking is one. A second is the possible advantageous governance strucure benefits of reciprocity. The two can be distinguished by the type of product being sold.

The tiebreaker explanation applies where firm B, which is buying specialized product from A, asks that A buy standardized product from B on the condition that B meets market terms. Other things being equal, procurement agents at A are apt to accede. F. M. Scherer notes, "Most of the 163 corporation executives responding to a 1963 survey stated that their firms' purchases were awarded on the basis of reciprocity only when the price, quality, and delivery conditions were equal" (1980, p. 344).

The more interesting case is where reciprocity involves the sale of specialized product to B conditioned on the procurement of specialized product from B. The argument here is that reciprocity can serve to equalize the exposure of the parties, thereby reducing the incentive of the buyer to defect from the exchange—leaving the supplier to redeploy specialized assets at greatly reduced alternative value. Absent a hostage (or other assurance that

[1]President's Task Force Report on Productivity and Competition, reprinted in Commerce Clearing House *Trade Regulation Reporter,* June 24, 1969, No. 419, p. 39.

the buyer will not defect), the sale by A of specialized product to B may never materialize. The buyer's commitment to the exchange is more assuredly signaled by his willingness to accept reciprocal exposure of specialized assets. Defection hazards are thereby mitigated.

The original (1968) Merger Guidelines of the U.S. Department of Justice took a wholly different approach. Although the subject was conglomerate mergers, the concern with reciprocity as a contracting practice was general. The language is instructive:

> (a) Since reciprocal buying (i.e., favoring one's customer when making purchases of a product which is sold by the customer) is an economically unjustified business practice which confers a competitive advantage on the favored firm unrelated to the merits of the product, the Department will ordinarily challenge any merger which creates a significant danger of reciprocal buying. . . .
> (c) Unless there are exceptional circumstances, the Department will not accept as a justification for a merger creating a significant danger of reciprocal buying the claim that the merger will produce economies, because, among other reasons, the Department believes that in general equivalent economies can be achieved by the firms involved through other mergers.

The Guidelines are noteworthy in several respects. For one thing, they plainly have origins in the inhospitality tradition: Reciprocity, like other nonstandard contracting practices, is an "economically unjustified business practice." Second, and related, the Guidelines are informed by the technological tradition: Reference is made to the "merits of the product" (a technological standard), but the "merits of the transaction" (a governance concern) go unmentioned. Third, the Guidelines assert that the relevant economies can be realized without posing reciprocity hazards: Socially valued (technological) economies can ordinarily be realized by finding substitute mergers for which reciprocity hazards are absent. The possibility that nonstandard contracting, of which reciprocity is a member, can yield valued economies is simply ignored. Such economies are evidently so implausible that potential contractual benefits do not even have to be admitted in principle before being dismissed.

Lon Fuller's interesting discussion of reciprocity, although posed in much more general terms than those set out here, is plainly apposite:

> I think we may discern three conditions for the optimum efficacy of the notion of duty. *First,* the relation of reciprocity out of which the duty arises must result from a voluntary agreement between the parties immediately affected; they themselves "create" the duty. *Second,* the reciprocal performances of the parties must in some sense be equal in value. Though the notion of voluntary assumption itself makes a strong appeal to the sense of justice, the appeal is reinforced when the element of equivalence is added to it. . . . *Third* . . . the relationship of duty must in theory and in practice be reversible. . . .

When we ask, "In what kind of society are these conditions most apt to be met?" The answer is a surprising one: in a society of economic traders. [Fuller, 1964, pp. 22–23]

Lest the hostage argument be uncritically considered a defense for reciprocal trading quite generally, note that it applies only where specialized assets are placed at hazard by *both* parties. Where only one or neither invests in specialized assets, the practice of reciprocity plainly has other origins.[2]

1.2 *Exchanges*

Although reciprocal trading among nonrivals may occasionally be justified, the exchange of product among nominal rivals is surely more puzzling and troublesome. Firms that are presumed to be in head-to-head competition ought to be selling product against one another rather than to one another. Inasmuch as neoclassical benefits are not plausibly imputed to the continuing exchange of product between rivals, public policy toward exchanges has been mainly negative and even hostile.

Several distinctions are useful in considering exchanges. First, trade among rivals—short-term or long-term, unilateral or bilateral—is feasible only if product is fungible. That is not true for many differentiated goods and services, so the issue of trade among rivals never arises for those. Second, short-term supply agreements are usefully distinguished from long-term. The former may be explained as an "occasional exception," whereby one rival will sell product to another on a short-term, gap-filling basis so as to provide temporary relief against unanticipated product shortfalls (occasioned by either demand or supply changes). Recognizing that the shoe may be on the other foot next time, otherwise rivalrous firms may assist one another for stopgap purposes. Public policy can presumably recognize merit in such trades and, so long as they lack a pattern, hence do not give rise to a "web of interdependence," will regard them as unobjectionable. Long-term trading among rivals is, however, much less consistent with the notion of effective head-to-head rivalry. At the very least, such arrangements warrant scrutiny.

Whether there are efficiency incentives for rivals to supply product to one another on a long-term basis turns initially on prospective realization of production cost savings. The realization of production cost savings through long-term trade between rivals requires that economies of scale be large in

---

[2]Possible trading objections are discussed by F. M. Scherer (1980, pp. 344–45). Another objection is that reciprocity becomes a bureaucratic habit that salesmen and purchasing agents find convenient, and outsiders are thereby disadvantaged in attempting to secure sales. See Williamson (1975, pp. 163–64).

relation to the size of geographic markets and, if they are, that firm-specific reputation effects extend across geographic market boundaries. The former is obvious since, absent economies of scale, every firm would presumably supply everywhere to its own long-term needs. Where scale economies are significant, however, each market will support only a limited number of plants of minimum efficient size.

But fungibility and scale economies do not establish that gains from trade will be realized from such sales. That will occur only if the value of (identical) product sold by rivals exceeds that sold by the local supplier. The issue here is whether valued reputation effects will go unrealized if rivals are unable to secure local product on favorable terms. Firms that possess valued reputations extending beyond their local market to include distant markets are thus the ones for which long-term supply by rivals will be attractive.[3]

Even supposing that fungibility, scale economy, and reputation effect conditions are satisfied, that merely establishes that *unilateral* long-term trade among rivals can yield economies. A justification for *bilateral* (exchange) agreements is not reached by the same arguments. Indeed, the usual defense for exchanges—that inefficient cross-hauling will occur if every firm is required to supply everywhere to its own needs—conveniently suppresses the obvious alternative, which is not the absence of trade at all but unilateral long-term trade. Failure to address such matters directly and demonstrate wherein exchanges enjoy comparative institutional advantages over more standard and familiar forms of unilateral trade presumably explains the suspect or hostile attitude with which exchanges are typically regarded. The argument that emerges from this chapter is that bilateral exchanges offer prospective advantages over unilateral trade *if* the resulting exposure of transaction-specific assets effects a credible commitment without simultaneously posing expropriation hazards.

The type of specific asset that is placed at hazard by unilateral long-term trade, but which a reciprocal long-term exchange agreement serves to protect, is that of a dedicated asset. Recall that dedicated assets were described as discrete additions to generalized capacity that would not be put in place but for the prospect of selling a large amount of product to a particular customer. Premature termination of the contract by the buyer would leave the supplier with a large overhang of capacity that could be disposed of only at distress prices. Requiring buyers to post a bond would check that hazard, but only by posing another: The supplier may contrive to expropriate the bond. More generally, the interests of the supplier in adapting efficiently to new circum-

---

[3]Reputation effect valuations may be illusory or real. Those that are real take the form of customer convenience (billing, contracting) or assured knowledge of product characteristics.

stances are not fully engaged. Reciprocal trading supported by separate but concurrent investments in specific assets provides a mutual safeguard against this second class of hazards. The hostages thereby created have the interesting property, moreover, that they are *never exchanged*. Instead, each party retains possession of its dedicated assets should the contract be prematurely terminated.

The usual argument that exchanges are justified because they avoid costly cross-hauling does not get to the issues described above and, by itself, is not an adequate justification for widespread use of exchanges. Were it only that transportation cost savings were realized, unilateral trading would suffice. Indeed, firms that buy from and sell product to rivals should be expected to create a central exchange in which supplies and demands were brought into correspondence by an auctioneer. Firms would end up selling to each other only by accident in such circumstances. Where dedicated assets are exposed, however, *the identity of the parties clearly matters*. Trades of that kind will not go through an auction market but will be carefully negotiated between the parties. Reciprocity in those circumstances is thus a device by which the continuity of a specific trading relation is promoted with risk attenuation effects.

2. The Hostage Model Extended

Assume that the two firms are engaged in tied bilateral trade and that both have made specific asset investments of k in support of each other. Assume further that each firm incurs redeployable costs of production of v_2 and that $\hat{p}$ is the price at which product is traded. In deciding whether to take delivery or cancel an order, a firm needs to consider not merely the net gain from procurement but also the net gain from supply. Let the net gain from buying and selling product be given by b_B and b_S, respectively. The combined gain from observing reciprocity is then given by $b_R = b_B + b_S$. Net benefits upon taking delivery in the purchase market will be given by

$$(1) \qquad b_B = p - \hat{p}$$

while net benefits from the simultaneous sale of product (given that specific assets in amount k have already been sunk) are given by

$$(2) \qquad b_S = \hat{p} - v_2.$$

The net benefits of noncancellation—that is, of continuing reciprocal trade (given that one's trading counterpart does not renege)—are then

$$(3) \qquad b_R = (p - \hat{p}) + (\hat{p} - v_2) = p - v_2$$

which will be positive so long as demand realization in the market for which product is purchased exceeds the marginal cost of own production.

Although the specific asset term, k, appears nowhere in these expressions, that does not mean it is irrelevant. Thus assume, as before, that demand in both markets is uniformly distributed over the interval 0 to 1. Then the expected net benefits of reciprocity will be positive only if the probability of trade under the reciprocal trading criterion (namely, $1 - v_2$) times the expected gain from remunerative exchange $(1 - v_2)/2$ exceeds the value of nonsalvageable assets, k. Thus the inequality $(1 - v_2)^2/2 - k > 0$ must be satisfied.

More significant is the fact that only if specific assets are committed in support of the exchange will the benefits from the sale of product be given by $b_S = \hat{p} - v_2$. If, for example, one of the parties to the exchange were to employ the general purpose technology T_1 instead, the net benefits from supplying product for which $\hat{p}$ is received would be $b'_S = \hat{p} - v_1$. The criterion for assessing whether to cancel or not would then be $b'_R = p - v_1$, which would call for cancellation in demand states where $p < v_1$. One party to the bilateral exchange would thus find cancellation attractive under circumstances where the other, because it has made specific asset investments, would want product to be traded. The symmetrical exposure of specific assets avoids that result.[4]

Alternatively, the issues can be presented as follows. As above, let $b_B = p - \hat{p}$ be the buyer's net benefits from unilateral trade if he decides to take delivery and $b_S = \hat{p} - v_2$ be the net gain to the seller from making delivery. Assume that $\hat{p} = 2$ and $v_2 = 1$ and that there are three possible state realizations: $p = 4$, $p = 2 - \epsilon$, and $p = 0$. It is the buyer's decision to accept delivery or refuse it. The payoffs associated with each decision, demand realization pair are:

	accept b_B, b_S	refuse b_B, b_S
$p = 4$	2, 1	0, 0
$p = 2 - \epsilon$	$-\epsilon$, 1	0, 0
$p = 0$	-2, 1	0, 0

[4]Symmetry is a sufficient but not a necessary condition for the parties to assess the net benefits of noncancellation identically. Other trading relations with this same property might conceivably be crafted. (If, for example, one of the parties invests more in specific assets than does the other, then an identical assessment of the net benefits of noncancellation could obtain if the party with the lesser degree of asset investment (whose redeployable costs $v_1 > v_2$) were to sell in a final product market where the distribution of demand, to be denoted by $p + \Delta$, was such that $p + \Delta - v_1 = p - v_2$.)

The efficient choice is for the seller to deliver in the two more favorable demand realization states and to shut down, thereby saving variable costs, if $p = 0$. If, however, the buyer consults only his own profits in deciding on whether to accept or refuse delivery, the buyer will take delivery only in the most favorable demand state and will refuse it if $p = 2-\epsilon$ or if $p = 0$, since $b_B < 0$ in both instances.

Enlarging the transaction from one of unilateral to bilateral trade changes the payoffs in such a way as to eliminate this inefficiency. Thus now the payoff to both parties is given by $b_R = p - v_2$. The corresponding payoffs faced by both parties are now identical and are given by:

	accept b_R	refuse b_R
$p = 4$	3	0
$p = 2-\epsilon$	$1-\epsilon$	0
$p = 0$	-1	0

Product will thus be traded in the two more favorable demand states, but production will be shut down if $p = 0$, which is the efficient result. Reciprocity can thus be regarded as a reaction to the inherent strains (and resulting inefficiencies) that would occur under a unilateral trading regime. Public policy insistence that anything other than unilateral trading is "unnatural" and presumptively antisocial is simply mistaken.

3. Petroleum Exchanges

"The task of linking concepts with observations demands a great deal of detailed knowledge of the realities of economic life" (Koopmans, 1957, p. 145). The phenomenon of petroleum exchanges has puzzled economists for a very long time. It routinely comes up in antitrust cases and investigations. The 1973 case brought by the United States Federal Trade Commission against the largest petroleum firms maintained the view that exchanges were instrumental in maintaining a web of interdependencies among those firms, thereby helping to effect an oligopolistic outcome in an industry that was relatively unconcentrated on normal market structure criteria.[5] The more recent study on *The State of Competition in the Canadian Petroleum Industry* likewise regards exchanges as objectionable.[6] The Canadian Study, moreover, produces docu-

[5]*FTC* v. *Exxon et al.* Docket No. 8934 (1963).

[6]Robert J. Bertrand, Q.C., Director of Investigation and Research, Combines Investigation Act, coordinated the eight-volume study *The State of Competiton in the Canadian Petroleum*

ments—contracts, internal company memoranda, letters, and the like—as well as deposition testimony to support its views that exchanges are devices for extending and perfecting monopoly among the leading petroleum firms. Such evidence on the details and purposes of contracting is usually confidential and hence unavailable. But detailed knowledge is clearly germane—and often essential—to a microanalytic assessment of the transaction cost features of contract.

3.1 The Evidence from the Canadian Study

Volume V of the Canadian Study deals with the refining sector. Arguments are advanced and supporting evidence is developed that interfirm supply arrangements permit the principal refiners to perfect oligopolistic restrictions in the following four respects:[7] (1) valuable knowledge about investment and marketing plans of rivals are disclosed by such agreements (p. 56); (2) leading firms are able to control lesser firms by manipulating the terms of exchange (pp. 49–50); (3) competition is impaired by conditioning supply on the payment of an "entry fee" (pp. 53–54); and (4) exchange agreements impose limits on growth and supplementary supply (pp. 51–52).

The first two fail to pass scrutiny of the most rudimentary comparative institutional kind. Thus assuming that trade between rivals is efficient and that unilateral supply agreements (if not exchange) will be permitted, the objectionable information disclosures attributed to exchanges would presumably continue—since investment and marketing plans will be unavoidably disclosed in the process. Accordingly, evaluated in comparative institutional terms, the information disclosure objection is properly regarded as an objection to long-term trade of any kind. Exchanges are not uniquely culpable.

The suggestion that exchanges are anticompetitive because they permit firms to realize unfair bargaining advantages is similarly misplaced. The correct view is that firms should always be expected to realize such bargaining advantages as their positions lawfully permit. Absent a showing that exchanges are different from unilateral trades in bargaining respects, that objection is properly disregarded also.

Industry (Quebec, 1981). All references in this chapter are to Vol. V, *The Refining Sector.* That study will hereinafter be referred to as the Canadian Study.

[7]The Canadian Study contends that "a close examination of the interest of the [major refiners] and their actions shows that refining arrangements were meant to restrict competition. The collection of information, the intent to control lesser firms, the imposition of an 'entry fee,' the use of restrictions on downstream growth are not characteristics that would be expected normally from a competitive market" (V: 76).

The entry fee and marketing restraint objections are more substantial, however, and warrant elaboration.

a.   ENTRY FEES

The entry fee objection to exchanges is that this has foreclosure consequences. That such fees are required as a precondition for trade, or at least the sale of product at favorable prices, is set out in the Canadian Study as follows (pp. 53–54; emphasis added):

> Evidence of an understanding that a fee relating to investment was required for acceptance into the industry can be found in the following quotation from Gulf:
>
> > "We do believe that the oil industry generally, although grudgingly, will allow a participant who has paid his ante, to play the game; the ante in this game being the capital for refining, distributing and selling products."
>
> (Document #71248, undated, Gulf)
>
> The significance of the quotation lies equally in the notion that an "entry fee" was required and in the notion that the industry set the rules of the "game." The meaning of the "entry fee" as well as the rules of the "game" as understood by the industry can be found in the actual dealings between companies where the explicit mention of an "entry fee" arises. These cases demonstrate the rules that were being applied—the rules to which Gulf was referring. Companies which had not paid an "entry fee," that is, companies which had not made a sufficient investment in refining capacity or in marketing distribution facilities would *either not be supplied or would be penalized in the terms of the supply agreement.* [Emphasis added]

b.   MARKETING RESTRAINTS

The Canadian Study notes that exchanges were made conditional on growth and territorial restraints and regards both as objectionable. The Imperial–Shell exchange agreement, under which Imperial supplied product to Shell in the Maritimes and received product in Montreal, is cited in both connections (p. 51):

> The agreement between Imperial and Shell, originally signed in 1963, was renegotiated in 1967. In July 1972, Imperial did this because Shell had been growing too rapidly in the Maritimes. In 1971/72, Imperial had expressed its dissatisfaction with the agreement because of Shell's marketing policies. Shell noted:
>
> > "There [sic] [Imperial's] present attitude is that we have built a market with their facilities, we are aggressive and threatening them all the time, and they are not going to help and in fact get as tough as possible with us."
>
> (Document #23633, undated, Shell)

Imperial renewed the agreement with Shell only after imposing a price penalty if expansion were to exceed "normal growth rates" and furthermore stipulated that "Shell would not generally be allowed to obtain product from third party sources" to service the Maritimes (p. 52).

Gulf Oil likewise took the position that rivals receiving product under exchange agreements should be restrained to normal growth: "Processing agreements (and exchange agreements) should be entered into only after considering the overall economics of the Corporation and should be geared to providing competitors with volumes required for the normal growth only."[8] It furthermore sought and secured assurances that product supplied by Gulf would be used only by the recipient and would not be diverted to other regions or made available to other parties (p. 59).

3.2 Interpretations

These practices are subject to several interpretations. One is that the entry fees and marketing restraints are both anticompetitive. A second is that efficiency purposes are arguably served, especially by the former. A third is that there are mixed effects.

a. THE INHOSPITALITY TRADITION

The two polar contracting traditions for evaluating nonstandard or unfamiliar contracting practices are the common law tradition and the antitrust or inhospitality tradition. Whereas contractual irregularities are presumed to serve affirmative economic purposes under the common law tradition, a deep suspicion of anticompetitive purposes is maintained by the antitrust (or inhospitality) tradition.[9]

The inhospitality tradition belongs to the monopoly branch of contract and is supported by the widespread view that economic organization is technologically determined. Economies of scale and technological nonseparabilities explain the organization of economic activity within firms. All other activity is appropriately organized by market exchanges. Legitimate market transactions will be mediated entirely by price; restrictive contractual relations signal anticompetitive intent.

The authors of the Canadian Study are evidently persuaded of the merits

[8]The Canadian Study (p. 59) identifies the source as Document #73814, January 1972, Gulf.

[9]See Chapter 1, footnote 9 and accompanying text.

of that tradition. Long-term trade among rivals of any kind is suspect. And exchanges, which represent an irregular if not unnatural contracting form, are especially objectionable. Not only do exchanges facilitate information disclosure and permit bargaining muscles to be flexed, but they are used punitively against nonintegrated independents who, because they have not paid an entry fee, are denied product on parity terms. Furthermore, the marketing restraints associated with exchanges are patently offensive.

b.   AN EFFICIENCY ASSESSMENT

Unlike the inhospitality tradition, the transaction cost approach is in the common law tradition. A comparative institutional orientation (Coase, 1964) is maintained. "Defects" are thus objectionable only where superior feasible alternatives can be described. Inasmuch as the information disclosure and bargaining concerns raised by the authors of the Canadian Study continue under unilateral trading, they are set aside, and attention is focused on entry fees and marketing restraints.

1. *Entry fees.* The entry fee issue is the matter of special interest to this chapter. Long-term exchange agreements permit firms to secure product in geographic markets where own production is not feasible because economies of scale are large in relation to their own needs. The amount of product in question may nevertheless be substantial. Firms with whom exchange agreements are reached will thus construct and maintain larger plants than they otherwise would. Specific investments in dedicated assets are made as a consequence of such agreements.

If supply agreements were of a unilateral kind and the buyer was unable or unwilling to offer a hostage, contracts of the kind described in Chapter 7 as type II would presumably be negotiated—whence the trading price would be $\bar{p} = v_2 + k/(1 - \bar{p})$. If instead the contract is extended to include bilateral rather than unilateral trade, the contract is converted to one of type III. Although exchange agreements stipulate the physical flows of product, the effective price is $\hat{p} = v_2 + k$, which is less than $\bar{p}$. Moreover, the parties have the incentive to exchange product so long as realized demand price in both regions exceeds v_2,[10] which is the marginal cost supply criterion. Assuming that demands in the two regions are highly correlated, the parties will normally reach common decisions on the desirability of trade.[11]

[10]This assumes common costs, which condition will normally be approximated in exchanges of product between firms within a single country where factor prices are very similar.

[11]The possibility that the contract will drift out of alignment nevertheless needs to be recognized. Should one of the firms in an exchange agreement operate much closer to its capacity limits than the other, the latter party would incur much higher costs of termination than would the former. Recognition of this may explain why "during the renegotiation of a reciprocal purchase/sale agreement covering Montreal and the Maritimes," Shell noted that Imperial advised it

2. *Marketing restraints.* The supply and growth restraints discussed by the Canadian Study can be looked at in three ways. First, they can be viewed as a means by which to protect the exchange agreement against unilateral defection. Second, such restraints may serve strategic market division purposes. Third, restraints may serve to regularize markets. These are not mutually exclusive.

Only the first purpose is consonant with an efficiency interpretation. The argument here is that marketing restraints help to preserve symmetrical incentives. Such symmetry could be upset if one of the firms were to receive product in its deficit region from third parties. Such a firm might then be in a position to play one supplier off against the other. Or symmetry could be placed under strain if one party were to receive product from the other such that it began to grow "in excess of normal"—in which event it might be prepared to construct its own plant and scuttle the exchange agreement. Marketing restraints that help to forestall such outcomes encourage parties to participate in exchanges that might otherwise be unacceptable.

c. A MIXED VIEW

Monopoly explanations are commonly advanced when economists, lawyers, or other interested observers come across contractual practices they do not understand. Inasmuch as "we are very ignorant [in this field], the number of ununderstandable practices tends to be very large, and the reliance on a monopoly explanation frequent" (Coase, 1972, p. 67). A rebuttable presumption that nonstandard contracting practices are serving affirmative economic purposes, rather than monopoly purposes, would arguably serve antitrust law and economics better than the inhospitality presumption, which until recently has prevailed.[12]

The presumption that exchanges have efficiency purposes could be chal-

---

that "they were not satisfied with the extent of Shell's investment in the Maritimes" (p. 54). In addition to the investment in refining in Montreal, which Shell interpreted as an investment "by exchange" in the Maritimes, Imperial wanted Shell to make direct investment in a Maritime distribution network (p. 54). Shell observed in that connection that although it had made no significant investment of its own in the Maritimes, "we have invested in Montreal and by exchange invested in the Maritimes so we have paid an entrance fee, although we have not paid for distribution network." The Canadian Study (p. 54) identifies the source as Document #23633, undated, Shell.

[12]To be sure, this oversimplifies. Antitrust has been loath to declare contractual constraints to be *per se* illegal. As discussed in Chapter 7, however, it came perilously close to taking this step in *U.S.* v. *Arnold, Schwinn & Co.,* 388 U.S. 365 (1967). The prevailing enforcement view toward contractual restraints in the 1960s is accurately characterized as inhospitable. The 1968 Merger Guideline treatment of reciprocity, which is quoted and discussed in 1.1 above, is illustrative.

lenged on any or all of three grounds. First, it might be argued that exchanges are merely a clever device by which to deny product to nonintegrated rivals. Refusals to sell to nonintegrated firms on $\bar{p}$ terms would support that contention. (It is plainly unrealistic, however, for buyers that have not made credible commitments to expect to receive product at $\hat{p}$.) Second, the market in question could be shown to have troublesome structural properties. The issue here is whether the requisite preconditions for market power—mainly high concentration coupled with high barriers to entry[13]—are satisfied. A third would be that the preconditions for efficiency are not satisfied. Factors favorable to the efficiency interpretation are the following: The exchange should be of a long-term kind; the amount of product exchanged should represent a significant fraction of plant capacity; but economies of plant scale should be large in relation to the amount of product traded. Exchanges for a small quantity of product where economies of scale are insubstantial are much more problematic.

To be sure, exchanges might simultaneously serve efficiency and anticompetitive or other antisocial[14] purposes. Here as elsewhere, where trade-offs are posed, they ought to be evaluated.

4. Concluding Remarks

These two chapters on credible commitments maintain and develop the viewpoint that private ordering is widely used to govern complex contractual relations. It thus takes issue with the legal centralism tradition. Rather than employ a legal rules approach to contract, the concept of contract as framework is emphasized instead. Disputes are not therefore routinely litigated; contract and the courts are used for ultimate appeal (Llewellyn, 1931). Such ultimate appeal affords protection against egregious abuses, of which "might is right" is an elementary example. But ultimate recourse does not imply a

[13]There is growing agreement that the structural preconditions that must be satisfied before claims of strategic anticompetitive behavior are seriously entertained are very high concentration coupled with barriers to entry (Williamson, 1977, pp. 292–93; Joskow and Klevorick, 1979, pp. 225–31; Ordover and Willig, 1981, pp. 307–8). See the discussion of these matters in Chapter 14.

[14]A possible antisocial use of exchanges that has recently come to light is the practice by California oil companies to use swaps as a means to underprice crude oil that was produced on public lands. It has been alleged that "the major oil companies went to great lengths to suppress the price of heavy crude, including the invention of a complicated barter arrangement by which the major companies could swap the underpriced crude oil among themselves without buying or selling it in a cash transaction that would reveal its true market value" (Jackson and Pasztor, 1984, p. 30). The oil companies insist that efficiency purposes were served.

capacity to make frequent and nuanced adjustments in continuing relations so as to restore the parties to a trading position on the shifting contract curve.

Rather than maintain the presumption that the courts "work well," therefore, the approach taken here acknowledges that court ordering often experiences severe limitations. Since the severity of those limitations varies with the circumstances, a discriminating approach to the study of contract will necessarily acknowledge differing governance capacities and needs. The study of contract is thus appropriately extended beyond legal rules to include a comparative assessment of transactions in relation to alternative governance structures. Of special interest is the use of bilateral governance structures to implement nonstandard contracts where the adaptation and continuity needs of the parties are especially great.

This chapter and the one preceding establish the following:

1. *Hostages.* Contrary to the prevailing view that hostages are a quaint concept with little or no practical importance to contemporary contracting, the use of hostages to support exchange is widespread and economically important. But hostage creation is only part of the story. Expropriation hazards and prospective maladaptation conditions also have to be considered. Complex governance structures, of which reciprocal trading is one, arise in response to such conditions.

2. *Asset specificity.* The organization of economic activity is massively influenced by the degree to which the transactions under examination are supported by assets that are specific to the parties. These chapters reaffirm the basic proposition that governance structures must be matched to the underlying attributes of transactions in a discriminating way if the efficiency purposes of economic organization are to be realized and establish that, as between two buyers, one of whom posts a hostage in support of specific asset investments by suppliers while the other does not, suppliers will offer better terms to the former, *ceteris paribus.*

3. *Contracting in its entirety.* Not every transaction poses defection hazards, and it may not be possible to safeguard all that do. Where the potential hazards that beset contracts are evident to the parties from the outset, however, studies of contract and of contracting institutions arguably start "at the beginning." This has ramifications for assessing the importance of the prisoners' dilemma and for understanding the administration of justice.

a. *Prisoners' dilemma.* The benefits of cooperation notwithstanding, the achievement of cooperation is widely thought to be frustrated by the relentless logic of the prisoners' dilemma. To be sure, it has always been evident that defection can be deterred if payoffs are appropriately altered. But that stratagem is held to be infeasible or is otherwise dismissed, on which account the dilemma persists or appeal is made to "exogenous norms of cooperative behavior [that are] adhered to by the actors" (Hirschman, 1982, p. 1470). I submit that the feasibility of crafting superior *ex ante* incentive structures warrants more attention. A leading reason for its neglect is that the study of the institutions of contract has occupied such a low place on the research agenda. Subtle incentive features incorporated in nonstandard contracting practices have gone undetected as a consequence of this nonchalance—hence the practical significance of the prisoners' dilemma to the study of exchange has been vastly exaggerated.

b. *Justice.* The notion that hostages are demanded as a condition for supplying product on favorable terms has the appearance of an arbitrary exercise of power: The stronger party "demands" a hostage from the weaker, who accedes because it has no other choice. In fact, a comparative institutional assessment of contractual alternatives discloses that efficiency purposes are often served by hostages and that it is in the mutual interest of the parties to achieve that result. Not only can producers be induced to invest in the most efficient technology, but buyers can be induced to take delivery whenever demand realizations exceed marginal cost. More generally, contracts ought to be examined *in their entirety,* with special attention to their governance features. Principles of justice or competition that look at the relation between the parties at the execution stage without examining the *ex ante* bargaining relation are at best incomplete and are frequently mistaken.[15] Parties to a contract should not expect to have their cake (low price) and eat it too (no hostage).

[15]Robert Nozick's views on justice are apposite: "[W]hether a distribution is just depends upon how it came about. In contrast, *current-time-slice* principles of justice hold that the justice of a distribution is determined by how things are distributed (who has what)" (1975, p. 153; emphasis in original). What he refers to as the current-time-slice approach to justice neglects *ex ante* bargaining and evaluates justice in terms of outcomes alone. Upon realization that justice is administered in this way, initial bargains will be struck on terms different from the terms if the parties were given assurance that the complete contract would be subject to review in evaluating the merits of a contracting relation.

Two difficult issues nevertheless remain if the comprehensive bargain orientation to justice is adopted: the initial distribution of resources and the competence of the parties to evaluate complex contracts. Only if wealth redistribution cannot more effectively be accomplished through direct means should contract be used for this purpose, and then only upon making allowance for the adaptive responses referred to above. Consumer protection may sometimes be warranted where information processing problems (real or contrived) are thought to be severe.

CHAPTER 9

The Organization of Work

The organization of work is the subject of this chapter and the next. The economic rationale for hierarchy is traced to transaction cost origins in this chapter. The governance structure safeguards that are associated with internal labor markets are examined in Chapter 10.

Those to whom the transaction cost advantages of simple hierarchy are obvious may wish to omit this chapter and go directly to the next.[1] It is nevertheless noteworthy that the economic merits of hierarchy have recently been disputed by Radical Economists and others. What was once taken for granted is thus usefully resubmitted to scrutiny. Since the Radical Economists are principally responsible for the charge that hierarchy lacks redeeming economic purpose, this chapter focuses on the issues set out and elaborated in that literature.

The Radical account of hierarchy is sketched in section 1. Missing transaction cost features are introduced in section 2. A description of six alternative work modes that differ in contractual, ownership, and hierarchical respects is set out in section 3. The efficiency attributes of those modes are then compared in section 4. Power approaches to the study of organization are examined in section 5.

[1]For an earlier discussion of simple hierarchy less extensive than that appearing here, see Williamson (1975, chap. 3).

1. The Radical Account of Hierarchy

The Radical account of hierarchy comes down to this: (1) All legitimate efficiency purposes of organization can be discerned by reference to the neoclassical theory of the firm; (2) neoclassical theory makes no provision for hierarchy; accordingly (3) the alternative hypothesis—namely, that hierarchy operates in the service of power—wins.

Original contributions by Stephen Marglin (1974) and Katherine Stone (1974) are central to the Radical critique.[2] Whether there is an efficiency justification for hierarchy is examined by Marglin both with reference to Adam Smith's treatment of the division of labor and in terms of the historical displacement of nonhierarchical by hierarchical modes. To the question "What do bosses do?" Marglin offers the reply: Bosses exploit workers, and hierarchy is the organizational device by which this result is accomplished.

1.1 *Pinmaking*

T. S. Ashton contends that examining the organization of work in the context of pinmaking is regretable:[3] Pinmaking is neither economically important nor technologically interesting. The pinmaking example nevertheless has several advantages. For one thing, the technology is simple. Not only are the tasks and tooling relatively uncomplicated, but successive stages of pinmaking are technologically separable. There is no occasion, therefore, to disallow certain types of nonhierarchical work modes at the outset because of the "imperatives of technology." Instead, a wide range of organizational modes are technologically feasible, and transactions rather than technology are arguably determinative.

Second, the pinmaking example has the advantage of being already familiar to social scientists. Indeed, it would be difficult to cite another case where the economies that accrue to the specialization of labor are thought to

[2]See Bowles and Gintis (1976, chap. 3) for a summary of the radical arguments where the Marglin and Stone papers are prominently featured.

[3]Ashton (1925, p. 281) observed that in "text-books and examination scripts the pin trade of a hundred or more years ago has been given a prominence which is far from justified by its true rank among economic activities. Babbage notwithstanding, the manufacture of pins does not afford the ideal illustration of the division of labor; and one may echo Dr. Clapham's regret 'that Adam Smith did not go a few miles from Kirkcaldy to the Carron Works to see them turning and boring their cannonades instead of to his silly pin factory.' "

be so clearly established. Not only does Smith discuss the production process in detail, but Charles Babbage (1835, pp. 175–83) and Ashton (1925) give even more complete descriptions. Third, and related, although Smith's use of the pinmaking example to illustrate the advantages of the specialization of labor was long thought to be uncontroversial, Marglin argues that Smith's discussion of alternative modes for organizing pinmaking is incomplete and is biased in favor of hierarchy. Whether pinmaking ought to be organized hierarchically is thus actively open to dispute.

Smith's discussion of the division of labor in the context of pinmaking is worth recounting in detail. He observed that

> . . . in the way in which this business is now carried on, not only the whole work is a peculiar trade, but it is divided into a number of branches, of which the greater part are likewise peculiar trades. One man draws out the wire, another straights it, a third cuts it, a fourth points it, a fifth grinds it at the top for receiving the head, to make the head requires two or three distinct operations; to put it on is a peculiar business, to whiten the pins is another; it is even a trade by itself to put them into the paper; and the important business of making a pin is, in this manner, divided into about eighteen distinct operations, which, in some manufactories, are all performed by distinct hands, though in others the same man will sometimes perform two or three of them. I have seen a small manufactory of this kind where ten men only were employed, and where some of them consequently performed two or three distinct operations. But though they were very poor, and therefore but indifferently accommodated with the necessary machinery, they could, when they exerted themselves, make among them about twelve pounds of pins in a day. There are in a pound upwards of four thousand pins of a middling size. Those ten persons, therefore, could make among them upwards of forty-eight thousand pins in a day. Each person, therefore, making a tenth part of forty-eight thousand pins, might be considered as making four thousand eight hundred pins in a day. But if they had all wrought separately and independently, and without any of them having been educated to this peculiar business, they certainly could not each of them have made twenty, perhaps not one pin in a day. [Smith, 1922, pp. 6–7]

The factors that are responsible for the advantages attributable to the division of labor are identified by Smith as follows:

> This great increase of the quantity of work which in consequence of the division of labour, the same number of people are capable of performing, is owing to three different circumstances; first, to the increase of dexterity in every particular workman; secondly, to the saving of the time which is commonly lost in passing from one species of work to another; and lastly to the invention of a great number of machines which facilitate and abridge labour, and enable one man to do the work of many. [p. 9]

Several things are noteworthy about those observations. For one thing, Smith is imprecise about the organizational and ownership relations that exist among the workmen in the small factory in question, though one may infer that the workmen were subject to an authority relation and that the plant and equipment was owned by a capitalist owner-manager who directed the work. Second, only a single alternative to factory organization of the kind described is considered. The alternative is for each man to work "separately and independently," each pin being crafted separately, start to finish, before work on the next is begun. Intentionally or not, the comparison is thereby rigged in favor of factory modes of organization.

As Marglin (1974, p. 38) points out, the separate crafting of each individual pin is absurd. Both dexterity and setup time economies can be realized by substituting batch processing for separate crafting: "It appears to have been technologically possible to obtain the economies of reducing setup time *without* specialization. A workman, with his wife and children, could have proceeded from task to task, first drawing out enough wire for hundreds or thousands of pins, then straightening it, then cutting it, and so on with each successive operation, thus realizing the advantages of dividing the overall production into separate tasks." Indeed, in Marglin's view, the "capitalist division of labor, typified by Adam Smith's famous example of pin manufacture, was the result of a search not for a *technologically* superior organization of work, but for an *organization* which guaranteed to the entrepreneur an essential *role* in the production process, as integrator of the separate efforts of his workers into a marketable product" (1974, p. 34; emphasis added).

1.2 *Power*

As indicated, the familiar neoclassical production function framework, whereby economizing is accomplished mainly by equating marginal rates of transformation with relative factor prices, is simply inimical to the proposition that organization form matters. Marglin recognizes this and appears to concede that hierarchical organization yields economies of other kinds. The success of the factory (hierarchy) over the putting-out system is thus described by Marglin as follows

> [T]he agglomeration of workers into factories was a natural outgrowth of the putting-out system (a result, if you will, of its internal contradictions) whose success had little or nothing to do with the technological superiority of large-scale machinery. The key to the success of the factory, as well as its aspiration, was the substitution of capitalists for workers' control of the production process; discipline and supervision could and did reduce costs *without* being technologically superior. [1974, p. 46; emphasis in original]

Additional or related productivity advantages of hierarchy, as compared with the putting-out system, are that hierarchy permits the benefits of innovation to be appropriated more completely (Marglin, 1974, p. 48) and serves to check "embezzlement and like deceits" (p. 51).

Despite productivity and efficiency consequences of those kinds, radical economists take the position that hierarchy lacks redeeming social purpose. For one thing, productivity gains that are attributable to discipline are involuntary. The disutility of work presumably more than offsets the output gains that result from discipline.[4] Second, although hierarchy may check transactional disabilities associated with nonhierarchical modes, those disabilities are evidently thought to be unimportant or are explained by institutional defects of a remediable kind. As an example of the latter, Marglin (1974, p. 49) contends that the patent system could be reshaped in ways that vitiate the innovative advantages the patent system currently assigns to hierarchy. Accordingly, his answer to the question, "Is hierarchical authority really necessary to high levels of production?" appears mainly to be negative: Although hierarchy may favor the accumulation of capital (p. 34), the coupling of the hierarchical organization of work with an extensive division of labor is artificial and has as its object the exploitative purpose of " 'divide and conquer' rather than efficiency" (p. 39).

Not only do radical economists argue that hierarchy lacks a compelling efficiency rationale, but they further contend that the history of hierarchy supports the alternative hypothesis, namely, hierarchy arose in the service of capitalist power over labor. Stone's (1974) interpretation of the transformation of the steel industry in the late nineteenth century develops that argument in a way that both Samuel Bowles and Herbert Gintis (1976) and Marglin (1974) find compelling. Also, radical economists take the position that not only are nonhierarchical work modes more efficient, but they result in greater work satisfaction (Bowles and Gintis, 1976, pp. 78–81).

The steel industry transformation is interpreted in transaction cost terms in section 5, while the matter of work satisfaction is deferred to the following chapter. The central issue, and my main interest here, is an assessment of alternative work modes in transaction cost terms. If, as alleged, hierarchy does not serve efficiency purposes, the power relationship hypothesis is more compelling. If, however, hierarchy serves to economize on transaction costs,

---

[4]This neglects the possibility that the benefits of supervision are perceived by the workers and that supervision is imposed by mutual consent so as to check free riding among the membership of an interdependent work force. Alchian and Demsetz (1972) motivate what they refer to as the "classical capitalist firm" on such mutual consent grounds.

then an alternative explanation for the historical events to which Marglin and Stone refer warrants serious consideration.

2. Transaction Cost Aspects

Recall that two branches of transaction cost economics are distinguished in the cognitive map of contract set out in Chapter 2: a governance branch, where the concern is with adaptive, sequential decision-making, and a measurement branch, where the problems are attributable to information impactedness. To be sure, the two conditions are commonly joined (Alchian, 1984, p. 39). My discussion of the organization of intermediate product markets deals principally with the governance side. If measurement problems exist, they are assumed to vary directly with asset specificity.

My discussion of labor organization and of corporate organizations in this chapter and those following makes greater provision for measurement aspects. As between the two, the governance side continues to be the main source of refutable implications. But express attention to measurement is more important and even essential.

2.1 The Fundamental Transformation

The Radical account of pinmaking and of work organization makes no provision for asset specificity and its organizational ramifications. Even supposing that the machines used to make pins were interchangeable, one factory to another, so that a condition of physical asset specificity was absent, the equipment in a pin factory had site specificity features (it was not "on wheels"). It is furthermore plausible that the workers developed firm-specific knowledge and skills.[5] Given nontrivial asset specificity in either site or human asset respects, successive stations would thereafter operate in an *ex post* bilateral trading relationship with each other. Despite what may have been a large numbers bidding condition at the outset, if the fundamental transformation thereafter took effect, then the eventual configuration would be one for which a specialized governance structure was needed.

[5]Pinmaking plainly involves the acquisition of special skills—to cut, point, straighten, etc. Whether these take much or little time is not obvious; I conjecture that the necessary skills are quickly learned. In any event, many of those skills are presumably transferable to rival pinmaking firms. If, therefore, the pin industry is unconcentrated, skill specialization need not stand as a strong impediment to human asset redeployment. Team features, however, can complicate that and favor a longer-term employment relation.

To be sure, radical economists are not uniquely culpable in their failure to acknowledge that condition and to recognize its organizational importance. But they were plainly in a better position to deal with such matters than were economists of orthodox persuasions. Marglin and others had already made the shift to a more microanalytic level of analysis in their efforts to assess the organization of work. Implicitly, the transaction had become the basic unit of analysis. The next step was to submit alternative feasible organizing structures to comparative institutional analysis. They pulled up short of that, however, and were content instead to assert that nonhierarchical modes of organization had good if not superior efficiency properties.

2.2 Measurement

The measurement difficulties of principal interest in this chapter and those following are attributable to a condition of information impactedness. One of the parties to a transaction has more complete knowledge than does the other, which asymmetry condition is costly to overcome and gives rise to a trading hazard. Sometimes markets fail for that reason (Akerlof, 1970). But that is not the only, or even the main, possibility. Organizational responses often occur that serve to mitigate the hazard.

Two responses can be distinguished: an incentive response and a metering response. The incentive response relaxes the connection between rewards and an imperfectly observed indicator of performance, thereby weakening the incentive for deceit. For example, workers on piece rate have stronger incentives to shade quality than do hourly workers. The metering response may entail redesigning the product or reorganizing the task. The object in either case is to display true attributes more accurately.

Although radical economists regard shirking, embezzlement, and quality shading as income redistribution effects, the fact is that numerous resource allocation consequences ensue. For one thing, investments in products and technologies that are more subject to such losses will be relatively disfavored. Second, the black markets on which embezzled product is traded are inefficient. Third, efforts to police against those losses involve the use of real resources. Further distortions occur because systems that are more subject to shirking and embezzlement will induce wage adjustments that penalize workers who are less given to such deceits. (It is not an accident that those with few scruples predominate in some occupations. Those with more scruples are simply nonviable.)

3. A Comparative Institutional Framework

3.1 *Assumptions*

Marglin contends that the nonexperimental nature of the social sciences contributes to the continuing neglect of internal organization. Were that not the case, alternative modes of organization, including egalitarian work modes, would be designed and tested experimentally (Marglin, 1974, pp. 33–34). While I agree that experimental testing of that kind has great merit, I submit that a great deal can be discovered about the efficacy of alternative work modes by an abstract assessment of their transactional properties. At the very least, *a priori* analysis of the transactional attributes of alternative modes should permit the empirical issues to be greatly delimited.

So that alternative modes will be on a parity in technological and locational respects, it will be useful first to specify the common manufacturing characteristics associated with each. One of the more serious problems with the work mode literature is that such assumptions are rarely made explicit. The following assumptions will be maintained in this and the next two sections and, except where noted to the contrary, will apply across all modes:

1. Specialized equipment, provided that it can be utilized at design capacity, facilitates low-cost pin manufacture. Nontrivial setup costs are incurred in putting the equipment in place.
2. Workers acquire dexterity by repeated operations of the same kind, though this is subject to diminishing returns.
3. It is economical, so as to save on transportation expense, that all pinmaking operations be completed at a common location, so that, the putting-out system excepted, all work is performed under one roof.
4. The common building is leased and, whatever the station ownership and utilization arrangements, no problems arise with respect to building lease payments.
5. Successive stages of manufacture are separable in the sense that placing a buffer inventory between them permits work at each stage to proceed independently of the other.
6. The production line is balanced in the following very special sense: Work stations are designed such that, absent untoward events, a steady flow of intermediate product between stations is assured by placing a single, fully occupied worker at each station.

7. Market transactions for intermediate product are very costly.
8. The workers employed under each mode are a random sample of the technically qualified population of which they are a part.
9. Replacement investment occurs routinely and investment for expansion purposes is ignored.

The first four assumptions are relatively uncontroversial. The fifth assumption (separability) means that differences among work modes turn on transactional rather than technological considerations. Coupling this with the one-man-each-station condition (assumption 6) effectively means that the technology associated with the putting-out system is not inferior; rather, the same technology is feasible for and is common to all modes.

As noted, the one-man-each-station assumption is very special. It serves to concentrate attention on transaction cost issues, which have hitherto been neglected, and suppresses technological considerations, the importance of which have previously been exaggerated. Redressing the imbalance by way of the one-man-each-station device scarcely yields a "representative" outcome. It is nevertheless noteworthy that the very same transaction cost attributes of work organization that this device serves to isolate also appear in the multiperson station context. The assumption will accordingly be retained throughout the chapter. Pat Hudson's remarks regarding organization and technology, made in conjunction with her assessment of proto-industrialization, are instructive—"considerable economies in costs could be achieved . . . without technical change" (1981, p. 46). Indeed she asserts, and thereafter demonstrates, that "much early factory development occurred in order to achieve organizational economies and efficiencies and not according to technological dictates" (Hudson, 1981, p. 46).[6]

The assumption that intermediate product markets work badly focuses attention on the transactional properties of *internal* organization. If market alternatives to internal exchange could be exercised at slight cost, choice among alternative internal modes becomes less important, since market relief can always be obtained when internal modes threaten to break down. Assumption 7 forecloses that possibility.

The assumption that the workers employed under each mode are a random sample of the population precludes the possibility that workers will match preferences toward work modes in a discriminating way. Thus although certain work modes may be competitively viable if they are staffed

---

[6]Hudson's views are usefully contrasted with those of another economic historian, S. R. H. Jones (1982). As set out elsewhere, I maintain that Jones's reliance on technology to explain work organization does not wash (Williamson, 1983). His noncomparative analysis is unpersuasive.

with workers with *special* attributes, that is foreclosed by the random assignment stipulation wherein all modes are assessed with respect to a common workforce.

Assumption 9 permits new investment issues to be set aside; attention is focused on the operating and adaptive attributes of alternative modes instead. That has two advantages. First, the investment properties of alternative ownership arrangements can be and have been investigated within the neoclassical framework. The studies of Vanek (1970), Meade (1972), and Furubotn (1976) all confirm that collective ownership models are beset with investment problems. Second, the operating and adaptive attributes of alternative work modes have been relatively neglected in the prior literature. Omitting investment from the performance attributes under scrutiny serves to compensate for that imbalance.

So much for the assumptions; I turn now to a description of alternative modes. Six different modes are described, first in ownership and then in contracting terms. Both for transaction cost purposes and for purposes of studying hierarchy, the latter is more basic. Ownership, however, is the more familiar way of describing work modes and will be employed first.

3.2 *Alternative Modes/Ownership*

Three types of station ownership relations—entrepreneurial, collective ownership, and capitalist—with two variants within each will be considered.

a. ENTREPRENEURIAL MODES

Entrepreneurial modes are ones in which each station is owned and operated by a specialist.

1. *Putting-Out system.* A merchant-coordinator supplies the raw materials, owns the work-in-process inventories, and makes contracts with the individual entrepreneurs, each of whom performs one of the basic operations at his home using his own equipment. Material is moved from station to station (home to home) in batches under the direction of the merchant-coordinator.

The Putting-Out system has been described by Landes as follows:

[M]erchant-manufacturers "put out" raw materials—raw wool, yarn, metal rods, as the case might be—to dispersed cottage labor, to be worked up into finished or semifinished products. Sometimes the household was responsible for more than one step in the production process: spinning and weaving were a typical combination. But the system was also compatible with the most refined division of labor, and in the cutlery manufacture of Solingen or Thiers or in the needle trade of Iserlohn, the manufacturing process was broken down into as many as a dozen stages, with each cottage shop specializing in one. Putting-Out was a major step on the path to industrial capitalism. For one thing, it brought industrial organization closer to the modern division between employers who own the capital and workers who sell their labor. To be sure, most domestic weavers owned their loom and nailers their forge. They were not, however, independent entrepreneurs selling their products in the open market; rather they were hirelings, generally tied to a particular employer, to whom they agreed to furnish a given amount of work at a price stipulated in advance. [Landes, 1966, p. 12]

2. *Federated.* Stations are located side by side in a common facility. Intermediate product is transferred across stages according to contract. So as to avoid the need for supervision or continuous coordination, buffer inventories are introduced at each station. Subject to the condition that buffer inventories do not fall below prescribed levels, in which event penalties are assessed, each worker proceeds at his own pace.

Whether this mode was ever widely used is uncertain and perhaps doubtful. Thus although Landes (1966, p. 14) observes that the practice of "leasing space and power in a mill to individual artisans, each conducting his own enterprise" was common in nineteenth-century England, it is unclear whether intermediate product was traded among stations or if each station was self-contained.

Hudson likewise observes that "the majority of early woolen mills were occupied and run, if not entirely financed, by small manufacturers . . . rather than by wealthy mercantile concerns" and explains this by "the fact that the size and cost of a competitive mill remained small in the woolen branch until well into the 19th century. More importantly, tenancy and multiple tenancy of mills was ubiquitous throughout the period" (1981, p. 48). Again it is unclear whether each tenant was self-contained or there was trade between stations. In principle, however, there could have been trade.

Moreover, it is useful to consider the Federated mode as an evolutionary development, even if only of a hypothetical kind. For one thing, it illustrates the use of comparative analysis of a microanalytic kind to investigate the properties of new forms of organization. Once an abstract mode has been described, its incentive and contracting properties, in relation to other modes, are relatively easy to establish. Additionally, the Federated mode has the attractive property that it preserves considerable worker autonomy.[7] Egalitarian work relations are presumably favored as a consequence.

---

[7]An alternative mode, of a less autonomous kind, would be to transfer the Putting-Out mode into the factory. Thus instead of each work station striking contracts with predecessor and successor stations, all contracts would be mediated instead by a central agent—the merchant-

b. COLLECTIVE OWNERSHIP

Work stations are here owned in common by the entire group of workers.

3. *Communal-emh.* Although stations are owned in common, every man has a claim to the output associated with his own labors. So as to facilitate the acquisition of dexterity and economize on setup costs, each worker engages in batch process manufacture. The orderly movement of product is accomplished by having workers move between successive stations at prescribed intervals (hourly, daily, weekly, or whatever appears most appropriate), each bringing his own work-in-process inventory with him and selling his final product in the market.

The suffix "emh" is used to emphasize that this is an every-man-for-himself system.[8] Thus although workers pool their resources with respect to the ownership of plant and equipment and orderly station moves are accomplished by calendar, there is no specialization among workers. Such a joining of common ownership with an every-man-for-himself rule is what Harold Demsetz (1967, p. 54) has described elsewhere as the communal mode. Unsurprisingly, the combination of community ownership with emh appropriability leads to mixed performance results. To conclude, however, that collective ownership is inferior to private ownership because of defects in the Communal-emh mode is unwarranted. If collective modes, such as the Peer Group, can be devised that have better properties than does Communal-emh, they presumably should be considered.[9]

4. *Peer Groups.* The same ownership arrangement obtains as in the communal-emh mode, but workers are not compensated on the basis of their own product but are paid the average product of the group instead.[10] Workers may rotate among stations or specialize at one or a few stations. Moreover, so as to avoid the need for full group discussion whenever an adaptation has to be made and/or to assure better coordination among the members with respect to work breaks, variable rates of production, and the like, Peer Groups may elect temporary "leaders," who make operating—but not strategic—decisions on

coordinator. Since, except in transportation expense respects, the simple efficiency properties of this mode are substantially identical to those of the Putting-Out system, the Federated mode, with bilateral contracting between stations, has more interesting properties. Freudenberger and Redlich (1964, p. 394) conjecture: "Very probably the first consolidated, centrally managed workshops were little more than concentrated Putting-Out arrangements."

[8]Alternatively, the suffix "eph/h" could be used, where this refers to every-person-for-his/herself. For purposes of economy, I use emh.

[9]Demsetz was concerned with land use rather than batch manufacturing in his discussion of communal ownership. I conjecture that the Peer Group typically has superior properties to the Communal-emh mode for land use as well.

[10]Specifying average group product is unnecessary. Any of a variety of nonmarginal product reward schemes will do.

behalf of the group. It is important, however, that leadership rotate among group members if rigid hierarchical relations are to be avoided.[11] Ernest Mandel's (1968, p. 677) proposal for self-management "in which everybody will take a turn to carry out administrative work in which the differences between 'director' and 'directed' will be abolished" is in that spirit. The joining of a nonmarginal productivity sharing rule with democratic decision-making is what characterizes Peer Group organization.[12]

c. CAPITALIST MODES

Inventories of all kinds (raw materials, intermediate product, finished goods) as well as plant and equipment are owned by a single party under capitalist modes.

5. *Inside Contracting.* The Inside Contracting mode of organization has been succinctly described by Buttrick in the following way:

> Under the system of inside contracting, the management of a firm provided floor space and machinery, supplied raw material and working capital, and arranged for the sale of the final product. The gap between raw material and finished product, however, was filled not by paid employees arranged in [a] descending hierarchy . . . but by [inside] contractors, to whom the production job was delegated. They hired their own employees, supervised the work process, and received a [negotiated] piece rate from the company. [Buttrick, 1952, pp. 201–2]

The Inside Contracting system permits a capitalist who has relatively little technical knowledge to employ his capital productively while limiting his involvement to negotiating contracts with inside contractors, inspecting and coordinating the flow of intermediate product, and taking responsibility for final sales.[13] Howard Gospel observes that Inside Contracting was widely used in batch process systems in the nineteenth century (undated, p. 7), but was never employed on the railways or continuous process industries (p. 9). Robert Eccles (1981) contends that the construction industry is even now organized on Inside Contracting principles.

6. *Authority Relation.* The Authority Relation mode involves capitalist ownership of equipment and inventories coupled with an employment relationship between capitalist and worker. The employment relation is, by design, an incomplete form of contracting. Flexibility is featured as the employee stands ready to accept authority regarding work assignments provided only that the behavior called for falls within the "zone of acceptance" of the

[11]Branko Horvat also features rotation in his discussion of the "socialist firm" (1982, p. 244). In fact, however, as discussed in Chapter 10, the rotation ideal is difficult to implement.

[12]For an elaboration, see Williamson (1975, chap. 3).

[13]For an evaluation of the limits of Inside Contracting, see Williamson (1975, pp. 96–99). Section 6.1 of Chapter 6 briefly discusses this condition.

contract. Joining an organization under the Authority Relation mode thus entails an agreement "that within some limits (defined both explicitly and implicitly by the terms of the employment contract) [the employee] will accept as premises of his behavior orders and instructions supplied to him by the organization" (March and Simon, 1958, p. 90). Rather than enjoy the contractual autonomy of an inside contractor, who is subject to only very loose performance constraints (e.g. that minimum quality standards be met and that buffer inventories not fall below prescribed levels more than a certain percentage of the time), the worker now is subject to much more detailed supervision.

3.3 *Alternative Modes/Contracting*

Contractual differences of two kinds should be distinguished. The first and more important compares alternative modes in terms of their degree of reliance on contractual detail to coordinate production. That is the distinction emphasized here and in section 4. The second has reference to the bargaining relation between the contracting agents. That aspect is examined under 3.4, below.

The six alternative modes under examination in this chapter differ significantly in the degree to which they rely on comprehensive contracting. For three of the modes, contracting (and recontracting) is the exclusive basis by which product is exchanged and interfaces are brought into adjustment. For the other three modes contract is used to provide framework, which is subject to reshaping at the contract renewal interval. Within the context of that framework, however, day-to-day operations are governed by an administrative process. The two different styles of organization will be referred to as continuous contracting and periodic contracting, respectively.

a. CONTINUOUS CONTRACTING

Both types of entrepreneurial modes (Putting-Out and Federated) as well as the Inside Contracting mode rely extensively on contracting. The putter-out and the capitalist serve as the common contracting agent in the first and third instances while the workers in the Federated mode engage in bilateral contracts with the owners of predecessor and successor stations. A common characteristic of contracting modes is that each worker maintains considerable autonomy and, once the terms of the contract are struck, lays claims to a distinct profit stream. Since the gains of one agent are frequently made at the expense of another, relations among the parties are of a highly calculative kind.

The problems with such contracting modes are of two kinds. First, can the requisite complex contract be described, negotiated, and enforced in a low-cost manner? Bounded rationality considerations preclude comprehensive contracting from being realized. Confronted with the infeasibility of such complete contracting, the hazards of incomplete contracting then have to be addressed.

Since bargaining relations between successive stations are necessarily of a small numbers kind, bilateral monopoly problems abound. To be sure, a long-term, recurring relationship between the parties is contemplated. Unrestrained, myopic subgoal pursuit is accordingly discouraged. But it is unrealistic to expect autonomous parties to adapt to unforeseen, hence unplanned, circumstances in a joint profit maximizing way without first settling their respective claims on profit streams through intensive, self-interested bargaining. Merely to transfer a transaction out of the market and organize it internally does not, without more, harmonize exchange. The prospect and actuality of such recurrent bargaining is a serious impediment to autonomous internal contracting work modes.

b. PERIODIC CONTRACTING

There is no exchange of intermediate product among members of Communal-emh firms, so there is little occasion for contracting under that mode. *Ad hoc* contracts might, however, be negotiated if workers were to become disabled, since work-in-process inventories would otherwise stand idle. Also, original investment, reinvestment, and maintenance agreements will have to be worked out. Although those are not trivial matters, the problems of recurring contracting that arise in connection with day-to-day operations in each of the contracting modes described previously do not appear.

Members of Peer Groups have even less need for contracting. Work left undone by a disabled worker would be completed by his associates. To be sure, membership affiliation and disaffiliation terms would have to be reached. But no bilateral contracting between successive stations on operating matters would occur. Democratic decision-making, effected by the rotating leader or by full group discussion, is used to bring station interfaces into adjustment.

Contracting under the Authority Relation is apt to be somewhat more complete, in that explicit and implicit understandings regarding the zone of acceptance of the employment relation (Barnard, 1938; Simon, 1957) need to be reached. Once agreement has been reached, however, this is an essentially noncontractual mode. Adaptations of an operating kind are made within the framework of that rather general contract, whereby boss and worker essentially agree to "tell and be told." Strategic decisions affecting the overall configuration of the enterprise are mainly left to the boss's discretion.

3.4 *The Degree of Hierarchy*

The degree of hierarchy is usually assessed in decision-making respects. Where the responsibility for effecting adaptations is concentrated on one or a few agents, hierarchy is relatively great. Where instead adaptations are taken by individual agents or are subject to collective approval, hierarchy is slight. A less common but nonetheless useful way to characterize hierarchy is in contractual terms. If one or a few agents are responsible for negotiating all contracts, the contractual hierarchy is great. If instead each agent negotiates each interface separately, the contractual hierarchy is weak.[14] Although there is a strong, positive rank correlation between the two ways of characterizing hierarchy for the work modes investigated here, the correlation is not perfect. What is perhaps more interesting is that ownership is imperfectly correlated with hierarchies of both kinds. Using E, Co, and Cap to denote entrepreneurial, collective, and capitalist modes respectively, and using braces to denote ties (or near ties), the rank ordering of modes from least to most hierarchical in contractual and decision-making respects is as follows:

DEGREE OF HIERARCHY (LEAST TO MOST)

Contractual		*Decision-making*	
(1)	{ Federated (E) Communal-emh (Co) Peer Group (Co)	(1)	{ Federated (E) Communal-emh (Co)
(2)	Putting-Out (E)	(2)	{ Putting-Out (E) Inside Contracting (Cap)
(3)	{ Inside Contracting (Cap) Authority Relation (Cap)	(3)	Peer Group (Co)
		(4)	Authority Relation (Cap)

There is no central contracting agent in the Federated, Communal-emh, or Peer Group modes of organization, so a contractual hierarchical relationship is altogether absent for them. By contrast, there is a central agent for

---

[14]Note in this connection that the term "contractual hierarchy" has reference to the relation between the contracting agents, not to the reliance on contracting to effect adaptations. Modes that are described above as periodic may (and some do) have strong hierarchical properties at contract renewal intervals.

the other three modes. Although characterizing the hierarchical relation between central agent and workers is not simple, a plausible case for the
relations shown between Putting-Out, Inside Contracting, and the Authority
Relation can be made in terms of bargaining strength of workers vis-à-vis the
central agent at the contract renewal interval. That varies with (1) the extent to
which workers have acquired firm specific skills and knowledge, (2) collective organization among workers, and (3) physical asset ownership.

Skill acquisition is the same under all three central agent modes, since
each involves specialization in identical degree. Collective organization may
be slightly stronger under the Authority Relation, since workers here are less
autonomous than under Putting-Out (where they are dispersed) and Inside
Contracting (where they appropriate separate profit streams). Physical assets
are owned by each worker under Putting-Out, but the central agent owns the
stations in both instances under the Authority Relation and Inside Contracting. The upshot is that the contractual hierarchy is weak for Putting-Out,
while the Authority Relation and Inside Contracting are somewhat stronger in
contractual hierarchy respects.

Consider now the decision-making hierarchy. There is no command
relation whatsoever between the members of the Federated and Communal-
emh modes. The former is governed by rules and bilateral contractual relations; the latter is governed by rules and democratic decision-making. A
relatively weak command relation exists for Inside Contracting and the Putting-Out modes. The central agent to the contracts can appeal to the workers
to adapt in coordinated ways to changed circumstances, but the contracts
govern as responsibility for operating matters has been extensively delegated.
Thus bargaining and bribes may be needed if interim changes favored by the
central agent are to be effected. The Peer Group acknowledges the benefits of
a command structure by designating a leader to coordinate day-to-day affairs.
The leadership position turns over regularly, however, and strategic decisions
are reached only after a full group discussion. Democratic decision-making
effectively prevails. The Authority Relation posits at the outset that a superi-
or–subordinate relation will govern in both operating and strategic respects.
To be sure, the zone of acceptance of the employment relation, within which
workers will accept orders without resistance, is limited by formal and informal agreement. But a command hierarchy is a prominent feature of the Authority Relation.

Although capitalist modes are more hierarchical than collective ownership modes from a contractual point of view, the more critical hierarchy for
performance purposes is the decision-making hierarchy. The observed relation between ownership and hierarchy is very weak in decision-making respects. The least hierarchical modes, Federated and Communal-emh, are of

different ownership kinds (entrepreneurial and collective ownership, respectively). The Peer Group, Putting-Out, and Inside Contracting modes have intermediate degrees of hierarchy, and each is from a different ownership class. Although the most hierarchical decision-making mode is the capitalist mode, the next strongest command hierarchy features collective ownership.

4. A Comparative Institutional Assessment

The issue to be addressed here is: Socioeconomic attributes of the enterprise aside, do alternative work modes differ systematically in efficiency respects? A set of simple efficiency criteria is proposed first. Crude rankings of work modes with respect to those criteria are then attempted.

4.1 *Simple Efficiency Criteria*

None of the eleven efficiency measures described below is unfamiliar. Not only will each be recognized as a relevant efficiency dimension, but, at one time or another, the ramifications of each for the organization of work have been discussed previously by others. What has been missing is an overview of the issues. No single mode has been systematically assessed with respect to all of the eleven criteria. Neither has there been an effort to make comparisons across modes in terms of the criteria.

The eleven efficiency indicators are usefully grouped into three types: attributes associated with the flow of product, the efficiency with which workers are assigned to tasks, and the incentive properties of alternative modes. Note that each of the eleven performance statements that follow is of a *ceteris paribus* kind.

    a. PRODUCT FLOW[15]

Transportation expense, buffer inventory requirements, and the "leakage" of product at successive processing stages are the matters to be evaluated here.

    1. *Transportation expense.* The physical transport of work-in-process inventories from one station to the next is costly. *Ceteris paribus,* modes that economize on transportation expense are favored.

[15]These product flow economies are often advanced as the reason for supplanting the Putting-Out system with the factory. See Babbage (1835, pp. 135, 213, 219) and Freudenberger and Redlich (1964, p. 395). As described below, however, there is much more to it than this.

2. *Buffer inventories.* Temporal separability between successive work stations is effected by creating a buffer inventory. Modes that economize on the level of buffer inventories are favored.

3. *Interface leakage.* Interface leakage has reference to actual or effective losses of product during manufacture. Modes are favored that, at low cost, discourage embezzlement and/or deter the disguise of the true quality attributes of intermediate product as product is transferred across stages.

b. ASSIGNMENT ATTRIBUTES

Assignment issues of three kinds arise. First, there is the matter of assigning workers to work stations. Second is the issue of leadership. Third is the matter of contracting with nonoperating specialists.

4. *Station assignments.* Talents will be effectively utilized to the extent that workers are assigned to tasks for which they are relatively well suited. This is a specialization of labor issue. In the normal case where workers are not equally skilled in every task, modes that make discriminating job assignments on the basis of comparative advantage are favored.

5. *Leadership.* Modes vary in the degree to which coordination is required and the efficacy with which leadership assignments are made. Modes that economize on coordination needs and make discriminating leadership assignments are favored.

6. *Contracting.* The capacity to aggregate demands and contract with specialists to serve the needs of many stations (e.g. maintenance specialists)[16] is the issue here. Modes in which such contracting is easily accomplished are favored.

c. INCENTIVE ATTRIBUTES

Differential steady state and intertemporal incentives give rise to performance differences. Of special interest are:

7. *Work intensity.* Work intensity refers to the amount of productive energy expended on the job. Modes that discourage workers from malingering are favored.

8. *Equipment utilization.* The issue is whether equipment is utilized

[16]Among the advantages of the factory identified by Baines (1835, p. 460) and Babbage (1835, pp. 214–15) was the fact that it allowed specialists to perform maintenance functions on a number of machines in a single location.

with appropriate care. Modes that disfavor equipment abuse and neglect are favored.

9. *Local shock responsiveness.* Local shocks are those which affect an individual work station. Work stoppages due to machine breakdown or worker illness are examples. Modes that facilitate quick recovery are favored.

10. *Local innovation.* Local innovations involve process improvements at individual stations. Modes that promote local cost economizing process changes are preferred.

11. *System responsiveness.* The capacity to respond to system shocks and to recognize and implement system innovations (of process, product, or organizational kinds) are the matters of interest here.[17] Modes that adapt easily to changing market circumstances and permit systems improvements to be made without requiring extensive contract renegotiation are favored.

4.2 *Efficiency Comparisons*

Although there are some dimensions for which best or worst efficiency ratings are easily made (e.g. the Putting-Out mode has the worst transportation expense features; the Communal-emh mode, where workers move successively across stations and appropriate the fruits of their own labors, has the best work intensity and interface leakage properties but is worst in equipment utilization respects; the Authority Relation has the best system responsiveness properties; and so on), there is little to be gained by using a fourfold ranking system (best, good, poor, worst) rather than a simpler bivariate ranking in which best or good modes are assigned the value 1 and poor or worst modes are rated 0.[18]

Bivariate assignments for each of the simple efficiency dimensions are reported in Table 9–1, where modes are grouped according to ownership type. Although no detailed rationale for the assignments is attempted here, one is reported elsewhere (Williamson, 1976, pp. 30–50). Most of the assign-

[17]These could be treated as separate performance categories. As it turns out, the rankings of modes across system shock and system innovation dimensions are substantially identical, hence the composite system responsiveness category.

[18]For an earlier rating scheme in which the fourfold assignments were used, see Williamson (1976). For earlier efforts to assess the efficiency of alternative organizing modes by rank ordering their efficiency properties, see S. H. Udy, Jr. (1970) and Amartya Sen (1975, chap. 3). Both are concerned with broader economic development issues (Udy from an anthropological point of view) than are of concern to me here; and both are of limited immediate relevance to an assessment of batch process manufacturing—though Sen might be extended in that direction.

Table 9–1. Simple Efficiency Properties of Alternative Modes, Ownership Grouping

Mode	Product Flow Attributes			Assignment Attributes			Incentive Attributes				
	Transportation Expense	Buffer Inventories	Interface Leakage	Station	Leadership	Contracting	Work Intensity	Equipment Utilization	Local Responsiveness	Local Innovation	System Responsiveness
Entrepreneurial											
Putting-Out	0	0	0	1	1	0	1	1	0	1	0
Federated	1	0	0	1	0	0	1	1	0	1	0
Collective											
Communal-emh	1	0	1	0	1	0	1	0	0	0	0
Peer Group	1	1	1	0	0	1	0	1	1	1	1
Capitalist											
Inside Contracting	1	0	0	1	1	1	1	0	0	1	0
Authority Relation	1	1	1	1	1	1	0	1	1	0	1

ments are nevertheless transparent or are evident from the discussions of ownership comparisons and contracting comparisons that appear below.

a. OWNERSHIP COMPARISONS

The Putting-Out and Federated modes, which are the entrepreneurial ownership modes, have rather poor product flow attributes, mixed assignment attributes, and are indistinguishable in incentive respects. Inasmuch as the Federated mode involves concentrating work stations at a common location, transportation expense economies are realized over the Putting-Out mode. Buffer inventories for each mode are high, however—though the reasons differ. For the Putting-Out mode, inventories are high because each station works on its own schedule (subject to daily or weekly output agreements), and product is moved in discrete shipments. Buffer inventories are high for the Federated mode so as to reduce the temporal dependence on predecessor stages, which are linked by bilateral contracts. Small buffer inventories would predictably result in numerous disputes if, as is commonly the case, it is costly to assess responsibility for delivery failures.

Interface leakage for both entrepreneurial modes is high. Chronic theft and quality problems are reported in connection with the Putting-Out mode (Babbage, 1835, pp. 135, 219; Freudenberger and Redlich, 1964, p. 395; Marglin, 1974, p. 51). Theft is not a problem with the Federated mode, but quality control is. Not only is there an incentive for each stage to shade quality, but there are complex attribution problems when complaints are registered.[19]

The Putting-Out mode has leadership advantages over the Federated mode since there is a central contracting agent. The dispersed location of the stages, however, makes it difficult for leadership to be exercised in contracting, local responsiveness, or system responsiveness respects—hence Putting-Out is rated no better than the Federated mode in those dimensions.

The two collective ownership modes have generally good product flow attributes, rather poor assignment properties, and very different incentive properties. The Communal-emh mode has higher buffer inventory requirements, since each worker moves successively across all stages, taking his own work-in-progress inventory with him. Assuming that setup costs are not negli-

---

[19]Thus if putting a head on a pin depends on the manner in which wire is drawn and straightened but not on pointing, if pointing precedes head attachment in order of progression, and if carelessness in the pointing operation can result in bent shafts, determining the responsibility for the condition of the shafts at the head attachment stage may not be easy: Was the straightening defective or are the bent shafts due to careless handling by the pointer?

gible, each worker will remain at each stage for a considerable period. Inventory requirements thus are correspondingly great.

The Communal-emh mode has excellent work intensity incentives, since every worker appropriates the fruits of his own labors. The Peer Group, by contrast, is subject to free rider abuses. (Although careful screening of candidates for Peer Group membership could serve to check such abuses, that would violate the random assignment assumption.) In other respects, however, the Peer Group has superior incentive properties to the Communal-emh mode. That is because the Peer Group is a cooperative mode whereas the Communal-emh mode is given to aggressive suboptimization.

Such suboptimization is especially evident in the case of equipment utilization. The benefits attributable to careful utilization of equipment are realized mainly by others, while the costs of intensive or careless utilization are shifted mainly to others; adverse incentives proliferate. A complex bargain would have to be struck and policed to alter that adverse outcome. Peer Group members, by contrast, experience no such myopic equipment use incentives. The suboptimization versus cooperative aspects of the two modes explain other incentive differences as well.

The Authority Relation has product flow attributes superior to the other capitalist mode, Inside Contracting. Absent penalties on excess work-in-process inventories, contractors have the incentive to accumulate such inventories so as to realize greater operating autonomy. By contract, the Authority Relation does not need to rely on pecuniary penalties to move inventories: fiat will do. And it can carry low inventories because of its superior responsiveness attributes. Interface leakage is also a problem with Inside Contracting, because contractors have an incentive to suboptimize (shade quality) that is not operative among hourly employees.[20]

Inside Contracting and the Authority Relation have uniformly good assignment attributes. They have very different incentive properties, however, mainly because inside contractors have greater autonomy, appropriate the fruits of their own labors more fully, and need to be bribed to adapt cooperatively, while employees working in an Authority Relation mode are less given to aggressive subgoal pursuit and do not resist adaptations because they do not possess the requisite property rights. Thus inside contractors work intensively and introduce local innovations, but respond to local or system adaptation requirements much less readily. Also since inside contractors do not own the equipment, malutilization may occur.

Specifically, the relevant time horizon to which inside contractors refer

[20]Piece rates for employees under the Authority Relation create worker incentives closer to that of Inside Contracting. More generally, piece rate workers have less incentive to act cooperatively than do hourly workers when adaptations are proposed. This type of limitation of piece rates has not received the attention it deserves.

is the contract termination date. Repairs generating benefits that more than recover costs within the contract interval will be made, but those for which the benefits can be recovered only if the contractor wins the bid for successive contracts will be deferred.[21] Equipment repairs of a major kind will thus be delayed and left to the capitalist at the contract renewal interval. Even minor repairs may be postponed as contract termination dates approach.

b. CONTRACTING COMPARISONS

Consider now Table 9–2, where the same rankings are displayed—only here the modes are grouped by contracting attributes. The striking features are: (1) Continuous contracting modes have generally poor product flow attributes and uniformly poor local and system responsiveness attributes; (2) continuous contracting modes are uniformly good in station assignment, work intensity, and local innovation respects; (3) periodic contracting modes have generally good product flow attributes; and (4) although some periodic contracting modes are good in assignment and incentive respects, no general statements can be made for periodic contracting modes as a group in either of those general categories.

c. AGGREGATION

Aggregation to obtain an overall efficiency rating for each mode requires that the relative importance of the eleven efficiency indicators be addressed. This will obviously vary across industries. Suppose, however, that all are weighted equally and a composite rating is obtained by taking the row sum for each mode. The following rankings then emerge:

Mode	Row sum
Communal-emh	4
Putting-Out	5
Federated	5
Inside Contracting	6
Peer Group	8
Authority Relation	9

Even allowing for the fact that the rankings are very rough, several interesting relations warrant comment:

[21]This assumes the inside contractors are neither compensated for repairs that yield benefits extending beyond the contract termination date nor reimbursed for idle time if the capitalist were to make repairs during the contract interval. The former poses serious benefit estimation problems, while compensating for idle time would set up incentives to utilize equipment carelessly.

Table 9–2. Simple Efficiency Properties at Alternative Modes, Contracting Grouping

Mode	Product Flow Attributes			Assignment Attributes			Incentive Attributes				
	Transportation Expense	Buffer Inventories	Interface Leakage	Station	Leadership	Contracting	Work Intensity	Equipment Utilization	Local Responsiveness	Local Innovation	System Responsiveness
Continuous Contracting Modes											
Putting-Out	0	0	0	1	1	0	1	1	0	1	0
Federated	1	0	0	1	0	0	1	1	0	1	0
Inside Contracting	1	0	0	1	1	1	1	0	0	1	0
Periodic Contracting Modes											
Communal-emh	1	0	1	0	1	0	1	1	0	0	0
Peer Group	1	1	1	0	0	1	0	1	1	1	1
Authority Relation	1	1	1	1	1	1	0	1	1	0	1

1. The Communal-emh mode, which accords workers the greatest degree of job variety and appears to be greatly favored by Marglin,[22] is the least efficient mode. Although it is possible to ascribe the nonexistence of the Communal-emh mode to pernicious efforts by vested interests to annihilate it, a more plausible explanation is that the Communal-emh mode is dragged down by its own efficiency disabilities.

2. The least hierarchical modes, in both contracting and decision-making respects (see subsection 3.4, above), have the worst efficiency properties. By contrast, both the Peer Group and the Authority Relation rely extensively on a decision-making hierarchy—which indeed goes far to explain the superior performance of each. Hostility to hierarchy thus lacks a comparative institutional foundation. There may be more and less preferred types of hierarchy; but hierarchy itself is unavoidable unless efficiency sacrifices are made.[23]

3. The Communal-emh mode aside, periodic contracting modes have efficiency properties superior to continuous contracting modes.

4. Modes are listed roughly in the same order as they appeared historically. Although it is possible to argue that later modes displaced earlier modes because the "interests" were determined to stamp out autonomy, an alternative hypothesis is that successor modes have superior efficiency properties to predecessor modes. The progression from Putting-Out to Inside Contracting to the Authority Relation is especially noteworthy in that respect.

5. Ranking the six modes in terms of power differentials between boss and workers is difficult for lack of a power metric. One nevertheless has the impression that there is a positive rank correlation between row sum efficiency and power. At the same time, that correlation is less than perfect. (Putting-Out, which accords the boss greater power than does the Peer Group or Federated mode, has worse efficiency properties than both.) The best evidence that power is driving organizational outcomes would be a demonstration that less efficient modes that serve to concentrate power displace more efficient modes in which power is more evenly distributed.[24]

5. Power Versus Efficiency

The argument that successive modes of organization represent efficiency advances on earlier modes poses for the radical economics literature a dilemma

---

[22]See Marglin's remarks quoted in section 2, *supra*.

[23]Louis Putterman, who would promote more extensive use of participatory modes, agrees (1982). For a brief discussion, see Williamson (1981); also see Macneil (1974, p. 699).

[24]The issues are discussed further in Chapter 10, where the Peer Group (socialist firm) and Authority Relation (capitalist firm) are examined. Horvat holds that it is necessary to prohibit capitalist firms because the socialist firm "cannot easily survive in a capitalist environment regardless of its *potential* efficiency" (1982, p. 455; emphasis in original).

that was apparent even in Karl Marx. I review some of the consequent tensions here.

5.1 Origins of the Division of Labor

Early in his chapter on the division of labor and manufacture, Marx describes an organization where a capitalist employs a number of artificers. Initially each artificer, with the help of one or two apprentices, "makes the entire commodity, and he consequently performs in succession all the operations necessary . . . in his old handicraft way" (Marx, 1967, p. 337). Except for workshop ownership, that appears to correspond with the Communal-emh mode of organization. This continues until external circumstances change. For example, an "increased quantity of the article has perhaps to be delivered within a given time" (p. 377). As a consequence of the changes, work is temporarily reorganized. "Instead of each man being allowed to perform all the various operations in succession, these operations are changed into disconnected isolated ones, carried on side by side; each is assigned to a different artificer. . . . This accidental repartition gets repeated, develops advantages of its own, and gradually ossifies into a systematic division of labor" (p. 337). The resulting division of labor thus appears to arise as an efficiency response to changing circumstances rather than as a capitalist scheme to divide and conquer.

5.2 The Demise of Putting-Out

Similarly, Harry Braverman reports that the early phases of industrial capitalism "were marked by a sustained effort on the part of the capitalist . . . to buy labor in the same way he bought his raw materials. . . . This attempt took the form of a great variety of subcontracting and 'Putting-Out' systems" (1974, pp. 60–61). Braverman then goes on to observe that the "subcontracting and 'Putting-Out' systems were plagued by problems of irregularity of production, loss of materials in transit and through embezzlement, slowness of manufacture, lack of uniformity and uncertainty of the quality of the product. But most of all, they were limited by their inability to change the processes of production" (p. 63). Unsurprisingly, those early forms of organization were supplanted by others that had better product flow, task assignment, and incentive attributes. Again, however, the changes are driven by efficiency; a pernicious scheme to divide and conquer is not needed to reach those results.

Hudson's account of the differences between the woolen and worsted branches of the textile industry in embezzlement and organizational respects is also instructive. She observes that frauds were responsible for "considerable inefficiencies and diseconomies" under the Putting-Out system in the late eighteenth century. They were more severe in the worsted branch than in woolens, mainly because there were fewer wage workers in woolens "and those there were, tended to be closely supervised in small workshops. In the worsted branch, however, woolcombers commonly embezzled their employers' wool and the spinners reeled 'false' or short yarn. Combinations of operatives were often successful in ensuring that these appropriations continued with impunity" (Hudson, 1981, p. 50). The differential ease of embezzlement contributed to the more rapid transition to factory production in the worsted branch (p. 52).

5.3 *Water Versus Handmills*

Marglin reviews the handmill–watermill controversy in feudal England and observes that the centralization of milling under watermills had contract enforcement advantages over the handmill: "It must have been extremely difficult to prevent the peasant from 'embezzling' the lord's 'rightful' portion of grain if the milling operation took place within the peasant's own home. Bloch mentions the 'lawsuits which grimly pursued their endless and fruitless course, leaving the tenants always the losers'—but *at great expense of time, effort, and money* to the lord as well" (1974, p. 56; emphasis added). Despite the aforementioned costs, Marglin interprets the prohibition of handmills as an exercise of power and a manifestation of class conflict (pp. 55–58) since the handmill was, in his judgment, on a technological parity with the watermill.

There are two problems. First, if the watermills had only policing benefits and offered no technological advantages over handmills, then the obvious way to mill grain would be to concentrate all of the handmills at a central location and insist upon their use there. Inasmuch as handmills were sunk costs, investment in new equipment would thereby be avoided. But second, and more important, assessing the choice of milling technique in technology versus power terms is unacceptable if transaction cost differences are operative—as they plainly were.

Transaction cost disabilities of two types can be associated with the local handmilling of grain. First, actual compensation will differ from reported compensation in favor of those in the peasant population who are most prepared to lie, cheat, and steal. Such a compensation scheme is, among other things, shot through with adverse selection incentives. Second, and related, the embezzlement of grain will elicit protective responses by lords, policing that is costly and is appropriately included in the social calculus.

That is not to say that metering is an unmixed blessing and cannot be taken to excess. It can be and sometimes is. The issues here, however, are not the ones addressed by Marglin but arise in conjunction with the economics of atmosphere (Williamson, 1975, pp. 37–38) and in distinguishing between perfunctory and consummate cooperation (pp. 69–70). Those are important matters with which the organization of work is legitimately concerned. They are briefly considered in Chapter 10, but a much more complete treatment is needed.

5.4 Inside Contracting in Steel

The principal historical study to which Bowles and Gintis (1976) refer is the article by Stone, in which the transformation of the steel industry is examined. According to Stone, the organization of the steel industry in the late nineteenth century corresponded approximately to the Inside Contracting system described and discussed above. The Amalgamated Association of Iron, Steel, and Tin Workers, which was the union to which the skilled workers belonged and was reported to be the strongest union of its day, gave "the skilled workers authority over every aspect of steel production" (Stone, 1974, p. 64). The costly haggling and inflexibility to which Inside Contracting is subject predictably resulted. Operating inefficiency developed, and innovations were suppressed. Examples cited by Stone (1974, pp. 64–65) include the following:

1. The consent and approval of the executive committee within each department was needed to fill a vacant position.
2. The details of the work were subject to recurring dispute.
3. Output per worker was restricted.
4. Production procedures were proscribed: The "proportion of scrap that might be used in running a furnace was fixed; the quality of pig-iron was stated; the puddlers' use of brick and fire clay was forbidden, with exceptions; the labor of assistants was defined."
5. Presumably to perfect and maintain their monopoly over jobs, skilled workers were prohibited from teaching other workers.
6. Changes in the physical plant could not be made without the approval of the executive committee of the union, which prevented the company from realizing greater labor productivity by reorganizing or mechanizing labor tasks.

7. Innovations of a labor-saving kind were discouraged: "The many innovations introduced between 1860 and 1890, of which the most notable was the Bessemer converter, increased the size and capacity of the furnaces and mills, but they generally did not replace men with machines."

The resulting inefficiencies were apparent to the companies. Andrew Carnegie and Henry Clay Frick resolved to challenge the union at Carnegie's Homestead mill, which was reputed to be the strongest lodge of the Amalgamated Association. A lockout was ordered in 1892, and Frick announced that the mill would thenceforth be operated nonunion. Violence resulted, with members of the union pitted against scabs and Pinkerton agents. The support of state and federal governments helped Carnegie and Frick prevail. Whether emboldened by the success of Carnegie and Frick or out of realization that their competitive viability rested on their being likewise able to disaffiliate with the Amalgamated Association, other steel companies challenged and beat the union as well. Association membership, which peaked at twenty-five thousand in 1892, was down to ten thousand in 1898. By 1910 the entire steel industry was nonunion. The effects of breaking the power of the skilled workers are summarized by Stone as follows:

> The decade that followed the Homestead defeat brought unprecedented developments in every stage of steelmaking. The rate of innovation in steel has never been equaled. Electric trolleys, the pig casting machine, the Jones mixer, and mechanical ladle cars transformed the blast furnace. Electric traveling cranes in the Bessemer converter, and the Wellman charger in the open hearth did away with almost all the manual aspects of steel production proper. And electric cars and rising-and-falling tables made the rolling mills a continuous operation. [Stone, 1974, p. 66]

Breaking the union's grip on procedures did not, however, assure the steel industry that its labor force would thereafter be organized efficiently. Such efficiency required that new institutional structures be devised. The objectives of the steps taken seem mainly to have been designed to (1) supply affirmative incentives for productivity, (2) tie the interests of the workers to the firm over the long term, (3) develop the requisite work skills among inexperienced workers, and (4) organize the work to preclude subsequent loss of control by the company. Stone interprets the various steps taken to realize those objectives as pernicious and evidence of a continuing class struggle between workers and employers. But there is another possibility: The incentive to challenge the union in the first place and the efforts to organize labor subsequently were principally geared to achieving efficiency, the rewards for which, once the new methods were imitated by rivals and rates of return were driven down to competitive levels, were diffused throughout society.

Put differently, were it not that the Amalgamated Association had prohibited efficiency gains and impaired efficiency incentives, Carnegie's challenge to the union is plausibly interpreted as a contest for raw power—its purpose being to redistribute income away from workers in favor of capital. Given, however, the large efficiency gains that Stone reports, the efficiency hypothesis (or a combined efficiency-power hypothesis) cannot be rejected. The efforts to organize labor in the post-Homestead era are also broadly consistent with the efficiency hypothesis.

Stone nevertheless asserts that the benefits of reorganization described above could have been realized without the adverse, oppressive effects of hierarchy. She contends that "a system of job rotation, one in which the workers themselves allocated work, would have been just as rational and effective a way of organizing production" (Stone, 1974, p. 66). While the details of such an organizational arrangement are not supplied, the rotation arrangement appears to correspond to the Communal-emh system[25] described in section 3 and evaluated above. That the Communal-emh mode has the worst efficiency properties of all six modes examined in this chapter might be arguable. But that it is shot through with adverse incentives and maladaptive attributes is, I think, beyond dispute.

5.5 *Forward Integration in Meatpacking*

The power approach to vertical integration appears to assume that everything that feasibly can be integrated will be—or at least that is the result that William Ouchi and I reached in attempting to interpret Charles Perrow's views on integration (Williamson and Ouchi, 1981, pp. 321–24). The belief, evidently, is that more integrated systems are more powerful than less. Branco Horvat's position on this is explicit: "Corporations strive for vertical integration in order to control prices and other conditions of supply. . . . Ever expanding corporations try to *internalize all* decisions concerning production, buying, selling, and financing" (1982, pp. 15–16; emphasis added).

The efficiency hypothesis, by contrast, is that vertical integration will occur selectively rather than comprehensively, that mistaken vertical integration can rarely be sustained, and that more efficient modes will eventually supplant less efficient modes—though entrenched power interests can sometimes delay the displacement. Evidence bearing on the selectivity hypothesis is developed in Chapter 5.

A particularly interesting confrontation between efficiency and power

[25]Possibly, however, Stone intends that a Peer Group with rotation arrangements be organized instead.

occurred in the meatpacking industry late in the nineteenth century. Here, moreover, power was aligned *against* integration.

Gustavus Swift believed that the practice of shipping Western cattle to Eastern markets alive rather than slaughtered and dressed was unnecessarily expensive. He proposed to realize economies by butchering the animals in the West and shipping the meat east in refrigerated cars, where it would be received and distributed from a network of refrigerated storage houses. Not only did this involve investments in specialized assets, the value of which would be limited should Swift's strategy fail, but it met determined opposition:

> Railroads, startled by the prospect of losing their livestock business, which was an even greater producer of revenue than grain on the west to east routes, refused to build refrigerated cars. When Swift began to construct his own, the Eastern Trunk Line Association refused to carry them. Only by using the Grand Trunk, then outside of the Association, was Swift able to bring his cars east. At the same time he had to combat boycotts by local wholesalers, who in 1886 formed the National Butchers' Protective Association to fight "the trust." These butchers attempted to exploit a prejudice against eating fresh meat that had been killed days or even weeks before, more than a thousand miles away. [Chandler, 1977, p. 300]

Despite the opposition from the railroads and butchers, Swift's "high quality and low prices" combined with "careful scheduling" prevailed (p. 300). Other packers soon thereafter realized that "if they were to compete with Swift in the national market they must follow his lead" (p. 301). Efficiency thus evidently swamped the resistance of entrenched power interests— though this is not to say that Swift won easily. Had the efficiency gains been much smaller or had the entrenched interests been better organized, power might well have defeated Swift. I submit, however, that *large* efficiency differences place entrenched interests under great strain. (The aphorism "if you can't beat them, join them" is often the way by which such interests secure relief.)

6. Concluding Remarks

Victor Goldberg observes that "conflict and struggle are . . . fundamental elements of the radical's world view, and it is, therefore, quite natural for issues of power to surface in their analyses." He further holds that the "lesson the nonradicals should draw from the radical account is to take issues of power seriously" (1980, p. 269). My own view is that there is merit in all explanations that add to our understanding of complex phenomena. The main problem with power is that the concept is so poorly defined that power can be and is invoked to explain virtually anything. Such an undisciplined approach to the study of complex social science phenomena is clearly unsatisfactory. A serious effort at operationalization is greatly needed if power is to be properly evaluated.

To be sure, efficiency analysis stands in need of refinement as well. A systematic strategy for assessing the transaction cost consequences of alternative modes of contracting has nevertheless been emerging. The comparative institutional assessment of alternative internal modes attempted here involves:

1. Ascertaining where trading is feasible and where it is not. This requires that tasks be described in sufficient microanalytic detail to disclose what parts of the task are technologically separable.
2. Identifying alternative work modes and describing their operation in sufficient detail to permit their transaction cost properties to be assessed.
3. Identifying the relevant set of performance dimensions with respect to which alternative modes are to be assessed.

This chapter demonstrates that each step can be implemented and that the piecemeal defects of prior studies (because interfaces were not identified, because mode comparisons were unnecessarily restricted, or because some of the relevant performance dimensions were omitted) can be avoided. Although I focus attention on a rather simple task—pinmaking—it is the obvious task to consider, given the history of the work mode literature. Indeed, failure to address pinmaking would certainly raise issues of noncomparability between my assessment and earlier studies.

The noncomparability of tasks ought not, however, to be exaggerated. The organization of any batch process manufacturing activity poses very similar transaction cost issues. Additionally, although technology may be either more (as with petroleum refining) or less (as with the organization of a legal office) determinative of work modes when other than batch process manufacturing is considered, the same microanalytic approach for evaluating work modes applies quite generally. It entails identifying the relevant transaction cost dimensions, describing alternative modes for organizing the transactions in question, and performing a comparative institutional assessment. Thus although both modes and transaction cost attributes will vary among activities, the same microanalytic and comparative institutional research strategy that is employed in this book has broad applicability.[26]

[26]I conjecture that this approach will make greatest headway among those students of organization who (1) are concerned with real organizational phenomena, (2) adopt a comparative orientation, and (3) believe that the microanalytics matter. Those, by contrast, who regard

One of the striking results of this chapter is that ownership is only weakly related to hierarchy. That holds both in contractual and command hierarchy respects. Additionally, if simple aggregation is permitted, the modes that have the worst performance attributes are those with the weakest hierarchical properties. The question of optimal work organization is thus poorly posed when it is put in terms of hierarchy or its absence. Attention ought to be shifted instead to whether reliance on hierarchy is excessive (generates adverse side effects) and whether appointments to hierarchical positions are made in a way that both promotes efficiency and commands general respect. My examination of those issues continues in the following chapter.

---

economic organization in noncomparative terms and who are not persuaded that the details matter are apt to remain skeptics. Raymond Russell's forthcoming article (''Employee Ownership and Internal Governance,'' *Journal of Economic Behavior and Organization*) and book (*Sharing Ownership in the Workplace*) are illustrative of the former. Russell is very much concerned with the particulars of work organization and has written to me as follows: ''Since I have spent most of the last twelve years researching employee-owned firms, I was eager to defend my field against some discouraging remarks and implications that I found in your work. The more I argued with you in successive drafts of the article, however, the more I myself began to see these organizations in transactional terms'' (personal communication). Needless to say, I am encouraged by such developments. As I report in a forthcoming book of my essays (titled *Economic Organization*), my own views on managerial discretion were deeply and permanently transformed when, in the late 1960s, I first read Alfred D. Chandler, Jr's. influential book, *Strategy and Structure*.

The forthcoming treatment of law firm organization by Ronald Gilson and Robert Mnookin (''Sharing Among the Human Capitalists: An Economic Analysis of the Corporate Law Firm and How Partners Share Profits,'' *Stanford Law Review*) also illustrates the application of comparative economic analysis of transactions to nonmanufacturing activity.

CHAPTER 10

The Organization of Labor

Inasmuch as neoclassical economics takes institutions as given, the manner in which labor is organized is mainly of interest only as it relates to monopoly power. Control over entry (through unions, licensure, and the like) is thus of interest, but the microanalytics of labor organization are beyond the purview of orthodox analysis. By contrast, both the transaction cost and the socialist approaches to labor organization maintain that the governance structures within which labor is organized have important economic and social ramifications. The transaction cost approach to labor organization is developed here.

Some of the central issues with which a theory of labor organization should be concerned are identified in section 1. Just as the dimensions of intermediate product market transactions are critical in assessing their governance needs, so likewise are the dimensions of labor market transactions critical to the study of labor organization. The underlying dimensions and governance needs of labor market transactions are examined in section 2. Labor unions are considered in sections 3 and 4. The producer cooperative dilemma is addressed in section 5. The matter of dignity is briefly considered in section 6. The principal implications of the transaction cost approach are summarized in section 7.

1. Central Issues

A central thesis of this book is that a common theory of contract applies to transactions of all types—labor market transactions included. The organization of labor is nevertheless a very complicated matter. No single approach to the study of labor organization is at present adequate—which is to say that the study of these matters is usefully informed from several points of view.[1] Transaction cost economics focuses on efficiency aspects. Among the areas in which potential benefits might be realized through collective organization are wage and benefit determination; the enhancement of productivity through human asset development; dispute settlement; efficacious adaptation; and regard for dignity.

A discriminating approach to labor organization will recognize that the magnitudes of those benefits vary with the circumstances. One of the purposes of this chapter is to ascertain how the potential gains vary. That leads to two related questions: What are the governance structure needs of different transactions? What are the ramifications for union organization? In addition to the benefits, the potential hazards of collective organization have to be considered. Those are briefly assessed as well.

2. An Abstract Approach

Although it is sometimes argued that there is a single preferred way by which to organize labor, casual inspection discloses that labor organization is highly varied. An explanation for the differences would plainly add to our understanding. The transaction cost approach rests on the proposition that governance structures for labor must be matched with the attributes of labor transactions in a discriminating way if transaction cost economizing is to be accomplished. To use a simple structure to govern a complex transaction will predictably have disruptive consequences—and possibly fracture the relationship—while to use a complex structure to govern a simple transaction is to incur excessive costs. The efficiency orientation employed here is broadly consistent with Frank Knight's view that

> . . . men in general, and within limits, wish to behave economically, to make their activities *and their organization* "efficient" rather than wasteful. This fact does deserve the utmost emphasis; and an adequate definition of the science of economics . . . might well make it explicit that the main relevance of the discus-

---

[1]Some of the leading approaches to labor organization that help to inform the issues are considered in Section 3.

sion is found in its relation to social policy, assumed to be directed toward the end indicated, of increasing economic efficiency, of reducing waste. [Knight, 1941, p. 252; emphasis added]

2.1 Dimensions

a. GOVERNANCE

Recall that the principal dimensions for describing transactions are frequency, uncertainty, and asset specificity. The transactions of interest here are ones of a recurring kind. Accordingly, frequency will be set aside and emphasis placed on uncertainty and asset specificity.

For the reasons given previously, the labor market transactions for which continuity between firm and worker are valued are those for which a firm-specific human asset condition develops. Note in this connection that skill acquisition is a necessary but not a sufficient condition for asset specificity features to appear. The nature of the skills also matters. Thus physicians, engineers, lawyers, and the like possess valued skills for which they expect to be compensated, but such skills do not by themselves pose a governance issue. Unless those skills are deepened and specialized to a particular employer, neither employer nor employee has a productive interest in maintaining a continuing employment relation. The employer can easily hire a substitute and the employee can move to alternative employment without loss of productive value.[2]

Mere deepening of skills through job experience does not by itself pose a problem either. Thus typing skills may be enhanced by practice, but if they are equally valued by current and potential employers there is no need to devise special protection for an ongoing employment relation. Knowledge of a particular firm's filing system, by contrast, may be highly specific (non-transferable). Continuity of the employment relation in the latter case is a source of added value.[3]

Thus whereas neoclassical reasoning links skills to productivity and

[2]This ignores transitional problems that may be associated with job relocation. All employees experience them, hence protection against arbitrary dismissal is sought. But the further question is what *additional* safeguards are warranted. That matter turns on human asset specificity.

[3]Alfred Marshall was aware of this condition:

> [T]he head clerk in a business has an acquaintance with men and things, the use of which he could in some cases sell at a high price to rival firms. But in other cases it is of a kind to be of no value save in the business in which he already is; and then his departure would perhaps injure it by several times the value of his salary, while probably he could not get half that salary elsewhere. [Marshall, 1948, p. 626]

compensation, transaction cost reasoning introduces organizational considerations. Specifically, skills that are acquired in a learning-by-doing fashion and that are imperfectly transferable across employers have to be *embedded in a protective governance structure* lest productive values be sacrificed if the employment relation is unwittingly severed.[4] The argument here is related to but is usefully distinguished from Gary Becker's (1962) argument that compensation structures vary systematically with human asset specificity. That is correct as far as it goes, but it ignores important organizational features of the employment relation. Rules governing ports of entry, job ladders, bumping, grievance procedures, and the like are all part of the employment relation broadly conceived (Doeringer and Piore, 1971) but are not treated by Becker. Transaction cost economics maintains that governance structures must be crafted more carefully as the degree of human asset specificity increases.

The second dimension on which the study of labor market transactions turns is that of uncertainty. As with intermediate product market transactions, an increase in parametric uncertainty is troublesome mainly for transactions in which human asset specificity is great. Possible transition costs aside,[5] neither party has a continuity interest in transactions in which asset specificity is negligible. Presumably, therefore, increases in parametric uncertainty will be reflected in the original terms upon which such bargains are struck. But the governance of transactions in which asset specificity is slight will otherwise be unaffected.

Transactions in which continuity is valued, by contrast, are placed under greater stress as parametric uncertainty increases. Such transactions will have to be adapted more frequently or extensively to restore a position on the shifting contract curve. Such contracts will therefore be negotiated more carefully. Also, as will be discussed in section 3 below, the contract renewal interval may be shortened. Whatever the length of the contract interval, management will have greater latitude of adjustment (e.g. be less encumbered by work rules) where uncertainty is great than would otherwise be the case. Lest such latitude be exercised irresponsibly, procedural safeguards to provide for the early and equitable disposition of grievances become more important.

The argument thus far mainly repeats that made earlier in conjunction

[4]The concern here is with what Knight has referred to as "the internal problems of the corporation, the protection . . . of members and adherents against each other's predatory propensities" (1965, p. 254).

[5]These transition costs are asymmetrically concentrated on the employee side of the transaction. They mainly arise in conjunction with the disruptive effects on family and social life that job termination and reemployment sometimes produces. Protection against arbitrary dismissals is thus warranted even for nonspecific jobs. Provided, however, that short notice requirements are respected, the firm cannot be said to have a symmetrical interest in preventing unexplained quits.

with intermediate product markets. The organization of labor, however, poses additional complications that have not previously been encountered. They arise in conjunction with the measurement of work product.

b. MEASUREMENT

Although measurement issues of both *ex ante* screening and *ex post* execution kinds are germane to the organization of labor, the latter are given principal emphasis here. The team organization problems to which Alchian and Demsetz (1972) refer and the issues dealt with by Ouchi in distinguishing between "behavior control" and "output control" (1978, pp. 174–75) are the matters of interest. The complication with which Alchian and Demsetz are concerned has its origins in a condition of technological nonseparability. The condition was earlier recognized by Marx (1967, vol. 1, chap. 13) and is illustrated by Alchian and Demsetz with the manual freight loading example:

> Two men jointly lift cargo into trucks. Solely by observing the total weight loaded per day, it is impossible to determine each person's marginal productivi-ty. . . . The output is yielded by a team, by definition, and it is not a *sum* of separable outputs of each of its members. [1972, p. 779]

Where tasks are nonseparable in that sense, individual productivity can-not be assessed by measuring output. An assessment of inputs is needed. Sometimes it may be inferred by observing the intensity with which an indi-vidual works, the aspect emphasized by Alchian and Demsetz. A monitor is created so as to discourage shirking. Often, however, the assessment of inputs is much more subtle than effort-accounting. Does the employee cooperate in helping to devise and implement complex responses to unanticipated circum-stances, or does he attend to own or local goals at the expense of the others?[6] Those concerns are especially great where the members of the team develop idiosyncratic working relationships with one another, in which case no single member can be replaced without having disruptive effects on the productivity

---

[6]Alchian and Demsetz discuss a related condition in the context of artists and professionals, where

> . . . watching a man's activities is not a good clue to what he is actually thinking or doing with his mind. . . . [I]t is difficult to manage and direct a lawyer in the preparation and presentation of a case. . . . [D]etailed direction in the preparation of a law case would require in much greater detail that the monitor prepare the case himself. [1972, p. 788]

The issue here is less nonseparability between workers than it is ambiguity in the creativity with which an individual applies himself. These metering problems become progressively more diffi-cult in higher reaches of the management hierarchy. They apply, however, in some degree almost everywhere. I effectively hold creativity constant in my treatment of work organization below. A more complete treatment would examine a three-way classification of work—asset specificity, separability, and creativity—rather than the two-way classification that I employ.

of the unit. More complex teams in which mutual motivation and internal monitoring are encouraged are apt to take shape in such circumstances.

c. A PROVISIONAL MATCH

Letting k_0 and k_1 represent low and high degrees of human asset specificity and S_0 and S_1 represent separable and nonseparable work relations, respectively, the following four-way classification of internal governance structures is tentatively proposed:[7]

1. k_0, S_0: internal spot market

Human assets that are nonspecific and separable are meeting market tests continuously for their jobs. Neither workers nor firms have an efficiency interest in maintaining the association. Workers can move between employers without loss of productivity, and firms can secure replacements without incurring start-up costs.[8] No special governance structure is thus devised to sustain the relation. Instead, the employment relation is terminated when dissatisfaction by either party occurs. An internal spot market labor relation may be said to exist. Examples include migrant farm workers and custodial employees. Professional employees whose skills are nonspecific (certain draftsmen and engineers) also fall in this category. Such jobs appear to be of the kind that Arthur Okun had in mind in his reference to the use of "brokers" to help supply labor where "the jobs at stake . . . require unskilled workers (like farm workers) or transitory workers (like office fill-ins) or involve formally graded skills (as is the case when unions certify craftsmen in construction, longshoring, and printing)" (1981, p. 63).

---

[7]Alchian's more recent treatment also makes provision for both separability and asset specificity features:

> Team production makes measurability of *marginal* products difficult, but not impossible. Even without team production, the contribution of one person in an exchange may not be economically measurable in all pertinent characteristics. If one party can gain by shirking in its performance, this *means* the other party is "specific" to the shirker by the circumstances. This mode of expression emphasizes the specificity of one resource to another, but it obscures the significance of measurement of performance. On the other hand, if measurement of performance is emphasized, then the significance of expropriability of coalition, interspecific resource quasi-rents is obscured. Even if measurement were no problem at all, opportunistic behavior can occur blatantly because contracts are not costless to enforce, though I presume that without substantial expropriable quasi-rents of specific resources, blatant defiant cheating is not likely to be a serious problem. [1984, p. 39]

One might therefore define the firm in terms of two features: the measurable detectability of *input* performance in team production *and* the opportunity for expropriation of quasi-rents of interspecific resources.

[8]Arthur Ross observes, "Until the 1920s, employers made no particular attempts to conserve manpower. . . . So long as the unskilled hand was replaceable, the employer suffered no great loss when the employee quit" (Ross, 1958, p. 911).

2. k_0, S_1: primitive team

Although the human assets here are nonspecific, individual output cannot be metered easily. This is the team organization to which Alchian and Demsetz refer (1972). Although the membership of such teams can be altered without loss of productivity, compensation cannot easily be determined on an individual basis. The simple brokerage role described above is thus extended to include supervision. As John Pencavel indicates, "the Italian padrone at the turn of the century . . . not only advanced credit to poorly-informed immigrants and occupied the role of the go between for laborers and employers, but also sometimes acted as foreman and paymaster" and the *jamadar* in India both "enlists and supervises workers for firms in the construction industry" (1977, pp. 251–52, n. 5). More generally, the coupling of employment with an oversight assignment is involved. The structure is referred to as a primitive team to distinguish it from the relational team described under 4, below.

3. k_1, S_0: obligational market

There is a considerable amount of firm-specific learning here, but tasks are easy to meter.[9] Idiosyncratic technological experience (as described, for example, by Doeringer and Piore, 1971, pp. 15–16), and idiosyncratic organizational experience (accounting and data processing conventions, internalization of other complex rules and procedures, and the like) both contribute to asset specificity. Okun's "toll model" of employment applies, in that sunk costs are incurred in qualifying a worker for productive employment in the firm (Okun, 1982, pp. 49–77). Both firm and workers have an interest in maintaining the continuity of such employment relations. Procedural safeguards and monetary penalties, such as severance pay, will thus be devised to discourage arbitrary dismissal. And nonvested retirement and other benefits will accrue to such workers so as to discourage unwanted quits (Mortenson, 1978).

4. k_1, S_1: relational team

The human assets here are specific to the firm and involve a significant team aspect. This approximates Ouchi's (1980b) "clan" form of organiza-

[9] The text implicitly assumes that output can be measured without difficulty. This is the assumption made in the principal-agent literature, where output is given by $X = X(a, \theta)$, where a is the actions taken by the agent and θ is the state of the world. The assumption that the quality of output is costlessly known is, of course, an analytical convenience. It is well-known that there are goods and services for which this assumption is not satisfied (March and Simon, 1958, p. 145; Barzel, 1982). Yoram Barzel (1982), Douglass North (1981), and Kenney and Klein (1983) attribute a great deal of nonmarket or market-assisted organization to quality measurement difficulties.

tion. The firm here will engage in considerable social conditioning to help assure that employees understand and are dedicated to the purposes of the firm, and employees will be provided with considerable job security, which gives them assurance against exploitation. Effective adaptation in a cooperative team context is especially difficult and important to achieve. A sense that management and workers are "in this together" furthers all of those purposes.

The Japanese corporation is said to have those attributes (Dore, 1973; Clark, 1979; Gibney, 1982) and both Ouchi (1981) and Fred Foulkes (1981) contend that some large American corporations have crafted the same. In addition to a governance structure in which employment safeguards are provided and respected, Foulkes contends that "fiercely egalitarian" practices— same parking lot, medical benefits, cafeteria, and spartan offices—for both management and labor contribute to "a high degree of employee loyalty, a low rate of turnover and absenteeism, and low degree of resistance to technological change" (1981, p. 90).

The above-described match of internal governance structures with internal transactional attributes is summarized in Figure 10–1. Admittedly, describing internal transactions in bivariate, binary terms simplifies considerably. The overall framework is nevertheless in place and refinements can be made as needed. (Thus mixed internal governance structures will presumably arise to service transactions that take on intermediate, rather than extreme, k and S values.)

The foregoing discussion makes no explicit reference to union organiza-

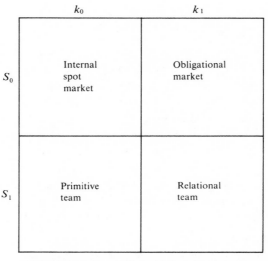

FIGURE 10–1. Efficient Work Organization

tion. It nevertheless has significant ramifications for both the attitude firms display toward unions and the structure of the employment relation among unionized employees. The issues here are developed in Section 3. Before turning to that, however, consider first whether the hazards of expropriation posed by workers vitiate the argument that market organization and internal organization differ in appropriability respects.

2.2 Expropriation by Workers

The mistaken argument is this: Shifting a transaction out of the market into the firm merely relocates an expropriation hazard but otherwise leaves the trading hazard intact. The reasoning here is that appropriable assets that are not exacted by trading opposites in an intermediate product market transaction are exposed to an equivalent expropriation hazard by employees of the firm should integration be attempted. There being no safe haven for specific assets, the transaction cost rationale for vertical integration collapses.

The issues will be clarified by breaking the argument down into parts:

1. Which assets are subject to expropriation?
2. In what ways, if any, do employment contracts differ from commercial contracts?
3. What are the ramifications for corporate governance?

Consider these seriatim.

a. ASSETS TO BE EXPROPRIATED

It is presumably beyond dispute that employees will bargain over their share of the quasi-rents that are embodied in human capital. That has a well-defined upper limit. The expropriation argument has reference not to that but to investments made by suppliers of capital (owners of equity; long-term debt holders). Site-specific investments in plant and equipment and idiosyncratic physical capital are both candidates.

The magnitude of those equity and debt supported assets could greatly exceed the amount of firm-specific human capital. Absent property rights to jobs, however, the upper limit of worker expropriation is the amount of firm-specific human capital. Employees risk—indeed, invite—termination should their demands exceed that limit.[10] Property rights considerations aside, therefore, the potentially appropriable quasi-rents to which employees have access

---

[10] To be sure, successor employees might repeat the exercise. Each new group of employees, however, can be terminated when its demands exceed the quasi-rents embodied in human capital.

are those reflected in human assets. Plainly this is a smaller magnitude than the total quasi-rent exposure, which includes transaction-specific physical capital.

b. EMPLOYMENT CONTRACTS

Employment contracts and commercial contracts differ in the following fundamental respect:

> Even where the collective agreement lists certain offenses or the parties negotiate plant rules, management may normally supplement the listed offenses or negotiated rules. Rules prescribed by management are subject to arbitrator review, but they carry a presumptive validity and will be upheld so long as they are reasonably related to achieving efficient operation and maintaining order and are not manifestly unfair or do not unnecessarily burden employees' rights.
>
> Management also is entitled to have its orders obeyed and may discipline employees for refusing to obey even improper orders. Arbitrators almost uniformly hold that an employee must obey first and then seek recourse through the grievance procedure, except where obeying would expose him to substantial risks of health and safety. [Summers, 1976, p. 502]

Procurement of the same good or service from an autonomous supplier ordinarily lacks that command and control aspect but requires mutual consent before adaptations can be affected.

Internal organization is thus able to adapt more effectively than can interfirm trading to changing market and technological circumstances. Not only do employment contracts contemplate such flexibility by providing for "zones of acceptance" within which orders will be implemented without resistance, but orders that exceed the scope of the authority relation can be implemented in extreme circumstances. Commercial agreements lack the same degree of responsiveness, since to write a commercial contract that awards buyers with effective control over the assets of a seller is to risk asset abuse if not expropriation. The issues here are akin to those addressed in Chapter 6.

The point can be made somewhat differently as follows: "When a number of persons are participating in a decision-making process, and these individuals have the same operational goals, differences in opinion will be resolved by predominately analytic processes. . . . But when goals are not shared . . . the decision will be reached by predominately bargaining processes" (March and Simon, 1958, p. 156). Acquiescence, if not goal sharing, is presumed for activities that fall within the zone of acceptance, so that analytical processes predominate. Bargaining is more prevalent between autonomous trading parties whenever efforts are made to restore the parties to a position on the shifting contract curve.

The upshot is that the opportunities to haggle rather than adapt are vastly greater for commercial contracts than they are for employment contracts. As a consequence the asserted advantages of internal organization as compared with market organization survive.

c. GOVERNANCE

Issues of corporate governance are discussed in detail in Chapter 12. Suffice it to observe here that corporate governance has to be sensitive to expropriation hazards. Property rights over jobs, the uses of corporate debt and the institution of bankruptcy, and control over the board of directors all have a bearing.

3. Union Organization

Unions are complex organizations, have many facets, and serve many purposes. Efficiency aspects are mainly emphasized here. They are examined from the standpoint of private ordering. Other aspects, however, are also considered, including a discussion of power.

3.1 *Private Ordering*

Katherine Stone has recently examined the development of American labor law in the period following 1945, with special attention to the "industrial pluralism" model, which holds that "collective bargaining is self-government by management and labor" (1981, p. 1511). She contends that this model distorts rather than clarifies issues because it is "based upon a false assumption: the assumption that management and labor have equal power in the workplace" (1981, p. 1511).

I submit that examining the development of labor law as a private ordering exercise is instructive. Although the industrial pluralists with whom Stone takes exception—especially professors Schulman and Cox among labor law scholars, Justice Douglas on the Supreme Court, and Arthur Goldberg as a labor lawyer—treat labor in a more aggregative way than I think adviseable, all appear to recognize the benefits of a private ordering orientation. Inasmuch, moreover, as an "equal power in the workplace" criterion is nowhere defined, I am unable to ascertain how labor markets would have been organized if the leading figures had adopted her preferred standard.

Schulman interprets the Wagner Act as a "bare legal framework" within which private ordering by labor and management can proceed (1955, p. 1000). To be sure, the Act made express reference to the desirability of creating "equality of bargaining power between employers and employees."[11] Stone views this as a call to political reform, whereby the law intervenes actively "to alter the definition of property rights in order to create true equality" (1981, p. 1580). Power equalization being an ambiguous criterion, the industrial pluralists concentrated instead on attainable goals: fashioning efficient and feasible reforms.

The institution of arbitration lies at the core of industrial pluralism. As Stone puts it:

> In the industrial pluralist model, disputes over breaches of collective agreements are not submitted to an administrative or judicial tribunal. Rather, they are submitted to the dispute resolution mechanism that the parties in this mini-democracy have established for themselves—private arbitration. . . .
> A corollary of this description of the industrial world is the prescription that the processes of the state—the courts and administrative tribunals—should keep out. The workplace . . . becomes . . . an island of self-rule whose self-regulating mechanisms must not be disrupted by judicial intervention or other scrutiny by outsiders. [Stone, 1981, p. 1515]

Stone goes on to observe, "Judicial resolution of labor disputes . . . was unacceptable because it imposed a noncontractual solution upon the parties" (1981, p. 1524). She contends, moreover, that the purported advantages of voluntary arbitration—special expertise of arbitrators, the informality of the arbitration procedures, the arbitrators' flexibility of remedy—could all have been realized by assigning this responsibility not to an arbitrator mutually chosen by the parties but to the National Labor Relations Board (Stone, 1981, p. 1531).

To be sure, the parties would lose control over the arbitrator in the process. But Stone does not regard that as a liability. She projects no adverse consequences because of her confidence in the NLRB bureaucracy[12] and because of her preference for a judicial result: "If arbitration serves the function of a judiciary in a mini-democracy, then in theory, the arbitrator is to interpret the language of the written agreement, *not please the parties*" (Stone, 1981, p. 1552, n. 238; emphasis in original).

But suppose that both the immediate parties and society at large benefit from a more efficient exchange relation. If the pleasure of the parties is promoted by restoring a position on the shifting contract curve, and if that is

---

[11]29 U.S.C. para 151 (1976).

[12]The possibilities that NLRB resolution of industrial disputes would be protracted, giving rise to a massive written record and bureaucratic posturing, with career civil servants giving vent to their political preferences rather than focusing on the needs of the parties, go unmentioned.

better realized by voluntary arbitration than by a legalistic (or black letter) approach to contract, then little wonder that the parties opted for private ordering.

Indeed, had the judicial model favored by Stone been adopted, the parties would presumably have recognized the problems and would have redefined their relationship appropriately. Rather than submit to the inefficiencies of legal centralism, the parties would attempt to craft private orderings. And if such efforts are resisted and defeated by the judiciary, the parties will then predictably respond by avoiding technologies and working relations in which continuity is valued.

The simple contracting schema set out in Chapter 1 is again relevant. Recall that the parties first have to reach a decision on whether or not to make specific investments. If $k = 0$, a discrete market contracting relation obtains. If instead a $k > 0$ decision is made, then a further decision has to be made on whether or not to safeguard the transaction with protective governance structure. The industrial pluralists believed that it was useful to "please the parties," hence a specialized governance structure designed to harmonize interests and promote continuity was devised. Stone rejects that in favor of litigation. If, however, insistence on the latter places an inefficiency burden on the parties, which it arguably does, efforts to void that result can be anticipated. Reverting to a nonspecific ($k = 0$) labor relation is one possibility.

3.2 The Many Facets of Unions

The dominant view of unions is that they are organizations whose main purpose is to raise wages—what Richard Freeman and James Medoff (1979) refer to as the monopoly face of unionism. There is a growing appreciation, however, that (1) unions serve other important purposes and (2) the functions served by unions *vary systematically with the nature of the task*. These are the matters of special interest here.

One of the reasons why the monopoly face of unionism has received so much attention in relation to other aspects is that monopoly analysis is congenial to neoclassical economics. A second reason is that confrontational wage bargaining is much more newsworthy than is reporting on humdrum, day-to-day governance. Neither, however, justifies the neglect of the other two faces of unionism: efficiency and voice. Efficiency raises governance issues of a transaction cost kind (Williamson, Wachter, and Harris, 1975), while voice has been addressed and elaborated by Freeman (1976) and Freeman and Medoff (1979). All three faces of unionism—monopoly, efficiency, and voice—have to be recognized if the organization of labor is to be accurately assessed. Furthermore, there are distinguishable facets within each of the three faces, the separate treatment of which will further contribute to a more informed assessment of unionism.

a. THE MONOPOLY FACE

Price discrimination aside, monopoly manifests itself as a condition of contrived scarcity. At least three distinguishable types of unions that aspired to raise wages, presumably by controlling supply, can be identified: class unions, craft unions, and industrial unions.

The first represented workers as a group in relation to employers as a group. Attempts in the United States in the nineteenth century to organize along those lines (National Labor Union, Knights of Labor) were not successful. A substantial problem with such an approach to unionism is that economic differences among workers and jobs are ignored or suppressed. Craft unions, by contrast, are organized along much narrower lines. The organizational features and wage bargaining attributes of the union can be adjusted to the nature of the job much more fully if the craft union model is adopted. Glenn Porter's examination of the early history of labor unions is instructive:

> [R]ailroad workers were the first to achieve genuine collective bargaining and grievance channels through their national unions, the railroad brotherhoods. Initially these unions, like many other early American labor organizations, were social and mutual benefit societies. By the 1870s, though, they were evolving into modern unions. Like many of the craft unions which formed the American Federation of Labor in the 1880s, the railway brotherhoods derived economic strength from the fact that their members had scarce and hard to replace skills. A strike by such a union was a real threat to employers, because it was extremely difficult to break the strike by bringing in outside workers ("scabs" in union parlance). Furthermore, the railway workers were additionally vital because they controlled the use and maintenance of expensive equipment. The unhappy history of unions that tried to include all the nation's working people, such as the National Labor Union and the Knights of Labor, indicated that it was very difficult, if not impossible, to create and maintain unions unless the members had scarce economic skills like the railroad workers and the members of the craft unions that made up the American Federation of Labor in the 1880s. The all-inclusive unions faced other difficulties as well. Gerald Grob's *Workers and Utopia* (1961) convincingly argued that the members and the leaders of such noncraft unions shared an ideological reluctance to accept the wage system. [Porter, 1973, pp. 34–55]

Industrial unions in the United States made their appearance after the passage of the Wagner Act. Requiring as they did the assistance of the political process, they evidently lacked natural advantages of either contrived scarcity or efficiency kinds. Unlike craft unions, industrial unions were organizing workers whose jobs required little skill. Controlling entry—e.g. through licensure—was for that reason difficult. Accordingly, incumbent workers in those industries were unable, without political assistance, to reach and enforce supracompetitive wage bargains—because "potential entrants" for their jobs would undo them. Additionally, industrial unions had relatively less to offer in the way of efficiency benefits, since simple governance structures are adequate to service the efficiency needs of the employment relation for jobs that entail little human asset specificity.

The monopoly face of unionism is thus one in which control over entry is emphasized. It can be effected selectively by licensure among craft unions or more generally with the support of the political process, as with industrial unions. Class unionism appears to be feasible, however, only by effecting more massive political change in which capitalism is supplanted by socialism. Both Stone (1981, pp. 1579–80) and Branko Horvat (1982) appear to be in agreement on this last.

b. EFFICIENCY

Unions can serve efficiency purposes in at least two respects. For one thing, unions can serve certain basic agency functions. In addition, and more important, unions can serve important governance purposes.

1. *Agency.* The union as agent argument has been set out by Joseph Reid and Roger Faith (1980) and has been discussed by Freeman and Medoff under the heading of personnel practices and employee benefits (1979, pp. 82–84). Unions can both serve as a source of information regarding employee needs and preferences (with respect, for example, to fringe benefits) and assist employees in evaluating complex wage and benefit offers. Thus whereas it is unlikely, not to say inefficient, for individual workers to evaluate alternative compensation packages, unions can and do "hire the lawyers, actuaries, and other experts necessary to perform these analyses" (Freeman and Medoff, 1979, p. 83).

An agency role for unions is a purely instrumental one that permits the parties to reach and enforce preferred bargains. Virtually all types of labor can benefit from use of an agent to perform those functions. Workers in non-unionized firms will ordinarily recognize the benefits and will often develop a machinery (including a collective means by which to cover the costs) so as to realize them.

2. *Governance.* Whereas the agency benefits of unions apply quite generally, the governance benefits apply in a more selective fashion. Indeed, this is the source of much of the predictive content of the transaction cost

approach. The basic argument is by now familiar: Continuity of the employment relation is valued by both employer and employee for tasks that involve the acquisition of significant transaction-specific skills, while tasks for which skill acquisition is insubstantial and/or general purpose do not create the same continuity interests.

Gary Becker, to whom much of the pioneering work on human capital is due, recognized that continuity interests would be manifested in incentive schemes. As he put it:

> A pension plan with incomplete vesting privileges penalizes employees who quit before retirement and thus provides an incentive—often an extremely powerful one—not to quit. At the same time pension plans "insure" firms against quits, for they are given a lump sum—the nonvested portion of payments—whenever a worker quits. Insurance is needed for specifically trained employees because their turnover would impose capital losses on the firm. [Becker, 1965, p. 18]

The issues here have subsequently been elaborated by Dale Mortensen (1978).

It was not, however, until 1975 that the collective organization ramifications were recognized. The basic argument is this:

> [A]lthough it is in the interest of each worker, bargaining individually or as a part of a small team, to acquire and exploit monopoly positions, it is plainly not in the interest of the system that employees should behave in this way. Opportunistic bargaining not only itself absorbs real resources, but efficient adaptations will be delayed and possibly forgone altogether. What this suggests, accordingly, is that the employment relation be transformed in such a way that systems concerns are made more fully to prevail and the following objectives are realized: (1) bargaining costs are made lower, (2) the internal wage structure is rationalized in terms of objective task characteristics, (3) consummate rather than perfunctory cooperation is encouraged, and (4) investments of idiosyncratic types, which constitute a potential source of monopoly, are undertaken without risk of exploitation. [Williamson, Wachter, and Harris, 1975, p. 270]

Collective organization can be made to serve each of those purposes.

The mutual interest between workers and firm in protecting the employment relation against exploitation by the other should have given rise to "company unions" in the pre–Wagner Act era. Although there evidently were some developments along those lines, they were scarcely widespread. Whether that reflected lack of knowledge of the benefits, apprehension over the potential monopoly uses of collective organization, or the fact that the efficiency benefits were rarely great is unclear.[13] In any event, if the potential benefits of collective organization vary directly with human asset specificity, then the firms in which human asset specificity were greater were those that confronted a tradeoff in contemplating company union formation. By con-

[13]See note 8, *supra*.

trast, firms in which human asset specificity was negligible experienced no such tradeoff: There were few gains to be realized, while the monopoly hazards were clear.

Two testable propositions thus emerge from examining collective organization in governance terms: (1) The incentive to organize production workers within a collective governance structure increases with the degree of human asset specificity, and (2) the degree to which an internal governance structure is elaborated will vary directly with the degree of human asset specificity. Transaction cost analysis thus predicts that unions will arise early in such industries as railroads, where the skills are highly specific, and will arise late in such industries as migrant farm labor, where skills are nonspecific. It further predicts that the governance structure (job ladders, grievance procedures, pay scales) will be more fully elaborated in industries with greater specificity than in those with less (steel versus autos is an example). The preliminary data appear to support both propositions. The quotation from Porter under 3.2a above is germane in the first of these respects. Cox's remarks about activating the arbitration machinery when disputes arise have a bearing on the second:

> [G]iving the union control over all claims arising under the collective agreement comports so much better with the functional nature of a collective bargaining agreement. . . . Allowing an individual to carry a claim to arbitration whenever he is dissatisfied with the adjustment worked out by the company and the union . . . discourages the kind of day-to-day cooperation between company and union which is normally the mark of sound industrial relations—a relationship in which grievances are treated as problems to be solved and contracts are only guideposts in a dynamic human relationship. When . . . the individual's claim endangers group interests, the union's function is to resolve the competition by reaching an accommodation or striking a balance. [Cox, 1958, p. 24]

Another aspect of arbitration, less widely remarked but also germane, is that arbitration "gives management . . . a low-cost method of ascertaining when low-level supervisors are failing to follow the wishes of upper management. If the [labor rules] to which the management has agreed do in fact increase productivity, it is important to the firm that they be followed" (Vogel, 1981, p. 24). Arbitrary and capricious behavior by foremen is at the expense of the firm's long-run interests. Practices that deter suboptimization will naturally be favored. More generally, "Employers who know that their actions are subject to arbitral review will seek to avoid unjustified discipline in the first instance by articulation of rules, instruction of foremen, careful investigation and other management controls" (Summers, 1976, pp. 507–8). Creating a governance unit to check myopic abuses is thus in the *mutual* interests of both labor and management.

c. VOICE

The political side of unionism is described by Freeman and Medoff (1979) under the heading of "voice"—which has its origins in Albert Hirschman's (1970) book in which he distinguishes exit and voice as alternative means of organizing economic activity. Hirschman regards exit as the usual economic means for expressing preferences, while voice is the relatively neglected political process for influencing outcomes. Consumers, workers, voters and the like vote with their pocketbook or with their feet in the former case. Voice, by contrast, involves dialog, persuasion, and sustained organizational effort.

Freeman and Medoff impute efficiency, distributional, and social organization effects to the collective-voice view of unionism. The efficiency benefits they ascribe to voice, however, are essentially those described above in conjunction with agency and governance. But there is a difference. Whereas the voice view of unionism attributes beneficial governance features to union organization quite generally, the transaction cost (or governance) approach predicts that they will vary with the continuity needs of the parties. As set out in section 2 above, those continuity needs are greatest where human assets are more highly specific. Spot market contracting will continue to be efficacious, however, where human asset skills are nonspecific and inputs are separable. The voice view of unionism evidently holds otherwise, in that it ascribes efficiency benefits to unions in all circumstances—spot market contracting included. In principle, a discriminating test of the governance versus voice approaches to unionism can thus be had by examining the efficiency benefits of collective organization associated with the k_0, S_0 cell (which is the case where assets are nonspecific and separable).

The merits of the voice view of unionism do not, however, turn entirely on efficiency ramifications. Distributional considerations also warrant attention. Effects of two kinds have been ascribed to unions. The first is the conventional monopoly distortion associated with union wage gains. The relatively neglected feature to which Freeman and Medoff call attention, which is distinctively associated with the voice view of unionism, is that income inequality—within a firm or within an industry—is reduced among organized workers.

The social effects of unions, according to the collective-voice approach, is that unions are political institutions that represent both the will of their members and the political interests of lower-income and disadvantaged persons. The latter effects might be disputed, but unions plainly are important to the political process—in health and safety as well as in other societal respects.

Those effects would be difficult to actualize under the agency view of unions, which locates union activity at a plant or firm level. The joining of union interests at political levels is apt to benefit from composite (or hierarchical) union organization, which the collective-voice view of unionism arguably supports.

3.3 Power

The claim or suggestion that power rather than efficiency is responsible for decisions to organize exchange relations one way rather than another runs through much of the social science commentary on labor organization. Rarely is power defined, however. Partly this is because it is widely believed that while power "may be tricky to define . . . it is not that difficult to recognize" (Pfeffer, 1981, p. 3). I submit, however, that much of what is "recognized" as power is the result of looking at individual contracts in an *ex post* state rather than, as comparative institutional analysis requires, considering the *set* of relevant contracts in their *entirety*.

Sometimes what is referred to as power reduces to a preference for an alternative distribution of income. Those who have fewer resources would have greater purchasing "power" if this were accomplished. But the organization of labor need not be affected on that account. To be sure, the mix of goods and services would probably change. But the way in which work is organized need not. Indeed, if efficiency is driving organizational outcomes, modes that are efficient under one distribution of income will normally remain efficient under another.[14] Since mutual gains are potentially available whenever a move from a less to a more efficient configuration is accomplished, the incentive to choose more efficient modes is transparent.

Issues that require clarification in evaluating the power literature include the following: (1) nondiversifiable risk, (2) reputation effects, (3) competitive process, and (4) worker control over the intensity and quality of the labor input. A common misconception that runs through much of the power literature is that aggregate power can be inferred by ascertaining which of two contestants will win in an *isolated* confrontation.

a. NONDIVERSIFIABLE RISK

Branko Horvat contrasts owners with workers in risk-bearing terms as follows: "The owner can spread the risks by acquiring a diversified portfolio

---

[14]See, however, Putterman's discussion (1982, pp. 156–57).

of shares, while the worker has just one labor power and one job'' (1982, p. 447). Several observations are relevant. First, there is a narrow technical sense in which the notion that labor is nondiversifiable is correct. Legal prohibitions against indentured servitude aside, a market in human capital in which risks are diversified through the buying and selling of shares in individual income streams is not viable. "One cannot, for example, sell a piece of oneself if one is a lawyer in Cincinnati and buy a portion of a carpenter in San Diego" (Gordon, 1974, p. 447).

But second, it is possible for workers to choose between general purpose and firm-specific skills. Workers who choose the former will be qualified to work for a large number of employers. Only those who invest very heavily in firm-specific skill acquisition are accurately described as "one labor power and one job." Even here, alternative employment, albeit at reduced levels of productivity, is ordinarily feasible. Furthermore, and more important, workers who accept employment of a firm-specific kind will presumably recognize the risks and insist upon surrounding such jobs with protective governance structures. One labor power and one job regarded nakedly and one labor power and one job embedded in a protective governance structure have very different connotations.

b. REPUTATION EFFECTS

The snapshot view of worker versus firm in power terms suppresses future consequences. Each confrontation is regarded separately, and the worker is inevitably the loser in each. The worker is terminated and has to find another job. The firm hires a replacement from the reserve army of the unemployed.

That scenario is defective in two respects. First, there is an implicit assumption that the firm experiences no dislocation costs when an employee is terminated. That is true, however, only if human asset specificity is negligible and any team effects are of the primitive team kind. Second, it assumes that workers have no employment options, hence do not choose among alternatives with an eye on different practices. But as Arthur Okun observes, "in the absence of an explicit contract, applicants will seek information from other workers about the employers' past performance. Applicants are obliged to judge the employer, in part, by reputation" (1981, p. 51). Those firms with better reputations will presumably be able to hire workers on better terms, *ceteris paribus*. (Again, the $\hat{p}$ versus $\bar{p}$ comparison of Chapter 1 is germane.)

Reputation effects are subtle matters, however. The possibility that the firm will use reputation in a strategic way presumably warrants consideration. Thus the argument that both workers and employers have a mutual interest in the continuity of the employment relation where investments in transaction-specific human assets are great might be disputed on the grounds that the worker is one of many and that the employer can and will realize strategic advantages by making an example of one or a few workers, thereby teaching a lesson to the many. The symmetry argument is thus mistaken, because it ignores this fundamental disparity. Put differently, the proposition that both parties stand to lose if an employee with significant transaction-specific skills quits or is terminated—the employee loses because he cannot turn to other employment without loss of productive value; the employer loses because of the costs of disruption and training that replacement entails—is correct as far as it goes, but it does not go far enough. It ignores the strategic aspects and for that reason must be supplanted by a strategic assessment of the employment relation in which asymmetries are recognized and explicitly taken into account.

The importance of reputation effects has been discussed by Christian von Weizsacker in conjunction with what he refers to as the extrapolation principle:

> One of the most effective mechanisms available to society for the reduction of information production cost is the principle of extrapolation. By this I mean the phenomenon that people extrapolate the behavior of others from past observations and that this extrapolation is self-stabilizing, because it provides an incentive for others to live up to these expectations. . . . By observing others' behavior in the past, one can fairly confidently predict their behavior in the future without incurring further costs. . . .
>
> [This] extrapolation principle is deeply rooted in the structure of human behavior. Indeed it is also available in animal societies. . . . The fight between two chickens does not only produce information about relative strengths in the present, but also about relative strength in the future. [Weizsacker, 1980b, pp. 72–73]

The issues have been developed more formally by David Kreps and Robert Wilson, who address the credibility of predatory threats. They show that where there is uncertainty about the dominant firm's payoffs and where the dominant firm is engaged in repeated play with a sequence of opponents, "none of whom have the ability to foster a reputation" (Kreps and Wilson, 1980, p. 58), punitive behavior becomes a much more attractive policy.

A series of parallels between dominant firm and small rivals on the one hand and the employer and numerous individual employees on the other invite the transfer of that reasoning to the employment context. Thus (1) the employer's resources are much more extensive than are those of the typical employee, (2) individual employees may well have difficulty in assessing the payoffs to employers of alternative bargains, and (3) individual employees maybe thought of as a sequence of opponents, each of whom is unable to develop a countervailing reputation. The parallels, however, are incomplete. Specifically, whereas the dominant firm is dealing with *rivals* and hopes to have no further dealings with the would-be entrant or his ilk, the employer is dealing with *suppliers* and has continuing needs to hire workers. That difference can be decisive.

That is not to say that an employer cannot successfully teach a lesson to many employees by making an example of one or a few. Inasmuch as all employees who have made transaction-specific investments are vulnerable to exploitation, an employer may, through selective but conspicuous punitive measures, induce all incumbents to accept inferior terms. Reference to incumbents, however, flags an important limit on that type of behavior. Among employers who plan to be in business on a continuing basis, successor generation employees may also learn—and the lesson here is very different from that of the incumbents.

Specifically, employers who have a reputation for exploiting incumbent employees will not thereafter be able to induce new employees to accept employment on the same terms. A wage premium may have to be paid; or tasks may have to be redefined to eliminate the transaction-specific features; or contractual guarantees against future abuses may have to be granted. In consideration of those possibilities, the strategy of exploiting the specific investments of incumbent employees is effectively restricted to circumstances where (1) firms are of a fly-by-night kind, (2) firms are playing end games, and (3) intergenerational learning is negligible. In circumstances, however, where firms are continuously in the employment market and successor generations learn, efforts to exploit incumbent employees are myopic and will predictably elicit protective reactions.

There are good reasons, nonetheless, for employees to organize in such a way as to forestall even one-time or mistaken efforts to exploit the transaction-specific investments of labor. For one thing, exposure to myopic or fly-by-night operators and to end games can thereby be reduced. Second, intergenerational reputation effects may more assuredly be brought to bear on continuing firms by creating an institutional machinery to record and communicate incidents of expropriation. Third, employers may recognize the merits of fair dealing with employees but be unable to impress them on first-line supervisors. The collective organization of workers (unions) has advantages in each of the three respects.

C. COMPETITIVE PROCESS

The suggestion that employers rather than employees or society at large is the gainer whenever more efficient work practices are implemented assumes that workers lack bargaining power and neglects the competitive process. Work rule changes made during a contract are normally subject to arbitration, however. And those made during contract renewal negotiations are part of a much larger package in which tradeoffs are worked out.

The neglect of the competitive process is especially regretable. Thus assume that a more efficient practice can be identified and suppose that the employer initially appropriates the whole of the efficiency gain. Even though workers are no better off (indeed, depending on the particulars, some may be released and need to find new employment), society stands to gain in two respects. First, the resources saved by the reorganization of work can be productively reemployed in alternative uses. Second, the immediate profits that accrue to the firm will rarely be durable. Instead, the scenario described earlier in conjunction with the steel industry[15] will normally obtain: significant reforms will be detected and imitated by others, and prices will fall as margins are restored to earlier levels.[16] Further allocative efficiency gains are realized as a consequence.

d. WORKER DISCRETION

The suggestion that workers' bargaining power is limited to one dimension—report for work or strike—is common but mistaken. Thus Stone observes, "The availability of injunctive relief to force a union to cease striking . . . meant that [the] union's alternative economic weapons were withdrawn" (1981, p. 1539). In fact, however, what "the firm wants when it hires an employee is productive performance. . . . It wishes to buy quality of work rather than merely time on the job" (Okun, 1981, p. 63).[17] Accordingly, exploited incumbent employees are not totally without recourse. Incumbent employees who are "forced" to accept inferior terms can adjust quality to the disadvantage of a predatory employer. The issues here have been addressed previously in distinguishing between consummate and perfunctory cooperation (Williamson, 1975, p. 69). Of necessity, the employment contract is an incomplete agreement, and performance varies with the way in which it is executed. Consummate cooperation is an affirmative job attitude whereby gaps are filled, initiative is taken, and judgment is exercised in an instrumental way. Perfunctory cooperation involves working

---

[15]See Chapter 5, section 4.2.

[16]An absence of monopoly power is not assumed. I merely assume that work organization changes do not add to preexisting market power, so profit margins will normally be restored to earlier levels when the adaptation has been completed.

[17]As Alfred Marshall remarked, "even if the number of [working] hours in the year were rigidly fixed, which it is not, the intensity of work would remain elastic" (1948, p. 438, n. 1).

to rules and in other respects performing in a minimally acceptable way. As Peter Blau and Richard Scott observe:

> [T]he contract obligates employees to perform only a set of duties in accordance with minimum standards and does not assure their striving to achieve optimum performance. . . . [L]egal authority does not and cannot command the employee's willingness to devote his ingenuity and energy to performing his tasks to the best of his ability. . . . It promotes compliance with directives and discipline, but does not encourage employees to exert effort, to accept responsibilities, or to exercise initiative. [Blau and Scott, 1962, p. 140]

In fact, most contracts—labor, intermediate goods, and other—are incomplete in significant respects, on which account suppliers enjoy discretion. Buyers thus "abuse" suppliers by demanding exacting performance in accordance with the letter of the contract only at hazard.

4.   Problematic Features of Union Organization

The foregoing emphasizes the benefits of collective organization. They are especially great in circumstances where the labor force acquires (or the management wishes to induce the workers to acquire) firm-specific human capital. But there are additional efficiency benefits, of a simple agency kind, that collective organization can provide in virtually all enterprises.

Unions are the prevailing form of collective organization in capitalist economies. That the union was not introduced earlier or was not received without resistance is presumably because, in addition to the aforementioned benefits, there are also prospective costs. Some of the more obvious are noted here.

4.1   *Monopoly Power*

Collective organization can permit workers to improve the bargains they strike with respect to the disposition of the quasi-rent attributable to firm-specific human capital. If, contrary to the argument in subsection 2.2, workers acquire secure property rights over jobs, further improvement in those bargains—at least in the short run—can be realized by expropriating sunk costs in physical plant and organizational infrastructure. Out of recognition of such an expropriation potential, firms and industries in which investments in durable nonhuman capital are greater will be more resistant to union organization, *ceteris paribus*.

4.2 Oligarchy

The Iron Law of Oligarchy holds: "It is organization which gives birth to the dominion of the elected over the electors, of the mandatories over the mandators, of the delegates over the delegators. Who says organization, says oligarchy" (Michels, 1962, p. 365). Efforts to weaken this Law notwithstanding, it has so far resisted repeal. As Seymour Lipset puts it, modern man is faced by an unresolvable dilemma: He "cannot have large institutions such as nation state, trade unions, political parties, or churches, without turning over effective power to the few who are at the summit of these institutions" (1962, p. 15). The leadership of unions, like the leadership of other large organizations, is thus often in a position to entrench itself and/or pursue its interests.

That is sometimes obvious, as when the union leadership squanders the retirement and hospitalization payments of the membership. It can also be subtle, however, and may be influenced by the institutional rules of the game. Aoki's recent discussion of the choice of contract renewal intervals is a possible example of the latter.

The issue is, What is the appropriate interval at which to renegotiate contracts? There are great advantages, from an efficiency point of view, in concentrating the hard bargaining aspects of the relation at the contract renewal periods and using analytic processes to effect adaptations during contract execution. Long-term contracts offer the apparent advantage of reducing bargaining and increasing analytic processes, but that can be misleading. If the basic contract gets out of alignment with the economic realities, one party or the other is apt to press for relief during contract execution. As a consequence the presumption that the parties will cooperate during the period between contract renewals is placed under strain.

Aoki nevertheless notes an interesting empirical regularity that distinguishes contracting practices in Germany and Japan from those in the United States: Contracts in the first two countries are typically renegotiated at one-year intervals, while in the United States the usual interval is three years (Aoki, 1984, p. 148). What explains the difference?

One possibility is that economic disturbances in Germany and Japan are larger and more frequent. That is the uncertainty explanation: Contracts that experience greater uncertainty should presumably come up for renegotiation more frequently than those that experience less. The explanation that Aoki favors, however, traces the difference to a National Labor Relations Board ruling. The "contract bar" doctrine prevents a challenge to the incumbent union from being filed "during the term of an existing contract, with a three year maximum in the case of contracts that run for more than three years" (1984, p. 148). Aoki contends that the resulting three-year contracts protect incumbents at the expense of efficiency (pp. 148–50). Whether that is correct or not, the possibility that oligarchical outcomes will influence the rules of the game warrants attention.[18]

4.3 *Heterogeneity*

More complex labor governance structures are needed as investments in firm-specific human capital deepen, *ceteris paribus*. In consideration of that, and given heterogeneity in the typical work force, it may be that a series of bargains rather than a single bargain applicable to the entire labor force should be struck. Among other things a single union operating under a uniform agreement will have difficulty aggregating the preferences of a disparate membership. To negotiate discriminating terms is at variance, however, with the egalitarian purposes of unions. Japanese firms and labor unions have mitigated the problem by spinning off divergent activities through extensive subcontracting and by the creation of subsidiaries (Aoki, 1984, p. 142). Those who would have United States firms and unions imitate their Japanese counterparts more closely but are not prepared simultaneously to accept Japanese subcontracting (and related practices that facilitate discrimination) should acknowledge the strains.

5. The Producer Cooperative Dilemma

This book is mainly preoccupied with assessing capitalist modes of organization. Although the underlying approach to the study of organization applies to noncapitalist modes as well, few such applications are attempted. The following brief discussion of producer cooperatives is no remedy. It merely poses issues for which further study is needed. The basic dilemma is this: If producer cooperatives mitigate the disabilities that many social scientists and social commentators associate with the Authority Relation, why is the record of producer cooperatives so weak?

A definitive answer to that query is not attempted here. Indeed, inasmuch as the producer cooperative mode is still undergoing refinements— witness the Mondragon experiment, which has been in progress in the Basque province of Spain for almost thirty years (Bradley and Gelb, 1980, 1982)—a final determination is unwarranted. The earlier history of producer cooperatives has nevertheless been disappointing. The high hopes with which they

---

[18]Another problematic feature of unionism is what William Fellner refers to as "Case 3 Oligopoly." Such a condition involves collusion among the firms within an industry (or among a subset of firms) supported by the "active aid of an outside agency" (Fellner, 1965, p. 47). For an illustration in which the United Mine Workers and the large bituminous coal mines appear to have been joined in such a relation, see Williamson (1968). This does not, however, appear to be a common outcome.

were launched have gone unrealized (Kanter, 1972; Manuel and Manuel, 1979). What have been the contributing factors?

Bowles and Gintis (1976, p. 62) observe that worker cooperatives offered a viable alternative to the Authority Relation and "were a widespread and influential part of the labor movement as early as the 1840s. . . . The cooperative movement reached a peak shortly after the Civil War but failed because sufficient capital could not be raised." They go on to quote Grob as follows:

> Even when funds were available the desire for profits often became so overwhelming that many cooperatives were turned into joint stock companies. Stockholders then became intent on paying low wages. Not unimportant were the discriminations practiced by competitors who feared the success of cooperative enterprises. [Bowles and Gintis, 1976, p. 62]

Ellerman describes the "degenerative tendencies" of employee-owned corporations in a similar way (1982, p. 39).

Horvat poses the dilemma directly: "If labor-managed firms are really more efficient than their capitalist . . . counterparts . . . why do they not outcompete the latter firms in the market?" (1982, p. 455). His answer is that "a labor-managed firm cannot easily survive in a capitalist environment regardless of its *potential* efficiency" (p. 455; emphasis in original). The reasons are three (p. 456): (1) Bank and trade credit are difficult for producer cooperatives to obtain, (2) cooperatives are unable to retain superior managers, who are induced to leave by offers of better pay in capitalist firms, and (3) successful cooperatives experience the above-described degeneration, since founders are unwilling to share the fruits of their success with newcomers.

Horvat offers a biological analogy in support of the first point—"capitalist economy behaves like an organism that has undergone an organ transplant: it spontaneously rejects the alien tissue" (1982, p. 456). I submit, however, that short-term bank and trade credit are more accurately described by a physical analogy. They are more nearly akin to iron filings in a magnetic field. The prospect of high (risk-adjusted) returns presents a well-nigh irresistible attraction to liquid reserves. To be sure, local exhortations to discriminate can be temporarily effective. But venture capitalists are unprincipled in their search for profit. Capital displays an inexorable tendency to equalize returns at the margin.

A more serious financial concern, which Horvat does not mention but Putterman (1982, p. 158) does, is access to long-term bank financing and equity capital. The issue is not that cooperatives are denied parity access to such funds, but the special hazards that the cooperative form poses. Track record and expropriation hazards must be distinguished. Only the latter are troublesome in the long run.

Considering the difficulties of evaluating the merits of any new enterprise *ex ante,* investors are always wary at the outset. But that is characteristic of all new firms. Starting small and growing through retained earnings is thus a common scenario. Since workers who are attracted to cooperatives will presumably work for a lower wage,[19] the oppressiveness of the Authority Relation having been removed, the greater profitability that thereby results is a decided advantage.[20] Once displayed, the above-described magnetic attraction of funds should materialize.

That assumes, however, that the cooperative firm and the capitalist firm do not pose distinguishably different expropriation hazards to long-term debt and, especially, to equity financing. Those issues are best developed in conjunction with the discussion of corporate governance in Chapter 12. Suffice it to observe here that whereas the capitalist form of organization can tolerate outside intervention, to include even the change of management through the concentration of equity ownership to effect a takeover, this is antithetical to the cooperative conception of the enterprise. *Ceteris paribus,* equity ownership is subject to greater hazard in the cooperative firm.[21] The cooperative form of organization experiences a serious (comparative) limitation on that account.

Horvat, however, offers two other reasons, both of which turn on the behavior of managers and are closely linked: the inability of cooperatives to retain good managers, and the unwillingness of founders to share. Putterman's recent treatment of management problems in worker-run enterprise is instructive. He observes that

> . . . while the market system will *permit* the existence of worker-run enterprises side by side with capitalist firms, worker-run firms may not be fully viable, and

[19]To be sure, worker buy-outs of failing businesses are special cases. Experienced workers in such circumstances may willingly sacrifice quasi-rents because of the grim alternatives. It is nevertheless instructive that the employees at National Steel Corporation's Weirton plant in West Virginia are expected to accept a 32 percent wage and benefit cut as a part of their buy-out effort: "Some 7,400 hourly workers represented by the Independent Steelworkers Union (ISU) would take a 14.1% wage cut and eliminate 6 of 11 holidays, a week of vacation pay, and other benefits. In addition, the union gave up a cost-of-living adjustment (COLA) provision in return for a profit sharing plan, which would provide the only compensation increases during a six-year wage freeze" (*Business Week,* September 5, 1983, p. 35).

[20]Putterman cautions that success may not be immediate because of startup problems (1982, pp. 150–51). Many producer cooperatives, however, got off to a good start. Their problems developed later.

[21]As Putterman puts it, "if equity-owners value their voting control over firm policies, and if worker-run firms cannot (on principle) share such control with their equity owners, then the costs of raising equity-capital will be higher for the worker-run firm" (1982, p. 158) One possible adaptation is for worker-managed firms to specialize in industries and technologies where the exposure of specific assets is limited.

are likely to be unable to attain their full possibilities, under such coexistence, so long as entrepreneurial talent has its best deal in the competing form. It may be necesssary for democratic control to become a fundamental social principle, implemented through legislation insofar as it is not established by the sheer weight of adoption as a social norm, before managerial talent is captured within the worker-run system, turned toward the wider benefit of the workforce as a whole, and brought to cooperate in the multiplication of skills and the education of the workforce which might make management itself less of a scarce resource, and thus promote the success of highly participatory organizational forms. In other words, worker-run enterprise could be better for most workers in the long-run, yet be unattainable as long as that minority of workers for whom this is *not* so are attracted to the service of capital. [Putterman, 1982, pp. 157–58]

The argument, evidently, is that skilled managers generate high externalities. Since few if any managers are prepared to make the personal sacrifices needed for the worker-run enterprise to be viable, legislative intervention is needed if social optimality is to be realized. The defects of human nature as we know it have to be corrected.

As with all proposals for reform, however, the issue is not whether there are defects but rather whether the defects are remediable. What is the prospect that the reform will yield net gains? Since feasible modes of socialist organization are already in place in Yugoslavia and elsewhere, a greater effort to evaluate their benefits and costs presumably ought to be made.[22]

6. Dignity

Assume, *arguendo,* that the political reforms favored by radical economists and others will not be implemented immediately. Are there other measures that can and should be taken to mitigate the oppressiveness of the Authority Relation in the meantime? My examination of that question is in two parts. The literature on job satisfaction and alienation is examined first. The more general issue of dignity is then considered.

6.1 *Job Satisfaction/Alienation*

One cannot read the literature of radical economists and the sociology of work without being impressed that work sometimes is oppressively organized and that efforts to remedy that condition are warranted. But much of the literature also has another quality: It suffers for want of reality testing. Thus when

---

[22]The comparative institutional assessment of work modes in chapter 9 disclosed that Peer Groups compare favorably, at least in small organizations. Scaling the size of Peer Groups up, however, unavoidably poses oligarchical strain.

confronted with a conflict between what workers say in response to questionnaires and what they do in the market place, many social commentators place inordinate weight on questionnaires.[23] Most economists, by contrast, would argue that preferences are revealed by actual choices. Consider the following study of assembly line workers at a General Motors assembly line plant in Massachusetts reported by Amitai Etzioni:

> An examination of their previous jobs indicates that by six criteria of job satisfaction, the workers were much better off on their previous job; 87.4 percent had formerly held a job where pace was determined individually; 72 percent had had nonrepetitive jobs; about 60 percent had had jobs requiring some skills and training; and 62.7 percent had been entirely or partly free to determine how their jobs ought to be done. . . . They chose to leave these jobs and take the frustrating assembly-line jobs basically because the new jobs offered a higher and more secure income. Three-quarters of the workers reported that the reasons bringing them to the new plant were primarily economic. Wage differences were about 30 percent. [Etzioni, 1975, pp. 34–35]

To be sure, better pay and better working conditions would be preferred by all. Confronted, however, with the need to make tradeoffs, valued attributes will be adjusted at the margin. Except as it can be demonstrated that work has been organized in an inferior manner, so that more satisfying work modes can be devised without sacrifice in efficiency, complaints about prevailing work practices, where workers have voluntarily sacrificed greater work satisfaction for greater pay, are of uncertain purpose.[24] Paul Blumberg nevertheless contends, "There is scarcely a study in the entire literature which fails to demonstrate that satisfaction is enhanced . . . or productivity

[23]See, for example, *Work In America* (1973, p. 13). One gets a sense that when some observers do not get the answer they are looking for at the outset, questions will be reshaped and answers reinterpreted until the desired result is realized (*Work In America*, 1973, pp. 14–15). Innovative programs such as Lincoln Electric's—which has a fifty-year history of success—are reported (pp. 107–8) without ever confronting such questions as whether Lincoln's employees are a random sample of the population or asking why Lincoln does not use this successful organizational innovation (or is not imitated by others) to diversify and become a large and decisive factor on the American business scene. Problems with "conventional" modes, such as General Motors experienced at Lordstown (*Work In America,* 1973, pp. 19, 38), are reported as though they are windows on the future. If, however, as at Lordstown, the problems abate, attention is directed elsewhere. Likewise, whereas reorganizing the process for assembling automobiles at Volvo's Kalmar plant received widespread coverage at the outset, its subsequent history has been much less widely reported.

[24]Inasmuch as automobile assembly is one of the more routinized of jobs, prior manufacturing employment for most automotive workers will, of necessity, rank more highly in job satisfaction respects. The basic point, however, is that composite evaluation of a job is a function of wages, job security, and job satisfaction. To focus only on the last is to ignore tradeoffs. The General Motors employees plainly did not accept inferior employment in job satisfaction respects without receiving compensating value in wage and job security terms. Although the adequacy of this compensation can be disputed on the grounds that the social valuation of job satisfaction exceeds the private valuation, that is a highly conjectural line of argument.

increases from a genuine increase in workers' decision-making power. Findings of such consistency, I submit, are rare in social research. . . . The participative worker is an involved worker."[25]

Curiously, the evidence relating job satisfaction to productivity discloses little or no association between the two (March and Simon, 1958, pp. 48, 50; Vroom, 1964, pp. 181–86; Katz and Kahn, 1966, p. 373; Gallagher and Einhorn, 1976, pp. 367, 371). Scott's survey of the empirical work brought on by the human relations school concludes with the blunt statement that "several decades of research have demonstrated no clear relation between worker satisfaction and productivity" (1981, p. 90). Gallagher and Einhorn conclude their survey of that literature with the observation: "We feel that job enlargement and enrichment can be useful tools for management. However, the important question that remains is not whether these programs work, but rather, *under what conditions* will they be most effective" (1976, p. 373; emphasis added). And Gunzberg's recent survey of work mode changes in Sweden concludes that the economic consequences of participative practices have been difficult to assess. Thus although they have, in his judgment, yielded social/psychological gains, they "do not add to the value of goods and services, and can add to their cost" (Gunzberg, 1978, p. 45).

Rarely, I submit, will optimum job design involve the elimination of hierarchy. Instead, it entails taking the rough edges off of hierarchy and affording those workers who desire it a greater degree of interested involvement. But it is no accident that hierarchy is ubiquitous within all organizations of any size. That holds not merely within the private-for-profit sector but among nonprofits and government bureaus as well. It likewise holds across national boundaries and is independent of political systems. In short, inveighing against hierarchy is rhetoric; both the logic of efficiency and the historical evidence disclose that nonhierarchical modes are mainly of ephemeral duration. Putterman, among others, evidently agrees (1982).

6.2 *Dignitary Values*

The foregoing discussion of participation benefits raises a serious doubt that efforts to effect participation can be justified on profitability grounds. That general conclusion might be challenged, however, by arguing that the studies to date are insufficiently discriminating. Even if participation does not yield detectable benefits in general, an examination of tasks in greater microanalytic detail will disclose that some tasks regularly benefit from participation. Moreover, some of the benefits of participation may show up in the social calculus even though the private calculus does not support them.

---

[25]The passage is cited in Bowles and Gintis (1976, pp. 79–80). Horvat also relies on Blumberg for his claim that "participation increases productivity" (1982, p. 207).

The more general issue is whether the inclusion of dignity as an underlying attribute of human nature is warranted. Why should it be? What are the refutable implications?

The issues here are beyond the scope of this treatise. I submit, however, that capitalism is prone to undervalue dignity and that institutional safeguards can sometimes be forged that help to correct the condition. Some of the procedural safeguards urged by labor law specialists (Summers, 1976, pp. 503–8, 519–22) are examples.

Jerry Mashaw observes that the unifying thread in the "natural rights" approach to due process "is the perception that the effects of process on participants, not just the rationality of substantive results, must be considered" (1985, p. 182). "At an intuitive level [w]e all feel that process matters irrespective of result. . . . We *do* distinguish between losing and being treated unfairly" (p. 183). Such intuition presumably lies behind Karl Llewellyn's observation: "In no legal system are all promises enforceable; people and courts have too much sense" (1931, p. 738).

Unpacking all this is not easy. Two levels of argument can, however, be distinguished. The lower level involves the profitability calculus and maintains that remediable suboptimization by managers (e.g. first-line supervisors) ought to be corrected. The higher level involves the Kantian moral imperative never to treat anyone as a mere means (Mashaw, 1985, p. 144; Pincoffs, 1977, pp. 175–79). The first of those purposes will be served by judicious use of institutional safeguards. Assuming that upper levels of the organizational hierarchy are aware of the earlier described behavioral tendencies of lower levels of management, myopia can be checked (in some degree) by using the firm's overall profitability calculus as a basis for deriving appropriate supervisory constraints. Purely calculative but informed upper-level decision-makers can be expected to implement such organizational reforms.

How far short of the Kantian moral imperative such reforms will fall is the remaining issue. Horvat expresses the socialist objection to capitalism as follows: "[R]elations between persons are expressed and experienced as relations between things. . . . Men evaluate each other as they evaluate objects" (1982, pp. 90–91). Economists, whose knowledge of capitalism and its nuances runs deep, ought to be involved in devising a thoughtful response. Safeguarding firm-specific values in human capital is easy. But what dignitary values beyond those warrant support? What are the comparative institutional ramifications? What are the tradeoffs?

7. Concluding Remarks

Recall the contracting schema in section 4 of Chapter 1, where nodes A, B, and C are distinguished. The main implications of the transaction cost approach to labor organization, as developed in this chapter, may be summarized with reference to that schema as follows:

1. Labor market transactions located at node A are ones for which human assets are nonspecific. Accordingly:
   a. Specialized governance structure for those labor transactions is unneeded. Discrete market contracting will characterize transactions of that kind. Migrant farm labor is an example.
   b. Since the organization of nonspecific (fungible) labor affords no economies, management (acting as the agent of capital) will normally resist efforts to unionize. Unions, if they appear at all, will be organized late in such industries and often will require the support of the political process.
   c. The governance structures (ports of entry, promotion ladders, grievance procedures, seniority rules, and the like) will be relatively primitive whether labor of this kind is organized or not.
2. Labor market transactions of the node B kind expose specialized human assets to expropriation hazards and are unstable.
   a. Workers will accept such jobs only upon payment of a wage premium.
   b. Jobs of this kind are apt to be redesigned. Either the idiosyncratic attributes will be sacrificed (in which case the job will revert to node A) or protective governance structure will be devised (the attributes will be protected under node C).
3. Labor market transactions of the node C kind are those for which collective organization (often in the form of a union) has been mutually agreed to. Such structure protects labor against expropriation hazards, protects management against unwanted quits, and permits adaptations to changing circumstances to be made in an uncontested (mainly cooperative) way.
   a. Jobs of this kind are candidates for early unionization, since mutual gains can thereby be realized.
   b. The governance structures associated with such jobs will be highly elaborated.

But while the transaction cost approach to labor organization is the source of numerous refutable implications, it is not by itself adequate to deal with all the relevant issues with which the study of labor organization is legitimately concerned. For one thing, the matter of power is underdeveloped. Additionally, while the importance of dignity is admitted, the calculative/efficiency-oriented approach maintained by transaction cost economics cannot encompass the full set of issues that a concern for dignity introduces. Finally, possible disequilibrium features are ignored.

CHAPTER 11

The Modern Corporation

There is virtual unanimity for the proposition that the modern corporation is a complex and important economic institution. There is much less agreement on what its attributes are and on how and why it has successively evolved to take on its current configuration. While I agree that there have been a number of contributing factors, I submit that the modern corporation is mainly to be understood as the product of a series of organizational innovations that have had the purpose and effect of economizing on transaction costs.

Note that I do not argue that the modern corporation is to be understood exclusively in those terms. Clearly there have been other contributing factors, of which the quest for monopoly gains is one and the imperatives of technology are another. Those mainly have a bearing on market shares and on the absolute size of specific technological units, however; the distribution of economic activity, as between firms and markets, and the internal organization (including both the shape and the aggregate size) of the firm are not explained, except perhaps in trivial ways, in those terms. Inasmuch as shape and composition are core issues, a theory of the modern corporation that does not address them is, at best, seriously incomplete.

Specifically, the study of the modern corporation should extend beyond vertical integration to concern itself with and provide consistent explanations for the following features of the organization of economic activity: What

economic purposes are served by the widespread adoption of divisionalization? What ramifications, if any, does internal organization have for the long-
standing dilemma posed by the separation of ownership from control? Can the
"puzzle" of the conglomerate be unraveled? Do similar considerations apply
in assessing multinational enterprise? Can an underlying rationale be provided
for the reported association between technological innovation and direct foreign investment?

Key legal features of the corporation—limited liability and the transferability of ownership—are taken as given. Failure to discuss them does not
reflect a judgment that they are either irrelevant or uninteresting. The main
focus of this chapter, however, is on the internal organization of the corporation. Since any of a number of internal structures is consistent with these legal
features, an explanation for the specific organizational innovations that were
actually adopted evidently resides elsewhere. Among the more significant of
those innovations, and the ones addressed here, are the development of line-
and-staff organization by the railroads; selective forward integration by manufacturers into distribution; the development of the divisionalized corporate
form; the evolution of the conglomerate; and the appearance of the multinational enterprise. The first three changes have been studied by business historians, the contributions of Chandler (1962; 1977) being the most ambitious
and notable.

Railroad organization in the nineteenth century is examined in section 1.
The multidivisional structure is described and interpreted in section 2. Conglomerate organization and multinational organization are treated in section 3.
The central proposition repeated throughout is this: Organization form
matters.

1. Railroad Organization

The 1840s mark the beginning of a great wave of organizational change that
has evolved into the modern corporation (Chandler, 1977). According to
Stuart Bruchey, the fifteenth-century merchant of Venice would have understood the form of organization and methods of managing men, records, and
investment used by Baltimore merchants in 1790 (1956, pp. 370–71). Those
practices evidently remained quite serviceable until after the 1840s. The two
most significant developments were the appearance of the railroads and, in
response, forward integration by manufacturers into distribution. Selective
forward integration is described and interpreted in Chapter 5. The experience
of the railroads has yet to be addressed.

Although a number of technological developments—including the telegraph (Chandler, 1977, p. 189), the development of continuous process machinery (pp. 252–53), the refinement of interchangeable parts manufacture (pp. 75–77), and related mass manufacturing techniques (chap. 8)—contributed to organizational changes in the second half of the nineteenth century, none was more important than the railroads (Porter and Livesay, 1971, p. 55). Not only did the railroads pose distinctive organizational problems of their own, but the incentive to integrate forward from manufacturing into distribution would have been much less without the low-cost, reliable, all-weather transportation afforded by the railroads.

The appearance and purported importance of the railroads have been matters of great interest to economic historians. But with very few exceptions the organizational—as opposed to the technological—significance of the railroads has been neglected. Thus Robert Fogel (1964) and Albert Fishlow (1965) "investigated the railroad as a construction activity and as a means of transport, but not as an organizational form. As with most economists, the internal workings of the railroad organizations were ignored. This appears to be the result of an implicit assumption that the organization form used to accomplish an objective does not matter" (Temin, 1981, p. 3).

The economic success of the railroads entailed more, however, than the substitution of one technology (rails) for another (canals). Rather, organizational aspects also required attention. As Chandler puts it:

> [The] safe, regular reliable movement of goods and passengers, as well as the continuing maintenance and repair of locomotives, rolling stock, and track, roadbed, stations, roundhouses, and other equipment, required the creation of a sizable administrative organization. It meant the employment of a set of managers to supervise these functional activities over an extensive geographical area; and the appointment of an administrative command of middle and top executives to monitor, evaluate, and coordinate the work of managers responsible for the day-to-day operations. It meant, too, the formulation of brand new types of internal administrative procedures and accounting and statistical controls. Hence, the operational requirements of the railroads demanded the creation of the first administrative hierarchies in American business. [1977, p. 87]

To be sure, that can be disputed. Markets, after all, can and do perform many of those functions. What is it about the "operational requirements" of the railroads that was responsible for the displacement of markets by hierarchies? Does similar reasoning apply to other transportation systems, such as trucking?

The "natural" railroad units, as they first evolved, were lines of about fifty miles in length. Those roads employed about fifty workers and were administered by a superintendent and several managers of functional activities

(Chandler, 1977, p. 96). That was adequate as long as traffic flows were uncomplicated and short hauls prevailed. The full promise of the railroads could be realized, however, only if traffic densities were increased and longer hauls introduced. How was that to be effected?

In principle, successive end-to-end systems could be joined by contract. The resulting contracts would be tightly bilateral, however, since investments in site-specific assets by each party were considerable. Contracting difficulties of two kinds would have to be faced. Not only would the railroads need to reach agreement on how to deal with a series of complex operating matters— equipment utilization, costing, and maintenance; adapting cooperatively to unanticipated disturbances; assigning responsibility for customer complaints, breakdown, and so on—but problems of customers contracting with a set of autonomous end-to-end suppliers would have to be worked out.

There were several possibilities. One would be to be patient: The marvel of the market would work things out. A second would be to move to the opposite extreme and coordinate through comprehensive planning. A third would be to evolve organizational innovations located in between.

David Evans and Sanford Grossman interpret the railroad response in market terms. They note that "market systems in which property ownership is dispersed among numerous self-interested businesses and individuals have demonstrated a remarkable ability to coordinate the provision of goods and services" (1983, p. 96), and they specifically apply this argument to the railroads:

> The experience of the railroads in the 19th century . . . demonstrates how the market system encourages physical coordination. Many separate companies built segments of our railroad system during the mid-19th century. By interconnecting with each other and enabling produce and passengers to transfer easily between railroads, these companies were able to increase revenues and profits. [Evans and Grossman, 1983, p. 103]

Evans and Grossman support this by reference to the study by George Taylor and Irene Neu, who reported that traffic between New York City and Boston moved easily over tracks owned by four different companies in 1861 (Taylor and Neu, 1956, p. 19). They also cite Chandler in support of their argument that "the market provides strong incentives for physical coordination without common ownership" (Evans and Grossman, 1983, p. 104, n. 22).

Evidently there is more to railroad organization than "physical coordination," however. Otherwise the natural railroad units of fifty miles in length would have remained intact. And there is also more to railroad organization than unified ownership. Thus the Western and Albany road, which was just over 150 miles in length and was built in three sections, each operated as a separate division with its own set of functional managers, experienced severe problems (Chandler, 1977, pp. 96–97). As a consequence a new organizational form was fashioned whereby the first "formal administrative structure manned by full-time salaried managers" in the United States appeared (pp. 97–98).

That structure was progressively perfected. The organizational innovation that the railroads eventually evolved is characterized by Chandler as the "decentralized line-and-staff concept of organization." It provided that "the managers on the line of authority were responsible for ordering men involved with the basic function of the enterprise, and other functional managers (the staff executives) were responsible for setting standards" (Chandler, 1977, p. 106). Geographic divisions were defined, and the superintendents in charge were held responsible for the "day-to-day movement of trains and traffic by an express delegation of authority" (p. 102). The division superintendents were on the "direct line of authority from the president through the general superintendent" (p. 106), and the functional managers within the geographic divisions—who dealt with transportation, motive power, maintenance of way, passenger, freight, and accounting—reported to them rather than to their functional superiors at the central office (pp. 106–7). That administrative apparatus permitted individual railroads to operate thousands of miles of track by 1893.[1]

To be sure, that falls well short of central planning. Moreover, the contractual difficulties posed by coordination and efficient utilization to which Chandler referred were not the only factors that elicited the large system response. Chandler also gives great weight to the strategic purposes served (1977, chap. 5). The latter, however, also has contractual origins: Unable to control prices and allocate traffic through interfirm organization, the railroads were driven to merger. Thus whereas there is a widely held view that express or tacit collusion is easy to effectuate—John Kenneth Galbraith opines that "the firm, in tacit collaboration with other firms in the industry, has wholly sufficient power to set and maintain prices" (1967, p. 200)—that is repeatedly refuted by the evidence. The history of cartel failures among the railroads is especially instructive. The early railroads evolved a series of progressively more elaborate interfirm structures in an effort to curb competitive pricing. The first involved informal alliances, which worked well until "the volume of through traffic began to fall off and competitive pressures increased." With the onset of the depression in 1873 there began an "increasingly desperate search for traffic. . . . Secret rebating intensified. Soon roads were openly reducing rates." The railroads thereupon decided to

---

[1]Each of the ten largest railroads opearated more than five thousand miles of track in 1893 (Chandler, 1977, p. 168).

"transform weak, tenuous alliances into strong, carefully organized, well-managed federations" (Chandler, 1977, pp. 134, 137). The membership of the federations was expanded, and other federations in other geographic regions appeared. As Albert Fink, who headed up the largest such federation realized, however, "the only bond which holds this government together is the intelligence and good faith of the parties composing it" (Chandler, 1977, p. 140). To rectify that weakness, Fink urged the railroads to seek legislation that would give the actions of the federation legal standing.

Lack of legal sanctions means that loyal members of the cartel must exact penalities against deviants in the market place. Unless such disciplinary actions (mainly price cuts) can be localized, every member of the cartel, loyalist and defector alike, suffers. That is a very severe (if little remarked) limitation on the efficacy of cartels. Inasmuch as national legislation was not forthcoming, Fink and his associates "found to their sorrow that they could not rely on the intelligence and good faith of railroad executives" (Chandler, 1977, p. 141). In the end, the railroads turned to merger. The high-powered incentives of autonomous ownership evidently presented too strong a temptation for cheating in an industry where sunk costs were substantial.

The railroad industry thus progressed from small, end-to-end units with fifty miles of track to systems of several hundred and, eventually, to several thousand miles of track. Market coordination was thus supplanted by administrative organization in substantial degree:

> The fast-freight lines, the cooperatives, and finally the traffic departments of the larger roads had completed the transformation from market coordination to administrative coordination in American overland transportation. A multitude of commission agents, freight forwarders, and express companies, as well as stage and wagon companies, and canal, river, lake, and coastal shipping lines disappeared. In their place stood a small number of large multi-unit railroad enterprises. . . . By the 1880s the transformation begun in the 1840s was virtually completed. [Chandler, 1977, p. 130]

To be sure, transaction cost economics does not predict the final configuration in detail. It is nevertheless noteworthy that (1) efficient technological units were very small in relation to efficient economic units in this industry, which is to say that organizational rather than technological factors were responsible for the creation of large systems; (2) transaction cost economics predicts that severe problems will arise in attempting to coordinate autonomous end-to-end systems that are characterized by site specificity by contract;[2] and (3) the limits of cartels also have organizational origins and are

---

[2]Other types of specific assets also influenced railroad organization. In particular, although steam locomotives were assets on wheels, they required an inordinate amount of preventive and corrective maintenance. A resale market in steam locomotives was impaired by the acquired knowledge embedded in the mechanics familiar with the idiosyncratic attributes of each. (The diesel locomotive, by comparison, was less idiosyncratic in maintenance cost respects.)

evident upon posing problems of interfirm organization in contracting terms. That the trucking industry, which does not have the same site specificity (mainly roadbed) features, should differ from the railroad industry in significant respects is furthermore predicted by transaction cost reasoning. (Indeed, the absence of site-specific investments in the trucking industry make it a much better candidate than the railroads to illustrate the Evans and Grossman argument that market coordination is a marvel.[3] If Chandler's account is accurate, the railroad industry illustrates the importance of hierarchy.)

Operating the large railroad systems was possible only upon solving administrative complexities which greatly exceeded those faced by earlier business enterprises. As discussed below, the hierarchical structure that the railroad managers crafted was broadly consistent with the principles of efficient hierarchical decomposition stated by Simon. Thus, support activities (lower-frequency dynamics) were split off from operations (higher-frequency dynamics), and the linkages within each of those classes of activity were stronger than the linkages between. That organizational innovation, in Chandler's judgment, paved the way for modern business enterprise.

2.   The M-Form Innovation

2.1   *The Transformation*

The most significant organizational innovation of the twentieth century was the development in the 1920s of the multidivisional structure. That development was little noted and not widely appreciated, however, as late as 1960. Leading management texts extolled the virtues of ''basic departmentation'' and ''line and staff authority relationships,'' but the special importance of multidivisionalization went unremarked.[4]

Chandler's pathbreaking study of business history, *Strategy and Structure,* simply bypassed this management literature. He advanced the thesis that ''changing developments in business organization presented a challenging area for comparative analysis'' and observed that ''the study of [organizational] innovation seemed to furnish the proper focus for such an investigation''

---

[3]Trucking is also a much better candidate for deregulation than the railroads. To be sure, no one is urging a return of the railroads to their regulatory status of 1980. That there is greater dissatisfaction with deregulation of the railroads than with trucking is, however, predictable upon examining their transaction cost features. See Christopher Conte, ''Push for Tighter U.S. Supervision of Railroads Is a Threat to Success of Reagan Deregulators,'' *Wall Street Journal,* January 7, 1985, p. 50.

[4]The treatment of these matters by Harold Koontz and Cyril O'Donnell (1955) is representative.

(Chandler, 1962 [1966 edition], p. 2). Having identified the multidivisional structure as one of the most important such innovations, he proceeded to trace its origins, identify the factors that gave rise to its appearance, and describe the subsequent diffusion of that organization form. It was uninformed and untenable to argue that organization form was of no account after the appearance of Chandler's book.

The leading figures in the creation of the multidivisional (or M-form) structure were Pierre S. du Pont and Alfred P. Sloan; the period was the early 1930s; the firms were du Pont and General Motors; and the organizational strain of trying to cope with economic adversity under the old structure was the occasion to innovate in both. The structures of the two companies, however, were different.

Du Pont was operating under the centralized, functionally departmentalized or unitary (U-form) structure. General Motors, by contrast, had been operated more like a holding company (H-form) by William Durant, whose genius in perceiving market opportunities in the automobile industry (Livesay, 1979, pp. 232–34) evidently did not extend to organization. John Lee Pratt, who served as an assistant to Durant and as chairman of the Appropriations Committee after Du Pont took an equity position in General Motors, observed that "under Mr. Durant's regime we were never able to get things under control" (Chandler, 1966, p. 154). A leading reason is that the Executive Committee, which consisted of Division Managers, was highly politicized: "When one of them had a project, why he would vote for his fellow members; if they would vote for his project, he would vote for theirs. It was a sort of horse trading" (Pratt, quoted by Chandler, 1966, p. 154).

Chandler summarizes the defects of the large U-form enterprise in the following way:

> The inherent weakness in the centralized, functionally departmentalized operating company . . . became critical only when the administrative load on the senior executives increased to such an extent that they were unable to handle their entrepreneurial responsibilities efficiently. This situation arose when the operations of the enterprise became too complex and the problems of coordination, appraisal, and policy formulation too intricate for a small number of top officers to handle both long-run, entrepreneurial, and short-run operational administrative activities. [1966, pp. 382–83]

The ability of the management to handle the volume and complexity of the demands placed upon it became strained and even collapsed. Unable meaningfully to identify with or contribute to the realization of global goals, managers in each of the functional parts attended to what they perceived to be operational subgoals instead (Chandler, 1966, p. 156). In the language of transaction cost economics, bounds on rationality were reached as the U-form structure labored under a communication overload while the pursuit of sub-goals by the functional parts (sales, engineering, production) was partly a manifestation of opportunism.

The M-form structure fashioned by du Pont and Sloan involved the creation of semiautonomous operating divisions (mainly profit centers) organized along product, brand, or geographic lines. The operating affairs of each were managed separately. More than a change in decomposition rules was needed, however, for the M-form to be fully effective. Du Pont and Sloan also created a general office "consisting of a number of powerful general executives and large advisory and financial staffs" (Chandler, 1977, p. 460) to monitor divisional performance, allocate resources among divisions, and engage in strategic planning. The reasons for the success of the M-form innovation are summarized by Chandler:

> The basic reason for its success was simply that it clearly removed the executives responsible for the destiny of the entire enterprise from the more routine operational activities, and so gave them the time, information, and even psychological commitment for long-term planning and appraisal. . . .
> [The] new structure left the broad strategic decisions as to the allocation of existing resources and the acquisition of new ones in the hands of a top team of generalists. Relieved of operating duties and tactical decisions, a general executive was less likely to reflect the position of just one part of the whole. [1966, pp. 382–83]

In contrast with the holding company—which is also a divisionalized form but has little general office capability and hence is little more than a corporate shell—the M-form organization adds (1) a strategic planning and resource allocation capability and (2) monitoring and control apparatus. As a consequence, cash flows are reallocated among divisions to favor high-yield uses, and internal incentive and control instruments are exercised in a discriminating way. In short, the M-form corporation takes on many of the properties of (and is usefully regarded as) a miniature capital market,[5] which is a much more ambitious concept of the corporation than the term "holding company" contemplates.

2.2 *An Information Processing Interpretation*

Most recent treatments of the corporation nevertheless accord scant attention to the architecture of the firm and focus entirely on incentive features instead. In fact, however, organization form matters even in a firm in which incentive

---

[5]Richard Heflebower (1960) and Armen Alchian (1969) also impute capital market resource allocation and control functions to the M-form corporation.

problems attributable to opportunism are missing. The studies of hierarchy by W. Ross Ashby (1960) and by Herbert Simon (1962) are germane.

Ashby established that all adaptive systems that have a capacity to respond to a bimodal distribution of disturbances—some being disturbances in degree; other being disturbances in kind—will be characterized by double feedback. The rudimentary model is shown in Figure 11–1. Disturbances in degree are handled in the primary feedback loop (or operating part) within the context of extant decision rules. Disturbances in kind involve longer-run adjustments in which parameter changes are introduced or new rules are developed in the secondary (or strategic) feedback loop. The second feedback loop is needed because the repertoire of the primary loop is limited—which is a concession to bounded rationality. Evolutionary systems that are subject to such bimodal disturbances will, under natural selection, necessarily develop two readily distinguishable feedbacks (Ashby, 1960, p. 131).

Simon's discussion of the organizational division of decision-making labor in the firm is in the same spirit. From "the information processing point of view, division of labor means factoring the total system of decisions that need to be made into relatively independent subsystems, each one of which can be designed with only minimal concern for its interaction with the others" (Simon, 1973, p. 270). That applies to both technical and temporal aspects of

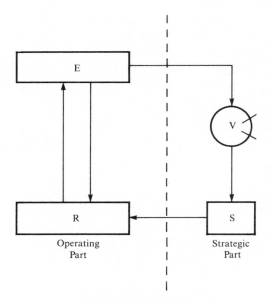

FIGURE 11–1.   Double Feedback

the organization. In both respects the object is to recognize and give effect to conditions of near decomposability. That is accomplished by grouping the operating parts into separable entities within which interactions are strong and between which they are weak and by making temporal distinctions of a strategic versus operating kind. Problems are thus factored in such a way that the higher-frequency (or short-run) dynamics are associated with the operating parts while the lower-frequency (or long-run) dynamics are associated with the strategic system (Simon, 1962, p. 477). Those operating and strategic distinctions correspond with the lower and higher levels in the organizational hierarchy, respectively. They furthermore correspond with the primary and secondary feedback loops to which Ashby referred.

2.3 *Governance*

Effective divisionalization requires more than mere decomposition. Otherwise the H-form would have been an adequate answer to the strains that appear as the (indecomposable) U-form structure was scaled up.

Indeed, in a team theory world in which managers are assumed to share identical preferences, the problem of organization is precisely one of decomposing the enterprise in efficient information processing respects (Marshak and Radner, 1972; Geanakoplos and Milgrom, 1984). As noted in Chapter 2, team theory combines the assumption of bounded rationality with non-self-interest-seeking. If, however, the managers of the firm are given to opportunism, additional problems of incentive alignment, decision review, auditing, dispute resolution, and the like must be confronted. Those who invented the M-form structure were aware of those needs and made provision for them.

Opportunism in the H-form enterprise can take several forms. For one thing, subsidiaries that have preemptive claims against their own earnings are unlikely to return those resources to the center but will "reinvest" to excess instead.[6] Additionally, since the secondary feedback loop has limited competence to evaluate performance, costs are apt to escalate. If subsidiaries enjoy relief from market tests because of corporate cross-subsidization, moreover, further cost excesses will appear. Finally, partisan decision-making of the kind that Pratt associated with General Motors in the Durant era may appear.

The M-form structure removes the general office executives from partisan involvement in the functional parts and assigns operating responsibilities

---

[6]To be sure, the H-form firm could encourage divisions to invest in one another. Serious problems of information display, evaluation, auditing, and the like are posed for which a central agency is apt to enjoy advantages, however—which is to say that internal resource allocation among divisions can benefit from the support of a general office.

to the divisions. The general office, moreover, is supported by an elite staff that has the capacity to evaluate divisional performance. Not only, therefore, is the goal structure altered in favor of enterprise-wide considerations, but an improved information base permits rewards and penalties to be assigned to divisions on a more discriminating basis, and resources can be reallocated within the firm from less to more productive uses. A concept of the firm as an internal capital market thus emerges.

Effective multidivisionalization thus involves the general office in the following set of activities: (1) the identification of separable economic activities within the firm; (2) according quasi-autonomous standing (usually of a profit center nature) to each; (3) monitoring the efficiency performance of each division; (4) awarding incentives; (5) allocating cash flows to high-yield uses; and (6) performing strategic planning (diversification, acquisition, divestiture, and related activities) in other respects. The M-form structure is thus one that *combines* the divisionalization concept with an internal control and strategic decision-making capability.

2.4 *An Isomorphism*

Although the economic correspondences are imperfect, it is nevertheless of interest that the U-form, H-form, and M-form structures bear a formal relation to the basic contracting schema set out in Chapter 1. Figure 11–2 displays the parallel relations.

Thus whereas the contracting schema was developed in terms of two production technologies ($k = 0$ and $k > 0$), the organizational distinction to be made is between two information processing technologies (centralized and decentralized, respectively). Given the requisite preconditions[7] and assuming the absence of opportunism, the $k > 0$/decentralized technologies will yield a superior result. But the $k > 0$/decentralized technologies also pose serious hazards of opportunism. Unless safeguards can be devised, the full benefits of the $k > 0$/decentralized technologies will go unrealized.

The $s = 0$ condition reflects a refusal to safeguard a contract for which nonredeployable assets are at hazard. The organizational correspondence is the H-form firm. The $s > 0$ conditions reflects a decision to provide protective governance. The M-form firm is the organizational counterpart for contractual safeguards. Thus the full benefits of the $k > 0$/decentralized organization are achieved only if $s > 0$/M-form governance is provided.

---

[7]The preconditions in the production technology case go to specifying the stochastic structure of demand. In the information technology case, the issue is one of firm size and complexity. (The M-form structure is unneeded in small and simple firms.)

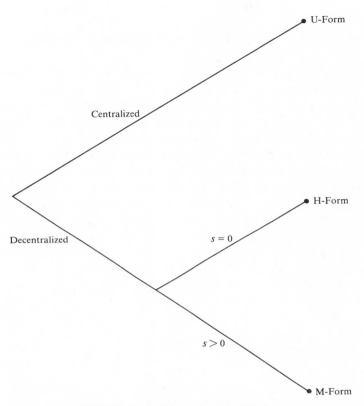

FIGURE 11–2.   Organizational Choices

Indeed, the contracting analogy can be carried further by regarding investors who supply capital to a firm as the counterpart of the suppliers of intermediate product in the nonstandard contracting context. Recall that suppliers of intermediate product were willing to employ any technology and would accept any contract for which expected breakeven could be projected. The same is true of suppliers of capital: They will invest in any firm with any organization form on terms such that a competitive (risk-adjusted) rate of return can be projected. This, however, merely reflects the outcome of a competitive market process. More germane to our purposes here is the following: Although firms that employ an inferior (U-form) information technology or that do not safeguard the superior technology against the hazards of opportunism (H-form) may still be able to raise capital if their product line is sufficiently strong (e.g. they enjoy patent protection), they could raise capital on better terms if a superior information technology supported by safeguards were to be employed—which is what the M-form structure adds to decentralization.

3. Applications: Conglomerate and Multinational Enterprise

As discussed in earlier chapters, the inhospitality tradition regarded nonstandard contracting practices as presumptively unlawful. Nonstandard internal forms of organization have also been regarded with deep suspicion. The same technological orientation to economic organization plainly informed both of those approaches. Unless a clear-cut technological justification for the contracting practices or organizational structure in question could be discerned, antitrust specialists were quick to ascribe antisocial purpose and effect. Transaction cost economics regards nonstandard forms of market and internal organization differently. For one thing, anticompetitive concerns ought to be reserved for the subset of conditions for which a condition of preexisting monopoly power exists. For another, the possibility that economies of transaction cost are realized ought to be admitted. Rather, therefore, than regard organizational innovations with suspicion and hostility, such innovations are assessed on the merits instead. Real economies of all kinds, transaction cost included, warrant respect.

3.1 *The Conglomerate*

The conglomerate form of organization has been subject to a variety of interpretations. Some of them are sketched here, after which a transaction cost interpretation is advanced. The matter of tradeoffs is then briefly addressed.

a. EARLIER INTERPRETATIONS

The antitrust enforcement agencies were among the first to venture an unfavorable assessment of the conglomerate. Thus the staff of the Federal Trade Commission held:

> With the economic power which it secures through its operation in many diverse fields, the giant conglomerate may attain an almost impregnable position. Threatened with competition in any one of its various activities, it may well sell below cost in that field, offsetting its losses through profits made in its other lines—a practice which is frequently explained as one of meeting competition. The conglomerate corporation is thus in a position to strike out with great force against smaller business. [U.S. Federal Trade Commission, 1948, p. 59]

Robert Solo subsequently characterized the conglomerate corporation as a "truly dangerous phenomenon" and argued that it "will probably subvert management effectiveness and organizational rationale for generations"

(1972, pp. 47–48). Others advised that the large conglomerate was a hazard to competition "in every line of commerce in every section of the country" (Blake, 1973, p. 567). Bogeyman economics became fashionable. Procter & Gamble, for example, was repeatedly described as a "brooding omnipresence" in a court of law.[8] Even those who regarded the conglomerate form more sympathetically referred to it as a puzzle (Posner, 1972, p. 204).

To be sure, Morris Adelman (1961) advanced a more favorable interpretation. He observed that the conglomerate form of organization had attractive portfolio diversification properties. But why should the conglomerate appear in the 1960s rather than much earlier? After all, holding companies, which long predated the conglomerate, can accomplish portfolio diversification. And individual stockholders, through mutual funds and otherwise, are able to diversify their own portfolios. At best the portfolio diversification thesis is a very incomplete explanation for the postwar wave of conglomerate mergers.[9]

b.   AN INTERNAL CAPITAL MARKET INTERPRETATION

As set out previously, Alfred P. Sloan, Jr., and his associates at General Motors were among the first to perceive the merits of the M-form structure. But while the divisionalization concept was well understood and carefully implemented within General Motors, those same executives were fixated on the notion that General Motors was an automobile company.

Thus Sloan remarked that "tetraethyl lead was clearly a misfit for GM. It was a chemical product, rather than a mechanical one. And it had to go to market as part of the gasoline and thus required a gasoline distribution system."[10] Accordingly, although GM retained an investment position, the Ethyl Corporation became a free-standing entity rather than an operating division (Sloan, 1964, p. 224). Similarly, although Durant had acquired Frigidaire and Frigidaire's market share of refrigerators exceeded 50 percent in the 1920s, the position was allowed to deteriorate as rivals developed market positions in

[8]The phrase was repeatedly used by expert economists for the plaintiff in *Purex* v. *Procter & Gamble*, which was a private antitrust suit in which Purex claimed that the resources of Procter & Gamble put a scare into Purex in its rivalry with Clorox. The district court decided against Purex. 419 F. Supp. 931 (C.D. Cal. 1976).

[9]Homemade diversification is not a perfect substitute for conglomerate diversification, because bankruptcy has real costs that the firm, but not individuals, can reduce by portfolio diversification. Bankruptcy costs have not sharply increased in the past thirty years, however, so those differences do not explain the appearance of the conglomerate during that interval.

[10]Quoted by Burton and Kuhn (1979, p. 6).

other major appliances (radios, ranges, washers, etc.) while Frigidaire concentrated on refrigerators. The suggestion that GM get into air conditioners "did not register on us, and the proposal was not . . . adopted" (Sloan, 1964, p. 361). As Richard Burton and Arthur Kuhn conclude, GM's "deep and myopic involvement in the automobile sector of the economy [prevented] product diversification opportunities in other market areas—even in product lines where GM had already achieved substantial penetration—[from being] recognized" (1979, pp. 10–11).

The conglomerate form of organization, whereby the corporation consciously took on a diversified character and nurtured its various parts, evidently required a conceptual break in the mind-set of Sloan and other prewar business leaders. That occurred gradually, more by evolution than by grand design (Sobel, 1974, p. 377), and it involved a new group of organizational innovators—of which Royal Little was one (Sobel, 1974). The natural growth of conglomerates, which would occur as the techniques for managing diverse assets were refined, was accelerated as antitrust enforcement against horizontal and vertical mergers became progressively more severe. Conglomerate acquisitions—in terms of numbers, assets acquired, and as a proportion of total acquisitions—grew rapidly with the result that "pure" conglomerate mergers, which in the period 1948–53 constituted only 3 percent of the assets acquired by merger, had grown to 49 percent by 1973–77 (Scherer, 1980, p. 124).

As developed more fully elsewhere (Williamson, 1975, pp. 158–162), the conglomerate is best understood as a logical outgrowth of the M-form mode for organizing complex economic affairs. Thus once the merits of the M-form structure for managing separable, albeit related, lines of business (e.g. a series of automobile or a series of chemical divisions) were recognized and digested, its extension to manage less closely related activities was natural. That is not to say that the management of product variety is without problems of its own. But the basic M-form logic, whereby strategic and operating decisions are distinguished and responsibilities are separated, carried over. The conglomerates in which M-form principles of organization are respected are usefully thought of as internal capital markets whereby cash flows from diverse sources are concentrated and directed to high-yield uses.

The conglomerate is noteworthy, however, not merely because it permitted the M-form structure to take that diversification step. Equally interesting are the unanticipated systems consequences that developed as a byproduct. Thus once it was clear that the corporation could manage diverse assets in an effective way, the possibility of takeover by tender offer suggested itself. The issues here are developed in Chapter 12.

C. TRADEOFFS

The term "M-form" is reserved for those divisionalized firms in which the general office is engaged in periodic auditing and decision review and is actively involved in the internal resource allocation process. Cash flows, therefore, are subject to an internal investment competition rather than automatically reinvested at their source. The affirmative assessment of the conglomerate as a miniature capital market presumes that the firm is operated in such a way. Not all conglomerates were. In particular, firms that in the 1960s were referred to as "go-go" conglomerates did not respect M-form principles. Their merits, if they had any, presumably resided elsewhere.

Inasmuch, however, as the organizational logic of the M-form structure runs very deep—serving, as it does, both to economize on bounded rationality (the information processing interpretation) and safeguard the internal resource allocation process against the hazards of opportunism (which is what the general office concept adds), the rationale for conglomerate structures in which M-form principles are violated is gravely suspect. Indeed, one would expect, and events have borne the expectation out, that the "go-go" conglomerates would become unglued when adversity set in—as it did in the late 1960s. Those firms found it necessary to reorganize along M-form lines, to simplify their product lines, or to do both.

Note in that connection that the M-form conglomerate engages in a depth-for-breadth tradeoff. As Alchian and Demsetz put it: "Efficient production into heterogeneous resources is not a result of having *better* resources but in knowing more *accurately* the relative productive performance of those resources" (1972, p. 789; emphasis in original). Plainly, diversification can be taken to excess. As the capacity to engage knowledgeably in internal resource allocation becomes strained, problems of misallocation and opportunism intrude. That conglomerate firms voluntarily engage in divestiture is presumably explained by that condition.

Lest I be misunderstood, I do not mean to suggest that opportunities to express managerial preferences in ways that conflict with the preferences of the stockholders have been extinguished as a result of the conglomerate form. The continuing tension between management and stockholder interests is reflected in numerous efforts that incumbent managements have taken to protect target firms against takeover (Cary, 1969; Williamson, 1979; Benston, 1980). Changes in internal organization have nevertheless relieved managerial discretion concerns. A study of the economic institutions of capitalism that makes no allowance for organization form changes and their capital market ramifications will naturally overlook the possibility that the

corporate control dilemma posed by Berle and Means has since been alleviated more by internal than it has by regulatory or external organizational
reforms.[11]

3.2 *Multinational Enterprise*

The discussion of the multinational enterprise (MNE) that follows deals mainly with recent developments and, among them, emphasizes organizational
aspects—particularly those associated with technology transfer in manufacturing industries. As Mira Wilkins has reported, direct foreign investment,
expressed as a percentage of GNP, was in the range of 7 to 8 percent in 1914,
1929, and 1970 (Wilkins, 1974, p. 437). Both the character of this investment
and, relatedly, the organization structure within which this investment took
place were changing, however. It is not accidental that the term MNE was
coined neither in 1914 nor in 1929 but is of much more recent origin.

Thus whereas the ratio of the book value of U.S. foreign investments in
manufacturing as compared with all other (petroleum, trade, mining, public
utilities) was 0.47 in 1950, that had increased to 0.71 in 1970 (Wilkins, 1974,
p. 329). Also, "what impressed Europeans about American plants in Europe
and the United States [in 1929] was mass production, standardization, and
scientific management; in the 1960s, Europeans were remarking that America's superiority was based on technological and managerial advantage [and]
that this expertise was being exported via direct investment" (Wilkins, 1974,
p. 436).

The spread of the multinational corporation in the post–World War II
period has given rise to considerable scrutiny, some puzzlement, and even
some alarm (Tsurumi, 1977, p. 74). One of the reasons for this unsettled state
of affairs is that transaction cost economizing and organization form issues
have been relatively neglected in efforts to assess MNE activity.[12]

---

[11]Hostility to the conglomerate form nevertheless continues. See Samuel Loescher (1984).
Also, the Antitrust Division of the United States Department of Justice argued in 1978 that
Occidental Petroleum should not be permitted to acquire the Mead Corporation because that
would permit Mead to make "efficient and cost effective" investments in greenfield plants to the
disadvantage of Mead's less efficient rivals. For a discussion of the government's use of "creative lawyering" to deter conglomerate mergers, see Williamson (1979, p. 69–73).

Antitrust caveats apply wherever an acquiring firm is properly characterized as one of a very
few most likely potential entrants (Williamson, 1975, pp. 165–70). Also, although very large
conglomerates might be regarded as objectionable from a populist political standpoint, such
arguments should be advanced in a frankly political way (rather than masqueraded in economic
garb) and treated in the context of giant-size firms quite generally.

[12]An important exception is the work of Buckley and Casson (1976).

Organization form is relevant in two related respects. First is the matter of U.S.-based as against foreign-based investment rates. Yoshi Tsurumi reports in this connection that the rate of foreign direct investments by U.S. firms increased rapidly after 1953, peaked in the mid-1960s, and has leveled off and declined since (Tsurumi, 1977, p. 97). The pattern of foreign direct investments by foreign firms, by contrast, has lagged that of the United States by about a decade (pp. 91–92).

Recall that the conglomerate uses the M-form structure to extend asset management from specialized to diversified lines of commerce. The MNE counterpart is the use of the M-form structure to extend asset management from a domestic base to include foreign operations. Thus the domestic M-form strategy for decomposing complex business structures into semi-autonomous operating units was subsequently applied to the management of foreign subsidiaries. The transformation of the corporation along M-form lines came earlier in the United States than in Europe and elsewhere. U.S. corporations were for that reason better qualified to engage in foreign direct investments at an earlier date than were foreign-based firms. Only as the latter took on the M-form structure did that multinational management capability appear. The pattern of foreign direct investments recorded by Tsurumi and reported above is consistent with the temporal differences of U.S. and foreign firms in adopting the M-form structure.

That U.S. corporations possessed an M-form capability earlier than their foreign counterparts does not, however, establish that they used it to organize foreign investment. John Stopford and Louis Wells have studied that issue. They report that while initial foreign investments were usually organized as autonomous subsidiaries, divisional status within an M-form structure invariably appeared as the size and complexity of foreign operations increased (Stopford and Wells, 1972, p. 21). The transformation usually followed the organization of domestic operations along M-form lines (p. 24). The adoption of a "global" strategy or "worldwide perspective"—whereby "strategic planning and major policy decisions" are made in the central office of the enterprise (p. 25)—could be accomplished only within a multidivisional framework.

Even more interesting than those organization form issues is the fact that foreign direct investments by U.S. firms have been concentrated in a few industries. Manufacturing industries that have made substantial foreign direct investments include chemicals, drugs, automobiles, food processing, electronics, electrical and nonelectrical machinery, nonferrous metals, and rubber. Tobacco, textiles and apparel, furniture, printing, glass, steel, and aircraft have, by comparison, done little foreign direct investment (Tsurumi, 1977, p. 87).

Stephen Hymer's "dual" explanation for the multinational enterprise is of interest in this connection. Thus Hymer observes that direct foreign investment "allows business firms to transfer capital, technology, and organizational skill from one country to another. It is also an instrument for restraining competition between firms of different nations" (Hymer, 1970, p. 443).

Hymer is surely correct that the MNE can service both of those purposes, and examples of both kinds can doubtless be found. It is nevertheless useful to ask whether the overall character of MNE investment, in terms of its distribution among industries, is more consistent with the efficiency purposes to which Hymer refers (transfer of capital, technology, and organizational skill) or with the oligopolistic restraint hypothesis. Adopting a transaction cost orientation discloses that the observed pattern of investment is more consistent with the efficiency part of Hymer's dual explanation.

For one thing, oligopolistic purposes can presumably be realized by portfolio investment coupled with a limited degree of management involvement to segregate markets. Put differently, direct foreign investment and the organization of foreign subsidiaries within an M-form structure are not needed to effect competitive restraints. Furthermore, if competitive restraints were mainly responsible for those investments, then presumably all concentrated industries—which would include tobacco, glass, and steel—rather than those associated with rapid technical progress, would be active in MNE creation. Finally, although many of the leading U.S. firms that engaged in foreign direct investment enjoyed "market power," that was by no means true for all.

By contrast, the pattern of foreign direct investments reported by Tsurumi appears to be consistent with a transaction cost economizing interpretation. Raymond Vernon's 1971 study of the *Fortune* 500 corporations disclosed that 187 of them had a substantial multinational presence. R&D expenditures as a percentage of sales were higher among those 187 than among the remaining firms in the *Fortune* 500 group. Furthermore, according to Vernon, firms that went multinational tended to be technological innovators at the time of making their initial foreign direct investments.

That raises the question of the attributes of firms and markets for accomplishing technology transfer. The difficulties with transferring technology across a market interface are of three kinds: recognition, disclosure, and team organization (Arrow, 1962; Williamson, 1975, pp. 31–33, 203–7; Teece, 1977).[13] Of those three, recognition is probably the least severe. To be sure, foreign firms may sometimes fail to perceive the opportunities to apply technological developments originated elsewhere. But enterprising domestic firms

---

[13]The material that follows is based on Williamson and Teece (1980). Our argument is similar to that advanced by Buckley and Casson (1976).

that have made the advance can be expected to identify at least some of the potential applications abroad.

Suppose, therefore, that recognition problems are set aside and consider disclosure. Attempts to transfer technology by contract can break down because of the "paradox of information." A very severe information asymmetry problem exists, on which account the less informed party (in this instance the buyer) must be wary of opportunistic representations by the seller.[14] Although sometimes the asymmetry can be overcome by sufficient *ex ante* disclosure (and veracity checks thereon), that may shift rather than solve the difficulty. The fundamental paradox of information is that "its value for the purchaser is not known until he has the information, but then he has in effect acquired it without cost" (Arrow, 1971, p. 152).

Suppose, *arguendo,* that buyers concede value and are prepared to pay for information in the seller's possession. The incentive to trade is then clear, and for some items this will suffice. The formula for a chemical compound or the blueprints for a special device may be all that is needed to effect the transfer. Frequently, however, and probably often, new knowledge is diffusely distributed and is poorly defined (Nelson, 1981). Where the requisite information is distributed among a number of individuals all of whom understand their speciality in only a tacit, intuitive way[15] a simple contract to transfer the technology cannot be devised.

Transfer need not cease, however, because simple contracts are not feasible. If the benefits of technology transfer are sufficiently great, exchange may be accomplished either by devising a complex trade or through direct foreign investment. Which will be employed depends on the circumstances. If only a one-time (or very occasional) transfer of techology is contemplated, direct foreign investment is a somewhat extreme response.[16] The complex contractual alternative is to negotiate a tie-in sale whereby the technology and associated knowhow are transferred as a package. Since the knowhow is concentrated in the human assets who are already familiar with the technology, this entails the creation of a "consulting team" by the seller to accompany the physical technology transfer—the object being to overcome

[14]Markets for information are apt to be especially costly and/or hazardous when transmission across a national boundary is attempted. Language differences naturally complicate the communication problem, and differences in the technological base compound those difficulties. If, moreover, as is commonly the case, cultural differences foster suspicion, the trust needed to support informational exchange may be lacking. Not only will contract negotiations be more complex and costly on that account, but execution will be subject to more formal and costly procedures than would occur under a regime of greater trust.

[15]On this, see Polanyi (1962).

[16]This is an implication of transaction cost reasoning in which the frequency dimension has explanatory power.

startup difficulties and to familiarize the employees of the foreign firm, through teaching and demonstration, with the idiosyncrasies of the operation.[17]

Inasmuch as many of the contingencies that arise in the execution of such contracts will be unforseen, and as it will be too costly to work out appropriate *ex ante* responses for others, such consulting contracts are subject to considerable strain. Where a succession of transfers is contemplated, which is to say when the frequency shifts from occasional to recurring, complex contracting is apt to give way to direct foreign investment. A more harmonious and efficient exchange relation—better disclosure, easier reconciliation of differences, more complete crosscultural adaptation, more effective team organization and reconfiguration—predictably results from the substitution of an internal governance relation for bilateral trading under those recurrent trading circumstances where assets, of which complex technology transfer is an example, have a highly specific character.

The upshot is that while puzzlement with and concerns over MNEs will surely continue,[18] a transaction cost interpretation of the phenomenon sheds insight on the following conspicuous features of multinational investment: (1) the reported concentration of foreign direct investment in manufacturing industries where technology transfer is of special importance; (2) the organization of those investments within M-form structures; and (3) the differential timing of foreign direct investment between U.S. and foreign manufacturing enterprises (which difference also has organization form origins).[19]

4. Concluding Remarks

There is widespread agreement, among economists and noneconomists alike, with the proposition that the modern corporation is an important and complex economic institution. Such agreement is mainly explained by the obtrusive

[17]On the importance of on-site observation and of teaching-by-doing, see Polanyi (1962), Doeringer and Piore (1971, pp. 15–16), and Williamson, Wachter, and Harris (1975).

[18]For recent summaries of and contributions to this literature, see Caves (1982) and Hennart and Wilkins (1983).

[19]The argument can be extended to deal with such observations as those of Mansfield, Romeo, and Wagner (1979), who report that firms use subsidiaries to transfer their newest technology overseas but rely on licensing or joint ventures for older technology. The transaction cost argument is that the latter are more well defined, hence are more easily reduced to contract, and require less firm-specific know-how to effect successful transfer.

size of the largest firms. The economic factors that lie behind the size, shape, and performance of the modern corporation, however, are poorly understood.

The puzzlement is not of recent origin. Edward Mason complained more than twenty years ago that ''the functioning of the corporate system has not to date been adequately explained. . . . The man of action may be content with a system that works. But one who reflects on the properties or characteristics of this system cannot help asking why it works and whether it will continue to work'' (1959, p. 4). The predicament to which Mason refers is, I submit, largely the product of two different (but not unrelated) intellectual traditions. The first holds that the structural features of the corporation are irrelevant. The neoclassical theory of the firm that populates intermediate theory textbooks is consistent with this view. Structural differences are suppressed as the firm is described as a production function to which a profit maximization objective has been assigned. The second has public policy roots—the inhospitality tradition to which I referred earlier. The distinctive structural features of the corporation are here believed to be the result of unwanted (anticompetitive) intrusions into market processes.

The transaction cost approach differs from both. Unlike neoclassical analysis, internal organization is specifically held to be important. Unlike the inhospitality tradition, structural differences are presumed to arise primarily in the service of transaction cost economizing.

The progressive evolution of the modern corporation records the imprint of transaction cost economizing at every stage. The railroads, which were the ''first modern business enterprises'' (Chandler, 1977, p. 120), devised the line-and-staff structure when coordination of end-to-end systems by contract broke down and older and simpler structures were unable to manage the resulting networks. Transaction costs rather than technology were plainly driving those developments. Forward integration out of manufacturing into distribution was widespread at the turn of the century. As discussed in Chapter 5, integration occurred selectively rather than comprehensively and in a manner that is broadly consistent with transaction cost reasoning.

The two leading corporate forms that were in place in 1920 were the functional (or U-form) and holding company (H-form) structures. Both experienced internal inefficiency and managerial discretion distortions as firms grew in size and complexity. Viewing internal organization within a nexus of contract perspective, the implicit contracts were too cumbersome on the one hand (the U-form case) and too incomplete on the other (the H-form condition). Faced with the need either to retrench or to develop a new set of internal contracting relationships, organizational innovators devised the M-form structure.

The resulting structure recognized essential decomposability, thus rectifying the overcentralization condition in the U-form enterprise. The M-form furthermore effected a split between operating and strategic decision-making and reserved the latter for the general office. Providing the general office with an internal incentive and control capability was required lest the potential benefits of the division of effort be dissipated. Such a capacity had been lacking in the H-form organization and contributed to problematic performance therein.

This argument bears a resemblance to the two technology problem discussed in earlier chapters. The two technologies under review here are the centralized and decentralized modes of organization. The first corresponds to the U-form; the second can be either H or M. The contractual difference between the latter two is that safeguards against opportunism are more fully developed in the M-form. Investors will presumably be prepared to supply capital on superior terms, therefore, to a large, diversified M-form corporation than they would to an equivalent H-form firm. In the degree to which the M-form is in fact the fitter, natural selection, which includes competition in the capital market, favors this result.

The M-form innovation introduced by General Motors and du Pont (and subsequently imitated by others) thus served both technical and internal governance purposes—in that it served both to economize on bounded rationality and attenuate opportunism. Specifically, operating decisions were no longer forced to the top but were resolved at the divisional level, which relieved the communication load. Strategic decisions were reserved for the general office, which reduced partisan political input into the resource allocation process. And the internal auditing and control techniques to which the general office had access served to overcome information impactedness conditions and permit fine tuning controls to be exercised over the operating parts.

The M-form structure, which was originally adopted by firms in relatively specialized lines of commerce, was subsequently extended to manage diversified assets (the conglomerate) and foreign direct investments (MNE). A breadth-for-depth tradeoff is involved in the former case, as the firm selectively internalizes functions ordinarily associated with the capital market. MNE activity has also been selective—being concentrated in the more technologically progressive industries where higher rates of R&D are reported and technology transfer arguably poses greater difficulties. This pattern of foreign direct foreign investment cannot be explained by a monopoly hypothesis but is consistent with transaction cost reasoning.

To be sure, the interpretation of the modern corporation set out in this chapter and elsewhere in this book deals only with salient features. There is both room for and need of refinement. It nevertheless makes headway against the rationality puzzlement to which Mason referred and which has troubled other students of the modern corporation. The basic proposition is this: Organization form deserves to be taken seriously. Once that is acknowledged, transaction cost economizing becomes a very large part of the argument.

CHAPTER 12

Corporate Governance

The simple contractual schema set out in Chapter 1, on which I have repeatedly relied, is applied here to corporate governance. The main issues with which this chapter is concerned are these: What governance needs, if any, are served by creating a board of directors? What are the consequences of broad representation by all of the "interested" constituencies on the board of directors? What is the relation between managerial discretion and organization form?

I deal with the first by examining the relation between the firm and each of its constituencies—labor, capital, suppliers, customers, the community, and management—in contractual terms. I argue that the board of directors should be regarded primarily as a governance structure safeguard between the firm and owners of equity capital and secondarily as a way by which to safeguard the contractual relation between the firm and its management. Although other constituencies may sometimes be invited onto the board for the limited purpose of sharing information in a timely and credible manner, to assign other and larger purposes to the board involves tradeoffs with doubtful net benefits. Most constituencies are better advised to perfect their relation to the firm at the contracting interface at which firm and constituencies strike their main bargain.

The general issue of corporate control and several proposals for expansive representation on the board of directors are described in section 1. The contractual approach is applied to each of the principal constituencies in section 2. The management's relation to the board is elaborated in section 3. Managerial discretion is examined in relation to organization form in section 4. Concluding remarks follow.

1. Background

Observers of the corporate scene have long struggled with the dilemma of corporate control. It was originally expressed in terms of the strain between diffuse ownership and management. It has subsequently been enlarged to consider the problems of creating a mechanism to ensure that corporate management does right by "labor, suppliers, customers, and owners while simultaneously serving the public interests" (Mason, 1958, p. 7).

Large corporate size was mainly responsible for Berle and Means's (1932) challenge to the view that the shareholders controlled the modern corporation. Since the large size of modern firms often resulted in diffuse ownership, management purportedly assumed effective control. Berle and Means thus inquired whether, under those circumstances, there was "any justification for assuming that those in control of a modern corporation will also choose to operate it in the interests of the owners" (1932, p. 121). The possibility that management might operate the corporation in its own interests could scarcely be dismissed.[1]

Other scholars broadened the inquiry and examined the role of other constituencies. Their views sometimes reflect political preferences, pure and simple. They are often buttressed, however, by implicit or explicit reference to market failure. Thus although the stockholders may at one time have had defensible exclusive claims on the board of directors, that has since become an anachronism—all the more so as markets in modern economies progressively deviate from the neoclassical ideal. Since imperfect markets afford

[1]If outsiders to whom equity shares are sold anticipate the behavioral consequences of the dilution of ownership, then the price at which equity is sold will reflect prospective managerial discretion. Some observers of the corporate scene thus conclude that the Berle and Means query is irrelevant. Managerial discretion is simply a cost of dilution, but one that is more than offset by the gains. There is an inconsistency, however, in admitting that managerial discretion is significant and to insist that firm behavior be modeled according to the postulate of profit maximization. If managerial discretion is real and varies, among other things, with organization form, this should be acknowledged, which is to say that the Berle–Means query remains important, *ex ante* anticipation notwithstanding.

very unsatisfactory relief against corporate malfunctions, all constituencies require direct access to corporate governance lest their legitimate interests be ignored or abused.

The market failure view of corporate governance has been elaborated by reference to the efficacy of stock markets as compared with factor markets. Thus E. C. B. Gower observes that "the workers form an integral part of the company," and laments that this condition is ignored by company law in Britain (1969, p. 10). He contends that a master-servant fiction is maintained by legal theory and that this "is unreal, in that it ignores the undoubted fact that the employees are members of the company for which they work to a far greater extent than are the shareholders whom the law persists in regarding as its proprietors" (Gower, 1969, p. 11). Masahiko Aoki similarly observes that "the association of individual shareholders . . . may not be enduring" and concurs that the "employees form an integral part of the firm for which they work to a far greater extent than" most shareholders (1983, p. 5). Summers concurs:

> If the corporation is conceived . . . as an operating institution combining all factors of production to conduct an on-going business, then the employees who provide the labor are as much members of that enterprise as the shareholders who provide the capital. Indeed, the employees may have made a much greater investment in the enterprise by their years of service, may have much less ability to withdraw, and may have a greater stake in the future of the enterprise than many of the stockholders. In a corporation, so conceived, employee directors have no more conflict of interest than shareholder directors. [1982, p. 170]

Application of that logic suggests that other constituencies with a long-term stake in the enterprise also deserve representation on the board of directors. This would go beyond E. Merrick Dodd's (1932) proposal that the directors of a corporation should serve as trustees for all the constituencies—shareholders, customers, suppliers, community—that have a stake in the corporation. What Robert Dahl has referred to as "interest group management" would expressly apportion seats on the board of directors to corporate constituencies: "Thus the board of directors might consist of one-third representatives elected by employees, one-third consumer representatives, one-third delegates of federal, state and local governments" (Dahl, 1970, p. 20).[2] Shareholders are conspicuously omitted from the proposal.

---

[2]Dahl does not favor this solution to corporate governance. His preferred solution is worker self-management. He nevertheless argues that "interest group management would be an improvement over the present arrangements, and it may be what Americans will be content with, if the corporation is to be reformed at all" (1970, p. 23).

2. A Contractual Assessment

The study of corporate contracting is complicated by interdependencies within and between contracts; changes in one set of terms commonly require realignments in others. It will nevertheless be more helpful to examine the contracts of corporate constituencies in a sequential rather than a fully interactive way. That completed, I shall then examine interaction effects.

2.1 *Framework*

Recall the two-technology schema in Chapter 1. One is the general purpose technology—technology that is useful over a broad range of transactions and therefore involves no exposure of transaction-specific assets. Such resources can be redeployed easily should either party terminate the contract. Special purpose technology, by contrast, incorporates transaction-specific assets. They cannot be redeployed easily or costlessly if the contract is prematurely terminated or if continuity of the exchange relation is otherwise upset. Using k as a measure of transaction-specific assets, transactions that use the general purpose technology are ones for which $k = 0$. When transactions use special purpose technology, $k > 0$. Such trades experience a fundamental transformation, hence take on the attributes of bilateral dependency.

Although classical market contracting suffices for transactions when $k = 0$, unassisted market governance poses hazards whenever transaction-specific assets are placed at risk, because parties then have a special incentive to safeguard investments. Let s denote the magnitude of any such safeguards. A situation in which $s = 0$ is one in which no safeguards are provided. A condition of complete safeguard will obtain if $s = k$. A refusal to provide a contractual safeguard will, of course, show up in the price. If $\bar{p}$ is the price at which the firm procures a good or service when $s = 0$, and if $\hat{p}$ is the price for the same good or service when $s > 0$, then $\bar{p} > \hat{p}$, *ceteris paribus*.

What is referred to in Figure 1–2 as a node A outcome obtains if $k = 0$. Node B is the $k > 0$, $s = 0$ result. And node C corresponds to $k > 0$, $s > 0$.

The above all relates to the governance branch of transaction cost economics. The measurement branch, however, is often relevant (and, as discussed below, is here). Thus, despite trading safeguards of a node C kind, there may be special circumstances where additional benefits would accrue if information pertinent to the exchange were more fully disclosed. Sometimes the disclosure will enable the recipient more successfully to anticipate future developments and plan accordingly. Sometimes such disclosure will reduce informational asymmetries which, if unrelieved, will cause the less informed party to disbelieve the representations of the more informed and lead to a costly contractual impasse.

It bears repeating, however, that such disclosures are not needed if assets are nonspecific. Investment plans do not turn on bilateral trading in such circumstances. And where neither party values continuity in its relationship with the other, a costly effort to reduce informational asymmetries serves no useful veracity purposes either.

2.2 Applications

Two classes of membership on the board of directors will be considered: voting membership and participation only to secure information. Voting membership invites a constituency to participate in what Eugene Fama and Michael Jensen (1983) refer to as the ratification of corporate decisions and the follow-on monitoring of corporate performance. Informational participation allows a constituency to observe strategic planning and to be apprised of the information on which decisions are based, but allows no vote on investments or management. Those responsibilities are reserved for the voting subset of the board.[3]

a. LABOR

Supporters of codetermination regard participation for informational purposes as inadequate. They maintain that codetermination should extend the influence of workers to include "general issues of investments, market planning, decisions about output, and so forth" (Schauer, 1973, p. 215).[4]

That argument is clearly mistaken as applied to workers with general purpose skills and knowledge (node A). Such workers can quit and be replaced without productive losses to either worker or firm.[5] Consider, there-

---

[3]Allowing only informational participation to a constituency could be implemented through two-tier boards, but more often it takes the form of implicit understandings among the members of the board. In principle, members are equals, but a subset understands that its useful participation is limited to supplying and receiving information. As Oliver Hart observes, complete information sharing is not assured by such a practice (1983, p. 23). However, this form of participation arguably assures more complete information sharing than nonparticipation.

[4]I do not mean to implicate Schauer, Gower, Aoki, and Summers in this expansive view of labor participation.

[5]This is an oversimplification. It assumes easy reemployment and ignores transitional costs, including the impact on the family. As Knight observes, "Laborers are attached to their homes and even to their work by sentimental ties to which market facts are ruthless" (1965, p. 346). I

fore, workers who make firm-specific investments and are located at nodes B or C. Ordinarily, it can be presumed that workers and firms will recognize the benefits of creating specialized structure of governance to safeguard firm-specific assets. Failure to provide such safeguards will cause demands for higher wages. Also, as discussed in Chapter 7, inefficient utilization decisions will result from node B outcomes. Accordingly, efficiency purposes will be served if labor of the $k > 0$ kind is located at node C by aligning incentives and crafting specialized bilateral governance structures that are responsive to the needs of firm and labor at this contracting nexus.

Consider therefore the relation of node C labor to the board of directors in informational respects. A chronic difficulty with long-term labor agreements is that misallocation will result if wages are set first and employment levels are unilaterally determined by management later. The inefficiency was first noted by Wassily Leontief (1946) and has since been elaborated upon by Robert Hall and David Lilien (1979) and by Masahiko Aoki (1984). Even if wages and employment are both established at the outset, the agreement may drift out of alignment during the contract's execution to the disadvantage of the less informed member of the contracting pair. Such a result might be avoided by imparting more information to labor. Labor membership on the board of directors for informational purposes is one means of achieving that result. Indeed, Aoki contends that the "true value of co-determination is to be found in its being an instrument through which important and accurate information is shared" (1984, p. 167).

Labor membership on boards of directors can be especially important during periods of actual or alleged adversity, especially when firms are asking workers for give-backs. Labor's board membership might mitigate worker's skepticism by promoting the exchange of credible information.[6] Douglas Fraser's inclusion on the Chrysler board during the company's recovery is an illustration.

The practice does not, however, enjoy widespread support. Some opponents fear that it will be difficult to resist the transformation of informational

---

will assume that those effects are constant across (or vary directly with) human asset specificity. Accordingly, the cutting edge is the degree of human asset specificity.

[6]As Hart observes, if only the firm and not workers can observe state of the world realizations, their "wages cannot be made to depend on the state directly. For if the contract says that wages should fall in bad times, then it is in the interest of the firm always to claim that times are bad" (1983, p. 3). To be sure, there are limits. As *ex post* information becomes available, firms that egregiously understate true conditions will become known and will thereafter carry a stigma. *Ex ante* terms will thereafter be adjusted to their disadvantage.

roles into decision-making participation. It is also possible, however, that the informational benefits of labor membership are not adequately appreciated.[7]

b. OWNERS

The term "owners" is usually reserved for stockholders, but debt-holders sometimes assume this status. However described, suppliers of finance bear a unique relation to the firm: The whole of their investment in the firm is potentially placed at hazard. By contrast, the productive assets (plant and equipment; human capital) of suppliers of raw material, labor, intermediate product, electric power, and the like normally remains in the suppliers' possession. If located at node A, therefore, these suppliers can costlessly redeploy their assets to productive advantage. Suppliers of finance must secure repayment or otherwise repossess their investments to effect redeployment.[8] Accordingly, suppliers of finance are, in effect, always located on the $k > 0$ branch. The only question is whether their investments are protected well (node C) or poorly (node B).

1. *Equity.* Although a well-developed market in shares permits individual stockholders to terminate ownership easily by selling their shares, it does not follow that stockholders as a group have a limited stake in the firm. What is available to individual stockholders may be unavailable to stockholders in the aggregate. Although some students of governance see only an attenuated relation between stockholders and the corporation, that view is based on a fallacy of composition. Stockholders as a group bear a unique relation to the firm. They are the only voluntary constituency whose relation with the corporation does not come up for periodic renewal. (The public may be regarded as an involuntary constituency whose relation to the corporation is indefinite.) Labor, suppliers in the intermediate product market, debtholders, and consumers all have opportunities to renegotiate terms when contracts are renewed. Stockholders, by contrast, invest for the life of the

---

[7]A recent law review note contends that informational benefits would accrue to the stockholders by including union membership on the board of directors. Note, *"An Economic and Legal Analysis of Union Representation on Corporate Boards of Directors,"* 130 U. Pa. L. Rev. 919 (1982). The author claims that such membership would purportedly "reduce the ability of management to run the corporation so as to further their own interests rather than those of the share holders." *Id.* at 956. If true, the question arises as to why some perceptive shareholders have not recognized the benefits and made provision for union participation. Is it ignorance of the gains? Are incumbent managements so well entrenched that they can defeat any such efforts? Or are the gains offset by unacknowledged costs?

[8]Suppliers of finance are, in effect, subject to two hazards: First, they supply general purpose purchasing power that can be embezzled or otherwise expropriated: and second, the funds can be used to support firm specific investments. Although suppliers of other firm specific inputs—labor, raw material, intermediate product—face hazards of the second kind, their exposure in the first respect is usually limited to the amount of short-term credit extended.

firm,[9] and their claims are located at the end of the queue should liquidation occur.

Stockholders are also unique in that their investments are not associated with particular assets. The diffuse character of their investments puts shareholders at an enormous disadvantage in crafting the kind of bilateral safeguards normally associated with node C. Given the enormous variety, the usual strictures on the feasibility of comprehensive *ex ante* contracting apply here in superlative degree. Inasmuch, moreover, as unanticipated events cannot be addressed and folded into the contract at contract renewal intervals, because the equity contract runs for the life of the firm, the parties appear to be at a contracting impasse. Absent the creation of some form of protection, stockholders are unavoidably located at node B.

Recall that suppliers located at node B demand a premium because of the hazard of expropriation that such contracts pose. That premium can be regarded as a penalty imposed on the firm for its failure to craft node C safeguards. The incentive of the firm to secure relief from the penalty is clear (Jensen and Meckling, 1976, p. 305). What to do?

One possibility would be for entrepreneurs to supply all of their equity financing directly—from their own funds or from friends and family who know and trust them and can apply sanctions that are unavailable to outsiders who are not members of friend or family networks. This would place a severe limit, however, on the amount of equity funding available. It is no solution, moreover, to increase the amount of debt financing to compensate for those restraints.[10]

A second possibility is to invent a governance structure that holders of equity recognize as a safeguard against expropriation and egregious mismanagement. Suppose that a board of directors is created that (1) is elected by the pro-rata votes of those who hold tradable shares, (2) has the power to replace the management, (3) has access to internal performance measures on a timely basis, (4) can authorize audits in depth for special follow-up purposes, (5) is apprised of important investment and operating proposals before they are implemented, and (6) in other respects bears a decision review and monitoring relation to the firm's management.[11] Such a governance structure

[9]The contract between the firm and the shareholders actually can be, and sometimes is, adjusted by making changes in the corporate charter. These changes appear, however, mainly to be initiated by the management and are frequently management-favoring in character. (See the discussion of golden parachutes in note 24 below.)

[10]Debt-holders, moreover, will be reluctant to invest in nonredeployable assets, hence the firm will invest more heavily in general purpose (redeployable) plant and equipment than it would if it could secure equity funding on node C terms.

[11]Fama and Jensen describe a four step in process: "1. *initiation*—generation of proposals for resource utilization and structuring of contracts; 2. *ratification*—choice of decision initiatives

arguably moves the node B relation that would otherwise obtain toward a node C result, with the attendant benefits that are associated therewith.

The board of directors thus arises endogenously, as a means by which to safeguard the investments of those who face a diffuse but significant risk of expropriation because the assets in question are numerous and ill-defined and cannot be protected in a well-focused, transaction-specific way. Thus regarded, the board of directors should be seen as a governance instrument of the stockholders. Whether other constituencies also qualify depends on their contracting relation with the firm.

Such protection for stockholders can be and often is supplemented by other measures. Corporate charter restrictions and informational disclosure requirements are examples. Firms recognize stockholders' needs for controls, and many attempt responsibly to provide them.[12] Some managements, however, play "end games" (undisclosed strategic decisions to cut and run before corrective measures can be taken), and individual managers commonly disclose information selectively or distort the data. Additional checks against such concealment and distortion can be devised to give shareholders greater confidence. Arguably, an audit committee composed of outside directors and a certification of financial reports by an accredited accounting firm promote those purposes. Another possibility is the required disclosure of financial reports to a public agency with powers of investigation. The efficacy of those devices is difficult to gauge.[13]

---

to be implemented; 3. *implementation*—execution of ratified decisions; and 4. *monitoring*—measurement of the performance of decision agents and implementation of rewards" (1983, p. 303). They assign the initiation and implementation steps to the management and the ratification and monitoring to the board of directors (p. 313). Also see the FitzRoy and Mueller discussion (1984) of the relation of stockholders to the corporation. As they point out, "If voting rights were removed from common shares, stockholders would demand a more explicit contractual statement of the conditions and amounts" of dividends (FitzRoy and Mueller, 1984, p. 40).

[12]Traders' interests in the disclosure of information is discussed in Diamond (1983). Corporate charter abuses are discussed in Williamson (1979).

[13]George Stigler has nevertheless made an interesting attempt to assess the impact of the SEC. He describes the basic test as "simplicity itself. . . . We take all the new issues of industrial stocks with a value exceeding $2.5 million in 1923–28, and exceeding $5 million in 1949–55, and measure the values of these issues . . . in five subsequent years . . . relative to the market average" (1964, p. 120). The pre-SEC versus post-SEC performance of new issues in relation to the market at one-year intervals is as follows (where the first figure is the pre-SEC mean and the second is post-SEC): after one year, 81.9 versus 81.6; after two years 65.1 versus 73.3; after three years, 56.2 versus 72.6; after four years 52.8 versus 71.9; and after five years, 58.5 versus 69.6. Stigler declares that since these differences are statistically significant only in the third and fourth years, the SEC had no effect.

There are, however, two problems with that argument. First, tests of statistical significance are not needed where, as in Stigler's case, the attributes of an entire population, rather than a

2. *Lenders.* In certain atypical circumstances, lenders may also deserve board representation. Unlike stockholders, lenders commonly make short-term loans for general business purposes or longer-term loans against earmarked assets. Proof that the firm is currently financially sound, coupled with short maturity, affords protection for short-term lenders. Such lenders do not need additional representation. Lenders who make longer-term loans commonly place preemptive claims against durable assets. If the assets cannot be easily redeployed, lenders usually require partial financing through equity collateral. Thus, long-term lenders usually carefully align incentives and protect themselves with safeguards of the sort associated with node C (Smith and Warner, 1979).

As Mervyn King observes, however, firms in countries where the stock market is poorly developed are forced to rely more extensively on debt (1977, p. 156). Adequate safeguards are more difficult to provide in such circumstances. As the exposure to risk increases, these debt-holders become more concerned with the details of the firm's operating decisions and strategic plans: With high debt–equity ratios the creditors become more like shareholders, and greater consultation between the management and its principal creditors results. A banking presence in a voting capacity on the board of directors may be warranted in those circumstances. More generally, a banking presence may be appropriate for firms experiencing adversity, but that should change as evidence of recovery progresses.

3. *A Digression on Optimal Finance.* The above discussion suggests that the manner in which an investment is financed will vary systematically with the attributes of the assets. For the reasons given in Chapter 2, the usual fixed cost–variable cost distinction will not do. Rather, the crucial matter is one of redeployability. Equity financing, according to the approach taken here, will vary directly with the degree to which assets are nonredeployable. Theories of finance that do not make the asset specificity distinction predict, by contrast, that there will be no such association. The Modigliani-Miller theorem (1958), which maintains that the cost of capital is independent of the capital structure in the firm, is thus at variance with the asset specificity/governance structure approach.

c. SUPPLIERS

Whether or not suppliers of raw material and intermediate product have a stake in a firm depends on whether they have made substantial investments in

---

sample thereof, are measured. Second, a more interesting test would be to ascertain whether rates of return on equity changed with regulation. Improved information disclosure should lead to lower average rates, *ceteris paribus*.

durable assets that cannot be redeployed without sacrificing productive value if the relationship with the firm were to be terminated prematurely. The mere fact that one firm does a considerable amount of business with another, however, does not establish that specific assets have thereby been exposed. At worst, suppliers located at node A experience modest transitional expenses if the relation is terminated. Neither specialized bilateral governance nor membership on the board of directors is needed to safeguard their interests. The protection afforded by the market suffices.

Suppliers who make substantial firm-specific investments in support of an exchange will demand either a price premium (as at node B, where the projected breakeven price is $\bar{p}$) or special governance safeguards (as at node C). Progress payments and the use of hostages to support exchange are illustrations of node C safeguards. An agreement to settle disputes through arbitration, rather than through litigation, is also in the spirit of node C governance. (The issues here are those developed in earlier chapters, where the governance relations between suppliers and buyers are examined.)

Considering the variety of widely applicable governance devices to which firms and their suppliers have access, there is no general basis to accord suppliers additional protection through membership on the board of directors. There could be exceptions, of course, where a large volume of business is at stake and a common information base is needed to coordinate investment planning.[14] Ordinarily, however, the governance structure that firm and supplier devise at the time of contract (and help to support through a web of interfirm relationships) will afford adequate protection. Membership on the board, if it occurs at all, should be restricted to informational participation.

d. CUSTOMERS

The main protection for customers located at node A is generally the option to take their trade elsewhere. Products that have delayed health effects are an exception, and consumer durables can also pose special problems. Membership on the board of directors is not, however, clearly indicated for either reason.

Health hazards pose problems if consumers are poorly organized in relation to the firm and lack the relevant information. If consumers can organize only with difficulty, because they are unknown to one another or

---

[14]The information advantage is that the supplier is made privy to the plans of the buyer and can satisfy himself on the merits of the internal decision-making process. One large Japanese manufacturer volunteered that it had a major supplier (who was close to a co-venturer) on the board for information sharing but not decision-making purposes. If minority votes are inconsequential while credible information disclosure is highly valued, there is little gain (indeed, some potential loss) to extending the franchise.

because of the ease of free-riding, then a bilateral governance structure between firm and consumers may fail to materialize. Protection by third parties may be warranted instead. A regulatory agency equipped to receive complaints and screen products for health hazards could serve to infuse confidence in such markets.

Whether consumer membership on the board would afford additional protection is problematic. Who are representative consumers? How do they communicate with their constituency? Token representation may create only unwarranted confidence.[15]

Similar problems of consumer organization and ignorance arise in conjunction with consumer durables. That is true whether the consumer durable requires no follow-on service or a great deal of such service.[16] Among the available types of consumer protection are brand names, warranties, and arbitration panels. Shoppers who choose node B are presumably looking for bargains. They will spurn the additional protections in favor of a lower price. Such customers implicitly accept a higher risk and should accept occasional disappointments. There are other consumers however, who value protections at node C. Some are prepared to pay a premium for a brand name item. Brand names effectively extend a firm's planning horizon and create incentives for the firm to behave "more responsibly."[17] (To be sure, customers must be wary against firms that build up a reputation, thereafter to expend it by taking advantage of lagging consumer perceptions.[18]) Warranties are explicit forms

[15]As Reinier Kraakman observes on a related matter of director selection, since "corporate managers are . . . largely free to control the selection and tenure of outside directors, lawyers, and accountants . . . it may be child's play for would-be offenders to select corrupt or captive outside participants in the firm" (1984, p. 863). Conceivably "professional" consumer advocates would relieve those concerns. But how to credentialize the subset of professionals who qualify poses difficult issues.

[16]A solid state radio that is replaced rather than repaired when it becomes defective is an example of the former; an automobile of the latter.

[17]Problems arise when established firms with apparent commitments to an industry decide to cut losses and terminate. The home computer market is a recent illustration. Andrew Pollack describes Texas Instruments' decision to terminate:

> The losing battle of Texas Instruments Inc. in the home computer market has taken a severe toll on the company's finances, its reputation and its employees. Yet more than one million other people—the owners of the Texas Instruments 99A home computers—will suffer as well.
> They are likely to find it much more difficult to get their machines repaired and to find new programs and peripheral equipment, such as data storage devices and printers, to use with the machines. [*"Texas Instruments' Pullout"* New York Times, October 31, 1983, at D1, col. 3]

The purchasers of the T199A, who had struck an implicit bargain with Texas Instruments but went uncompensated when the decision to terminate was made, were the losers.

[18]For a general discussion of consumer information issues, see Beales, Craswell, and Salop (1981).

of follow-on protection, and many are available on optional terms. The recently introduced consumer arbitration panels are likewise responsive to concerns over consumer protection. Consumers concerned about fair play during the service period will presumably concentrate their purchases on brands for which arbitration is available.

Further innovations to offer consumer protection on a discriminating basis may be needed. With the possible exception of large customers with special informational needs, however, a general case for inclusion of consumers on the board of directors is not compelling.

e. THE COMMUNITY

Community interest in the corporation is a very large subject. I consider two concerns here: externalities and the hazards of appropriation.

Externalities commonly arise where the parties in question do not bear a contracting relation to each other. Pollution is one example. Corrections can be interpreted as an effort by the community to impose a contract where none existed. For example, the community may place a pollution tax (price) on the firm, or it may stipulate that pollution abatement regulations must be satisfied as a condition for doing business.

A chronic problem in this area is to secure the knowledge on which to base an informed pollution control policy. Firms are often in possession of the necessary knowledge and may disclose it only in a selective or distorted manner. Public membership on the board of directors could conceivably reduce misinformation. But the remedy would come at a high cost if the corporation were thereby politicized or deflected from its chief purpose of serving as an economizing instrument. Penalties against misinformation coupled with moral suasion may be more effective. It is an area in which there may simply be no unambiguously good choices.

The hazards of expropriation are even less of a justification for public membership on boards. Communities often construct durable infrastructures to support a new plant or renewal investments by old firms. Expropriation is possible if the firm is able to capitalize these public investments and realize a gain upon selling off the facility. Such concerns are much greater if the firm makes general purpose rather than special investments. Communities that make investments in support of a firm should therefore scrutinize the character of the investments that the firm itself makes.

As elsewhere, expropriation hazards will be mitigated if the parties can locate themselves at node C. Insistence that the firm make specialized investments is akin to the use of hostages to support exchange. In general, specially crafted node C protection, rather than public membership on the board of directors, has much to commend it as the main basis for safeguarding community investments.

c. THE MANAGEMENT

There is one constituency that curiously goes unmentioned in most discussions of corporate governance: the management. Perhaps analysts assume that management is appropriately assigned a mediation role between contesting constituencies.[19] And some critics maintain that management is already overrepresented in the affairs of the firm: Management participation on the board of directors is the problem, not the solution. The issues here are developed in section 3, below.

2.3 *Contracting in Its Entirety*

Suppose, *arguendo,* that voting membership for node B constituencies is granted. Suppose further that constituencies located at node C ask for voting participation. Two arguments might be advanced in support of the proposal: A spirit of generosity warrants node C inclusion, and democratic purposes would be served by broadening the board in that way. What are the costs?

One obvious cost is that of supplying information. Huge educational needs arise if specialized constituencies are to be informed participants on the board. Representatives of each specialized constituency would need to learn a great deal about the overall character and agenda of the corporation. Such participation also risks deflecting strategic decision-makers from their main purposes by forcing them to redress operating-level complaints. That squanders a valuable resource. More serious, however, is the prospect that the inclusion of partisan constituencies on the board invites opportunism. A constituency that had reached a bilateral bargain with the corporation would, if it participated in board level decisions, gain leverage to extract additional concessions from the corporation during the execution of the contract. Opportunism is especially likely where many partisan constituencies are represented on the board and logrolling is feasible. Also, and related, corporate assets may be dissipated in the support of "worthy causes" with which specialized constituencies sympathize.

"Unwarranted" participation in the decisions of the board of directors by such poorly suited constituencies will, moreover, cause subsequent adaptation by other parties who deal with the firm. For one thing those who are

---

[19]This is the position of Aoki (1984, ch. 8). Also see Berle (1959, p. 8).

asked to provide general purpose corporate funding will adversely adjust the terms under which corporate finance will be made available. Moreover, the bilateral contracts affected by the deflection, distortion, and dissipation of corporate assets will be realigned. Not only will the original terms (price) differ in anticipation of later efforts by a constituency to strike "better" deals, but also bilateral safeguards are apt to be reduced. Node C governance will thus move toward node B. In extreme cases special purpose technologies and involvements will give way to general purpose ones, and node A governance will result. Since membership on the board of directors by constituencies located at node A lacks economic purpose, it is naive to believe that the board of directors' franchise can be extended without cost.

Broadening the franchise is not, therefore, a simple matter of effecting a redistribution of wealth away from those who had the franchise previously in favor of those to whom it is newly awarded. Absent the prospect that a contractual defect will be corrected by awarding a place on the board of directors to a previously unrepresented constituency, broadening the franchise will have two adverse effects: Future terms of finance will be adversely adjusted, and the terms of the bilateral bargain between the firm and the affected constituency are apt to deteriorate. Here as elsewhere, contracting must be examined not at a point in time but in its entirety.

Informational participation does not appear, however, to pose equally serious concerns. In the degree, therefore, that informational participation promotes contracting confidence and deters possible abuses (of the kind discussed in 3.4, below), such participation has much to commend it.

3. Management as a Constituency

3.1 *Management Contracting*

A large difficulty in treating management's contract with the corporation like those of other constituencies is that management is thought to be in effective control of the corporation. Rather than being responsive agents of the stockholders, managers operate the firm with a keen eye to their own interests. Any proposal to improve their terms of employment is automatically suspect, because managers are presumed merely to be adding another layer of down to their already well-feathered nests. This section will suspend judgment on that matter and treat managers like other constituencies: What attributes does the management–corporation contract have, and what ones should it have?

Since no firm-specific human assets are exposed by managers located at node A, no specialized governance is needed. Like any other constituency with attributes of node A, such managers look to the market for basic protection. Managers who develop a firm-specific asset relationship with the firm, however, are located at nodes B or C.

Those managers who contract with the firm in a node B manner will receive higher current compensation than those accorded internal governance protection of a node C kind. That is the familiar $\bar{p} > \hat{p}$ result. To what types of governance protection do managers located at node C have access? The answers are unclear, partly because the proposition that governance structures can and do promote the mutual interest of contracting parties is relatively novel. Such structures have either been ignored or, as in the case of labor unions, treated as instruments of power whereby labor improves the wage bargain *at the expense of the firm*. To be sure, that sometimes occurs. But the collective organization of workers can also reduce hazards of contracting, to the benefit of both parties, if workers develop firm-specific skills in the course of their employment.

The same general approach applies to the study of contractual relations between management and firm, but there are added difficulties. Whereas labor organization has been the subject of repeated studies, and much of the relevant microanalytics there has been carefully described,[20] contracting by management has received much less systematic attention. There are several reasons. Management contracts tend to be crafted individually rather than collectively, and they are not subject to public scrutiny. The protections or procedures to which an aggrieved manager turns are usually not formally organized and are more difficult to study for that reason. Further, treating the firm and its management as separate contracting entities is progressively more difficult as higher echelons of management come under review. Unless an independent compensation committee exists, for example, an understanding of the contract between firm and manager is complicated by the fact that managers apparently write their own contracts with one hand and sign them with the other. Also, management is often encouraged, for good reason, to think of itself and the firm as one. As Alan Fox puts it, "High level managers and administrators whose decisions cannot be easily or quickly monitored are treated as members of a high-trust fraternity," lest their moral involvement deteriorate (1974, pp. 170–71). It would not sit well with that conception for managers to develop a formal grievance machinery to which they could turn for relief and redress.

---

[20]See Doeringer and Piore (1971).

It is nonetheless true that managers who are asked to make firm-specific investments will presumably strike different (better) terms if they locate at node C than at node B. What kinds of protection are available?

3.2 Compensation Schemes

Both the firm and its managers should recognize the merits of drafting compensation packages that deter both hasty dismissals and unwanted departures. Requiring firms to make severance payments upon dismissal and managers to sacrifice nonvested rights should they quit can serve to safeguard specific assets. The recent phenomenon of "golden parachutes" is germane to the assessment of compensation in several respects.

Golden parachutes are severance payments to senior managers that are contingent upon an "adverse" change in the ownership of common shares in the firm, usually as a result of unfriendly takeovers. The appearance and refinement of takeover techniques expose managers to new risks. Senior managers are often dismissed after takeovers. Even if the managers are kept on, the takeover often upsets their career expectations. Upon recognizing those hazards, managers will attempt to renegotiate their contracts to reflect the risks.

The golden parachute can be thought of as such a response. If an adverse change of ownership occurs, the senior management does not have to wait to be dismissed in order to receive severance pay. Instead, the management can trigger the award itself. Managers are thus provided with the option of "bail out" and collect a larger severance award than they would be entitled to after a "normal" dismissal (one independent of an ownership change). Without such protection the post-takeover management could give demeaning assignments to incumbent managers and force them to quit, thus denying them any severance award.

Granting the merit of self-initiated severance pay, what explains a severance premium? The defense for such a premium presumably resides in the differences between dismissals from normal employment and dismissals that occur in conjunction with takeovers. Dismissals from normal employment are generally for cause, and they activate some protection (albeit diffuse) under an internal due process machinery.[21] After takeovers, an atmosphere of mutual suspicion and hostility often exists, and the successful bidders are concerned that incumbents will sabotage the transition. Dismissals after takeovers are commonly unrelated to job performance and relatively unprotected by an

[21]The issues are briefly discussed in Chapter 6, where the manner in which informal organization helps to support internal due process is briefly examined.

internal machinery.[22] Because of the added risks, larger severance awards for terminations that occur in conjunction with takeovers are arguably warranted.[23]

That explanation, however, merely establishes that golden parachute awards will exceed those that attend normal terminations. Some perspective on the magnitude of golden parachutes is needed. Golden parachutes ought to vary directly with the extent of the firm-specific investment that a manager has placed at risk. The absolute value of the pension and other benefits that an executive sacrifices should he voluntarily quit is one measure of those investments. Absence of penalties for voluntary quitting is *prima facie* evidence that the management skills are general purpose rather than firm-specific. Golden parachute protection for such managers is unwarranted and probably reflects self-dealing.[24]

[22]Takeover effectively suspends many of the due process benefits of internal organization until a new set of implicit bargains is struck.

[23]Jensen expresses puzzlement with "golden parachute contracts . . . [which] pay off only when the manager leaves his job and thus creates an unnecessary conflict between shareholders and executives. Current shareholders and the acquiring company will want to retain the services of a manager who has valuable knowledge and skills. . . . A company can eliminate this problem by making the award conditional on the transfer of control and not on the manager's exit from the company" (1984, p. 118).

I am troubled with this proposal. It appears to assume that (1) incumbent managers will not be disaffected by a takeover or (2) if disaffected they will either (a) behave in an unchanged fashion or (b) can be bribed to behave in an unchanged fashion in the post-takeover era. Golden parachutes would not be offered at all if either (1) or (2a) were to obtain. Accordingly, (2b) is the operative assumption. Lacking mechanics, it is not obvious how lump sum, golden parachute awards made payment upon changes of control would reliably induce unchanged behavior. To the contrary, this seems most unlikely—whence current golden parachute practice is an altogether rational response to the employment tensions which attend takeover.

[24]Executives in specialized firms (monopolies or firms that are serving very special niches) are more apt to qualify for golden parachutes than those in competitively organized industries where experience in one firm partly transfers to another.

A systematic assessment of the variety of golden parachute terms is sorely needed. Considerable variety in golden parachute provisions is evident from the following *Wall Street Journal* article:

> The modest plan of AVX Corp., a Great Neck, N.Y. electronic components maker, would provide Chairman Marshall Butler with nine months pay of about $100,000 if he is ousted in a takeover. Beneficial Corp.'s plan, on the other hand, covers 250 "key" executives and provides each with three years' pay and benefits if they determine their jobs have been altered after a change of control; the diversified financial services concern refuses to estimate the potential total cost of its plan but its five top executives alone earned almost $1.6 million in fiscal 1982 and it could easily exceed $40 million.
>
> A few plans cover directors as well as executives. Just before Brunswick Corp. fought off a takeover bid by Whittaker Corp. earlier this year, its board approved parachutes for outside directors 55 years of age or older with five years' service. It voted to pay them their annual retainers ($22,000) and company benefits for life if they chose to "retire" in connection with a hostile acquisition; the health, recreation and technology company's 11 top officers, some of whom also were directors, received parachutes guaranteeing them up to five years' pay in the same package. . . .

Note that failure to craft a node C response for managers located on the $k > 0$ branch will elicit a new node B bargain. To be sure, incumbent managers, whose human assets are committed, may be unable to insist that their compensation be adjusted to reflect the added risks. But successor generation managers who are asked to take assignments on the $k > 0$ branch are not similarly encumbered. If a node C bargain is not struck, they will insist that compensation at node B be increased to reflect the takeover hazard. Such managers will then have a great deal at stake should a takeover threat materialize. Not only do they lack golden parachute relief, but their large node B salaries will now be placed in jeopardy. Accordingly, those managers will expend inordinate energies to defeat a takeover effort. It is not, therefore, in the interests of the stockholders that golden parachute terms be denied to $k > 0$ managers.

3.3 Board Membership

Suppose that the appropriate incentive alignments have been worked out. Can the firm realize additional improvements by including the management on the board of directors? Putting the issue that way presumes that the central function of the board is to safeguard the interests of the stockholders. Such a conception of the board has been described by others as the ''monitoring model.'' Kenneth Andrews characterizes the monitoring model as simplistic, overformal, and self-defeating (1982, pp. 44–46). Paul MacAvoy and his collaborators contend that serious efforts to implement the monitoring model could have a ''pervasive negative effect . . . on risk taking'' (MacAvoy et al., 1983, p. c-24).

Both, of course, may be correct. But neither Andrews nor MacAvoy and his collaborators advance an alternative conception of the board in which a clear sense of contractual purpose is described. Andrews's favored model is what he refers to as the ''participative board.'' The outside board members are invited to join with the management to enhance the quality of strategic

---

Companies give various reasons for instituting golden parachutes. While most at least imply that their plans will ensure that top executives won't arbitrarily oppose takeover bids that would reward shareholders, a few advance them frankly as anti-takeover measures. For example, last year directors of Grey Advertising Inc. gave its chairman and president, Edward H. Meyer, a $3 million parachute as part of a number of changes it said ''may make the company less susceptible to a successful takeover attempt'' by making a takeover more expensive. At the time it was adopted, Mr. Meyer's parachute was worth about 8% of the value of all the company's common stock. [Klein, 1982, p. 56]

That all of these plans are equally meritorious is surely doubtful. Managerial/directorial self-dealing strikes again?

decisions. Such involvement can come at a high cost, however, if objectivity is thereby sacrificed. As Donald Campbell remarks, if an "administrative system has committed itself in advance to the correctness and efficacy of its reforms, it cannot tolerate to learn of failure" (1969, p. 410). That defensive propensity is the origin of the tendency to throw good money after bad. A less informed but more skeptical posture by outsiders may well be superior.

Since managers enjoy huge informational advantages because of their full-time status and inside knowledge, the participating board easily becomes an instrument of the management. Notwithstanding the variety of checks against managerial discretion described by MacAvoy and his collaborators,[25] the interests of the stockholders—indeed, of all principal constituencies[26]— are apt to be sacrificed as a consequence.

Rejection of the participating model in favor of a control model of the decision ratification and monitoring kind does not, however, imply that the management should be excluded altogether. So long as the basic control relation of the board to the corporation is not upset, management's participation on the board affords three benefits. First, it permits the board to observe and evaluate the process of decision-making as well as the outcomes. The board thereby gains superior knowledge of management's competence that can help to avoid appointment errors or correct them more quickly. Second, the board must make choices among competing investment proposals. Management's participation may elicit more and deeper information than a formal presentation would permit. Finally, management's participation may help safeguard the employment relation between management and the firm—an important function in view of the inadequacy of formal procedures for grievance.

According to the contractual conception advanced here, however, those are supplemental purposes. To the extent that management participation permits reviews on the merits to be done more responsibly and serves to safeguard an employment relationship that would otherwise be exposed to excessive risk, management may be added to the core membership. But the principal function of the board remains that of providing governance structure protection for the stockholders. Management participation should not become so extensive as to upset that basic board purpose. Where it does, managerial

---

[25]For a critique of the *ex post* settling up process on which MacAvoy relies, see FitzRoy and Mueller (1984).

[26]Viewing contracting in its entirety, all major constitutencies have a viability interest in the enterprise. As Alchian puts it, "[A]nyone vulnerable to [a] threat of loss [if the coalition is impaired] will seek to preserve not only the coalition but also to reduce the possibility of that threat from the other members of the coalition to expropriate the quasi-rent of the specific resource" (1983, p. 9).

discretion is apt, sooner or later, to manifest itself in self-dealing or subgoal pursuit.

3.4 *Management Centrality*

That management is centrally implicated in all contracts is scarcely evident from the above. Instead, the fiction that all contracts are struck with a legal entity called "the firm" is maintained. Not only is the contractual relation between the firm and each constituency assessed in an instrumental way, but a symmetrical orientation is maintained throughout. The very same contractual apparatus is thus uniformly applied to each constituency. Upon disclosing its attributes, the appropriate contractual node to which to assign a constituency follows directly.

That the management's relation to the firm is largely, much less wholly, instrumental is widely disputed. More often the management is regarded as the locus of power. Strategic rather than instrumental considerations are thus brought under scrutiny. Managerial discretion and abuses are made the focus of attention.

This book principally employs and traces out the consequences of an efficiency (instrumentalist) perspective. That this is instructive is illustrated by the numerous insights that this viewpoint afford—illustrated most recently by the interpretation of golden parachutes set out above. But just as it is possible to insist that markets are marvels and to concede market failures (even comparative market failures) in the same breath—"markets, albeit imperfect, are marvels"—so too is it possible to adopt an efficiency orientation, yet make concessions to strategic behavior. Such concessions are specifically needed in assessing the management's contractual relation to the firm.

The aforementioned centrality of the management distinguishes it from all other constituencies. This difference has been acknowledged before and is responsible for much of the managerialist literature set in motion by Berle and Means (1932). The main point here is this: Strategically situated as it is, the management is able to present (screen, digest, distort, manipulate) information in ways which favor its own agenda. Albeit subject to limitations of the kinds discussed in section 4 below, managerial discretion is not for nought (Williamson, 1964; Alchian, 1965).

A somewhat narrower but previously neglected ramification of centrality is emphasized here. This involves the possibility that a constituency which strikes what it believes to be a well-informed, bilateral deal with the corporation is thereafter exposed to undisclosed hazards because the management subsequently strikes bilateral deals with other constituencies in a strategic manner.

Thus suppose that labor is asked to make firm specific investments in human capital and that a node C bargain (with a wage of $\hat{w}$ and safeguards s) is struck as a consequence. Assume that an employment agreement is also reached between the firm and the management and that this agreement features high-powered incentives. Extensive profit sharing is thus provided. And assume finally that a contract between the firm and its customers of a $\bar{p}$ kind is negotiated. This is a troublesome triad.

Thus rather than require customers to provide safeguards (which would serve both to deter the likelihood of cancellation and to mitigate the losses which attend cancellation) in exchange for a lower ($\hat{p}$) price, the management of the supply firm agrees to accept the high risks that a node B bargain entails. If adverse demand realizations do not occur, the customer will take delivery at the price of $\bar{p}$ and the seller will show a large profit. If, however, adversity does appear, then delivery will be canceled and the full costs will be borne by the seller. Low profits will result.

Given high-powered incentives, the management will participate handsomely when favorable outcomes obtain, and it will evidently be penalized when adversity materializes. Considering, however, the specific asset commitments of the labor, labor may be vulnerable to requests for give-backs, thereby to save its jobs. The profit consequences of adversity would then be buffered by labor rather than borne by management—whence the resulting set of contracts would place the management in a "heads I win, tails you lose" posture.

This outcome is more likely in the degree to which (1) labor contracts are long term, (2) human assets are more highly firm specific, and (3) the management is believed to be more opportunistic. This last may sometimes be inferred from earlier experience—although, as discussed in Chapter 15, reputation effects can be elusive. Plainly, however, where management incentives are of a more high-powered kind, greater precautions are indicated. Insistence upon contractual disclosure and contract reopeners so as to deter strategic inconsistencies across successive contractual interfaces may be warranted in such circumstances. Informational participation could materialize.

4.   Managerial Discretion and Organization Form

Enthusiasts of laissez-faire capitalism are loath to confront, and are sometimes schizophrenic on the subject of, managerial discretion. Focusing on any given time, they commonly deny the existence of managerial discretion. Comparing current practices with the past, however, those same enthusiasts point with pride to the development of new techniques that have brought managerial discretion under more effective control.

To be sure, the earlier condition may have been irremediable: The corrective instruments to which investors earlier had access could have been, indeed arguably were, fully deployed. But it is inconsistent to employ the *very same* neoclassical model—whereby the firm is characterized as a production function to which unrestricted profit maximization is continuously ascribed—at both the earlier and later dates. A conception of the firm in which opportunities for managerial discretion are expressed as a function of the control instruments is needed instead. Such a conception leads to greater respect for successive organizational innovations that have superior control properties and that attenuate managerial discretion.

Managerial discretion can take numerous forms, some very subtle. Individual managers may run slack operations; they may pursue subgoals that are at variance with corporate purposes; they can engage in self-dealing. Such distortions become more severe where there is logrolling. These and other manifestations of managerial discretion were well-known to Berle and Means, Mason, and other observers of the corporate scene. What went unnoticed, however, was the vast transformation of the corporate form between 1930 and 1960 and the consequences that had on managerial discretion. The earlier, centralized, functionally organized, unitary (or U-form) structure of the corporation was progressively supplanted by the multidivisional (or M-form) structure.

The direct effects of the M-form innovation on corporate performance are described in Chapter 11. For one thing, the shift from a functional to a divisional form served to rationalize decision-making. The confusion of purposes that characterized the U-form firm, where causality and responsibility were difficult to trace, was supplanted by a divisionalized structure where separability among quasi-autonomous parts was emphasized. Sharper definition of purpose and savings in informational costs resulted.

Disengaging the general office from operating affairs also improved incentives. What had been short-run, partisan involvements by the top executives who had previously been heads of functional activities (e.g. manufacturing, marketing, finance) gave way to longer-run, strategic decision-making. The general office gave precedence to objectives of the enterprise over functional responsibilities. A competence to monitor the performance of the divisions, allocate resources to high-valued uses, and use internal incentives and controls in a discriminating way was perfected. The M-form organization thereby attenuated managerial discretion in what had previously been U-form firms.

The attenuation of managerial discretion does not, however, imply its elimination. Rather, the argument is comparative. Albeit in reduced degree, continuing managerial discretion can be expected to survive those direct effects. Interestingly, however, the M-form innovation also had indirect effects that operate on managerial discretion through competition in the capital market.[27]

It has often been noted that tender offers increasingly replaced proxy contests as a takeover technique beginning in the late 1950s.[28] What explains this? Gregg Jarrell and Michael Bradley contend that the costs of proxy contests were increased by new regulations.[29] Takeovers are thus explained as the response to a regulation-induced change in the relative price of the methods for gaining control.

That is an interesting hypothesis, but it would be more compelling if proxy contests actually had been widely and successfully used to challenge incumbent managements before those rule changes. In fact, proxy contests were never numerous and were usually unsuccessful. Moreover, although the regulation of proxy contests could encourage greater reliance on a takeover, why should a switch to this (previously inferior) device be associated with a larger number of contests for corporate control and a greater degree of success?

In principle, takeover by tender offer was always feasible. I submit that the reason why it was not employed earlier is that a corporate structure conducive to takeover was not yet in place. Specifically, reorganization of the corporation from a functionally departmentalized to a divisionalized structure had profound consequences for corporate control. Conceiving of the firm as a governance structure rather than as a production function is the key to understanding the phenomenon of takeover by tender offer.

The main advantage of an M-form firm over a U-form enterprise in takeover respects is the ability of an M-form acquirer to "digest" its acquisition. The acquired firm is normally assigned profit center status and thereafter

[27] Henry Manne's classic treatment (1965) of the market for corporate control is germane.

[28] As Greg Jarrell and Michael Bradley observe, "Cash takeover bids were very rare in the United States prior to the 1960's, but they burst onto the financial scene in the mid-1960's, a period of much corporate conglomeration" (1980, p. 371, n. 1).

[29] They cite the work of Peter Dodd, who:

. . . associated the sudden emergence of cash tender offers as a takeover device with the successive expansions in 1955 and 1964 (Securities Acts Amendment) by the SEC of its rules governing proxy contests . . . [T]hese changes in proxy rules increased insurgents' costs of assuming corporate control via the proxy and, therefore, increased usage of the cash tender offer to achieve a change in management. [Jarrell and Bradley, 1980, p. 371, n. 1].

In fact, however, the proxy contest had never been an effective instrument. As Henry Manne puts it (1965, p. 114): "The most dramatic and publicized of the take-over devices is the proxy contest; it is also the most expensive, the most uncertain, and the least used of the various techniques." From 1956 to 1960, only nine of the twenty-eight proxy fights for control were fully successful (Hayes and Taussig, 1967, p. 137). Proxy contests that aim less for control than for bargaining advantages seem to have come into vogue more recently.

becomes subject to the corporation's internal incentive, control, and resource allocation processes. The firm does not attempt to integrate comprehensively the new assets with the old. Inasmuch as M-form firms separate operating from strategic decision-making, the general office neither seeks nor requires the same familiarity with the operating parts that managers in U-form firms must have. The greater competence of the large M-form firm to manage extant assets thus applies to the management of acquired assets as well.

To be sure, managerial preferences and stockholder preferences do not become perfectly consonant as a result of M-form organization and the associated activation of the capital market. The continuing tension between management and stockholder interests is evident in the numerous efforts that incumbent managements have taken to protect target firms against takeover (Cary, 1969; Easterbrook and Fischel, 1981). Changes in internal organization have nevertheless relieved legitimate concerns with managerial discretion. To characterize the corporation as a production function, rather than as a governance structure, misses those consequences. The vitality of the modern corporation, and its importance as an economic institution of capitalism, is thereby undervalued.

5. Concluding Remarks

The composition and functions of the board of directors have been the subject of controversy at least since the exchange between Dodd and Berle in 1932.[30] Recent commentary shows little signs of convergence. Thus Andrews (1982) favors the participatory model, whereby the board becomes implicated in the management of the firm, and characterizes the monitoring model as legalistic. And Dahl would radically shift the composition of the board in favor of the employees. The contractual approach takes exception with both.

Thus consider Dahl's views on the composition of the board:

> I do not see why a board of directors elected by the employees could not select managers as competent as those selected by a board of directors chosen by banks, insurance companies, or the managers themselves. The board of a self-governing firm might hire a management team on a term contract in the way that a board of directors of a mutual fund often does now—and also fire them if they are incompetent. If the ''profit motive'' is all that it has been touted to be, who would have more at stake in improving the earnings of a firm than employees, if the management were responsible to them rather than to stockholders? [Dahl, 1970, p. 21]

[30]Dodd opened the exchange with his 1932 article, ''For Whom Are Corporate Managers Trustees?'' Whereas Dodd favored a broad conception, Berle did not.

Dahl evidently assumes that mutual funds and manufacturing firms are equivalent. The possibility that workers can and will craft superior governance structures at the contractual interface between workers and firm goes unmentioned. And the expropriation risks that Dahl's procedures would introduce are ignored.

The contractual approach views those matters differently. Thus mutual funds are distinguished by the facts that ownership can be instantly liquidated at objective market values and mutual fund performance assessments are easy. The price of shares in a manufacturing enterprise, by contrast, is supported not by a diversified portfolio of separately priced securities but by its own performance prospects. Comparative assessments of those prospects are often difficult. Also, whereas workers are often able to craft a sensitively attuned bilateral governance structure at the contractual interface between firm and workers, that is much more difficult for holders of equity. Lacking control over the board, equity holders are vulnerable to expropriation. Some economists and many noneconomists nevertheless maintain the view that "not by logic but by history, owners of capital have become the owners of the enterprise" (Lindblom, 1977, p. 105). The prevailing view notwithstanding, Richard Cyert and James March invite us to consider economic organization more symmetrically: "Why is it that in our quasi-genetic moments we are inclined to say that in the beginning there was a manager and he recruited workers and capital?" (1963, p. 30). Paul Samuelson's remarks on the symmetry between capital hiring labor and labor hiring capital, made in the context of Marxian models with technical change, are even stronger: "In a perfectly competitive market it doesn't really matter who hires whom: so have labor hire 'capital' " (1975, p. 894).

Whether there is a contractual logic to corporate governance can usefully be assessed by adopting a Cyert and March/Samuelson orientation. Thus suppose that a group of workers wish to create opportunities for employment without themselves investing equity capital in the enterprise. Suppose further that the business in question has the need for a series of inputs, of which investments in nonredeployable durable assets are included. We can imagine the workers approaching a series of input suppliers and asking each to participate. General purpose inputs contract easily and without hazard. Special purpose inputs offer a supply on $\bar{p}$ or $\hat{p}$ terms, depending on whether or not governance safeguards are crafted. Considering the above described problems of crafting a well-focused safeguard for equity capital (which, by definition, is used to finance diffuse but specific assets), the equity suppliers initially offer to hold debt at a price of $\bar{p}$. Upon realizing that this is a very inefficient result, the workers who are organizing the enterprise thereupon invent a new general purpose safeguard, name it the Board of Directors, and offer it to the suppliers of equity. Upon recognizing that expropriation hazards are thereby reduced, the suppliers of equity capital lower their terms of participation to $\hat{p}$. They also become the "owners" of the enterprise. Not by history but by logic does this result materialize.

By way of summary, the argument advanced in this chapter comes down to this:

First, Those who are associated with the firm in a node A relation have no need for supportive governance, whether it be of a board-connected kind or otherwise. Instead, market mediation suffices for such parties.

Second, those who are associated with the firm in a node C relation have already crafted bilateral governance that is attuned to the idiosyncratic needs of the transaction. Unless there are significant gaps or defects in the bilateral governance, board participation is unnecessary. The main occasion for those with node C governance to be included on the board of directors is for information purposes. Labor may sometimes qualify, especially when a firm is experiencing difficulties and is asking for givebacks. Suppliers who are engaged in a large-scale firm-specific project and very large customers may also qualify.

Third, those whose contracting relation is of a node B kind are in the greatest need of remedial governance. By its very nature, the contractual relationship between the shareholders and firm is difficult to safeguard. Providing stockholders with an ability to monitor the affairs of the firm and to replace the management in a crisis will arguably facilitate obtaining equity financing on superior terms. For that reason the board of directors should be regarded principally as a governance instrument of the shareholders. Viewed in the context of all contractual relations, moreover, it is in the interests of all constituencies that voting board membership be reserved for those whose contractual relation to the firm is of a node B kind.

It is difficult to craft governance structures for managers whose relation to the firm is highly specific. Management's presence on the board can improve the amount and quality of information and lead to superior decisions. But such a presence should not upset the board's basic control relation with the corporation.

The manner in which boards of directors in most large corporations are constituted and operated is broadly consonant with that prescription. Yet there are significant differences. The management often plays a larger role in governance than the contractual framework dictates; boards are often pressed to go beyond a monitoring role to adopt a participative one; and corporations have been under economic and political pressure to extend voting board membership to various interest groups. In theory, the first two of those phenomena may be explained by the efficacy of *ex post* settling-up (Fama, 1980). An alternative explanation is that the deviations are a reflection of the continuing presence of managerial discretion: Incumbent managements feel more secure and have greater latitude in participative boards which they dominate.

Note with respect to this last that I have assumed throughout that, once struck, all node C bargains will thereafter be respected. That ignores the possibility that circumstances will change and that departure from the spirit, if not the letter, of the contract will sometimes follow. For example, the resolve of a regulatory commission to set rates at a level that yields a fair rate of return may weaken if regulated firms do not have recurring needs to resort to capital markets for expansion and renewal capital.[31] The same applies to stockholders in a firm that has no need for equity financing. Although management may have enthusiastically supported governance structure safeguards for the stockholders at the time that initial equity financing was secured in order to benefit from more favorable terms, it may subsequently prefer relief from the monitoring pressures that such a node C bargain implies. If additional equity capital is not needed, the composition and character of the board may be altered to the disadvantage of the shareholders.[32] To be sure, there are checks against such distortions. But as FitzRoy and Mueller (1984) observe, assertions that *ex post* settling-up processes are always and everywhere fully efficacious strain credulity.[33]

[31]Accordingly, a public utility that is financed by intermediate-term debt that is continuously rolled over is less subject to punitive rate setting than is an otherwise equivalent public utility that uses very long-term debt and has no need for renewal financing. In other words, how the rate setting process will be affected is a factor that should enter the calculus of the public utility.

[32]A recent potentially troublesome development that warrants scrutiny in corporate governance respects is the use of Employee Stock Ownership Plans (ESOPs) to repurchase company stock and place it in safe hands. This practice is done at the behest of management and with the consent of its employees (or, at least, of the leadership of the company's employees). The apparent object is to deter hostile takeovers, thereby to relieve the management of competition in the capital market pressures. This has dubious social benefits. It would appear to be an unintended and antisocial use of ESOPs, which currently enjoy tax advantages.

[33]For a recent treatment of this issue, see Holmstrom and Ricart i Costa (1984).

CHAPTER 13

Franchise Bidding
for Natural Monopoly

Although monopoly supply is commonly efficient where economies of scale are large in relation to the size of the market, it also poses organizational difficulties. As Milton Friedman observes, "There is unfortunately no good solution for technical monopoly. There is only a choice among three evils: private unregulated monopoly, private monopoly regulated by the state, and government operation" (1962, p. 128).

Actually, a fourth solution has been proposed. It was the result of an imaginative series of papers that originated at Chicago.[1] That Friedman characterized private unregulated monopoly as an evil is because he assumed private monopoly ownership implied pricing on monopoly terms. The Chicago response—as successively developed by Demsetz (1968), Stigler (1968), and Posner (1972)—is that monopoly price is not a necessary consequence of a private unregulated monopoly condition. Such an outcome can be avoided by using *ex ante* bidding to award the monopoly franchise to the firm that offers to supply product on the best terms.

This chapter examines the contractual details that attend efforts to implement franchise bidding, both in general and with respect to cable television

[1]Surprisingly, those papers and this fourth solution go unmentioned in Melvin Reder's recent survey of "Chicago Economics," where he recounts numerous instances in which economic (and even noneconomic) issues were reformulated to good advantage within the Chicago tradition (Reder, 1982).

326

(CATV). As with most complex economic problems of organization, it turns out that there is no single, all-purpose, best solution. Rather, the efficacy of franchise bidding as an organizational response to the problems posed by natural monopoly varies with the circumstances—chief among which, not surprisingly, is the condition of asset specificity.

My discussion of franchise bidding for natural monopoly is in five parts. Some background is sketched in section 1. The simple franchise bidding scheme as proposed by Demsetz is described in section 2. Contractual difficulties with implementing such a scheme for CATV are considered in section 3. The study of complex issues of economic organization through the use of case studies is treated in section 4 (and in the appendix). Concluding remarks follow.

1. Introduction

The case for a comparative institutional approach to regulation was succinctly put by Coase twenty years ago:

> Contemplation of an optimal system may provide techniques of analysis that would otherwise have been missed and, in certain special cases, it may go far to providing a solution. But in general its influence has been pernicious. It has directed economists' attention away from the main question, which is how *alternative arrangements will actually work in practice*. It has led economists to derive conclusions for economic policy from a study of an abstract of a market situation. It is no accident that in the literature . . . we find a category "market failure" but no category "government failure." Until we realize that we are choosing between social arrangements which are all more or less failures, we are not likely to make much headway. [Coase, 1964, p. 195; emphasis added]

Largely as a result of criticisms of this kind, much of it originating at Chicago, the study of regulation has been considerably reshaped. Thus whereas reference to market failures was once thought to be a sufficient condition for government intervention, there has been a growing realization that regulation is beset with problems of its own. Moreover, the limits of markets are now perceived to be less severe than was true of the interventionist era of the 1960s. The study of contracting in its entirety, in which both *ex ante* contracting and *ex post* implementation are considered, discloses that complex contracts can often be devised that are responsive to the needs of the parties.

The franchise bidding for natural monopoly literature acknowledges the limits of regulation but deals with the issues of contracting in a very incomplete way. Specifically, it either does not examine how "alternative arrangements will actually work in practice'' or does so in a highly sanguine way. As a consequence, the enthusiasts of franchise bidding claim too much for the efficacy of that organizational alternative. Applications that are supportable in one context (namely, where asset specificity is slight) are uncritically extended to circumstances where they are not (namely, where asset specificity is substantial).

That the franchise bidding for natural monopoly literature is flawed does not, however, mean that it has had an undesirable public policy impact. The deregulation of trucking and airlines arguably benefited from the viewpoint advanced in the franchise bidding literature. The investments in question here really are "assets on wheels," hence lack specificity. But similar deregulation reasoning does not, without more, carry over to electric power generation or cable television systems. Given that the assets in question for electric power and cable are both long-lived and immobile, specific attention to the attributes of the enabling contracts is needed before a decision is reached to go forward with deregulation.

Thus although the limits of regulation are manifold, merely to show that regulation is flawed does not establish that regulation is an inferior mode of organizing economic activity. Not only do the disabilities of regulation vary with both the type of activity regulated and the form of regulation attempted, but there is an obligation to assess the properties of the proposed alternative— not only in general but also specifically with respect to the activity in question. If the proposed mode is flawed in similar or different respects, the purported advantages of shifting out of regulation may be illusory.

Among the factors that are relevant to an assessment of alternative modes of organizing natural monopoly services are the following: (1) the costs of ascertaining and aggregating consumer preferences through direct solicitation; (2) the efficacy of scalar bidding; (3) the degree to which technology is well developed; (4) demand uncertainty; (5) the degree to which incumbent suppliers acquire idiosyncratic skills; (6) the extent to which specialized, long-lived equipment is involved; and (7) the susceptibility of the political process to opportunistic representations and the differential proclivity, among modes, to make them. (Of special relevance in that last connection is the tendency for regulation, once put in place, to assert ancillary powers, thereby to expand its jurisdiction, often with dysfunctional consequences. Indeed, I conjecture that creeping "ancillariness" is one of the more severe disabilities to which regulation is subject.) The more confidence one has in contracting and in the efficacy of competition—both at the outset and at contract renewal intervals—the more one tends to favor market modes. Conformably, regulation, in some form, is relatively favored when one is dubious that incomplete contracting will yield desired results and when competitive processes are prone to break down.

Since variants within both market and regulatory modes exist, discriminating assessments within as well as between modes are indicated. Also, a once-for-all verdict with respect to the supply of a particular natural monopoly service is unwarranted. The better mode at an early stage of an industry's development may no longer be better later on when a lesser degree of uncertainty prevails. To the extent that difficult transition problems are apt to be posed in shifting from one mode to the other, this should be acknowledged and taken expressly into account at the outset.

2. The Simple Franchise Bidding Scheme

Demsetz contends that even though efficiency considerations may dictate that there be only one supplier in a natural monopoly industry, the unregulated market price need display no elements of monopoly. Conventional analysis is flawed by a failure to distinguish between the number of *ex ante* bidders and the condition of *ex post* supply. Even though scale economies may dictate that there be a single *ex post* supplier, large numbers competition may nevertheless be feasible at the initial bidding stage. Where large numbers of qualified parties enter noncollusive bids to become the supplier of the decreasing cost activity, the resulting price need not reflect monopoly power. The defect with conventional analysis is that it ignores this initial franchise bidding stage.

Franchise bids that involve lump-sum payments should be distinguished from those where the franchise is awarded to the bidder who offers to supply at the lowest per unit price. Awarding an exclusive franchise to the non-collusive bidder who will pay the largest lump-sum fee to secure the business effectively capitalizes the monopoly profits that thereafter accrue. But the product or service for which such a franchise is granted will be priced on monopolistic terms. To avoid that outcome, the franchise award criterion of lowest per unit price is favored. Stigler, among others, evidently finds the argument persuasive (1968, pp. 18–19; 1974, p. 360).

Demsetz illustrates the argument by examining a hypothetical example in which the state requires automobile owners to purchase automobile license plates annually, where the plates in question are produced under decreasing cost conditions. To simplify the argument he strips away "*irrelevant complications,* such as durability of distribution systems, uncertainty, and irrational behavior, all of which may or may not justify the use of regulatory commissions but none of which is relevant to the theory of natural monopoly; for this theory depends on one belief only—price and output will be at monopoly levels if, due to scale economies, only one firm succeeds in producing the product" (1968, p. 57; emphasis added).[2] Provided that there are many qualified and noncollusive bidders for the annual contract and that the contract is awarded to the party that offers to supply at the lowest per-unit price. "the winning price will differ insignificantly from the per-unit cost of producing license plates" (Demsetz, 1968, p. 61).

Demsetz and others evidently believe, moreover, that the argument is not vitiated when the simple case is extended to include such complications as equipment durability and uncertainty. Equipment durability need not lead to wasteful duplication of facilities since, should a potential supplier offer superior terms, trunk line distributional facilities can be transferred from the original supplier to the successor firm (Demsetz, 1968, p. 62). Whether regulation is warranted as a means by which to cope more effectively with uncertainty is met with the observation that "[l]ong-term contracts for the supply of [nonutility services] are concluded satisfactorily in the market place without the aid of regulation" (p. 64).

The dominant theme that emerges, occasional disclaimers to the contrary notwithstanding,[3] is that franchise bidding for natural monopolies has attractive properties. It is a market solution that avoids many of the disabilities of regulation. Demsetz's concluding remarks, in which he registers his "belief that rivalry of the open market place disciplines more effectively than do the regulatory processes of the commission" (1968, p. 65), are plainly in this spirit.

2.1   The Marginal Cost Pricing Objection

Lester Telser takes issue with Demsetz's treatment of natural monopoly on the grounds that franchise bidding gives no assurance that output will be priced efficiently on marginal cost terms:

> [Demsetz] leaves readers with the impression that he is content with a situation in which the firm is prevented from obtaining a monopoly return and he does not

[2]To the extent that Demsetz's treatment of natural monopoly is limited to a critique of elementary textbook discussions, the argument goes through. Plainly, however, Demsetz and others also contend that it has real world relevance. The "irrelevant complications" referred to in the text are conspicuously present when this latter application is attempted. As will be apparent, the purported superiority of franchise bidding is a good deal more difficult to establish when these conditions are present.

[3]Demsetz is somewhat more cautious about the merits of franchise bidding and highlights the qualifications to his argument in his reply to Telser's critique (Demsetz, 1971).

raise the question of efficiency. Hence he implies that direct regulation of an industry subject to decreasing average cost is unnecessary if it is prevented from obtaining a monopoly return. . . . This misses the point. The controversy concerns regulation to secure efficiency and to promote public welfare. It does not concern the rate of return. [Telser, 1969, pp. 938–39]

Another way of putting it is that Demsetz does not identify the relevant social welfare function or evaluate his results in welfare terms. Failure to do so, coupled with the prospect that franchise bidding will not lead to efficient marginal cost pricing, is, in Telser's view, a critical shortcoming of Demsetz's approach.

Demsetz has responded to those criticisms by observing that marginal cost pricing was of secondary importance to his paper (1971, p. 356). Although a complete treatment of the natural monopoly problem would require that efficient pricing be addressed, his original article did not pretend to be complete (p. 356). He furthermore considers it doubtful that regulation leads to more efficient pricing than an appropriately elaborated bidding scheme (pp. 360–61).

I suggest, for the purposes of this chapter, that the marginal cost pricing issue be set aside and that the frictions associated with franchise bidding, which are glossed over in previous treatments, be examined instead. To the extent that filling the *lacunae* in Demsetz's "vaguely described bidding process"—which Telser (1971, p. 364) mentions but does not investigate—involves the progressive elaboration of an administrative machinery, the advantages of franchise bidding over regulation are uncertain. If, despite such machinery, the price-to-cost tracking properties of regulation are arguably superior to those of franchise bidding, the purported advantages of franchise bidding are further suspect.

2.2 *Irrelevant Complications*

The irrelevant complications to which Demsetz, refers—equipment durability and uncertainty—and dismisses in the context of his automobile license plate example are really the core issues. To be sure, steady state analysis of the type he employs sometimes yields fruitful insights that have wide-reaching applications. I submit, however, that the interesting problems of *comparative institutional choice,* are largely finessed when the issues are posed in steady state terms. Frank Knight's admonitions to this effect, although expressed in a different institutional context (1965, pp. 267–68), have general application. The basic argument, which applies both to Knight's interest in whether internal organization matters and to Demsetz's concern with market modes of contracting, is this: Rates of convergence aside, any of a large variety of organizing modes will achieve equally efficient results if steady state conditions obtain.[4] In circumstances, however, in which the operating environment is characterized by a nontrivial degree of uncertainty, self-conscious attention to both the *initial* and *adaptability* attributes of alternative modes is warranted.

Demsetz's treatment of franchise bidding emphasizes the initial supply price aspect and, as developed below, treats the matter of adaptability in a rather limited and sanguine way. As will be apparent, franchise bidding for public utility services under uncertainty encounters many of the same problems that the critics of regulation associate with regulation; as Goldberg (1976) argues, the problems inhere in the circumstances.

3. Franchise Bidding Elaborated

It will be useful to examine franchise contracts of three types: once-for-all contracts, which appear to be the type of contract envisaged by Stigler; incomplete, long-term contracts, which are favored by Demsetz; and recurrent short-term contracts, which Posner endorses.

3.1 *Once-For-All Contracts*

Stigler's views on franchise bidding are limited mainly to an endorsement of Demsetz's prior treatment of those matters. He observes simply that "[n]atural monopolies are often regulated by the state. We note that customers can auction off the right to sell electricity, using the state as the instrument to conduct the auction, and thus economize on transaction costs. The auction . . . consists of a promise to sell cheaply" (1968, p. 19). Since he gives no indication to the contrary, Stigler apparently intends that such bidding be regarded as a serious alternative to regulation under actual market circumstances—which is to say under conditions of market and technological uncer-

---

[4]Consider in this connection whether, from an allocative efficiency point of view, it really matters if franchises are awarded on the basis of a lump-sum fee rather than a lowest supply price criterion. I submit that the monopoly distortions commonly associated with the former mode of contracting will tend to vanish if steady state conditions obtain. The reasoning here is that steady state conditions facilitate low-cost price discrimination, in which event the marginal customer is supplied on marginal cost terms, and/or that customers can more effectively organize their side of the market and bargain to an efficient result.

tainty. Failure to refer to recurrent bidding also suggests that the bidding scheme proposed is of the once-for-all variety.[5]

Once-for-all contracts of two types can be distinguished: complete contingent claims contracts and incomplete contracts. The former require that each prospective franchisee specify the terms (prices) at which he is prepared to supply service now and, if price changes are to be made in response to uncertain future events, the conditional terms under which he will supply service in the future. It is generally appreciated that complete contracts of this kind are impossibly complex to write, negotiate, and enforce (Radner, 1968). The underlying transactional disabilities have been discussed in earlier chapters.

Given the infeasibility of complete contingent claims contracts, incomplete once-for-all contracts might be considered. Contractual incompleteness, however, is not without cost. Although incomplete once-for-all contracts are feasible in the sense that bounded rationality constraints are satisfied, such contracts pose hazards by increasing the risk of opportunism. The problems here are substantially those discussed below in conjunction with incomplete long-term contracts.

3.2 Incomplete Long-Term Contracts

Demsetz evidently has in mind that franchise awards be of a long-term kind in which adaptations to unanticipated developments are accomplished by permitting renegotiation of terms subject to penalty clauses (1968, pp. 64–65). Such renegotiation would be unnecessary, of course, if the parties to the contract could agree, at the outset, to deal with unanticipated events and to resolve conflicts by employing a joint profit maximizing decision rule, thereafter to share the gains of the resulting adaptation. General agreements to that effect are not self-enforcing, however, unless the profit consequences are fully known to both of the parties and can be displayed, at low cost, to an impartial arbitrator. Absent this, each party will be inclined, when the unanticipated events occur, to manipulate the data in a way that favors its interests.

To be sure, aggressive self-interest seeking of a myopic kind is attenuated both by the existence of informal sanctions and by an appreciation between the parties that accommodation yields long-run benefits (Macaulay, 1963). But the hazards of opportunism scarcely vanish on those accounts. Among the problems to be anticipated when incomplete long-term contracts

[5]Possibly, however, Stigler intends that Demsetz's discussion of renegotiation and/or rebidding should apply. Demsetz's treatment of these matters appears below.

are negotiated under conditions of uncertainty are the following: (1) the initial award criterion is apt to be artificial or obscure; (2) execution problems in price-cost, in other performance, and in political respects are apt to develop; and (3) bidding parity between the incumbent and prospective rivals at the contract renewal interval is unlikely to be realized. Consider these several conditions *seriatim*.

a. ARTIFICIAL OR OBSCURE INITIAL AWARD CRITERION

The promise to "supply cheaply" is scarcely a well-defined commitment unless the quality of service is well specified and scalar valued bids possess economic merit. Posner recognizes the former and proposes that subscriber preferences regarding quality be ascertained by a preaward solicitation. The mechanics involve

> . . . an "open season" in which all franchise applicants were free to solicit the area's residents for a set period of time. This would not be a poll; the applicants would seek to obtain actual commitments from potential subscribers. At the end of the solicitation period, the commitments received by the various applicants would be compared and the franchise awarded to the applicant whose guaranteed receipts, on the basis of subscriber commitments, were largest. In this fashion the vote of each subscriber would be weighted by his willingness to pay, and the winning applicant would be the one who, in free competition with the other applicants, was preferred by subscribers in the aggregate. To keep the solicitation process honest, each applicant would be required to contract in advance that, in the event he won, he would provide the level of service, and at the rate represented, in his solicitation drive. [Posner, 1972, p. 115]

The comparability problems that would otherwise be posed if both price and quality were permitted to vary at the final competition stage are thus avoided. The preaward solicitation not only prevents the quality level from being set by a political body, but also relieves the need to choose among disparate price-quality mixes, on grounds that are uncertain, at the final competition.

However imaginative this preaward solicitation process of Posner, it is not obviously practicable. For one thing, it assumes that subscribers are able to assess quality-price packages abstractly and have the time and inclination to do so—which poses a bounded rationality issue.[6] For another, it aggregates

---

[6]To observe that "customers face and overcome [such problems] daily in choosing among products that differ in quality as well as price" (Posner, 1972, p. 115) is scarcely dispositive. Issues peculiar to the supply of natural monopoly services are not even raised. For example, quality variability of electricity supply is apt to entail voltage variations or prospective supply interruptions, the implications of which are apt to be difficult to assess. Second, variable load pricing issues, with which most consumers have little familiarity, may be posed. Third, collective choice issues which do not appear for most consumer goods must be faced in deciding on

preferences in a rather arbitrary way.[7] Finally, it assumes that subscribers will demand that winners provide the level of service at the rate represented or can otherwise obtain satisfaction for failure to perform. This poses execution issues and is discussed under b below.[8]

If, additionally, the prices at which service is supplied are to vary with periodic demands—a measure that often has efficient capacity rationing properties for public utility services—a complex variable load pricing schedule, rather than a single lowest bid price, must be solicited. Vector valued bids clearly pose award difficulties.

The upshot is that, although franchise awards can be reduced to a lowest-bid price criterion, that is apt to be artificial if the future is uncertain and the service in question is at all complex. Such awards are apt to be arbitrary and/or pose the hazard that "adventurous" bids will be tendered by those who are best-suited or most inclined to assume political risks. Again, this gives ries to execution issues, to which we now turn.

b. EXECUTION PROBLEMS

Even if contract award issues of the kinds described above either were absent or could be dismissed as *de minimis,* we would still have to face problems of contract execution. It is at the execution stage and in conjunction with contract renewal that the convergence of franchise bidding to public utility regulation is especially evident.

I assume, for the purposes of this subsection, that there is a strong presumption that the winner of the bidding competition will be the supplier of the public utility service over the entire contract period. Only in the event of egregious and persistent malperformance would an effort be made to replace the winning franchisee.

The assumption is supported by the following considerations. First, the award of a long-term contract plainly contemplates that the winner will be the supplier over a considerable period. A leading reason to make the contract

---

electricity supply. Fourth, long-term interaction effects between electricity price and substitutes and complements are rather strong, albeit difficult to sort out in the context of hypothetical solicitations.

[7]Thus, if price-quality package A wins the competition, on Posner's criterion, over price-quality mixes B, C, D, and E, where A is a high-price, high-quality mode and B through E are all variants on a low price-quality mix, does it follow that package A is socially preferred?

[8]Similar problems arise with respect to the matter of who in the community is to be supplied service and at what connection costs: Connect everybody who requests it at a flat charge? Only those who live in areas where connected service exceeds some threshold? Anyone who bears his own incremental costs? Although a single standard can be stipulated by the contracting agency, is this optimal and ought such a connection standard to remain fixed for the duration of the contract?

long term is to provide the supplier with requisite incentives to install long-lived assets.[9] If any slight failure to perform in accordance with the franchisor's expectations would occasion rescission of the franchise, the long-term contract would be a fiction and its investment purposes vitiated.

The prospect of litigation delays and expenses also discourages an effort to displace a franchisee. Moreover, even if such an effort were successful, nontrivial transition costs would be incurred. (They are discussed further under c below.) Finally, franchise award agencies, like other bureaucracies, are loath to concede or be accused of error. As Eckstein puts it, publicly accountable decision-makers "acquire political and psychological stakes in their own decisions and develop a justificatory rather than a critical attitude towards them" (1956, p. 223). Since displacement may be interpreted as a public admission of error, franchise award agencies predictably prefer, when faced with malperformance, to negotiate a "compromise" solution instead.

In circumstances in which long-term contracts are executed under conditions of uncertainty, fixed price bids are apt to be rather unsatisfactory. If the environment is characterized by uncertainty with respect to technology, demand, local factor supply conditions, inflation, and the like, price-cost divergences and/or indeterminacies will develop.

To be sure, some of these divergences can be reduced by introducing price flexibility by formula (Fuller and Braucher, 1964, pp. 77–78; Goldberg, 1976b, p. 439). Adjustment for changes in the price in response to some index of prices is one possibility. It is, however, a relatively crude correction and unlikely to be satisfactory where there is rapid technical change or where local conditions deviate significantly from the index population. More precise tracking of prices to costs will be realized if, instead of fixed price contracts, cost plus (or cost sharing) contracts are negotiated. All of the difficulties associated with the execution of defense contracts of the cost sharing kind then appear, however (Scherer, 1964; Williamson, 1967a). Problems of auditing and of defective incentives are especially severe. (Those, it will be noted, are disabilities associated with regulation. Franchise bidding is designed to overcome them.)

A lack of specificity in the contract with respect to the quality of service and a failure to stipulate monitoring and accounting procedures accords latitude to franchisees during contract execution. Despite *ex ante* assurances to the contrary, franchisees can rarely be made to fulfill the spirit of an agreement if net revenues are enhanced by adhering to the letter of the contract only

---

[9]The short-term contracting procedure favored by Posner contemplates the transfer of long-lived assets from the winning franchisee to a successor firm. Appropriate investment incentives would thereby be realized. For the reasons developed under c below, I am skeptical of the properties of the asset transfer procedure described by Posner.

(CTIC, 1972a, p. 11). Moreover, technical standards by themselves are not self-enforcing; enforcement requires that a policing apparatus be devised (CTIC, 1973, p. 7). Since individual consumers are unlikely to have the data or competence to evaluate the quality of service in a discriminating way (Goldberg, 1976) and since both setup cost and specialization of labor economies will be realized by assigning the quality evaluation function to a specialized agency, centralization is indicated. But again, the convergence toward regulation should be noted.[10]

It may not be sufficient, moreover, merely to specify a common quality standard for all bidders. Thus, suppose that one bidder proposes to achieve the specified quality target by installing high-performance, long-lived equipment, that a second proposes to have backup equipment ready in the event of breakdown, and that the third claims that he will invest heavily in maintenance personnel. Although only one of them may fully satisfy the requirements, both subscribers and the franchising agency may lack the *ex ante* capacity to discern which. Granting the franchise to the low bidder only to discover that he is unable to perform as described is plainly unsatisfactory. Although penalty clauses in contracts can help forestall such outcomes, it is often the case—as the history of defense contracting suggests—that successful bidders are able to have terms renegotiated to their advantage.

Accounting ambiguities coupled with the disinclination of franchising agencies to allow winning bidders to fail permit franchisees to use accounting data in a strategic way—to include the threat of bankruptcy—during renegotiations. The introduction of monitoring and accounting control techniques can prevent such outcomes, but that measure then joins the winning bidder and the franchising agency in a quasi-regulatory relationship.

In circumstances where renegotiation is common and perhaps vital to the profitable operation of a franchise, political skills assume special importance. Prospective suppliers who possess superior skills in least cost supply respects but who are relatively inept in dealing with the franchising bureaucracy and in influencing the political process are unlikely to submit winning bids.[11] To the extent that political skills override objective economic skills, the advantages of franchising over regulation are placed in question.

[10]The Cable Television Information Center expresses the issue as follows:

[T]echnical standards do not enforce themselves. Enforcement requires testing the system, evaluation of the tests, and deciding upon corrective actions required. These activities add to the administrative burden of regulation. A franchising authority should not adopt standards unless it is willing to shoulder the burden of enforcement. [CTIC, 1973, p. 7]

[11]Note that a merger between parties who possess economic qualifications and those with political skills yields private and probably social gains in these circumstances. Such a merger actually occurred in the case study reported in the appendix to this chapter.

Indeed, if franchisees are subject to less stringent profit controls than regulated firms (where the latter are subject to rate of return constraints), it may well be that franchising encourages greater political participation. The argument here is that the incentive to invest private resources to influence political decisions varies directly with the degree to which the resulting advantages can be privately appropriated—and that franchised firms have an appropriability advantage in this respect.[12]

C. BIDDING PARITY AT CONTRACT RENEWAL

Bidding parity at contract renewal intervals will be upset if winners realize substantial advantages over nonwinners. Award advantages of three kinds can be distinguished: economic, administrative, and political. The economic advantages have their origins in the fundamental transformation—a contracting phenomenon that was first introduced in Chapter 2 and has made its appearance in a variety of contracting contexts since. The administrative advantages arise in conjunction with asset valuation and related problems that would attend a franchise transfer. Issues of both kinds are discussed in subsection 3.3 below.

CATV is still a young industry, and many communities have yet to solicit renewal bids. Predictably, interest in securing immunity from rivalry at the franchise renewal date has been building among incumbent franchisees. Original agreements to submit to the discipline of competition and the hypothetical benefits of competition are mere contrivances; the reality is that competition is a hair shirt. Incumbency advantages notwithstanding, why submit to the threat of nonrenewal and to the scrutiny that such a renewal bidding competition would entail? Skeletons will unavoidably be exposed. Considering the administrative difficulties and legal challenges that would attend a nonrenewal, why go through the exercise? Such concerns have struck a responsive political chord. The U.S. Senate has passed a bill that would give "substantial preference to the initial franchisee" in return for leased access to channel capacity for up to 15 percent of the system (Price, 1983, p. 32). Whether this or some variant eventually becomes public law, the prospect that politicians will permit unrestrained competition on the merits at franchise renewal time is surely doubtful (Cohen, 1983). Only political innocents would claim otherwise. The Oakland, California franchise experience reported in the appendix is corroborative.

---

[12]This assumes that regulation is not a farce and that management engrossing is strictly limited under regulation. Note also that the argument assumes that the *marginal* net gains of influencing the political process are greater under the franchise mode. For a discussion of politics and regulation, see Alfred Kahn (1971, pp. 326–27).

3.3 *Recurrent Short-Term Contracts*

A leading advantage of recurrent short-term contracting over long-term contracting is that short-term contracts facilitate adaptive, sequential decision-making. The requirements that contingencies be comprehensively described and appropriate adaptations to each worked out in advance are thereby avoided. Rather, the future is permitted to unfold and adaptations are introduced, at contract renewal intervals, only to those events which actually materialize. Put differently, bridges are crossed one (or a few) at a time, as specific events occur. As compared with the contingent claims contracting requirement that the complete decision tree be generated, so that all possible bridges are crossed in advance, the adaptive, sequential decision-making procedure economizes greatly on bounded rationality.

Additionally, under the assumption that competition at the contract renewal interval is efficacious, the hazards of contractual incompleteness that beset incomplete long-term contracts are avoided. Failure to define contractual terms appropriately gives rise, at most, to malperformance during the duration of the current short-term contract. Indeed, recognizing that a bidding competition will be held in the near future, winning bidders may be more inclined to cooperate with the franchising authority, if specific contractual deficiencies are noted, rather than use such occasions to realize temporary bargaining advantages.[13] Opportunism is thereby curbed as well.[14]

The efficacy of recurrent short-term contracting depends crucially, however, on the assumption that *parity among bidders at the contract renewal interval is realized.*[15] Posner faces and disposes of this issue:

[13]This assumes that winning bidders are not fly-by-night operators, but instead are interested in remaining in the business on a continuing basis. Other things being equal, the franchising authority can be expected to continue with the current supplier or shift to a new supplier at the contract renewal interval depending on its experience with the current winner during the contract period.

[14]Similar considerations have a bearing on the performance of the franchising agency. Posner puts the argument as follows:

> [If] the duration of the franchise . . . is long, the parties may not have foreseen all of the circumstances that might require modification of its terms. Although this is a problem common to all contracts, the peculiarity here is that one of the contracting parties is not a true party in interest but a public body charged with overseeing the interest of the other parties (subscribers). Experience with regulatory agencies suggests that one cannot assume such a body will represent the consumer interest faithfully. When the cable company asks for a modification of the contract by virtue of an unforeseen change in circumstances, the public body may react ineffectually or perversely. [Posner, 1972, pp. 115–16]

With short-duration contracts, "no modification of . . . terms need be entertained" (p. 116), in which event the distortions referred to are avoided.

[15]For prior discussions of bidding parity and its absence at contract renewal intervals, see Peacock and Rowley (1972, p. 242) and Williamson (1975, pp. 26–35).

> [T]he fact that the cable company's plant normally will outlast the period of its franchise raises a question: Will not the cable company be able to outbid any new applicant, who would have to build a plant from scratch? And will not the bargaining method therefore be ineffective after the first round? Not necessarily: in bidding for the franchise on the basis of new equipment costs, new applicants need not be at a significant disadvantage in relation to the incumbent franchisee. For example, once a new applicant is franchised he could negotiate to purchase the system of the existing franchisee, who is faced with the loss of the unamortized portion of his investment if his successor builds a new system. Insofar as the economic life of a cable plant is considered a problem when the franchise term is short, it can be solved by including in the franchise a provision requiring the franchisee, at the successor's option, to sell his plant (including improvements) to the latter at its original cost, as depreciated. [Posner, 1972, p. 116]

I find these views overly sanguine. For one thing, equipment valuation problems are apt to be rather more complex than Posner's remarks suggest. Secondly, Posner focuses entirely on nonhuman capital: the possibility that human capital problems also exist is nowhere acknowledged. To be sure, human asset benefits that accrue during contract execution and that give incumbents an advantage over outsiders will, if anticipated, be reflected in the original bidding competition. But "buying in" can be risky, and the price tracking properties of such strategies are easily inferior to average cost pricing in resource allocation respects. The upshot is that recurrent bidding (at, say, four-year intervals) is riddled with contractual indeterminacies.

Concern over plant and equipment valuation is, of course, mitigated if the investments in question are relatively unspecialized. I conjecture that this is the case for Demsetz's automobile license plate example. If, with only minor modifications, general purpose equipment (for the cutting, stamping, painting, and so on) can produce license plates efficiently, then a franchisee who fails to win the renewal contract can productively employ most of this same equipment for other purposes, while the new winner can, at slight cost, modify his own plant and equipment to produce the annual requirement efficiently.

Alternatively, concern over plant and equipment poses no problem if its useful life is exhausted during the contract execution interval. As Posner's remarks suggest, however, and as is generally conceded, it is inefficient to install utility plant and equipment of such short duration.

Unlike Demsetz's license plate manufacturers, moreover, most utility services (gas, water, electricity, telephone) require that *specialized* plant and equipment be put in place. The same is true of CATV. Since the construction of parallel systems is wasteful and since to require it to be done would place outside bidders at a disadvantage at the contract renewal interval, some method of transferring assets from existing franchisees to successor firms plainly needs to be worked out.

Posner contends that it can be handled by stipulating that plant and equipment be sold to the successor firm, at its option, at the original cost less depreciation of the predecessor franchisee. Consistent with his emphasis on fundamental policy choices, Posner declines to supply the details. Unfortunately, however, the details are troublesome.

For one thing, original cost can be manipulated by the predecessor firm. For another, even if depreciation accounting procedures are specified under the original franchise terms, implementation may still be contested. Third, original cost less depreciation at best sets an upper bound—and perhaps not even that, since inflation issues are not faced—on the valuation of plant and equipment. The successor franchisee may well offer less, in which case costly haggling ensues. Finally, even if no disputes eventuate, Posner's procedures merely provide a legal rule for transferring assets. He does not address the economic properties of the procedures in investment incentive and utilization respects.

Whether the accounting records of original costs can be accepted as recorded depends in part on whether the equipment was bought on competitive terms. The original franchisee who is integrated backward into equipment supply or who arranges a kickback from an equipment supplier can plainly rig the prices to the disadvantage of rival bidders at the contract renewal interval. Furthermore, and related, the original cost should also include the labor expense of installing plant and equipment. To the extent, however, that the allocation of labor expense between operating and capital categories is not unambiguous, the original winner can capitalize certain labor expenses to the disadvantage of would-be successors. Auditing can be employed to limit those distortions, but that has the appearance of regulation. Even if carefully done, moreover, the results are apt to be disputed. Inasmuch as information on true valuation is asymmetrically distributed to the disadvantage of outside parties, the burden of showing excess capitalization falls heavily on the would-be new supplier.

Reaching agreement on depreciation charges, which are notoriously difficult to define (especially if obsolescence is a problem and maintenance expenditures can be manipulated in a strategic manner), poses similar problems. Therefore, costly arbitration, for both original equipment valuation and depreciation reasons, is apt to ensue.[16] Rate base valuations of a regulatory kind thereby obtain.

Indeed, the valuation of physical assets is predictably more severe under franchise bidding than under regulation. For one thing, earnings in the regulated firm are a product of the rate base and the realized rate of return.

[16]The City of Los Angeles anticipated such difficulties in its ordinance on franchise award and execution (Ordinance No. 58,200). The ordinance stipulates that the City has a right to purchase the property of a franchise or find a purchaser therefor and further provides that

Clearly, the regulated firm can be conciliatory about the rate base if in exchange it receives allowable rate of return concessions. Additionally, the regulatory agency and regulated firm are prospectively joined in a long series of negotiations. Errors made by either party on one round are less critical if they can be remedied at the next rate review interval (or if, in a crisis, interim relief can be anticipated). More is at stake with asset valuation under franchise bidding, since degrees of freedom of both rate of return and intertemporal kinds are missing. Accordingly, more contentious bargaining leading to litigation is to be expected.

. . . in the event said franchise shall expire by operation of law, said city shall have the right, at its option, declared not more than one (1) year before the expiration of the franchise term as herein fixed, which right an option is hereby reserved to said city, to purchase and take over the property of such utility, and in the event that said city shall so exercise its right under such option the said city shall pay to the said grantee the fair value of the property of such utility as herein provided. (d) The term ''fair value'' as used herein shall be construed to mean the reasonable value of the property of such utility having regard to its condition of repair and its adaptability and capacity for the use for which it shall have been originally intended. The price to be paid by the City for any utility shall be on the basis of actual cost to the utility for the property taken, less depreciation accrued, as of the date of purchase, with due allowance for obsolescence, if any, and the efficiency of its units to perform the duties imposed on them; no allowance shall be made for franchise value, good will, going concern, earning power, increased cost of reproduction or increased value of right of way or allowance for damages by reasons of severance. (e) That the valuation of the property of such utility proposed to be purchased upon the termination of said franchise as herein provided, or otherwise, shall be determined by a board of three arbitrators of whom one shall be appointed by the city, one by the grantee, and the third by the two arbitrators so appointed. Said arbitrators shall be appointed within thirty days after the declaration by the city of its option to purchase said property of such utility, or to find a purchaser therefor. In case said arbitrators fail to make and file an award within the time hereinafter limited, a new board of three arbitrators shall be appointed as hereinbefore prescribed. The board of arbitrators shall immediately upon the appointment of its members enter upon the discharge of its duties. Any vacancy in the board of arbitrators shall be filled by the party who made the original appointment to the vacant place. (f) In the event the grantee shall fail to appoint an arbitrator within thirty days after the declaration by the city of its option to purchase the property of such utility or to find a purchase therefor, or in the event of the death or resignation of such arbitrator so appointed and such grantee, its successors or assigns, shall fail to appoint an arbitrator to fill such vacancy within ten (10) days thereafter, or in the event the two arbitrators appointed by the city and grantee, as hereinbefore provided, shall fail to appoint a third arbitrator within sixty (60) days after the declaration of the city of its option to purchase the property of such utility, or to find a purchaser therefor, then upon application made either by the city, or by said grantee after (5) days' notice in writing to the other party, such arbitrator shall be appointed by the presiding Judge of the Superior Court of the State of California, in and for the County of Los Angeles, and the arbitrators so appointed shall have the same powers and duties as though he had been appointed in the manner hereinabove prescribed. (g) The award of the arbitrators must be made and filed with the City Clerk of said city within three (3) months after their appointment, and a majority of the arbitrators who agree thereto may make such award.

For a discussion of franchise valuations of a similar kind in connection with New York City's award of CATV franchises, see CTIC (1972a, pp. 16–17).

A related difficulty with Posner's physical asset valuation scheme is that it merely sets an upper bound. Inasmuch, however, as procurement on those terms is left to the successor firm's option, there is little reason to expect that figure to prevail. Without stipulating more, the successor firm would presumably offer to buy the specialized plant and equipment at its value in its best alternative (nonfranchised) use. That will normally be a small fraction of the depreciated original cost. Predecessor and successor firms thus find themselves confronted with a wide bargaining range within which to reach an exchange agreement. Since competitive forces sufficient to drive the parties to a unique agreement are lacking, additional haggling (which is a social cost) can be anticipated. Albeit vexing, the details, which are neglected by Posner, nevertheless matter; the frictionless transfer on which he appears to rely is simply not to be had on the terms described.

Conceivably superior asset valuation and franchise bidding schemes can be devised to mitigate those problems.[17] It is patently incumbent, however, on those who believe that large numbers competition can be made effective at the contract renewal interval to come forward with the requisite operational details. Without such specificity, one must consider dubious the contention that low-cost resassignment of physical assets can be effected at the contract renewal interval for franchised services that require specialized and long-lived plant and equipment to be installed. Rather, nontrivial haggling and litigation expenses appear to infect Posner's proposal.

Moreover, human asset problems, which Posner and Demsetz fail even to mention, also must be faced. Again, the matter of fungibility arises. To the extent that the skills of operating the franchise are widely available or, alternatively, that employees of the incumbent firm deal with rival bidders and the incumbent's owners on identical terms, no problems of this kind appear. If, however, nontrivial specialized skills and knowledge accrue to individuals and small groups as a result of on-the-job training and experience, the first of those conditions is violated. If, additionally, employees resist transfer of ownership in the bidding competition, rivals are put to a disadvantage.

The matter of nonredeployability of labor has been discussed in earlier chapters. As set out there, significant differences sometimes develop between experienced and inexperienced workers in the following respects: (1) Equip-

---

[17]One possibility is for each willing bidder, at the contract renewal interval, to indicate his asset valuation at the time he enters his bid on the quality and price of service. The problem here is that asset valuations and service bids are not independent. Franchisees will be prepared to pay dearly for assets if in the process they can charge a high price.

Other schemes might be explored (see note 16 *supra*) and possibly some can be shown to have attractive properties. It is plainly the case, however, that a good deal of hard thinking about the mechanics of the asset valuation process is needed before the rebidding scheme can be considered complete.

ment idiosyncracies, due to highly specialized or incompletely standardized, albeit common, equipment, are "revealed" only to experienced workers; (2) processing economies of an idiosyncratic kind are fashioned or "adopted" by managers and workers in specific operating contexts; (3) informal team accommodations, attributable to mutual adaptation among parties engaged in recurrent contact, develop and are upset, to the possible detriment of group performance, when the membership is altered; and (4) communication idiosyncracies evolve (with respect, for example, to information channels and codes) but are of value only in an operating context where the parties are familiar with each other and share a common language.

As a consequence, it is often inefficient fully or extensively to displace the experienced labor and management group employed by the winner of the initial franchise award. Familiarizing another group with the idiosyncrasies of the operation and developing the requisite team production and communication skills are costly. Accordingly, incumbent employees, who alone possess idiosyncratic knowledge needed to realize least-cost supply, are powerfully situated to block a franchise reassignment effort.

The cost disadvantage referred to will obtain, however, only insofar as incumbent employees deal with the current ownership and outside bidders differently. The strategic advantage they enjoy in relation to inexperienced but otherwise qualified employees can be exercised against both the current owner and his bidding rivals alike. The issue thus comes down to whether current and prospective owners are treated differently at the contract renewal interval.[18] I conjecture that they will be. The main reason is that *informal* understandings (with respect to job security, promotional expectations, and other aspects of internal due process) are much easier to reach and enforce in familiar circumstances than in unfamiliar ones.[19]

This is not to say that employees cannot or will not strike bargains with outsiders, but rather than such bargains will be more costly to reach because

[18]Relevant in this connection is the following issue: Why have incumbent employees failed to exploit fully their idiosyncratic advantage over inexperienced employees during the contract execution period—in which event there is no unliquidated idiosyncratic gain to be differentially awarded at the contract renewal interval? A distinction between moving equilibrium and discrete bargaining behavior is relevant in this connection. For one thing, there may be adjustment lags in the system, which are tolerated during the operating period but for which correction is possible at the contract renewal interval. For another, collective action is necessary to appropriate the idiosyncratic gains. Enterprise owners may work out a *modus vivendi* with managers and labor representatives in which management and labor, in exchange for ownership support (including job security, emoluments, and so on), consciously decline to absorb the full idiosyncratic gain. Out of recognition that the "leadership" is in this together, a reserve of unliquidated idiosyncratic gain has strategic advantages.

[19]For a sociological discussion of some of the problems of succession, see Gouldner (1954). Macneil observes that "the elements of trust demanded by participant views or relations make identity important, and simple transfer therefore unlikely" (1974, p. 791).

much more attention to explicit detail will be required, or there is greater risk associated with an informal (incompletely specified) agreement with outsiders. Where additional detail is sought, outsiders will be at a disadvantage in relation to insiders, because the costs of reaching agreement are increased. If, instead, employees are asked to trust the outsider to behave "responsibly" or, alternatively, the outsider agrees to accept the interpretation placed on incomplete agreements by the employees when unanticipated events not expressly covered by the employment contract develop, the implied risks are great and corresponding premiums will find their way, directly or indirectly, into the bid price. As a consequence, idiosyncratic employment attributes coupled with the inability of outsiders to reach equivalent agreements at equal expense place original franchisees at an advantage at the contract renewal interval. Thus human capital considerations compound the bidding difficulties that physical asset valuation problems pose. To contend that bidding parity can be expected at the contract renewal interval is accordingly suspect for this reason as well. Put differently, if original winners of the bidding competition realize nontrivial advantages in informational and informal organizational respects during contract execution, bidding parity at the contract renewal interval can no longer be presumed. Rather, what was once a large numbers bidding situation, at the time the original franchise was awarded *is converted into what is tantamount to a small numbers bargaining situation* when the franchise comes up for renewal. A fundamental transformation thus obtains.

It might be argued, of course, that the incumbency advantage will be anticipated at the outset, in which event discounted certainty equivalent profits will be bid down to zero by large numbers competition for the original award. That is not, however, an entirely satisfactory answer. For one thing, to come in at a price below cost for the initial award (perhaps even a negative price) and to set price at the level of alternative cost at contract renewal intervals easily result in resource utilization of an inferior kind. Additionally, buying-in strategies are risky. The alternative supply price can be influenced by the terms the franchisor sets on subsequent rounds, including terms that may obsolete the learning-by-doing advantages of incumbents.

3.4 *A Summing Up*

Once-for-all bidding schemes of the contingent claims contracting kind are infeasible and/or pose execution hazards. Incomplete long-term contracts of the type envisaged by Demsetz alleviate the first of those problems but aggravate the second. A whole series of difficulties long familiar to students of defense contracting and regulation appears. The upshot is that franchise bidding for incomplete long-term contracts is a much more dubious undertaking than Demsetz's discussion suggests.

Posner's proposal that franchise terms be kept short is designed to overcome the adaptability problems associated with incomplete long-term contracts, but his discussion is insufficiently microanalytic and/or critical of the disabilities of short-term contracts to expose their shortcomings. The fundamental limitation of the argument is that, despite Posner's procedural stipulations (1972, p. 116), bidding parity at the contract renewal interval between the original winner and rival successor firms cannot safely be presumed. To the contrary, there are reasons to doubt such parity, in which case the adaptability and price to cost properties that Posner associates with recurrent contracting[20] are not to be had on the frictionless (or low-cost) terms he describes.

To be sure, some of the difficulties that infect the Posner proposal can be mitigated by introducing an extensive regulatory/arbitration apparatus. Assessing plant and equipment installations, auditing related accounting records, and arbitrating disputes between incumbent and rival firms over physical asset valuations are illustrative. But then franchise bidding and regulation differ only in degree.

It is perhaps unsurprising, in view of the foregoing, that Posner's recurrent bidding proposal has not been widely adopted. Rather, most CATV franchise awards are for ten to fifteen years, and contractual incompleteness has been handled by progressively elaborating a regulatory structure (CTIC, 1972c, pp. 9–12)—a result that conceivably reflects a desire by CATV operators to insulate themselves from the rigors of competition. I submit, however, that the drift toward regulation is also explained by performance defects associated with CATV franchise awards which are caused in part by contractual incompleteness (CTIC, 1972c, p. 9).

Still the contractual incompleteness defects described above might conceivably be remedied by progressively refining CATV awards in the future. Stipulating appropriate penalties for unsatisfactory performance and setting out complex conditional responses to contingent events may serve to promote efficient adaptation and mitigate haggling expenses. Elaborating the contract in these respects is not costless, however, and franchising agencies often lack the resolve to exact penalties as prescribed.[21] Many of the limits of franchise

[20]The basic argument is that ''[e]ach bidder would submit a plan of service and schedule of rates. As long as there was more than one bidder and collusion among the bidders was prevented—conditions that ought not to be insuperably difficult to secure—the process of bidding subscriber rates down and quality of service up would eliminate monopoly pricing and profits'' (Posner, 1972, p. 115).

[21]Note, moreover, that not only are contract remedies ''among the weakest of those the legal system can deliver, [b]ut a host of doctrines and techniques lies in the way even of those

bidding described above were evident to students of regulation some eighty years ago:

> Regulation does not end with the formulation and adoption of a satisfactory contract, in itself a considerable task. If this were all, a few wise and honest men might, once in a generation supervise the framing of a franchise in proper form, and nothing further would be necessary. It is a current fallacy and the common practice in American public life to assume that a constitution or a statute or a charter, once properly drawn up by intelligent citizens and adopted by an awakened public, is self-executing and that the duty of good citizens ends with the successful enactment of some such well matured plan. But repeated experience has demonstrated—what should have been always apparent—the absolute futility of such a course, and the disastrous consequences of reliance upon a written document for the purposes of living administration. As with a constitution, a statute, or a charter so with a franchise. It has been found that such an agreement is not self-enforcing. [Moreover, the] administration may ignore or fail to enforce compliance with those essential parts of a contract entrusted to its executive authority; and legal proceedings . . . are frequently unavoidable long before the time of the franchise has expired. [Fisher, 1907, pp. 39–40]

At the risk of oversimplification, regulation may be described contractually as a highly incomplete form of long-term contracting in which (1) the regulatee is assured an overall fair rate of return, in exchange for which (2) adaptations to changing circumstances are successively introduced without the costly haggling that attends such changes when parties to the contract enjoy greater autonomy. Whether net gains are thereby realized turns on the extent to which the disincentive effects of the former (which may be checked in some degree by performance audits and by mobilizing competition in the capital market forces) are more than offset by the gains from the latter. This is apt to vary with the degree to which the industry is subject to uncertainties of market and technological kinds.

4. A Case Study

The requisite level of detail for assessing the efficacy of an organizational mode will vary with the circumstances. There plainly are regulatory matters for which detail of the kind developed above is unnecessary. The level of detail at which much of the regulatory dialog is conducted is often too aggregative, however, to ascertain "how alternative arrangements will actually

---

remedies'' (Macneil, 1974, p. 730). Until franchisers and the legal system can be persuaded to believe otherwise, it is fatuous to contend that franchisees can be induced to behave in ideal ways by the introduction of a complex set of penalty clauses.

work in practice"—which Coase identifies as the "main question" in the quotation that appears at the outset.

Enthusiasts of franchise bidding do not see it that way. Thus Posner declares that to expound "the details of particular regulations and proposals . . . would serve only to obscure the basic issues" (1972, p. 98). More generally, the "economic approach to the law" with which Posner is associated and has done so much to advance is characteristically deficient in microanalytic respects. The economic approach that Posner favors traces its intellectual origins, in antitrust respects at least, to Aaron Director and his students (Posner, 1975, p. 758, n. 6). As I have observed elsewhere, this tradition relies heavily on the fiction of frictionlessness and/or invokes transaction cost considerations selectively (Williamson, 1974a; 1974b). However powerful and useful it is for classroom purposes and as a check against loose public policy prescriptions, it easily leads to extreme and untenable "solutions."[22] What Arthur Leff has referred to as a "legal approach to economics" (1975), in which transaction costs are more prominently and systematically featured, is a necessary supplement to (and sometimes substitute for) the Director–Posner tradition.

Tests of three kinds can be applied in assesssing whether microanalytic analysis of the kind attempted here has merit. One is to ask whether, as a consequence of such efforts, our understanding of a complex economic phenomenon is deeper than and/or different from what it had been previously. Second, we can inquire whether the explanation fits within a general schema or has been crafted in what appears to be an *ad hoc* way to fit the circumstances. This is that pattern-seeking test of knowledge to which Hayek referred (1967, pp. 40, 50–58). Although the particulars differ, vertical integration, nonstandard contracting for intermediate goods, the employment relation, corporate governance, and regulation are all, according to the argument developed in this and preceding chapters, variations on a theme. Finally, one can appeal to the data.

Microanalytic analysis yields implications at both aggregative and sub-aggregative levels of detail. For example, the theory predicts that collective organization will appear earlier in firms where workers acquire firm-specific human capital (or in concentrated industries, where workers acquire industry-specific human capital). That is a reasonably aggregative prediction. It also predicts that more finely crafted governance structures for labor will be ob-

[22]Posner regards Coase's classic paper "The Problem of Social Cost" (1960) as the entering wedge to the "new law and economics field" (1975, p. 760). It is noteworthy that this important and influential paper is in two parts: The first part features frictionlessness; the second qualifies the earlier discussion to make allowance for frictions. Much of the follow-on literature, including franchise bidding, is largely or wholly preoccupied with frictionlessness or deals with frictions in a limited or sanguine way.

served in unions where human asset specificity is great than where it is slight. That is a more microanalytic implication.

Microanalytic implications can sometimes be tested through the use of proxy variables that, for whatever reason, happen to be available. But examining the phenomenon in question at a level of detail that corresponds with the level of analysis has obvious advantages. It will often require that case studies be undertaken. As P. T. Bauer and A. A. Walters observe, "the complexity, instability, and local variation of many economic phenomena imply that the establishment or understanding of relationships requires that analysis be supplemented by extensive observation, and also that the inquiry must often extend beyond statistical information to direct observation and use of primary sources" (1975, p. 12). The case study of CATV franchising in Oakland, California, as reported in the appendix to this chapter, is in that spirit. The complexity of this contracting problem exceeds that of Demsetz's automobile license plate example by several orders of magnitude. That a different understanding of franchise bidding obtains is unsurprising.

The Oakland CATV case study is not only microanalytic but a case study with a focus. Potential observations proliferate when microanalytic features are brought under scrutiny. Which should be recorded and which are left out? An analysis that develops the contractual details germane to the theory is plainly more instructive. Although sometimes such details may appear serendipitously, as in the Canadian study of petroleum exchanges in Chapter 8, it is better that they be sought out deliberately.

The Oakland CATV case is not, however, representative. To the contrary, more problems were encountered in Oakland than is usual. Does that vitiate the study? I think not. As remarked earlier, the "study of extreme instances often provides important leads to the essentials of the situation" (Behavioral Sciences Subpanel, 1962, p. 5). Subject to the conditions that only qualitative inferences are to be attempted and that the system is observed to respond to disturbances in a coherent way, such observations offer a relatively economical way by which to secure insights into the properties of a complex organization. The case study reported here is used only for gross inference purposes, and the bureaucratic/political process is neither corrupt nor out of control. The case study thus introduces a hitherto missing element of reality testing into the evaluation of franchise bidding for natural monopolies.

Of course, just as one swallow does not make a spring, a single case study does not settle franchise bidding for CATV definitively. But neither is such a study merely "one observation." Not only are the data germane, because they are collected with the needs of the theory foremost in mind, but a set of observations that can be examined for internal consistency can be developed in a focused case study. It is responsive to the spirit of Koopmans's observation that while economics is handicapped in relation to the natural sciences in conducting "meaningful experimentation, the opportunities for direct introspection by, and direct observation of, individual decision makers are a much needed source of evidence which in some degree offsets the handicap" (Koopmans, 1957, p. 140).

5. Concluding Remarks

Whatever their origins, the cost of good intentions needs to be evaluated. The comparative institutional approach to the study of economic organization is precisely designed to do that.

This chapter examines the efficacy of franchise bidding schemes as an alternative to regulation in the provision of public utility services in circumstances where there are nontrivial economies associated with monopoly supply. Granting that regulation is highly imperfect, assessed in terms of an abstract ideal, what are the conditions under which franchise bidding is a vastly superior solution to the supply of "traditional" public utility services?

Surely no one would dispute that the "correct way to view the problem is one of selecting the best type of contract" (Demsetz, 1968, p. 68). But one also needs to be instructed on how to proceed. Although it may be possible to disallow some contracting modes on static allocative efficiency grounds,[23] the more interesting cases involve an examination of the efficiency properties of alternative contracts executed under conditions of uncertainty. Contrary to normal practice, attention to transactional detail is needed if the real issues are to be exposed. Additionally, a check on the operational properties of abstract contracting modes is usefully made *by examining one or more actual cases* in which different modes are being employed.

Microanalytic assessments of the abstract contracting attributes of franchise bidding yield a mixed verdict. Where significant investments in durable specific assets are required and contracts are subject to technological and market uncertainties, franchise bidding in practice requires the progressive elaboration of an administration apparatus that differs mainly in name rather than in kind from that which is associated with the regulation that it is

---

[23]For example, awarding a franchise to the bidder who will pay the largest lump-sum amount will serve to capitalize the monopoly profits but, at least transitionally, will lead to a higher price and lower output than will an award of the franchise to the bidder who offers to supply at the lowest price.

intended to supplant.[24] It is elementary that a *change in name lacks comparative institutional significance.*[25]

This is not, however, to suggest that franchise bidding for goods or services supplied under decreasing cost conditions is never feasible or to imply that extant regulation or public ownership can never be supplanted by franchise bidding with net gains. Considering the ease with which physical assets can be redeployed, trucking deregulation would appear to have merit. Franchise bidding might also be warranted for local service airlines and, possibly, postal delivery. The winning bidder for each can be displaced without posing serious asset valuation problems, since the base plant (terminals, post offices, warehouses, and so on) can be owned by the government, and other assets (planes, trucks, and the like) will have an active secondhand market. It is not, therefore, that franchise bidding is totally lacking in merit, but that those who have favored it have been insufficiently discriminating in their endorsement of it.[26]

Applications of the general approach that have since been made include Paul Joskow and Richard Schmalensee's recent assessment of deregulation proposals for electric power generation (1983). Claims that such deregulation can be effectuated with ease are submitted to careful comparative institutional scrutiny. Characterized as much of the industry is by durable, transaction-specific assets, Joskow and Schmalensee conclude that unassisted franchise bidding is not a viable organizational alternative. Forcing deregulation scenarios through the screen of microanalytic analysis is the device by which analytical leverage is purchased. The same strategy is available more generally.[27]

[24]A distinctive limitation of regulation, to which franchise bidding is presumably less subject, is the proclivity of regulators progressively to expand the reach of regulation to include "ancillary" activities. More generally, the greater autonomy and degree of specialization associated with regulation, as compared with franchise bidding agencies, may have unfavorable long-run rigidity consequences. In particular, regulatory authorities are apt to resist vigorously anything that threatens their demise.

[25]As Donald Dewey has observed, the "disdain and contempt for regulation [by economists] is nearly universal" (1974, p. 10). Although much of regulation is indeed contemptible, I submit that *some* of the problems for which regulation has been devised are really intractable—in the sense that *all* of the feasible modes of organization are beset with difficulties. Arguments favoring market modes in which those difficulties are not squarely faced should accordingly be regarded with skepticism.

[26]William Baumol and Robert Willig not only agree with the general argument but also use airlines and postal delivery as examples of industries with "capital on wheels" so that "their fixed costs may considerably exceed their sunk costs" (1981, p. 407), and the economic difficulties that attend nonmobile fixed cost industries are greatly relieved. Inasmuch as Baumol and Willig's use of sunk costs corresponds, in the lexicon of transaction cost economics, to an asset specificity condition, there appears to be growing agreement over the circumstances where franchise bidding can be presumed to be efficacious and where it is not. (The fact that I restrict the argument to local service airlines while they include trunk lines is perhaps noteworthy, but the difference is mainly one of degree.)

[27]Railroad deregulation is an obvious candidate. See Chapter 11, note 3.

The Oakland CATV Franchise Bidding Experience

Although the case study reported below cannot claim to be representative, it does reveal that many of the franchise concerns disscused in Chapter 13 are not purely imaginary.[1] The study both indicates the importance of evaluating proposals to scrap regulation in favor of market alternatives in more micro-

---

[1] It is also noteworthy that many of the franchising concerns reported by the Cable Television Information Center are consonant with those set out in Section 3. Among the concerns and recommendations of the CTIC are the following (CTIC, 1972a):

1. The renewal period has proven to be a period of great pressure on the city, with the cable operator often threatening to discontinue service immediately unless renewal is promised (p. 16).
2. The franchising authority will . . . want to include buyback provisions as part of its effort to insure continuity of service. The provision should include . . . a method of evaluation or termination (S. 4, p. 6).
3. [The] right of transfer should be limited at the initial stages of the systems' development, and perhaps flatly forbidden before construction, to avoid trafficking in franchise awards (p. 17).
4. Results of system performance and tests should be submitted periodically to ensure the system's quality (p. 24).
5. [Day to day regulation involves] considering consumer complaints and passing on requests for rate increases (p. 25).
6. Once a procedure has been developed for considering rate changes, the proposed changes are to be measured against the standard of what is fair to the system and to the subscribing public (p. 30).

analytic terms and discloses that, in practice, franchise bidding for CATV (and presumably other public utility services) has many of the qualities of regulation.

1. The Record

On June 19, 1969, the Council of the City of Oakland, California, passed a city ordinance that provided for the granting of community antenna television franchises. The main features of the ordinance, for the purposes of this appendix, were:[2]

1. The frachise award was to be nonexclusive.
2. The franchise duration was not to exceed twenty years.
3. The City was authorized to terminate a franchisee for non-compliance after thirty days' notice and a public hearing.
4. The franchisee was directed to supply a complete financial statement to the City annually and the City was given the right to inspect the franchisee's records.
5. The City had the right to acquire the CATV system at the cost of reproduction.
6. The City Manager was authorized to adjust, settle, or compromise any controversy that might arise among the City, the franchisee, or subscribers, although aggrieved parties could appeal to the City Council.
7. Failure to comply with time requirements of the franchise were grounds for termination.
8. Inasmuch as failure to comply with time requirements would result in damages that would be costly to assess, an automatic fine of seven hundred and fifty dollars per day would be imposed for each day beyond the three-year target completion date that the franchisee took to install the system.
9. Any property of the franchisee that was abandoned in place would become the property of the City.
10. A surety bond of one hundred thousand dollars was to be obtained by the franchisee and renewed annually.
11. Property of the franchisee was to be subject to inspection by the City.
12. The CATV system was to be installed and maintained in accordance with the "highest and best accepted standards" of the industry.

---

7. One of the most neglected areas in ordinances has been enforcement. Mechanisms such as arbitration, provision for leaseback, and the ability to seek court action will aid in achieving the type of Cable system the community wants (p. 45).

[2]City of Oakland, Ordinance No. 7989 C.M.S., June 19, 1969.

1.1 *Operationalizing the Bidding Process*

The above constituted the basic legislative authority and ground rules. Rather, however, than solicit bids immediately, the Department of General Services engaged instead in a set of preliminary discussions with prospective franchisees.[3] Simultaneously, community groups were requested to advise the City on the types of services to be offered. The resulting dialogue was intended to elicit information regarding cost, demand characteristics, technical capabilities, and so on, and would help define the "basic service," which would then be stipulated in the contract. Comparability among bids for a standardized service would thereby be facilitated.

Ten months later, on April 30, 1970, the City of Oakland apprised five applicants that the City would receive their amended applications to construct, operate, and maintain a nonexclusive CATV system franchise within the City. The main features, for the purposes of this appendix, of the invitation to bid were:[4]

1. Two systems were to be provided:
   a. System A, which is the basic system, would permit the subscriber to receive the entire FM radio band plus twelve TV channels distributed as follows: nine local off-the-air channels; one or more newly created local origination channels; and one channel assigned to the City and School District. Payment of a monthly charge of "X" plus connection charges (see item 5 and 6, below) would permit the subscriber to receive System A.
   b. System B would provide special programming and other services. The mix of programming and other services were left unspecified, however. The charges for System B were to be determined later by the franchisee with the approval of the City Council.
2. All areas within the city limits of the City of Oakland were to be served.
3. Franchise duration was set at fifteen years.
4. The franchisee was to make annual payments to the City of 8 percent of gross receipts or $125,000, whichever was greater.[5]
5. Connection charges for each of four customer classes[6] were stipulated, and thus common for all bidders. It was further stipulated that no additional fee be charged to the subscriber for switches or converters needed to receive System A.

[3]The dialogue period was described to me by Mark Leh, Assistant Manager of Electrical Services of the Department of General Services, Oakland.

[4]City of Oakland, "Invitation to Submit Amended Applications for a Community Antenna Television System Franchise," April 30, 1970.

[5]The $125,000 figure was built up in successive $25,000 annual increments, starting with zero in 1970 and reaching $125,000 in 1975, thereafter to continue at this level.

[6]The four customer classes were: noncommercial housed in buildings with less than four living units; noncommercial housed in multiple unit apartments, motels, hotels; commercial; and special, including low-density users. The installation charge was $10 for noncommercial subscribers housed in buildings with less than four living units.

6. The basic bid consisted of designating the monthly fee "X," which would be charged to each subscriber for the first TV and FM outlet connected in his living unit, with an additional monthly charge of $0.2X$ to be paid for each additional outlet in his living unit. This would entitle the subscriber to receive System A.
7. The franchisee was to provide the City and School District with certain free connections and services, including studio facilities for originating programming for up to twenty hours per week.
8. The system to be installed was to be a dual cable system, and each of the cables was to be capable of carrying the equivalent of thirty-two video channels. A series of minimum technical specifications concerning signal quality, cable characteristics, installation methods, automatic controls, and so forth were stipulated.
9. Service requirements were described in general terms. The details were to be defined by the franchisee subject to Council approval.
10. The system was to be 25 percent complete within eighteen months of franchise acceptance, with an additional 25 percent being completed in each succeeding six-month period, so that the system would be fully completed in three years.
11. Proposals to raise rates to subscribers could be submitted annually. (No indexing or other criteria were offered in this connection.)

1.2 Bid Acceptance

Bids were made on July 1, 1970, the lowest being the bid of Focus Cable of Oakland, Inc., which stipulated an "X" (see items 1 and 6, above) of $1.70 per month.[7] The next lowest bid was by Cablecom-General of Northern California, which set a rate of $3.48.[8] The Tele Promp Ter Corporation bid was $5.95 (Libman, 1974, p. 34).

Focus Cable apprised the City at the time of its bid that TeleCommunications, Inc. of Denver, Colorado, whose participation had been vital to the qualification of Focus as an applicant, had elected to withdraw from the Focus Cable proposal.[9] Focus Cable reorganized the corporation under the laws of California and included a copy of the Articles of Incorporation, dated July 1, 1970, with its bid. Inasmuch as Focus had entered the lowest bid (by a factor of two), was the only local bidder, and represented an ethnic minority,[10] the City was reluctant to reject their bid for lack of financial capability and technical qualifications. However, awarding the franchise to Focus plainly posed hazards.

[7]Amended Application for a Franchise to Construct, Operate and Maintain a Community Antenna Television System within the City of Oakland submitted by Focus Cable of Oakland, Inc., July 1, 1970.

[8]Memorandum from the City Manager to the City Council, dated September 28, 1970, p. 3.

[9]See note 7 *supra*.

[10]Minority group involvement in cable—in ownership, employment, and programming respects—is prominently featured in the CATV literature (CTIC, 1972c, p. 13). The FCC requires cable operators to establish affirmative action plans (CTIC, 1972a, p. 34).

It appeared that these were greatly mitigated when Tele Promp Ter Corporation proposed on July 16, 1970, to enter into a joint venture with Focus Cable to construct and develop the Oakland franchise. As a part of the joint venture, Tele Promp Ter agreed to provide all needed financing for the project.[11] Why Tele Promp Ter was prepared to do this at a monthly charge less than 30 percent of its own bid was not disclosed. Presumably, however, the prospect of earning substantial returns on System B was a contributing factor.[12] Focus Cable advised the City of Oakland, in a letter dated July 21, 1970, that "the proposed financing of Focus by Tele Promp Ter can and will provide the ideal marriage of local investors, CATV expertise, and over-all financial strength to best develop the CATV franchise in Oakland."[13] The Focus contribution to this ideal marriage was its local investor attributes.

The agreement between Focus and Tele Promp Ter provided that each should have equal ownership at the outset but that Tele Promp Ter would convert this to a majority interest immediately and could exercise options after the first year which gave it ownership of 80 percent of the capital stock outstanding.[14] The joining of Tele Promp Ter with Focus was thought to warrant completing the negotiations. A report to the City Council from the City Manager and the City Attorney, dated September 28, 1970, concluded as follows:[15]

> Part of the concept of Systems A and B in the specifications was, by competitive applications, to obtain a rate sufficiently low on System A which would encourage the early development of System B. It is staff opinion that the low rate submitted by Focus would motivate such a development. Also, the low rate will assure the widest utilization of System A by families of all economic means.
>
> Focus is the applicant which has submitted the lowest basic monthly subscriber rate. The question has been raised as to whether Focus meets the specifications due to changes in its organization. From a legal standpoint, the organizational change does not disqualify Focus from further Council consideration. It is staff opinion that the proposed agreements between Focus and Tele Promp Ter, with the additional guarantees by Tele Promp Ter, will result in a useful combination of initial local respresentation with one of the largest and best qualified CATV firms in the United States.

Focus Cable and Tele Prompt Ter Corporation entered into a Subscription Agreement on September 21, 1970, in anticipation of being awarded the

[11]Letter from Leonard Tow, Vice President of Tele Promp Ter, Inc., to Harold Farrow of Focus Cable, dated July 16, 1970.

[12]The rate on System B was not included in the original bid but was to be negotiated later. As things worked out, and probably ought to have been anticipated, most subscribers elected to receive System B—at a considerably higher rate than System A.

[13]Letter from Focus Cable to the City Manager of Oakland, dated July 21, 1970.

[14]Stock Transfer Restriction and Purchase Agreement, dated September 21, 1970, Appendix A to Focus Cable of Oakland, Inc., Subscription Agreement.

[15]See note 8 *supra*.

franchise. Two hundred shares at ten dollars per share were to be paid for by the organizers of Focus.[16] Additionally, the Agreement provided:

> The Corporation shall purchase equipment and products from TPT [Tele Promp Ter] for use in its business in preference to other sources to the extent that the quality and workmanship of such equipment and products are comparable to such other sources. If TPT shall sell any such equipment or products to the Corporation, the price to be charged shall not exceed an amount which would be reasonably comparable to the charge for like equipment and products if obtained from an independent supplier dealing on an arm's length basis.[17]

The Subscription Agreement also set out the Tele Promp Ter option to acquire an 80 percent ownership position at an option price per share of $10.[18] The purchase of eight hundred shares at ten dollars per share would thus give Tele Promp Ter an 80 percent ownership position for an outlay of eight thousand dollars.

The Council of the City of Oakland awarded the CATV franchise to Focus Cable on November 10, 1970.[19] Focus Cable accepted the franchise on December 23, 1970.[20]

1.3 *Execution of the Franchise*

A rate for System B of $4.45 per month was requested by Focus Cable on March 10, 1971, and was approved on March 11, 1971.[21] The combined rate for System A and System B thus came to $6.15 per month.

Construction, which was due to be completed on December 28, 1973, did not go as quickly as the franchise specifications called for, fewer households subscribed to the service than anticipated, and costs escalated. Focus Cable appealed to the City to renegotiate the terms of the franchise. A reduction in the penalty period and the penalty fee was sought; a stretch-out of the construction period was requested; and a downgrading of the cable requirement was proposed. The Staff of the Office of General Services summarized the requested changes as follows:

> Focus is requesting that: further construction be limited to a dual trunk/single feeder cable configuration; a two-year construction extension be granted; only 90% of the households be served at the end of the two years with the remaining 10% to be served only under specified conditions; activation of the dual cable system be deferred until adequate demand develops; damage payments for con-

[16]See Subscription Agreement, note 14 *supra,* p. 2.

[17]*Ibid.,* p. 12.

[18]See note 14 *supra,* p. 6.

[19]City of Oakland Ordinance No. 8246 C.M.S., November 10, 1970.

[20]Statement from Leonard Tow, Treasurer, Focus Cable of Oakland, to City of Oakland, dated December 23, 1970.

[21]Oakland City Council Resolution No. 51477 C.M.S., Dated March 11, 1971.

struction delays be waived; rates of $1.70 for basic services and $6.15 for extended services continue but that additional set rates be increased; extended service subscribers be reduced from 38 to 30 channels; and that reductions be made in the city and school spectrum allocations.[22]

The Staff then considered four alternatives: (1) insist that the terms of the original franchise be met; (2) negotiate a revised agreement with Focus; and terminate the franchise, in which event (3) proposals from other commercial cable operators would be invited, or (4) shift the franchise to public ownership. The first was rejected because it would require great effort by the City "to obtain a satisfactory result from a recalcitrant operator. Citizen complaints about service will proliferate and require enormous effort to resolve. Litigation may result."[23] The third was rejected because other operators were thought unlikely to provide any more than the "minimum requirements of the 1972 Cable Television Report and Order"—"28-Channel capacity, some two-way capacity, three channels for local use, and 'significant' local programming"—offerings which were characterized as "significantly less than would be provided by Focus' recommended plant revisions."[24] Furthermore, public ownership was rejected for philosophical and financial reasons.[25] The second alternative, which the Staff characterized as the compromise solution, was accordingly proposed.[26]

In the course of reviewing Focus Cable's problems, the Staff reported that Focus claimed to have invested $12,600,000 to date and that Focus estimated that this would increase to $21,400,000 if the dual system were to be completed. The Staff disputed these figures and offered its own estimate of $18,684,000 as the completed capital cost of the dual system. The original Focus estimate, by contrast, was $11,753,000. The Staff attributed the increase over the initial estimate to "possible mismanagement of construction activities; inflation, which was compounded by Focus's not meeting the original construction schedule; and an underestimate by Focus of the mileage and unit costs necessary to build the Oakland system."[27]

Since 437 miles, or 55 percent of the system, were already completed and furnished with dual cable, the Staff recommended that the system be completed as a dual cable system. The second cable, however, would not be energized until a later date. Since only the one cable was to be energized, a reduction of channel capacity on System B resulted, and a reduction of city and school spectrum allocations was proposed. The subscriber to the extended

[22]Inter-Office Letter from Office of General Services to Office of the City Manager, dated April 5, 1974, p. 1.

[23]*Ibid.*, attachment, p. 4.

[24]*Ibid.*, attachment, p. 5.

[25]*Ibid.*, attachment, p. 5.

[26]*Ibid.*, attachment, p. 8.

[27]*Ibid.*, attachment, p. 8.

service (now designated A/B) would receive 12 channels on System A and 18 channels on System B.[28] Also, the Staff was agreeable to the proposal that a construction extension of two years be granted and that only 90 percent rather than 100 percent coverage be attempted.[29] Additionally, the Staff recommended that Focus pay the City $240,000 for lost revenues, due to the delay, during the period 1973 to 1976 and that any delays beyond December 1976 be assessed at the rate of $250 rather than $750 per day.[30] Finally, the Staff recommended that the monthly rate for the initial System A connection remain at $1.70 and that the initial System B connection remain at $4.45 (so that System A/B remained at $6.15), but that the monthly rate on additional outlets for System A be increased from $.34 to $1.70 and that the rate for additional System B outlets be set at $3.00.[31]

The "compromise" that finally emerged and was approved by City Council had the following provisions.[32] (1) A shift from the dual to a single cable system was permitted with the understanding that additional transmission capacity would be put in place within one year after it was ascertained that the "additional transmission capacity will attract sufficient revenues to provide a per annum rate-of-return on the gross investment required, over a 10-year period, equivalent to ten percent."[33] (2) The minimum franchise fee was increased by $25,000 in 1974 and each year thereafter. (3) Damages were assessed at the rate of $250 per day from December 18, 1973, until the first reading of the amended franchise—which resulted in a penalty of $36,000—rather than $750 per day for the entire period from December 18, 1973, until system completion—a penalty which would have been greater by a factor of 20 or more and which might have precipitated bankruptcy. (4) A deferred construction schedule was approved. Finally, (5) the monthly rate on additional connections was increased from $.34 to $1.70 per month on System A and was set at $3.00 per month on System B.

The City passed an ordinance on May 30, 1974, to reflect most of those changes.[34] Attorneys for Focus forwarded Letters of Acceptance by Focus and Tele Promp Ter on June 14, 1974, and sent a check from Tele Promp Ter Corporation made payable to the City of Oakland in the amount of $36,000.

[28]*Ibid.*, attachment, pp. 10–11.

[29]*Ibid.*, attachment, pp. 8–9.

[30]*Ibid.*, attachment, pp. 11–12.

[31]*Ibid.*, attachment, pp. 12–13.

[32]Memorandum from Office of General Services to Office of City Manager summarizing actions taken by the City Council at work sessions concerning Focus Cable, dated April 22, 1974.

[33]*Ibid.*, attachment I.

[34]City of Oakland, Ordinance No. 9018 C.M.S., Amending Ordinance No. 8246 C.M.S., and Ordinance No. 7989 C.M.S., Relating to the Community Antenna Television System Franchise, dated May 30, 1974. The only significant exceptions from the compromise described in the text are the following: The additional connection rate for System B was set at $1.30 per month, and it was stipulated that System B should provide not less than 18 video channels.

Focus Cable filed a progress report on November 15, 1974, which showed that 11,131 subscribers were connected. Of those, 770 took the basic service at $1.70 per month (of which 206 had additional outlets), and 10,361 had the extended service at $6.15 per month (of which 974 had additional outlets). That represented an overall penetration rate of 36 percent.[35] The Office of General Services recommended that Cable Dynamics, Inc. of Burlingame, California, be retained as consultants to "devise and perform tests to establish the degree of compliance" with technical requirements of the franchise.[36] Cable Dynamics estimated that the costs from Autumn 1974 to June 1976 would be approximately $10,750.[37] Focus agreed to reimburse the City for these costs up to an amount not to exceed $10,750.[38]

2. An Evaluation

The franchising procedures employed by the City of Oakland, especially at the initial reward stage, are not without merit. As compared, for example, with those in New York City, which awarded noncompetitive, twenty-year contracts to Manhattan Cable TV and to Tele Promp Ter to supply CATV in Manhattan,[39] the Oakland exercise had the appearance of a genuine bidding competition. Franchise specifications were standardized and, with respect to System A at least, carefully described. Bidding competition in terms of a simple promise to sell cheaply (by designating the value "X" at which System A services would be supplied) was thereby facilitated. However, numerous problems, many of which were anticipated in the discussion of incomplete long-term contracts, developed. Thus, consider each of the previously described disabilities which sometimes infect franchise awards: (1) the artificiality or obscurity of the initial award criterion; (2) the development of execution problems in price-cost, other performance, and political respects; and (3) the absence of bidding parity at the contract renewal interval.

2.1 Initial Award

Awarding the franchise on the basis of the lowest bid of "X" to supply System A service simplified the award criterion, but the promise to supply cheaply proved to be specious. The lack of attention to System B (which was

[35]Attachment to City of Oakland Inter-Office Letter from Office of General Services to City Manager, dated November 20, 1974.

[36]Letter, *ibid.*, p. 2.

[37]Attachment to letter, *ibid.*

[38]Letter, see Note 25 *supra*, p. 2.

[39]*New York Times*, July 29, 1970, p. 1.

treated as a futuristic service and, except for capacity requirements, was left relatively undefined) in both quality and price respects may well have contributed to "adventurous" bidding on the part of Focus. Trafficking in the franchise award quickly ensued.

To have regarded System A, which essentially supplies improved off-the-air signals, as the "basic system" was misguided. Over 90 percent of the subscribers took the combined A/B service, although the additional service thereby obtained was relatively mundane (mainly the import of distant signals). The rate on the combined service, however, was three-and-a-half times as great as the basic System A service. Surely a more careful effort to assess subscriber preferences at the outset would have revealed that System A lacked appeal. Indeed, inasmuch as most of the prospective franchisees were experienced in supplying CATV services in other areas, it is difficult to understand the preoccupation with System A services during the extended precontract discussion between the franchisor and the prospective franchisees. The possibility that the Staff was gullible and deliberately misled during these precontract discussions cannot be dismissed.[40]

Whatever the case—given the demand and technological uncertainties associated with CATV (CTIC, 1972c, pp. 5, 12) and the complexity of the service, in quality and product mix respects—reducing the award criterion to the lowest bid price for System A resulted in a strained and perhaps bogus competiton.

2.2 Execution Difficulties

a. PRICE-COST RELATIONS

Whether the Focus bid of $1.70 per month for System A can be regarded as close to "per unit production cost" is doubtful in view of the following factors: (1) The disparity among bid prices raises a question as to whether an economically meaningful competition was conducted; (2) System B prices, which appear to be the more relevant dimension, were negotiated subsequent to the bidding competition; and (3) true cost levels are difficult to ascertain—partly because the vertically integrated supply relation obscures them, partly because inflation rates during the construction period have been abnormally high, and partly because the Staff lacks an auditing capability. What is evident is that Focus and the Staff of the Office of General Services are, together with the City Council, involved in a long-term bargaining relationship over prices and costs in which political interests, bureaucratic interests, and franchise viability all play a role.

---

[40]As Posner surmised, it is hazardous to permit a public agency by itself to declare subscriber preferences for service.

b. OTHER PERFORMANCE ATTRIBUTES

The stipulation that the CATV system be installed and maintained in accordance with the "highest and best accepted standards" of the industry coupled with technical specifications did not yield a well-defined quality outcome.[41] Sufficient customer complaints over quality have been registered with the Staff of the Office of General Services[42] that the Staff, unable itself to assess the quality of service, has arranged for a consultant to test the degree of compliance of service with technical requirements.

c. POLITICS

Whether the winning bid by Focus involved "buying in" is uncertain. An inference that buying in did occur is supported by the following considerations. (1) The next lowest bid was double the Focus bid, while the Tele Promp Ter bid was more than triple the Focus bid. (2) The timing and nature of the Focus reorganization suggest a foot-in-the-door strategy—the object being that, once in, the franchising authority would be inclined to work with Focus and its affiliates in an accommodating manner. (3) Focus's local bidder status was affirmatively regarded by the franchising authority and evidently supported politicking.[43] Finally, (4) the extensive renegotiations undertaken by Focus, with evident success—the Staff acceded to most of Focus's requests and the City Council approved a "compromise" in which energizing of the second cable was deferred (with a cutback in System B services to eighteen channels); the annual franchising fee was increased slightly; damages were reduced drastically; construction deadlines were extended; and rates on additional System A and B connections were increased—reinforce this judgment.

2.3 Frictionless Takeover or Transfer

Although the enabling ordinance provided for buying up of the plant and equipment of the franchisee, the City was plainly not prepared to upset the

[41]Partly this may be because "[a]n initial high signal quality may, over time, slowly degrade, to the point where the signal quality is not acceptable" (CTIC, 1973, p. 9); partly it is that signal quality is multidimensional and varies with the capability of the system to receive off-air and microwave signal as well as headend and cable attributes (CTIC, 1973, pp. 19–24).

[42]The existence of customer complaints regarding quality of service was disclosed in an interview with Mark Leh (see note 8 *supra*).

[43]Libman (1974) reports that the award of the Oakland CATV franchise to the Focus group, despite its lack of expertise and adequate financing, and the subsequent implementation of the franchise appear to have been influenced by political considerations. A more spectacular and unambiguous case is afforded by the CATV competition in Johnstown, Pennsylvania, where Irving Kahn, the former chief executive and chairman of Tele Promp Ter, the nation's largest operator of cable TV, was tried and convicted of bribery and perjury. Kahn has also admitted

original award. The reasons appear to be that incumbents are strategically positioned to bargain—both in terms of service interruptions and the litigating and other expenses which franchise termination would entail—and, relatedly, because franchising agencies lack resolve. This lack of resolution appears to be attributable to the reward structure in bureaus. Unable to appropriate the gains that reassignment of the franchise would prospectively yield and unwilling to concede error, the bureaus favor "accommodation" whenever contract execution difficulties appear.

The interruptions and expenses which franchise termination would experience are presumably explained, in part at least, by physical and human asset problems of the kinds discussed in Section 3. Absent rules for valuing the CATV plant and equipment that are at once rational, unambiguous, and inexpensive to employ, physical asset valuation problems predictably arise.[44] Inasmuch as such rules had not been devised (and, realistically, perhaps could not have been devised) for the Oakland franchise, litigation expenses and delays would attend any effort to take over the physical plant in question.

The risk of service interruptions and related malfunctions would be compounded if the human assets associated with the franchise had acquired, in a learning-by-doing process, nontrivial task idiosyncrasies. Given that the Staff lacked qualifications in the CATV area and was evidently unwilling to solicit bids from other experienced CATV operators (possibly because the Staff was unwilling to accept the risk of embarrassment should the new operator also prove to be deficient), the transfer of human assets would need to be worked out if City ownership were to be attempted. The incentive to displace the original franchisee would be attenuated to the extent that a frictionless transfer of such human assets could not be anticipated.

The upshot is that, good intentions to the contrary notwithstanding, *unassisted* franchise bidding for CATV conducted and executed under conditions of uncertainty has dubious properties. The franchising authority that assumes an accommodating posture is merely legitimating monopoly, while a concerted effort to exercise control requires the agency to adopt a regulatory

---

bribing public officials in Trenton, New Jersey, to secure their votes. Politics appears also to have been a decisive factor in the award of CATV franchises in New York City. (See note 39 *supra*.) Whether this holds for CATV awards in large cities more generally is uncertain. The incidence of corruption with respect to franchise awards for other types of services is also an open question.

[44]Indeed they did arise. Witness that the completed system estimate by Focus exceeded the Staff's estimate by almost three million dollars. Note also that it is ill-advised to permit the franchisee to become affiliated with a firm that supplies equipment and products for the construction of the plant. The risk here is that the procurement costs of these items will be overstated, thereby to build up the rate base of the franchisee and improve its bargaining position during rate negotiations. Despite claims that equipment will be procured on competitive terms, this is costly to check and violations are difficult to prove conclusively. The Oakland Staff suspects unwarranted equipment cost escalation in the estimates by Focus of plant valuation, but admits that it has no definitive proof.

posture. The purported dichotomy between "regulatory controls" on the one hand and "natural economic forces" on the other is accordingly strained. It confuses the issues to characterize market solutions as "natural" where these are actually supported by an administrative apparatus of considerable complexity.[45]

[45]Posner employs this dichotomy in his 1969 discussion of natural monopoly, in which he urges that "even in markets where efficiency dictates monopoly we might do better to allow natural economic forces to determine business conduct and performance subject only to the constraints of antitrust policy" (1969, p. 549). He declines, however, to handle the CATV issue in this way but instead favors the market assisted bidding scheme described in section 3, the administrative problems associated with which are formidable.

CHAPTER 14

Antitrust Enforcement

Antitrust enforcement has been massively reshaped in the past twenty years. Much of that is a result of persistent economic criticism that has its origins in received microtheory. The demise of the leverage theory of tie-ins is an illustration (Posner, 1979, p. 929). Some reforms are attributable to a growing appreciation for transaction costs. Public policy toward firm and market organization is unavoidably transformed as the concept of the firm as a governance structure takes hold and by efforts to assess complex contracts in a comparative institutional way.

Transformations of public policy toward mergers are described in section 1. Nonstandard contracting reforms are discussed in section 2. Some of the novel and difficult issues of analysis and enforcement posed by strategic behavior are addressed in sections 3 and 4. Concluding remarks follow.

1. Merger Policy

Changes in public policy toward vertical and conglomerate mergers have been described in Chapters 4 and 11. They do not require repeating here. The proposition that public policy toward mergers had undergone significant transformation is difficult to appreciate, however, without a statement of specifics. I attempt to give some background here.

1.1 *The 1960s*

The 1960s was the era when market power analysis flourished. Partly that was due to recent theoretical, empirical, and policy studies in which the importance of barriers to entry was featured. But it was also because antitrust economics was sorely lacking in two other respects. First, there was a general undervaluation of the social benefits of efficiency. Second, there was a widespread tendency to regard efficiency very narrowly—mainly in technological terms. An awareness of transaction costs, much less a sensitivity to the importance of economizing thereon, had scarcely surfaced. Instead, the firm was held to be a production function to which a profit maximization objective had been assigned.[1] The efficient boundaries of firms were thought to be determined by technology. Accordingly, efforts to reconfigure firm and market structures that violated those "natural" boundaries were believed to have market power origins.

The prevailing state of affairs is indicated by the Federal Trade Commission's opinion in *Foremost Dairies,* where the Commission ventured the view that necessary proof of violation of Section 7 "consists of types of evidence showing that the acquiring firm possesses significant power in some markets *or* that its over-all organization gives it a decisive advantage in efficiency over its smaller rivals."[2] Although Donald Turner, among others, was quick to label that as bad law and bad economics (1965, p. 1324), in that it protects competitors rather than promoting the welfare benefits of competition, the Commission carried its reasoning forward in *Procter & Gamble* and linked it with barriers to entry in the following way:

> In stressing as we have the importance of advantages of scale as a factor heightening the barriers to new entry into the liquid bleach industry, we reject, as specious in law and unfounded in fact, the argument that the Commission ought not, for the sake of protecting the "inefficient" small firms in the industry, proscribe a merger so productive of "efficiencies." The short answer to this argument is that, in a proceeding under Section 7, economic efficiency or any other social benefit resulting from a merger is pertinent only insofar as it may tend to promote or retard the vigor of competition.[3]

[1]The period 1950–70 has been described by Coase as the applied price theory era in industrial organization. The leading texts were preoccupied with "the study of pricing and output policies of firms, especially in oligopolistic situations (often called a study of market structure)" (Coase, 1972, p. 62). The firm, for those purposes, was essentially viewed as a production function.

[2]In re *Foremost Dairies, Inc.,* 60 F.T.C. 944, 1084 (1962), emphasis added.

[3]Quoted from Bork (1978, p. 254).

The emphasis on entry barriers and the low regard accorded to economies also appear in the Supreme Court's opinion. Thus the Court observed that Procter's acquisition of Clorox may

> . . . have the tendency of raising the barriers to new entry. The major competitive weapon in the successful marketing of bleach is advertising. Clorox was limited in this area by its relatively small budget and its inability to obtain substantial discounts. By contrast, Procter's budget was much larger; and, although it would not devote its entire budget to advertising Clorox, it could divert a large portion to meet the short-term threat of a new entrant. Procter would be able to use its volume discounts to advantage in advertising Clorox. Thus, a new entrant would be much more reluctant to face the giant Procter than it would have been to face the smaller Clorox.
>
> Possible economies cannot be used as a defense to illegality.[4]

The low opinion and perverse regard for economies went so far that beleaguered respondents disclaimed efficiency gains. Thus Procter & Gamble insisted that its acquisition of Clorox was unobjectionable because the government was unable definitively to establish that any efficiencies would result:

> [The Government is unable to prove] any advantages in the procurement or price of raw materials or in the acquisition or use of needed manufacturing facilities or in the purchase of bottles or in freight costs. . . . [T]here is no proof of any savings in any aspect of manufacturing. There is no proof that any additional manufacturing facilities would be usable for the production of Clorox. There is no proof that any combination of manufacturing facilities would effect any savings, even if such combination were feasible.[5]

This upside-down assessment of economies was bound to change, and it did—but not before Justice Stewart, in a dissenting opinion in 1966, recorded that the "sole consistency that I can find is that in [merger] litigation under Section 7, the Government always wins."[6]

1.2 Subsequent Developments

The reforms of antitrust enforcement in the 1970s had their origins in critiques of the 1960s. Those include (1) the insistence of the "Chicago School" that antitrust issues be studied through the lens of price theory; (2) related critiques of the entry barrier approach; (3) application of the partial equilibrium welfare

---

[4]*Federal Trade Commission* v. *Procter & Gamble Co.*, 386 U.S. 568, 574 (1967).

[5]The disclaimer of efficiencies appeared in Procter & Gamble's brief as Respondent in the Clorox litigation. See Fisher and Lande (1983, p. 1582, n. 5).

[6]*United States* v. *Von's Grocery Co.*, 384 U.S. 270, 301 (1966) (Stewart, J., dissenting).

economics model to assess the tradeoffs between market power and efficiency; and (4) a reformulation of the theory of the modern corporation whereby transaction cost economizing considerations were brought to the fore. An additional contributing factor was the reorganization of the economics staff of the Antitrust Division. Whereas previously the staff economists were used almost exclusively to support the legal staff in the preparation and litigation of cases, it was now asked to assess the economic merits of cases before they were filed.

The Chicago School approach has been set out by Richard Posner (1979) elsewhere. Although it is possible to quibble with Posner's rendition of Harvard versus Chicago (as these were viewed in the 1960s), it is nevertheless clear that the leverage theory approach to nonstandard contracting has progressively given way to the price discrimination interpretation favored by Aaron Director (and his students and colleagues).

The preoccupation of merger policy with entry barriers was also criticized by Chicago. Objectives of two kinds were registered. The first held that the basic entry barrier model, as set out by Bain (1956) and elaborated by Franco Modigliani (1958), purported to be but did not qualify as an oligopoly model. As Stigler put it, the entry barrier models solved the oligopoly problems by murder: "The ability of the oligopolists to agree upon and police the limit price is apparently independent of the sizes and numbers of oligopolists" (1968, p. 21). Put differently, the model did not address itself to the mechanics by which collective action was realized. Instead, it simply assumed that the requisite coordination to effect a limit price result would appear. As discussed below, recent models in the entry barrier tradition have avoided that problem by explicitly casting the analysis in a "sitting monopolist"/duopoly framework. Addressing the issues of entry in this more limited context has analytical advantages, but applications outside of the dominant firm context are appropriate only upon a showing that the necessary preconditions to effect oligopolistic coordination are satisfied.

The other objection to entry barrier analysis relates to public policy misuses of entry barrier reasoning. That the condition of entry is impeded is neither here nor there if no superior structural configuration—expressed in welfare terms—can be described. However obvious that may be on reflection, it was not always the case. Rather, there was a widespread tendency to regard barriers of all kinds as contrary to the social interest. But as Robert Bork has put it, "The question for antitrust is whether there exist *artificial* entry barriers. These must be barriers that are not forms of superior efficiency and which yet prevent the forces of the market . . . from operating to erode market positions not based on efficiency" (1978, p. 311; emphasis added).

The distinction between remediable and irremediable entry impediments thus becomes the focus of attention. Little useful public policy purpose is served, and a considerable risk of public policy mischief results, when conditions of an irremediable kind are brought under fire. Mistaken treatment of economies of scale illustrates what is at stake. Thus suppose that economies of scale exist and that the market is of sufficient size to support the larger of two technologies. Since superior outcomes will be attributable to the less efficient technology only in very unusual conditions, net social benefits ought presumably to be attributed to the scale economy conditions. To describe such economies as "barriers to entry," however, does not invite that conclusion; to the contrary, mistaken welfare judgments are encouraged.

That efficiency benefits were held in such low regard in the 1960s is partly explained by the widespread opinion that, as between two structural alternatives—one of which simultaneously presents greater market power and greater efficiency than the other—the more competitive structure is invariably to be preferred. That view was supported by the implicit assumption that even small anticompetitive effects would surely swamp efficiency benefits in arriving at a net valuation. The FTC opinion that "economic efficiency or any other social benefit [is] pertinent only insofar as it may tend to promote or retard the vigor of competition"[7]—where competition is defined in structural terms—is a clear indication of such thinking.

Application of the basic partial equilibrium welfare economics model to an assessment of market power versus economies tradeoffs disclosed that to sacrifice economies for reduced market power came at a high cost (Williamson, 1968). Although the merits of that framework remain open to dispute (Posner, 1975, p. 821), the general approach, if not the framework itself, has since been employed by others. Bain was among the first to acknowledge the merits of an economies defense in assessing mergers (1968, p. 658). Wesley Liebeler (1978), Robert Bork (1978), and Timothy Muris (1979) have all made extensive use of the partial equilibrium tradeoff model in their insistence that antitrust enforcement that proceeds heedless of tradeoffs is uninformed and contrary to the social interest.

A common argument against tradeoff analysis is that the courts are poorly suited to assess economic evidence and arguments of this kind (Bork, 1978). In fact, however, a simple sensitivity to the merits of economies is sufficient to avoid the inverted reasoning of *Foremost Dairies*. And although errors of the *Schwinn* kind are avoided only upon recognizing that economies can take transaction cost as well as technological forms, the mistakes of the "inhospitality tradition" also become less likely once that step has been

[7]See note 3 *supra*.

taken. The upside-down assessment of economies in the 1960s appears thoroughly to have been vanquished by the economies as an antitrust defense literature (Fisher and Lande, 1983).

Indeed, not only are economies no longer regarded as an anticompetitive feature, but the 1984 Merger Guidelines of the Department of Justice expressly declare that "some mergers that the Department otherwise might challenge may be reasonably necessary to achieve significant net efficiencies. If the parties to the merger establish by clear and convincing evidence that a merger will achieve such efficiencies, the Department will consider those efficiencies in deciding to challenge the merger" (U.S. Department of Justice, 1984, Sec. 3.5). In effect, firms that are proposing a merger are now invited to present evidence of efficiencies as support for the merger—rather than suppress such evidence (the market power standard) or deny that any efficiencies exist (the perverse condition to which merger enforcement had fallen in the 1960s). Economies of both technological and transaction cost kinds will be entertained (Sec. 3.5 and 4.24).

Although such an approach to merger enforcement accords what some may regard as excessive discretion to an administrative branch of the government, there are no costless choices. Only time will tell whether the lawyers and economists in the Antitrust Division will be able to sort real from contrived claims of efficiency and thus permit the merger statutes to be enforced with net social gains. I am nevertheless cautiously optimistic of such a result.[8]

2. Nonstandard Contracting

The inhospitality tradition to which I referred earlier[9] held that nonstandard modes of contracting were presumptively anticompetitive. The argument, moreover, was very sweeping. No effort was made to delimit applications to a subset of activity where the anticompetitive concerns were thought to be especially severe. Rather, customer, territorial, and related contract restraints were held to be presumptively unlawful, without qualification.

That policy position was based on two lines of argument. The affirmative argument was that rivals, distributors, customers, and so on are somehow "disadvantaged" when nonstandard contracting is employed. That was but-

---

[8]Although I would not encourage that a full-blown economies defense be presented and actively contested in a court if the Department decides to challenge a merger and the case is brought to trial, permitting the respondent to present economies to the court as part of its rationale for a merger could have salutory effects. That proposal, and some of the complications that attend it, are discussed elsewhere (Williamson, 1968, pp. 113–14, and 1977, pp. 727–29).

[9]See the text at note 9 in Chapter 1, where a bold statement of the inhospitality position is advanced.

tressed by the view that true economies take a technological form, hence are fully realized within firms. Since there is nothing to be gained by introducing nonstandard terms into market-mediated exchange, the use of contract restraints was presumed to have anticompetitive purpose and affect.

Both lines of argument are related and mistaken. The notion that all relevant economies have technological origins is the more obviously mistaken of the two. At best it is a convenient fiction, as is surely evident from the contracting schema in Chapter 1 (to which reference has been made repeatedly throughout the book).

To prohibit contract restraints for trades that are supported by specific investments is to insist, in effect, that all $k > 0$ contracts be of a node B kind. That is patently inefficient in circumstances where effective contractual safeguards of a node C kind can be fashioned. It bears repeating, moreover, that price and governance structure are determined simultaneously, in an internally consistent relation to each other.

That last introduces contracting in its entirety considerations. It is easy to conclude, upon examining a contract at a point in time, that one of the parties to the exchange is disadvantaged by the restraint—in the sense that the restrained party would behave differently if the restraint were removed. Thus franchisees would frequently exercise the option to buy supplies (product; replacement parts) from unauthorized suppliers if that were permitted. That supposedly demonstrates that manufacturer insistence that purchases be made only from authorized suppliers is one-sided and anticompetitive.

Such a myopic conception fails to recognize that the terms under which the original franchise was struck reflect the associated restraints. It is understandably attractive to have your cake (low price) and eat it too (no restrictions). But both the theory and the practice of contract preclude that.

The *Schwinn* case, which was argued in 1966 and decided in 1967, reflects those confusions. The main arguments and their premises are examined in section 6 of Chapter 4. With one exception, they will not be repeated here. Consider, however, the government's views on vertical integration versus vertical restraints—"a rule that treats manufacturers who assume the distribution function themselves more leniently than those who impose restraints on independent distributors merely reflects the fact that, although integration in distribution sometimes benefits the economy by leading to cost savings, agreements to maintain resale prices or to impose territorial restrictions of unlimited duration or outlet limitations of the type involved here have never been shown to produce comparable economies."[10] The clear preference for internal over market modes of organization is consonant with the

[10]Brief for the United States at 58, *United States v. Arnold, Schwinn & Co.*, 388 U.S. 365 (1967).

then prevailing preoccupation with technological features and the corresponding disregard for transaction costs.

That orientation did not withstand subsequent criticism. The mistaken reasoning of *Schwinn* was corrected only a decade later when the Supreme Court decided the *GTE-Sylvania* case. The Court held that

> [vertical] restrictions, in varying forms, are widely used in our free market economy. [Moreover, while] there is substantial scholarly opinion and judicial authority supporting their economic utility, [t]here is relatively little authority to the contrary. Certainly there has been no showing in this case, either generally or with respect to Sylvania's agreement, that vertical restrictions have or are likely to have a "pernicious effect on competition" or that they "lack . . . any redeeming virtue." . . . Accordingly, we conclude that the per se rule in *Schwinn* must be overruled.[11]

The intellectual basis for assessing the merits of alternative modes of organization evidently experienced substantial changes in the ten-year interval between those two opinions. Public policy was transformed as a consequence.[12] Subsequent revisions in public policy toward price discrimination, franchise restrictions, reciprocity, basing point systems, block booking, and the like are also to be anticipated if recent scholarship on those matters is equally persuasive.[13]

Lest the affirmative case for vertical restrictions become the new orthodoxy, however, it should not be concluded that such restrictions are unproblematic. For one thing, there is the usual caveat that vertical restrictions can be and sometimes are used to support horizontal cartels. Resale price maintenance, for example, can serve dealer cartel purposes; and vertical

---

[11]*Continental T.V. Inc. et al.* v. *GTE Sylvania Inc.* 433 U.S. 36, 45 (1977). Both Richard Posner and Donald Turner, who had played major notes in briefing and arguing *Schwinn* before the Supreme Court, were persuaded that their earlier views were incorrect and were instrumental in persuading the Court to reverse itself in *GTE-Sylvania*.

[12]George Stigler holds otherwise. Thus he observes: "Economists have their glories, but I do not believe that the body of American antitrust law is among them. . . . Some cases seem sophisticated and sensible (for example, the widely acclaimed Sylvania decision), but why shouldn't this happen with random fluctuation?" (Stigler, 1982, p. 7).

A distinction between coin flipping and reasoned decisions needs to be made. Were it that the Supreme Court merely decided cases and did not write opinions, random fluctuations might properly be inferred. Students on multiple choice exams, after all, sometimes guess correctly. But students who write essay exams are subject to a further and deeper check.

Developing measures of statistical significance for those deeper types of evidence is not easy. But it is surely the case that a closely reasoned argument is entitled to greater credence than a "single observation" of the coin flipping or multiple choice genre. (Poorly reasoned but correct decisions, by contrast, may well be an indication of random fluctuation: correct decisions and mere words will not do.)

[13]See the discussions in Chapters 7 and 8 on Robinson–Patman, franchise restrictions, and reciprocity. See David Haddock (1982) on basing points. See Kenney and Klein (1983) on block booking.

restrictions can also serve to regularize a manufacturers' cartel (the facilitating practices doctrine). But the issues go deeper than that.

Thus consider a vertical restriction that has two effects: It helps to mitigate free rider effects, and thus restores incentives to engage in valued promotional and related sales and service activity, *and* it serves as a device by which to price discriminate. The first effect is generally in the public interest. The second may be, but it need not. As I have discussed elsewhere, efforts to monetize consumers' surplus can yield net private gains and net social losses if the transaction costs that attend those efforts are substantial (Williamson, 1975, pp. 11–13). Specifically, three effects of price discrimination have to be distinguished: (1) What had been consumers' surplus in a uniform pricing regime is monetized (let this be V_1); (2) net revenue is further augmented by the sale of added product made possible by price discrimination (let this be V_2, and assume, for convenience, that price discrimination is perfect); and (3) transaction costs are incurred in introducing and policing the practice by which perfect price discrimination is achieved (let this be T). Net private gains will then obtain if $\Delta\pi = V_1 + V_2 - T > 0$, but a social gain will be realized only if $\Delta W = V_2 - T > 0$. The possibility that $\Delta\pi > 0$ and $\Delta W < 0$ must thus be admitted. The monetization of consumers' surplus on intramarginal product is the troublesome factor that yields this mixed result.[14]

3. Strategic Behavior

The study of strategic behavior—by which I mean efforts by established firms to take up advance positions in relation to actual or potential rivals and/or to respond punitively to new rivalry—is enormously complex. The early entry barrier models emphasized *ex ante* positioning.[15] More recent work on predatory pricing has emphasized *ex post* responses.[16]

---

[14]To be sure, the overall social gain is understated by V_2 - T; the social benefits realized by eliminating free riding need to be added in. Suppose, however, that upon making that correction a net social loss still obtains. Ought a vertical restriction that yields a net social loss in comparison with the discrete market contracting standard of exchange be prohibited? Not necessarily. For one thing the discrete market contracting standard may not be the appropriate one. If the denial of one restriction does not result in uniform pricing but elicits the use of an inferior restriction that has even worse welfare properties, then the prohibition is counterproductive. For another, a *per se* rule permitting all vertical restrictions might be warranted if, from a statistical decision theory point of view, a rule of reason is too costly and other efforts to define filters (of the kind proposed by Easterbrook [1984]) are problematic. In no event is a return to the inhospitality tradition warranted by reason of the "complications" to which I refer above.

[15]This was the main emphasis, but behavioral assumptions about price-making in the post-entry period necessarily played a role.

[16]It should be recognized, however, that *ex post* responses vary with *ex ante* investments.

Objections that have been or could be leveled at early entry barrier models and related applications to predatory pricing include: (1) The structural preconditions are not carefully stated; (2) whether it is more attractive to bar rather than accept entry is assumed but not demonstrated; (3) attention is focused on total costs, but the composition of costs and the characteristics of assets matter crucially and have been neglected; (4) the incentives to engage in predation are weak; and (5) cost asymmetries between established firms and potential entrants are asserted but rarely addressed. Recent work has made headway with each objection.

3.1 Structural Preconditions

As discussed above, the early entry barrier models purported to be oligopoly models. But the question of how oligopolists managed to achieve effective concurrence of market action—with respect to price, output, investment, and so on—was not addressed. The relevance of such models outside of the dominant firm context was thus questionable.

Recent models in the entry barrier tradition have essentially abandoned the oligopoly claim. The issues are posed instead in a duopoly context between a "sitting monopolist" and a potential entrant. Those who would apply those models to oligopoly presumably have the heavy burden of demonstrating their transferability.

Similar care has been taken in assessing claims of predation. The hazard here is that the legal process will be misused to discourage legitimate rivalry. There is growing agreement that the structural preconditions that must be satisfied before claims of predation are seriously entertained are very high concentration coupled with barriers to entry (Williamson, 1977, pp. 292–93). Joskow and Klevorick (1979, pp. 225–31) and Ordover and Willig (1981) concur and propose a "two-tier" test for predatory pricing. The subset of industries for which strategic behavior warrants public policy scrutiny would thus appear to be the following: (1) the sitting monopolist/duopolist situation; (2) regulated monopolies; (3) dominant firm industries; and (4) what William Fellner has referred to as "Case 3 oligopoly" (1949, pp. 47–49), an industry where an outside agency (e.g. a union) enforces collective action.[17]

3.2 Rationality of Preentry Deterrence

In principle, entry can be deterred in any of three ways: (1) by expanding output and investment in the preentry period, thereby to discourage the incen-

---

[17]It has been argued that the United Mine Workers performed this function in the bituminous coal industry (Williamson, 1967b).

tive to enter; (2) by threatening aggressive postentry responses; and (3) by imposing cost disadvantages on rivals. The latter two are addressed below. The first is in the spirit of Bain and Modigliani and has been dealt with more recently by Avinash Dixit, who models the entry problem in a duopoly context (1979, 1980). That permits him simultaneously to display and assess the profitability and feasibility of having the sitting monopolist adopt any of three postures: (1) behave in an unconstrained monopoly fashion; (2) expand output and investment so as to deter entry; and (3) accept entry by taking up a Stackelburg leadership position vis-à-vis the entrant. Dixit demonstrates that entry deterrence is optimal when fixed costs—actually, durable investments of a firm-specific kind—are of "intermediate" degree, whence the complaint that entry deterrence is an imposed rather than derived result can be dismissed if the requisite conditions are satisfied.

3.3 Costs, Assets, and Credibility

The standard entry barrier model assumes that potential entrants have access to the same long-run average total cost curve as do established firms. But the composition of costs, as between specific and nonspecific, is ignored. That poses the following anomaly: Extant firms and potential entrants are indistinguishable if all costs are nonspecific. The only "effective" entry deterring policy in circumstances where all costs are nonspecific is to set price equal to total cost, which is to say that entry deterrence is without purpose. The crucial role of sunk costs in entry deterrence is evident from an examination of Dixit's (1979) formulation of the entry problem.

Even granting that entry deterrence sometimes is optimal, a further question arises as to how large a monopoly distortion can develop by reason of temporal asymmetry (the sitting monopolist has assets in place at the outset) and fixed cost conditions. Schmalensee has recently addressed the issue and shows that the preentry present value of excess profits that can be realized by established firms "cannot exceed the capital (start-up) cost of a firm of minimum efficient scale" and that scale economies are therefore of little quantitative importance from a welfare standpoint (1980, pp. 3, 8). That result is questionable, however, because it ignores the reputation effect incentives discussed under 3.4 below.

A related issue that has come under scrutiny is the matter of credible threats. This goes to the issue of what postentry behavior is appropriately imputed to the sitting monopolist. As Curtis Eaton and Richard Lipsey observe (1980, p. 721), both credible and posturing threats take the same form—namely, "If you take action X, I shall take action Y, which will make you regret X." But credible and noncredible threats are distinguishable in that the party issuing the threat will rationally take action Y only if credibility conditions are satisfied. If the Nash response to X is indeed to take action Y, the threat is credible. But if, despite the threat, X occurs and the net benefits accruing to the party issuing the threat are greater if he accommodates (by taking action Z rather than Y), then the threat will be perceived as posturing rather than credible. Since such threats will be empty, Eaton and Lipsey have urged that analysis of strategic behavior focus entirely on threats for which credibility is satisfied. The translation of that argument into investment terms discloses that the sitting monopolist must invest in durable, *transaction-specific assets* if he is to preempt a market and deter entry successfully.

3.4 *Reputation Effects*

Robert Bork's original assessment of the benefits of predation, the Areeda–Turner criterion for assessing predation, Schmalensee's measure of welfare distortion, and the Eaton and Lipsey treatment of credible threats all address the issue of entry and predation in a very narrow context. A large, established firm is confronted with a clearly defined threat of entry, and its response is assessed entirely in that bilateral context. The rationality of killing a rival (Bork, 1978) or of deterring an equally efficient firm (which has not yet made irreversible commitments) becomes the focus of attention (Eaton and Lipsey, 1980; 1981). If, however, punitive behavior carries signals to that and other firms—in future periods, in other geographic areas, and, possibly, in other lines of commerce—such analyses may understate the full set of effects on which the would-be predator is relying in his decision to discipline a rival. Assessing this requires that the issue of predation be addressed in a richer context in which information asymmetries and reputation effects are admitted.

Although their analyses do not make reference to the composition of costs—in particular, the specific versus nonspecific cost distinction is ignored—and for this reason are incomplete, recent articles by David Kreps and Robert Wilson (1982) and Paul Milgrom and John Roberts (1982) make considerable headway with those issues. As Milgrom and Roberts put it

> [P]redation emerges as a rational, profit-maximizing strategy . . . not because it is directly profitable to eliminate the particular rival in question, but rather because it may deter future potential entrants. The mechanism by which this deterrent effect comes about is that by practicing predation the firm establishes a reputation as a predator. [1982, p. 281]

They develop the argument in an intertemporal game theoretic framework in which the usual assumption of complete information is relaxed.

Crucial to their argument is that potential entrants be uncertain as to how to interpret the behavior of the established firm. As they observe:[18]

> There are numerous reasons why this element of uncertainty should exist. On the one hand, the entrants could be [unsure] about the game being played. For example, it might be that the established firm could actually be involved in some bigger game. . . . A second possibility is that in the game actually being played, the established firm may be able to precommit itself to an aggressive course of action and may have done so. Other scenarios involve the entrants allowing that the firm is not behaving as a fully rational game theorist. [Milgrom and Roberts, 1982, p. 303]

And they conclude with the observation that acts of "predation will only rarely need to be practiced. The credible threat of predation will deter all but the toughest entrants" (Milgrom and Roberts, 1982, p. 304).

The claim that predation is irrational and can be dismissed is thus evidently mistaken—or at least that would appear to be the judicious view to maintain until such time as those of the nonpredation persuasion can demonstrate wherein the recent treatments to which I refer are defective.

Applications pose the question of whether the circumstances where reputation effect incentives are strong can be recognized. An important consideration is whether local entry is being attempted into a small sector of the total market where the established firm enjoys dominance. Exploratory entry into a local geographic market or into one or a few products in a much broader line of related products would presumably enhance the appeal of sending a predatory signal. The likelihood that the observed behavior is strategic is increased in the degree to which (1) the response is intensively focused on the local disturbance (is carefully crafted to apply only to the market where entry is attempted) and (2) goes beyond a simple defensive response (e.g. holding output unchanged in the face of entry) to include a punitive aspect (e.g. increasing output as the reply to entry).

3.5 *Cost Asymmetries*

Areeda and Turner (1975) take the position that the "predatory impact" of a price reduction by a dominant firm can be judged by whether such a reduction will exclude an equally efficient rival. As I have argued elsewhere, that is a peculiar criterion for assessing the welfare benefits of contingent increases in

---

[18]Kreps and Wilson express it as follows: "[I]f the situation is repeated, so that it is worthwhile to develop a reputation, and if there is some uncertainty about the motivations of one or more of the players, then that uncertainty can substantially affect the play of the game. There need not be much uncertainty for this to happen" (1982, p. 275).

output—"now it's there, now it isn't, depending on whether an entrant has appeared or perished" (Williamson, 1977, p. 339). I did not, however, comment on the costs incurred by the entrant except in passing (pp. 296, 303–4). In consideration of the series of strategic cost disadvantages that an entrant experiences or may be made to bear in relation to an established firm, that is a regrettable oversight.

There are two points here, the first of which is that history matters in assessing costs. Temporal cost differences can arise in operating cost, cost of capital, and learning curve respects. The second and more significant point is that the established firm may by its own actions be responsible for added cost differences of all of those kinds.

Many of the issues here have been developed elsewhere (Williamson, 1968; Spence, 1981), and some are discussed in earlier chapters. Suffice it to observe here that the equally efficient rival criterion is primarily suited to static circumstances where historical differences and contrived cost asymmetries may be presumed to be absent.[19] To the extent that actual circumstances are not accurately described in that way, allowance for cost differences may be necessary if an informed assessment of predation is to be realized.[20]

4. Unresolved Dilemmas

The study of strategic behavior has made remarkable progress during the past five years. A number of troublesome problems nevertheless remain. These include (1) whether efforts to curb predation should focus primarily on price and output or if other aspects of rivalry should be included; (2) inasmuch as rules governing predation set up incentives for established firms to preposition, should allowance be made for prepositioning in assessing the merits of alternative rules; and (3) whether victims of "mistaken predation" should be accorded protection.

[19]Although a consensus on the issue has not yet developed, there is widespread concern that a marginal cost pricing standard is defective because it appeals to static welfare economics arguments for support while predatory pricing is unavoidably an intertemporal issue. As William Baumol succinctly puts it, static analysis of the kind on which Areeda and Turner rely is "inadequate because it draws our attention from the most pressing issues that are involved. . . . Williamson had identified the nub of the problem in his emphasis on the intertemporal aspect of the situation" (Baumol, 1979, pp. 2–3).

[20]F. M. Scherer observes: "Entry at or near the minimum optimal scale into significant oligopolistic markets is [rare]. Indeed, it is sufficiently rare that it usually receives considerable attention in the relevant trade press" (1980, p. 248). Many models of predatory pricing ignore that and argue that only output produced by an equally efficient rival is socially valued.

4.1 *Dimensions*

Although they are not independent, the study of strategic behavior is usefully split into *ex ante* and *ex post* parts. *Ex ante* behavior takes the form of preentry investment (in capacity, R&D, promotion, the offer of multiple brands, and so on), while *ex post* behavior involves specific adaptations by dominant firms contingent upon rival behavior—especially new entry. As between the two, aggressive strategic behavior in *ex post* respects is widely believed to be the more reprehensible, but there are complicating factors here as well.

Christian von Weizsacker's work on innovation is instructive in that regard. He distinguishes between progressive and mature industries and observes that the positive externalities of innovation are especially strong in a progressive industry due to the "possibility of generating the next innovation" (1981, p. 150). A welfare assessment of the intertemporal incentives to engage in innovation in a progressive industry leads Weizsacker to conclude that "a pricing action by an incumbent, which by reasonable standards is not considered a predatory action in a nonprogressive industry, [*a fortiori*] cannot be called a predatory action in a progressive industry" (1981, p. 210).

A somewhat different aspect is emphasized by Ordover and Willig, who contend that *ex post* "manipulation of the product set can frequently be more effective than price cutting as an anticompetitive tactic" (1981, p. 326). Two types of tactics are examined. The first entails "the introduction of a new product that is a substitute for the products of the rival firm and that endangers its viability by diverting its sales. The second tactic is employed in the context of systems rivalry. It consists of the constriction in the supply of components that are vital to consumers' use of the rival's product, coupled with the introduction of systems components that enable consumers to bypass their use of the rival's products" (Ordover and Willig, 1981, pp. 326–27). Although both their criterion for assessing predation and the practicability of implementing their rules for components complementary to a rival may be disputed, the issues have nevertheless been structured in a useful way. Follow-on studies will surely make use of that framework.

But what should be done in the meantime when the law is confronted with problems that run well ahead of the theory? Thus SCM Corporation asked for compulsory licensing relief in its complaint that Xerox had excluded SCM from the plain copier market.[21] And Berkey Photo argued that unannounced product innovations by Kodak placed it at an unfair disadvantage.[22]

[21]*SCM Corp.* v. *Xerox Corp.* (DC Conn 1978) 1978-2 Trade Cases, Par. 62, 392.

[22]*Berkey Photo, Inc.* v. *Eastman Kodak Co.* (DC NY 1978) 1978-1 Trade Cases, Par. 62,092.

The FTC has also brought some rather ambitious strategic behavior suits. A collusive strategy of brand proliferation formed the basis of its complaint against the principal producers of ready-to-eat cereals (Kellogg, General Mills, General Foods, and Quaker Oats).[23] And the FTC subsequently charged du Pont with making preemptive investments in the titanium dioxide market.[24]

Except for cases that are patently protectionist (and some of these have a protectionist flavor), there are no happy choices. Put differently, tradeoffs proliferate and our capacity to evaluate them is very primitive. Thus although some reject those suits with the observation that plaintiffs' "arguments in the high technology cases of the 1970s rest implicitly on an atomistic theory of competition which posits an organized economy with no changes in technology, no shifts in consumer tastes, no change in population—and no future that is essentially different from the past" (Conference Board, 1980, p. 18), that is really a red herring. Strategic behavior is an interesting economic issue *only* in an intertemporal context where uncertainty is featured. The high-technology cases are plainly of that kind and arguably involve strategic calculations in which private and social valuations differ. The courts have been understandably cautious in moving ahead in that area. Assuming that those are matters that can be reexamined as a deeper understanding of the issues and capacity to make informed tradeoffs develops, that would appear to be the responsible result.

Such caution in enforcing Section 2 of the Sherman Act against complaints of unlawful strategic behavior are usefully joined, however, with greater vigilance in enforcing Section 7 of the Clayton Act. Although the present primitive state of the art makes it very difficult to prove conclusively that strategic moves made by established firms are in fact predatory, such an admission does not imply that strategic behavior is unproblematic. To the contrary, it is deeply troubling and recent scholarship demonstrates that it may be even more subtle and serious than had previously been imagined. Accordingly, any merger that poses antitrust concerns when evaluated in normal (nonstratetgic) terms becomes all the more worrisome if strategic concerns would be deepened if the merger were to be approved. The prophylactic use of Section 7 in such circumstances would appear to be the judicious interim response—awaiting resolution of the Section 2 issues referred to above.

[23]*FTC* v. *Kellogg* et. al., Docket No. 8883.

[24]*FTC* v. *E.I. du Pont de Nemours & Co.*, Complaint, Dkt. 9108, April 5, 1978 CCH Trade Regulation Reporter, transfer blinder, Federal Trade Commission Complaints and Orders, 1976–1979, Par. 21,407.

4.2 *Prepositioning*

A primary focus on *ex post* price and output behavior does not, however, mean that *ex ante* investments should be ignored entirely. Indeed, if comprehensive comparisons of the welfare ramifications of alternative predatory pricing rules are to be attempted, differential *ex ante* consequences, if they exist, should presumably be included.

The ways by which firms will preposition in relation to different rules have been addressed by Spence (1977), Salop (1979), Dixit (1979; 1980), and Eaton and Lipsey (1980; 1981) in relation to entry deterrence in general and by Williamson (1977) as entry deterrence applies to predation. The general argument here is that an "established firm can alter the *outcome* to its advantage by changing the initial conditions. In particular, an irrevocable choice of investment allows it to alter its post-entry marginal cost curve, and thereby the post-entry equilibrium" (Dixit, 1980, p. 96). That line of reasoning has been applied to the study of predation with the following result: Each predatory pricing rule predictably gives rise to "pre-entry price, output, and investment adjustments on the part of dominant firms whose markets are subject to encroachment. To neglect the incentives of rules whereby dominant firms make *pre-entry adaptive responses of a strategic kind* necessarily misses an important part of the problem" (Williamson, 1977, p. 293; emphasis in original).[25]

4.3 *Mistaken Predation*

A troublesome question arises where predatory pricing is attempted in circumstances where the structural preconditions described in section 3 are not satisfied. I shall refer to that class of events as "mistaken predation," in that even if the predator is successful in driving a rival from the market, it will fail to realize anything but very transient market power benefits. A significant excess of price over cost cannot be supported for any but a short period of time where rivals are many and entry is easy. Where that obtains, an attempt at predation is mistaken because a correct assessment of the net benefits of "successful" predation will disclose that they are negative.

[25]There is less than unanimity, however, over whether these prepositioning effects should be taken into account. Recent supporters of the marginal cost/equally efficient rival pricing rule (McGee, 1980; Ordover and Willig, 1981) ignore the prepositioning ramifications of alternative rules. Whether that is because they believe them to be unimportant or beyond the purview of responsible analysis is unclear. For the moment, the matter of prepositioning incentives and their relevance for rule assessment is under dispute.

The fact that attempted predation is mistaken does not, however, guarantee that it will never occur. Where it does, should the victims be entitled to relief by bringing suit and recovering damages? Applying the type of reasoning employed by Joskow and Klevorick would suggest a negative answer. The hazard is that many of the suits brought by firms in competitive industries would have the purpose of relieving those firms from legitimate rivalry rather than attempted predation. Since mistaken predation will presumably be rare or at least not repeated, the "false positive errors—that is . . . errors that involve labeling truly competitive price cuts as predatory" (Joskow and Klevorick, 1979, p. 223) would appear to be high and augurs against allowing suits of that kind. Some firms would be victimized as a result, however, and other students of predation may assess the hazards differently.

Assistant Attorney General (now, once again, Professor) William Baxter counsels the courts to move cautiously in the strategic behavior areas. Subtle and sophisticated though much of the recent work has been, the issues are enormously complex. Even if rules of law—with respect, for example, to predatory pricing—could be agreed to, formidable problems of implementation would have to be faced (Baxter, 1983).

Caution on these matters does not mean, however, that strategic behavior is forever beyond the competence of antitrust. I anticipate that there will be further developments on these matters and that, albeit limited, some applications will be made.

5. Concluding Remarks

The 1960s was a decade when nonstandard modes of economic organization were presumed to have monopoly purpose and effect. Antitrust was preoccupied with measures of concentration and entry barriers. Such a narrow formulation facilitated easy enforcement, but sometimes at the expense of an informed welfare assessment of the issues. Three factors contributed to this condition. First, it was widely believed that oligopolistic collusion was easy to effectuate. Second, wherever entry barriers were discovered they were held to be anticompetitive and antisocial, there being a great reluctance to acknowledge tradeoffs. And third, the business firm was thought to be adequately described as a production function to which a profit maximization objective had been assigned.

These views had two unfortunate consequences. For one thing, anything that contributed to market power—offsetting benefits notwithstanding—was held to be unlawful. For another, nonstandard or unfamiliar business practices that departed from autonomous market contracting were also held to be presumptively unlawful. If the "natural" way by which to mediate transactions between technologically separable entites was through markets, surely any effort by the firm to extend control beyond its natural (technological) boundaries must be motivated by strategic purpose.

Matters changed in the 1970s as a greater appreciation for efficiency benefits developed and as the conception of the firm as a governance structure took hold. The perverse hostility with which efficiency differentials were once regarded gave way to an affirmative valuation of efficiency benefits.[26] And business practices that were previously suspect, because they did not fit comfortably with the view of the firm as a production function, were reinterpreted in a larger context in which—implicitly, if not explicitly—transaction cost economizing was introduced. As a consequence, antitrust errors and enforcement excesses that characterized the treatment of nonstandard contracting in the 1960s were removed or reversed in the 1970s.

Despite progress with these matters, antitrust cannot settle back to a quiet life. Other difficult antitrust issues relating to strategic behavior have recently surfaced, and existing criteria for assessing the lawfulness of strategic practices are actively under dispute. Significant headway with a number of strategic behavior issues has nevertheless been made and more is in prospect. The study of strategic behavior has been clarified in the following significant respects: (1) Severe structural preconditions in both concentration and entry barrier respects need to be satisfied before an incentive to behave strategically can be claimed to exist; (2) attention to investment and asset characteristics is needed in assessing the condition of entry—specifically, nontrivial irreversible investments of a transaction specific kind have especially strong deterrent effects; (3) history matters in assessing rivalry—both with respect to the leadership advantage enjoyed by a sitting monopolist as well as in the incidence and evaluation of comparative costs; and (4) reputation effects are important in assessing the rationality of predatory behavior.

This last has a bearing on two crucial aspects of strategic behavior. For one thing, those who argue that strategic behavior can be disregarded unless "full information" credible threat conditions are fulfilled have overstated the case. This is not to suggest that the study of credible threats cannot usefully inform the analysis of strategic behavior. But if knowledge is imperfect, then

---

[26]Vigilance is nevertheless necessary lest retrogression occur. Thus the government's lead attorney advised the court in *U.S.* v. *Occidental Petroleum* (Civil Action No. C-3-78-288) that the acquisition of Mead by Occidental was objectionable because it would permit Mead to construct a large greenfield plant, which was "the most efficient and cost effective investment," and that this would disadvantage Mead's rivals.

One of the advantages of the Merger Guidelines is that they serve to discipline the creative lawyering of the government's attorneys. The mistakes of Mead will presumably not be repeated so long as the 1984 Merger Guidelines remain in place.

dominant firms can alter expectations by posturing (as well as by objectively fulfilling credibility conditions), in which event pre-commitments need not be as extensive as the credible threat literature would indicate. Second, myopic assessments of strategic behavior understate the incentives to engage in predation. Those who focus on the incentive to kill a specific rival are ignoring what may often be the stronger incentive—namely, to develop a reputation that will subsequently help to deter this and other firms in later periods, in other geographic markets, and in other lines of commerce.

CHAPTER 15

Conclusions

The economic institutions of capitalism are endlessly varied. Although this book is concerned with some of the more important of those institutions, many others have not been mentioned, much less assessed.

Considerable variety notwithstanding, the economic institutions of capitalism examined in earlier chapters display many common elements. Indeed, much of vertical integration, many vertical market restrictions, the organization of work, labor union organization, the modern corporation (including conglomerate and multinational aspects), corporate governance, regulation and much of antitrust turn out to be variants on a theme. The very same contracting schema—whereby technology, price, and governance are all joined—applies repeatedly. This is gratifying, since pattern repetition reinforces confidence in functional arguments that might otherwise appear ad hoc.

Not everything fits, however. Other patterns are awaiting discovery. Nevertheless, I conjecture that the general microanalytic strategy employed here will apply elsewhere. This entails making the transaction the basic unit of analysis, ascertaining the underlying attributes of transactions, and aligning institutions (incentives, controls, governance structures) in a discriminating way.

A brief overview of transaction cost economics is sketched in section 1. Some of the issues in economics, law, and organization for which further study is needed are presented in sections 2 through 4. A postscript follows.

1. Transaction Cost Economics

John R. Hicks advises that since economics is concerned with a changing world, "a theory which illumines the right things now may illumine the wrong things another time. [Accordingly], there is . . . no economic theory which will do for us everything we want all the time. . . . We may [someday] reject our present theories not because they are wrong, but because they have become inappropriate" (1976, p. 208). By the mid-1960s, if not earlier, the changing world to which Hicks referred was posing strains of two kinds.

One took the form of public policy excesses.[1] As Justice Stewart put it in 1966, "The sole consistency that I can find is that in [merger] litigation under Section 7, the Government always wins."[2] Although the excesses of both antitrust and regulation in the 1960s are now generally conceded, the limits of public policy were then obscured by the prevailing optimism that "the most intractable problems would give way before the resolute assault of intelligent, committed people" (Morris, 1980, p. 23). The comparative institutional approach admits to and attempts to assess "failures" of all kinds. Transaction cost economics is in that spirit.

Strains were also developing over the growing disjunction between pure theory and applications. George Feiwel quotes from and summarizes Michio Morishima's position on that as follows

> [Morishima] attributes the continuous frustration which has beset the development of economic theory over the last thirty years or more to 'failure of economic theorists to carry out sweeping, systematic research into the actual mechanisms of the economy and economic organization, despite being aware that their own models are inappropriate to analysis of the actual economy.' [Feiwel, 1983, p. 48A]

To be sure, Morishima's advice that economic theorists "make a serious effort in the direction of the institutionalization of economics, in the sense of slowing the speed of all development toward mathematization and developing economic theory in accordance with knowledge of economic organizations, industrial structure and economic history"[3] would be disputed by some. Still, there is growing agreement that a better balance will be struck by bringing institutions more prominently into the picture.[4] Transaction cost economics is

---

[1]Themes of "reindustrialization" and "industrial policy" that in an earlier era would have been heard as clarion calls are thus regarded skeptically and are submitted instead to tough-minded criticism. Good intentions no longer suffice.

[2]*United States* v. *Von's Grocery Co.* 384 U.S. 270, 301 (1966) (Stewart, J., dissenting).

[3]Quoted from Feiwel (1983, p. 118A).

[4]This is especially true in the public policy arena. Coase thus asserts that "we have less to

expressly institutional in character. It nevertheless maintains a strong commitment to intended rationality, and it holds out the prospect of progressive formalization. It appears to be broadly consonant with the research enterprise that Morishima contemplates.

1.1 *Rudiments*

Transaction cost economics is a comparative institutional approach to the study of economic organization in which the transaction is made the basic unit of analysis. It is interdisciplinary, involving aspects of economics, law, and organization theory. It has relatively broad scope and application. Virtually any relation, economic or otherwise, that takes the form of or can be described as a contracting problem can be evaluated to advantage in transaction cost economics terms. Most explicit contracting relations qualify; many implicit contracting relations do also.

As compared with other approaches to the study of economic organization, transaction cost economics (1) is more microanalytic, (2) is more self-conscious about its behavioral assumptions, (3) introduces and develops the economic importance of asset specificity, (4) relies more on comparative institutional analysis, (5) regards the business firm as a governance structure rather than a production function, and (6) places greater weight on the *ex post* institutions of contract, with special emphasis on private ordering (as compared with court ordering). A large number of refutable implications obtain upon addressing problems of economic organization in this way.

As indicated, transaction cost economics maintains the rebuttable presumption that organizational variety arises primarily in the service of transaction cost economizing. That approach is to be distinguished not merely from the technological approach to economic organization but also from power approaches, which ascribe nonstandard forms of organization to monopoly purposes or class interests. To be sure, organizational variety sometimes serves several purposes simultaneously. That is not, however, to say that all explanations are on a parity. Assuming that alternative hypotheses are to be evaluated with reference to the touchstone of refutable implications, the transaction cost hypothesis will presumably be judged according to that comparative standard. The basic strategy for deriving refutable implications— repeated, with variations, throughout the book—is this: Transactions, which

---

fear from institutionalists who are not theorists than from theorists who are not institutionalists''
(1964, p. 296).

differ in their attributes, are assigned to governance structures, which differ in their organizational costs and competencies, so as to effect a discriminating (mainly transaction cost economizing) match.

Transaction costs of both *ex ante* and *ex post* kinds are distinguished. The *ex ante* costs are those incurred in drafting and negotiating agreements. They vary with the design of the good or service to be produced. The *ex post* costs include the setup and running costs of the governance structure to which monitoring is assigned and to which disputes are referred and settled; the maladaptation costs that are incurred for failure to restore positions on the shifting contract curve; the haggling costs that attend adjustments (or the lack thereof); and the bonding costs of effecting secure commitments. Although the conditions of uncertainty to which the transactions are subject and the trading context (customs, mores, habits, legal institutions) in which the trans-actions are located influence both the *ex ante* and *ex post* costs of contracting, those features are mainly taken as given. (Further implications can, however, be realized by relaxing that restraint.)

Those simplifications notwithstanding, the resulting approach to contract is enormously complex. That is often reflected in the piecemeal character of the analysis. Repeated efforts are nonetheless made to locate and assess contracts (and the contracting process) in their entirety.

1.2 *A Digression on Risk Neutrality*

The two behavioral assumptions to which transaction cost economics makes repeated reference are bounded rationality and opportunism. The first main-tains that human agents are intendedly rational but only limitedly so. That is manifestly true and massively influences the manner in which the subject of contract is conceived. The second holds that human agents will not reliably self-enforce promises but will defect from the letter and the spirit of an agreement when it suits their purposes. That somewhat dismal view of human nature alerts contracting parties (and those who would study contracting prac-tices) to be wary of the hazards. To be sure, suspicions and precautions can be and sometimes are taken to excess (see 1.3b below). But a healthy regard for opportunism is essential to an understanding of the purposes served by com-plex modes of economic organization.

A third behavioral assumption that is also employed but to which refer-ence is less frequently made warrants separate attention. That is the assump-tion of risk neutrality. Unlike the other two assumptions, this one is patently counterfactual.

Counterfactual assumptions are commonly justified by the fruitfulness of the resulting model (Friedman, 1953). That is part of the justification here. But the main argument is really different.

Indeed, there are really three defenses for the assumption of risk neutrality. For one thing, this book places a great deal of emphasis on intermediate product markets. Those are transactions between firms rather than individuals. Not only do most firms diversify in some degree, but owners of firms can usually diversify their financial holdings easily. At least with respect to this class of activity, therefore, the risk neutrality assumption may be a close approximation.[5] Second, and related, if the penalties for incapacity to bear risk are great, parties have strong incentives to craft structures with superior risk-bearing properties. Where the assumption of risk neutrality both facilitates analysis and captures central tendencies, outliers can presumably, or at least often, be dealt with separately.

But third, and the most compelling reason for invoking risk neutrality, is that this assumption helps to disclose core efficiency features that go unnoticed or are misconstrued when risk aversion assumptions are employed. Contrast, for example, the transaction cost approach to labor market organization with that of the implicit contracting tradition (Azariadis, 1975; Baily, 1974; Gordon, 1974). The latter invokes risk aversion to explain sticky wages but is completely silent regarding the manner in which labor markets are organized and has no parallel explanation for sticky prices in intermediate product markets. The risk neutral/transaction cost account treats wages and prices symmetrically and addresses itself, as it must, to the governance structures of wage and price determination (Wachter and Williamson, 1978).

Or consider Robert Townsend's (1982) interesting treatment of multiperiod contracts in intermediate product markets. He introduces the basic model as follows: "Consider an economy with just two . . . agents, one risk averse" (p. 1170). Absent differential risk aversion, multiperiod contracting in his model vanishes.[6] Plainly, however, multiperiod contracting will appear in a risk neutral world in which specific assets are placed at risk.[7] The governance structures that arise in support of multiperiod contracts are also brought under scrutiny when the attributes of transactions, rather than the risk attitudes of transactors, are made the focus of attention. It is not accidental

---

[5] To be sure, this ignores the risk attitudes of managers—which for some purposes can be of utmost importance, especially for transactions that are organized internally. For a brief discussion, see Chapter 6, section 4.

[6] Townsend actually develops the argument in two stages: The first assumes differential risk aversion and full information; the second assumes differential risk aversion and private information. Multiperiod contracts arise in his model only for the second condition.

[7] See, for example, Chapters 4 through 8.

that studies of legal doctrine (Landes and Posner, forthcoming) and of economic organization that eschew the assumption of risk aversion and employ transaction cost reasoning are more concerned with institutional features than those that do not.

The third justification thus comes down to this: Risk aversion often deflects attention from core efficiency purposes and related institutional features that are more readily discerned and more accurately assessed if, at this early stage in the development of the New Institutional Economics at least, a risk neutrality assumption is maintained.

1.3 *Some Limitations*

Limitations of three kinds are noteworthy: transaction cost economics is crude, it is given to instrumentalist excesses, and it is incomplete. Consider each *seriatim*.

a. CRUDENESS

The crudeness of transaction cost economics shows up in at least four ways: The models are very primitive, the tradeoffs are underdeveloped, measurement problems are severe, and there are too many degrees of freedom.

That the models are primitive is partly explained by the fact that comparative institutional analysis often requires that only basic distinctions be made and that simple comparisons be performed. Formal models of verbal arguments that lose in the translation are scarcely to be counted as gains (Simon, 1978, pp. 8–9). Formalization is not wanted at any cost.

Sometimes, however, efforts at formalization disclose gaps or ambiguities that the verbal argument did not. The tradeoffs between production cost economies (where the market often enjoys the advantage), governance cost economies (where the advantage accrues to internal organization as commitments to bilateral trading progressively deepen) and high-powered incentives (where the market again moves to the fore) have to be addressed not sequentially but in a fully simultaneous fashion. Although efforts along those lines have been progressing (Masten, 1982; Riordan and Williamson, forthcoming; Grossman and Hart, 1984; Mann and Wissink, 1984; Hart and Moore, 1985), much more remains to be done. The factors that are responsible for tradeoff differences—technology (economies of scale or scope); the nature of rivalry, including progressiveness; customer attributes, including competencies to evaluate product; incentive and control efficacy; market vagaries and uncertainties—all, at some stage, must be taken into account.

The three main dimensions in describing transactions are frequency, uncertainty, and the condition of asset specificity. None of them is easy to measure, although empirical researchers have found crude or proxy measures for each. Even should experience disclose ways by which to utilize accounting and other business or government records to better advantage, a great deal of original data collection will be needed. (As between breadth—more observations—and depth—fewer but more relevant data—the needs of transaction cost economics, at least in the near term, are apt to be better served by the latter.)

Each of the above features—primitive models, underdeveloped trade-offs, measurement difficulties—contributes to the excessive degrees of freedom enjoyed by transaction cost economics. One way of dealing with that is to eschew appeal to omitted or unmeasured factors when confronted by conditions where the data and the models do not line up. Anomalies and contradictions can and should push those who employ transaction cost analysis to develop better models.

b. INSTRUMENTALISM

As with economic models more generally, the human agents who populate transaction cost economics are highly calculative. That is plainly not an attractive or even an accurate view of human nature. Economics is thought to be a dismal science partly for that reason. But insistence on rationality is also the great strength of economics (Arrow, 1974). To be sure, rationality can be and sometimes is overdone. Hyperrationality is mainly a fiction and/or a pathology. But one does not need to assert that the only reliable human motive is avarice to recognize that much of the success of economics in relation to the other social sciences occurs because calculativeness is presumed to be present in nontrivial degree.

As compared with orthodoxy, the human agents of transaction cost economics are both less and more calculative. They are less calculative in the capacity to receive, store, retrieve, and process information. They are more calculative in that they are given to opportunism. Taken together, that appears to correspond more closely with human nature as we know it. Still, it is plainly a narrow prescription. It makes little provision for attributes such as kindness, sympathy, solidarity, and the like. Indeed, to the extent that such factors are acknowledged, their costs, rather than their benefits, are emphasized. (Thus, as discussed in Chapter 6, propensities for forgiveness are held to be responsible for limitations on firm size.) The human agents who populate the economic institutions of capitalism are lacking in compassion.

This unattractive view of human nature nevertheless generates numerous refutable implications. The view that individuals are opportunistic does not, moreover, preclude the possibility that they will forge durable alliances. Large numbers of otherwise anomalous contracting and organizational practices predictably appear upon imputing a capacity for semi-farsightedness to opportunistic parties who are engaged in trade. Upon realization that the benefits of cooperation will reliably come about only if alliances are buttressed by mutual assurances, efforts to provide credible commitments will predictably be made.

To be sure, those alliances are imperfect and sometimes break down. Also, they are more costly to forge in a low-trust than in a high-trust society. But bounded rationality plus opportunism does not imply myopia. A great deal of "middle range" credible contracting is consonant with 20–50 (or even 20–500) foresight.[8] As discussed in section 4 below, however, a richer theory of economic organization awaits deeper behavioral insights.

c. INCOMPLETENESS

Transaction cost economics is incomplete in at least three significant respects. For one thing, the models are very partial rather than general. Here, as elsewhere, general models are to be preferred to special models, *ceteris paribus*. But where the *cetera* are not *paria,* and if prediction is the touchstone to which we insistently refer, then General Theories of Action that make vague reference to utility maximization, property rights foundations, and the like, but which are largely tautological, come at an unacceptably high cost. By contrast, more general models that yield more and deeper implications are always to be encouraged.

Another aspect of incompleteness to which I would call special attention is the underdeveloped state of the theory of bureaucracy. As compared with the market failure literature, the study of bureaucratic failure is very primitive. What are the biases and distortions to which internal organization is given? Why do they arise? How do they vary with organization form? An adequate understanding of economic organization plainly requires more atten-

---

[8]Its limitations notwithstanding, to characterize capitalist man in terms of bounded rationality and opportunism is arguably more accurate than a utopian insistence upon "sincerity, for a complete unity between the individual and social roles, the notion that somehow in an ideal society there would be no conflict between one's demand on oneself and one's responses to the demands of society" (Arrow, 1974, pp. 15–16). Problems of economic organization would be vastly simplified if such tensions were missing. The iron law of oligarchy speaks to the errors of that conception. The hazards of suboptimization and the needs for veracity checks are similar in socialist and capitalist systems alike.

tion to those issues. Again, however, I would emphasize that comparative institutional standards should be maintained.

Although transaction cost economics insistently addresses both *ex ante* and *ex post* conditions of contract (sometimes referred to as the study of contracting in its entirety), it normally examines each trading nexus separately. Albeit useful for displaying the core features of each contract, interdependencies among a series of related contracts may be missed or undervalued as a consequence. Greater attention to the multilateral ramifications of contract is sometimes needed. (The discussion of unbargained-for risk shifting in Chapter 12 is an illustration.)

2. Economics

Transaction cost economics acknowledges that technology and ownership of assets are both important, but it maintains that neither is determinative of economic organization, nor are both together. Rather, the study of economic organization has to go beyond technology and ownership to include an examination of incentives and governance. Transaction cost economics maintains that the transaction is the basic unit of analysis and gives special emphasis to the study of governance.

Thus, even holding technology constant, three things happen when a transaction is transferred out of the market and is placed under unified ownership: Ownership changes, incentives change, and governance structures change. The first—ownership change—occurs by definition. Even if the formal incentive rules (e.g. transfer pricing) are held constant between firm and market, the *effective* incentives change as a consequence of a change in asset ownership. Accordingly, the formal rules are apt to be adapted. New governance structure will appear in either event to support the integrity of the internal exchange relation. All of the above, moreover, will vary as a function of the nature and degree of asset specificity. Plainly, the study of economic organization is a much more complex undertaking than a production function formulation contemplates.

2.1 *Prospective Applications*

As is evident from earlier chapters, transaction cost economics applications have been made in the fields of industrial organization, labor economics, and the study of the modern corporation. Those scarcely require recounting here. Of greater interest are applications made in other areas.

One of the more obvious and natural of them is the application of transaction cost economics to comparative economic systems. Stephen Sacks's recent book (1983) on Yugoslav self-management is an illustration. As Horvat's 1972 survey of Yugoslav economic reforms in the postwar period discloses, the links between the microanalytics of capitalism and socialism are numerous and important. Sacks's treatment confirms that. But as he points out, a great deal remains to be done.

To be sure, linkages can be discovered at several levels. Koopmans, for example, regards the "pre-institutional character" of activity analysis as one of its attractions: "Technology and human needs are universal. To start with just these elements has facilitated and intensified professional contacts and interactions between market and socialist countries" (Koopmans, 1977, pp. 264–65). I submit, however, that exclusive reliance on technology and human needs can foreshorten the inquiry. The study of human needs is usefully joined with the study of human nature. Additionally, albeit difficult to orchestrate, contacts between capitalist and socialist countries regarding the study of governance structures—with attention to both similarities and differences—hold considerable promise for deepening our understanding of those matters.

Applications of transaction cost economics to business history also hold out considerable promise. This is not to suggest that successive organizational innovations should be assessed exclusively in this way. But viable modes of economic organization—those that endure, are imitated by rivals, diffuse to other sectors, are successively refined and perfected, and do not depend on the political process for protection against alternative modes—ordinarily possess an efficiency advantage.[9]

Other applications on which headway has already been made but for which further inquiry is warranted include the study of family organization (Ben-Porath, 1980; Pollak, 1983), and nonprofit forms of enterprise (Hansmann, 1982; Fama and Jensen, 1983).

An area in which Klein and his associates have made significant headway[10] and for which more is in prospect is the economics of the middleman: the merchant, the dealer, the franchisee. A vast number of contractual irregularities that occur at that level of organization appear to have the purpose and effect of economizing on transaction costs.

An area to which transaction cost economics has made only limited contributions but that holds out considerable promise is public finance. To be sure, aspects of defense contracting have been examined in terms that are akin

[9]A joinder of transaction cost with evolutionary economics is needed to assess this more carefully.

[10]See Kenney and Klein (1983) and the references cited therein.

to the transaction cost approach (Williamson, 1967a). And the difficult problems of information that have a bearing on R&D policy have also been examined in semi-microanalytic terms (Arrow, 1971; Nelson, 1984). But if the choice and design of institutions is what public finance is all about, then countless applications of transaction cost economics have yet to be made. Problems of incentives and governance are enormously difficult in a political context. Tolerance for greater variance in relation to private sector efficiency assessments is likely to be needed.

2.2 *Research Needs*

a. INCENTIVE ASSESSMENTS

Given the requisite preconditions, quasi-market and internal modes of organization realize governance benefits in relation to autonomous market trading. The high-powered incentives of markets are unavoidably compromised, however, when a transaction is placed under unified ownership. As between the two, this book gives disproportionate attention to the governance as compared with the incentive features of capitalist modes of economic organization.[11]

Attention to both, however, is essential if the economic institutions of capitalism are to be accurately assessed. Among other things, ways by which to enhance the incentive efficacy of internal organization—by effecting semi-decomposability (which is a leading purpose of the M-form structure); by surrounding operating rules and procedures with credible commitments, thereby to enhance reliance—require concerted study. Comparative institutional assessments of proposals to enhance incentive efficacy will be realized only when the relevant microanalytic details of market, quasi-market, and administrative modes are set out. Partly that is a conceptual exercise. Partly it is empirical. An enormous amount of work plainly needs to be done.

b. REPUTATION EFFECTS

Reputation effects will deter defection from the letter and the spirit of an agreement in the degree to which (1) defections can be made public knowledge, (2) the consequences of defection can be fully ascertained (which will permit, among other things, real versus contrived claims of defection to be

---

[11]To describe capitalism as a gale of creative destruction (Schumpeter, 1942) reverses this emphasis.

distinguished), and (3) parties who experience or observe defection penalize the offender and/or his successors in "full measure."

None of those conditions is easy to satisfy. With respect to the first, it is costly to advertise defections. Even if a simple announcement could be costlessly made, moreover, it is further necessary to supply the details. Is it a bogus claim? What is the magnitude of the damages? Did the plaintiff take appropriate steps to mitigate the damages? What were the alternatives and when did they become known? Information at this second level becomes enormously costly to supply and evaluate.

Fly-by-night operators aside, the third condition guarantees that full penalties will be extracted from offending parties. A firm under one ownership/management cannot escape the penalties assigned to an earlier ownership/management by asking for forgiveness. Instead, the sins of the fathers are assuredly visited on the sons—in which event the asset valuations of an enterprise will continuously reflect prior behavior (Kreps, 1984).

The issues here go to the behavioral attributes of human actors and are discussed further in section 4. Suffice it to observe here that reputation effects are no contracting panacea. The limits as well as the powers of those effects need to be studied (Carmichael, 1984).

c. CONSUMER

Any discussion of the economic institutions of capitalism that does not deal with final product markets is egregiously incomplete. This is a very large and complicated topic. An informed assessment of final product market practices will require a great deal of detailed knowledge of those practices. Although I am confident that the approach herein developed has considerable generality and am furthermore encouraged that my opinion is shared by others,[12] an application to final product markets is beyond the scope of this book.

Strong commonalities notwithstanding, the correspondence between intermediate product markets and final product markets is inexact. Some of the differences are attributable to the differential ease with which hierarchical organizations can relieve bounds on rationality as compared with small groups (families) and individuals.

Purchasing and contracting functions in large organizations can be and commonly are assigned to specialists who are deeply knowledgeable of the

---

[12]I am especially gratified that marketing specialists have shown an interest in this approach. A marketing conference organized jointly by the Marketing Science Institute and the Center for the Study of Organizational Innovation was held at the University of Pennsylvania in October 1983 to explore these matters. Also, see Anderson and Schmittlein (1984).

technical, market, and contractual features of each of the many goods and services bought and sold. Information asymmetries between the parties are greatly relieved as a consequence. Individual consumers, by contrast, are unable to delegate in the same way and therefore rely much more on market signals to infer product attributes.

Branding and advertising serve signaling purposes. But the signals can be and sometimes are used strategically,[13] which complicates the welfare assessment. The possibility that consumers can be provided with more reliable, compact, economical signals warrants sympathetic study. Truth in lending is in that spirit. Can egregious cases be identified for which truth in advertising efforts are warranted?[14]

A further feature of the consumer market that warrants comment is the evident incapacity of the average individual to make probabilistic choices in a consistent way. The biases to which large numbers of individuals are subject in dealing with probabilistic matters have been documented repeatedly (Tversky and Kahneman, 1974). They are especially evident when low-probability events are being evaluated (Kunreuther et al., 1978). That most individuals possess those biases and limitations does not, however, imply that most organizations will also display them. If more and less competent probabilists can be distinguished, and if responsibility for processing and displaying the consequences of probabilistic choices is concentrated on the more competent types, then economies of specialization will be realized. But whereas organizations (corporations) can effect such specialization easily, individual consumers are much more limited. Again, the possibility of public policy intervention to yield (on average) improved consumer decisions when confronted with probabilistic choice suggests itself. Insurance is an obvious candidate.

3. Law

Ronald Gilson advances the novel and controversial view that business lawyers should be thought of as "transaction cost engineers" (1984). Such an approach ascribes value enhancement to the job of transaction design, which is a theme advanced repeatedly in this book.[15] It emphasizes and gives content to the

---

[13]Strategic uses of branding and advertising can be directed at consumers or at rivals.

[14]Health warnings on cigarettes are an illustration.

[15]Gilson (1984) maintains that describing the business lawyer's job as transaction cost engineer has ramifications (1) for understanding the relationship between what is typically seen as "lawyer's work" and the transactional functions typically assigned other professions, (2) for improving the competitive position of business lawyers among the professions, (3) for restructur-

affirmative side of lawyering. Transaction cost economics will figure more prominently if those views are adopted (Gilson, 1984, pp. 127–29).

Transaction cost economics also resonates with Robert Clark's recent methodological commentary on legal scholarship. Thus Clark favors an "interdisciplinary study of legal evolution" that is more microanalytic than the usual historical accounts of legal change. Such an approach "should be more institutional and doctrinal than is some of the interesting recent theoretical work by economic analysts on the evolution of the common law: its analysis of systems of legal rules and nonlegal practices should be *detailed* in its systematic attention to particular institutions and doctrines" (Clark, 1981, p. 1238, emphasis added).[16]

That aspects of antitrust, regulation, corporate governance, and labor law all benefit from adopting a microanalytic point of view in which transaction costs are emphasized is, I hope, evident from earlier chapters. More can and I am sure will be done—to refine extant applications and address additional issues—in each of those areas. My remarks here, however, focus on the research needs of transaction cost economics in the area of contract—which, after all, is the unifying concept of organization that illuminates all of those areas.

3.1 The Governance Mix

Although contract law scholarship has repeatedly and vigorously taken exception to the fiction that contracts are enforced literally and that disputes are routinely presented to and settled by the courts (Llewellyn, 1931; Macaulay, 1963; Macneil, 1974; Galanter, 1981; Kronman, 1985), this tradition retains a firm grip on legal and, even more, on economic research. That is partly explained by the fact that the fiction of pure legal centralism is an enormous

---

ing business law education, and (4) for understanding the current round of cross-cultural criticism of American lawyers.

[16]Eli Devon's remarks on the role of the economist and those of Iredell Jenkins in his approach to the law are also germane. Thus Devon counsels that "there are many complex problems of policy to which the economist does not know the answer. . . . On such questions there might be more understanding if economists exercised self-restraint and confined themselves to attempting to explain the nature and complexity of problems, rather than providing conflicting and widely divergent solutions" (Devon, 1961, p. 46). And Jenkins maintains that the study of the law will benefit from efforts to "expose the complexity of the problem and the framework within which it must be resolved, to clarify the issues at stake, to direct attention to repercussions and consequences that are not immediately apparent, and to protect deliberation against the appeals of sentiment and expediency while guiding it toward an outcome that is reasoned and principled" (Jenkins, 1980, p. 62).

analytical convenience. But the absence of a well-specified alternative theory of contract is probably the main culprit.

Recent economic scholarship has, however, made headway with models of contract in which court ordering is eschewed altogether. Pure private ordering maintains that the parties cannot turn to the courts or to other third parties but must look to the self-enforcing features of the contract alone (Telser, 1981; Klein and Leffler, 1981). The hostage model in Chapter 7 is in that tradition. Albeit instructive, this rival tradition is also a fiction. Contract in practice is rarely located at either of those extremes.

To be sure, it is sometimes argued that models of polar extremes are wholly adequate.[17] But the relevant test, presumably, is whether middle-range phenomena can better be understood and refutable implications derived by studying these matters directly. As matters stand at present, contracts in the middle range are notoriously intractable. But if that is where the main contracting action resides, more attention to mixed transactions is arguably warranted.[18] Transaction cost economics should help to inform such an undertaking.

The basic strategy is that described and employed in earlier chapters. Thus if transactions differ in their attributes, if governance structures are aligned to the needs of transactions in a discriminating way, and if private ordering and court ordering can be used in combination rather than separately, then the study of contract will benefit from an effort to identify the *mix* of private and public structures that best serve the purposes of the parties (Kronman, 1985). Deep knowledge of institutional structures, as well as the objective needs of contract, will be needed to conduct the exercise (Gilson, 1984).

[17]Friedman's views on the adequacy of "two 'ideal' types of firms: atomistically competitive firms, grouped into industries, and monopolistic firms" (1953, p. 35) are illustrative.

[18]Patrick Atiyeh also maintains that this is where the contract law action resides:

[T]here has been a shift in the paradigm of contractual relationship from the single, discrete transaction, to relationships, the tendency is for the risks of future change to be adjusted by some kind of quasi-administrative process, rather than by standing by the letter of some original contract.

The result of these and other factors has been that, in practice, contractual relations tend increasingly to be concerned with executed or part-executed transactions. The law has become increasingly dominated by what contracting parties do, and less by what they originally agreed. A breach of contract is, increasingly, treated as something more akin to an accident than to a willful refusal to accept a bargained-for risk. It is a misfire situation, a case where something has gone wrong, and where some equitable adjustment has to be made in order to resolve a conflict. Inevitably this process has led to a return in various respects to older ideas underlying contractual liability. The decline of the executory model, and the rise of the part-executed contract, has involved the revival of the importance of the twin elements of benefit and reliance. The notion that benefits should be fairly recompensed, and the notion that reasonable reliance should be protected, have come once again into greater prominence, as the idea of the executory contract, and of promise-based liability, have declined. [Atiyeh, 1979, pp. 713–14]

3.2 *Contract Law Doctrine*

Llewellyn observes: "In no legal system are all promises enforceable; people
and courts have too much sense" (1931, p. 738). That is evidently supported
by considerations of fairness: "When we approach constructive conditions
bottomed on the unforeseen, [n]ot agreement, but fairness, is the goal of the
inquiry. This holds of impossibility, and of frustration; it holds of mistake"
(p. 746). The contract exceptions to which Macneil refers presumably have
similar origins:

> A less than total commitment to the keeping of promises is reflected in countless
> ways in the legal system. The most striking is the modesty of its remedial
> commitment; contract remedies are generally among the weakest of those the
> legal system can deliver. But a host of doctrines and techniques lies in the way
> even of those remedies: impossibility, frustration, mistake, manipulative in-
> terpretation, jury discretion, consideration, illegality, duress, undue influence,
> unconscionability, capacity, forfeiture and penalty rules, doctrines of substantial
> performance, severability, bankruptcy laws, statutes of frauds, to name some;
> almost any contract doctrine can and does serve to make the commitment of the
> legal system to promise keeping less than complete. [Macneil, 1974, p. 73]

Although I am persuaded that the fairness to which Llewellyn refers
motivates each of those doctrinal matters, those doctrines also reflect considerations of efficiency. The basic argument is this: As between a contracting
regime in which agreements are strictly enforced, at the insistence of either
party, and a regime where insistence upon strict enforcement by one party
would impose "undue" hardship on the other, the latter regime will be
preferred—assuming that undue hardship exceptions can be distinguished
without difficulty.

Such an approach to contract invites the courts to develop contract law
doctrines in which exceptions to the normal presumption of strict enforcement
are provided. It asks that contracts be embedded in a governance structure in
which the parties have greater confidence. Upon realization that the contracting *process* will be impaired (some contracts will not be reached; other agreements will be negotiated only at great expense) if the private net benefit
calculus is everywhere permitted to be fully determinative in the *ex post*
period, the contracting population asks that literal enforcement be prohibited
where the requisite conditions obtain. The object is to effect compromise,
conciliation, or forgiveness where outcomes judged to be harsh or punitive
would otherwise result. Although that can be (and is) interpreted as an effort
by the people and the courts to review promise with reference to fairness and
justice, the provision for such exceptions is also consonant with an extended

efficiency rationale. Embedding contract in a framework in which outliers are truncated yields efficiency benefits of the above-described systems kind.

Inasmuch as there are numerous sources of contract disappointment, and not all are accorded relief, the critical question is, Which hardships are undue? Very preliminary efforts to deal with that query are reported elsewhere (Williamson, forthcoming). Suffice it to observe here that while appeal to transaction cost reasoning helps to organize the issues, a great deal remains to be done before doctrinal consistency and clarity can be claimed.

3.3 *Contracting in Its Entirety*

It is rudimentary that people cannot have their cake and eat it too. Insistence upon studying contracting in its entirety serves to avoid that fallacy—which comes up repeatedly in the study of contract. Consider Charles Fried's treatment of *Batsakis* v. *Demotsis,* where "the defendant, desperate for money soon after the German occupation of Greece, borrowed an amount of Greek currency, which in those chaotic circumstances may have been the equivalent of as little as fifty dollars, against her promise to repay two thousand dollars plus normal interest from funds she controlled in the United States" (Fried, 1981, p. 109). Fried declares that such a bargain is "offensive to decency" and asserts that "Batsakis had a duty to share with his destitute countrymen." Fried hesitates "not . . . at all to deny the bad Samaritan his unjust profit" (1981, pp. 109–11).

Such a view of contract may withstand scrutiny if the special preconditions to which it applies can be carefully delimited. It comes close, however, to inviting borrowers to have their cake (a timely loan) and eat it too (*ex post* reform of terms in their favor). Upon realization that loans will be subject to such reform, bad Samaritans will decline to make them. Unless we are prepared to compel Batsakis to share, which Fried is unwilling to do (1981, p. 111), such an approach to contract will deny resources to those in the dire *ex ante* straits to whom Fried would thereafter accord *ex post* contract relief.

Suppose, *arguendo,* that the merits of contracting in its entirety are granted. Surely, however, there are limits to that approach to contract enforcement. When does the reasoning break down?

Some of the issues here are raised, but are scarcely disposed of, by my discussion of corporate governance dilemmas at the end of Chapter 12. The issues also overlap those that arise in attempts to bring order into the study of contract doctrine, as discussed in 3.2 above. But a sharper appreciation for the limits of contracting in its entirety will benefit by considering disequilibrium contracting issues of the kind discussed in section 4.5 below.

4. Organization

Unlike economists, sociologists have long been concerned with the puzzle, "Why are there so many kinds of organization?" (Hannan and Freeman, 1977, p. 936). Although numerous interesting explanations for organizational variety have resulted, the explanation favored here—namely, organizational variety arises in the service of transaction cost economizing—was not natural to and is still resisted by many organization theory specialists.

I nevertheless submit that transaction cost economics is pertinent to many of the matters of interest to organization theory.[19] A richer theory of organization would appear to be in prospect by harnessing, refining, and delimiting transaction cost analysis. But gains also flow in the reverse direction. Transaction cost economics stands to benefit from the infusion of greater organizational content. More generally, economics should both speak and listen to organization theory.

Coase's remarks on economics and contiguous disciplines are germane. He observes that the "success of economists in moving into the other social sciences is a sign that they possess certain advantages in handling the problems of those disciplines. One is, I believe, that they study the economic system as a unified interdependent system" (1978, p. 209). He goes on, however, to remark: "Once some of these practitioners have acquired the simple, but valuable, truths which economics has to offer . . . economists who try to work in the other social sciences will have lost their main advantage and will face competitors who know more about the subject matter than they do" (Coase, 1978, p. 210).

The research opportunities sketched out below are ones for which organization theory specialists would appear to enjoy the advantage.

4.1 Observational Advantages

The empirical needs of transaction cost economics are much more microanalytic than those of applied price theory. Taking microanalytic observations can be tiresome, however, and requires special skills. Koopmans nevertheless maintains that

> . . . we have to exploit all the evidence we can secure, direct and indirect. If, in comparison with some other sciences, economics is handicapped by severe and

---

[19]This view is shared by others—see, for example, William Ouchi (1976) and W. Richard Scott (1981)—though it is probably a minority opinion.

possibly insurmountable obstacles to meaningful experimentation, the opportunities for direct introspection by, and direct observation of, individual decision makers are a much needed source of evidence which in some degree offsets the handicap. [Koopmans, 1957, p. 140]

Organization theory specialists who are trained in making microanalytic observations plainly enjoy the advantage for such an effort.

Implementing that in a way responsive to the needs of transaction cost economics may not be easy, however. For one thing, organization theory frequently emphasizes organizational pathologies to the neglect of anatomy and physiology. To be sure, all are important. Furthermore, transaction cost economics has to be sensitized in pathological respects. But if efficiency plays the central role that I ascribe to it, then the anatomy and physiology of organization will require greater attention. Second, the microanalytic features of organization that are of special interest to transaction cost economics involve asset specificity, information asymmetry, uncertainty (especially surprise), formal and informal governance apparatus, and incentives. Few studies of organization address those matters with the needs of transaction cost economics in mind. Is a remedy feasible? Is the effort warranted?

4.2 *Incentive Disabilities*

The question, Why can't a large firm do everything that a collection of small firms can do and more? is posed in Chapter 6. The answer I advance is that internal organization is unable to replicate the high-powered incentives of markets and is subject to bureaucratic disabilities. The factors that lie behind those conditions, however, are only scratched. The ways in which firms can improve their incentive and bureaucratic competencies in relation to markets also warrant more self-conscious attention.

The question of who manages the managers (Dalton, 1959) is germane, but it is also important to inquire into such mundane matters as how the accounting conventions and procedures are decided. Are the incentive alignments right? What biases do they introduce? What assumptions about information and its processing are maintained? Are they reasonable? What trade-offs are set up? Are they recognized? What is the effective limit of incentive differentials within a firm? Why? What are the organizational ramifications?

Those are plainly matters with which economists (including specialists in comparative systems) have a great interest but for which organization theory specialists would appear to enjoy the advantage.

4.3 *Organizational Innovation*

Although perceptions are changing, the study of organizational innovation has never been more than a poor second cousin to the study of technological innovation. To be sure, Joseph Schumpeter included organizational innovation among the driving forces of capitalism: "The fundamental impulse that sets and keeps the capitalist engine in motion comes from the new consumers' goods, the new methods of production or transportation, the new markets, the new forms of industrial organization that capitalist enterprise creates" (Schumpeter, 1942, p. 83). And Arrow observes, "Truly among man's innovations, the use of organization to accomplish his ends is among both his greatest and his earliest" (1971, p. 224). Arthur Cole, moreover, held that "if changes in business procedures and practices were patentable, the contributions of business change to the economic growth of the nation would be as widely recognized as the influence of mechanical innovations or the inflow of capital from abroad" (Cole, 1968, pp. 61–62). Chandler evidently agrees. In his judgment, "far more economies result from the careful coordination of flow through the processes of production and distribution than from increasing the size of producing or distributing units in terms of capital facilities or number of workers" (Chandler, 1977, p. 490). Aside, however, from the Research Center in Entrepreneurial History at Harvard, which was established in 1948 and closed its doors a decade later, there has not been a concerted effort to work through and establish the importance of organizational innovation.

The record of organizational innovations is therefore sparse. Much of it is linked to and focuses on technology. A systematic effort to identify organizational innovations—both successes and failures—would be an enormous research resource.

Note the reference to successes *and failures.* Neglect of the latter is altogether understandable. Failures are unlikely to be long-lived or widely imitated; and innovators may prefer to bury their mistakes rather than have them recorded. Focusing attention on failures, however, would help to avoid the mistaken conclusion that the modern business enterprise is an uninterrupted sequence of successful refinements. What were the aberrations? Were the failures predictable, in that organizational flaws could have been identified *ex ante,* or were the innovations undone by events of an unforeseeable kind? The role of competition in sorting out innovations according to their economic merits also warrants more complete treatment. The link to evolutionary economics (Nelson and Winter, 1983) will be especially instructive.

4.4 *Dignitary Values and Trust*

Both lawyers and organization theory specialists are more sensitive to dignitary values, especially as they are embedded in the governance process, than are most economists. Although dignity is uncommonly difficult to operationalize, the importance of deepening our knowledge of economic organization in dignitary respects is enormous.[20]

Instrumentalist excesses of two kinds are of concern. One is that capitalist man is a nonhumanist. That is not a flattering or fully accurate description of human nature. The second is that transaction cost economics must be placed in perspective, lest it become dehumanizing. Thinking about economic organization exclusively in an instrumentalist way can spill over into a treatment of individuals as instruments. Such excesses of instrumentalism have to be checked.

For one thing, as Leon Mayhew puts it in his interpretation of Talcott Parsons, "behind utilitarian markets stand an authentic society, a society that is prior to and regulates utilitarian contracts between individuals. . . . The social arrangements behind utilitarian agreements justify criticizing and limiting—that is, constraining—private contracts in the name and in the interests of a larger society" (Mayhew, 1984, p. 1289). Economizing, after all, is a means not an end.

Second, calculativeness can get in the way of trust. As Arrow has repeatedly argued, trust has an important bearing on economic organization (1969, p. 62; 1971, p. 207; 1973, p. 24; 1974, p. 23). Thus he observes that

> . . . ethical elements enter in some measure into every contract; without them, no market could function. There is an element of trust in every transaction; typically, one object of value changes hands before the other one does, and there is confidence that the countervalue will in fact be given up. It is not adequate to argue that there are enforcement mechanism, such as police and the courts; these are themselves services bought and sold, and it has to be asked why they will in fact do what *they* have contracted to do. [Arrow, 1973, p. 24]

He furthermore observes: "Trust and similar values, loyalty or truthtelling, are . . . not commodities for which trade on the open market is technically possible or even meaningful" (1974, p. 23).

[20]My own efforts along this line are at best suggestive (Williamson, 1975, pp. 37–39; 1984a, pp. 210–12). The calculative orientation that economists bring to bear advantageously on other matters may be a disability on this. Organization theory specialists, being less committed to the rational spirit, have less baggage to contend with.

Those are important observations. But operationalizing trust has proved inordinately difficult. A noncalculative orientation may help to unpack the issues.[21] Organization theorists would appear to be well suited to the task.

4.5 *Labor Contracting*

The study of the employment relation is complicated by family considerations that are not expressly included in the transaction cost economics calculus. If workers with generalized skills are not really mobile, because of the dislocation costs that moving would impose on other members of the family, then workers may develop demands for job security, due process, and the like that the earlier job calculus disregarded. To be sure, firms have incentives to respect security preferences of every kind—whether these have job or family origins. But the problem of studying labor organization in a discriminating way is plainly more complicated when family considerations are introduced.

A second difficulty concerns the efficacy of reputation effects. There are several potential problems. The most obvious is whether contemporary observers and successor generations are apprised of contracting difficulties in sufficient detail to make informed assessments. Idiosyncratic experience between buyer and seller that is known only to the immediate parties plainly poses a serious impediment. A second problem is competency bias. If, with the benefit of hindsight, observers can "see through" the particular difficulties of the transaction in question, and if they believe themselves to be too clever to make such a mistake themselves, then observers may discount the experience of others excessively.[22]

Still more difficult problems arise if penalties for poor conduct in contract execution must be exacted not by contemporaries but by future genera-

---

[21]Note in this connection that trust places real strains on the basic contracting schema. Trust is unneeded at node A. It is patently absurd, moreover, to associate trust with node B. (The payments here are up front and contemplate defection. To inquire "How much must I pay you to love me with deep affection?" is consonant with node B but is patently ridiculous.) The mutual offer and receipt of credible commitments is in the spirit of node C and is more consonant with trust. It nevertheless preserves a quasi-calculative orientation, more calculative than the term "trust" normally contemplates. Attention to behavioral and governance features that transcend bargaining frameworks of even the node C kind may be needed. Organization theorists would appear to have the advantage for such an undertaking.

[22]The tendency to discount the experiences of others has two sources: (1) a propensity to overestimate own-competencies (consider the difficulty of human agents conceding that they are below the median), and (2) errors attributable to 20–20 hindsight, which is to say a propensity to oversimplify. Thus although observers may be able to recognize the same difficulty should it recur, they do not perceive the general problem of which it is a part and will not be able to cope equally well with variants.

tions. Breakdowns of at least three kinds can be described. One is due to simple failure of memory. Reputation effects are at best imperfect if the relevant institutional memories are embedded in players who have retired or have otherwise been relocated. Also, successor generations of sellers may ask, sometimes with cause, that they not be held accountable for the sins of their fathers. But if those to whom forgiveness is warranted cannot be distinguished from false claimants, and if there is a propensity to err on the side of charity, then forgiveness may permit contracting errors to be repeated.[23] Finally, successor generations may depend on leaders to represent them. If the leaders have been co-opted or corrupted, wherein do the reputation effect penalties obtain?

The upshot is that if human nature as we know it is subject to propensities of the kinds described above, then sellers can and sometimes will escape the penalties of opportunistic behavior during contract execution. Accordingly, appeal to reputation effects does not obviously warrant that private ordering outcomes be regarded as determinative. The issues need to be delimited.

5. Postscript

Schumpeter posed the question ''Can capitalism survive'' to which he ventured the opinion, ''No. I do not think that it can'' (1942, p. 61). Lack of intellectual support for—indeed, prevailing intellectual skepticism regarding—the merits of capitalist modes of organization was among the factors that led to that negative assessment (Schumpeter, 1942, chap. 13).

Forty years is not a long period in the evolution of economic organization. Schumpeter's negative assessment may be borne out yet. Plainly, however, the demise of capitalism is not imminent. It is furthermore noteworthy that intellectual opinion has improved over the interval. Partly that is explained by a deeper appreciation for the purposes served by complex economic institutions; but the intervening record of economic accomplishment has probably been the more important factor. Whatever the explanation, earlier intellectual skepticism regarding the merits of capitalism has given way to qualified respect.

Inasmuch as no complex form of economic organization, capitalist or otherwise, is unproblematic, qualified respect is all that any deserves. It is not therefore inconsistent to regard some economic institutions as marvels, even

---

[23]Forgiveness may also complicate intragenerational as well as intergenerational trade. More generally, if sellers can repeatedly gull buyers, then efforts to restrain fraud or deceit warrant assessment. Contractual protection for minors is an example.

as awesome, and simultaneously to express real concerns. To the contrary, any other posture is injudicious.

Grudging respect is warranted for another reason as well: It reinforces the perspective that economic institutions are always means and never ends. Rarely does any mode of organization dominate another in all relevant performance respects. Choice among alternative modes—at least among the "finalists" under review—always involves tradeoffs: Improvements in one or more performance measures are realized only at the sacrifice of others. That is true even when the comparison is among efficiency attributes.[24] It applies *a fortiori* when sociopolitical features are introduced.

Preferences among alternative modes thus may differ not because performance is judged to be different on any particular performance dimension, but because individuals use different weighting schemes in reaching an aggregate assessment. Efficiency sacrifices that are voluntarily and knowledgeably made so as to accomplish some other valued purpose are "merely costs." Involuntary or non-knowledgeable sacrifices, however, are another matter.

Transaction costs economics holds that microeconomic institutions play a crucial, subtle, and relatively neglected role in explaining differential economic performance—over time, within and between industries, within and between nation states and sociopolitical systems. The huge valuation disparity between technological and organizational factors, to which Hayek referred with dismay in 1945, is still awaiting redress.

Transaction cost economics helps to inform the study of economic organization by requiring the analyst to examine those microanalytic attributes of organization where the relevant comparative institutional action resides, by disclosing hitherto neglected transaction cost features, and by insisting that assessments be made not abstractly but in comparative institutional terms. "Flawed" modes of economic organization for which no superior feasible mode can be described are, until something better comes along, winners nonetheless.

---

[24]This is especially evident in the comparisons among modes in Chapter 9.

Bibliography

ADELMAN, M. A. 1961. "The antimerger act, 1950–1960," *American Economic Review, 51* (May): 236–44.

AKERLOF, GEORGE A. 1970. "The market for 'lemons': Qualitative uncertainty and the market mechanism," *Quarterly Journal of Economics, 84* (August): 488–500.

AKERLOF, GEORGE A., and HAJIME MIYAZAKI. 1980. "The implicit contract theory of unemployment meets the wage bill argument," *Review of Economic Studies, 47* (January): 321–38.

ALCHIAN, ARMEN. 1950. "Uncertainty, evolution and economic theory," *Journal of Political Economy, 58* (June): 211–21.

––––––. 1959. "Costs and outputs." In M. Abramovitz et al., *The Allocation of Economic Resources: Essays in Honor of Bernard Francis Haley.* Stanford, Calif.: Stanford University Press, pp. 23–40.

––––––. 1961. *Some Economics of Property.* RAND D-2316. Santa Monica, Calif.: RAND Corporation.

––––––. 1965. "The basis of some recent advances in the theory of management of the firm," *Journal of Industrial Economics, 14* (December): 30–41.

––––––. 1969. "Corporate management and property rights." In H. G. Manne, ed., *Economic Policy and Regulation of Corporate Securities.* Washington, D.C.: American Enterprise Institute for Public Policy Research, pp. 337–60.

––––––. 1982. "First National Maintenance *vs.* National Labor Relations Board." Unpublished manuscript.

———. 1983. "Specificity, specialization, and coalitions." Draft manuscript, February.

———. 1984. "Specificity, specialization, and coalitions," *Journal of Economic Theory and Institutions, 140* (March): 34–49.

ALCHIAN, ARMEN, and H. DEMSETZ. 1972. "Production, information costs, and economic organization," *American Economic Review, 62* (December): 777–95.

———. 1973. "The property rights paradigm," *Journal of Economic History, 33* (March): 16–27.

ALDRICH, HOWARD E. 1979. *Organizations and Environments.* Englewood Cliffs, N.J.: Prentice-Hall.

ANDERSON, ERIN, and DAVID SCHMITTLEIN. 1984. "Integration of the sales force: An empirical examination," *The Rand Journal of Economics, 15* (Autumn): 385–95.

ANDREWS, KENNETH. 1982. "Rigid rules will not make good boards," *Harvard Business Review, 60* (November–December): 34–40.

AOKI, MASAHIKO. 1983. "Managerialism revisited in the light of bargaining-game theory," *International Journal of Industrial Organization, 1:* 1–21.

———. 1984. *The Cooperative Game Theory of the Firm.* London: Oxford University Press.

AREEDA, PHILIP. 1967. *Antitrust Analysis.* Boston: Little, Brown.

AREEDA, PHILIP, and D. F. TURNER. 1975. "Predatory pricing and related practices under Section 2 of the Sherman Act," *Harvard Law Review, 88* (February): 697–733.

ARMOUR, H. O., and D. TEECE. 1978. "Organizational structure and economic performance," *Bell Journal of Economics, 9:* 106–22.

ARROW, KENNETH J. 1959. "Toward a theory of price adjustment." In Moses Abramovitz et al., eds., *The Allocation of Resources.* Stanford, Calif.: Stanford University Press, pp. 41–51.

———. 1962. "Economic welfare and the allocation of resources of invention." In National Bureau of Economic Research, ed., *The Rate and Direction of Inventive Activity: Economic and Social Factors.* Princeton, N.J.: Princeton University Press, pp. 609–25.

———. 1963. "Uncertainty and the welfare economics of medical care," *American Economic Review, 53* (December): 941–73.

———. 1964. "Control in large organizations," *Management Science, 10* (April): 397–408.

———. 1969. "The organization of economic activity: Issues pertinent to the choice of market versus nonmarket allocation." In *The Analysis and Evaluation of Public Expenditure: The PPB System.* Vol. 1. U.S. Joint Economic Committee, 91st Congress, 1st Session. Washington, D.C.: U.S. Government Printing Office, pp. 59–73.

———. 1971. *Essays in the Theory of Risk-Bearing.* Chicago: Markham.

———. 1973. *Information and Economic Behavior.* Stockholm: Federation of Swedish Industries.

———. 1974. *The Limits of Organization.* First ed. New York: W. W. Norton.

ASHBY, W. ROSS. 1956. *An Introduction to Cybernetics*. New York: John Wiley & Sons.

———. 1960. *Design for a Brain*. New York: John Wiley & Sons.

ASHTON, T. S. 1925. "The records of a pin manufactory—1814–21," *Economica* (November): 281–92.

ATIYAH, P. S. 1979. *The Rise and Fall of Freedom of Contract*. Oxford, Eng.: Clarendon Press.

AUERBACH, JERROLD. 1983. *Justice Without Law?* New York: Oxford University Press.

AXELROD, ROBERT. 1983. *The Evolution of Cooperation*, New York: Basic Books.

AZARDIADIS, C. 1975. "Implicit contracts and underemployment equilibria," *Journal of Political Economy, 83* (December): 1183–1202.

BABBAGE, CHARLES. 1835. *On the Economy of Machinery and Manufactures*. 4th ed. enl. Repr. of 1835 ed., the addition of *Thoughts on the Principles of Taxation* [3d. ed.] (1982), New York: A.M. Kelley, 1971. From a series, *Reprints of Economic Classics*.

BAILY, M. N. 1974. "Wages and unemployment under uncertain demand," *Review of Economic Studies, 41* (January): 37–50.

BAIMAN, STANLEY. 1982. "Agency research in managerial accounting: A survey," *Journal of Accounting Literature, 1:* 154–213.

BAIN, JOE. 1956. *Barriers to New Competition*. Cambridge, Mass.: Harvard University Press.

———. 1958. *Industrial Organization*. New York: John Wiley & Sons.

———. 1968. *Industrial Organization*. 2d ed. New York: John Wiley & Sons.

BAINES, E. 1835. *History of the Cotton Manufacture in Great Britain*. 2d ed., illus.: 1966. London: Biblio Distributors.

BANFIELD, E. C. 1958. *The Moral Basis of a Backward Society*. New York: Free Press.

BARNARD, CHESTER. 1938. *The Functions of the Executive*. Cambridge: Harvard University Press (fifteenth printing, 1962).

BARTLETT, F. C. 1932. *Remembering*. Cambridge, Eng.: The University Press.

BARZEL, YORAM. 1982. "Measurement cost and the organization of markets," *Journal of Law and Economics, 25* (April): 27–48.

BAUER, P. T., and A. A. WALTERS. 1975. "The state of economics," *Journal of Law and Economics, 18* (April): 1–24.

BAUMOL, W. J. 1959. *Business Behavior, Value and Growth*. New York: Macmillan.

———. 1968. "Entrepreneurship in economic theory," *American Economic Review, 58* (May): 64–71.

———. 1979. "Quasi-permanence of price reductions: A policy for prevention of predatory pricing," *Yale Law Journal, 89* (November): 1–26.

BAUMOL, W. J., and R. D. WILLIG. 1981. "Fixed costs, sunk costs, entry barriers, and sustainability of monopoly," *Quarterly Journal of Economics* (August): 405–31.

412 / THE ECONOMIC INSTITUTIONS OF CAPITALISM

BAUMOL, W. J.; JOHN PANZER; and ROBERT WILLIG. 1982. *Contestable Markets.* New York: Harcourt Brace Jovanovich.

BAXTER, WILLIAM. 1983. "Reflections upon Professor Williamson's comments," *St. Louis University Law Review, 27:* 315–20.

BEALES, HOWARD; RICHARD CRASWELL; and STEVEN SALOP. 1981. "The efficient regulation of consumer information," *Journal of Law and Economics, 24* (December): 491–540.

BECKER, G. S. 1962. "Investment in human capital: Effects on earnings," *Journal of Political Economy, 70* (October): 9–49.

———. 1965. "Theory of the allocation of time," *Economic Journal, 75* (September): 493–517.

BEHAVIORAL SCIENCES SUBPANEL, PRESIDENT'S SCIENCE ADVISORY COMMITTEE. 1962. *Strengthening the Behavioral Sciences.* Washington, D.C.: U.S. Government Printing Office.

BEN-PORATH, YORAM. 1980. "The F-connection: Families, friends, and firms and the organization of exchange," *Population and Development Review, 6* (March): 1–30.

BENSTON, GEORGE J. 1980. *Conglomerate Mergers: Causes, Consequences and Remedies.* Washington, D.C.: American Enterprise Institute for Public Policy Research.

BERLE, ADOLPH A. 1959. *Power Without Property: A New Development in American Political Economy.* New York: Harcourt, Brace.

BERLE, ADOLPH A., and G. C. MEANS. 1932. *The Modern Corporation and Private Property.* New York: Macmillan.

BLAIR, ROGER, and DAVID KASERMAN. 1983. *Law and Economics of Vertical Integration and Control.* New York: Academic Press.

BLAKE, HARLAN M. 1973. "Conglomerate mergers and the antitrust laws," *Columbia Law Review, 73* (March): 555–92.

BLAU, P. M., and R. W. SCOTT. 1962. *Formal Organizations.* San Francisco: Chandler.

BLUMBERG, PAUL. 1969. *Industrial Democracy.* New York: Schocken Books.

BOK, D. 1960. "Section 7 of the Clayton Act and the merging law and economics," *Harvard Law Review, 74* (December): 226–355.

———. 1983. *Annual Report to the Board of Overseers, Harvard University.* Cambridge, Mass.

BORK, R. H. 1954. "Vertical integration and the Sherman Act: The legal history of an economic misconception," *University of Chicago Law Review, 22* (Autumn): 157–201.

———. 1978. *The Antitrust Paradox,* New York: Basic Books.

BOWLES, SAMUEL, and HERBERT GINTIS. 1976. *Schooling in Capitalist America: Educational Reform and the Contradictions of Economic Life.* New York: Basic Books.

BRADLEY, KEITH, and ALAN GELB. 1980. "Motivation and control in the Mondragon experiment," *British Journal of Industrial Relations, 19* (June): 211–31.

————. 1982. "The replicability and sustainability of the Mondragon experiment," *British Journal of Industrial Relations, 20* (March): 20–33.

BRAVERMAN, HARRY. 1974. *Labor and Monopoly Capital: The Degradation of Work in the Twentieth Century.* New York: Monthly Review Press.

BRENNAN, GEOFFREY, and JAMES BUCHANAN. 1983. "Predictive power and choice among regimes," *Economic Journal, 93* (March): 89–105.

BRENNON, TIMOTHY, and SHELDON KIMMEL. 1983. "Joint production and monopoly extension through tying," EPO Discussion Paper 84-1, U.S. Department of Justice, Washington, D.C., November.

BREYER, STEPHEN. 1982. *Regulation and Its Reform.* Cambridge, Mass.: Harvard University Press.

BRIDGEMAN, PERCY. 1955. *Reflections of a Physicist.* 2d ed. New York: Philosophical Library.

BROCKMAN, ROSSER H. 1980. "Commercial contract law in late nineteenth century Taiwan." In Jerome Alan Cohen, R. Randle Edwards, and Fu-mei Chang Chen, eds., *Essays on China's Legal Tradition.* Princeton, N.J.: Princeton University Press, pp. 76–136.

BROWN, D. 1924. "Pricing policy in relation to financial control," *Management and Administration, 1* (February): 195–258.

BRUCHEY, STUART W. 1956. *Robert Oliver, Merchant of Baltimore, 1783–1819.* Baltimore: John Hopkins Press.

BUCHANAN, JAMES. 1975. "A contractarian paradigm for applying economic theory," *American Economic Review, 65* (May): 225–30.

BUCKLEY, P. J., and M. CASSON. 1976. *The Future of Multi-National Enterprise.* New York: Holmes & Meier.

BULL, CLIVE. 1983. "Implicit contracts in the absence of enforcement and risk aversion," *American Economic Review, 73* (September): 658–71.

BURTON, R. H., and A. J. KUHN. 1979. "Strategy follows structure: The missing link of their intertwined relation," Working Paper No. 260, Fuqua School of Business, Duke University, May.

BUTTRICK, J. 1952. "The inside contracting system," *Journal of Economic History, 12* (Summer): 205–21.

CALABRESI, GUIDO. 1970. *The Cost of Accidents.* New Haven, Conn.: Yale University Press.

CAMPBELL, DONALD T. 1958. "Systematic error on the part of human links in communication systems," *Information and Control, 1:* 334–69.

————. 1969. "Reforms as experiments," *American Psychologist. 24* (April): 409–29.

CARLTON, D. W. 1979. "Vertical integration in competitive markets under uncertainty," *Journal of Industrial Economics, 27* (March): 189–209.

CARMICHAEL, H. L. 1984. "Reputations in the labor market," *American Economic Review, 74* (September): 713–25.

CARY, W. 1969. "Corporate devices used to insulate management from attack," *Antitrust Law Journal, 39* no. 1 (1969–1970): 318–33.

CAVES, RICHARD E. 1980. "Corporate strategy and structure," *Journal of Economic Literature, 18* (March): 64–92.

―――. 1982. *Multinational Enterprises and Economic Analysis.* New York: Cambridge University Press.

CAVES, RICHARD E., and MICHAEL PORTER. 1977. "From entry barriers to mobility barriers," *Quarterly Journal of Economics, 91* (May): 230–49.

CHANDLER, A. D., JR. 1962. *Strategy and Structure.* Cambridge, Mass.: MIT Press. Subsequently published in New York: Doubleday & Co., 1966.

―――. 1977. *The Visible Hand: The Managerial Revolution in American Business.* Cambridge, Mass.: Harvard University Press.

CHANDLER, A. D., JR., and H. DAEMS. 1979. "Administrative coordination, allocation and monitoring: Concepts and comparisons." In N. Horn and J. Kocka, eds., *Law and the Formation of the Big Enterprises in the 19th and Early 20th Centuries.* Gottingen: Vandenhoeck & Ruprecht, pp. 28–54.

CHEUNG, STEVEN. 1969. "Transaction costs, risk aversion, and the choice of contractual arrangements," *Journal of Law and Economics, 12* (April): 23–45.

―――. 1983. "The contractual nature of the firm," *Journal of Law and Economics, 26* (April): 1–22.

CLARK, ROBERT. 1981. "The four stages of capitalism: Reflections on investment management treatises," *Harvard Law Review, 94* (January): 561–83.

CLARK, RODNEY. 1979. *The Japanese Company.* New Haven, Conn.: Yale University Press.

CLARKSON, KENNETH W.; ROGER L. MILLER; and TIMOTHY J. MURIS. 1978. "Liquidated damages v. penalties," *Wisconsin Law Review,* pp. 351–90.

COASE, RONALD H. 1952. "The nature of the firm," *Economica N.S., 4* (1937): 386–405. Repr. in G. J. Stigler and K. E. Boulding, eds., *Readings in Price Theory.* Homewood, Ill.: Richard D. Irwin.

―――. 1959. "The Federal Communications Commission," *The Journal of Law and Economics, 2* (October): 1–40.

―――. 1960. "The problem of social cost," *Journal of Law and Economics, 3* (October): 1–44.

―――. 1964. "The regulated industries: Discussion," *American Economic Review, 54* (May): 194–97.

―――. 1972. "Industrial organization: A proposal for research." In V. R. Fuchs, ed., *Policy Issues and Research Opportunities in Industrial Organization.* New York: National Bureau of Economic Research, pp. 59–73.

―――. 1978. "Economics and contiguous disciplines," *Journal of Legal Studies, 7:* 201–11.

―――. 1984. "The new institutional economics," *Journal of Institutional and Theoretical Economics, 140* (March): 229–31.

COCHRAN, T. C. 1948. *The Pabst Brewing Company.* New York: New York University Press.

―――. 1972. *Business in American Life: A History.* New York: McGraw-Hill.

COHEN, LESLIE P. 1983. "Cable-television firms and cities haggle over franchises that trail expectations," *Wall Street Journal,* December 28, p. 34.

COLE, A. H. 1968. "The entrepreneur: Introductory remarks," *American Economic Review, 63* (May): 60–63.

COLEMAN, JAMES. 1982. *The Asymmetric Society.* Syracuse, N.Y.: Syracuse University Press.

COMMONS, JOHN R. 1934. *Institutional Economics.* Madison: University of Wisconsin Press.

———. 1970. *The Economics of Collective Action.* Madison: University of Wisconsin Press.

CONFERENCE BOARD. 1980. *Strategic Planning and the Future of Antitrust.* Antitrust Forum, no. 90.

COX, A. 1958. "The legal nature of collective bargaining agreements," *Michigan Law Review, 57* (November): 1–36.

CTIC. 1972a. *How to Plan an Ordinance.* Washington, D.C.

———. 1972b. *A Suggested Procedure.* Washington, D.C.

———. 1972c. *Cable: An Overview.* Washington, D.C.

———. 1973. *Technical Standards and Specifications.* Washington, D.C.

CYERT, R. M., and J. G. MARCH. 1963. *A Behavioral Theory of the Firm.* Englewood Cliffs, N.J.: Prentice-Hall.

DAHL, R. A. 1968. "Power." In *International Encyclopedia of the Social Sciences.* New York: Free Press, *12:* 405–15.

———. 1970. "Power to the workers?" *New York Review of Books,* November 19, pp. 20–24.

DALTON, MELVILLE. 1957. *Men Who Manage.* New York: Wiley.

DAVIS, LANCE E., and DOUGLASS C. NORTH. 1971. *Institutional Change and American Economic Growth.* Cambridge, Eng.: Cambridge University Press.

DE ALESSI, LOUIS. 1983. "Property rights, transaction costs, and X-efficiency," *American Economic Review, 73* (March): 64–81.

DEBREU, GERHARD. 1959. *Theory of Value.* New York: Wiley.

DEMSETZ, H. 1967. "Toward a theory of property rights," *American Economic Review, 57* (May): 347–59.

———. 1968a. "The cost of transacting," *Quarterly Journal of Economics, 82* (February): 33–53.

———. 1968b. "Why regulate utilities?" *Journal of Law and Economics, 11* (April): 55–66.

———. 1969. "Information and efficiency: Another viewpoint," *Journal of Law and Economics, 12* (April): 1–22.

———. 1971. "On the regulation of industry: A reply," *Journal of Political Economy, 79* (March/April): 356–63.

DEVON, ELI. 1961. *Essays in Economics.* London: Allen & Unwin.

DEWEY, D. J. 1974. "An introduction to the issues." In H. J. Goldschmid, H. M. Mann, and J. F. Weston, eds., *Industrial Concentration: The New Learning.* Boston: Little-Brown, pp. 1–14.

DIAMOND, DOUGLAS. 1983. "Optimal release of information by firms," University of Chicago Center for Research in Security Prices, Working Paper No. 102.

DIAMOND, P. 1971. "Political and economic evaluation of social effects and externalities: Comment." In M. Intrilligator, ed., *Frontiers of Quantitative Economics*. Amsterdam: North-Holland Publishing Company, pp. 30–32.

DIAMOND, P., and ERIC MASKIN. 1979. "An equilibrium analysis of search and breach of contract," *Bell Journal of Economics, 10* (Spring): 282–316.

DIRECTOR, AARON, and EDWARD LEVI. 1956. "Law and the future: Trade regulation," *Northwestern University Law Review, 10:* 281–317.

DIXIT, A. 1979. "A model of duopoly suggesting a theory of entry barriers," *Bell Journal of Economics, 10* (Spring): 20–32.

––––––. 1980. "The role of investment in entry deterrence," *Economic Journal, 90* (March): 95–106.

––––––. 1982. "Recent developments in oligopoly theory," *American Economic Review, 72* (May): 12–17.

DODD, E. MERRICK. 1932. "For whom are corporate managers trustees?" *Harvard Law Review, 45* (June): 1145–63.

DOERINGER, P., and M. PIORE. 1971. *Internal Labor Markets and Manpower Analysis*. Lexington, Mass.: D. C. Heath.

DORE, RONALD. 1973. *British Factory—Japanese Factory*. Berkeley: University of California Press.

––––––. 1983. "Goodwill and the spirit of market capitalism," *British Journal of Sociology, 34* (December): 459–82.

DOWNS, ANTHONY. 1967. *Inside Bureaucracy*. Boston: Little, Brown.

EASTERBROOK, FRANK. 1984. "The limits of antitrust," *Texas Law Review, 63* (August): 1–40.

EASTERBROOK, FRANK, and DANIEL FISCHEL. 1981. "The proper role of a target's management in responding to a tender offer," *Harvard Law Review, 94* (April): 1161–1204.

EATON, C., and R. G. LIPSEY. 1980. "Exit barriers are entry barriers: The durability of capital," *Bell Journal of Economics 11* (Autumn): 721–29.

––––––. 1981. "Capital, commitment, and entry equilibrium," *Bell Journal of Economics, 12* (Autumn): 593–604.

ECCLES, ROBERT. 1981. "The quasifirm in the construction industry," *Journal of Economic Behavior and Organization, 2* (December): 335–58.

ECKSTEIN, A. 1956. "Planning: The National Health Service." In R. Rose, ed., *Policy-Making in Britain*. London: Macmillan, pp. 221–37.

ELLERMAN, DAVID P. 1982. "Theory of legal structure: Worker cooperatives." Unpublished manuscript. Industrial Cooperative Association, Somerville, Mass.

ELSTER, JON. 1979. *Ulysses and the Sirens*. Cambridge, Eng.: Cambridge University Press.

ETZIONI, A. 1975. *A Comparative Analysis of Complex Organizations*. New York: Free Press.

EVANS, DAVID, and SANFORD GROSSMAN. 1983. "Integration." In D. Evans, ed., *Breaking Up Bell*. New York: North-Holland Publishing Co., pp. 95–126.

FAMA, EUGENE F. 1980. "Agency problems and the theory of the firm," *Journal of Political Economy, 88* (April): 288–307.

FAMA, EUGENE F., and MICHAEL C. JENSEN. 1983. "Separation of ownership and control," *Journal of Law and Economics, 26* (June): 301–26.

FEIWEL, GEORGE. 1983. "Some perceptions and tensions in microeconomics." Unpublished manuscript.

FELDMAN, J., and H. KANTER. 1965. "Organizational decision making." In J. March, ed., *Handbook of Organizations*. Chicago: Rand McNally, pp. 614–49.

FELDMAN, MARTHA S., and JAMES G. MARCH. 1981. "Information in organizations as signal and symbol," *Administrative Science Quarterly, 26* (April): 171–86.

FELLER, DAVID E. 1973. "A general theory of the collective bargaining agreement," *California Law Review, 61* (May): 663–856.

FELLER, W. 1957. *An Introduction to Probability Theory and Its Application.* New York: John Wiley & Sons.

FELLNER, W. 1949. *Competition Among the Few.* New York: Alfred A. Knopf.

FISHER, ALAN, and ROBERT LANDE. 1983. "Efficiency considerations in merger enforcement," *California Law Review, 71* (December): 1580–1696.

FISHER, STANLEY. 1977. "Long-term contracting, sticky prices, and monetary policy: Comment," *Journal of Monetary Economics, 3:* 317–24.

FISHER, W. L. 1907. "The American municipality." In Commission on Public Ownership and Operation, ed., *Municipal and Private Operation of Public Utilities*, Part I, New York, I: 36–48.

FISHLOW, ALBERT. 1965. *American Railroads and the Transformation of the Antebellum Economy.* Cambridge, Mass.: Harvard University Press.

FITZROY, FELIX, and DENNIS MUELLER. 1985. "Cooperation and conflict in contractual organizations," *Quarterly Review of Economics and Business, 24* (Winter): 24–49.

FLAHERTY, T. 1981. "Prices versus quantities and vertical financial integration," *Bell Journal of Economics, 12* (Autumn): 507–25.

FOGEL, R. 1964. *Railroads and American Economic Growth: Essays in Econometric History.* Baltimore: Johns Hopkins Press.

FOULKES, FRED. 1981. "How top nonunion companies manage employees," *Harvard Business Review* (September–October): 90–96.

FOX, A. 1974. *Beyond Contract: Work, Power, and Trust Relations.* London: Faber & Faber.

FRANKO, LAWRENCE G. 1972. "The growth and organizational efficiency of European multinational firms: Some emerging hypotheses," *Colloques international aux C.N.R.S.,* pp. 335–66.

FREEMAN, R. B. 1976. "Individual mobility and union voice in the labor market," *American Economic Review, 66* (May): 361–68.

FREEMAN, R. B., and J. MEDOFF. 1979. "The two faces of unionism," *Public Interest* (Fall): 69–93.

FREUDENBERGER, H., and F. REDLICH. 1964. "The industrial development of Europe: Reality, symbols, images," *Kyklos 17:* 372–403.

FRIED, CHARLES. 1981. *Contract as Promise.* Cambridge, Mass.: Harvard University Press.

FRIEDMAN, L. M. 1965. *Contract Law in America.* Madison: University of Wisconsin Press.

FRIEDMAN, MILTON. 1953. *Essays in Positive Economics.* Chicago: University of Chicago Press.

―――. 1962. *Capitalism and Freedom.* Chicago: University of Chicago Press.

FULLER, LON L. 1963. "Collective bargaining and the arbitrator," *Wisconsin Law Review* (January): 3–46.

―――. 1964. *The Morality of Law.* New Haven: Yale University Press.

FULLER, LON L., and WILLIAM PERDUE. 1936. "The reliance interest in contract damages," *Yale Law Journal, 46:* 52–124.

FULLER, LON L., and R. BRAUCHER. 1964. *Basic Contract Law.* St. Paul: West Publishing Co.

FURUBOTN, E. 1976. "Worker alienation and the structure of firm." In S. Pejovich, ed., *Governmental Controls and the Free Market.* College Station: Texas A. and M. University Press, pp. 195–225.

FURUBOTN, E., and S. PEJOVICH. 1972. "Property rights and economic theory: A survey of recent literature," *Journal of Economic Literature, 10* (December): 1137–62.

―――. 1974. *The Economics of Property Rights.* Cambridge, Mass.: Ballinger.

GALANTER, MARC. 1981. "Justice in many rooms: Courts, private ordering, and indigenous law," *Journal of Legal Pluralism,* no. 19, pp. 1–47.

GALBRAITH, J. K. 1967. *The New Industrial State.* Boston: Houghton-Mifflin.

GALLAGHER, W. E., JR., and H. J. EINHORN. 1976. "Motivation theory and job design," *Journal of Business, 49* (July): 358–73.

GAUSS, CHRISTIAN. 1952. "Introduction" to Machiavelli (1952), pp. 7–32.

GEANAKOPLOS, JOHN, and PAUL MILGROM. 1984. "Information, planning, and control in hierarchies." Unpublished paper, March.

GEORGESCU-ROEGEN, NICHOLAS. 1971. *The Entropy Law and Economic Process.* Cambridge, Mass.: Harvard University Press.

GETSCHOW, GEORGE. 1982. "Loss of expert talent impedes oil finding by new Tenneco unit," *Wall Street Journal,* February 9.

GIBNEY, FRANK. 1982. *Miracle by Design.* New York: Times Books.

GILSON, RONALD. 1984. "Value creation by business lawyers: Legal skills and asset pricing," Law and Economics Program Working Paper No. 18, Stanford University, Stanford, Calif.

GOETZ, CHARLES, and ROBERT SCOTT. 1981. "Principles of relational contracts," *Virginia Law Review, 67:* 1089–1151.

―――. 1983. "The mitigation principle: Toward a general theory of contractual obligation," *Virginia Law Review, 69* (September): 967–1024.

GOFFMANN, E. 1969. *Strategic Interaction.* Philadelphia: University of Pennsylvania Press.

GOLDBERG, JEFFREY. 1982. "A theoretical and econometric analysis of franchising." Unpublished Ph.D. dissertation, University of Pennsylvania.

GOLDBERG, VICTOR. 1976a. "Toward an expanded economic theory of contract," *Journal of Economic Issues, 10* (March): 45–61.

———. 1976b. "Regulation and administered contracts," *Bell Journal of Economics, 7* (Autumn): 426–52.

———. 1980. "Bridges over contested terrain," *Journal of Economic Behavior and Organization, 1* (September): 249–74.

GOLDBERG, VICTOR, and JOHN E. ERICKSON. 1982. "Long-term contracts for petroleum coke," Department of Economics Working Paper Series No. 206, University of California, Davis, September.

GORDON, DONALD. 1974. "A neoclassical theory of Keynesian unemployment," *Economic Inquiry, 12* (December): 431–59.

GORT, MICHAEL. 1962. *Diversification and Integration in American Industry.* Princeton, N.J.: Princeton University Press.

GOSPEL, HOWARD. Undated. "The development of labour management and work organization in Britain: A historical perspective." Unpublished manuscript, University of Kent, England, Business History Unit.

GOULDNER, A. W. 1954. *Industrial Bureaucracy.* Glencoe, Ill.: Free Press.

———. 1961. "The norm of reciprocity," *American Sociological Review, 25* (May): 161–79.

GOWER, E. C. B. 1969. *Principles of Modern Company Law.* London: Stevens & Sons.

GRANOVETTER, MARK. 1985. "Economic action and social structure: A theory of embeddedness," *American Journal of Sociology.*

GREEN, JERRY. 1984. "Information in economics." In Kenneth Arrow and Seppo Honkapohja, eds., *Frontiers of Economics.* London: Basil Blackwell.

GRETHER, DAVID, and CHARLES PLOTT. 1979. "Economic theory of choice and the preference reversal phenomenon," *American Economic Review, 69* (September): 623–38.

GROSSMAN, SANFORD J., and OLIVER D. HART. 1982. "Corporate financial structure and managerial incentives." In John J. McCall, ed., *The Economics of Information.* Chicago: The University of Chicago Press, pp. 107–40.

———. 1984. "The costs and benefits of ownership: A theory of vertical integration." Unpublished manuscript, March.

GUNZBERG, D. 1978. "On-the-job democracy," *Sweden Now, 12:* 42–45.

HADDOCK, DAVID. 1982. "Basing point pricing: Competitive vs. collusive theories," *American Economic Review, 72* (June): 289–306.

HALL, ROBERT, and DAVID LILIEN. 1979. "Efficient wage bargains under uncertain supply and demand," *American Economic Review, 69* (September): 868–79.

HAMBURG, D. 1963. "Invention in the industrial laboratory," *Journal of Political Economy, 71* (April): 95–116.

———. 1966. *R&D: Essays on the Economics of Research and Development.* New York: Random House.

HANNAN, MICHAEL T., and JOHN FREEMAN. 1977. "The population ecology of organizations," *American Journal of Sociology, 82* (March): 929–64.

HARRIS, MILTON, and ARTHUR RAVIV. 1976. "Optimal incentive contracts with imperfect information," Working Paper #70-75-76, Graduate School of Industrial Administration, Carnegie-Mellon University, April (revised December 1977).

HARRIS, MILTON, and ROBERT TOWNSEND. 1981. "Resource allocation under asymmetric information," *Econometrica, 49* (January): 33–64.

HART, OLIVER. 1983. "Optimal labour contracts under asymmetric information: An introduction," *Review of Economic Studies, 50* (February): 3–36.

HART, OLIVER, and JOHN MOORE. 1985. "Incomplete contracts and renegotiation," January. Unpublished manuscript.

HAYEK, F. 1945. "The use of knowledge in society," *American Economic Review, 35* (September): pp. 519–30.

———. 1967. *Studies in Philosophy, Politics, and Economics.* London: Routledge & Kegan Paul.

HAYES, S. L., III, and R. A. TAUSSIG. 1967. "Tactics of cash takeover bids," *Harvard Business Review, 46* (March–April): 136–47.

HEFLEBOWER, R. B. 1960. "Observations on decentralization in large enterprises," *Journal of Industrial Economics, 9* (November): 7–22.

HEIMER, RONALD. 1983. "The origin of predictable behavior," *American Economic Review, 73* (September): 560–95.

HENNART, JEAN-FRANÇOIS, and MIRA WILKINS. 1983. "Multinational enterprise, transaction costs and the markets and hierarchies hypothesis." Unpublished manuscript, Florida International University.

HICKS, JOHN R. 1976. " 'Revolution' in Economics." In S. J. Latsis, ed., *Method and Appraisal in Economics.* Cambridge, Eng.: Cambridge University Press, pp. 207–18.

HIRSCHMAN, ALBERT O. 1970. *Exit, Voice and Loyalty.* Cambridge, Mass.: Harvard University Press.

———. 1982. "Rival interpretations of market society: Civilizing, destructive, or feeble?" *Journal of Economic Literature, 20* (December): 1463–84.

HIRSCHMEIER, J., and T. YUI. 1975. *The Development of Japanese Business, 1600–1973.* London: George Allen & Unwin.

HOBBES, THOMAS. 1928. *Leviathan, or the Matter, Forme, and Power of Commonwealth Ecclesiastical and Civil.* Oxford, Eng.: Basil Blackwell.

HOLMSTROM, B. 1979. "Moral hazard and observability," *Bell Journal of Economics, 10* (Spring): 74–91.

———. 1984. "Differential information, the market, and incentive compatibility." In Kenneth Arrow and Seppo Hankapohja, eds., *Frontiers in Economics.* London: Basil Blackwell.

HOLMSTROM, BENGT, and JOAN E. RICART I COSTA. 1984. "Managerial incentives and capital management." Yale School of Organization and Management Working Paper, Series D, No. 4.

HORVAT, BRANKO. 1982. *The Political Economy of Socialism.* New York: M. E. Sharpe.

HUDSON, PAT. 1981. "Proto-industrialization: The case of the West Riding World Textile Industry in the 18th and early 19th centuries," *History Workshop, 12* (Autumn): 34–61.

HURWICZ, LEONID. 1972. "On informationally decentralized systems." In C. B. McGuire and R. Radner, eds., *Decision and Organization.* Amsterdam: North-Holland Publishing Company, pp. 297–336.

————. 1973. "The design of mechanisms for resource allocation," *American Economic Review, 63* (May): 1–30.

HYMER, S. 1970. "The efficiency (contradictions) of multinational corporations," *American Economic Review, 60* (May): 441–48.

INKELES, ALEX. 1969. "Making men modern: On the causes and consequences of individual change in six developing countries," *American Journal of Sociology, 75* (September): 208–25.

JACKSON, BROOKS, and ANDY PASZTOR. 1984. "Court records show big oil companies exchanged price data," *Wall Street Journal,* December 17, pp. 1, 30.

JARRELL, GREGG, and MICHAEL BRADLEY. 1980. "The economic effect of federal and state regulation of cash tender offers," *Journal of Law and Economics, 23* (October): 371–94.

JENKINS, IREDELL. 1980. *Social Order and the Limits of the Law.* Princeton, N.J.: Princeton University Press.

JENSEN, MICHAEL. 1983. "Organization theory and methodology," *Accounting Review, 50* (April): 319–39.

JENSEN, MICHAEL, and WILLIAM MECKLING. 1976. "Theory of the firm: Managerial behavior, agency costs, and capital structure," *Journal of Financial Economics, 3* (October): 305–60.

————. 1979. "Rights and production functions: An application to labor-managed firms", *Journal of Business, 52* (October): 469–506.

JEWKES, J.; D. SAWERS; and R. STILLERMAN. 1959. *The Sources of Invention.* New York: St. Martin's Press.

JOHANSEN, LEIF. 1979. "The bargaining society and the inefficiency of bargaining," *Kyklos, 32:* 497–521.

JONES, S. R. H. 1982. "The organization of work: A historical dimension," *Journal of Economic Behavior and Organization, 3* (June): 117–38.

JÖRESKOG, KARL G., and DAG SÖRBOM. 1982. *LISREL V: Analysis of Linear Structural Relationships by Maximum Likelihood and Least Squares Methods.* Chicago: National Educational Resources.

JOSKOW, P. L. 1980. "The political content of antitrust: Comment." In O. E. Williamson, ed., *Antitrust Law and Economics.* Houston, Tex.: Dame Publishers, pp. 196–204.

————. 1985. "Vertical integration and long-term contracts," *Journal of Law, Economics and Organization, 1* (Spring).

JOSKOW, P. L., and A. K. KLEVORICK. 1979. "A framework for analyzing predatory pricing policy," *Yale Law Journal, 89* (December): 213–70.

JOSKOW, P. L., and RICHARD SCHMALENSEE. 1983. *Markets for Power.* Cambridge, Mass.: MIT Press.

KAHN, ALFRED E. 1971. *The Economics of Regulation: Vol. 2. Institutional Issues.* New York: John Wiley & Sons.

KANTER, ROSABETH MOSS. 1972. *Community and Commitment.* Cambridge, Mass.: Harvard University Press.

KATZ, DANIEL, and ROBERT KAHN. 1966. *The Social Psychology of Organizations.* New York: John Wiley & Sons.

KAUPER, THOMAS E. 1983. "The 1982 horizontal merger guidelines: Of collusion, efficiency, and failure," *California Law Review, 71* (March): 497–534.

KENNEY, ROY, and BENJAMIN KLEIN. 1983. "The economics of block booking," *Journal of Law and Economics, 26* (October): 497–540.

KESSEL, RUBIN A. 1958. "Price discrimination in medicine," *Journal of Law and Economics, 1:* 20–53.

KING, MERVYN. 1977. *Public Policy and the Corporation.* London: Chapman & Hull.

KIRZNER, ISRAEL M. 1973. *Competition and Entrepreneurship.* Chicago: University of Chicago Press.

KITAGAWA, ZENTARO. 1980. "Contract law in general." In *Doing Business in Japan.* Vol. 2. Tokyo.

KLEIN, BENJAMIN. 1980. "Transaction cost determinants of 'unfair' contractual arrangements," *American Economic Review, 70* (May): 356–62.

KLEIN, BENJAMIN; R. A. CRAWFORD; and A. A. ALCHIAN. 1978. "Vertical integration, appropriable rents, and the competitive contracting process," *Journal of Law and Economics, 21* (October): 297–326.

KLEIN, BENJAMIN, and K. B. LEFFLER. 1981. "The role of market forces in assuring contractual performance," *Journal of Political Economy, 89* (August): 615–41.

KLEIN, BENJAMIN; ANDREW MCLAUGHLIN; and KEVIN MURPHY. 1983. "The economics of resale price maintenance: The Coors case." Unpublished working paper, UCLA Economics Department.

KLEIN, FREDERICK C. 1982. "A golden parachute protects executives, but does it hinder or foster takeovers?" *Wall Street Journal,* December 8, p. 56.

KLEINDORFER, PAUL, and GUNTER KNIEPS. 1982. "Vertical integration and transaction-specific sunk costs," *European Economic Review, 19:* 71–87.

KNIGHT, FRANK H. 1941. "Review of Melville J. Herskovits' 'Economic anthropology,'" *Journal of Political Economy, 49* (April): 247–58.

———. 1965. *Risk, Uncertainty and Profit.* New York: Harper & Row.

KOHN, MELVIN. 1971. "Bureaucratic man: A portrait and an interpretation," *American Sociological Review, 36* (June): 461–74.

KOONTZ, H., and C. O'DONNELL. 1955. *Principles of Management: An Analysis of Managerial Functions.* New York: McGraw-Hill.

KOOPMANS, TJALLING. 1957. *Three Essays on the State of Economic Science.* New York: McGraw-Hill.

———. 1974. "Is the theory of competitive equilibrium with it?" *American Economic Review, 64* (May): 325–29.

———. 1977. "Concepts of optimality and their uses," *American Economic Review, 67* (June): 261–74.

KORNAI, J. 1971. *Anti-equilibrium.* Amsterdam: North-Holland Publishing Company.

KRAAKMAN, REINIER. 1984. "Corporate liability strategies and the costs of legal controls," *Yale Law Journal, 93* (April): 857–98.

KREPS, DAVID M. 1984. "Corporate culture and economic theory." Unpublished manuscript, Graduate School of Business, Stanford University, Stanford, Calif.

KREPS, DAVID M., and ROBERT WILSON. 1980. "On the chain-store paradox and predation: Reputation for toughness." GSB Research Paper No. 551, June, Stanford, Calif.

———. 1982. "Reputation and imperfect information," *Journal of Economic Theory, 27* (August): 253–79.

KRONMAN, ANTHONY. 1985. "Contract law and the state of nature," *Journal of Law, Economics and Organization, 1* (Spring).

KRONMAN, ANTHONY, and R. A. POSNER. 1979. *The Economics of Contract Law.* Boston: Little, Brown.

KUHN, THOMAS S. 1962. *The Structure of Scientific Revolutions.* Chicago: University of Chicago Press.

KUNREUTHER, HOWARD, ET AL. 1978. *Protecting Against High-Risk Hazards: Public Policy Lessons.* New York: John Wiley & Sons.

LANDES, D. S., ED. 1966. *The Rise of Capitalism.* New York: n.p.

LANDES, WILLIAM, and RICHARD POSNER. 1985. "A positive economic analysis of products liability," *Journal of Legal Studies.*

LANGLOIS, RICHARD H. 1982. "Economics as a process," *R.R. 82–21,* New York University.

———. 1984. "Internal organization in a dynamic context: Some theoretical considerations." In M. Jussawalla and H. Ebenfield, eds., *Communication and Information Economics.* Amsterdam: Elsevier Science Publishers, pp. 23–49.

LARSON, H. M. 1948. *Guide to Business History.* Cambridge, Mass.: Harvard University Press.

LEFF, A. A. 1975. "Teams, firms, and the aesthetics of antitrust," draft manuscript, February.

LEIBENSTEIN, H. 1968. "Entrepreneurship and development," *American Economic Review, 58* (May): 72–83.

LEONTIEF, WASSILY. 1946. "The pure theory of the guaranteed annual wage contract," *Journal of Political Economy, 54* (August): 392–415.

LEVIN, RICHARD. 1982. "The semiconductor industry." In Richard R. Nelson, ed., *Government and Technical Progress.* New York, Pergamon Press, pp. 9–100.

LEWIS, TRACY. 1983. "Preemption, divestiture, and forward contracting in a market dominated by a single firm," *American Economic Review, 73* (December): 1092–1101.

LIBMAN, J. 1974. "In Oakland, a cable-TV system fails to live up to promises," *Wall Street Journal,* September 25, p. 34.

LIEBELER, W. C. 1978. "Market power and competitive superiority in concentrated industries," *UCLA Law Review, 25* (August): 1231–1300.

LIFSON, THOMAS B. 1979. "An emergent administrative system: Interpersonal networks in a Japanese general trading firm,'' Working Paper 79-55, Harvard University, Graduate School of Business.

LINDBLOM, CHARLES E. 1977. *Politics and Markets: The World's Political-Economic Systems.* New York: Basic Books.

LIPSET, SEYMOUR M. 1962. "Introduction" to Michels (1962).

LITTLECHILD, STEPHEN. 1985. "Three types of market process." In R. Langlois, ed., *Economics as a Process.* Cambridge, Eng.: Cambridge University Press.

LIVESAY, H. C. 1979. *American Made: Men Who Shaped the American Economy.* Boston: Little, Brown.

LLEWELLYN, KARL N. 1931. "What price contract? An essay in perspective," *Yale Law Journal, 40* (May): 704–51.

LOESCHER, SAMUEL. 1984. "Bureaucratic measurement, shuttling stock shares and shortened time horizons," *Quarterly Review of Economics and Business, 24* (Winter): 8–23.

LOWE, ADOLPH. 1965. *On Economic Knowledge: Toward a Science of Political Economics.* New York: M. E. Sharpe. Repr. 1983.

LOWRY, S. TODD. 1976. "Bargain and contract theory in law and economics," *Journal of Economic Issues, 10* (March): 1–19.

MACAULAY, S. 1963. "Non-contractual relations in business," *American Sociological Review, 28:* 55–70.

MACAVOY, PAUL; SCOTT CANTOR; JIM DANA; and SARAH PECK. 1983. "ALI proposals for increased control of the corporation by the board of directors: An economic analysis." In *Statement of the Business Roundtable on the American Law Institute's Proposed Principles of Corporate Governance and Structure: Restatement and Recommendations.* February.

MACHIAVELLI, NICCOLÒ. 1952. *The Prince.* New York: New American Library.

MACNEIL, I. R. 1974. "The many futures of contracts," *Southern California Law Review, 47* (May): 691–816.

————. 1978. "Contracts: Adjustments of long-term economic relations under classical, neoclassical, and relational contract law," *Northwestern University Law Review, 72:* 854–906.

MALMGREN, H. 1961. "Information, expectations and the theory of the firm," *Quarterly Journal of Economics, 75* (August): 399–421.

MANDEL, EARNEST. 1968. *Marxist Economic Theory.* Trans. B. Pearce. Rev. Ed. Vol. 2. New York: Monthly Review Press.

MANN, DOUGLAS, and JENNIFER WISSINK. 1984. "Inside vs. outside production," CSOI Discussion Paper No. 170, University of Pennsylvania, June.

MANNE, HENRY G. 1965. "Mergers and the market for corporate control," *Journal of Political Economy, 73* (April): 110–20.

MANSFIELD, EDWIN. 1962. "Comments on inventive activity and industrial R and D expenditure." In *The Rate and Direction of Inventive Activity.* Princeton, N.J.: Princeton University Press.

MANSFIELD, EDWIN; A. ROMEO; and S. WAGNER. 1979. "Foreign trade and U.S. research and development," *Review of Economics and Statistics, 61* (February): 49–57.

MANUEL, FRANK E., and FRITIZIE P. MANUEL. 1979. *Utopian Thought in the Western World.* Cambridge, Mass.: Harvard University Press.

MARCH, JAMES G. 1973. "Model bias in social action," *Review of Educational Research, 42:* 413–29.

————. 1978. "Bounded rationality, ambiguity, and the engineering of choice," *Bell Journal of Economics, 9* (Autumn): 587–608.

MARCH, JAMES G., and HERBERT A. SIMON. 1958. *Organizations.* New York: Wiley.

MARGLIN, STEPHEN A. 1974. "What do bosses do? The origins and functions of hierarchy in capitalist production," *Review of Radical Political Economic, 6:* 33–60.

————. 1984. "Knowledge and power." In Frank A. Stephen, ed., *Firms, Organization and Labour.* London: Macmillan.

MARRIS, R. 1964. *The Economic Theory of Managerial Capitalism.* New York: Free Press.

MARRIS, R., and D. C. MUELLER. 1980. "The corporation and competition," *Journal of Economic Literature, 18* (March): 32–63.

MARSCHAK, J. 1968. "Economics of inquiring, communicating, deciding," *American Economic Review, 58* (May): 1–18.

MARSCHAK, J., and R. RADNER. 1972. *The Theory of Teams.* New Haven, Conn.: Yale University Press.

MARSHALL, ALFRED. 1948. *Principles of Economics.* Eighth ed. New York: Macmillan.

MARX, K. 1967. *Capital.* Vol. 1. New York: International Publishers.

MASHAW, J. 1985. *Due Process in the Administrative State.* New Haven, Conn.: Yale University Press.

MASON, EDWARD. 1958. "The apologetics of managerialism," *Journal of Business, 31:* 1–11.

————. 1959. *The Corporation in Modern Society.* Cambridge, Mass.: Harvard University Press.

MASTEN, SCOTT. 1982. *Transaction Costs, Institutional Choice, and the Theory of the Firm.* Unpublished Ph.D. dissertation, University of Pennsylvania.

————. 1984. "The organization of production: Evidence from the aerospace industry," *Journal of Law and Economics, 27* (October): 403–18.

MAYER, THOMAS. 1980. "Economics as a hard science," *Economic Inquiry, 18* (April): 165–78.

MAYHEW, LEON. 1984. "In defense of modernity: Talcott Parsons and the utilitarian tradition," *American Journal of Sociology, 89* (May): 1273–1305.

MAYHEW, LEON. 1984. "In defense of modernity: Talcott Parsons and the utilitarian tradition," *American Journal of Sociology, 89* (May): 1273–1305.

MCCLOSKEY, DONALD. 1983. "The rhetoric of economics," *Journal of Economic Literature, 21* (June): 481–517.

MCGEE, J. S. 1980. "Predatory pricing revisited," *Journal of Law and Economics, 23* (October): 289–330.

MEADE, J. E. 1971. *The Controlled Economy.* London: George Allen & Unwin.

————. 1972. "The theory of labour managed firms and of profit sharing," *Economic Journal, 82* (Spring): 402–28.

MENGER, KARL. 1963. *Problems in Economics and Sociology.* Trans. F. J. Noch. Urbana: University of Illinois Press.

MERTON, ROBERT. 1936. "The unanticipated consequences of purposive social action," *American Sociological Review, 1:* 894–904.

MICHELS, R. 1962. *Political Parties.* Glencoe, Ill.: Free Press.

MILGROM, PAUL, and JOHN ROBERTS. 1982. "Predation, reputation, and entry deterrence," *Journal of Economic Theory, 27* (August): 280–312.

MIRRLEES, J. A. 1976. "The optimal structure of incentives and authority within an organization," *Bell Journal of Economics, 7* (Spring): 105–31.

MISES, LUDWIG VON. 1949. *Human Action: A Treatise on Economics.* New Haven, Conn.: Yale University Press.

MNOOKIN, ROBERT H., and LEWIS KORNHAUSER. 1979. "Bargaining in the shadow of the law: The case of divorce," *Yale Law Journal, 88* (March): 950–97.

MODIGLIANI, F. 1958. "New developments on the oligopoly front," *Journal of Political Economy, 66* (June): 215–32.

MODIGLIANI, FRANCO, and MERTON MILLER. 1958. "The cost of capital, corporation finance, and the theory of investment," *American Economic Review, 48* (June): 261–97.

MONTEVERDE, KIRK, and DAVID TEECE. 1982. "Supplier switching costs and vertical integration in the automobile industry," *Bell Journal of Economics, 13* (Spring): 206–13.

MORGENSTERN, OSKAR. 1976. "Perfect foresight and economic equilibrium." In Andrew Schotter, ed., *Selected Economic Writings of Oskar Morgenstern.* New York: NYU Press, pp. 169–83.

MORRIS, CHARLES. 1980. *The Cost of Good Intentions.* New York: W. W. Norton.

MORTENSON, DALE T. 1978. "Specific capital and labor turnover," *Bell Journal of Economics, 9* (Autumn): 572–86.

MURIS, T. J. 1979. "The efficiency defense under Section 7 of the Clayton Act," *Case Western Reserve Law Review, 30* (Fall): 381–432.

MYERSON, ROGER. 1979. "Incentive compatibility and the bargaining problem," *Econometrica, 47* (January): 61–73.

NADER, R.; M. GREEN, and J. SELIJMAN. 1976. *Taming the Giant Corporation.* New York: Norton.

NELSON, RICHARD R. 1972. "Issues and suggestions for the study of industrial organization in a regime of rapid technical change." In V. R. Fuchs, ed., *Policy Issues and Research Opportunities in Industrial Organization.* New York: Columbia University Press, pp. 34–58.

————. 1981. "Assessing private enterprise: An exegesis of tangled doctrine," *Bell Journal of Economics* (Spring).

————. 1984. "Incentives for entrepreneurship and macroeconomic decline," *Review of World Economics, 120:* 646–61.

NELSON, RICHARD R., and S. G. WINTER. 1982. *An Evolutionary Theory of Economic Change.* Cambridge, Mass.: Harvard University Press.

NORTH, DOUGLASS. 1978. "Structure and performance: The task of economic history," *Journal of Economic Literature, 16* (Septemer): 963–78.

_____. 1981. *Structure and Change in Economic History.* New York: W. W. Norton.

NOZICK, ROBERT. 1974. *Anarchy, State, and Utopia.* New York: Basic Books.

OKUN, A. 1975. "Inflation: Its mechanics and welfare costs," *Brookings Papers on Economic Activity, 2:* 351–90.

_____. 1981. *Prices and Quantities: A Macroeconomic Analysis.* Washington, D.C.: The Brookings Institution.

OLSON, MANCUR. 1982. *The Rise and Decline of Nations.* New Haven, Conn.: Yale University Press.

ORDOVER, J. A., and R. D. WILLIG. 1981. "An economic definition of predatory product innovation." In S. Salop, ed., *Strategic Views of Predation.* Washington, D.C.: Federal Trade Commission, pp. 301–96.

OUCHI, WILLIAM G. 1977a. "Review of *Markets and Hierarchies,*" *Administrative Science Quarterly, 22* (September): 541–44.

_____. 1977b. "The relationship between organizational structure and organizational control," *Administrative Science Quarterly, 22:* 95–113.

_____. 1978. "The transmission of control through organizational hierarchy," *Academy of Management Journal, 21:* 248–63.

_____. 1980a. "Efficient boundaries." Mimeographed. Los Angeles: University of California, Los Angeles.

_____. 1980b. "Markets, bureaucracies, and clans," *Administrative Science Quarterly, 25* (March): 120–42.

_____. 1981. *Theory Z.* Reading, Mass.: Addison-Wesley Press.

PALAY, THOMAS. 1981. "The governance of rail–freight contracts: A comparative institutional approach." Unpublished Ph.D. dissertation, University of Pennsylvania.

_____. 1984. "Comparative institutional economics: The governance of rail freight contracting," *Journal of Legal Studies, 13* (June): 265–88.

_____. 1985. "The avoidance of regulatory constraints: The use of informal contracts," *Journal of Law, Economics and Organization, 1* (Spring).

PANZAR, JOHN C., and ROBERT D. WILLIG. 1981. "Economies of scope," *American Economic Review, 71,* no. 2 (May): 268–72.

PARSONS, DONALD O., and EDWARD RAY. 1975. "The United States Steel consolidation: The creation of market control," *Journal of Law and Economics, 18* (April): 181–219.

PASHIGIAN, B. P. 1961. *The Distribution of Automobiles: An Economic Analysis of the Franchise System.* Englewood Cliffs, N.J.: Prentice-Hall.

PEACOCK, A. T., and C. K. ROWLEY. 1972. "Welfare economics and the public regulation of natural monopolies," *Journal of Public Economics, 1:* 227–44.

PENCAVEL, JOHN. 1977. "Work effort, on-the-job screening, and alternative methods of remuneration." In R. G. Ehrenberg, ed., *Research in Labor Economics,* Vol. 1. Greenwich, Conn.: JAI Press, pp. 225–58.

PENROSE, EDITH. 1959. *The Theory of Growth of the Firm.* New York: John Wiley & Sons.

PERROW, CHARLES. 1983. *Normal Accidents: Living with High-Risk Technologies.* New York: Basic Books.

PFEFFER, JEFFREY. 1978. *Organizational Design.* Northbrook, Ill.: AHM Publishing Corp.

———. 1981. *Power in Organizations.* Marshfield, Mass.: Pitman Publishing.

PHILLIPS, ALMARIN. 1970. *Technological Change and Market Structure.* Lexington, Mass.: D. C. Heath.

PINCOFFS, EDMUND. 1977. "Due process, fraternity, and a Kantian injemation," *Due Process, Nomos, 28:* 160–95.

POLANYI, MICHAEL. 1962. *Personal Knowledge: Towards a Post-Critical Philosophy.* New York: Harper & Row.

POLLACK, ANDREW. 1983. "Texas Instruments' pullout," *New York Times,* October 31, p. D1.

POLLAK, ROBERT. 1983. "A transaction cost approach to households." Unpublished manuscript, September.

PORTER, G. 1973. *The Rise of Big Business, 1860–1910.* Arlington Heights, Ill.: AHM Publishing Corp.

PORTER, G., and H. C. LIVESAY. 1971. *Merchants and Manufacturers: Studies in the Changing Structure of Nineteenth Century Marketing.* Baltimore: Johns Hopkins Press.

POSNER, R. A. 1969. "Natural monopoly and its regulation," *Stanford Law Review, 21* (February): 548–643.

———. 1970. "Cable television: The problem of local monopoly," RAND Memorandum RM-6309-FF, May.

———. 1972. "The appropriate scope of regulation in the cable television industry," *The Bell Journal of Economics and Management Science, 3,* no. 1 (Spring): 98–129.

———. 1974. "Theories of economic regulation," *The Bell Journal of Economics and Management Science, 5,* no. 2 (Autumn): 335–58.

———. 1975. "The economic approach to law," *Texas Law Review, 53,* No. 4 (May): 757–82.

———. 1976. *Antitrust Law.* Chicago: University of Chicago Press.

———. 1977. *Economic Analysis of Law.* Boston: Little, Brown.

———. 1979. "The Chicago School of antitrust analysis," *University of Pennsylvania Law Review, 127* (April): 925–48.

PRESCOTT, EDWARD, and MICHAEL VISSCHER. 1980. "Organizational capital," *Journal of Political Economy, 88* (June): 446–61.

PRESTON, LEE. 1965. "Restrictive distribution arrangements: Economic analysis and public policy standards," *Law and Contemporary Problems, 30:* 506–34.

PRICE, MONROE E. 1983. "Cable interests aren't so wired into competition now," *Wall Street Journal,* October 18, p. 32.

PUTTERMAN, LOUIS. 1982. "Some behavioral perspectives on the dominance of hierarchical over democratic forms of enterprise," *Journal of Economic Behavior and Organization, 3* (June): 139–60.

―――――. 1984. "On some recent explanations of why capital hires labor," *Economic Inquiry, 22:* 171–87.

RADNER, ROY. 1968. "Competitive equilibrium under uncertainty," *Econometrica, 36* (January): 31–58.

RAWLS, JOHN. 1983. "Political philosophy: Political not metaphysical." Unpublished manuscript.

REDER, M. W. 1982. "Chicago economics: Permanence and change," *Journal of Economic Literature, 20* (March): 1–38.

REID, J. D., and R. C. FAITH. 1980. "The union as its members' agent." CE 80-9-6, Center for Study of Public Choice, Blacksburg, Virginia.

RICHARDSON, G. B. 1972. "The organization of industry," *Economic Journal, 82* (September): pp. 883–96.

RIKER, W. J. 1964. "Some ambiguities in the notion of power," *American Political Science Review, 58* (June): 341–49.

RILEY, JOHN G. 1979a. "Informational equilibrium," *Econometrica, 47* (March): 331–53.

―――――. 1979b. "Noncooperative equilibrium and market signaling," *American Economic Review, 69* (May): 303–7.

RIORDAN, MICHAEL, and OLIVER WILLIAMSON. 1986. "Asset specificity and economic organization," *International Journal of Industrial Organization.*

ROBBINS, LIONEL, ED. 1933. *The Common Sense of Political Economy, and Selected Papers on Economic Theory, by Philip Wicksteed.* London: G. Routledge and Sons, Ltd.

ROBINSON, E. A. G. 1934. "The problem of management and the size of firms," *Economic Journal, 44* (June): 240–54.

ROMANO, ROBERTA. 1984. "Metapolitics and corporate law reform," *Stanford Law Review, 36* (April): 923–1016.

ROSS, ARTHUR. 1958. "Do we have a new industrial feudalism?" *American Economic Review, 48* (December): 668–83.

ROSS, S. 1973. "The economic theory of agency: The principal's problem," *American Economic Review, 63:* 134–39.

―――――. 1977. "The determination of financial structure: The incentive signaling approach," *Bell Journal of Economics, 8* (Spring): 23–40.

ROTHSCHILD, MICHAEL, and JOSEPH STIGLITZ. 1976. "Equilibrium in competitive insurance markets," *Quarterly Journal of Economics, 80* (November): 629–50.

SACKS, STEPHEN. 1983. *Self-Management and Efficiency.* London: George Allen & Unwin.

SALOP, S. 1979. "Strategic entry deterrence," *American Economic Review, 69* (May): 335–38.

SALOP, S., and D. SCHEFFMAN. 1983. "Raising rival's costs," *American Economic Review, 73* (May): 267–71.

SAMUELSON, PAUL. 1947. *Foundations of Economic Analysis.* Cambridge, Mass.: Harvard University Press.

———. 1957. "Wage and interest: A modern dissection of Marxian economic models," *American Economic Review, 47* (December): 884–912.

SCHAUER, H. 1973. "Critique of co-determination." In G. Hunnius, G. Garson, and J. Case, eds., *Worker's Control.* New York: Random House, pp. 210–24.

SCHELLING, THOMAS C. 1956. "An essay on bargaining," *American Economic Review, 46* (June): 281–306.

SCHERER, F. M. 1964. *The Weapons Acquisition Process: Economic Incentives.* Boston: Division of Research, Graduate School of Business Administration, Harvard.

———. 1980. *Industrial Market Structure and Economic Performance.* Chicago: Rand McNally.

SCHMALENSEE, R. 1973. "A note on the theory of vertical integration," *Journal of Political Economy, 81* (March/April): 442–49.

———. 1978. "Entry deterrence in the ready-to-eat breakfast cereal industry," *Bell Journal of Economics, 9* (Autumn): 305–27.

———. 1979. *The Control of Natural Monopolies.* Lexington, Mass.: Lexington Books.

———. 1980. "Economies of scale and barriers to entry." Sloan Working Paper No. 1130-80, June, Cambridge, Mass.

———. 1981. "Economies of scale and barriers to entry," *Journal of Political Economy, 89* (December): 1228–38.

SCHNEIDER, L. 1963. "Preface" to Karl Menger (1963).

SCHUMPETER, J. A. 1942. *Capitalism, Socialism, and Democracy.* New York: Harper & Row.

———. 1947. "The creative response in economic history," *Journal of Economic History, 7* (November): 149–59.

———. 1961. *The Theory of Economic Development.* New York: Oxford University Press.

SCHWARTZ, LOUIS B. 1983. "The new merger guidelines: Guide to government discretion and private counseling or propaganda for revision of the antitrust law," *California Law Review, 71* (March): 575–603.

SCOTT, K. 1983. "Corporation law and the American Law Institute's Corporate Governance Project," *Stanford Law Review, 35* (June): 927–53.

SCOTT, RICHARD. 1981. *Organizations.* Englewood Cliffs, N.J.: Prentice-Hall.

SELZNICK, PHILIP. 1948. "Foundations of the theory of organization," *American Sociological Review, 13* (February): 25–35.

SEN, AMARTYA. 1975. *Employment, Technology and Development.* Oxford, Eng.: Oxford University Press.

SHACKLE, G. L. S. 1961. *Decision, Order, and Time.* Cambridge, Eng.: Cambridge University Press.

SHAVELL, STEVEN. 1980. "Damage measures for breach of contract," *Bell Journal of Economics, 11* (Autumn): 446–90.

SHEPHERD, W. G. 1984. "Contestability vs. competition," *American Economic Review, 74* (September): 572–87.

SHULMAN, HARRY. 1955. "Reason, contract, and law in labor relations," *Harvard Law Review, 68* (June): 999–1036.

SIMON, HERBERT A. 1957. *Models of Man.* New York: John Wiley & Sons.

———. 1959. "Theories of decision making in economics and behavioral science," *American Economic Review, 49* (June): 253–58.

———. 1961. *Administrative Behavior.* 2d ed. New York: Macmillan. Original publication: 1947.

———. 1962. "The architecture of complexity," *Proceedings of the American Philosophical Society, 106* (December): 467–82.

———. 1969. *The Sciences of the Artificial.* Cambridge, Mass.: MIT Press.

———. 1972. "Theories of bounded rationality." In C. B. McGuire and Roy Radner, eds., *Decision and Organization.* New York: American Elsevier, pp. 161–76.

———. 1973. "Applying information technology to organization design," *Public Administrative Review, 33* (May–June): 268–78.

———. 1978. "Rationality as process and as product of thought," *American Economic Review, 68* (May): 1–16.

———. 1983. *Reason in Human Affairs.* Stanford: Stanford University Press.

SLOAN, A. P., JR. 1964. *My Years with General Motors.* New York: MacFadden.

SMITH, A. 1922. *The Wealth of Nations.* London: J. M. Dent & Sons.

SMITH, CLIFFORD, and JEROLD WARNER. 1979. "On financial contracting: An analysis of bond covenants," *Journal of Financial Economics, 7:* 117–61.

SMITH, V. 1974. "Economic theory and its discontents," *American Economic Review, 64* (May): 320–22.

SOBEL, R. 1974. *The Entrepreneurs.* New York: Weybright & Talley.

SOLO, ROBERT. 1972. "New maths and old sterilities," *Saturday Review,* January 22, pp. 47–48.

SOLTOW, J. H. 1968. "The entrepreneur in economic history," *American Economic Review, 58* (May): 84–92.

SPEIDEL, RICHARD E. 1981. "Court-imposed price adjustments under long-term supply contracts," *Northwestern University Law Review, 76* (October): 369–422.

SPENCE, A. M. 1977. "Entry, investment and oligopolistic pricing," *Bell Journal of Economics, 8* (Autumn): 534–44.

———. 1981. "The learning curve and competition," *Bell Journal of Economics, 12* (Spring).

———. 1983. "Contestable markets and the theory of industry structure: A review article," *Journal of Economic Literature, 21* (September): 981–90.

SPENCE, A. M., and RICHARD ZECKHAUSER. 1971. "Insurance, information, and individual action," *American Economic Review, 61* (May): 380–87.

SPILLER, PABLO. 1985. "On vertical mergers," *Journal of Law, Economics, and Organization, 1* (Fall).

STIGLER, GEORGE J. 1949. *Five Lectures on Economic Problems*. London: London School of Economics.

———. 1951. "The division of labor is limited by the extent of the market," *Journal of Political Economy, 59* (June): 185–93.

———. 1963. "United States *v.* Loew's, Inc.: A note on block booking," *Supreme Court Review*, pp. 152–64.

———. 1964. "Public regulation and the security markets," *Journal of Business, 37* (March): 117–32.

———. 1968. *The Organization of Industry*. Homewood, Ill.: Richard D. Irwin.

———. 1974. "Free riders and collective action," *Bell Journal of Economics, 5* (Autumn): 359–65.

———. 1982. "The economists and the monopoly problem," *American Economic Review, 72* (May): 1–11.

———. 1983. Comments in Edmund W. Kitch, ed., "The Fire of Truth: A Remembrance of Law and Economics at Chicago, 1932–1970," *Journal of Law and Economics, 26* (April): 163–234.

STIGLITZ, JOSEPH. 1974. "Incentives and risk sharing in sharecropping," *Review of Economic Studies, 41* (June): 219–57.

———. 1975. "Incentives, risk, and information: Notes towards a theory of hierarchy," *Bell Journal of Economics, 6* (Autumn): 552–79.

STINCHCOMBE, ARTHUR L. 1983. "Contracts as hierarchical documents." Unpublished manuscript, Stanford Graduate School of Business.

STOCKING, GEORGE W., and WILLARD F. MUELLER. 1957. "Business reciprocity and the size of firms," *Journal of Business, 30* (April): 73–95.

STONE, K. 1974. "The origins of job structures in the steel industry," *Review of Radical Political Economics, 6* (Summer): 61–97.

———. 1981. "The post-war paradigm in American labor law," *Yale Law Journal, 90* (June): 1509–80.

STOPFORD, JOHN M., and LOUIS T. WELLS, JR. 1972. *Managing the Multinational Enterprise: Organization of the Firm and Ownership of the Subsidiaries*. New York: Basic Books.

STUCKEY, JOHN. 1983. *Vertical Integration and Joint Ventures in the Aluminum Industry*. Cambridge, Mass.: Harvard University Press.

SUMMERS, CLYDE. 1969. "Collective agreements and the law of contracts," *Yale Law Journal, 78* (March): 537–75.

———. 1976. "Individual protection against unjust dismissal: Time for a statute," *Virginia Law Review, 62* (April): 481–532.

———. 1980. "Worker participation in the U.S. and West Germany: A comparative study from an American perspective," *American Journal of Comparative Law, 28* (June): 367–93.

———. 1982. "Codetermination in the United States: A projection of problems and potentials," *Journal of Comparative Corporate Law and Security Regulation*, pp. 155–83.

TAYLOR, GEORGE, and IRENE NEU. 1956. *The American Railroad Network*. Cambridge, Mass.: Harvard University Press.

TEECE, D. J. 1976. *Vertical Integration and Divestiture in the U.S. Oil Industry.* Stanford, Calif.: The Stanford University Institute for Energy Studies.

———. 1977. "Technology transfer by multinational firms," *Economic Journal, 87* (June): 242–61.

———. 1980. "Economies of scope and the scope of the enterprise," *Journal of Economic Behavior and Organization, 1,* no. 3 (September): 223–45.

———. 1981. "Internal organization and economic performance: An empirical analysis of the profitability of principal firms," *Journal of Industrial Economics, 30* (December): 173–200.

———. 1982. "Towards an economic theory of the multiproduct firm," *Journal of Economic Behavior and Organization, 3* (March): 39–64.

TELSER, LESTER. 1960. "Why should manufacturers want fair trade?" *Journal of Law and Economics, 3:* 86–104.

———. 1965. "Abusive trade practices: An economic analysis," *Law and Contemporary Problems, 30* (Summer): 488–510.

———. 1969. "On the regulation of industry: A note," *Journal of Political Economy, 77* (November/December): 937–52.

———. 1971. "On the regulation of industry: Rejoinder," *Journal of Political Economy, 79* (March/April): 364–65.

———. 1981. "A theory of self-enforcing agreements," *Journal of Business, 53* (February): 27–44.

TELSER, LESTER, and H. N. HIGINBOTHAM. 1977. "Organized futures markets: Costs and benefit," *Journal of Political Economy, 85,* no. 6: 969–1000.

TEMIN, P. 1981. "The future of the new economic history," *Journal of Interdisciplinary History, 12,* no. 2 (Autumn): 179–97.

THOMPSON, JAMES D. 1967. *Organizations in Action.* New York: McGraw-Hill.

TOWNSEND, ROBERT. 1982. "Optimal multiperiod contracts and gain from enduring relationships under private information," *Journal of Political Economy, 90:* 1166–86.

TSURUMI, Y. 1977. *Multinational Management.* Cambridge, Mass.: Ballinger.

TULLOCK, GORDON. 1965. *The Politics of Bureaucracy.* Washington: Public Affairs Press.

TURNER, D. F. 1965. "Conglomerate mergers and Section 7 of the Clayton Act," *Harvard Law Review, 78* (May): 1313–95.

TVERSKY, AMOS, and DANIEL KAHNEMAN. 1974. "Judgment under uncertainty: Heuristics and biases," *Science, 185:* 1124–31.

UDY, S. H., JR. 1970. *Work in Traditional and Modern Society.* Englewood Cliffs, N.J.: Prentice-Hall.

UNWIN, G. 1904. *Industrial Organization in the Sixteenth and Seventeenth Centuries.* Oxford, Eng.: Oxford University Press.

U.S. DEPARTMENT OF JUSTICE. 1982a. *Merger Guidelines—1968.* Commerce Clearing House, Trade Regulation Reports. July 9, para. 4510.

———. 1982b. *Merger Guidelines—1982.* Commerce Clearing House, Trade Regulation Reports. July 9, para. 4500.

U.S. FEDERAL TRADE COMMISSION. 1948. *Report of the Federal Trade Commission on the Merger Movement: A Summary Report.* Washington, D.C.: U.S. Government Printing Office.

VANEK, JAROSLAV. 1970. *The General Theory of Labor-Managed Market Economies.* Ithaca, N.Y.: Cornell University Press.

VERNON, J. M., and D. A. GRAHAM. 1971. "Profitability of monopolization by vertical integration," *Journal of Political Economy, 79* (July/August): 924–25.

VERNON, R. 1971. *Sovereignty at Bay.* New York: Basic Books.

VOGEL, EZRA F. 1981. *Japan as Number One: Lessons for America.* New York: Harper & Row.

VROOM, VICTOR. 1964. *Work and Motivation.* New York: John Wiley & Sons.

WACHTER, MICHAEL, and O. E. WILLIAMSON. 1978. "Obligational markets and the mechanics of inflation," *Bell Journal of Economics, 9* (Autumn): 549–71.

WALKER, GORDON, and DAVID WEBER. 1984. "A transaction cost approach to make-or-buy decisions," *Administrative Science Quarterly, 29* (September): 373–91.

WALL, JOSEPH F. 1970. *Andrew Carnegie.* Oxford, Eng.: Oxford University Press.

WALTON, R. E. 1980. "Establishing and maintaining high commitment work systems." In J. R. Kimberly and R. H. Miles, eds., *The Organizational Life Cycle.* San Francisco: Jossey-Bass, pp. 208–90.

WARREN-BOULTON, F. R. 1967. "Vertical control with variable proportions," *Journal of Political Economy, 75* (April): 123–38.

WAYNE, L. 1982. "The airlines: Stacked up in red ink," *New York Times,* February 14, Sec. 3, pp. 1, 6.

WEICK, K. E. 1969. *The Social Psychology of Organizing.* Reading, Mass.: Addison-Wesley.

WEIZSACKER, C. C. VON. 1980a. "A welfare analysis of barriers to entry," *Bell Journal of Economics, 11* (Autumn): 399–421.

———. 1980b. *Barriers to Entry.* New York: Springer-Verlag.

WHITE, HARRISON. 1981. "Where do markets come from?" *American Journal of Sociology, 87* (November): 517–47.

WILKINS, MIRA. 1974. *The Maturing of Multinational Enterprise: American Business Abroad from 1914 to 1970.* Cambridge, Mass.: Harvard University Press.

WILLIAMSON, O. E. 1964. *The Economics of Discretionary Behavior: Managerial Objectives in a Theory of the Firm.* Englewood Cliffs, N.J.: Prentice-Hall.

———. 1967a. "The economics of defense contracting: incentives and performance." In *Issues in Defense Economics.* New York: National Bureau of Economic Research, pp. 217–56.

———. 1967b. "Hierarchical control and optimum firm size," *Journal of Political Economy, 75* (April): 123–38.

———. 1968a. "Wage rates as a barrier to entry: The Pennington case in perspective," *Quarterly Journal of Economics, 82* (February): 85–116.

———. 1968b. "Economies as an antitrust defense: The welfare tradeoffs," *American Economic Review, 58* (March): 18–35.

_____. 1970. *Corporate Control and Business Behavior.* Englewood Cliffs, N.J.: Prentice-Hall.

_____. 1971. "The vertical integration of production: Market failure considerations," *American Economic Review, 61* (May): 112–23.

_____. 1973. "Markets and hierarchies: Some elementary considerations," *American Economic Review, 63* (May): 316–25.

_____. 1974a. "Patent and antitrust law: Book review," *Yale Law Journal, 83* (January): 647–61.

_____. 1974b. "The economics of antitrust: Transaction cost considerations," *University of Pennsylvania Law Review, 122* (June): 1439–96.

_____. 1975. *Markets and Hierarchies: Analysis and Antitrust Implications.* New York: Free Press.

_____. 1976. "Franchise bidding for natural monopolies—in general and with respect to CATV," *Bell Journal of Economics, 7* (Spring): 73–104.

_____. 1977. "Predatory pricing: A strategic and welfare analysis," *Yale Law Journal, 87* (December): 284–340.

_____. 1979a. "Transaction-cost economics: The governance of contractual relations," *Journal of Law and Economics, 22* (October): 3–61.

_____. 1979b. "Review of Bork, 'The Antitrust Paradox: A Policy at War with Itself,' " *University of Chicago Law Review, 46* (Winter): 526–31.

_____. 1979c. "Assessing vertical market restrictions," *University of Pennsylvania Law Review, 127* (April): 953–93.

_____. 1979d. "On the governance of the modern corporation," *Hofstra Law Review, 8* (Fall): 63–78.

_____. 1980. "The organization of work," *Journal of Economic Behavior and Organization, 1* (March): 5–38.

_____. 1981a. "Cost escalation and contracting," Center for the Study of Organizational Innovation, University of Pennsylvania, Discussion Paper #95, January.

_____. 1981b. "The economics of organization: The transaction cost approach," *American Journal of Sociology, 87* (November): 548–77.

_____. 1981c. "The modern corporation: Origins, evolution, attributes," *Journal of Economic Literature, 19* (December): 1537–68.

_____. 1982. "Antitrust enforcement: Where it has been; where it is going." In John Craven, ed., *Industrial Organization, Antitrust, and Public Policy.* Boston: Kluwer-Nijhoff Publishing, pp. 41–68.

_____. 1983a. "Organizational innovation: The transaction cost approach." In J. Ronen, ed., *Entrepreneurship.* Lexington, Mass.: Heath Lexington, 101–34.

_____. 1983b. "Organization form, residual claimants, and corporate control," *Journal of Law and Economics, 26* (June): 351–66.

_____. 1983c. "Credible commitments: Using hostages to support exchange," *American Economic Review, 73* (September): 519–40.

_____. 1984. "The economics of governance: Framework and implications," *Journal of Theoretical Economics, 140* (March): 195–223.

————. 1984. "Corporate governance," *Yale Law Journal, 93* (June).

————. 1984. "Perspectives on the modern corporation," *Quarterly Review of Economics and Business, 24* (Winter): 64–71.

WILLIAMSON, O. E., and WILLIAM G. OUCHI. 1981. "The markets and hierarchies program of research: Origins, implications, prospects." In William Joyce and Andrew Van de Ven, eds., *Organizational Design.* New York: Wiley.

WILLIAMSON, O. E.; MICHAEL L. WACHTER; and JEFFREY E. HARRIS. 1975. "Understanding the employment relation: The analysis of idiosyncratic exchange," *Bell Journal of Economics, 6* (Spring): 250–80.

WILLIAMSON, SCOTT R. 1980. "A selective history of the U.S. labor movement," B.A. thesis, Yale University.

WILSON, R. 1968. "The theory of syndicates," *Econometrica, 36:* 119–32.

WINTER, R. 1978. *Government and the Corporation.* Washington, D.C.: American Enterprise Institute for Public Policy Research.

WINTER, S. G. 1971. "Satisfying, selection, and the innovating remnant," *Quarterly Journal of Economics, 85* (May): 237–61.

WORK IN AMERICA. 1973. Report of a Special Task Force to the Secretary of Health, Education, and Welfare. Cambridge, Mass.: MIT Press.

Author Index

437

Subject Index

Aerospace industry, 117
Agency, 21, 27, 28, 254, 257
Aluminum industry, 127
Amalgamated Association of Iron, Steel, and
   Tin Workers, 234, 235
American Federation of Labor, 253
American Tobacco, 111, 120*n*
American tobacco industry, 108
Antitrust, 19, 25, 99, 100, 104, 197, 200,
   348, 366, 368, 385, 386, 398
Antitrust Division, United States Department
   of Justice, 290*n*, 368, 370
Antitrust enforcement, 17, 189, 286, 288
Antitrust law, 26, 202
Applied price theory, 26, 65, 66, 366*n*, 402
Arbitration, 10, 34, 60, 70, 71, 75, 114,
   115, 165, 178, 251, 252, 256, 262,
   308–310, 353*n*
Arbitrators, 29, 249, 251, 333
Arbuckle, John, 111
Arnold, Schwinn & Co., 183; *see also*
   Schwinn case
Asset specificity, 18, 29–32, 42, 52–56, 60,
   72, 78, 79, 83, 86, 90–96, 103, 104,
   106, 113, 114, 119, 129, 131, 132,
   137*n*, 139–141, 143, 144, 153, 163,
   173, 174, 180, 204, 211, 242, 243,
   307, 327, 328, 391, 393, 403

human, 137, 243, 245, 254–256, 259,
   303*n*, 349
Assets, 143, 151, 172, 173, 248, 389
   dedicated, 55, 95, 96, 137, 194, 195, 201
   firm-specific, 137, 138, 242, 303, 313
   specialized, 178–180, 191–193
   transaction-specific, 30, 32–34, 60–62,
      79, 137, 143, 169, 190, 194, 260, 301
Assignment attributes, 224, 227, 228
Audits, 154, 155*n*
Authority Relation, 218–222, 225, 229, 231,
   265–268
Automobile industry, 87*n*, 110, 120, 157,
   280

Bargaining, 125, 255, 262
Black letter law, 10
Block booking, 19, 25, 29, 372
Board of directors, 250, 298–300, 303, 305,
   306, 308–312, 317, 322–324
   membership of, 302, 316
Bonding costs, 21, 388
Boundaries, 4, 9, 26, 141, 155, 383
   efficient, 96–98, 116, 366
Buffer inventories, 224, 227
Bureaucracy, 148, 149, 153, 392
Bureaucratic failure literature, 149, 153, 392
Business history, 11, 16*n*, 394
Business history literature, 104

Unitary structure, 95, 280, 320
United Mine Workers, 265n, 374n
United States, 122, 264, 291
Utopian modes of organization, 50–52

Vertical Merger Guidelines (1968, 1982, 1984), 85, 98–102, 192, 202n, 370, 383
Vertical restrictions (restraints), 184, 185, 372
    effects of, 373
Voice, 252, 253, 257
Volvo, 269n

Wagner Act, 9, 250, 253
Watermill–handmill controversy, 233
Western Union, 160
Wholesaling, 108, 114
Work intensity, 224, 225, 228, 229
Work mode literature, 213–214, 238
Work modes, 210, 213–216, 220, 221, 223, 238

Work organization, 29, 262n, 385
Work satisfaction, 210
Worker autonomy, 216, 219
Worker buy-outs, 267n
Worker cooperatives, 266
Worker discretion, 262
Worker self-management, 300n
Worker-run enterprise, 268
Workers, 36, 38, 124, 213–219, 222, 224, 228, 231, 235, 236, 246, 247, 253, 258, 259, 262, 263, 267, 269, 272, 300, 302, 303, 323, 344, 406

Xerox, 379

Yugoslav self-management, 394
Yugoslavia, 268

Zones of acceptance, 218, 220, 222, 249